Waves of Global Change

A Holistic World History

Second Edition

Dr. Denise R. Ames

Published in 2015 by The Center for Global Awareness

ISBN: 978-1-943841-01-1

Book Design by Daryl S. Fuller and Jeanine McGann

The principal text of this book was composed in Adobe Garamond Pro.

The Center for Global Awareness
Albuquerque, New Mexico, USA
www.global-awareness.org

Acknowledgments

I have many people who I would like to thank in helping to bring this book to completion. The project has been completed in two phases: first, as a thesis and doctoral dissertation and second, as an experiential model used in the classroom and in professional development workshops.

In the first phase, I would especially like to thank Dr. Joseph Grabill, history professor emeritus of Illinois State University. Without his unwavering inspiration, support, and advice during the phases of writing my master's thesis and doctoral dissertation, this project would not have been imagined or completed. I would also like to thank the late Dr. Lawrence McBride, secondary education social studies professor at Illinois State University, who helped me adapt the holistic concept of world history into a comprehensive teaching model. Thanks to the faculty, staff, and students who I worked with at Illinois State University in the years 1991-1998. A special thanks to my family during this time: to my children, Dennis and Mia Beurskens, and to Frank Beurskens for his many years of encouragement and listening.

In the second phase of the book project, I am especially grateful to Nancy Harmon, my partner in our non-profit organization the Center for Global Awareness. Her crisp editing and encouragement have helped make this book a reality. Thanks to Stephanie Hiller who spent many hours making suggestions and editing. I appreciate the many students, educators, and reviewers, who have read part or all of the book in the 2000s and made helpful comments and criticisms. I would like to single out my former student and reviewer, Christina Durano, who has been particularly supportive. Thanks to graphic designer Daryl Fuller who has taken on the immense project of turning this book into reality, and Jeanine McGann who has been responsible for the second edition. And last, my heartfelt gratitude for the love and support of my partner, Jim Knutson.

Denise R. Ames
Albuquerque, New Mexico, USA

Contents

Chapter 3
Our Collective Story: Human Commonalities

Chapter 4
People as Nomadic Foragers: The Communal Wave

Chapter 5

People as Village Farmers: The Agricultural Wave

Chapter 6
People Create Civilizations: The Urban Wave

Chapter 7
People Multiply and Dominate the Globe: The Modern Wave

Chapter 8
People Creating a Future: The Global Wave

PREFACE

Waves of Global Change: A Holistic World History

It all started in the fall of 1992, when I embarked upon what would be a life-changing project. The project occurred to me in an intuitive flash. I was visiting a class taught by a popular history professor, Joseph Grabill, who would become my advisor and close friend. He was explaining religious change over time through what he called "eco-waves." In just a short moment, something clicked, and I knew what I wanted to do.

I was a "non-traditional" (meaning older) graduate student at Illinois State University in Normal, Illinois, and had been toying with ideas for my thesis topic, but nothing was exciting me. I had put forward a draft proposing to compare first ladies Rosalyn Carter and Eleanor Roosevelt. Yet, the books I had checked out from the library sat by my reading chair for weeks on end, un- opened and collecting dust. At the moment, the thesis seemed a daunting and uninspiring task.

On the fateful intuitive-flash day something changed. I would now develop a teaching model for world history borrowing Joe's "waves" as the organizing principle. Now, this idea excited me! I didn't know for sure if the model would work, but from my research and experience, I somehow intuitively surmised that this was a feasible ap- proach. After class, I rushed to the front of the classroom to share with Joe what to me was a fabulous idea. At first he looked perplexed as I babbled on about ideas I knew nothing about. He pondered for a moment then said "why not?" I was elated. As students filtered in for the next class, we made an appointment later in the week to discuss the idea in more depth.

I knew Joe from his dedicated work as the President of the Bloomington/Normal, Illinois and Vladimir, Russia/Canterbury, England Sister Cities program. He spearheaded the travel of a group of local student athletes to Vladimir, Russia (Soviet Union at the time) in the fall of 1989, to help with the dedication of their sports stadium. My son participated in the track meet, and I helped him with the planning. At least he knew I wasn't as flaky as I appeared when babbling on and on about world history after class that fateful day. In our meeting, I sketched out my rough plan for a thesis based on a model for teaching world history. I asked him to be my advisor. After an initial quizzical look he exclaimed, SURE! That was it. He loved the scheme and now we were both hooked.

I had no idea what I was getting into or the magnitude of the project. As I reflected on my decision, I realized I didn't really know that much about world history. My mother forced me to take a world history class in 9th grade; it certainly wasn't my choice. But I did like the class. Yet, there was a yawning gap between taking a 9th grade world history class and writing a thesis on the topic! In my defense, I did know something about the world. I taught world geography in grades 7-9. I also, was very interested in world affairs and keep fairly current with world developments. I was lucky enough to travel to different parts of the world and learned a lot from my travels. But still, my ignorance was probably a blessing in disguise, since if I really understood the scope of world history I may have retreated from this daunting undertaking.

I ceremoniously dumped my "first ladies" books into the library return bin. I then immediately and enthusiastically started researching and reading about world history. No dust accumulated on these books. I always had a head for "big picture" thinking, while the details could be summarily shuffled aside, but this was really a big, big picture! Although doubts surfaced, and the question of "was I really competent to do this" often discouraged me, Joe was an infallible supporter. I trudged on, trying to figure out how to organize this monstrosity of a subject.

In the early 1990s, as I was working on my thesis, the newly formed and expanding field of world history meant that lots of debate about how to organize it circulated. Ideas flew about, while consensus was not an option. It was truly exciting to read about different ways to interpret, teach, and understand world history. I loved the wide-open discussions and innovative ideas that were challenging the traditional western civilization approach that had become embedded in the nation's classrooms. I was inspired by the feeling that my ideas were as valid as some of the "big names" in world history, although certainly not as well researched or accepted at this point. I also zealously dove into applying anthropology, sociology, psychology, political science, economics, and geography principles in helping to broaden my holistic model. I enlisted the advice of the late Dr. Lawrence McBride in the social science education department at Illinois State University to be my advisor as well. He was always telling me: you got to "flesh out" the model, just keep "working it." It was a tremendous help to have two strong supporters to encourage me in developing my model of world history.

The thesis was successfully defended, and even won an award. The doctoral program was my next big step. Through my five years in working on my doctoral degree, I continued with my research, writing, and teaching of world history at Illinois State University. In the beginning, I stumbled through my teaching of introductory world history classes. I pity the students in my first class. As luck would have it, I had Illinois State's top undergraduate, a Bone Student Scholar recipient, as one of my students! Luckily she was sympathetic and actually loved the model; she also gave me valuable feedback for improvement.

Gradually, the model started to coalesce and by the time I taught my last world history class at Illinois State I felt more comfortable with its progress. I took a year off of teaching to write my dissertation and concentrated on filling gaping holes in my model. I met weekly with Joe and occasionally with my other advisers, and can honestly say it was a wonderful experience. Joe and I wrestled with the quandary that the world history model, by its very nature, would never be definitively "done." It was a constantly evolving project—a process, as one of my students astutely observed. Yet, a finalized copy was necessary for the doctorate to be awarded and I was ready to move on. I submitted the 450+ page tome to the proper committees, and with margins and footnotes correctly formatted I still needed the approval of the chair of the doctoral program: Dr. John Freed. He was a professor of European history, and always a skeptic about world history, (he constantly asked how does Europe fit in). A look of doubt colored his face as I rambled on to him that this was an evolving project and there were parts that needed more research but after all this was world history, an enormous project, and I thought 450+ pages was more than sufficient for a dissertation. Begrudgingly, and with some arm twisting from Joe, he agreed, with the provision that I would consent to fix some grammar and correctly spell some names (unfortunately they were European historians' names and he was a preeminent European historian). As noted earlier, never an eye for detail, I finally fixed up the grammar and spelled names correctly and happily scheduled my dissertation defense.

I had the cute little dissertation defense announcements printed up and sent out to anyone and everyone. I was actually looking forward to the defense and calmly seated myself among the imposing all male committee. The defense got off to a strange start, with actually a heated debate about world history between two of the members, and I wasn't included! I calmly interrupted them and asserted that we needed to get back to the task at hand; it was my defense and I was going to make the most of it. I answered the question of how Europe fits into world history before 1500 and many other thorny questions with ease. It went well and I was congratulated as Dr. Ames at the conclusion. Joe proclaimed that "I was now the expert." Although wary about the expert label, the title doctor felt right and well deserved.

After receiving my doctorate, I moved to Albuquerque, New Mexico. I always loved New Mexico; also, my mother lived there and my two adult children lived in Tempe, Arizona. I taught at various colleges and universities, but most of my classes were at Central New Mexico Community College. I taught everything from World History, to U.S. History, Western Civilization, Cultural Studies, and Global Issues. I was able to further test the model in the classroom.

In the early 2000s I became more interested in global issues, a topic I had always found fascinating. I started to do workshops in Albuquerque on topics such as globalization, in particular economic globalization. I decided to form an organization that would help disseminate information about globalization and the Center for Global Awareness was born in 2003. I continued with the workshops for the general public, and enjoyed interacting with adults. I even expanded to do some workshops around the nation. But then I started to reconsider my efforts. Many people encouraged me to expand my teaching to try to reach as many people as possible. I thought; why not conduct professional development workshops for educators. It put to use my years as a secondary social studies teacher, my training in world history education, my college teaching experience, and my independent research. It was a great idea. The most interesting workshop that I did was for educators in Singapore; they are required to teach about globalization.

It was with my new focus on professional development training that I decided to revive my holistic world history model. Although I had continued using the model in my teaching during the 2000s, I had lapsed in revising my dissertation for publication. I did several workshops for teacher organizations and seminars on the holistic world history model. It was greeted with interest and encouragement. I found that teachers and students found the model to be very beneficial as a "map" to world history. They said it was a comprehensive way to organize and understand world history; to simplify an often over-whelming subject into a graspable whole. There were many requests for materials, other than my handouts, on using this model in the classroom. They were always asking if I had materials on my model, and I had to respond with, "nothing commercially available, but I'll send you something for free." Many replied remonstratively "you need to get this published, just don't give your ideas away!"

I decided it was time to heed their advice and take the next step. In the spring of 2008 I taught my last two classes at the community college and turned to working on developing a holistic world history survey for students in grades 9-14.

I deliberated on the best way to market the world history book, as I was undergoing the revisions and further research. It was a painstaking process. I corresponded with a number of publishers, who expressed interest in the project, but either I didn't feel comfortable with them or they didn't feel comfortable with me. I also looked at the big picture—I wanted the world history survey to be the cornerstone book in a whole series of publications looking at various global issues and cultural topics. It seemed like an overwhelming project in the initial stages. I also had doubts if I was up to the task. But Joe Grabill's words were still inspirational to me, he would say "why not" or "you're the expert now." So I decided to carry through with my plan.

As luck would have it, I reconnected with a fellow educator Nancy Harmon in 2009. We first met at a globalization study group in 2003. We then both served on the board of directors of a local organization called PeacePal in 2009, where she wrote a wonderful peace curriculum for the organization. After many years teaching in various capacities and locations, she was ending her formal teaching career at the close of 2009. She was looking for another challenge. She was very interested in my plans for the Center for Global Awareness. Having a master's degree in multicultural education, she has always been interested in cultural topics, global issues and curriculum development. It was a perfect match. We decided to form a partnership and incorporate the center as a non-profit organization.

The primary goal of the center is dedicated to encouraging the education of globally aware citizens who, using 21st century skills, strive to participate in creating a more sustainable, equitable, peaceful, and culturally aware world community. The survey of world history would serve as the cornerstone piece in a series of books that would complement and expand upon the central premises of the holistic model. This lofty goal is implemented through what I have called (cleverly I think) the Global Awareness Program series or GAPs. The series is designed to fill in the "gaps" of a traditional educational curriculum with a thought-provoking and engaging, globally-focused alternative. The series of soft-cover books, each approximately 25 to 200 pages, offers an experiential, standards-based curriculum geared for students in grades 9-14. In addition to the holistic world history survey, *Waves of Global Change: A Holistic World History*, GAP curriculum includes *Waves of Global Change: An Educator's Handbook for Teaching a Holistic World History, The Global Economy: Connecting the Roots of a Holistic System, Connecting the Roots of the Global Economy: A Holistic Approach, Brief Edition, Financial Literacy: Wall Street and How it Works, International Folktales For English Language Learners*, and *Human Rights: A Universal Values System.* The curriculum addresses crucial issues and ways of understanding and thinking necessary for a more interdependent world and a more just, hopeful, and sustainable future. That should keep Nancy and me busy and challenged for the rest of our conscious lives!

I often ask myself "why do I want to embark upon such a formidable undertaking?" But recognizing that I am and I will probably always be an idealist and optimist, it just seems right that I contribute in whatever way I can to help shift our consciousness to different paradigmatic thinking and understanding of the world. As many of you are probably aware, I am not an alarmist who is overstating the fact that we are facing a mounting crisis in our world community; our future existence as a species on this planet is in severe jeopardy. We cannot continue on the path of exploitation of the planet's resources indefinitely; our days on this trajectory are numbered. But I refuse to be fatalistic about our chances for a viable future; after all, human choice has played a crucial part in constructing our past and plays an even more critical role in our future. As educators we know that we have a responsibility to help the next generation gain the tools and skills to fashion a future that is healthful, enriching and sustainable. yet, to paraphrase Einstein, we cannot use the same kind of thinking to solve problems that was used to create the problems in the first place. In other words, it is my firm belief that we need to think about and understand our world in a more holistic way.

I feel a profound calling to share my thoughts, research, and experience in helping our students and educators look at the world in a different way. With the celebrity of youth in our culture, we often ignore the wise council of elders. It is time for us elders to speak up and help guide the next generation, drawing on our trial and error experiences and our wisdom accumulated over the years. It is with this intention that we are developing the GAP series and hope that it will contribute in at least in a small way to this overarching goal of "saving the planet" (I always liked lofty goals). Although I am still uncomfortable with Joe Grabill's assertion as I earned by doctoral degree that "I was now the expert," I do feel more at ease in sharing what I have learned over the years with others. I hope my efforts in this world history you are about to read and the GAP series will contribute to helping you teach or think about issues, perspectives, and understandings that give you or your students a different way to look at the world.

Denise R. Ames
founder and president:
Center for Global Awareness

Organization of *Waves of Global Change: A Holistic World History*

This book, *Waves of Global Change: a Holistic World History,* is divided into eight chapters. The first chapter—An Introduction to a Holistic World History—introduces the holistic approach used in this world history. Holistic is when all the cultural traits—economic, technological, social, political, cultural—reinforce all others. The chapter explains how the development of humans across time and space forms a periodization framework that is organized into five critical turning points or waves: Communal, Agricultural, Urban, Modern, and Global. It also outlines a system thinking approach used in this world history. The chapter examines five worldviews—indigenous, modern, fundamentalist, globalized, and transformative—that inform our ways of thinking today.

Chapter two—The Universe to Human Emergence—sets the "big picture" of human history within our physical and biological history from the big bang through the evolution of our species. Woven into this chapter's narrative are five flows—interdependence, paradox, creative and destructive forces, change and continuity, and commonalities and diversity—that help create the Universe, generate life on Earth, and shape human story.

The third chapter—Human Commonalities—examines human universal behaviors that are organized into five comparative patterns or what I call currents. These five currents are drawn from an interdisciplinary perspective and integrated into a historical framework. The five currents—Relationship to Nature: Ecosystem Currents; Ways of Living: Techno-Economic Curreents; Human Networks: Social Currents; Establishing Order: Political Currents; and Human Expressions: Cultural Currents—each contain five sub-currents and are repeated, with different content, in each wave.

In the fourth chapter, The Communal Wave, people gather/hunt or forage for food and live together in small communal, nomadic bands bound together through strong kinship ties. This wave encompasses the emergence of modern humans around 40,000 years ago and continues today with very small numbers still practicing, although in an altered form, a foraging way of life. Also presented is a case study of the !Kung people in southwest Africa.

In chapter five—The Agricultural Wave—some people change from foraging for food to agricultural food production and a sedentary, village way of life. People begin to make this change in some, but not all, areas of the world approximately 10,000 BCE. This transition also occurs at later time periods whenever a group begins to adopt an agricultural way of life. Some people today continue to live in small villages and retain some Agricultural Wave characteristics similar to earlier people. A section on chiefdoms and a case study of Cahokia is included.

Chapter six—The Urban Wave—begins in Mesopotamia around 3500 BCE, when some groups of people evolve out of sedentary agricultural villages to develop more populous and complex urban societies. This wave marks a transition to what we call civilization and all its accompanying characteristics. Some people in the world today continue to practice conventions that are characteristic of the Urban Wave, especially its religious traditions. A section on nomadic/pastoral people is also included. The Urban Wave is further examined in three historical periods: ancient, classical, and post-classical civilizations.

The Modern Wave, chapter seven, emerges around 1500 CE when some Western European countries rise to prominence, beginning with the conquest of the Western hemisphere and followed by interaction with and subjugation of societies throughout the world. Modern characteristics, shaped largely by Western Europeans, diffuse around the world after 1500. The Modern Wave is arranged into the early modern era, the modern industrial era, and the modern 20th century.

Chapter eight—The Global Wave—is presently developing across the world. Humans in this wave create globally interconnected communication, transportation, financial, commercial, and trade networks and they use sophisticated technological innovations. The five worldviews—indigenous, modern, fundamentalists, globalized, and transformative—are further explained.

Features of *Waves of Global Change: A Holistic World History*

This book is organized as a framework for teaching and learning about world history. It is not an all-inclusive, voluminous, expensive textbook. The purpose of this holistic approach to world history is to provide a model or overall organization, in which all of the materials connect and relate to each other. One of the advantages of this world history survey is its flexibility, it can be adapted to a course's allotment of time, and a students' interest and ability levels. As I see it, many world history textbooks are too costly, contain too much detail, are rigid in their applications, and lack a coherent theme. This survey of world history addresses all these problems; it is very affordable, highlights general concepts instead of over-whelming detail, is flexible, and has a coherent theme! For example, when studying the Urban Wave, students and instructors may wish to explore more about the Roman Empire or the Mayans. The free, on-line resources provide additional materials on a variety of subjects that each individual class may choose in order to customize their particular study of world history. It is my intention that with this approach to world history, no two world history courses need to be identical!

You will notice that in each of the eight chapters there are two recurring features: "Questions to Consider" and "Insights." The Questions to Consider feature has been designed for the reader to take a pause and reflect on questions that connect the reading material to his/her own life. The Insights are designed for the reader to think about the reading in a different light. The Insights are purposely provocative, and not intended to have a right or wrong answer, but merely to spur critical and creative thinking about the topics.

As with any world history book, I, as the author, have a particular perspective. This holistic world history is no exception. I clearly state that I am recounting world history from a holistic perspective, further informed, as you will see, through a transformative worldview. Although my worldview is clear, it is not my intention to discourage dialogue and debate about the merits of this approach. In fact, many students and educators may disagree and prefer a more traditional or entirely different approach. My reason for using a holistic perspective is not to foist my ideas on others, but merely to help fill in the gaps of the traditional approach to world history with an alternative perspective. I hope you will explore this approach to world history with an open and inquiring mind; questioning not only my ideas and perspective, but your own as well. I wish you the best in this journey.

Accompanying Book for Educators

Accompanying this world history survey is a separate book *Waves of Global Change: An Educators Handbook for Teaching a Holistic World History*. This book provides helpful suggestions and strategies for teaching a holistic world history, and it is useful for teaching other history, social studies, and humanities courses. There are also on-line resources accompanying this handbook.

Bibliography, Endnotes, and Glossary

In order to conserve space and reduce the cost of the book, the full bibliography and expanded glossary are available on-line. The expanded glossary defines numerous terms related to world history—including highlighted terms in the book. A glossary that gives definitions of only terms highlighted in bold in the book is included at the back of the book.

On-line Resources

www.global-awareness.org/worldhistory

This book has free, on-line resources for instructors and students. Each of the eight chapters will include some or all of the following resources:

A. study questions
B. activities, critical thinking, research suggestions
C. charts and puzzles
D. additional resources
E. power point slides
F. maps
G. media
H. suggested reading
I. national world history standards
J. assessment suggestions

Instructors are invited to customize these on-line resources or use their own materials for their individual courses. We also invite instructors to contribute to our expanding on-line resource base with their own suggestions. As always, we invite your questions, comments, and suggestions. Please email info@global-awareness.org or visit our website at www.global-awareness.org.

The Second Edition

This book is the second edition to the first edition published in 2011. This edition has a new chapter 8: The Global Wave that incorporates the most recent developments.

Kind Regards,
Denise R. Ames
Center for Global Awareness
Albuquerque, New Mexico, USA

Chapter 1

A Holistic World History: An Introduction

"The significant problems we face cannot be solved at the same level of thinking we were at when we created them."

— Albert Einstein

TOKI GAWA: A LIFE OF CHANGE

Deep in the Amazon rainforest in a remote village along the river lives Toki Gawa, her lined face and hunched over backbone indicate her advanced age. She has seen many changes in her lifetime. As a girl she lived with her ancestral people the Wobi, an indigenous group of hunting and gathering or foraging people. Toki doesn't know her exact age. She has no need to know, but missionaries who have visited her people told her that she is probably 90 years old. One thing Toki does know—she has experienced many disruptions in her lifetime, some that she thinks are good and some that made her angry. She probably has experienced more changes than humans from any other period of time in history.

As a youngster Toki's people foraged for food in the dense rain forest. Her mother was very knowledgeable about all the edible plants that were just footsteps away from their camp. Toki's mother delighted in teaching her all she knew about the best edible foods and ways to make them into a meal. Toki was a fast learner and in particular she knew what plants, if prepared correctly, could cure whatever ailment someone might have, from bug bites to stomach pain. This was important since deadly diseases and infections could cut short her fellow foragers' lives very quickly. Most did not live beyond 40 years old. Life was precarious for all of them.

Toki's nomadic band of foragers moved their campsite several times during the year, but would always come back to the same sites the next year. Toki loved the campsite, which was a constant source of amusement and where storytelling and gossip enlivened their leisure time. It was at the campsite that Toki and others participated in exuberant dances and precise rituals. They believed the jaguar was one of the greatest spirits of the forest and they were careful not to disturb the spirits. If they did, they believed there could be retribution of some kind, such as not being able to locate the best nuts in the forest. She and others greatly respected the natural world and felt the spirits in the trees, river, animals, and sky enveloped them like a cocoon. Toki's life was filled with wonder, awe, superstition and fear of the spirits.

As a young girl Toki treasured her few personal possessions, a hair comb made out of bone, and necklaces out of shells. But Toki didn't think of herself as poor, since she didn't know what poor meant. She had all she needed: family, shelter, amusement, enough food, and the challenge of learning all the plants of the forest.

When Toki was a teenager, she encountered another group of people in a clearing in the tropical forest who had just moved into the area. Although the Wobi people had occasional contact with other foraging people, they had never seen people who lived in huts that couldn't be easily moved or fields of grain. They cautiously approached the strangers, who were not surprised to see them. Unbeknownst to Toki, she had encountered farmers for the first time. Some of the elders of Toki's group began to communicate as best they could with these strange farming people; soon the distrust dissolved and they were invited to a meal. Toki didn't think the food was very tasty; lots of grain and no monkey meat, but she enjoyed meeting the people. Toki's group decided to stay awhile with the villagers. Soon Toki was informed that the elders had decided that she, who was of marriageable age, should stay in the village and marry one of the eligible young men, since there were no eligible men in her foraging band. Although Toki did not want to do this, she was assured that her mother and family would visit often. She finally agreed. The elaborate and joyous marriage ceremony was planned for the next week; they would all participate in it.

Toki and her husband lived in a small hut and soon she became a mother of two daughters and a son. Toki found that being a farmer was much harder than gathering plants. Every day she had to get up very early to feed the animals and tend to the garden. But still there was time for playing with her children and the other children of her village. True to their word, her mother and family visited regularly. Toki was able to take the knowledge that she acquired as a gatherer and apply these skills to the growing of grains, vegetables, and tubers. Her fellow villagers also relied on her for treating their various ailments with herbs and medicines that she collected from the nearby forest. But if someone broke a leg she was powerless to help; the victim would limp for the rest of her life and often die young from the complications.

Toki was also able to make many things such as pottery and baskets, which were needed as storage devices for surplus crops, and jewelry, which was for adornment. Although Toki still did not know she was poor, on occasion, when there was a drought or insect infestation, the villagers would be hungry in the winter months since their stored food supplies would run out. Some in the village would die of starvation. Toki thought that it was strange that the villagers worshipped a goddess, believing that it was the female power that brought life not only to children but also to the crops as well. The villagers believed the goddess would ward off crop failure and ensure enough to eat through the lean winter months. She went along with what to her was a different religion, since the villagers were her family now.

It was one beautiful spring afternoon when Toki encountered another group of very different people than she had ever met before. The pale looking people came down the river in canoes laden with all kinds of goods. The people didn't speak her language but they had someone with them who could say some words in a language she understood. Who were these strange looking people, she wondered. She soon found out. The villagers welcomed the guests and treated them respectfully. The guests were also very respectful and interested to know more about Toki and her fellow villagers, especially about the way they worshipped the goddess and all the different rituals and ceremonies they performed to show their awe and respect for her. Soon Toki and the villagers learned that the newcomers preferred their god to the goddess. They called themselves Christian missionaries and preached that a man called Jesus was the savior god. They suggested that Toki and the villagers worship their god. Toki and the others liked the new people and said they would go along with their kind of religion, but secretly they also continued to worship the goddess and perform their secret rituals and ceremonies. Now Toki knew about and followed three different religious practices!

Soon more Christians came to live in the village and they built new houses, schools and churches for the villagers. Toki liked the Christians, but sometimes she thought they were too bossy and told her things that she should do when she liked her ways better. One thing she liked was that they taught her to read and write. She liked to read about people in different lands. She was also happy to have her children learn to read as well, and they received an education in the school the missionaries built. She was also happy that the Christians brought doctors to help heal people. She was amazed that the medicines they used to treat such diseases as malaria actually worked and that the operations they performed on people with broken bones really helped them. Other villagers, like herself, were living longer lives thanks to their medicine and doctors. But Toki got angry when they said she should not do the farming anymore; they said it was a man's job to do the outside work and he was the head of the family. They insisted that she should take care of the children and the house. She thought this was crazy since she was the one who knew the most about farming. As more Christians came to visit and tell the villagers about their religion, some of them went with the Christians to faraway places. Some never returned.

What came next for Toki and her villagers was even more change. Shortly after the Christians arrived more pale people came to visit. They didn't call themselves Christians though; as it was explained to her they were business people looking for minerals. She thought it was very strange that these business people wanted to buy the land from the villagers and take out minerals from Mother Earth. First of all, Toki had no idea what "buy the land" meant. She said that the land belonged to all the villagers and no one could "own" Mother Earth. But the business people insisted. Toki and the other villagers decided they had no choice but to let the business people take some of the land for the minerals, although they had no idea what they would use the minerals for. After the business people started to mine Toki and the villagers were very sorry that they agreed to let them come in and take the land. Big machines that she had never seen before rolled over their land and started to dig into Mother Earth. They were noisy and created a mess wherever they went. The miners used chemicals to extract the minerals from the ore and it left poison on the ground. Soon the rivers had a funny smell and many of the villagers became sick and died. Toki was very angry. When the miners wanted to dig for more minerals, Toki joined the other villagers in a protest against their actions. Soon the miners were forced to leave, although a great deal of damage had already been done.

Her children, who were now grown, had decided to leave the village and go to the city where they could find work, since they didn't want to be farmers. They said it was too much work to be a farmer. Toki was too old to go to the city and she wanted to stay in the village. Even though her children returned to visit her, she sadly realized her children had changed a great deal and were now part of the modern world. The Christians seemed to like the business people and told her that the mining would bring prosperity to their village. They would soon get money for the minerals taken from the Earth, and she would be rich. Toki said she would be rich if she could live with her family again.

Once the mining was all done, another group of business people came to see Toki and the villagers. By now Toki was the elder of the village and greatly respected by those who still remained. The new visitors said they were medical researchers and wanted to harvest medicinal plants from what was left of the forest. They thought that these plants could be made into medicines that would save millions of people's lives around the world. Toki thought this was a good idea so she agreed to help them find the plants. She told them many of her ancient ways of identifying medicinal plants. They promised her that she would get lots of money from these patented plants. She had no idea what a patent meant, since she never did understand how individual people could own pieces of Mother Earth, and she was leery about promises of money, since she had no need for it. She later found out that the research laboratory that harvested the plants made millions of dollars off of the knowledge that she shared with them; she was happy that she was able to help save millions of people's lives. Indeed, she was now a great healer of many people.

Now that many of the plants that she knew and loved had been harvested by the medical researchers, another strange occurrence for Toki came about. In faraway lands she was known as a wise elder woman of the forest. She was now famous. People from faraway wanted to come and visit her and have her share her wisdom with them. She agreed and the village where she had lived for years became an eco-tourist site. Hundreds of people came to visit and the tour operators set up camps for the visitors to live in. They took walks in the remaining forest and looked at the birds and wild life. They would ask her lots of questions and she would patiently answer. They also took lots of pictures of her and the few remaining elders of the village. It was annoying to pose for so many pictures, but the visitors seemed happy when she agreed. The visitors said they loved the way she lived so close to the land. She replied, "You can live close to the land if you want but it is hard work." Toki didn't think the visitors really wanted to live off the land, since their lives were pretty easy compared to the farmers of her village. She was surprised to learn that most of their work was done through little metal objects that they held in their hands and always looked at and talked into. But she liked the visitors and was glad to share all she knew about living as a forager and farmer. One visitor said her way of life was very different from theirs and that she should be featured in a magazine called National Geographic. She wondered if this was good or bad. But she good-naturedly agreed and her face adorned the cover of the magazine.

As Toki looked back over her life she was amazed at all the different changes that she experienced. She met some very nice people, who were kind to her. But she couldn't help wondering if all the changes she experienced made her life any better. She chuckled to herself and thought: "it all depends on what better means." Each group of people she met had a different way in which they thought their lives could be better. The foraging band thought it was best to have leisure time and sit around the campfire telling stories; the villagers thought it was best to plant crops to have enough to eat and worship the goddess; the Christian missionaries thought it was best to worship their god Jesus and learn to read and write; the business people thought it was best to take minerals from the earth to make things to make life easier and make money; the medical people thought it was best to invent medicine to cure millions of people of disease; and the tourists thought it was best to learn as much as possible about all kinds of things. Which one was best? She really didn't know. One thing she did know for certain is that life is all about change, and indeed she was the queen of changes and that being able to adapt helped her survive.

Toki is not an actual person. However, there are a handful of people in our lifetime that could have lived a life such as Toki's. Her fictitious way of life is unusual because it represents the transformative changes that have occurred throughout the world in our human history. Although these changes have taken place over thousands of years, Toki's character has lived through "five waves of change" that are the subject of this world history book. The five waves are the Communal Wave, Toki's foraging way of life; the Agricultural Wave, where Toki lived as a village farmer; the Urban Wave, where Toki encountered the Christian missionaries, which grew out of the universal religions of that time period; the Modern Wave, where the business people mined for minerals to fuel industrialization; and the Global Wave, where the medical researchers and eco-tourist companies took Toki's indigenous wisdom for knowledge and profit. Although Toki is not real, her life story is real; we can keep her in our thoughts as we learn about our human story through the five waves of global change.

AN INTRODUCTION TO A HOLISTIC WORLD HISTORY

Tsunami-wave shifts are occurring in our world today. We live in an increasingly interdependent world, and we are grappling with rapid changes that are dramatically affecting our lives. We are attempting to sort out what paths to follow today and into the future, while also trying to make sense of the momentous changes affecting our fragile planet. Global problems of monumental proportion are battering us at such an alarming frequency that we are often paralyzed into fear and inaction. These global problems require a collective effort to solve, something that we have never had to undertake in the past and for which there is no template. The question is where to begin? Perhaps one way to better understand the enormity of the issues and consequences of our actions that our collective species faces today is to draw upon lessons from the past. This holistic world history offers us valuable insights that we can learn from the past. Therefore, this history is a contribution to helping us sort-out and put into perspective where we have come from and where we are heading as a human species.

World History. The very concept seems overwhelming. There is no way we can know everything about the past. Many of us are intimidated by the vastness of the subject and never have been able to fully grasp the extent of its scope. It is an immense subject. But instead of casting the whole subject aside as insurmountable, I would like to share with you a different way of learning about world history. After all, our more interdependent and complex world necessitates that we have an understanding of the world around us. I call my approach a holistic world history. This approach simplifies world history into an understandable framework that can help you better comprehend what is happening in the world today and in the past. I have devoted many years to the development and teaching of this holistic approach and now have pulled all the research and experimenting together into this book.

The term **holistic** is used to describe this approach to world history. Holistic in this context means that as all a society's cultural traits—political, economic, technological, cultural, religious, social, values, attitudes, environmental—reinforce and support each other. A change in any cultural trait influences the others. This means that a society's economy reflects its political policies, its treatment of the environment reflects the values of its citizens, its technology reflects its economic characteristics, and so forth. For example, in the U.S. a brown

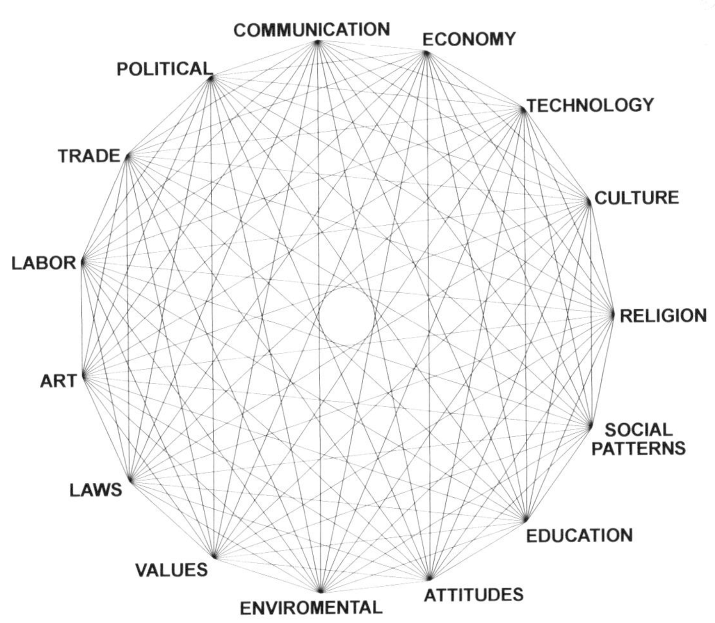

smog from car emissions often hangs over a large city such as Los Angeles, California. Obviously this brown smog is unhealthy and if cars were outlawed, the hazardous smog would be gone. However, the entire U.S. economy is dependent upon fossil fuels to run its transportation system and therefore, the smog is a necessary by-product of this system as it currently operates. The term holistic emphasizes the full range of relations among the cultural traits of a system and the ways the operation of those parts helps to perpetuate the whole system.

This **holistic world history** model studies the world's past by viewing it as a system of interactions instead of as separate, unrelated parts. We tstudy the whole system to see how the individual parts, events, and people of history relate to the whole. With this holistic perspective history is viewed in the broadest possible context in order to understand interconnections and interdependence. This approach offers a "big picture" vision of the past drawn from various disciplines—history, sociology, anthropology, political science, geography, economics, psychology, religion, ecology, the humanities, and the sciences. With this holistic model we gain a deeper appreciation of the world we live in today, how this present time is connected to our shared human past, and how we might help create a life-enhancing future. And the model helps to connect seemingly disparate strands of the past and present into a holistic process that provides a workable, intelligible framework for understanding our shared history.

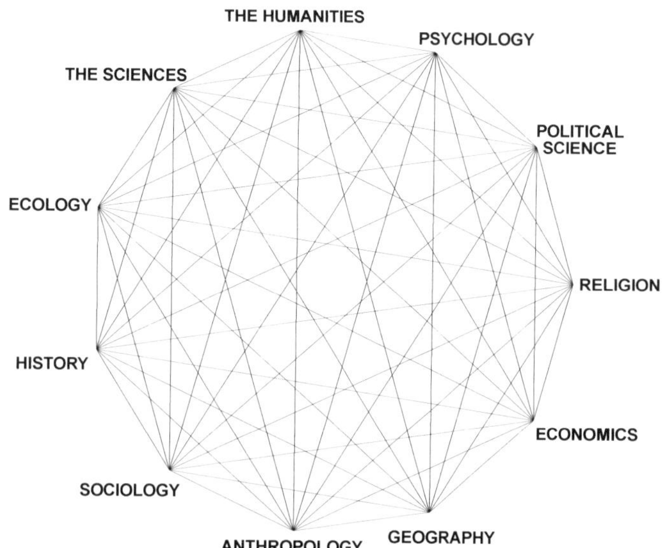

This holistic world history offers an alternative to the more familiar chronological and linear approach to history that I call traditional history. Most history analyzes just parts of history. For example, a traditional study of the French Revolution analyzes the separate events but usually fails to connect that turmoil with the broader context that gives rise to political revolutions in the Western hemisphere and England. Since the connections and patterns in history are ignored, valuable opportunities to learn lessons are denied. In the case of the French Revolution, one lesson to be learned is that the old system of feudalism in which the landed aristocracy, authority of the church and the absolute right of kings was giving way to the modern system in which constitutional rights and capitalism were hailed as the new institutions.

If we pay attention, our history can teach us valuable lessons from the past that can be applied to our life today. History needs to be more than a dry collection of interesting but unconnected facts about the past; instead it can be a rich gift from generations long ago to the present generation. Our study of history can provide a worthy experience relevant to our lives today from which wisdom and guidance can be gleaned, not only for making informed decisions about the present but also to gain valuable knowledge for fashioning a viable, healthy, stable and sustainable future.

The increasing complexity and interdependence of the world today calls for a new perspective. Our global community faces a long list of problems—climate change, resource depletion, poverty, wars, terrorism, inequality, population pressures, political corruption, and many others. Although the list hasn't changed much over the past few decades, the problems have significantly accelerated and intensified and, obviously, have not been solved. The current mode of thinking, which looks at only parts of issues and problems in isolation, will not move us forward to create a more livable, stable, and hopeful future. Instead of looking at each isolated part of world history, we need to understand the whole world as a system. This holistic approach to world history is a step in that direction. But this holistic approach, which sees a society's cultural traits reinforce each other, is part of a larger approach called systems thinking. In systems thinking individual elements of world history are part of a puzzle that, when pieced together, can give greater meaning to the whole panoramic picture of our world. By examining the past more holistically and through a systems thinking lens, we can gather wisdom that will be useful in addressing and solving some of the critical global issues that are begging for immediate attention. To understand systems thinking, let us next turn to a description of it.

Questions to Consider

1. List several issues or problems in your school or community that would benefit from a holistic approach in trying to solve them.
2. In the above text, I state that "If we pay attention, our history can teach us valuable lessons from the past that can be applied to our life today." What do you think we can learn from the past?

SYSTEMS THINKING: A DIFFERENT APPROACH TO HISTORY

Systems thinking informs this world history. But first, let's look at what is a system. A **system** is defined as something that maintains its existence and functions as a whole through the interaction of its parts. To put it another way, a system is a collection of parts that interact with each other to function as a whole and continually affect each other over time. Systems are not only interconnected, they are logically organized around a shared purpose. For example, the human body is a system; each part of the body affects another. A school is a system as well. Relationships and the mutual influence of the parts are more important than the number or size of the parts. These relationships and systems can be simple or complex.[1]

This holistic model of world history draws upon the field of systems thinking that is currently being applied to business, the sciences, health, medicine, and other fields. **Systems thinking** looks beyond what appear to be isolated and independent events to identify deeper structures within the system. The whole system and the interrelationship of the parts to the whole are the focus, not just the isolated basic building blocks. Seeing the connections between events is a basic

HOLISTIC AND SYSTEMS THINKING APPROACH

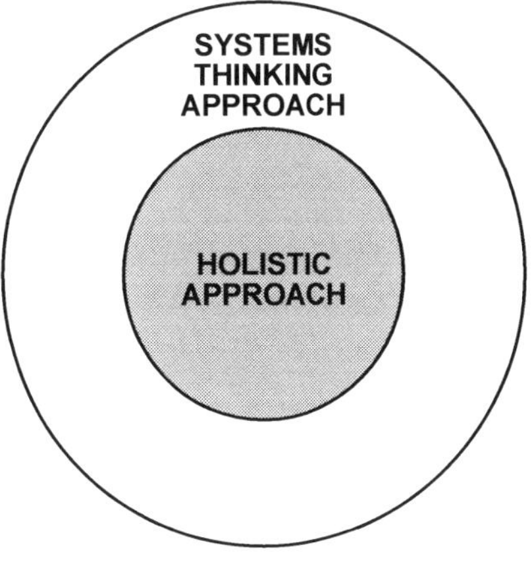

principle of systems thinking, where connections and the larger, context inform the subject. In other words, as the saying goes: "see the forest, not just the trees."

Systems thinking views issues and problems in the context of the larger whole; it is complementary to analytical thinking. Analysis means taking something apart in order to understand it and to see how the pieces work individually. But a system—such as world history—cannot be understood by analysis alone. The complement of analysis is synthesis, which means relating the parts to the harmonious whole. Deeper understanding is gained through synthesis and analysis, rather than analysis alone.[2]

Conventional Thinking

If systems thinking is so wonderful, why haven't we been using this type of thinking all along? Good question. Changing the way we see the world or our worldview does not happen easily or quickly; conventional ways of thinking have deeply entrenched roots that resist change. When using **conventional thinking**, sometimes called traditional, linear or mechanistic thinking, people tend to see simple sequences of cause and effect that are limited in time and space, which assumes that cause and effect occur within a close time frame. But the causes and effects may be far apart in time and space. For example, industrial pollutants have accumulated over a 200 year time period since the beginning of the Industrial Revolution around 1800, but the effects are only beginning to be felt today in the phenomenon known as climate change or commonly referred to as global warming.

Conventional thinking segments issues, events, and even world history into small divisible parts for careful analysis and scrutiny. The world is seen as a collection of separate objects while the relationships are secondary. In a systems view, networks of relationships are nested into larger networks. Relationships are primary while the

Conventional Thinking

- separates and divides people, nations, events, cultures and actions.
- sees simple sequences of cause and effect that are limited in time and space.
- uses only causes and effects to explain historical events.
- zeroes in to fault and blame an individual or group.
- applies analysis not synthesis.

In a system...

- parts are interconnected and function as a whole.
- a complex web of relationships unifies the parts.
- the system is changed by addition or subtraction of parts.
- arrangement of the pieces is crucial.
- behavior depends on total structure: change the structure and the behavior changes.

Aspen trees, all the roots are connected.
Photo by Denise Ames

objects are secondary.[3] An example of conventional thinking is when school officials administer standardized tests to students, who earn a score that ranks them with other students. This isolated score does not take into consideration the whole student: his/her relationship to other students, teachers, or parents, his/her contribution to the community, or even the student's ability to think about the subject beyond the questions in the test. The test score only represents one aspect of the student's ability, yet is given undue significance in classifying a student's abilities.

Conventional thinking continues to shape Western society in many ways. One example is the way in which schoolroom desks are arranged in linear straight rows; this arrangement reflects linear or hierarchical thinking in which the teacher is given a position of authority at the front of the classroom. Individual housing patterns in suburbs that are separated into "little boxes" and unconnected to each other through community space signifies compartmentalized thinking. Medical treatment of a patient's isolated symptoms with medications or surgery without recognizing the impact on the entire body is an example of conventional thinking. The way the international political structure is organized into separate, autonomous nations exemplifies conventional ways of organizing the world. And even in world history, individual regions or nations and events are usually separately studied, while general themes or patterns that connect the nations and regions are secondary or ignored all together. All these examples represent how conventional thinking is expressed in our daily lives. This way of thinking is habitual, familiar deeply embedded, and hard to change.

Questions to Consider

1. Think of and write down several ways in which conventional thinking is used in your school or community. How might systems thinking change these situations?

REASONS TO USE SYSTEMS THINKING IN WORLD HISTORY

Our daily lives are dramatically changing, even though we might not want to acknowledge it, while our future at this point looks uncertain, insecure and unpredictable. Although many of us wish to hide our heads in the sand and pay no attention to our critical situation, the reality is that we urgently need to address crucial global issues which are adversely impacting all our lives and threatening our future well-being. But the complexity of the situation requires that a different way of learning, thinking, teaching, and communicating be used to even address, let alone solve, these urgent issues such as climate change and resource depletion. Although it can be argued that conventional thinking served us fairly well for centuries (if you overlook wars, genocide, species eradication, and environmental devastation) this type of thinking cannot cope with the monumental problem-solving challenges that face us in an interconnected world. Therefore, it behooves us to be aware of a systems thinking approach and consider it as a viable alternative method that may be successfully applied in many different areas and situations, including world history.

Secondly, a detailed analysis of any specific problem or issue in isolation limits understanding of its complexity and ramifications. A look beyond individual issues towards a broader perspective is necessary, where an individual issue is seen as part of a coherent whole. Studying something in isolation, separate from the context in which it exists, restricts understanding because it does not include the effect one part has on another, or on the whole. But when systems thinking is used, the relationships among problems are primary and any proposed adjustment or correction to the system takes into consideration how all aspects affect the whole situation. For example, when planning for the development and growth in cities and suburbs, consideration of the availability of fresh water should be given high priority.

Third, we can't solve any of the problems on our own because only one perspective is not enough to wholly understand a problem; we need to be aware of as many different perspectives as possible. Therefore, it is useful to have people from diverse ethnic, racial, class, and gender perspectives working together on an issue, as well as people who have different personality types and worldviews. Those holding different perspectives provide unique angles for looking at problems and are instrumental in contributing to more effective solutions to problems.

Fourth, a systems thinking perspective enables us to understand why simply fault-finding is such a futile activity. Singling out the decisions or actions of participants to establish culpability for the cause of a problem is often limiting, as most blame is misdirected. A problem is usually not just one person's fault, for most people are usually doing the best they can within the system they are working. The structure of the system, not the effort of the people, has created most of the problems and determines the outcome. Just listen to a television or radio newscast and recount how many times the interviewer asks someone, "And who is to blame for this or that failure?" Systems thinkers progress beyond simply seeing the events and mishaps in isolation to seeing patterns of interaction and the underlying structures or worldviews that are accountable for the problems. Systems thinking is always process thinking; it explains things in terms of their context or situation.

World history is a system. And world history will be studied as a system in this book. It might not be easy to think of it as a system, it might seem strange or unfamiliar at first, but as we practice this type of thinking and apply it, the benefits will hopefully be recognized. There is nothing to lose and everything to gain from looking at world history from this different perspective.

Benefits of Systems Thinking[4]

1. recognizes episodes or patterns that underlie events.
2. sees underlying structures that are responsible for the episodes or patterns.
3. learns from history by discerning patterns so that we are not doomed to repeat the same problem.
4. predicts events and prepares for them, rather than being helpless in their wake.
5. appreciates how our thinking is inseparable from the problems we encounter.
6. understands obvious explanations and majority views are not always right.
7. goes beyond blaming others or one's self.
8. challenges, probes, and clarifies our own habitual ways of thinking.
9. encourages long term thinking.
10. predicts unintended consequences.

Questions to Consider

1. In what ways would systems thinking benefit you in your life? In your studies?
2. Do you think a systems thinking approach is a beneficial way to study world history? Explain.

THE INTERACTING PARTS OF A SYSTEM

Systems are quite complex and contain many different interacting components. It will be helpful to next examine how the system actually works.

The stability of a system—whether it changes or remains steady—depends on many factors, including the size, number and variety of the subsystems within it and the type and degree of connectivity between them. A large complex system is not necessarily an unstable one. Many complex systems are remarkably stable and resist change.

Examples of Stable Systems

- habits
- Supreme Court
- celebration of Christmas
- Judaism
- a lifelong marriage
- the Catholic Church
- Islam
- families

Overall, stability is a positive aspect, but it comes with a price: resistance to change. When a stable system does change, it can change rapidly and quite drastically. There is a threshold beyond which a system will suddenly change or break down. If it is under a lot of pressure a small trigger can cause collapse— the proverbial "straw that breaks the camel's back." Or, systems can change instead of collapsing. For example, with just the right combination of steps, smart leaders can sometimes initiate change with surprising ease. This is the principle of leverage. **Leverage** doesn't mean piling on the pressure, but knowing where to intervene so that a small effort can get a huge result. How do you apply leverage? First ask what stops the change, and then look at the connections that are holding in place the part you want to change. Cut or weaken these

The straw that broke the camel's back

connections and the change may be easy. Applying strategic leverage to initiate change is a key principle of systems thinking.[5]

Feedback loops are integral components of a system. The parts in a **feedback** system are all interconnected directly or indirectly, and when change occurs in one part it ripples out to affect all the other parts. The new parts change and the effect of this change ripples back to affect the original part. The original part then responds to the new influences and the influences then come back or feed back to the original part in a modified way, making a loop, not a straight line.

Reinforcing feedback is when changes in the whole system feed back to amplify the original change. Change goes through the system, pro-

FEEDBACK LOOP

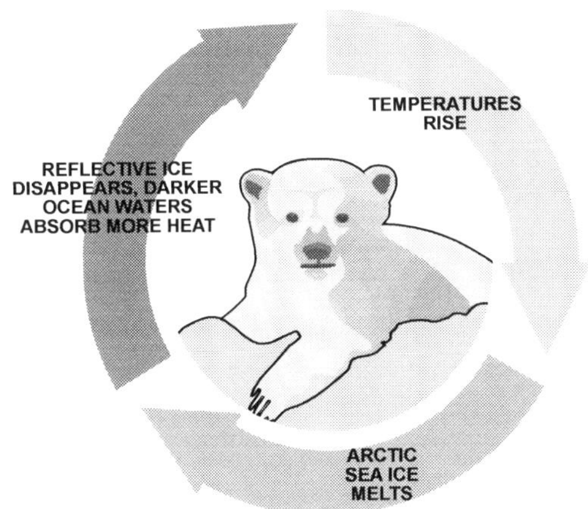
TEMPERATURES RISE
REFLECTIVE ICE DISAPPEARS, DARKER OCEAN WATERS ABSORB MORE HEAT
ARCTIC SEA ICE MELTS

REINFORCING FEEDBACK LOOP

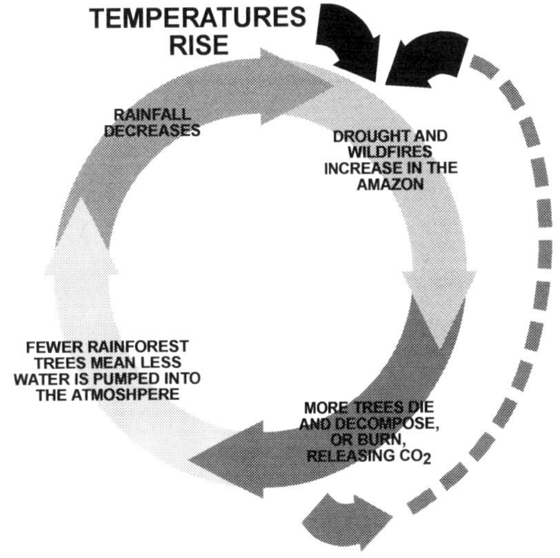
TEMPERATURES RISE
RAINFALL DECREASES
DROUGHT AND WILDFIRES INCREASE IN THE AMAZON
FEWER RAINFOREST TREES MEAN LESS WATER IS PUMPED INTO THE ATMOSHPERE
MORE TREES DIE AND DECOMPOSE, OR BURN, RELEASING CO2

ducing more change in the same direction as the initial change. Reinforcing feedback drives a system in the way it is going. Reinforcing feedback is more commonly referred to as positive feedback but this can be confusing since not all feedback is positive or beneficial. Reinforcing feedback may lead to growth or decline, depending on the starting conditions. We use several reinforcing feedback metaphors in everyday conversation to help describe this process: we're on a roll, jump on the bandwagon, it's downhill all the way, spiraling into oblivion, the sky's the limit, a ticket to heaven, can do no wrong, on the way up, on the slippery slope, snowballing out of control, and nothing lasts forever. [6]

The second type of feedback, **balancing feedback**, limits, restricts, and impedes change and keeps the system stable. Although more commonly called negative feedback, it is neither good nor bad but merely means the system resists change. All systems have balancing feedback loops to stay stable because all systems have a goal, even if it is to remain as they are. Balancing feedback loops keep our environment steady, such as in a rainforest, prairie, coral reef, desert, or marsh. However, today climate change is disrupting the balancing feedback loops and creating change in the atmosphere. Other examples of balancing feedback are bodily healing, body temperature, air conditioning, a car's cruise control, predator and prey relationships, food and population balance, supply and demand, and election cycles.

The more dynamically complex the system, the longer the feedback takes to travel around the network connection. When there is a time delay between cause and effect we often assume there is no effect at all. This delay may fool us into adjusting too late or too much. Many scientists believe this is the case with climate change: what we are doing to correct climate change is too little too late. The feedback delays in signaling climate change have been too far apart in time for us to recognize that the main cause is industrial pollutants and the burning of fossil fuels. Hopefully, we can make the needed adjustments.

Questions to Consider

1. Think of examples in your life where you might use reinforcing feedback. Balancing feedback.

WORLDVIEWS: THE WAY WE LOOK AT THE WORLD

Systems thinking is a viable method for solving the myriad of problems that we face and an interesting way of looking at world history. But the question remains, if we all know what the problems are and we have known for decades, why haven't we been able to solve the problems? In fact, why have they gotten worse? Why isn't systems thinking within our radar screen as a problem solving approach? Quite simply, I would argue, because these global problems are caused in large part by the ways we think, communicate,

Ways to Use Systems Thinking

- Look at the whole system, not just its parts.
- Appreciate how our thinking is inseparable from the problems we encounter.
- Transform the thinking that led to the problem in the first place.
- Scan the big picture context.
- Challenge the idea that you can judge a person's behavior/actions independent of the system s/he is in.
- Use circular or cyclical and deep thinking, more than just linear, vertical, or horizontal thinking.
- Apply maps, models, and visual images that make it easier to see connections, relationships, and patterns.
- Draw on diverse perspective when viewing chaotic events.
- Apply systems thinking to your own way of thinking because our beliefs are themselves a system.

learn, and understand! Our way of thinking or worldview heavily determines the kind of political, economic and social structures that we create, and those, in turn, create the patterns and events occurring in the world. You might respond and say that if we had a better president or more responsible corporations then the problems could be solved; or you might blame governmental and economic roadblocks for the impasse—after all, Congress moves at a snail's pace. However, the real roadblocks are not material but mental. Remember one of the systems thinking principles states that placing blame on individuals does not solve the problem; it is the underlying structures that create the problems in the first place.

If the ways of thinking that got us to this point are inadequate for coping with the future, we need to purposely learn to explore new ways of thinking. Let us first try to understand the nature of the problem. Systems thinkers often use an iceberg as an analogy for looking at a problem. At the tip of the iceberg, the 10-20 percent seen above the surface represents events. These events are reported on the television news, headlined in the newspaper, or featured on the Internet. But looking beneath the surface level of the iceberg's events are the patterns. For example, we see the event of Hurricane Katrina on the news,

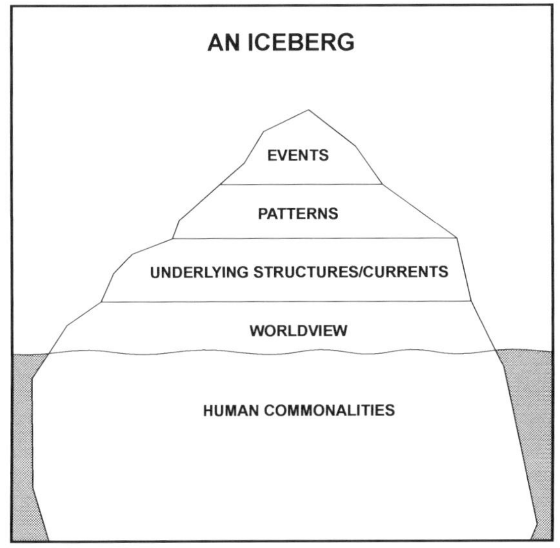

but the hurricane is not an isolated event; it is part of larger patterns of hurricanes and extreme weather that are wreaking havoc across the world. And if we look further below the surface of the iceberg's patterns, we see that the political, economic, technological, social, environmental, and cultural structures (I call these structures currents later in this world history) create these patterns. Many scientists attribute such violent and extreme weather conditions as Hurricane Katrina to climate change, which is caused by the burning of fossil fuels. The modern economic system, the underlying structure or current, is based on the burning of fossil fuels for energy consumption to drive our modern way of life, while the environmental impact of burning fossil fuels is an unfortunate but necessary byproduct.Farther down towards the base of the iceberg, lies what I call the worldview. This worldview, in turn, influences the underlying structures (currents), patterns, and events.[7] Our worldview is fashioned around the idea that unlimited economic growth is the unquestioned path to prosperity and well-being. However, the environmental repercussions of this worldview are finally revealing the unintended consequences of this unquestioned belief in unlimited growth. Finally, at the very base of the iceberg are our human behaviors, the universal human commonalities that shape who we are as a species (more on human commonalities in chapter 3). Therefore, if we want to change the events and patterns we must change the underlying structures (currents) that create them; this means we need to modify the way we think, learn and communicate. In other words we must transform our behaviors or worldview.

A Worldview

What is a worldview? A **worldview** is an overall perspective from which one sees and interprets the world; a set of simplifying suppositions about how the world works and what is seen and not seen. It is an internal collection of assumptions, held by an individual or a group that are firmly believed to be self-evident truths. These assumptions shape an individual's beliefs, ideas, attitudes, and values, which, in turn, affect behaviors and actions. A worldview is a paradigm, a fundamental way of looking at reality which functions as a filter. It admits information that is consistent with our deeply held expectations about the world while guiding us to disregard information that challenges or disproves these expectations. When we look through a filter we usually see through it, rather than seeing it—so it is with worldviews. A worldview acts as a built-in "operating system," even though most people are unaware that their perceptions are filtered through it. Worldviews are rarely brought out into the light of day, so people are not usually aware of them. They are hidden deep in our human consciousness, all the while quietly shaping our reactions to new ideas and information, guiding our decisions, and ordering expectations for the future. Every book read, policy statement enacted, vote cast, the way children are raised, the way solutions are made, a particular method of teaching, opinions about globalization, a religious sermon, and even the approach used to write and teach world history are shaped as much, if not more, by our worldview as by any objective data or analysis.[8] But if worldviews are so important in influencing what we do, what are the prevailing worldviews that we all hold so dearly?

Contemporary Worldviews

A unique period of human history is occurring at this time, a fifth turning—what I have called the Global Wave—that is transforming our human story as this new millennium dawns. Within the Global Wave there is not one all-pervasive, homogenous way of thinking and perceiving reality. Instead I have identified five often contentious and conflicting worldviews, with contradictory ways of knowing and understanding the world, each promoting dissimilar visions for the present and future. In the United States and throughout the world, most people identify with one or another of these worldviews. The following is a brief summary of the five major worldviews: indigenous, fundamentalist, modern, globalized, and transformative. (Chapter 8: also addresses the five worldviews.)

Five Worldviews

1. Indigenous
2. Modern
3. Fundamentalist
4. Globalized
5. Transformative

Indigenous Worldview

The indigenous worldview is held by very few people today. **Indigenous** peoples are any ethnic group who share a similar ethnic identity and inhabit a geographic region with which they have the earliest known historical connection.[9] The adjective indigenous has the common meaning of "from" or "of the original origin." Therefore, in a sense any given people, ethnic group or community may be described as being indigenous in reference to some particular region or location. Indigenous peoples are usually a politically underprivileged group, whose ethnic identity is different from the nation in power and who have been an ethnic entity in the locality before the present ruling nation took over power.[10] Other terms used to describe indigenous peoples are aborigines, first people, native people, aboriginal, or Native Americans or Indians in the U.S. However, the preferred term, indigenous peoples, appears to be used by different international agencies such as the United Nations and will be used here.

Indigenous societies are found in every inhabited climate zone and continent of the world from small, farming villages in India and Africa, to Native American pueblos in the Southwestern United States, to farming and herding communities high in the Himalayas, to nomadic groups in the African savannah, and to remote groups in the far Arctic reaches of Canada and Alaska.

Indigenous societies range from those who have been significantly exposed to modern influences such as the Maya peoples of Mexico and Central America to those who as yet remain in comparative isolation from any external influence such as the Sentinelese and Jarawa of the Andaman Islands in the Bay of Bengal to the east of India.

The total world population of indigenous peoples is hard to estimate given the difficulties of identification and inadequate census data, but recent estimates range from 300 million to 350 million as of the start of the 21st century. This would be just under 6 percent of the total world population. This total number includes at least 5,000 distinct peoples in over 72 countries.[11] Indigenous peoples today survive in populations ranging from only a few dozen to hundreds of thousands or more. Many groups have undergone a dramatic decline and some have even gone extinct, while others remain threatened. Some groups have also been assimilated by other modern populations, while in other cases indigenous populations are undergoing a recovery or expansion in numbers. Some indigenous societies no longer live on the land of their ancestors, because of migration, relocation, forced resettlement or having their land taken by others. In many cases, the changes for indigenous groups are ongoing, and include permanent loss of language, loss of lands, intrusion onto traditional territories, pollution of traditional lands, and disruption in traditional ways of life.

In the past and even today, many indigenous peoples have been subject to intense discrimination by Europeans or other people holding a modern worldview. The modern societies, who held superior warfare technology and immunity to deadly diseases, derisively labeled indigenous people as primitive, inferior, savage, uncivilized, backward, undeveloped, ignorant, and other derogatory terms. Through education and greater awareness, these labels have been largely jettisoned and replaced with terms such as indigenous peoples, which do not hold an evaluative judgment of superior or inferior.

Even though their numbers are small, and the modern perception of inferiority still continues among some, inclusion of their worldview is important in the Global Wave. Since they have successfully survived for thousands of years, compared to modern society that has continued for a mere 500 years; they have much wisdom to share with all of us.

One of the main characteristics of indigenous people is that they reached a social and technological plateau hundreds to thousands of years ago, although many have recently adopted modern technology. Characteristics common across many indigenous groups is that they rely upon subsistence-based production based on pastoral (herding), horticultural (simple agriculture) and/or hunting and gathering techniques. They are also predominantly non-urbanized societies. Indigenous societies may be either settled in a given locale or region or follow a nomadic lifestyle. The indigenous worldview is explained in more de-

!Kung woman making jewelry. Photo by Isla K. Bardavid

tail in the Communal and Agricultural Waves in chapters 3 and 4.

Modern Worldview

The **modern worldview** traces its historical origins back more than 500 years to the expansion of Western European power and its influence and/or ultimate dominance around the world. The modern worldview has been especially powerful over the last two centuries and has today expanded to the farthest reaches of the world.

The Modern Worldview
extols scientific reasoning
exalts individualism
treats nature as a commodity
promotes modern political traditions
separates church and state
promotes industrial production
embraces socialism or capitalism
places faith in technology

According to the modern worldview the world operates as a giant machine, often referred to as a Newtonian mechanistic view of the Universe. The modern worldview has ushered in a host of astonishing achievements such as the equality of women, medical breakthroughs, educational progress, and advancement of human rights, as well as appalling failures such as values of rampant consumerism, cut-throat competition, unlimited economic growth, the use of punishment as a way to correct behaviors, and military force to resolve conflict. One of the challenges of the 21st century is how to draw on the achievements produced from a modern worldview, and rethink or discard the darker elements. Chapter 7 describes the modern worldview.

Fundamentalist Worldview

Fundamentalism is the term I will be using in this book to describe the people who embrace the third worldview. **Fundamentalism** refers to a belief in a strict adherence to a set of basic principles (often religious in nature), sometimes as a reaction to perceived compromises with modern social, ideological and political life.[12] Many who hold to fundamentalist ideas wish to preserve what they see as traditional beliefs of the past and seek continuity with traditional religious ways. Fundamentalists follow religious traditions that were formed during the Urban Wave, a time when civilizations and universal religions emerged that continue today. However, those who follow a fundamentalist worldview are not following the exact traditions of the past, this would be impossible in a modern society; instead their ideas have grown out of a rejection of modern ideas coupled with a response to the disrupting influences of globalization.

Fundamentalism is a rejection of and reaction to the modern concepts of secularism and humanism. They see their religion as true and others as false, which usually results in a denouncement of alternative religious practices and interpretations. There are fundamentalist sects in almost all of the world's major religions: Christianity, Islam, Buddhism, Hinduism and Judaism. Across cultures, fundamentalism is characterized by a cluster of common characteristics including a literal interpretation of scripture, a suspicion of outsiders, a sense of alienation from the secular culture, a distrust of liberal elites, and the belief in the historical accuracy of their own interpretation of their religious scriptures. Also, religious fundamentalists are often politically active, and strive to shape the social order in line with their beliefs, and many feel that the state should be administered according to religious principles.

Fundamentalism is a movement through which its followers attempt to rescue their religious identity from inclusion into modern, secular Western culture. They have thus created a separate identity based on their particular religious community and upon the fundamental or founding principles of their religion. This formation of a separate identity is deemed necessary as a defensive measure to stem the real and perceived assault from the modern world. Often they see the choices for the organization of their nation as limited to a modern society or a traditional society. Since they reject a modern society, the only other choice they see is the preservation of their traditional ways. Also, many people in modern nations find that traditional values give resolute comfort and reassurance in a fluctuating and inexplicable world. Therefore, many people from the Middle East, to India, to the United States find that the familiar traditions of the past give meaning, identity, and steadfastness to their lives. Although the fundamentalist worldview is very diverse and not unchanged from the past, the essence of many of these beliefs continues today and is zealously held by millions, if not billions, of people throughout the world.

Although fundamentalism has largely retained its religious references, the term has more recently been generalized to mean strong obedience to any set of beliefs in the face of criticism or unpopularity. Some refer to any literal-minded philosophy with the pretense of being the sole source of objective truth as fundamentalist, regardless of

Iranian women in traditional dress at an Islamic shrine. Photo by Denise Ames

whether it is called a religion. For example, some people hold the belief—called market fundamentalism—that market capitalism is best and can correct all of society's ills. Some fundamentalists attempt to build an entire approach to the modern world based on strict commitment to their principles. Many have strong opinions about social and political values and voice their opinions in a forceful and sometimes violent manner. The application of the term fundamentalist to both a religious and social-political approach and actions seems appropriate.

The Globalized Worldview

A third worldview, the **globalized worldview**, is sweeping the world today. **Globalization** is a complex, multi-dimensional phenomenon that interconnects worldwide economic, political, cultural, social, environmental, and technological forces that transcend national boundaries. Greatly intensifying since the 1980s, it reflects the many ways in which people on an increasingly populated planet have been drawn together not only by their own movements but also through the flow of goods, services, capital, labor, technology, ideas, and information. Through globalization the world becomes a single place that serves as a frame of reference, which influences the way billions of people around the world conduct their everyday lives.

One of the most important dimensions of globalization is **economic globalization**. Economic globalization is the increasing integration and expansion of the global economy around the world, particularly through trade, financial flows, business, and the movement of labor, technology, and information across national borders. This expansion has reduced the significance of local and national economies and has folded the globe into an integrated economic system governed by capitalist principles. The globalization process and, in particular, economic globalization, has both negative and beneficial aspects. Although globalization has "opened up" the world in many positive ways—communication networks, especially the Internet, transportation linkages and travel opportunities, sophisticated technology, medical breakthroughs, and comfortable living standards for some—critics condemn its corporate dominance, unbridled consumerism, expedient business climate, ravaged environment, and uncertain future.

Transformative Worldview

At this point in time, diverse people are actively challenging the negative parameters of the four other worldviews. A different worldview, some say a different story, is urgently needed in order to assure the continuation of our human species and life as we know it on Earth. Leaders from diverse fields—religious leaders, business entrepreneurs, international political leaders, indigenous farmers, political activists, environmentalists, entertainers, scientists, working people, artists, writers, academics, educators, economists, concerned citizens, and others—are contributing to the creation of what I call a **transformative worldview**. Those who adhere at least in part to this worldview assert that diverse paths are possible and attainable and that the globalized worldview is not an inevitable or desirable scenario of how the future will or should be played out. Millions of people around the world are promoting alternative ideas and diverse options for a different worldview and voicing their convictions in a forceful, yet usually peaceful fashion.

Critics contend that none of the above worldviews seem sufficient to meet the complex, interrelated challenges of the 21st century and each has glaring detriments with the potential to harm our planet and undermine our future life. For example, some people advocating a transformative worldview admire the sense of local place and the importance of the environment that many indigenous peoples have connected with for millennia without losing a shared consciousness as global citizens. Critics contend that the rigid dogma and intolerance of fundamentalism will not generate a more inclusive and culturally tolerant worldview in an increasingly interracial environment. Others argue that we need to move beyond the mechanistic, segmented order of the modern worldview without sacrificing the value of scientific inquiry, secularism and rational, logical thought. Some people advocating a transformative worldview admire the modern advances in technology, transportation and communication, while rejecting the despoiling of our planet through environmental exploitation. Transformative supporters draw upon the idea that we are all global citizens, heralded in the globalized worldview, yet we need to take steps to limit the dominance of the world's economy by giant, multinational corporations.

Elements in the formation of a transformative worldview come from diverse sources; some are positive aspects of the other worldviews. For example, highly regarded from the indigenous worldview is the wisdom of indigenous people who call upon the wise council of their elders, respect and connect with nature, and value the strong relationship with territorial place. From the fundamentalist worldview many want to preserve the sense of shared meaning and universal values such as compassion and love that universal religions offer and the importance of family connections. From the modern worldview the ideals of democracy, the advancement of scientific inquiry, medical improvements, beneficial technological innovations, public-supported education, and the expansion of human rights to include women and people of color are all noteworthy accomplishments. The globalized worldview's stunning technological developments, especially high-speed, integrated computer networks and reasonably-priced, global transportation, have provided instantaneous communication linking diverse people around the globe. Even some indigenous people in remote villages are linked to the Internet and use appropriate scientific knowledge for enhancing their goal of achieving self-sufficiency in food production. And some supporters would say that the globalized worldview's vision of "opening up" the world to unfettered trade has benefited many people with a more materially comfortable standard of living than ever experienced before.

Yet the transformative worldview is in a process of evolution. Its many proponents offer alternatives to prevailing notions of cultural uniformity, corporate dominance, consumer-driven values, unchecked individualism, oligarchic concentration of wealth and power, and environmental destruction. Although this diverse array of thoughts, beliefs, ideas, theories, lifestyles, choices, and actions defies rigid categorization, these visionary conceptions share common characteristics that define the transformative worldview.

Even though the modern and globalized worldviews are the dominant paradigms at this point in time, the transformative worldview is challenging their sway and offering viable options for a sustainable, more equitable future. Which worldview or combination of worldviews will we as global citizens choose for our future? We all have a voice and a critical stake in the future outcome.

Now that we are aware of systems thinking and the five worldviews that are currently informing our Global Wave, it is time to turn to a description of this holistic world history model.

Questions to Consider

1. What worldview do you most closely identify with? Explain your choice. (There is certainly no right or wrong answer to this question).

WAVES OF GLOBAL CHANGE: A HOLISTIC WORLD HISTORY

World History from a Transformative Worldview

Each generation narrates its version of history through its particular lens or worldview, which filters how its members see the past; in other words, the present influences how the past is constructed. Through our worldview lens, the past is interpreted, the present is acted out, and the future is determined. Today different interpretations recount an incomprehensibly complex and diverse past, each vying with one another for authenticity and authority. Each world history author may interpret the past quite differently.

When using the phrase "traditional" approach to history, I am referring to interpretations of the past that are largely filtered through the prevailing, mainstream or modern, fundamentalist, or globalized worldview. My holistic approach to world history is seen through a particular lens as well. My version of world history offers a different lens from which to view the past, act upon the present, and visualize the future. I am using the term holistic in this world history to reflect the growing alternative perspective that sees the past, present, and future as a synergistic, interdependent process, not as a separate collection of unconnected events and actions. Through this holistic lens a different world history is told.

Many ideas, beliefs, ways of thinking, and values from the transformative worldview have inspired and informed my writing and teaching of a holistic world history. Although today many of us celebrate our political freedoms and enjoy material abundance, paradoxically, we are also witness to the insensitive abuse of nature, the perilous promotion of consumerism, threats to participatory democracy, and a push to homogenize and commodify world culture. These trends, among others, need to be seen in the larger context of our long and varied human history.

If we can look at the "big picture" of our past, we can more deeply understand the enormity of our present-day actions and recognize what I consider to be many destructive and unsustainable practices that our society is currently following and promoting around the world. The purpose of this book and this holistic model of world history is to shed light, through a holistic lens, on the history of our human species, and see how and why we have arrived at the point we have reached today. With this holistic perspective of our history we are able to acquire a deeper, richer, and clearer understanding of our shared human past that, in turn, helps us connect that past to our present life, enabling us to make more informed decisions about the crucial choices that we need to make not only today but in the future as well.

This holistic approach to world history is an attempt to write and convey a different history from the traditional history that is customarily written and taught in our schools. Our human story is not a static subject rigidly fixed in a set canon; rather it is a dynamic, flexible, and unfolding process. This holistic approach explores our story from a systems perspective in which interconnections and interactions among humans across the globe are communicated.

Organization of a Holistic World History

When writing about and teaching world history, the first logical question to ask is where does our story begin? A few historians argue that a true "big picture" history commences with the story of the "big bang" and the creation of the Universe, the Milky Way Galaxy, the solar system, the formation of life on Earth, and the evolution of our human species. I agree with this approach and have included a brief survey of these topics in the second chapter. I believe that this inclusion places humans within a larger historical and universal context. The themes or what I call flows (to be discussed below) that intertwine with our human history also exist and weave together the story of our Universe, Earth, and human evolution.

I suggest starting a narration of our human story around 40,000 BP (before the present) or 40,000 years ago when our rich tapestry of culture began to emerge and humans differentiated themselves as modern. Although some point out that our modern human species—homo sapiens sapiens—evolved earlier, around 100,000 BP, the 40,000 BP mark is a compelling time in which human artistic and technological expressions became more innovative and sophisticated denoting a clear break from earlier developments.

When describing this "big picture" of our 40,000 year story simplicity is of utmost importance. A chronological, historical narrative is typically the master organizer of most traditional history. However, in this holistic world history I have selected a different approach. The development of humans through history shapes this fairly simple periodization plan. **Human development**, in this holistic context, means the common ways in which humans fashion their ways of living, interact with the environment, cultivate political, economic, and social systems, and create cultural and religious expressions. Thus, the development of people, rather than a chronological narrative, is the master organizer in this world history.

With human development as the master organizer, we can steer away from the typical assumption that people have marched in triumphal steps towards "progress" by means of increasingly complex technology, culminating in what is assumed to be our superior modern society. Using human development as the master organizing principle also frees us from thinking in strictly chronological terms, which might impede our ability to view simultaneous occurrences around the world. However, I will use chronology within the development framework, since development is not stagnant and implies movement through time. This organizational framework encourages us to think more creatively and to examine more fully and without cultural judgment the world's peoples at various points of their development, seeing both the amazing accomplishments and the appalling shortcomings of our species.

> **Questions to Consider**
>
> 1. How is using the human development organization method different than the chronological method for organizing world history? How does this method change our view of history? Why?

WAVES OF GLOBAL CHANGE

As we consider our 40,000 year span of history, it can readily be seen that our species has fashioned very diverse ways of living. To clearly identify the distinct patterns of human development, I have arranged it into five major human transformations called **waves**, which are critical turning points or watersheds that represent deep structural change in the historical process. These developmental waves are organic metaphors and do not follow strict chronological dates, but they have approximate beginning dates and no ending dates. The beginning date of each wave indicates where the earliest known expression of that wave gets underway in a specific area of the world, but the ending dates are left open because all five waves continue, albeit in altered form, even today.

Waves are an easy image to envision, especially for visual learners, who can readily identify the ebb and flow of the waves and the fluidity with which waves change and adapt to their surroundings and new stimuli. Waves are both a description of what happened and a historical methodology for understanding our past. Although these waves denote change, it is important to remember that at a foundational level, universal human behaviors or commonalities lie below the surface and signify unifying continuity. Yet despite this continuity, paradoxically, change does occur. When change occurs within a wave, due to a combination of complex and interacting factors, ripples of change radiate and overlap to act upon all parts or patterns of human society. Deeply embedded within each wave is a paradigm or over-arching worldview that shapes the political, social, eco nomic, technological, intellectual, ecological, and cultural patterns, or what I call currents, of society. Waves can accommodate significant shifts in their currents without changing their essential worldview. But if change alters all the currents within a wave, it will cause a crucial shift in the fundamental paradigm or worldview inherent in the wave; thus a new wave is created or return to a different wave takes place.

Since paradigm-altering change is rare, only five waves of change are proposed in this world history. The five paradigmatic waves of change are the Communal, Agricultural, Urban, Modern, and Global. On the next page is a brief description of each wave.

Each wave represents a momentous transformation in all facets of human development—political, economic, social, technological, cultural, spiritual, ecological, and worldview. Hence, each wave is holistic. When some people begin to move into a different wave, this does not mean that all people throughout the world change simultaneously. Therefore, within a spe-

Waves

cific time in history, people throughout the world are at different developmental junctures. In other words, the occurrence of a new wave denotes that people in a core area or areas are making a transformation to a different way of life, a new wave, but not all the people throughout the world make the transition at the same time, while others may never change significantly at all. Hence, we find throughout the world diverse ways of living occurring simultaneously by societies in different waves of social development.

The core area or areas that make such a shift may only comprise a minority of the world's people at any given time, but these areas represent momentous change, despite their relatively small early numbers. For example, as the Modern Wave begins around 1500, the vast majority of the people in the world continue to live within the Communal, Agricultural, or Urban Waves. The changes labeled modern are only beginning to take root in specific parts of Western Europe, and only among a small number of people. But enough variables are interacting at this time to stimulate change among other people, and this change compounds and spreads to other areas of Europe and beyond. As these dominant changes radiate outward from the core area in the Modern Wave, more areas are enveloped into the Modern Wave system and assimilate its characteristics either voluntarily or through force and conquest. Usually those in the new wave have more sophisticated military technology than the other waves, which facilitate their subjugation of weaker groups. For example, some people in the Urban and Modern Waves use their complex warfare apparatus to overtake those in the less complex Communal and Agricultural Waves with relative ease.

On the other hand, some societies or regions do not necessarily move in lock-step fashion from the Communal, to the Agricultural, and onward to the Urban, Modern, and Global Waves. They

Five Waves of Global Change

1. **Communal Wave** In this wave people gather/hunt or forage for food and live together in small communal, nomadic bands bound together through strong kinship ties. This wave encompasses the emergence of modern humans around 40,000 years ago and continues today with very small numbers still practicing, although in an altered form, a foraging way of life.
2. **Agricultural Wave** With this wave people change from foraging for food to agricultural food production and a sedentary, village way of life. People begin to make this change in some, but not all, areas of the world beginning approximately 10,000 BCE.[13] This transition also occurs at later time periods whenever a group begins to adopt an agricultural way of life. Some people today continue to live in small villages and retain some Agricultural Wave characteristics similar to earlier people.
3. **Urban Wave** During this wave, beginning in Mesopotamia around 3500 BCE, groups of people evolve from sedentary agricultural villages to develop more populous and complex urban societies. This wave marks a transition to what we call civilization and all its accompanying characteristics. Some people in the world today continue to practice conventions that are characteristic of the Urban Wave, especially its religious traditions.
4. **Modern Wave** This wave emerges around 1500 CE when some Western European countries rise to prominence, beginning with the conquest of the Western hemisphere and followed by interaction with and subjugation of societies throughout the world. Modern characteristics, shaped largely by Western Europeans, diffuse around the world after 1500.
5. **Global Wave** This wave is presently developing across the world. People in this wave create globally interconnected communication, transportation, financial, commercial, and trade networks and they use sophisticated technological innovations.

may move from one wave to a different wave because of a number of interacting variables. For example, after the "fall" of the Roman Empire in the Urban Wave, many people fled the city and picked up a way of life characteristic of the Agricultural Wave, a less complex way of life more in keeping with their situation. The same occurrence happened with the collapse of the Mayan civilization in the Western hemisphere. Evidence suggests that most people were propelled into the Agricultural Wave from the Urban Wave for reasons beyond their control.

The MAP is not the TERRITORY

A cautionary reminder is needed here. This world history model is only the map, not the actual territory. A full account of the vast diversity of our human history through such a vast span of time and space can never be made; only a partial understanding, an approximation, can be achieved. World history, by its very nature, makes generalizations about people that do not always apply to every specific society or culture. With these generalizations comes the caveat that diversity is more prevalent than generalizations indicate and the use of generalizations is merely a convenient tool to explain the collective experience.

Questions to Consider

1. What do you think about the wave model by which this holistic world history is organized? Does this make sense to you?

Holistic Currents

This study of world history emphasizes differences, but a story of our human species cannot dwell exclusively on differences without becoming overwhelmed by detail. In this holistic approach human similarities or commonalities are recognized as well as differences, for one does not exist independently of the other. Human commonalities, which are what link us together as a species,

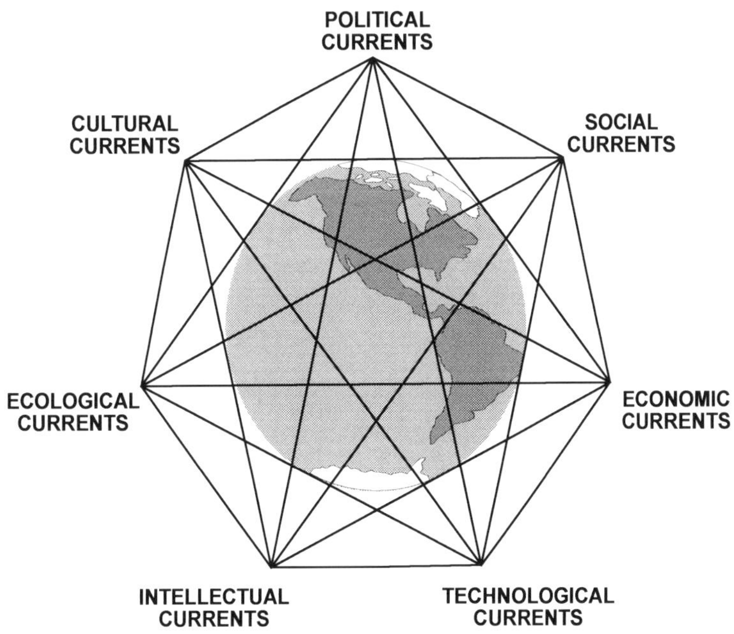

provide the foundation for this holistic approach. Therefore, I have organized these human commonalities into five patterns or, in keeping with our wave metaphor, what I call currents that are repeated in each of the five waves.

These five currents are the background on which cultural diversity is imprinted. Each current—ecosystems currents, techno-economic currents, social currents, political currents, and cultural currents—is further differentiated into five sub-currents for a total of 25 sub-currents. This organizational tool is repeated in each of the waves, although some of the sub-currents may be emphasized more than others, some may be ignored, or others added depending upon the circumstances. Yet this grouping of currents and sub-currents is intended to provide a sense of continuity and order that help us to remember significant information, concepts, and the flow of history. The currents concept is introduced here, although a full description of the five currents and sub-currents is in chapter 3. The currents and sub-currents are a mental organizer that can help us contextualize world history or, in other words, something for us to "hang our hat on."

Flows Through World History

Along with the five waves, five currents, and 25 sub-currents, this holistic world history has interwoven five key "flows" throughout the narrative. In the study of the formation of the Universe and Earth, the evolution of life on Earth, the emergence of humans, and our ensuing history, certain flows emerge as significant and recurring motifs. In this holistic history these motifs are woven into five dynamic and interconnected flows.

Currents

Five Flows in World History

- interdependence
- creative and destructive energies
- paradox
- commonality and diversity
- change and continuity

These intangible yet ever-present flows are manifested throughout history and from them are woven the events and processes, the behavior of humans and our fellow species, the global environment, and space and time itself, into an interdependent web.

These five flows are abstract and not always readily apparent but they are embedded within the deep processes of the Universe, the superficial and exterior occurrences of ordinary history, and in everyday human life. When they are repeatedly identified throughout history we can begin to grasp their significance, recurrence, and connection to our own lives. We are constantly reminded that we can learn from history; after all, that is why we study it. By identifying and connecting the five flows to real life situations and historical events, we can see their repeating motifs. We can learn from the past by circumspectly and judiciously applying what we have learned from these flows through history to our present situations. The following is a brief explanation of the five key, reoccurring flows coursing through this holistic world history.

1. Interdependence

For the past five centuries the Western worldview has regarded humans as separate, isolated superior entities set apart and above other forms of life. This segmented, Newtonian, differentiated, modern worldview is currently being challenged by proponents of holistic thinking, who see our human species as intricately connected to all other forms of life, each a part of an interdependent web of life on Earth. Humans are also inextricably connected to each other in a dynamic interplay of interactive relationships and exchange.

2. Creative and Destructive Energies

Both creative (constructive) and destructive energies are simultaneously at play within the Universe, in life on Earth, in the human experience, and in world history. Tension between creative and destructive energies is what creates change throughout the Universe and in our own history as well. In this holistic study, creative and destructive energies do not have normative values attached to them, but are seen as vital interacting processes.

3. Paradox

Paradox lies at the heart of the Universe, the natural world, and within human events and actions. A double edged sword, paradox cuts both ways. Paradox is expressed as an apparently true statement that appears to lead to a contradiction or to circumstances that defy common sense or intuition. The human story is a tale of contradictions and tensions that do not necessarily have a solution. Holding the tension of paradox and

CURRENTS AND SUB-CURRENTS IN WORLD HISTORY

Currents in World History	Sub-Currents in World History
Relationship with Nature Eco-system Currents	1. geography 2. environment 3. human populations 4. natural populations 5. human and nature interaction
Ways of Living Techno-Economic Currents	1. daily life 2. economic systems 3. technology 4. exchange and trade 5. patterns of labor
Human Networks Social Currents	1. human groups and institutions 2. the family 3. gender 4. prestige and social status 5. socialization and education
Establishing Order Political Currents	1. political systems 2. forms of leadership 3. customs, rules/laws and punishment 4. migration and interaction 5. conflict and cooperation and warfare
Human Expressions Cultural Currents	1. worldview/beliefs 2. spirituality/religion 3. communication 4. identity and belonging 5. aesthetic expression

controversy without feeling the need to resolve it is part of systems thinking. For every solution to a problem there are repercussions. No clear right and wrong appears to exist in history, as paradoxical as that may seem, but humans link normative values to paradoxical forces. Uncovering paradoxes and contradictions that continuously flow through our history and our everyday life is part of the mystery we observe and attempt to record here.

4. Commonalities and Diversity

Humans throughout the world share many similar characteristics, behaviors, and physical and genetic make-up. An exploration of human commonalities connects humans to a world community where we all share a common history. At the same time, humans are culturally diverse. As unique individuals and groups, we celebrate the cultural differences that give each of us a sense of identity and expression. In this history, diverse ways of living are represented in each of the five waves, while commonalities are expressed through our universal human behaviors.

5. Change and Continuity

Change and continuity are vital processes in history as in our daily lives. Change involves increasing or decreasing complexity, but it does not necessarily mean progress. Parallels between biological change and continuity on the one hand, and cultural change and continuity on the other, are evident in our human history and link us to our fellow species in the natural world.

It is difficult to understand and explain why some people change from one wave to another, and why continuity or slower change characterizes other human situations. A traditional world history approach usually explains change as cause and effect. For example, as it is usually explained, the construction of complex irrigation networks in China causes its civilization to develop. As historian Ross Dunn explains, most world history is a "serial study of several civilizations, stressing chronological strings of causation within each, with one cause creating the effect."[14]

When using a systems approach, change is viewed as an interacting feedback system in which numerous variables combine to create change. When change takes place, one variable or several variables are stimulated by various factors that disrupt continuity and accelerate change. Once disruption of previously stable variables takes place, the feedback loop system is set in motion, with one variable affecting another, which in turn stimulates change in others. For example, when one current within a wave—the economy, technology, society, politics, religion, or cultural expressions—is stimulated to change intensely, it can stimulate other elements to change as well. When change is forceful, the repercussions are exacerbated and the whole system changes. The

CREATIVE AND DESTRUCTIVE ENERGIES			
Destructive Energies in World History	**Creative Energies in World History**	**Destructive Behaviors to the Human Spirit**	**Creative Behaviors to the Human Spirit**
entropy, contraction, extinction of life forms, collapse and decline of civilizations, disorder, war, disease and conquest	expansion of the Universe, creation of life on Earth, evolution of our human species, spiritual connections, kinship bonds, human relationships, peace movements and artistic expressions	anger, apathy, avarice, boredom, conceit, despair, egotism, envy, fear, gluttony, greed, hate, indifference, jealousy, lust, narcissism, selfishness, self-indulgence, self-pity, and vanity	acceptance, altruism, appreciation, charity, compassion, empathy, forbearance, forgiveness, hope, gratitude, love, mercy, patience, self-control, selflessness, tolerance, and understanding

process of change can actually appear to be quite random, since all the variables involved may not be obvious.

A wave in this holistic world history is a fluid metaphor that signifies major human transformations. Major change in history is compared to waves in an ocean. Under the right conditions a tiny ripple in the ocean grows into a swell that becomes a wave, and helps to create even larger waves, until the whole process can either dissipate or grow to such proportions that it creates havoc and destruction in its wake. The creation of a new wave implies the destruction of one wave and a change in the way of life for the people living through the transformation.

Although this is not an exhaustive list, several variables help stimulate change:

Variables Creating Change

soil depletion
drought
climate change
interaction among strangers
military overreach
biological invasions
military invasions,
chance happenings
individual choice
religious ferment
creative individuals
forceful leaders
technological innovation
population increases
physical adaptations

These variables most likely differ from place to place, with some having greater influence in certain areas than in others. In order to explain change more fully, I have identified six basic types (*see next page*).

In this world history change is understood not as mono-causal and autonomous, but is composed of dynamic components influencing each other, which is best described with an interlooping feedback system. When change occurs, through the various causalities explained above, one variable or several variables are stimulated by assorted factors that disrupt continuity and accelerate change. Once disruption of previous variables takes place, a feedback loop system is activated with variables affecting each other. When one element or current within a wave is stimulated to change, the other currents—relationship to environment, economy, technology, social order, political organization, and cultural expressions—change to some degree as well. When change is dynamic enough, the repercussions are exaggerated and the whole system changes,[16] and from that, a new wave develops or a transition to another wave occurs. For example, technological and economic changes (the techno-economic current) have accelerated dramatically around the world in the last few decades. Innovative technologies such as the Internet and high speed computers are just two breakthrough variables that have stimulated other variables to change as well. By using this interacting feedback system to explain change, our history is seen as an interdependent, layered process rather than a surface-level chain of cause/effect events. When cultural change occurs in human societies, its members respond in a number of ways.

Continuity is coupled with change in this holistic world history. **Continuity** is the persistence of cultural elements in a society. If change is placed on a continuum, periods of relative stability or continuity also appear; this does not mean that no change occurs, but rather that change is superficial, not deeply structural. Continuity means the variables are balanced; secondary or non-structural changes can be accommodated by minor adjustments in the patterns. Long-term stability or continuity does not imply backwardness or stagnation; rather, it indicates a certain type of success. A society must effectively satisfy its members' physical and psychological needs if it is to endure, and in order to satisfy these needs a certain degree of stability and continuity is required. Cultural continuity persists not because certain cultural elements of a society are superior or more efficient than former elements, but because they provide uniformity and familiarity.

Rapid change disrupts a society's uniform and familiar way of life, which exacts a financial and psychological toll on its members. Change in one area of society likely means change in other areas as well. New information and accompanying

Six Types of Change	
1. Random Change or Chance Chance is analogous to biological mutation. In this type of change, apparently random historical circumstances or abrupt climatic events influence change.	**2. Regional Differentiation** When species are isolated, they change and develop their own adaptations in concert with their local environmental setting. Human societies that develop in diverse isolated or partially isolated settings adapt unique cultural customs and traditions that fit their particular circumstances. For example, on the island of New Guinea, an area in which humans were isolated until recently, linguists have identified over 1,000 spoken languages today out of a total of 5,000 recognized languages throughout the world.[15]
3. Cultural Change Cultures, like organisms, are typically not totally isolated, and they interact, in varying degrees, with others. When interaction occurs, diffusion takes place between interacting cultures; hence, cultural diffusion or cultural interaction occurs, with each culture involved in the interaction. Cultural interaction abounds in world history with the interaction between nomadic and urban societies just one of many recurring examples. The principles of cultural change are also applicable to biological change	**4. Innovative or Material Change** This usually occurs rather abruptly, especially when compared to longer periods of relative continuity. A few examples of material change include the development of new subsistence strategies, a technological innovation, or population increases
5. Cumulative Change Material change may be cumulative. An example of cumulative change is readily visible today; astounding technological advancements developed over decades have resulted in a comfortable material standard of living that many people in the West are accustomed to today. But cumulative change is not necessarily continuously progressive in an unbroken chain of upward advancement; cumulative advancement ends at some point. When cumulative change turns towards decline in cultural evolution, a civilization collapses or weakens. Similarly, at some point cumulative change may finally lead to biological involution and extinction occurs.	**6. Human Choice** Innovative cultural change is stimulated by human agency or choice, which, it can be argued, plays a role in biological change as well. Creative individuals, usually about 10 percent of the total population, or charismatic leaders, may be agents of either positive or negative historical change. Adolph Hitler, leader of Germany during World War II, has been called the most evil leader of the 20th century, while Mahatma Gandhi, the national and civil rights leader from India, epitomizes a compassionate leader. Paradoxically, both were instrumental in effecting change, but one produced destructive change while the other promoted constructive change.

Societal Responses to Change

1. Assimilation

One response is to assimilate or accept the new social and cultural elements that are introduced into a society. Assimilation can be accomplished when the recipients of change voluntarily absorb and accept new cultural elements, or when change is forced upon recipients by coercion, or by some combination of forces along an assimilation continuum. When assimilation occurs, most of the societal elements are replaced by new elements and older elements become secondary. An example of assimilation is the experience of immigrants in the "melting pot" of the United States during the 20th century. Many second generation immigrants no longer speak the family's language, and cultural traditions from the "old country" have given way to Americanized traditions.

2. Synthesis

A second response to change is when certain elements are preserved and sustained by combining old and new elements,[17] often called synthesis. In some cases, even if change is abrupt, the replaced culture's symbols, values, and beliefs may continue to exist in differing degrees and forms. This is the case with many Native Americans who accepted the Catholic religion imposed by the Spanish conquerors around 1500, but synthesized many of the Catholic saints and religious symbols into their indigenous religious beliefs.

3. System Breaks Down

A third response is when too much change occurs too rapidly; the system breaks down and panic and disorder prevail. An example of this third response is the 1979 Islamic Revolution in the nation of Iran. During this time deep changes in the form of a theocratic Islamic state were ushered in with Islam installed as the official religion and strict adherence to cultural traditions of the past was legally enforced. Today in Iran, many of the nation's young people under 30—who make up more than 70 percent of the population—are resisting imposition of this theocratic order in overt and subtle ways. Their elders may also wish to change the theocratic order since 1979 but remember the disruption and chaos of earlier changes and would rather not endure the hardships once again; thus, they resist or do not embrace change. When devastating social disruption occurs, a country's social values, traditions, and customs break down with alienation, despair, and violent behaviors expressed. Usually periods of rapid change are followed by periods of disorder, and then followed by long periods of continuity.

changes in daily routine are threatening to many people, who may be anxious or uncomfortable with its consequences. Not surprisingly, the elderly, who tend to be more conservative and less eager for change, strive to maintain stability, as do farmers, land-owners, ruling elites, and religious leaders. Informal and formal processes of socialization, such as education, also help maintain continuity in the midst of change. Socialization instills the society's cultural values and provides a rationale for members to believe their culture is worth preserving and continuing. We can think of United States history classes as an example of this process, or any history course that extols a particular nation or way of life. Socialization is very effective; cultural elements become embedded in our minds and hearts and we therefore automatically assume them to be true.

Questions to Consider

1. Which of the five flows do you most identify with? Explain.

FEATURES OF A HOLISTIC WORLD HISTORY

The following ten points (not necessarily in the order of importance) will further explain the advantages of this holistic world history model.

1. A "Big Picture" Periodization Plan

This holistic world history has a well defined and well developed periodization plan. As described above, the plan uses waves as a metaphor for human development and change. This plan begins world history with the "Big Bang," while human history begins approximately 40,000 years ago with the Communal Wave. While the categories of the five currents and sub-currents remain the same in each of the five waves, the content of the currents in each of the five waves changes.

2. Five Universal Flows

Our human story is often portrayed as separate and unconnected to the universal flows found within the resplendency of the Universe, the formation of our Milky Way galaxy, the solar system, and planet Earth, the unfolding of life on Earth, and the evolution of our human species. Yet, these five flows connect us together into this awe-inspiring process. Uncovering these flows that connect humans interdependently with the world tells us about ourselves and helps explain our often puzzling actions, behaviors, events, and ideas that all flow together into our paradoxical human story.

3. Recognition of Human Commonalities

Our species exhibits common characteristics that differentiate us from other species. These solidly rooted, underlying psychological and biological human commonalities provide a foundation that unites our diverse families, groups, clans, tribes, and nations across time and place. To discover our commonality, we set our story within a larger framework that stretches over a long 2.5 million years. During this long period of time, humans developed deeply rooted instincts, behaviors, and habits that have served our species well for our survival and proliferation. Among these hard-wired instincts are a shortsighted outlook of the future, concern for the welfare of the proximate group, and responsibility for the local environs.

As we coexist today with billions of our fellow humans on a finite planet, these narrowly focused behaviors that helped our ancestors endure over the millennia are paradoxically creating havoc for our species today. But along with our survival-based, shortsighted instincts, we also possess self awareness: the faculties of reason, reflection, the capacity to learn and understand, and a sense of our own personal and collective identity—in other words, consciousness. Along with all of these traits, we, as a species, have the remarkable ability to transform—that is, to change our own detrimental, deep-seated behaviors to life-sustaining behaviors and actions that will enhance the continuation of our species and countless other fellow life forms within our larger, complex ecosystem.

4. Five Currents

The commonalities described above are differentiated into currents—ecosystem, techno-economic, social, political, and cultural—and then into sub-currents as a way of sorting and organizing the material. Instead of exclusively organizing history by particular cultures or societies or using a chronological approach, observing currents provides a way to make a large amount of information intelligible.[18] In a chronological approach, names, dates, events, and other factual detail lead the organization, which is summed up in the humorous expression, "history is just one darn thing after another." This approach includes factual information but boils down a great deal of that information to a manageable level.

Each of the currents roughly carries equal weight in each of the waves. Political history, which emphasizes military campaigns, leaders, laws, elites, and dates, is usually over-emphasized in world history and leads to information overload. When focusing exclusively on political history, the depth and complexity of history is overlooked. Political history usually excludes or de-emphasizes women and non-elites, while men and elites are highlighted. In this holistic approach military history is largely reduced, as well, since wars and military heroes are often overly romanticized in world history and the realistic portrayal of horrific suffering and violence of warfare is disregarded. Alternative forms of conflict resolution are encouraged; therefore, a constant reference to wars reinforces the notion that only through military force can disputes be resolved. This holistic model includes political history but reduces the emphasis on political actors, events, and wars and gives equal balance to social, cultural, environmental and economic factors.

5. A Holistic/Systems Approach

One of the hallmarks of this model is that it uses systems thinking as a foundation for understanding history. With systems thinking the whole system is studied—all the parts and the connections between the parts—in order to more fully understand the parts in relationship to the whole system of world history.

6. Transdisciplinary Perspective

In keeping with a holistic approach, this world history uses an interdisciplinary or transdisciplinary perspective in which diverse subjects—history, anthropology, psychology, geography, economics, sociology, the humanities, ecology, political science, and the sciences—are woven into the historical framework. By scanning across the disciplines we can see emerging conditions, paradigm shifts, and change, while the artificial boundaries separating academic disciplines fall away.

7. A Global Format

This history follows a global format in which an attempt is made to give equal credence to diverse areas of the world, instead of following the familiar "Western civilization approach," more commonly found in traditional world history. In the West, Western civilization is the foundation of most of our values, institutions, beliefs, and worldview. From this Eurocentric vantage point, the West emerges as the influential agent with non-Western societies merely responding passively to its influence. The assumption is that Western values, goals, and worldview are an appropriate yardstick for comparing and judging the entire world. In that kind of curricular orientation, history is organized according to an ancient, medieval, modern timeline that fits the West. This holistic approach does not exclude or overly glorify Western civilization but balances it and integrates it into a larger framework.

Another approach often used in world history is based on a national history format. From this vantage point, world history is narrated as the sum of all national histories, which are merely compiled together on the assumption that a global picture will magically emerge. This format is reflective of modern worldview thinking in which separate, distinct national parts are treated as autonomous and unrelated. But in reality, human history is not the sum of disparate national history parts but an integrated process.

World history told from a regional plan jumps from region to region across the world, yet fails to find underlying commonalities connecting these regions together as an interdependent system. In a regional approach, each region signifies separate cultures or demarcated civilizations that have unique characteristics, cultural attributes, and histories. Interaction of regions is largely minimized, except when wars force regions into contact. Although the regional approach has some beneficial attributes—indeed regions often have distinctive characteristics—a regional approach alone does not provide a satisfactory holistic approach.

This holistic world history chooses a format that embraces global interaction, human commonalities, and regional commonalities and diversity rather than one based solely on Western civilization, or national or regional exclusivity.

8. A Female Voice

World history books are typically authored by male professional historians. Although I am certainly not discounting their rigorous, scholarly work, as a female author I believe a balancing female voice in world history is instrumental to a fuller understanding. I also have emphasized the role of females, family, and children in all five of the waves. I maintain that the female viewpoint is supportive of a holistic and thematic approach where patterns are the unifying factor. Less emphasis is placed on wars, political elites, and military history than in most world histories authored by men.

Educator Johnny Johnson, a Navajo man from Arizona,[19] commented at a conference that he feels that the male part of being human has come to dominate our educational system with its rigid hierarchies and emphasis on acquiring information. In order to save the planet he says we need a balancing female voice in our educational system as well as in our everyday lives. The male influence in education enforces hierarchy, "deadly" specialization, and exploitation; "like we are just a job shell." He believes that the female influence, on the other hand, would encourage gathering in a circle to foster the cooperative spirit, egalitarian relationships, and being more human. Western culture is male, but the Earth is female. He and others feel that we need to write and tell new stories that emphasize the female to balance our lives. I agree.

9. Non-State Peoples

History is traditionally about people who live in urban civilizations, empires, states, or nations with an inordinate emphasis on their "achievements." I have included in this holistic world history what are often called "non-state" peoples. Often derisively labeled "backward" or "primitive," these are people who have lived on the margins of civilizations, states, or nations, and have traditionally been excluded from the spotlight of history. The nomadic people of Asia, for example, are usually portrayed in history as the "barbarians" who attack and threaten to destroy civilization. Yet their nomadic culture and society is rich, diverse, and interesting. They and other marginalized groups ought to be represented in history, and, where possible, their stories have been woven into this holistic world history.

10. Insights: Learning from the Past

History can be an excellent way to learn valuable lessons from the past that in turn can be applied to our everyday lives. History must be more than a dry collection of interesting but colorless information about the far-removed past. We can incorporate history into our life experiences, making the study more personally relevant and valuable. Therefore, I have included what I call insights throughout the book that highlight valuable lessons that we can learn from the past and apply to our own experiences. Along with insights, as you have already seen, I have also included "Questions to Consider" at the end of most of the sections. These reflective questions offer the reader an opportunity to pause and reflect on what you have learned.

Questions to Consider

1. Rank the 10 features listed above that describe this holistic world history in the order that you think are most important. Describe your top two choices.
2. What other features do you think are more important than the ones listed? Why?

Insights: Learning from the Past

AN INTRODUCTION TO A HOLISTIC WORLD HISTORY: CONCLUDING INSIGHTS

This holistic model offers an alternative approach for understanding and learning about world history. It provides a realistic portrayal of world history; for example, we are made aware of the creation of new societies and the collapse and decline of them as well. This model encourages systems thinking and critical and creative thinking that I believe are valuable perspectives for well-informed and engaged global citizens to explore. This integrative approach offers a foundation for understanding other subjects, helping to put contemporary issues into context while connecting seemingly disparate strands of the past and present into a holistic process. It provides a workable, intelligible model that synthesizes an appreciation of our species in which we can gain a deeper admiration of the world in which we live today.

This approach does not purport to address all the issues and details about our human history, but it does attempt to provide a "big picture," global perspective for greater understanding. Thankfully, human history has many perspectives and interpretations, each contributing to a fuller understanding of a complex, interdependent global system. Varied perspectives can be a part of a puzzle that when pieced together will give greater meaning to the whole picture of our world. It is my intention that this holistic approach to world history will contribute to the development of new ways of thinking about how to interpret our shared past, our present human experiences, and the importance that our future decisions will have on us, our fellow species, and the Earth as a whole. It is with this purpose that I offer this holistic world history for your consideration.

Questions to Consider

1. In your opinion, what are the main weaknesses of this holistic world history model? Strengths of the model?

Before jumping into a discussion of the five waves in this holistic world history, we next turn to a brief survey of the Universe and human emergence. This chapter offers a big picture in which to contextualize a history of our human species and shows how the five flows are intertwined within events in the Universe, on Earth, and our species.

Endnotes

1. Joseph O'Conner, and Ian McDermott. *The Art of Systems Thinking: Essential Skills for Creativity and Problem Solving.* (London: Thorsons, 1997), p. 3-13 and John Goekler, "Teaching for the Future: Systems Thinking and Sustainability." *Green Teacher 70*, Spring 2003, p. 8-14.
2. Fritjof Capra. *The Web of Life: A New Scientific Understanding of Living Systems.* (New York: Anchor Books, Doubleday, 1996), p. 30.
3. Please see the modern worldview in this book to understand how mechanistic ways of thinking emerged.
4. O'Conner, *Systems Thinking*, p. xv-xvi
5. O'Conner, *Systems Thinking*, p. 19-21.
6. O'Conner, *Systems Thinking*, p. 32, 37
7. Goekler, *Green Teacher*, p. 8-14.
8. Donella and Dennis Meadows, Jorgen Randers, Jorgen. *Limits to Growth: The Thirty Year Update.* (White River Junction, Vermont: Chelsea Green Publishing Company, 2004), p. 4.
9. National Geographic Society, peoples of the world.
10. "United Nations Declaration on the Rights of Indigenous Peoples". United Nations. UNPFII. *http://www.un.org/esa/socdev/unpfii/documents/DRIPS_en.pdf.*
11. Indigenous Peoples and the United Nations System. Office of the High Commissioner for Human Rights, United Nations Office at Geneva. *http://www.unhchr.ch/html/racism/indileaflet1.* doc. and "Indigenous issues". International Work Group on Indigenous Affairs. *http://www.iwgia.org/sw155.asp.*
12. Benjamin Beit-Hallahmi, "Fundamentalism," *Global Policy Forum*, May 2000.
13. I will use the time designation BCE, before the Common Era, and CE Common Era for time, instead of BC and AD which stem from a Eurocentric approach to world history. I will dispense with the customary periods after the designations.
14. Ross Dunn, "Central Threads for World History," *Historical Literacy*, (New York: Macmillan Publishing Company, 1989), p. 227.
15. Jared Diamond, *The Third Chimpanzee: The Evolution and Future of the Human Animal.* (New York: Harper Perennial, 1992), p. 6.
16. Ruth Whitehouse and John Wilkins, T*he Making of Civilization*, (New York: Alfred A. Knopf, 1986), p. 51.
17. Gerhard and Jean Lenski, *Human Societies: An Introduction to Macrosociology* (New York: McGraw-Hill, 1982), p. 69.
18. Ross Dunn, "Central Threads World History," *Historical Literacy*, p. 219 and Jean Elliott Johnson, "Patterns and Comparison," The History Teacher, Vol. 20, No. 4 (1987), p. 436.
19. Comments made by Johnny P. Johnson, Fort Defiance, Arizona, at the New Mexico Conference on Aging, Albuquerque, New Mexico August, 29, 2007.

Chapter 2

The Universe to Human Emergence: A Story of Becoming

"When we try to pick out anything by itself, we find it hitched to everything else in the universe."

— John Muir

THE ROOTS OF BECOMING

Humans wonder about our origin, our place on Earth, and the mysteries of the Universe. People past and present have a deep desire to understand these perplexing and profound unknowns by creating elaborate stories as explanations, but the explanations vary according to worldview, geographic location, and place in time. For example, a story familiar to Westerners is the Biblical account of Genesis, in which God created the world and then, as his crowning achievement, gave life to Adam and Eve. Other creation stories abound the world over. In a Native-American creation story, humans emerged from a hole in the Earth called a *sipapu* which linked the real or surface world with a creative underworld. The hole in the Earth can be said to represent the birth canal and, like a female giving birth, the Earth gave birth to the human species.

Through the lens of a modern, rational worldview, the story of our beginning is based on scientific explanations about the origins of the Universe. Although scientists are able to answer many of the complex, methodological questions of how and when the Universe began, they have not been able to answer the question of why the Universe exists. Scientist Stephen Hawking, who says he cannot answer that question either, states: "Although science may solve the problem of how the Universe began, it cannot answer the question: Why does the Universe bother to exist?"[1] Even though scientists have amassed a vast accumulation of cosmological knowledge, there is still an element of mystery as to why we are here.

Scientific knowledge painstakingly assembled over time needs to be incorporated into new stories of the Universe, life on Earth, and the evolution of our species. In this world history I blend a scientific account into our holistic story that also reflects the deep mysteries of the Universe. This story enables us to not only appreciate the accomplishments of the scientific community but also allows us to surrender our rational mode of thinking to the uncontrollable and indeterminable mystery of the Universe. Knowledge is power and control, yet as humans we cannot control all aspects of nature. Instead we are participants, interdependent with all of Earth's community. Changing our way of thinking and acting from one that seeks control to an appreciation of our interdependence can contribute to our sense of well-being and may help ensure the survival of our human species and that of other life systems on Earth as well.

In this world history, humans are placed within a larger context of time and space than is typical of a traditional approach to history. To understand humans in this broader context, a survey of our place within the Universe and on Earth is offered. The purpose of understanding humans in this larger context is to gain a fuller recognition and appreciation of the five interconnected flows introduced in chapter 1—interdependence, commonality and diversity, change and continuity, destructive and creative energies, and paradox—that not only shape our human lives but all life on Earth as well.

Insights: Learning from the Past

ROOTS OF BECOMING

The recurring flow of creative and destructive energies plays a paramount role in this chapter, from the creation and destruction of stars to the evolution and extinction of species of life. At the core of this flow is an incongruous interplay between the different forms in which matter manifests and then disintegrates. All the energy in the Universe is present at all times; even at the time of the Big Bang, matter exists as potential. All subsequent developments are different forms of the original energy that is present forever. Hence, there is no real beginning or end to anything, as paradoxical as that may seem. For example, the potential of flowers, stars, or even humans has always been present, even though at a certain point in time that energy may be reconfigured or recycled into another form. In a giant paradoxical cosmic dance of creation and destruction, reconfiguration and recycling, evolution and extinction—our Universe exists. The human species evolves within this larger context of the unfolding Universe, the formation of our galaxy and solar system, and the generation of life on Earth. A good place to begin this journey of understanding is with the Big Bang.

Questions to Consider

1. What does the following statement mean to you: In a giant paradoxical cosmic dance of creation and destruction, reconfiguration and recycling, evolution and extinction—our Universe exists.

A STORY OF THE UNIVERSE

About 15 billion years ago an originating power, a singularity, more commonly known as the **Big Bang**, exploded into the Universe from a vacuum or void.[2] Each and every thing in the Universe has its roots in this originating force. The inflationary scenario of the Hot Big Bang explains the origin of the Universe.[3] According to this theory, all structures in the Universe evolved from minuscule, primordial fluctuations in density imprinted at the dawn of time. From these infinitesimal fluctuations everything in the Universe, including our Earth, unfolded.[4] A singularity is time zero or the beginning of time as we know it, a state of infinite density where the classical laws of physics and space/time break down. Chaos and randomness reigned during the early hot phase of the Big Bang since physical laws of the Universe

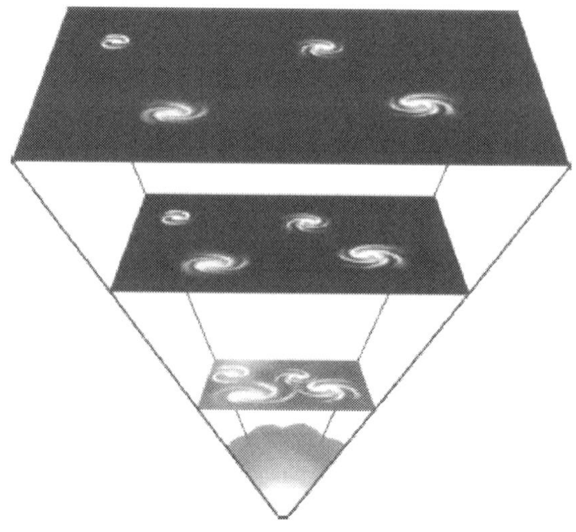

Universe expansion

were, as yet, entirely unpredictable. Singularity energy processes were created and then spewed forth into the Universe. No sooner than it appeared, the pinpoint cosmos started to expand. As the cosmos expanded, at about 10 -35 seconds after the Big Bang, the temperature plummeted and conditions snapped swiftly from one state to another. Within microseconds previously unified forces separated, new particles appeared and old ones vanished. In this instant the Universe cooled enough to allow gravity to harden from undifferentiated energy. However, the gravitational force was turned inside out as the rate of expansion, instead of slowing, accelerated explosively. Before the Universe was a second old, it was the size of the solar system. During the next five minutes after the Big Bang, a major transition occurred. The Universe cooled enough to allow for the creation of atoms.[5] New particles appeared. From a raging inferno of incomprehensible magnitude at the time of the Big Bang, the Universe continued to expand and cool with no significant transitions for about one million years. The explosive changes of one era slowed dramatically as a period of relative continuity ensued.

Stars Burst Forth

The Universe's active, creative energies burst forth into stars that were composed of gas and dust. A million years after the Big Bang, the primeval plasma fog lifted and radiation fields freed the plasma from its previously unrelenting grip. The neutralization of the primordial plasma allowed larger structures of hydrogen atoms to gather into great clouds that were the predecessors of galaxies. After swirling for several billion years, the great clouds of hydrogen and helium collapsed into **stars**. In star formation, it is theorized, a cloud of cold gas condenses under its own weight. During this time a proto star contracts, heats up, and emits electromagnetic radiation.[6] Once the temperature in its core rises above a certain degree, nuclear reactions, a reliable source of heat, take place and a star is born. During the greater part of its life a star burns hydrogen in its core. Once a star's hydrogen supply is exhausted, its core contracts and heats up, enabling helium fusion to commence. As the core burns helium, its luminosity brightens in a spectacular display. After the star's helium supply is depleted, it swells up like a balloon and becomes a "red giant." Our own Sun's fate is to become a red giant in five billion years, and the Earth will be engulfed into its fiery blaze.[7]

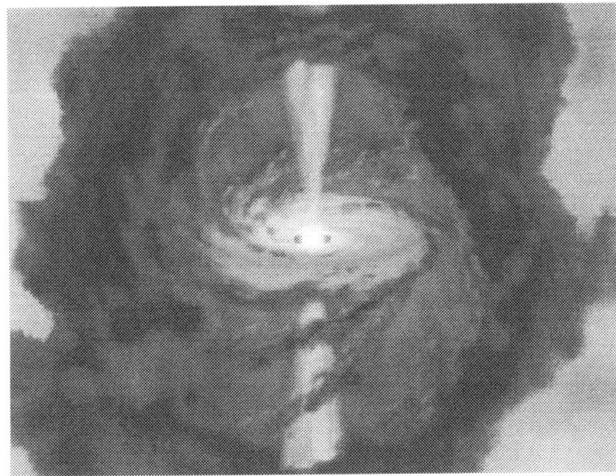

Birth of a Star

A neutron star is a massive star that collapses when its helium supply is exhausted. Physicist Joseph Silk explains, "A neutron star is a giant atomic nucleus, full of neutrons at nuclear density, a density so high that one teaspoonful of neutron star material weighs a billion tons." Most neutron stars explode as supernovas, spewing elements into the Universe. A supernova burns brighter than a billion suns. Eventually a star's eliminated elements mix together with hydrogen and recycle into a new generation of stars.[8] Basically, the method of star formation is tension between entropy and gravity. Gravitational forces generally tend to pull things together and entropy tends to spread things out.[9] Star formation is the manifestation of creative and destructive energies weaving a cyclical pattern of generation, expansion, contraction, and extinction.

Stars are not alone and do not evolve "in splendid isolation," but they are part of an inter-

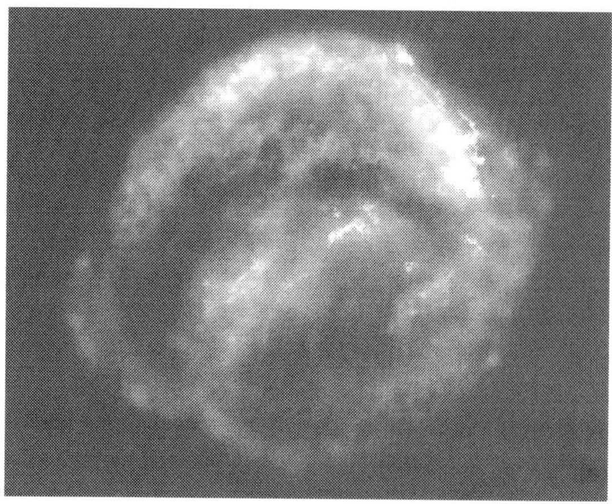

Supernova

dependent network of interstellar activity. Stars congregate in galaxies, clusters, and looser groups that all interact and shape each other. Galaxies are not strewn randomly throughout the Universe but are distributed in lacy patterns and dense clusters separated by a void brimming with non-measurable energy. Clusters form the largest self-gravitating groups of matter in the Universe. Our Sun is a mere speck in the Virgo Cluster, a self-contained clump of a thousand separate galaxies, including our Milky Way. The Milky Way and Andromeda galaxies form a small "Local Group" that is an outlying member of the Virgo Cluster.[10] The Milky Way is located 28,000 light years from Virgo's galactic center, and two-thirds the distance from the system's edge. The nearest galaxy comparable to the Milky Way is the Andromeda, two million light years away. Our Sun is just one of a hundred billion stars nestled in a bonded community known as the Milky Way Galaxy.[11]

Galaxies repeatedly invaded and absorbed their neighbors, resembling the actions of neighboring tribes or nations. Galaxies can be described as "sticky" systems, since a close encounter between two galaxies traveling at a sufficiently low speed invariably leads to a merger. Evidence of mergers is rarer today than in the past.[12] Discoveries by Hubble Space Telescope researchers reveal that our Milky Way is swallowing a dwarf galaxy, Sagittarius, and in another 200 million years the Milky Way will have absorbed Sagittarius' ten million stars.[13] Scientists theorize that the Milky Way is in a state of equilibrium or continuity, not expanding like the Universe, nor contracting like a collapsing interstellar gas cloud.

The darkest, coldest, and densest interstellar gas clouds are observed to be the sites of star formation throughout the Milky Way. Much of the hydrogen gas evident in the early Universe is recycled and then condensed to birth new stars. Young and forming stars are concentrated in our galaxy's spiral arms—Orion, Centaurus, Sagittarius, and Perseus—where thick clouds of gas condense and light their nuclear fires. Stars that coalesced early in our Universe's history seem indistinguishable in many respects from stars forming today. In a flow of continuity, many of these ancient stars are still with us today.[14]

Globular clusters are compact clumps containing anywhere from 100,000 to several million stars. Our Milky Way has about 150 globular clusters. Clusters are about twelve billion years old but also contain new stars, as discovered from data accumulated by the Hubble Space Telescope. Apparently violent stellar collisions are occurring in these ancient assemblages of stars, in which new stars are recycled from the ashes of stellar destruction.[15]

Milky Way Galaxy

Black holes are another source of wonder in the Universe. **Black holes** are thought to be a replication of the state of the Universe before the Big Bang. According to theoretical speculation, black holes form when the core of a star cluster or the nucleus of a galaxy becomes unstable and collapses. Black holes are the end states of very immense stars with masses equal to thousands, millions, or even billions of solar masses. When stars are densely packed together they sometimes collide with one another, spewing debris into the Universe that eventually accumulates into a giant black hole.[16] A black hole's extremely compact body contains such dense matter that not even light can escape from its gravitational force. Hubble Space Telescope researchers claim black holes "grow like weeds in the cosmic garden." In the center of every galaxy examined looms a voracious black hole swallowing burning gas equivalent to one million suns every year. The gas grows hot as it spirals toward the center of the disk and the resulting burp of radio waves shows up as a quasar.[17] Some scientists suggest that black holes may not last forever and in essence evaporate, while others state that only the smallest black holes evaporate. Albert Einstein's general theory of relativity postulates that black holes live forever.[18]

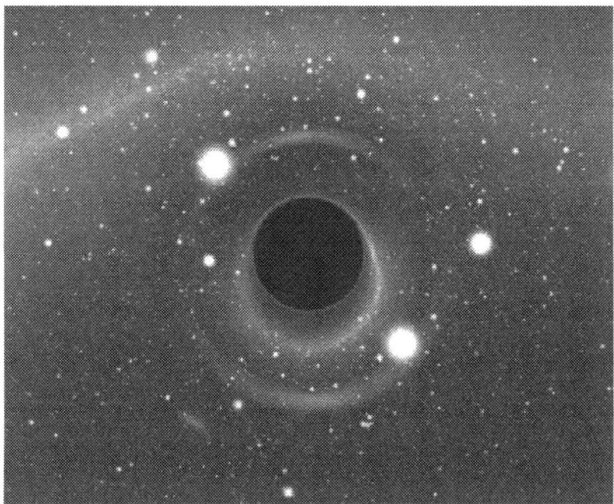

Black Holes

> **Questions to Consider**
>
> 1. Invasion and absorption are themes in the formation of stars. In what ways can we see this theme carried out by humans?

Our Solar System

Our solar system formed amidst unimaginable violence about 4.6 billion years ago. According to one theory, a supernova exploded near an interstellar cloud of condensed dust and gas particles and the explosion's shock swept through the clouds, compressing them to the point of gravitational collapse. One of the dense clumps thus formed contained the raw materials—hydrogen, helium, and heavier elements—necessary for the birth of our solar system. Gravity pulled the dense clump together and attracted hurling debris of dust particles and interplanetary gas that swirled close enough to be absorbed by the large mass. The clump slowly contracted into a disk, rotating faster and faster around a growing concentration of matter. As this concentration of matter grew, it heated up and transformed into our Sun.[19]

The young Sun evolved. The Sun was a fairly ordinary star, microscopic on a cosmological scale, somewhat above average in its mass and luminosity. It is located near the inner edge of the Orion Arm, approximately 30,000 light years from the center of the Milky Way Galaxy. Opposing gravitational and centrifugal forces locked the Sun into a near circular orbit around the central bulge of the galaxy. The Sun sped at nearly one million kilometers per hour, and every 250 million years it logged one complete galactic circuit. Our Sun is now middle aged, less than half way through its history as a luminous star. The chaos of its youth is now very rare and its former violent activity has largely been replaced with more order and precision.[20]

OUR EARTH AND THE UNFOLDING OF LIFE

Planets Form

Densely packed dust particles orbiting around the Sun frequently collided with each other and eventually joined together into growing bodies that rapidly reached the size of planetesimals, or "little planets." Planetesimals collided, split into fragments, merged, grew, and swept other small bodies into their orbital paths, eventually evolving into the planets of our solar system. Our Earth evolved as part of this complex and interdependent physical state.

Before the solar system settled into an orderly network, the Earth began to coalesce. The Earth, the third planet from the Sun, accumulated in darkness about 4.5 billion years ago. Although the primitive Sun blazed, there was so much gas and dust between the Earth and Sun that at first no light seeped through. The Earth was embedded in a black cocoon of interplanetary debris. The newly formed Earth was a churning, boiling inferno with heavy metals falling to its center forming a massive molten core. In the Earth's core the agitating motions in the liquid iron and nickel generated a strong magnetic field. Lighter rocky material drifted toward the surface to form a mantle and crust that was primarily responsible for containing Earth's high internal temperature.[21] As the Earth slowly cooled, the rock solidified and Earth's thin, fragile crust thickened and hardened; it became rounder and less lumpy. Most of the heat radiating from the surface of the infant Earth emanated from gravitational energy that was released when planetesimals collided and fell together. According to one theory, in one spectacular collision a sizable piece of matter struck the Earth so forcibly that it blasted considerable chunks into nearby space. The resulting ring of orbiting debris gradually united to form our moon.[22]

At first the solar system was enshrouded in darkness until winds swept away gas, dust, and random debris. The trapped heat within Earth's massive atmosphere began to dissipate. The Sun filtered through, warming the Earth's surface; water vapor cooled and condensed forming droplets of liquid water that trickled down to fill lowlands. Torrents of rain carved out multitudes of water configurations that even today cover two-thirds of our Earth's surface.[23]

The Earth had all the ingredients for the unfolding of life. Although each ingredient was not particularly extraordinary, the countless number and variety of random encounters among the various ingredients resulted in a chaotic association of parts that together combined to create life. The unfolding of life on Earth appears to have been highly improbable. The number of random possibilities for life's primeval ingredients to converge and create organic life was actually a highly implausible event; but it happened nonetheless.[24]

Life on Earth

Organic life on Earth began its unlikely existence about four billion years ago. All the ingredients were in balance, Earth was the proper size, enabling gravitational and electromagnetic equilibrium; it was in a perfect position from the Sun, ensuring a steady temperature range for complex molecules to form; it had a solid surface

Solar System

and the correct mass to retain an atmosphere of moderate depth; the right kinds and an ample supply of chemical raw materials; and suitable conditions for a variety of chemical reactions.[25] All the variables were in balance for the process of biological evolution on Earth.

Living organisms are made of ordinary matter and all have the same basic biochemical make-up. The atoms of these life forms are no different from those found in rocks, stars, or interstellar space; thus they are subjacent to the laws of physics. Biological evolution does not occur in isolation, but is a multi-faceted and interdependent process containing numerous feedback loops. All life is part of an ecosystem that never remains static but changes or evolves through time.[26]

After an intensely violent phase during Earth's early formation, its surface layers began to reach relative equilibrium. Large quantities of water, carbon dioxide, molecular nitrogen, and many other molecules formed the first atmosphere and youthful oceans. Energy from sunlight, lightning, volcanic heat, and meteorites sparked inorganic molecules to react chemically, which produced a variety of organic molecules—amino acids, sugars, lipids, and the bases of nucleic acids. Gradually these molecules accumulated in Earth's waters in what is euphemistically known as a "primordial soup."[27] Although what exactly took place is not perfectly understood, G. S. Kutter maintains "that the simple organic molecules assemble into larger and more complex molecules similar to those found in today's organisms." He continues, "Short strands of RNA are the first molecules in the primordial soup that carry information, and are regarded as the starting point of the evolution toward cellular life."[28] A universal characteristic of all cellular life on Earth is that it shares the same genetic codes in its RNA and DNA. These codes are fashioned from a particular set of biochemicals that are common to all organisms from simple bacteria to a chimpanzee.[29] From this set of biochemicals a diversity of energy forms is manifested.

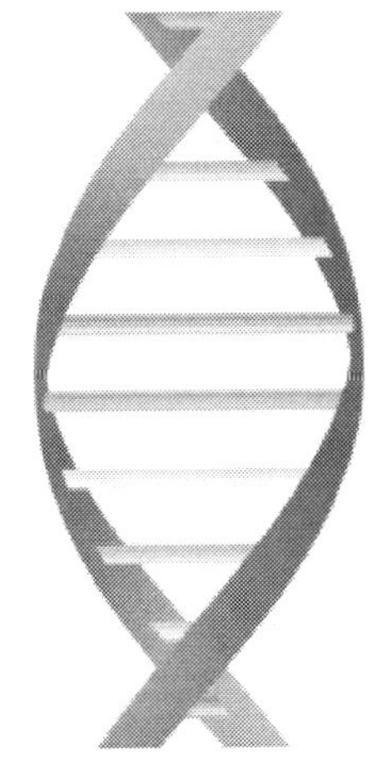
DNA (deoxyribonucleic acid) is in all known life.

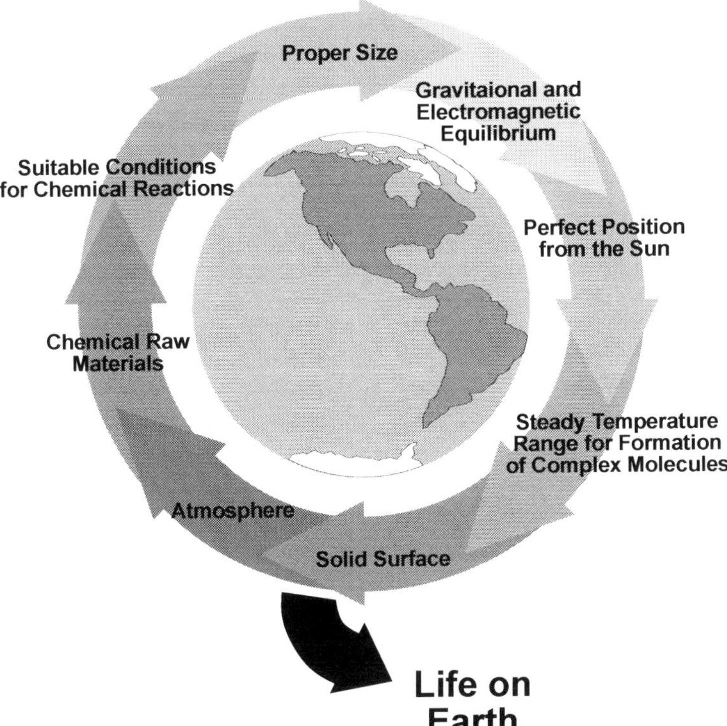

A new era in the evolution of energy forms unfolded. The physical laws were no longer solely guiding the course of events, but the laws of biology were influential as well. Over the eons, some early organisms became more complex and diversified, spreading to all corners of our planet. A worldwide ecosystem became firmly established and the greening of the Earth got underway.[30]

Two fundamentally related factors enabled organisms to form, thrive, continue, and evolve: genetic mutation and natural selection. Genetic mutations are random modifications introduced into offspring designs. Genes are the units of selection, which are inherited, selected, or eliminated. These mutations are spontaneous differentiations that occur in the genetic structure of living organisms. Though there are various forms of mutations, they all involve the appearance of a newly ordered sequence of the genetic materials of the DNA.[31]

While mutations apparently occur according to chance, **natural selection** is a self-selecting process by individual organisms, which select characteristics most advantageous for their survival. Natural selection steers the addition of design modifications over generations according to reproductive success. In short, evolution involves both random occurrences (chance) and natural selection (choice), assuring that offspring will deviate, ever so slightly, in attributes from their ancestors.[32] Evolution by natural selection generates a variety of creatures, but apparently it works according to probabilities and not a set plan. Evolution occurs according to the conditions and circumstances present at the time and the available materials. A new species buds off from its ancestors most often during times of environmental stress when many species are driven to extinction. Evolution and extinction go hand-in-hand. For example, if not for dramatic climate change 65 million years ago, the dinosaurs could still be with us![33] Instead mammals begin their evolutionary process. Time and chance play a role in the interaction of change and continuity with choice also a factor in the evolutionary process. For example, the members of an individual species decide by choice with whom they will mate, where to make their nests, or whether they will enter a new environment. Choice is a factor, to an unknown degree, in shaping genetic materials.[34]

The key component of biological organization is the cell. Cells are small, membrane-enclosed bodies filled with a concentrated solution of chemicals, each containing all the biochemical ingredients required for its metabolism and reproduction.[35] There are two basic kinds of cells: eukaryotes and prokaryotes.

Prokaryotes, meaning "prenuclear," lack nuclear membranes; their body organization is single-celled, and they usually reproduce asexually. Members of this realm[36] are commonly known as bacteria. The first organisms formed are of this type, which consists of around 5,000 identified species. They are the hardiest creatures on Earth and can live in boiling water, frozen rock, and possibly even on Mars. They form the core of Earth's community of life; a mere spoonful of soil holds an estimated 50 billion bacteria.[37] Eukaryotes, means "true nuclei." Multicellular life is only found in the eukaryotes cells that include the members of the other four realms: protista, fungi, plants, and animals. Since this story is

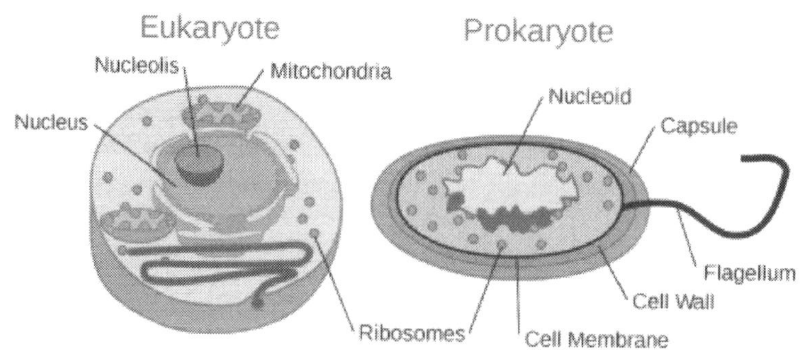

The cells of eukaryotes (left) and prokaryotes (right)

primarily about our human history, we turn our attention directly to the animal realm.

Questions to Consider

1. How do you feel about the statement in the text: "The number of random possibilities for life's primeval ingredients to converge and create organic life was actually a highly implausible event; but it happened nonetheless?"
2. How do you feel about the statement: "All life is part of an ecosystem that never remains static but changes or evolves through time?"

The Animal Realm

We humans are just one member of the animal realm that comprises from one to two million species. Animals are multicellular organisms possessing a high degree of structural differentiation, reproduce primarily sexually, and have developed capacities for digestion. Insects dominate the largest subgroup in the animal realm, with 850,000 species; there are an estimated 500,000 species of round worms, and 40,000 vertebrate species. Among the vertebrates are 9,000 species of birds, 6,000 reptile species, and 4,500 mammalian species.[38]

Animal life showed up in the fossil record 700 million years ago and exploded around 530 million years ago. Plants ventured onto land before animals. By 425 million years ago, fishes evolved from jawless creatures and populated the sea and fresh inland waters. Other water animals had difficulty with air and gravitation, but eventually clambered onto land's rocky surface. The animals that succeeded in the transition from water onto land found the forests a friendly habitat. They met the challenge of living on land by growing an exoskeleton that kept water within; in a sense, they were living, mobile ponds. Insects proliferated as they entered and adapted to a diverse number of new environments. Dragonflies grew wingspans of eighteen inches and millipedes expanded to eight feet in length. One scorpion was large enough to kill and devour small vertebrate animals, when they later appeared.[39] By about 250 million years ago, insects achieved such subtle adaptations that they never needed to significantly change. They attained biological continuity.

Vertebrates joined the march onto land. One theory suggests that vertebrates moved unto land mainly because of fluctuations in the climate. Amphibians, a branch of the fish family, generated lungs and became highly successful land-dwellers. Even today, amphibians still lay their eggs in water, a part of their ancient fish strategy adopted millions of years ago. An abundance of plant food covered the land, since no other vertebrates existed to compete for the plentiful food. An "age of amphibians" reigned for over 100 million years, from 410 million years ago when they first appeared until 285 million years ago when their dominance ebbed.[40]

The thriving animal world was virtually destroyed 245 million years ago due to shattering climatic shifts. Perhaps comets collided with the Earth and drastically altered its fragile atmosphere. When the dust settled and the extinction spasm was complete, a vastly impoverished animal world remained. Violent realities and destructive forces of the Universe were evident. The Earth slowly repopulated her animal realm, with

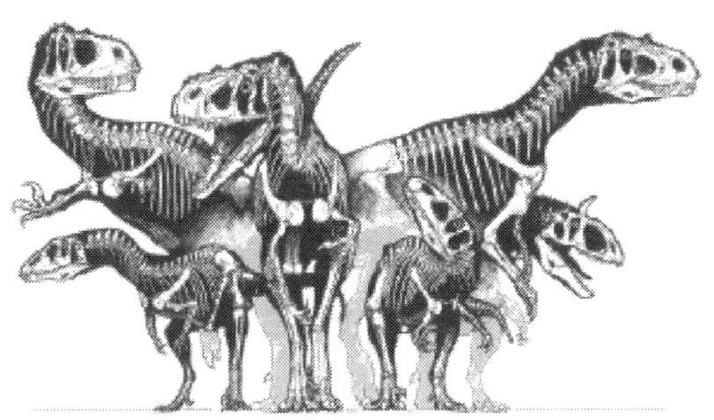

Assemblage of Dinosaurs

Saber Tooth tiger, now extinct

new species creating innovative ways of adapting to the new realities.[41]

After the mass extinction, reptiles, a newly evolved species, crowded out amphibians to become the predominant terrestrial vertebrate at the time. Shelled eggs, a crucial reptilian invention, ensured their dominance. Reptiles fertilize their eggs internally, and females cleverly lay their precious eggs on land far from predators who would feed upon them. After a period of incubation, fully formed baby reptiles peck their way out of their protective shells. With their watertight skin, reptiles roamed farther inland, even into deserts, areas amphibians could never reach.

Beginning around 200 million years ago and continuing for over 100 million years, dinosaurs held sway as the most prevalent vertebrate form. Ranging in size from a few feet to 100 feet in length, dinosaurs, which were social animals, traveled, hunted, and grazed in groups. They deftly buried their eggs, bonded with their young after they hatched, and nourished them towards independence. These tender parental behaviors were traits previously unknown to the reptilian world. Birds, which are direct descendants of the dinosaurs, first appeared around 150 million years ago.

Mammals entered the dinosaur-dominated landscape around 245 million years ago. However, the governing dinosaurs and other reptiles completely overshadowed their small mammal neighbors for more than 100 million years. These earliest mammals were actually quite small and resembled today's shrew. One mammal-like reptile, Pelycosaurs, appeared 220 to 175 million years ago; its features indicated it crossed the threshold that arbitrarily divides mammals from reptiles. Around 125 million years ago, the first marsupial mammals turned up. They were small nocturnal, smell-oriented animals that differed from dinosaurs by growing body fur instead of scales, gave live birth instead of laying eggs, and nursed their young with milk secreted by a female's special mammary glands.[42]

The "age of the dinosaurs" catastrophically halted 65 million years ago as another destructive mass extinction extinguished 96 percent of all species.[43] One theory posits the Earth and an asteroid or comet collided with such force that dust and steam in the upper atmosphere obliterated the Sun's rays and enveloped the Earth in total darkness for about six months. Temperatures plummeted to well below freezing. Thus, in a short period of time, the tyrannosaurus, the brontosaurus, and the triceratops deferred to smaller mammals, such as the newly evolved horses, cattle, rabbits, bats, walruses, whales, elephants, lions, rodents, and primates. Smaller animals, whose varied diet consisted of nuts, seeds, nectars and new forms of insects, survived and thrived after this devastating mass extinction. But the plant world was relatively unaffected by the mass extinction of animals at the close of the Mesozoic era 65 million years ago, and by 37 million years ago plants evolved into the forms that we recognize today as our flora.[44]

The "age of mammals" dawned. They rapidly moved into and prolifically adapted to the ecological niches created from the dinosaur's mass annihilation. Mammals are endothermic, which means they are able to maintain a warm body—commonly referred to as "warm blooded"—which helped them thrive in the face of a cold outer world. The fossil record suggests that

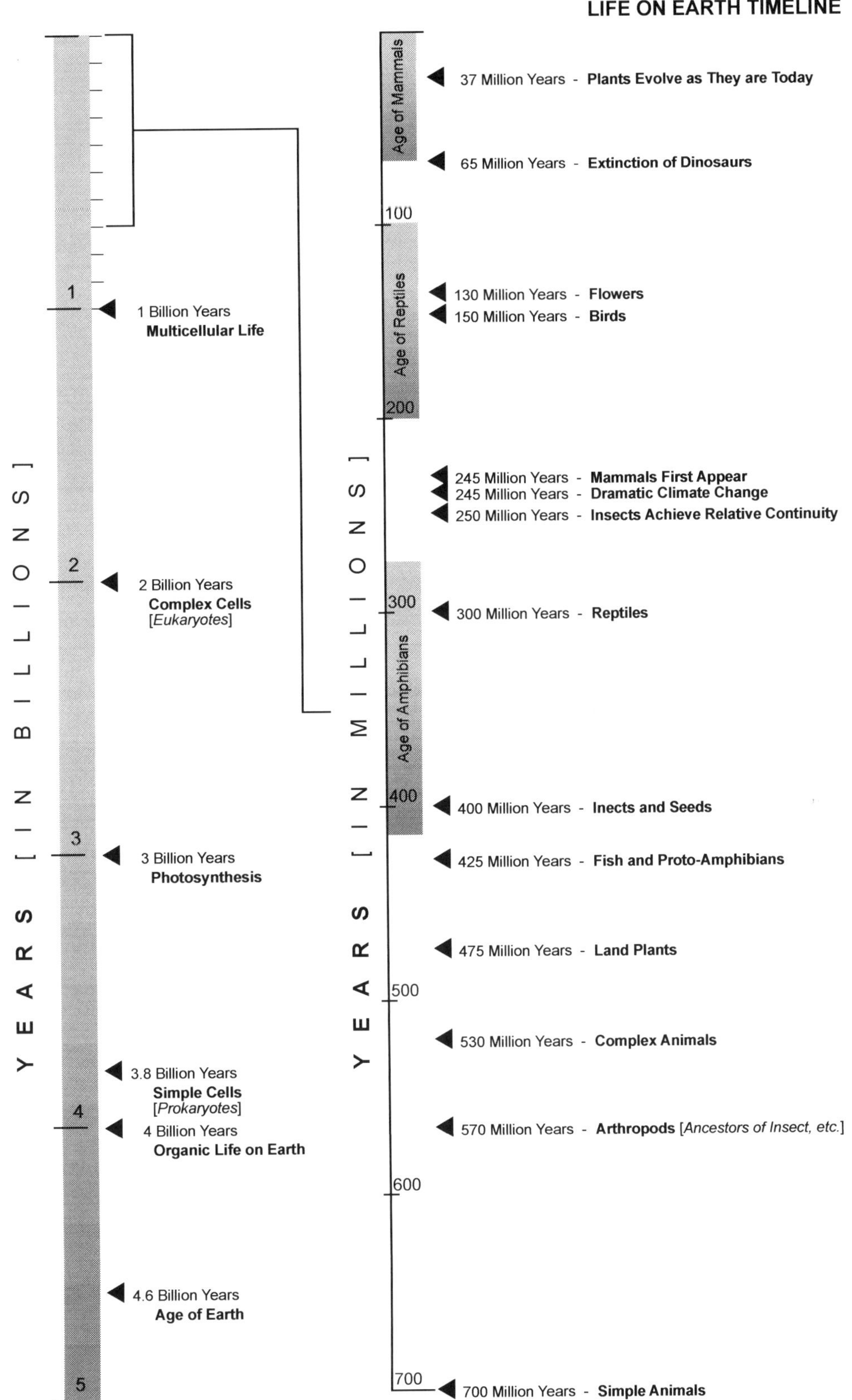
LIFE ON EARTH TIMELINE
YEARS [IN BILLIONS]
1
1 Billion Years
Multicellular Life
2
2 Billion Years
Complex Cells
[Eukaryotes]
3
3 Billion Years
Photosynthesis
3.8 Billion Years
Simple Cells
[Prokaryotes]
4
4 Billion Years
Organic Life on Earth
4.6 Billion Years
Age of Earth
5
YEARS [IN MILLIONS]
Age of Mammals
Age of Reptiles
Age of Amphibians
100
200
300
400
500
600
700
37 Million Years - Plants Evolve as They are Today
65 Million Years - Extinction of Dinosaurs
130 Million Years - Flowers
150 Million Years - Birds
245 Million Years - Mammals First Appear
245 Million Years - Dramatic Climate Change
250 Million Years - Insects Achieve Relative Continuity
300 Million Years - Reptiles
400 Million Years - Inects and Seeds
425 Million Years - Fish and Proto-Amphibians
475 Million Years - Land Plants
530 Million Years - Complex Animals
570 Million Years - Arthropods [Ancestors of Insect, etc.]
700 Million Years - Simple Animals

throughout the Cenozoic era, from 65 million years ago to the present, each species of mammals existed for an average of around a million years before becoming extinct or evolving into something else. Throughout mammalian history about 200,000 species have been identified, while there are about 4,300 mammalian species on Earth today. Thus, over 97 percent of mammalian species have become extinct.

Given the immense number of organisms and the limited supply of accessible matter, evolution could not have sustained itself for the nearly four billion years of life without recycling critical elements. Energy expert Vaclav Smil notes, "And these cycles—embracing the synthesis of new biomass, the death of tissues and organisms, their decomposition, and the return of elements to inorganic stores—must be relatively rapid." Without such recycling the largest planetary stores would be exhausted and organic life would cease to exist.[45]

Several significant theories of biological evolution bear mentioning. Darwinian evolutionary theory, a view that has prevailed in the scientific community for over a century, sees change as a slow, gradual process that occurs incrementally over vast reaches of time. But another view, articulated by scientists Stephen Jay Gould and Niles Eldredge, maintains the process of evolution takes place in punctuated bursts separated by long periods of stasis or no change. In this theory, known as punctuated equilibrium, once species appear for the first time, they do not change much during the remainder of their histories, which may go on for hundreds of thousands or even millions of years.[46] The theory of punctuated equilibrium has significant merit and reflects the theme of change and continuity in this holistic world history.

Questions to Consider

1. What does the following statement mean to you: "Given the immense number of organisms and the limited supply of accessible matter, evolution could not have sustained itself for the nearly four billion years of life without recycling critical elements?"

Insights: Learning from the Past

Our Earth and the Unfolding of Life

Biologists have classified over two million species of life on Earth, but they speculate that over the course of Earth's history there may have been 10 to 30 million species altogether. Millions of species have existed and millions, even perhaps billions have become extinct; thus extinction is the fate of 99.9 percent of all species that have ever existed.[47] The number and diversity of primate species that have evolved, changed, and gone extinct in the last 65 million years exceeds our imagination. Even though 200 primate species live today and 250 have been identified from fossil records, this is only 3.8 percent of the estimated 6,500 primate species that have existed.[48]

The underlying cause of nearly all extinctions today is the destruction of habitat, wiping out about 27,000 species a year.[49] It is surmised that the largest number of species that have ever lived on the Earth existed at the time humans first evolved. Like life on our planet, there is no guarantee that a species will continue forever. Creation and extinction are an inseparable and constant part of life's story.

It is becoming clear that something or someone is always becoming something or someone else. As we comprehend this phenomenon and

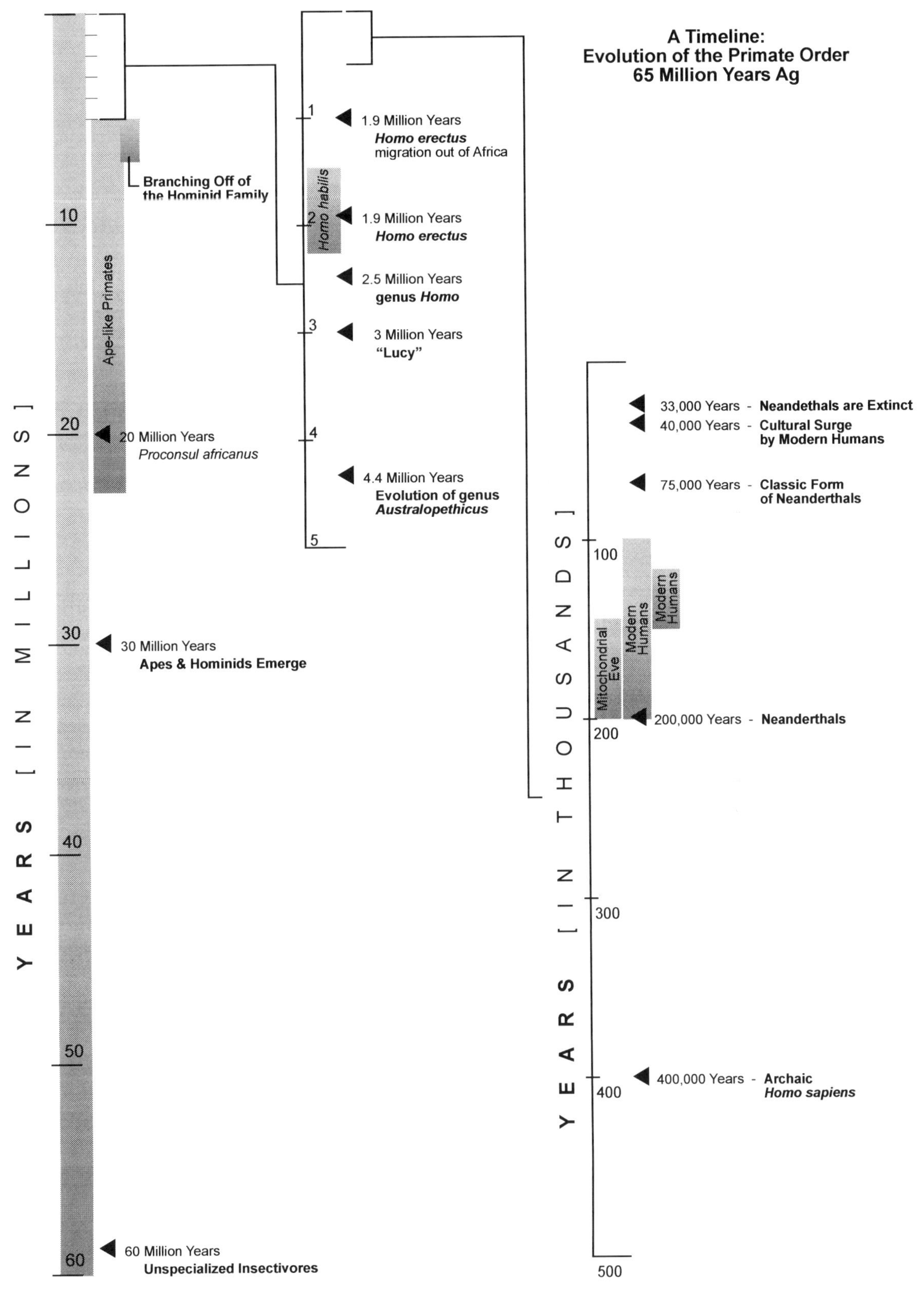

A Timeline:
Evolution of the Primate Order
65 Million Years Ag
YEARS [IN MILLIONS]
10
20
30
40
50
60
Ape-like Primates
Branching Off of the Hominid Family
20 Million Years
Proconsul africanus
30 Million Years
Apes & Hominids Emerge
60 Million Years
Unspecialized Insectivores
1
2
3
4
5
Homo habilis
1.9 Million Years
Homo erectus
migration out of Africa
1.9 Million Years
Homo erectus
2.5 Million Years
genus Homo
3 Million Years
"Lucy"
4.4 Million Years
Evolution of genus
Australopethicus
YEARS [IN THOUSANDS]
100
200
300
400
500
33,000 Years - Neandethals are Extinct
40,000 Years - Cultural Surge
by Modern Humans
75,000 Years - Classic Form
of Neanderthals
Mitochondrial Eve
Modern Humans
Modern Humans
200,000 Years - Neanderthals
400,000 Years - Archaic
Homo sapiens

see it unfold in our Universe, in the animal realm, and among mammals, it becomes evident that the same process unfolds in our everyday lives as well. The flow of creative and destructive energies helps us understand that we are all enfolded into this mysterious process. It is to the primates, an order in the animal realm and an integral part of this extinction and generation process, that we now turn.

Questions to Consider

1. Why have so many extinctions occurred in the history of life on Earth? Is this a surprise to you?

OUR HUMAN EVOLUTIONARY PATH

Humans are not just cultural beings, as is often depicted, but biological beings as well. We 21st century humans are often deaf to the deep rhythms that play within the Earth's ecosystem and sound across the millions of years of life on Earth. These deep rhythms lie beneath the surface of our outward behaviors, actions, and the thin guise of culture. To appreciate these deep rhythms we look at where they come from and how they have evolved over the millennia.

A story of human evolution is often told as a carefully planned, destined trajectory of the triumphal march of human progress. According to this story, humans progress in a gradual, purposeful way from simple, humble, primitive origins to our current level of complexity and superiority among all other life forms. This holistic approach tells a different story about human evolution. It is not a teleological, upward path of advancement; instead it is a story of tangled, interdependent paths with many blind alleys, detours, and random occurrences along the way. If environmental circumstances or particular events had gone differently at any divergent marker—for example, if the climate had not changed as it did or if a certain gene pool in a specific place had not been exposed to a particular pressure—then we humans, or perhaps our entire lineage, might not have appeared or would have evolved quite differently.[50] Humans are not the final destination in this tangled journey but part of an interdependent, evolutionary process. We came into being the same way everything else did: we evolved.

Human evolution mirrors environmental changes. A setting for our primate evolution developed amidst momentous climatic changes that took place around the globe 120 million years ago. A hot and humid climate settled over the world as the super-continent Pangaea fractured into the continents we know today. A warm and placid world encouraged the spread of enormous tropical forests that encompassed much of Africa and North America, extending farther north and south than where they presently exist.[51]

As our tangled, evolutionary path meanders, it encounters five significant turning points: first, evolution of our primate order over 65 million years ago; second, a branching off of the hominid family between 5 and 7 million years ago; third, evolution of the genus Australopithecus; fourth, evolution of the genus Homo around 2.5 million years ago; and fifth, the evolution of our own species, Homo sapiens about 150,000 years ago. Our primate order unfolded over the past 60 million years from rather unspecialized insectivores to ape-like primates around 5 million years ago.

After the mass extinction that eliminated the dinosaurs 65 million years ago, a primate order of mammals carved out their niche in a tropical arboreal setting. Arboreal primates distinguished themselves from other terrestrial mammals by a combination of related features: five fingers and toes on both fore and hind limbs, all with grasping capabilities; flexible limbs to manipulate food items and for climbing; a reduced reliance on the sense of smell, hence a shorter snout; and highly developed frontal vision. Since tree climbing under a forest canopy required quick decision-

Ring-tailed Lemurs

making skills, the primate's brain tended to be larger than terrestrial mammals of comparable size.[52]

Fossil evidence from 65 million years ago suggests that primates lived in trees because of intense competition on land, while a rich, plentiful food source awaited them in the canopy of trees. These primates, who resembled the modern tree shrew, ranged in size from a small field mouse to a large domestic cat. Many of these primates became extinct after 35 million years, while a new group emerged around 50 million years ago that was even better adapted to an arboreal way of life.[53] Unlike our ancestral primates, these primates were similar to today's promisians, lemur and tarsier-like animals that still live in Africa and Asia. Compared with other mammals of similar size, they housed notably enlarged brains and they foraged in tree branches. In the Eocene epoch 40 million years ago, fossils from two primates are evidence which suggests an early monkey or ape-like animal.[54]

About 30 million years ago during the Oligocene epoch, a large quantity of fossil evidence unearthed in the Fayum depression west of the Nile River in Egypt, clearly showed that apes and hominids emerged. Fossils of these primates showed that they had frontal vision and an expanded cranium which indicated they had evolved from small-bodied nocturnal to large-bodied diurnal animals. These primates enjoyed a diverse diet of fruits, pods, and seeds. Along a broad belt north and south of the equator the weather remained tropical and provided an ideal habitat for primate evolution.[55]

From the Miocene epoch 23 to 5 million years ago, evidence shows that ape-like primates of African origin had occupied areas ranging from Europe to Asia. Climate shifts transformed tropical forests to woodlands that encouraged our ancestors to, at least occasionally, descend from the trees onto the forest floor.[56] A significant specimen of this group of Miocene primates is the 20 million year old remains of Proconsul africanus. The 1948 recovery of Proconsul by Mary and Louis Leakey at a site on the western edge of Kenya indicated that descendants of Proconsul are ancestral to both the modern African apes and the first hominids, in other words, ancestral to us.[57]

One theory maintains that big leaps in evolution generally take place when an ecosystem shifts abruptly. Certain lineages are able to adapt to these abrupt changes, and others become extinct. Starting 10 million years ago, environmental changes ushered in a thinner forest cover across the African terrain. Heavily forested conditions favored those who could easily traverse dense forest cover by swinging from branches and living in trees. With a thinning forest, natural selection opted for those who exhibited a more efficient method of locomotion across a less forested landscape. A novel environmental adaptation, **bipedalism**, the ability to walk on two legs, appeared among fossil remains between 5 and 8 million years ago.[58]

An abrupt climate change occurred five million years ago in the late Miocene. Temperatures fell and an increase in aridity cooled and dried the Earth. Retreating forests turned into modest woodlands and grasses as a vast extinction of mammals occurred. During this global climate change, an ape-hominid split happened between four and seven million years ago. Anthropologist Richard Leakey believed the earliest hominid species evolved about seven million years ago, although a commonly used average is five million years ago.[59] These early humans formed troops of 30 individuals or so, much like today's savanna baboons. They foraged cooperatively and returned to a favorite sleeping site, such as a cliff or clump of trees, at night. Mature females and their offspring formed the nucleus of the troop. The dominant males achieved the most mating success, while immature and low-ranking males dwelt on the troop's periphery.[60]

Humans and apes share a common ancestor. Our nearest living relatives are two species of chimpanzees in the genus Pan, and gorillas in the genus Gorilla. The chimpanzees and gorillas are classed together with orangutans in the Pongo family, while humans and their extinct relatives form a separate Hominid family. DNA tests reveal a 99 percent biochemical overlap between our "cousins," the modern chimpanzee, and ourselves, which is only slightly less with gorillas.[61] Native to equatorial Africa, chimpanzees sleep and feed in trees. On the ground they walk on all fours, using their knuckles for support; they are rarely bipedal. They possess highly dexterous hands and use them for grooming, nest building, and tool handling. Chimpanzees are intelligent, inquisitive, and display a wide range of facial expressions, hand gestures, body postures, and vocal sounds.[62]

Climate changes sparked the evolution of a new genus, **Australopithecus**. The first fossil evidence appeared only 4.4 million years ago. The Australopithecus genus included an estimated six

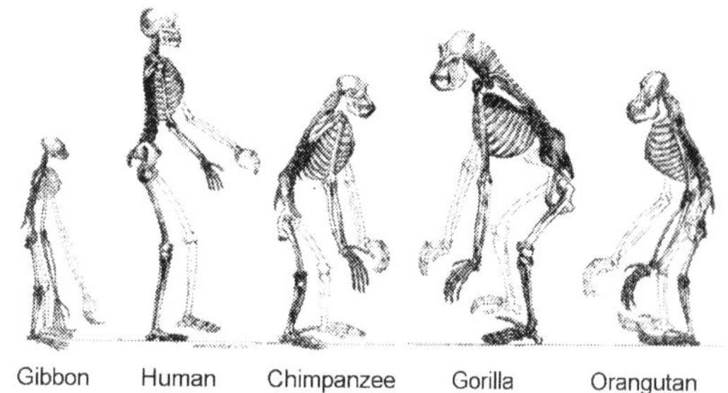

Ape Skeletons

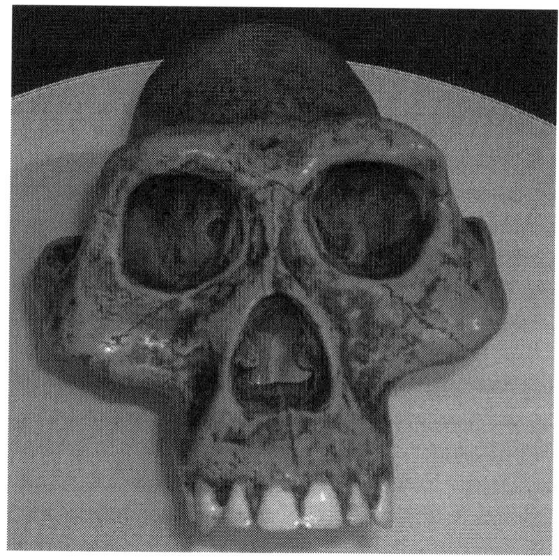

Skull of Australopithecus

species spanning a period between 4.4 and one million years ago. But the primate fossil record remains spotty and probably more than the six presently known species existed.[63] Environmental changes influenced physical changes in the Australopithecus genus. These hominids were bipedal and their style of locomotion on the ground was more similar to ours than either the chimpanzee's or the gorilla's. They did, however, retain specific tree-climbing capabilities, and probably continued to use trees as a place for refuge and sleep. Their woodland existence explains how bipedalism evolved—they lived a double life, half in trees and half on the ground. When climate changes ushered in a more grassland environment, they had the unique ability to fully adapt to bipedal land walking. Australopithecines had a small brain case indicating that their vocalizations were probably rudimentary. They grew big molar teeth but did not have projecting canine teeth like other primates. The anatomy of their jaws and teeth suggests a mainly vegetarian diet of seeds, roots, berries, nuts, tubers, and bird's eggs. Males were about 4½' to 5' tall and weighed between 60 and 80 pounds. Females were perhaps half the physical size of males. The color of their skin is unknown but was probably dark and lightly covered with fine hair. Their facial projections were similar to an ape's: no chin, protruding jaw, a wide and flat nose, low and sloping forehead, bony ridges above prominent eyes, and a large forward-thrusting face.[64]

Climate changes and physical adaptations combined to create shifts in the daily life of the Australopithecines. Anthropologists have cautiously pieced together what their daily life may have been like. They lived in small groups on the edge of a forest or on an open plain, just a day's walk to water. In addition to simple vocalizations they communicated via varied gestures, facial expressions, and body movements. They walked and ran on two legs and had a keen sense of sight enabling them to prey upon lizards, hares, rats, insects, and other small animals. They might have even stalked a sick or crippled animal, snared a newborn calf, or scavenged another animal's kill to add to their largely vegetarian diet. According to estimates, Australopithecines, like modern chimpanzees, obtained no more than 10 percent of their calories from meat.[65] They were not immune to being stalked themselves, and frequently fell prey to lions, leopards, hyenas, and the now extinct saber-toothed cat. Hence, they protected their group if threatened and wielded sticks, bone clubs, and chipped rocks for defensive purposes. Australopithecines manufactured tools, such as flake tools and pebble choppers, for scavenging and butchering meat. Evidence collected from animal bones and scattered stone tools suggests meat was brought to a site, butchered, and eaten.[66]

There were three species of Australopithecus (A.), — A. ramidus, A. afarensis, and A. africanus. Several notable and highly publicized recoveries are significant. At 4.4 million years old, A. ramidus was presumed to be the oldest of the Australopithecus species. Fossils of 17 A. ramidus individuals, who possessed both ape and human characteristics, were found in Ethiopia in 1992.[67] Another noted recovery was made by anthropologist Mary Leakey at the Laetoli Beds just south of Olduvai, in northern Tanzania. Along with fragments of skulls, jaws and teeth, she found perfectly preserved hominid, members of the human family, and animal footprints in volcanic ash. The footprints of hominids, giraffes, saber-tooth cats, and an extinct primitive horse date between 3.5 and 3.9 million years ago. Apparently the hominid footprints belong to the A. afarensis species of Australopithecus. The two footprint trails preserved in the ash were traced for more than 30 feet as the pair walked side by side. The couple stood 4' and 4'8" tall and strode like modern humans.[68]

Donald Johanson and his team made one of the most sensational recoveries in archaeology in the fall of 1974 at Hadar in Ethiopia. Over 40 percent of an A. afarensis skeleton was called Lucy, after the Beatle's song "Lucy in the Sky with Diamonds." Lucy was an instant celebrity. Living about three million years ago, Lucy was a mature adult in her early twenties when she died. Essentially bipedal, Lucy stood barely 3' tall, had long, slim arms and short legs. Her male counterpart was more robust and was probably double her size. Over 80 percent of Lucy's skeleton was reconstructed with additional fossils found at nearby Hadar sites.[69]

In an incredible recovery near Kimberley, South Africa in 1925, Raymond Dart found a fossilized child's cranium that was around two million years old. A member of the A. africanus species, the bipedal child stood around 4' tall, weighed 100 pounds, and housed a brain of 450 cc. Dart returned to excavations in the area and collected sufficient fossil material to identify an even smaller, more lightly built, graceful form of A. africanus, the oldest of which are three million years old. Some anthropologists see the species A. africanus as ancestral to the genus Homo.[70]

Emergence of genus **Homo** coincided with another significant global cooling and drying trend

Reconstruction of homo habilis

that unfolded between 2.7 and 2.5 million years ago. The emergence of a panoply of new species followed another massive extinction.[71] Around 2.5 million years ago two forms of hominid adaptation took place: first Homo, a large brained species, and second a small-brained adaptation of Australopithecus. Australopithecines, native to woodlands, were unable to adapt successfully over the long-term and became extinct about one million years ago. Evolving either from A. afarensis, A. africanus, or perhaps another species, the line of hominids survived. Homo, the new surviving species native to grasslands, appeared about 2.5 million years ago, soon after global cooling turned much of the woodland to savanna.[72] Early signs of Homo were found in earthen layers approximately 2.2 to 1.5 million years old. Jonathan Leakey recovered an individual specimen of the newly evolved Homo genus from Olduvai Gorge in Tanzania and dubbed it Homo habilis. This 1.8 million year old fossil had a larger brain size and more coordinated manual skills than its Australopithecine ancestors.

Along with physical adaptations to environmental change, Homo added cultural adaptation to the mix. Cultural developments were part of the evolutionary process that helped the species survive. Because of these significant cultural developments and physical adaptations, we often trace our human lineage to the emergence of the genus Homo. In essence, our human history spans over 2.5 million years. Three factors—environmental changes, physical adaptations, and cultural development—were instrumental in shaping who we are as a species.

Prior to 2.5 million years ago there is no convincing evidence of a systematic material culture, but by 2.5 million years ago our Homo ancestors utilized tools and left an enduring archaeological legacy. Found near fossil remains of the Homo species were animal bones and altered stones—choppers and scrappers—which were flaked on one side and served as cutting and pounding instruments in the preparation of vegetable foods and meat. Tools of this type marked the beginning of the Paleolithic era 2.5 million years ago and lasted until 12,000 years ago.[73] Toolmakers fashioned most of the flake tools from basalt, a fine-grained igneous rock common in the volcanic-rich East African rift region. Scratch marks on these flake tools were consistent with their function as cutting tools, some of which were utilized to cut grasses and others used on hides and meat.[74]

Was Homo a hunter? Probably Homo was a marginal scavenger at best. It appears that Homo coupled rudimentary hunting techniques with already acquired foraging and scavenging skills. He also employed cold-weather survival strategies by building substantial shelters and wearing protective clothing.[75] Homo's agile and efficient bipedalism released its arms and hands for aid in locomotion and to perform such tasks as carrying infants, transporting items, and assembling effective tools.

Infant care exemplified the link between Homo's physical changes and cultural development. A key to these changes was the 600 cc brain size of Homo, an increase from Australopithecus' 500 cc. Hominid infants had a disproportionately large brain compared to the size of other animals, and because of bipedalism females had a comparatively narrow pelvis, making it difficult to give birth to a mature infant. Thus, hominid infants were, in essence, born "too soon." Virtually helpless, an infant experienced a prolonged childhood, and in order to survive needed intense and constant motherly care. Because mothers undertook the crucial demands for constant childcare, the homo lineage developed fitting cultural adaptations. Small supportive cooperative groups proved to be essential for the survival of Homo's offspring, as a tightly knit social group provided a survival buffer between early hominids and their natural environment. Since Homo's open grassland locality exposed him/her as likely prey for other animals, s/he adapted defensive mechanisms to ward off predacious animals. Along with protecting their members from predators, groups provided mutual access to food supplies, and insulated each other from the natural elements.[76] By adapting an intricate web of social responsibilities, group members also assisted mothers with childcare obligations.

Environmental factors, such as expanding grasslands, combined with Homo's use of tools, bipedalism, and cooperative behavior, formed a feedback loop system that stimulated an increase in brain size. Although it is commonly assumed that natural selection favored big brains, this was not the case; big-brained animals command a disproportionate share of their body's energy compared pound for pound to smaller-brained creatures. Natural selection cannot favor this extravagance unless the brain provides a commensurate payoff. Big brains proved useful only if they aided in survival of the species, and they did prove useful. The fossil record suggests that in just a few hundred thousand years, many factors combined to stimulate a feedback loop system in which large brained species continued their development.[77]

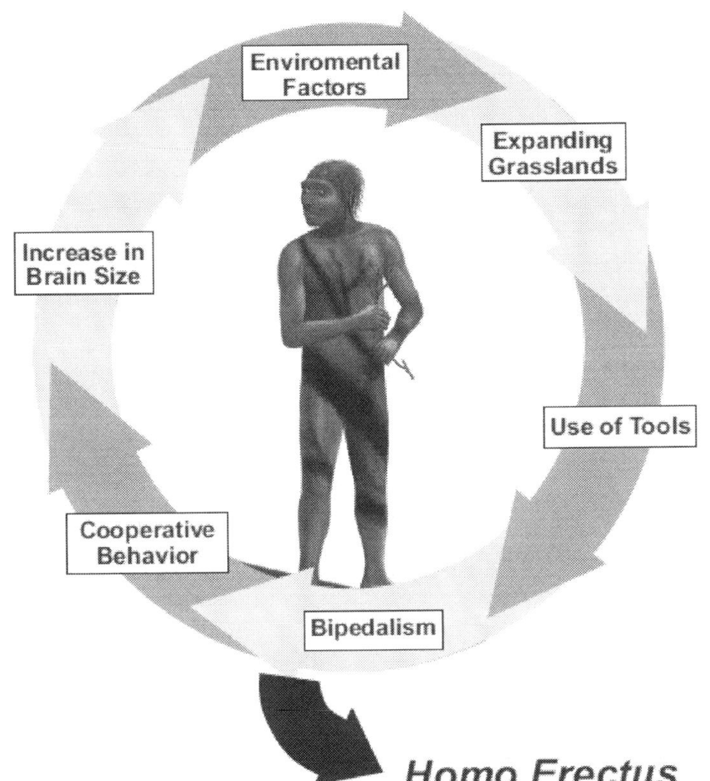

Another member of the Homo lineage, the species **Homo erectus**, appeared in eastern Africa around 1.9 million years ago and survived in many areas until roughly 300,000 years ago. Homo erectus, fully adapted to upright, bipedal walking, displayed a 900 cc. size brain, an increase from Homo's 600 cc. Homo erectus used this increase in brain capacity and other physical changes to create new cultural developments such as handy and efficient stone tools, most notably hand axes. This tool technology endured relatively unchanged for over a million years. Whether Home erectus used tools for hunting or scavenging is still debated, but whatever their method of acquisition, their meat intake increased to perhaps 20 percent of their total caloric consumption.[78]

Some anthropologists postulate that Homo erectus established **home bases**, where either hunting or scavenging and foraging activities were centered. From these home bases rich cultural developments evolved. Some anthropologists speculate that Homo erectus communicated through an elementary spoken language and the home base served as an ideal place to cultivate this language.[79] Communication likely centered on food foraging strategies, relaying the day's events, and planning for the future. These developments enhanced Homo erectus' ability to communicate and survive.

Homo erectus discovered and controlled fire. Their manipulation of fire was a significant survival tool and cultural development. Archaeologists excavated evidence of fire in hearths in both China and France dating from 480,000 years ago. More controversial evidence was unearthed in Ethiopia, where anthropologists claimed fire use dated from 1.1 million years ago.[80] In any case, the discovery of fire had many practical applications. Homo erectus ignited fires to burn off grasslands, which, in turn, created new growth. Fire served as a light source that extended the length of the day; it helped keep out nocturnal predators and provided warmth against cold temperatures and possibly the means for cooking foods. Fire served as the focal point at an agreed upon campsite where group members gathered and communicated.[81] Homo erectus increasingly relied on cultural developments to separate from and control the natural world.

Fire aided hominid travelers in their first venture out of Africa and their subsequent dispersal across the African/Eurasian landmass. A common date for Homo erectus' migration is one million years ago, although recent finds dating from 1.6 million years ago may indicate an earlier departure than previously assumed.[82] Whatever the date, campfires provided warmth and protection enabling Homo erectus to journey as far north as the Eurasian steppes during a frigid glacial era.

Migration of Homo erectus populations from their African homeland leads to puzzling questions concerning the ancestry of modern humans. The debate about where modern humans originated can be summarized in two different views. In the **multiregional evolutionary model**, Homo erectus populations migrated out of Africa close to two million years ago and settled throughout Eurasia. Genetic continuity was maintained by gene flow between local populations so that an evolutionary trend towards modern humans occurred wherever populations of Homo erectus existed. According to this view, there was little population migration, no population replacement, and populations remained separate for as many as two million years. In this model modern races have deep genetic roots.

In a second evolutionary model called **Out of Africa**, Homo erectus, as well as subsequent species of Homo sapiens, dispersed out of Africa. Actually three migrations occurred: first Homo erectus, second archaic Homo sapiens, and later modern Homo sapiens. Eventually the travelers from Africa replaced existing populations of Homo erectus and archaic Homo sapiens. Populations thus have shallow genetic roots and all derive from a single evolved population in Africa.[83]

The second evolutionary model appears to have the most support among anthropologists. Evidence from tests conducted by population geneticists, suggestively entitled a **Mitochondrial Eve** hypothesis, gives credence to an Out of Africa theory. The thesis of this argument is that all living populations derive their mitochondrial DNA from a hypothetical Homo sapiens woman, "Eve," who lived in Africa sometime between 150,000 and 200,000 years ago. Mitochondrial

Stone Tools

DNA is inherited entirely from the maternal side, and can be traced along matrilineal lines through many generations. Interbreeding between different homo species that lived side by side in different areas, if it occurred at all, was infinitesimal.[84] This model also suggests that anatomically modern humans arose somewhere in sub-Saharan Africa, before the population dispersed. A majority of population geneticists support this hypothesis as the most biologically plausible, and fossil evidence seems to support their theory.[85]

The tangled path of human evolution took another turn around 400,000 years ago when fossil records from Africa, Asia, Europe, and the Middle East turned up a likely new species, **archaic Homo sapiens**. Once again environmental changes, physical adaptations, and cultural development interacted to form a new species. Several important physical characteristics distinguished archaic Homo sapiens from their predecessors. Although archaic Homo sapiens has a bigger brain than Homo erectus and is ancestral to modern humans, this species differs from modern humans. Archaic Homo sapiens possessed less brain capacity than modern humans, but larger brains than the Homo erectus lineage. Archaic Homo sapiens showed erectus-like facial features with prominent brow ridges and protruding faces. Some anthropologists conclude that archaic Homo sapiens emerged gradually from erectus, with a vague borderline dividing the species. Fossil evidence shows only Homo erectus remains dating from 700,000 years ago, but by 200,000 years ago there is evidence of archaic Homo sapiens remains.[86] Mostly likely archaic Homo sapiens led to the rise of Neanderthals around 200,000 years ago and to modern humans around 120,000 years ago.[87]

Archaic Homo sapiens made important cultural developments beginning around 250,000 years ago. After more than a million years of relative technological stasis, the simple hand axe industry of Homo erectus gave way to a more complex technology in which tools were fashioned from large flakes. Flake tools—side-scrappers, knives, hand-axes, and points—were all of a standard shape and size, which were then further shaped.[88] Archaic Homo sapiens apparently crafted some of the oldest surviving wooden artifacts—wooden spears, digging sticks and clubs. It is difficult to estimate the first use of wood as a material for tools because it decayed more quickly than stone tools. But apparently wood served as the first tool material and was used for constructing the protective surroundings of a group's encampment. Tools recovered that are older than a few hundred thousand years were made of stone.[89] These cognitive and technological developments coincided with the biological shift from Homo erectus to archaic sapiens.

Reconstruction of a Neanderthal man

Increasingly sophisticated technology had often been assumed to be the selective pressure that stimulated an increase in brain size, but now many scholars believe that development of a spoken language sparked brain expansion. Studies show that simple speech requires more brain tissue than tool making. Skills necessary for successful social interaction lead to an increase in brain expansion. Although it is hard to draw conclusions about the effects of the development of language on brain size in the absence of traceable evidence, we can say that an increase in brain capacity and a greater reliance on cultural developments appear to have stimulated each other in a feedback loop of interaction.[90]

Archaic Homo sapiens were ancestors to both Homo sapiens sapiens (modern humans) and Neanderthals. **Neanderthals** are often portrayed as stereotypical, dim-witted, hairy, slouching beasts emerging from a dark cave, then tramping across a bleak and frozen tundra wielding a club in one hand while dragging his equally dim-witted female companion by the hair with the other. Despite this negative image, it is now believed they were a distinct group that evolved from archaic stock of Homo sapiens. Classified as Homo sapiens neanderthalis, this subspecies of Homo sapiens lived from 200,000 to 35,000 years ago and reached its classic form around 75,000 years ago during the last ice age that lasted until 10,000 years ago.[91] Neanderthals featured a stocky and muscular build, strong front teeth, a protruding, wide nose, and heavy brow ridges. They were well equipped to successfully survive the harsh northerly latitudes of the Ice Age. Formidable hunters, Neanderthals refined their tool-making skills to prey upon big herbivores, such as mammoths, rhinoceros, bison, and horses. Neanderthals needed great strength to hunt these large animals; an adult male could hoist as much as 700 pounds.[92] For protection against the harsh elements they fashioned clothing and tents from animal skins and sought sanctuary in caves and rock shelters. For warmth they built hearths, and they were perhaps the first to pioneer the use of fire for cooking and preparing meat, a mainstay of their diet. Neanderthals buried their dead. From the presence of pollen and other artifacts in their graves, we can infer that they performed funeral ceremonies to honor their dead.[93] Although older species may have practiced some sort of religious ceremony, the Neanderthal grave artifacts are the first evidence found of religious observances, an important cultural development that added a new dimension to their lives.

Neanderthals disappeared around 33,000 years ago. Speculation suggests that modern Homo sapiens invaded their territory and killed them off in war-like encounters. Others theorize that perhaps modern humans adapted more quickly and adroitly to environmental changes and eventually replaced the Neanderthals. The last argument has more merit, since Neanderthals and modern Homo sapiens lived side by side in many areas for as many as 60,000 years. Also, a computer simulation of the two populations showed that if Neanderthals had as little as a 2 percent lower birth rate due to contact with modern humans, this would result in their disappearance in a few thousand years. Whatever the reason for their demise, by 33,000 years ago in Western Europe, their last and main bastion of existence, Neanderthals joined millions of other species in becoming extinct.[94] Homo sapiens perhaps showed an early proclivity for invading an alien ecosystem, exploiting it, and hastening the extinction of a species. Neanderthals were perhaps the first victims of Homo sapiens' invasion and exploitation, a story that continues throughout our long history and into our own time.[95]

Evidence suggests modern humans—**homo sapiens sapiens**—emerged in sub-Saharan Africa just over 100,000 years ago, although some evidence dates the first evidence of our species to 195,000 years ago in Ethiopia. Modern humans traversed the world in another great migration over the next 60,000 years, replacing existing Neanderthals and archaic populations.[96] A theory of an African origin of modern humans has strong evidence to support it. Whereas the Neanderthals' anatomy was stocky with short limbs and a muscular build, the first modern humans in the same part of the world were tall, slight, and long-limbed. The body stature of modern humans was more suited to a tropical or temperate climate than a northerly clime. Excavation of two caves located in South Africa has yielded the earliest known modern human fossils, furnishing further evidence of our African origins.

From fossil evidence it appears that over 100,000 years ago humans attained their full brain size of approximately 1200 cc. Modern humans used their increased brain size to develop cultural innovations such as more sophisticated tool use. It seems likely that natural selection favored higher intelligence even within this limited time period. There is significant evidence for cultural developments during the last 100,000 years and phenomenal acceleration within the last 40,000 years.[97]

Questions to Consider

1. Do you think there is a tension between our animal and cultural selves that existed in the past and continues to the present day? Why or why not?

Insights: Learning from the Past

THE UNIVERSE TO HUMAN EMERGENCE CONCLUDING INSIGHTS

The key to our ability for cultural adaptation is the brain's capacity to think and our human gift to be self-aware and self-conscious. Why did this evolve? Niles Eldredge argues that the mind "provides a handy short-cut, a quick reference point to help each member of a social group figure out what's going on with everyone else."[98] Culture is a human adaptive strategy, an all-enveloping cocoon, a protective web that enables us to survive and thrive in the natural world. With the evolution of Homo sapiens sapiens, culture began to dominate over purely physical factors in our response to the natural environment in which we found ourselves. Through a series of evolutionary events, we began to rely more heavily on culturally learned behavior in our strategies for survival. But a tension between our animal and cultural selves existed then and continues to the present day.

Through a path of human evolution our species called Homo sapiens sapiens meanders. We modern humans have unique and species-specific characteristics, but we continue to be connected to our evolutionary past and to an interdependent network of living beings that constitutes the world.

Questions to Consider

1. What does the following statement mean to you: "We modern humans have unique and species-specific characteristics, but we continue to be connected to our evolutionary past and to an interdependent network of living beings that constitutes the world?"

In the next chapter we examine the universal commonalities that humans share with each other and how cultural diversity shapes our individual uniqueness.

ENDNOTES

1. Stephen Hawking, *Black Holes and Baby Universes and other Essays* (New York: McGraw Hill, 1993), p. 99.
2. Stuart Clark, *Towards the Edge of the Universe: A Review of Modern Cosmology* (West Sussex England: John Wiley & Sons, 1997), p. 173. Estimates of this date vary between 10 and 20 billion years.
3. Edward Wright, "The Origin of the Universe," in *The Origin and Evolution of the Universe*, eds. Ben Zuckerman and Matthew A. Malkan (Sudbury, MA: Jones and Bartlett Publishers, 1996), p. 1.
4. Joseph Silk, *A Short History of the Universe* (New York: Scientific American Library, 1994), p. 172.
5. Silk, *Short History of Universe*, p. 66, 172, and 233; Time Life Books, eds. Voyage Through the Universe: The Cosmos (Alexandria: Time Life Books, 1988), p. 12, 119 and 130.
6. Silk, *History of Universe*, p. 233 and Marc Lachieze-Rey, *Cosmology: A First Course* (Cambridge: Cambridge University Press, 1995), p. 7.
7. Silk, *History of Universe* 19; and Lachieze-Rey, *Cosmology*, p. 7.
8. Silk, *History of Universe*, p. 41.
9. Fred Adams, "The Origins of Stars and Planets," in *Origins and Evolution of Universe*, p. 37.
10. Silk, *History the Universe*, p. 122 and 194; and Lachieze-Rey, *Cosmology*, p. 10.
11. Brian Swimme and Thomas Berry, *The Universe Story* (New York: Harper Collins Publishers, 1991), p. 34-45; Carl Sagan and Ann Druyan, *Shadows of Forgotten Ancestors* (New York: Ballantine Books, 1992), p. 13; and Silk, *History of Universe*, p. 6.
12. Silk, *History of Universe*, p. 228-230.
13. Sharon Begley, "When Galaxies Collide," *Newsweek* Vol. 130, No. 18 (Nov. 3, 1997), p. 34.
14. Silk, *History of Universe*, p. 215 and 221.
15. Begley, "Galaxies Collide," *Newsweek*, p. 33.
16. Silk, *History of Universe*, p. 146-147.
17. Begley, "Galaxies Collide," *Newsweek*, p. 33-34; and Silk, *History of Universe*, p. 148-149.
18. Silk, *History of Universe*, p. 74 and 174.
19. G. Siefired Kutter, *The Universe and Life: Origins and Evolution* (Boston: Jones and Bartlett Publishers, Inc., 1987), p. 168; and Roger J. Taylor, *The Hidden Universe* (New York: Ellis Horwood, 1991), p. 17.
20. Kutter, *Universe and Life*, 168; and Taylor, *Hidden Universe*, p. 17.
21. Sagan and Druyan, *Shadows*, p. 22; and Kutter, *Universe and Life*, p. 306.
22. Sagan and Druyan, *Shadows*, p. 21-22.
23. Sagan and Druyan, *Shadows*, p. 22-23.
24. J. E. Lovelock, *Gaia: A New Look at Life on Earth*, (Oxford: Oxford Univ. Press, 1979), p. 14.
25. Swimme and Berry, *Universe Story*, p. 84; and Kutter, *Universe and Life*, p. 254.
26. Kutter, *Universe and Life*, p. 255, 256, and 258.
27. Kutter, *Universe and Life*, p. 304.
28. Kutter, *Universe and Life*, p. 305.
29. Christopher P. McKay, "The Origin and Evolution of Life in the Universe," in *Origin and Evolution of Universe*, p. 110.
30. Kutter, *Universe and Life*, p. 340.
31. Swimme and Berry, *Universe Story*, p. 125; and Barkow, Jerome H., Cosmides, Leda, Tooby, John, "Introduction: Evolutionary Psychology and Conceptual Integration," in *The Adapted Mind: Evolutionary Psychology and the Generation of Culture* (New York: Oxford University Press, 1992), p. 84

32. Barkow, Cosmides, and Tooby, "Evolutionary Psychology," in *Adapted Mind*, p. 51-52.
33. Colin Tudge, *The Time Before History: Five Million Years of Human Impact* (New York: Scribner, 1996), p. 111; and Niles Eldredge, *Dominion* (New York: Henry Holt and Company, 1995), p. 55.
34. Swimme and Berry, *Universe Story*, p. 129-130.
35. Kutter, *Universe and Life*, p. 256.
36. I have replaced the term kingdom with a gender neutral term, realm.
37. Swimme and Berry, *Universe Story*, p. 139.
38. Kutter, *Universe and Life*, p. 260-263; McKay, "The Origin and Evolution of Life in the Universe," in *Origin and Evolution of the Universe*, p. 110; and Swimme and Berry, *Universe Story*, p. 139-140.
39. Niles Eldredge, *Dominion* (New York: Henry Holt and Company, 1995), p. 19; Kutter, *Universe and Life*, p. 45; and Swimme and Berry, *Universe Story*, p. 116 and 117.
40. Kutter, *Universe and Life*, p. 429 and 455; and Swimme and Berry, *Universe Story*, p. 117.
41. Swimme and Berry, *Universe Story*, p. 119 and Eldredge, *Dominion*, p. 128.
42. Swimme and Berry, *Universe Story*, p. 122; and Kutter, *Universe and Life*, p. 476 and 486.
43. Eldredge, *Dominion*, p. 128.
44. Swimme and Berry, *Universe Story*, p. 123-124; and Kutter, *Universe and Life*, p. 477 and 496.
45. Vaclav Smil, *Cycles of Life: Civilization and the Biosphere* (New York: Scientific American Library, 1997), p. 9.
46. Eldredge, *Dominion*, p. 25; Clive Gamble, *Timewalkers: The Prehistory of Global Colonization* (Cambridge, MA: Harvard University Press, 1994), p. 11, 36-37 and 76.
47. Richard Leakey, T*he Origin of Modern Humans* (New York: Basic Books, 1994), p. 58.
48. Tudge, *Time Before History*, p. 113 and 170.
49. Eldredge, *Dominion*, p. 127.
50. Tudge, *Time Before History*, p. 176.
51. Kutter, *Universe and Life*, p. 516.
52. Brace, *Stages Evolution*, p. 78.
53. Kutter, *Universe and Life*, p. 517; and Tudge, *Time Before History*, p. 171.
54. Kutter, *Universe and Life*, p. 517-51; and Campbell, *Humankind Emerging*, p. 101 and 106.
55. John A. Gowlett, *Ascent to Civilization: The Archaeology of Early Humans* (New York: McGraw Hill, 1993), p. 20.
56. Gowlett, *Early Humans*, p. 20; and Kutter, *Universe and Life*, p. 528.
57. Brace, *Stages of Evolution*, p. 81, 83-84; and Campbell, *Humankind Emerging*, p. 113.
58. Roger Lewin, *The Origin of Modern Humans* (New York: Scientific American Library, 1993), p. 21.
59. Tudge, *Time Before History*, p. 189-190; and Campbell, *Humankind Emerging*, p. 218-220.
60. Leakey, *Origin Humans*, p. 20.
61. Tudge, *Time Before History*, p. 177-178.
62. Kutter, *Universe and Life*, p. 506-507.
63. Tudge, *Time Before History*, p. 199-200.
64. Tudge, *Time Before History*, p. 192.
65. Tudge, *Time Before History*, p. 197.
66. Brace, *Stages of Evolution*, p. 97-112.
67. Tudge, *Time Before History*, p. 189.
68. Brace, *Stages of Evolution*, p. 105-106; and Campbell, *Humankind Emerging*, p. 214.

69. Brace, *Stages of Evolution*, p. 102; and Gowlett, *Early Humans*, p. 26.
70. Alan Bilsborough, *Human Evolution* (London: Blackie Academic & Professional, 1992), p. 68-71 and 102; and Tudge, *Time Before History*, p. 189.
71. Eldredge, *Dominion*, p. 58.
72. Tudge, *Time Before History*, p. 190; Lewin, *Origin of Humans*, p. 25; and Kutter, *Universe and Life*, p. 532.
73. Tudge, *Time Before History*, p. 204 and p. 207-208; Kutter, *Universe and Life*, p. 534. The Paleolithic is divided into the Lower Paleolithic, 2.5 million years ago to 200,000 years ago; the Middle Paleolithic, 200,000 to 40,000 years ago; and the Upper, 40,000 to 12,000 years ago.
74. Eldrege, *Dominion*, p. 51-52.
75. Lewin, *Origin of Humans*, p. 34; and Kutter, *Universe and Life*, p. 532.
76. Linda Caporael and Marilynn B. Brewer, "Reviving Evolutionary Psychology: Biology Meets Society," *Journal of Social Issues* Vol. 47, No. 3 (1991), p. 190-191; Leakey, *Origin of Humankind*, p. 45; and Campbell, *Humankind Emerging*, p. 305.
77. Tudge, *Time Before History*, p. 206.
78. Gowlett, *Early Humans*, p. 62; and Tudge, *Time Before History*, p. 210.
79. Kutter, *Universe and Life*, p. 536-537.
80. Tudge, *Time Before History*, p. 259.
81. Brace, *Stages of Evolution*, p. 138. It is debatable whether Homo erectus cooked food. Some suggest Neanderthals pioneered this development.
82. Tudge, *Time Before History*, p. 210; and Lewin, *Origin of Humans*, p. 15.
83. Leakey, *Origin of Humankind*, p. 87-88; and Lewin, *Origin of Humans*, p. 63-87.
84. Gowlett, *Early Humans*, p. 101; and Leakey, *Origin of Humankind*, p. 96-97.
85. Leakey, *Origin of Humankind*, p. 90; and Eldredge, *Dominion*, p. 81.
86. Gowlett, *Early Humans*, p. 84.
87. Tudge, *Time Before History*, p. 214.
88. Lewin, *Origin of Humans*, p. 118.
89. Gowlett, *Early Humans*, p. 94.
90. Lewin, *Origin of Humans*, p. 32.
91. Tudge, *Time Before History*, p. 214-219; and Brace, *Stages of Evolution*, p. 141-143.
92. William F. Allman, *The Stone Age Present* (New York: Simon & Schuster, 1994), p. 194.
93. Tudge, *Time Before History*, p. 215-216 and 219; and Kutter, *Universe and Life*, p. 538-539.
94. Tudge, *Time Before History*, p. 219; Eldredge, *Dominion*, p. 86; and Allman, *Stone Age*, p. 189.
95. Eldredge, *Dominion*, p. 86.
96. Lewin, *Origin of Humans*, p. 117; Leakey, *Origin of Humankind*, p. 90; Eldredge, *Dominion*, p. 78; and Gowlett, *Early Humans*, p. 100.
97. Brace, *Stages of Evolution*, p. 78; and Gowlett, *Early Humans*, p. 104.
98. Eldredge, *Dominion*, p. 23.

Chapter 3

Our Collective Story: Human Commonalities

"A human being is part of the whole, called by us Universe, a part limited in time and space. He experiences himself, his thoughts and feelings as something separated from the rest—a kind of optical delusion of his consciousness. This delusion is a kind of prison for us, restricting us to our personal desires and to affection for a few persons nearest to us. Our task must be to free ourselves from this prison by widening our circle of compassion to embrace all living creatures and the whole of nature in its beauty."

— Albert Einstein

HUMAN COMMONALITIES: AN INTRODUCTION

We are physically connected with all forms of life, an interdependent part of the Earth and the Universe. In the course of our evolution we have acquired unique characteristics that both unite us as a species and distinguish us from other species. Despite variations in time and space, it is mystifying to see that we as a species have reacted to events, constructed our cultures, and conducted our ordinary ways of life in fairly consistent ways. Why is this so? Before we turn to the five waves of our human history, let's first explore the characteristics that demonstrate our human commonality, the many similarities that we all share through our long human story.

We can look at our common features from two perspectives: the individual level and the group level. First, at an individual level, humans through history exhibit numerous behaviors that are common to us all. This does not mean that all humans behave identically, but it does affirm that all humans share similar psychological and physical processes. Anthropologist Donald Brown asserts that the human mind "is fundamentally the same in all human populations."[1] Since as individuals we have many basic qualities in common, we can infer that we also share similarities at a group level. Regardless of where or when they occurred, human societies responded similarly to events and particular environments. These social and cultural responses are called group commonalities, an essential ingredient in this holistic approach.

Our interdisciplinary study of human commonalities draws in particular on the fields of psychology, sociology, and anthropology in order to explore what connects us as a species. **Evolutionary psychology**, a field of study that merges the disciplines of psychology and anthropology, helps explain individual and group commonalities. The inherited framework of the human mind has evolved through our 2.5 million year hominid and human existence.[2] We share a fundamental human psychology, or human nature, despite the disparate types of societies and cultures in which we live. This human nature is shaped by our history as foragers, our interaction with environmental influences, our genetic make-up and other factors. Natural selection plays a vital role by selecting psychological behaviors that are conducive to our way of life.[3] At a deep-seated level human emotions and behaviors are universal, but at a superficial level they vary according to culture.[4] In other words, there is a psychological unity of all humankind.

Cultural Diversity
Universal Human Commonalities

Psychologist Carl Jung's study of the collective unconscious, synchronicity, and other phenomena offers an insightful explanation of a universal human nature and provides a logical and comprehensive framework for this holistic history. Jung questions the perception that the human mind is a "blank slate" allowing humans to behave according to their own free will. Instead, he reasons that each human possesses a universal, inherited, unconscious that is manifested through raw images or archetypes and expressed through dreams, art, mythology, and other forms. **Archetypes** are universal, collective, primordial images or concepts that, together with instincts, form the collective unconscious. Archetypes are not fully developed pictures in the mind, but can be compared to a photograph waiting to be developed by an individual's experiences. A few of the many examples of archetypes are the hero, the villain, the trickster, the mother, and a deity. The archetypes expressed are a reflection of an individual's particular geographic location and worldview, but the universality of the archetypes connects individuals to our primordial ancestors and to humans around the world, regardless of cultural differences or experiences.[5] The repository of these inherited psychic characteristics Jung calls the **collective unconscious**, which is the cumulative experience we inherit from our ancestors regardless of cultural and individual differences.[6]

In this holistic world history, we see the role played by such variables as physical surroundings, social environment, and various experiences that combine to create diverse human cultures. **Culture** is briefly defined here as a system of learned behaviors, symbols, customs, beliefs, institutions, artifacts, and technology characteristic of a group and transmitted by its members to their offspring. Culture is manifested from a combination of common human behaviors, responses to the physical environment, and individual and collective experiences; it is not disembodied from a universal human nature but is inextricably linked with it.

Questions to Consider

1. What is your reaction to Albert Einstein's quote at the beginning of this chapter?

Individual Commonalities

By synthesizing various sources I have developed a ten dimensional Human Commonalities Model that explains our universal human nature.[7] The value of this model is that it shows how humans, because of certain universal human behaviors, historically develop similar institutions, artistic expressions, political organizations, and religious views. These commonalities provide a foundation for the construction of this holistic world history.

HUMAN COMMONALITIES MODEL

Dimension 1
The Physical and Physiological Dimension

All humans share physical senses: radiation senses—response to sight and temperature, feeling senses—hearing, making sounds, touch, and sense of balance, space, and rhythm, and chemical senses—(smell, taste, appetite, hunger, eating, and thirst.[8] Along with shared physical senses, humans have common physiological needs. A need is a force provoked by either external or internal events that triggers actions to satisfy it. In this dimension humans strive to satisfy such basic, physical needs as food, shelter, sleep, and water. According to Abraham Maslow, these basic needs must be satisfied before other needs are fulfilled.

Dimension 2
The Pleasure and Pain Dimension

Individuals generally focus on finding pleasurable sensations and activities. Sex is a pleasurable sensation along with forming bonds of community. An affinity to music and dance, and the taste of food and drink are pleasurable sensations. Other pleasurable sensations and activities include smoking, alcohol, and drugs. All pleasurable sensations can possibly become addictive. Sexual jealousy, grief, anxiety, and insecurity are but a few examples of painful emotional experiences.[9]

Dimension 3
The Survival Dimension

In this dimension an individual devises methods to obtain food for survival. This includes an ability to gather or grow food, and to identify edible foods. Because of this survival sense, many humans can be preoccupied with practical, everyday occurrences and meeting basic physical needs.

Dimension 4
The Territorial Dimension

Humans have a sense of territoriality that propels them to secure and protect a defined territory they designate as their own and to defend that territory from encroachment by others. This territorial sense when threatened has contributed to destructive conflict and war through history.

Dimension 5
The Power Dimension

Those who crave power aim to consume, to master, to conquer, to use violence, and to force their views on others.[10] Individuals have the capacity to react to circumstances and events by repelling, intimidating, exploiting, domesticating, conquering, and fighting. Emotions elicited include envy, fear, revenge, hate, terror, vindictiveness, anger, disapproval, and contempt. Individuals strive to dominate people and situations, increase their prestige and wealth, protect their pride, manipulate and control others and nature, and form hierarchical structures with themselves at the top.

Dimension 6
The Safety Dimension

Individuals strive to achieve personal safety and work to obtain life's basic needs in order to feel a sense of security and comfort. Safety needs include structure, security, order, stability, protection, comfort, avoidance of pain, and freedom from fear or chaos. The need for order and stability are heightened when the future is unpredictable or when political stability or the social order is threatened.[11] If safety needs are met, emotions expressed include trust, commitment, ease, and contentment. If safety needs are not met, emotional reactions may be mistrust, disapproval, fear, anger, anxiety, apprehension, or insecurity.

HUMAN COMMONALITIES MODEL

Dimension 7

The Belonging Dimension

Individuals look to satisfy the need to belong to a group and seek affection and friendship. People possess a cooperative nature that includes a capacity to share and reciprocate. We also have a need for self-esteem and self-respect, which includes the desire to feel competent and worthwhile, and to be recognized by others. A failure to be accepted by one's self and by others may lead to feelings of inferiority, alienation, insecurity, distress, mistrust, or discouragement. But when accepted, humans experience love and compassion, and feelings of harmony and acceptance. Although very few people are able to fulfill this dimension, those who do can feel compassion for suffering, and begin to love and accept others and themselves unconditionally. Pleasant emotions are associated with this dimension: delight, affection, love, happiness, sense of humor, play and sport, surprise, exultation, forgiveness, approval, admiration, passion, tenderness, commitment, and trust. Along with pleasant, belonging emotions, there are painful or unpleasant emotions that are also part of the human experience: sadness, sorrow, distress, grief, sadness, loss, and displeasure.

Dimension 8

The Consciousness Dimension

Individuals possess a sophisticated cognitive ability—consciousness. **Consciousness** is a feature of the mind usually associated with subjectivity, self-awareness, sentience, the capacity to perceive one's relationship with one's environment, and the ability to reflect upon these.[12] All humans have a consciousness with the following attributes: intuition, reasoning, capacity for logic and science, psychic capacity, hypnotic power, capacity for language and communication, the development of values and behavior that is inquisitive, reflective, and synthesizing.

Dimension 9

The Self-Actualization Dimension

In this dimension an individual directs his/her attention to discover or rediscover his/her inner world. S/he experiences a deep connection with the world, a continuous enjoyment of the here and now, impartially observes social roles free from fear and vulnerability, and non-judgmentally witnesses the drama of life.[13] When other needs are satisfied, for some rare individuals a new discontent or restlessness develops that demands attention. At this point an individual may ask, What do I want out of life, where is my life headed, what do I wish to accomplish? Answers to these self-reflective questions differ with each individual and particular society, but generally an individual has a need to realize his/her heart-felt potential. Most people direct some attention to self-actualization goals, but few adults actualize their goals.[14]

In this dimension individuals may exhibit an aesthetic sense that is expressed through a need to create artistic works and appreciate beauty, order, and symmetry.[15] Aesthetic expression is displayed through such different mediums as music, dance, sculpture, oral traditions, written works, song, dress, and personal adornment.

Dimension 10

The Spiritual Dimension

Humans embody a spiritual dimension that is often ignored in the study of world history. Materialists argue a spiritual capacity in humans is non-quantifiable, intangible, unknowable, and therefore does not exist. The following elements characterize the spiritual dimension: a conscience; ecstasy or joy; a connection between good and evil; sacrifice; a spiritual vision; a cosmic consciousness; a merging of mind, body, and spirit; and a mystical sense. A spiritual need is basic to our biological life and constitutes our essential humanity.

Carl Jung addresses humanity's spiritual dimension by asking a question: Why is there an entity similar to the idea of the Judeo-Christian God found in other cultures? He answers that question and others by theorizing that there is a spirit archetype that is inherited in our collective unconscious. Spiritual images surface in dreams, folklore, artwork, and experiences of people everywhere. Humans, in other words, are born with an unconscious predisposition to a spiritual dimension. Our spiritual inclinations are inherited, like our biological and mental capacities. But an individual's spiritual sense manifests itself differently according to a one's own personality, particular cultural experiences, environment, and historical circumstances.

Humans often form religious institutions to satisfy their spiritual needs. These institutions provide followers with a sense of purpose, feelings of security and belonging, a framework for dealing with the dualistic aspects of good and evil, and a community of support.

We tend to think in terms of contrasts and opposites such as black and white, good and evil, female and male, culture and biology. Dualistic thinking can be linked with our right/left brain behaviors that is in turn linked to brain symmetry and cerebral specialization. Dualistic thinking is a significant aspect of human thought since it conditions our cultural responses and influences our construction of religious ideas.[16]

Chenrezig sand mandala, which is Sanskrit for circle; a mandala is considered a sacred space by Hindus and Buddhists.

For many people, God, in one form or another, is the reality, and not just a handy concept. In the full expression of the spiritual dimension an individual loses all sense of separation and becomes one with all things. S/he identifies with both inner and outer worlds, and reaches a state beyond all categories, visions, sentiments, thoughts, and feelings. An individual connects to a cosmic consciousness dimension transcending individual self-awareness or ego. An individual feels at one with peace, love, wisdom, energy, beauty, clarity, and oneness.[17]

This model offers a brief compilation of human commonalities. When dwelling upon the many differences that exist from one society to another and from one time period to another, it is comforting to remember that beneath the layer of superficial differences are underlying commonalities that humans can acknowledge and celebrate as interconnected members of the same human species.

Questions to Consider

1. What is your reaction to the Human Commonalities Model? Do you think it adequately explains human behaviors? Explain.

Group Commonalities: Currents in World History

At the group level, commonalities are expressed and manifested in the formation of distinct human patterns or what I call currents in this world history. For example, the individual human need to belong can be connected to a response that is reflected in the formation of kinship groups and the family. A drive for power and control results in the formation of rules and laws to order society. There is an intricate relationship between individual human commonalities and the ways in which humans construct their society. In this world history, individual and group commonalities are organized into five currents.

The table below explains ways in which individual commonalities connect to the five currents and group commonalities. The five currents presented in this table are further developed in the rest of this chapter, and are presented in each of the five waves.

Human Commonalities and the Five Currents

CURRENTS	HUMAN COMMONALITIES
Relationship with Nature: Ecosystem Currents:	
1. geographic location 2. environment 3. human populations 4. natural populations 5. human and nature interaction	1. survival needs 2. need to grow food
Ways of Living: Techno-Economic Currents	
1. daily life 2. economic systems 3. technology 4. exchange and trade 5. patterns of labor	1. need for food, shelter, sleep, and water 2. horticulture sense 3. need for comfort 4. survival needs
Human Networks: Social Currents	
1. groups and institutions 2. family 3. gender roles 4. prestige and social status 5. socialization and education	1. sexual and reproductive needs 2. need to belong 3. cooperative sense 4. need to share and reciprocate 5. compassion 6. need for love 7. friendship 8. self-respect 9. kinship ties
Establishing Order: Political Currents	
1. political systems 2. forms of leadership 3. customs, rules/ laws and punishment 4. migration and interaction 5. conflict/cooperation and warfare	1. drive for power, mastery, control 2. conflict 3. sense of territoriality 4. needs of safety and security 5. need for stability
Human Expression: Cultural Currents	
1. worldview and ideology 2. spirituality and religion 3. communication 4. identity and belonging 5. aesthetic expression	1. sense of rhythm 2. aesthetic sense 3. identity 4. need for language/communication 5. sense of belonging 6. need for self-actualization 7. spiritual sense

Group Commonalities and Five Currents
1. relationship with nature: ecosystem currents 2. ways of living: techno-economic currents 3. human networks: social currents 4. ways of establishing order: political currents 5. human expressions: cultural currents

Currents in our human story are evidence of continuity that link us to one another and provide a foundation for understanding this holistic world history. But the five currents as they are expressed in each of the five waves—communal, agricultural, urban, modern, and global—show the transformation that people have undergone. The rest of this chapter includes a description of the human commonalities and an explanation of terms and concepts that are used in subsequent chapters.

RELATIONSHIP WITH NATURE: ECOSYSTEM CURRENTS

In this holistic world history an **ecosystem** is defined as the interacting community of all the organisms in an area—including humans and the non-human world—and their physical environment. Geography, the environment, human populations, natural populations, and interaction of humans and nature are all interrelated sub-currents in the ecosystem current.

Geography

Geographical factors are important variables that help shape a society's cultural manifestations. The following model summarizes the Earth's geography and is organized according to: Hot/Cold regions, Wet/Dry regions and High/Low regions.[18]

Environment

Environmental factors affect world history. The environmental factors affecting humans are water, climate, natural disasters, natural resources, soil, air quality and vegetation patterns. For

HOT AND COLD REGIONS	
HOT REGIONS	**COLD REGIONS**
1. Scrub forests between coasts and mountains that have mild, wet winters and hot, dry summers. These areas represent only 1% of the landmass, but hold 5% of the world's population. 2. Tropical forests are regions such as the Amazon basin of Brazil that have warm climates and abundant rainfall. They cover 10% of the Earth's surface with 28% of our human population occupying these regions.	1. Heavily wooded areas dominated by coniferous trees that have cold climate conditions, and occupy areas of northern North America and Eurasia. These forests represent 10% of the Earth's land surface, but only 1% of the world's population resides in these areas. 2. Polar lands near the north and south poles are characterized by three environments: • ice-zones, regions of permanent snow and ice; • tundra, undulating treeless plains in the arctic and subarctic regions of northern climes; • taigas, swampy coniferous forests of the northern lands south of the tundra. Polar lands represent 16% of the Earth's land area but are home to less than 1% of the Earth's people.

example water, the essence of life, covers 70 percent of the Earth's surface, but it is not evenly distributed across the globe. Humans interact with others for use and control of the world's watered areas. About half of the Earth's land surface is composed of arid deserts, rugged mountain ranges, and frigid tundra that cannot sustain a substantial human population. Therefore, human population is concentrated in a relatively small, often contested area of the Earth's surface near oceans, rivers, and lakes.

Human Populations

The size, density, composition, and dispersal of human populations signify an important

WET AND DRY REGIONS	
WET REGIONS	**DRY REGIONS**
• Lakes and coastal lands, river valleys, and mixed forests of conifers and broadleaf trees. • These areas have the highest population density and the most fertile soils. • Wet regions have temperate climates with moderate rainfall, and are characterized by rolling plains and open areas. • Although wetland regions make up approximately 7% of the Earth's land surface they currently house 43% of the world's population	• Grasslands cover 26% of the Earth's surface, but only 10% of the world's population inhabits these regions. • Three basic types of grassland differ in climate and type of grass: steppes, prairies, and savannas. • Steppes, such as the vast treeless expanse of southeast Europe and Asia, host dry climates and extreme temperature changes. The grasses are short, hardy varieties that tolerate dry climates. • Prairies, such as the North American Great Plains, have wetter climates, and support taller types of grasses. • Found in tropical areas, savannas, such as the treeless plains in East Africa, grow tall grasses and drought-resistant undergrowth. • Arid lands or deserts like the Sahara in northern Africa have low annual rainfall with much of the land sparsely covered by various grasses, low-growing desert shrubs, or devoid of plant life altogether. • Deserts comprise 18% of the world's landmass while only 6% of its people live in these forbidding regions.

HIGH AND LOW REGIONS	
HIGH REGIONS	**LOW REGIONS**
• Mountain lands with complex landforms and a variety of environments within close distance of each other. • Mountain lands represent 12% of the globe's land area, and home to 7% of the world's people.	• Low regions include river valleys, lake and coastal lands described above.

variable that affects cultural change. As human populations grow, social relationships become more complex and new ways of organizing society result. Populations are not evenly distributed around the globe but are concentrated in clusters. These clusters of intense population density do not remain static and may shift over time. Historically, four dense clusters of people are located in Asia: China's valley of the Huang He (Yellow) and Chang Jiang (Yangtze) Rivers; and South Asia's river valleys of the Ganges and Indus. Along with the older Asian centers, four contemporary dense population areas include western Europe, eastern North America, and parts of Africa and coastal areas of South America.[19]

Natural Populations

This sub-current examines the natural populations—flora and fauna—in a particular wave and how they are affected by humans. **Carrying capacity** is an important concept that is discussed in each wave. The term means the maximum number of individuals of a species that an area, region, or the whole Earth can support. In other words, it refers to the size of a population that can live indefinitely in an environment without doing that environment any harm. The term applies to plants, animals and people.

Human and Nature Interaction

Humans depend on nature to supply all basic needs and interact constantly with their environments. Our ancestors adapted and evolved in natural settings, where they reacted to changing environmental conditions. With the advent of agriculture 10,000 years ago, our relationship with nature began to change. Living within nature's limits, once the norm throughout our evolutionary past, began to change in the direction of increasing human control over other humans, animals, and the environment. Instead of participating with nature, cultural developments such as agriculture separated our species from nature. The fissure with nature can be placed on a continuum; with greater cultural and technological complexity, our awareness of and our reliance on nature diminishes.

Sahara Desert in Libya, north Africa

Our relationship with nature fluctuates from destructive to creative. As a creative force in human life, nature provides material resources for human survival and is the matrix that connects the human psyche to the wider cosmos. However, when nature disrupts human life, causing death and devastation, it is considered a destructive force. Our species strives to manipulate and control nature's destructive forces in order to enhance human survival as exemplified in the building of dams to prevent flooding. Although destructive and creative energies are neutral to nature, with no troublesome duality; humans may prescribe a moral judgment, such as good or evil, to these natural actions and events. Thus, humans denote a drought or flood as destructive, but it is merely a neutral act carried out by nature as part of its continuous process that has no moral meaning. When humans exert too much control over nature, such as when they divert too much water for irrigation purposes, they unduly upset the delicate balance with nature, which may ultimately create destruction such as soil salinity. On the other hand they may harness nature in a way that results in benefits for humans, at least in the short term.

Questions to Consider

1. What does the following quote mean to you? "Although destructive and creative energies are neutral to nature, with no troublesome duality; humans may prescribe a moral judgment, such as good or evil, to these natural actions and events."

WAYS OF LIVING: TECHNO-ECONOMIC CURRENTS

Daily life, economic systems, technology, exchange and trade, and patterns of labor all form the techno-economic currents. Humans fashion a way of life to create optimal conditions for survival and ingeniously devise methods for realizing this goal. Methods for satisfying survival needs vary with different environmental influences, acquired knowledge, and experience. Technological changes are an important factor in stimulating changes in other currents.

Daily Life

Through history humans have migrated to every area of the globe and call the frigid Arctic reaches of the North Pole to the steaming equatorial jungles home. The environment presents limits and possibilities in the form of natural resources that humans extract for food, clothing, and shelter. People create a domestic sphere that includes a dwelling space or shelter, a place for preparation and consumption of food, cleaning and grooming, a place for body adornment, an area for sleep and sexual activity, and a place for rearing infants and children.[20] Diverse forms of food, clothing, and shelter give a particular culture its unique and distinctive way of life.

Economic Systems

An **economic system** is a method by which people procure, distribute, and consume valued food, material goods, and services. An economic system includes subsistence methods that are related to the production of food and other needed goods, as well as the customs or rules that control how goods are utilized once they are produced. Types of economic systems vary with the complexity of a society and environmental influences. Economist Karl Polanyi classifies economic systems that distribute material resources into three types: reciprocity, redistribution, and the market system.[21] These different types are explained further in the five waves.

Technology

Humans use technology to transform nature, both physically and biologically, for their own use. **Technology** is defined as information for converting material resources of the environment to satisfy human needs. Humans are a mobile species and use various forms of transportation in their long treks across the globe. Anthropologist Leslie White considers technological activities related to survival—food, shelter, and defense—as the most significant influence on societal orga-

Traditional Iroquois longhouse

nization. According to White, the character of a particular society will be most directly influenced by its subsistence technology—the tools and techniques that are used by humans to obtain food.[22] Technological adaptation has a significant influence on human society, but caution should be taken against deterministic views in which technology is seen as the only factor in shaping a society's configuration. Technology is an important variable in fashioning society but not the only variable.

Patterns of Labor

Labor is a term that denotes work or physical and mental exertion to complete a specific task. For efficiency, work is usually divided according to gender and age. Until recently in world history, female labor tended to be more routine and domestic, with women's work usually carried out near a domestic center and concentrated on tasks more easily resumed after interruption due to pregnancy and the demands of childrearing. Women direct child-care responsibilities more often than men, and their other tasks are frequently associated with child-care.[23] Women are more than likely involved in the essential task of providing food for the family or group. This task varies from gathering foods in the Communal Wave to shopping for food in a grocery store in the Modern and Global Waves.

Male labor often involves physical strength, utilizing rapid and high bursts of energy, frequent travel at some distances from home, and responsibilities that have a high degree of risk and danger.[24] Males engage in dangerous work since they are considered more expendable members of society than females who bear children. Although biology and physical factors are significant in ascertaining specific tasks and divisions of labor, this does not mean that gender roles are fixed and unchangeable, as will be noted in the Global Wave.

Questions to Consider

1. Through much of world history, labor has been divided according to gender. Why do you think it has changed in our present, modern society?

Exchange and Trade

Exchange refers to a common human pattern of giving and receiving valuable objects, commodities, and services. The movement of resources or goods from where they are located or produced to where they are used is called **distribution**. Even when there is no formal means of exchange, distribution of food, goods and services takes place. Objects of exchange vary widely in different societies, and what is identified as a valuable commodity also differs. It is common for humans to participate in gift-giving and exchanging food.[25] When exchange becomes more formalized, the institution of trade develops. **Trade**, more complex than simple exchange, involves money, merchants, and rules that govern the transactions.

HUMAN NETWORKS: SOCIAL CURRENTS

Most people are not isolated hermits, but live together in some form of social configuration. People create diverse social organizations to maintain a stable, orderly society, which further ensures survival. Humans prefer to quell change and promote continuity whenever possible. Change disrupts society; the social patterns we form tend to instill and perpetuate continuity rather than promote change. Networks—groups and institutions, family, gender, prestige and social status, and socialization and education—are all parts of our social currents.

Groups and Institutions

The most basic human group configuration is based on kinship. **Kinship** is a set of interpersonal relations which unite individuals on the basis of descent and marriage and which are maintained by a system of socially recognized obligations, rights, and customs. Groups formed on the basis of kinship are called **kinship groups**; they consist of people who are related to each other through descent or marriage. Kinship groups are often defined by a certain locality or claim a specific territory, and are materially, culturally, and cognitively attached to the environment in which they live. As a rule, kinship groups think of themselves as a distinct people, and judge others on their own terms.[26] Their particular group is the **in-group**, or "us," and those outside their group is the **out-group**, or "other."

An **institution** is a system of social relationships and cultural elements that develops in a society in response to some set of basic and persistent needs. It is a formal organization that carries out social functions in a procedural manner. Institutions are formed when societies become more complex, such as in the Urban, Modern, and Global Waves.

> **Questions to Consider**
> 1. Do you belong to a network of kinship relations? Describe it.

Family

A **family** is a basic and enduring form of human organization found in diverse domestic settings around the world. The particular family type is related to its social, historical, and environmental circumstances. Families provide such valuable functions as protecting the mother during her long pregnancy and childcare years, and acculturating family members with the group's values, beliefs, and worldview. There are two types of family units: nuclear and extended. A **nuclear family** generally includes one male, one or more females, and dependent children. The family, in turn, is part of a larger and more inclusive kinship group known as an extended family. An **extended family** is a domestic group that includes various combinations of brothers, sisters, their spouses, nieces, nephews, aunts, uncles, grandparents, cousins, unmarried children, and others. **Households** consist of families whose members may or may not be related but who cooperate in activities related to economic production, food preparation, child rearing, and shelter construction. They often share a common residence.[27]

Humans, like other animals, mate. The sexual bond formed between humans varies: some mate for life and some do not, some mate with a single individual usually of the opposite sex, a few mate with members of the same sex, while others mate with several individuals. A cross-cultural study shows a near universal pattern in which males prefer younger, physically attractive females, while females select slightly older, ambitious males who are industrious and have good prospects for providing resources. Males exhibit visible signs of their resourcefulness and ability to provide for a family, while females accentuate their fertility by highlighting their attractiveness and youth. Males, and females to a lesser extent, demonstrate sexual jealousy or mate guarding, which is an emotional response to male rivalry.[28]

Marriage is a cross-cultural response to the common human need to belong. It is a reproductive alliance that has a mutual obligation of parental investment in their children, is recognized by people in the larger community, and is backed by customs, rules, or laws. The marriage institution publicly recognizes sexual access by males to childbearing females.[29] Human societies need to control sexual activity in order to prevent its potential disruptive influence on society. Marriage bonds stabilize society by officially restricting sexual activity to members of the marriage bond, reducing public promiscuity, and lessening aggression between males. Marriage also joins two unrelated families into a social relationship bound together through kinship ties. In

Hindu Marriage Ceremony

essence, unrelated in-laws become de facto kin. Marriage is an attempt to remedy disruptions and ensure a society's stability and continuity.[30]

Societies have customs or rules that regulate sexual relations, pregnancy, birth, and child rearing. Violators of society's customs and rules are usually reprimanded in some way. For example, in many societies adultery—sexual transgression of the marriage bond—entails certain forms of societal recrimination. Women in the Urban and Modern Waves who commit these transgressions are more severely punished than males. Therefore, those who violate the marriage bonds are usually private about their extramarital, promiscuous behavior in order to avoid possible punishment and social disapproval.[31] Marriage between members of the same family is widely prohibited. Certain forms of marriage, such as a father-daughter or a mother-son marriage, are generally barred. Although not universal, brother-sister marriage, which was acceptable in ancient Egypt and among the Inca elite, is usually forbidden.[32]

There are several types of marriages. **Monogamy**, in which an individual has a single spouse, or serial monogamy, in which marriage is followed by divorce and remarriage, is found in most human societies. Even though monogamy is not universal among humans, many favor it because it assures that males share significantly in raising offspring, it reduces helter-skelter competition for mates, it provides a forum for sexual gratification, and it limits the size of a kinship network. Anthropologist Robert Russell states, "Monogamy is a grand biological and cultural illusion of faithfulness to a single mate. The illusion works. Monogamous consort bonds, no matter how temporary, produce the most human offspring with the least social disruption."[33]

Another form of marriage is **polygamy**, or plural marriage, where a person is permitted to have more than one spouse at the same time. Although less common than monogamy, it is widely accepted in some parts of the world. There are two forms of polygamous marriages: **polygyny**, in which a husband is married to more than one wife; and a less common form, **polyandry**, in which a wife is married to more than one husband.[34] Studies show that relatively successful men who have more prestige and power than others often have polygamous marriages, whether simultaneously with several wives, with a wife and a mistress or concubine, or serially by multiple single marriages. Polygamous men and those who have multiple spouses are often socially, and sometimes legally, required to financially provide for more than one wife and their numerous children. In some urban societies extreme polygyny and sequestering of women is often practiced, and men who gain despotic power often hoard large numbers of childbearing women, wives, and concubines.[35]

Numerous people in a community are involved in childcare, even though the mother has this primary responsibility. A biological mother is usually a social mother as well, but that does not mean that she provides all the care for a child.[36] A mother is generally the primary care giver for the first few years of her child's life, but after her child is weaned both parents and other group members or institutions typically care for, protect, and teach children. Women carry out other responsibilities in addition to childcare, but those responsibilities are usually intertwined with childcare. Care of children by institutions such as daycare and schools is a recent phenomenon in the Modern and Global Waves.

Fatherhood is a relatively recent and variable role for males; active participation in child rearing is not a universal behavior that all fathers share. According to Russell, "The precise role of fatherhood is poorly defined and varies greatly between different cultures."[37] He states that the role of the father in conception was not known to our remote ancestors and "it is doubtful that human fathers associated the sex act with genetic progeny until less than 100,000 years ago." Fatherhood is "simply too new to have developed significant biological roots" and, "conforms to whatever role is deemed appropriate by a particular culture."[38] Male participation in parental care is more variable than female involvement.[39]

Population control has been practiced throughout our history. When children are considered assets, they increase a family's productivity and wealth, but if children are regarded as a burden they can be considered expendable. Historically, children deemed a burden are often abandoned or **infanticide**, the practice of killing newborn infants, is carried out.[40] This does not mean that those carrying out population control have no affection for children, but the practice is predicated on whether a child can be properly cared for and whether an additional child is detrimental to overall group survival. Throughout human history, females widely practice different forms of birth control to limit the size of their families and to ensure the maximum well-being for all members.

Questions to Consider

1. Why do you think families have been such a long-lasting institution in our human history?

Gender

Males and females relate to one another and to the world at large differently. **Gender** is a set of characteristics distinguishing between male and female. An important distinction is made between sex, which is biological, and gender, which is cultural. In our 2.5 million year human history, gender differences have developed in response to biological and physical differences. Societies construct and perpetuate male and female roles and form social institutions based on them in order to maintain order and stability, and to perform functions efficiently. But gender roles are not rigid or unchangeable and are expanded upon in each of the waves.

One question that perplexes humans today is: Why has there been such widespread devaluation of females and their role in our history? Although devaluation is more likely to take place in the Urban and Modern Waves, anthropologist Ernestine Friedl addresses this question by asserting that there is a degree of male dominance that exists. She defines male dominance as a "situation in which men have highly preferential access, although not always exclusive rights, to those activities in which the society accords the greatest value, and the exercise of which permits a measure of control over others." She maintains that the "subsistence technology of a society and its social and political organization have crucial consequences for the sexual division of labor, the differential allocation of power and recognition to men and women, and the quality of the relationship between the sexes."[41] In other words, a particular subsistence technology influences a female's status in her society; therefore, if a female plays an important role in providing food, she gains more status. Although this explanation may be more a reflection of today's emphasis on economic answers to complex problems than a universal characteristic of human society, it does offer one plausible theory.

Another interesting explanation for the diminished status of women in many cultures is the devaluation of nature in comparison to culture. Females and their activities are assumed to be closer to nature than culture, and, therefore, devalued compared to the activities of males, which are more associated with culture.[42] For example, women's ritualistic practices commemorating nature in ancient Greece were devalued over time, and, instead, the rational and logical practices of the ancient philosophers, such as Socrates and Aristotle, were extolled.

This holistic approach takes the position that biology plays a part in shaping male and female differences and some of the roles they perform in society, although this does not translate into rigid and unchanging female behaviors and roles. As we will see in each of the waves, biology is not the sole determining factor as to the status of females in a particular society. Variables such as historical precedence, religious doctrines, individual experiences, economic reasons, and other factors all significantly contribute to the behaviors, status, and social views of females.

Questions to Consider

1. What do you think is more important in shaping gender roles: biology or culture? Why?

Prestige and Social Status

In human societies certain individuals possess more prestige than others. **Prestige** is the reputation, influence, or high standing arising from success, achievement, rank, or other favorable attributes that an individual may hold. Those attaining prestige exhibit certain respected characteristics that are highly regarded: generosity, courage, selflessness, and good character. A subtle difference exists between the terms prestige and status. When an individual attains **status**, it means a culturally defined relationship in which one individual has greater stature in the group than another. Some societies give special privileges or rank to those who have more prestige. **Rank** refers to differences in prestige but not difference in political power. In ranked societies prestige is rarely translated into power or control over others, but has responsibilities along with the privileges.[43] Rank achieved through abilities and personality cannot be inherited.

Societies in which there is little differentiation between groups, either by age, sex, or kinship, are called **egalitarian**. To ensure equal status among its members, egalitarian societies employ **leveling mechanisms** which are societal obligations compelling members to distribute goods and services equally and preventing certain members from gaining too much recognition. The object of leveling mechanisms is to ensure that no one individual accumulates more wealth than anyone else, and thus secures a more stable society. Although wealth is equally distributed in an egalitarian society, certain individuals may achieve slightly more prestige than others. An objective in egalitarian societies is to ensure that a different level of prestige among its members does not significantly disrupt the group.

Societies in which individuals have more prestige than others, and use that prestige to gain

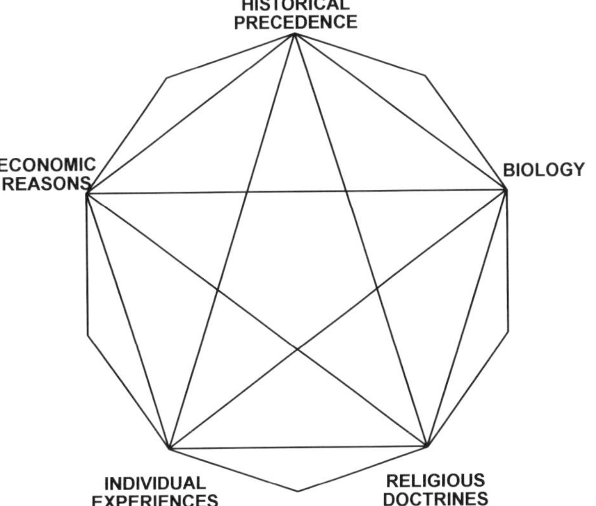

higher status, are called **stratified societies**, which are found in more complex agricultural societies, and in the Urban, Modern, and Global Waves. In stratified societies individuals with higher social status exercise real power over individuals of lower status, which is typically displayed in the political, social, and economic arenas. As a result, low-status individuals have less access to the material fruits of society. They may be forced into actions that benefit the higher status social group. Inequality may also be more or less passively accepted as a fact of life. Stratification occurs when people in one group are compared with those in another, and marked differences in privileges, rewards, restrictions, and obligations are apparent. Social stratification signifies institutionalized inequality.

Two types of status in human societies are ascribed and achieved. Status based on the social positions that one is assumed to occupy by virtue of the group into which one happens to be born—for instance, one's sex, race, age, or kinship—is called **ascribed status**. Ascribed status is found in both stratified societies and egalitarian societies. **Achieved status** in which division is based on criterion such as wealth, hereditary, and special abilities, is primarily found in stratified societies. Rules of succession are attached to status and it is also a method for maintaining social order.[44] Societies fall somewhere on a continuum between egalitarian and stratified social structures.

Questions to Consider

1. What forms of prestige do you have in your society today? Why do you have these particular forms?

Socialization and Education

To ensure their continuation, societies educate and socialize their members by transmitting the culture from one generation to the next. **Socialization** is a continuing process whereby an individual acquires a personal identity and learns the norms, values, and social skills appropriate to his social position and that of his/her society. The first agents of the socialization process are members of a newborn's family. As a child matures, individuals outside the family, such as other kin and peer group members, share in the socialization process. One way children learn is by watching and copying elders. In more populated and complex societies professionals share in the socialization process by educating children through formal instruction in educational institutions.[45] **Educational institutions** are formal organizations with the primary function of educating society's members into its specific worldview. For example, religious training is conducted for the purpose of inculcating the religious worldview.

Questions to Consider

1. Are you socialized into your society? How? Give examples.

ESTABLISHING ORDER: POLITICAL CURRENTS

Ways of establishing order—political systems, forms of leadership, customs, rules/laws and punishment, migration and interaction, conflict or cooperation, and war—are all part of our human political currents.

Political Systems

Societies form political processes to maintain internal order and manage affairs with other societies. The five political systems that have developed in the five waves range from decentralized and informal organizations such as bands and tribes to centralized and formal organizations, such as chiefdoms, states, empires, and nations.[46] Although these political systems will be explained more fully in each of the waves, a brief overview of them follows. A **band** is a small autonomous group found in the Communal Wave, in which members' needs are met by informal, decentralized political processes. A **tribe** is a decentralized political system consisting of groups of bands that occupy a specific region, speak a common language, share a common culture, and are integrated by other unifying factors. Tribal societies are mainly characteristic of the Agricultural Wave way of life, but continue through history to today. A **chiefdom** is a political unit of permanently allied tribes and villages under one recognized leader. Chiefdoms are found in complex agricultural societies in the Agricultural Wave and in nomadic societies that will be covered in the Urban Wave. Chiefdoms continue today. A **state** is a formal, centralized political organization in which political power is legitimately used to regulate the affairs of its citizens and relations with other states. State political systems are characteristic of societies in the Urban Wave and also in the Modern and Global Waves. **Empires** are states that expand beyond their city or provincial boundaries to encompass expansive territories. Usually these territories are conquered by a centralized military and annexed to the empire's center both politically and economically. An empire consists of diverse groups of people without a common language, customs, religion, or history, but held together through sheer military force. **Nations** are imagined political systems characteristic of the Modern and Global Waves. A nation is a political body composed of a group of people who exercise control over a specific territory, and usually share similar customs, traditions, ethnic origins, a history, and language. Citizens of a nation unite under a formal, centralized government in which various bureaucratic officials have administrative duties.

Questions to Consider?

1. What political system best describes where you live? Explain.

Forms of Leadership

Humans generally have a propensity to select leaders who exhibit generosity, courage, charismatic appeal, and good character, traits that humans universally admire. The extent of power and authority a leader exerts varies in the different waves. Often we see, especially in more complex societies in the Urban, Modern, and Global Waves that a dominant male power coalition, or oligarchy, controls an entire social group. An **oligarchy** is rule by the few and is composed of competitive subgroups all vying for power. Usually this internal strife is non-violent, but on occasion it can turn violent and civil war may result.[47]

Customs, Rules, Laws and Punishment

Humans have an innate aversion to disorder and insecurity and create customs and rules to avoid disruptions. Societies in the Communal and Agricultural Waves maintain group order with such informal means of social control as **customs**, informal norms that define desirable or acceptable behavior in the group, and help to clarify an individual's rights and obligations. In more complex societies social order is institutionalized into the formation of rules and laws, another form of social control. **Laws** are codified formal sanctions that have the intent of regulating human behavior. Many laws proscribe violent acts such as murder. Murder is defined as an unjustified taking of human life, although rules have been devised that permit taking another person's life in such circumstances as self-defense, capital punishment or war. If an individual violates any of the proscribed laws, group members may exercise a form of punishment. Before punishment is inflicted, the use of negotiation is often employed. Negotiation uses argument and compromise with the involved parties in an attempt to arrive at a satisfactory agreement for all. If negotiations fail, offenders can be punished for their infractions. Those guilty of violating laws are often removed from society either by expulsion, incarceration, ostracism, or execution.[48]

Customs, rules, and laws regulate the human sense of territoriality. Social regulations decide which valuable land resources are allocated to whom and how these resources are delineated. Property ownership is a temporary right to use and a right to deny use to others. Ownership is held even when the owner does not use the property and it can be given, bought, exchanged, or sold. Ownership of other possessions varies from a few, personal items owned by people in the Communal Wave to a wide variety of possessions accumulated by members of modern, industrial nations.[49]

Even though there are rules and laws to distinguish territorial rights, conflict can break out due to boundary disputes. Humans are territorial animals who are known to defend to the death a scrap of land that might appear perfectly worthless to an outsider. Problems arise whenever territorial ownership shifts over time due to invasion by another group or other factors. Those displaced from their territorial home can seek revenge in their effort to reclaim their homeland. Disputes over territory are recurring causes for conflict and war.

Questions to Consider

1. Why are disputes over territory a recurring cause for conflict and war?

Migration and Interaction

Since cultures change and evolve, interaction across cultural boundaries is an important process. An explanation of the term culture is warranted at this point. Culture was briefly described above as a system of learned behaviors, symbols, customs, beliefs, institutions, artifacts, and technology characteristic of a group, trans-

Political Organization in the Five Waves

The Wave	Political form	Characteristics
Communal	band	small, autonomous informal, decentralized
Agricultural	tribe	decentralized, occupy a specific region, speak a common language, share a common culture, unit in times of stress such as war
Agricultural Urban	chiefdom	political unit of permanently allied tribes and villages, under one recognized leader
Urban Modern	state	formal, centralized, political power is legitimately used to regulate the affairs of its citizens and relations with other states
Urban Modern	empires	states that expand beyond their city or provincial boundaries to encompass expansive territories, conquered by a centralized military and annexed to the empire's center both politically and economically.
Modern Global	nation states	imagined political systems, composed of a group of people who exercise control over a specific territory, usually share similar customs, traditions, ethnic origins, a history, and language.
Global	world organizations NGOs	world political organizations such as the United Nations, World Court, etc, and non-governmental organizations that exercise governance over nation states.

mitted by its members to their offspring. Yet, culture is a multi-faceted term that has many layers of meaning. The term culture can convey an image of bounded entities with distinct boundaries, each unique and separate from one another. But cultures are imagined constructs and do not have rigid boundaries. People living within its presumed boundaries do not have fixed identities; they change and their identities reconfigure. Imagined cultural boundaries are porous, and ideas, goods, and people flow easily in and out. Using the term culture is analogous to using a map; the map is merely a tool and not the actual territory.

The MAP is not the TERRITORY

Humans interact with new environments both biologically and culturally. When foreign species thrust themselves into a novel environment it is called biological invasion, like the spread of disease. Cultural interaction takes place through human migrations, expansion by military conquest, and interaction through trade or religious missions.[50] Humans respond to interaction in several ways: by peaceful assimilation of new ways, by extinction of the original society and replacement with a new culture, by means of coercion, and by rejection of or resistance to new ways introduced.

Questions to Consider

1. What does the following statement mean to you: cultures are imagined constructs and do not have rigid boundaries? Do you think this is a true statement?

Conflict, Cooperation and Warfare

Humans exhibit contradictory behaviors in their struggle to survive; selfishness and aggression may co-exist with cooperation, altruism, and sacrifice. Through our 2.5 million-year history, our selfish and aggressive behaviors have been necessary for our survival. Yet we form tight-knit, long-lasting, cooperative bonds with kin and non-kin alike that require sacrifice and altruistic behaviors, which are also essential for survival.[51] Both behaviors, paradoxically, exist within our human species.

Members of a society strive to preserve order and prevent disruption. Order is maintained through social controls that are internalized or "built into" an individual, or externalized in the form of sanctions. Internalized controls rely on such restraints as personal shame and fear. Gossip, criticism, fear, and frequently fright of supernatural reprisal, are forms of chastisement that help to ensure that members of a society behave in a socially acceptable manner. **Sanctions**, externalized social controls, are more formalized and enforced by official political regulations called laws.[52]

Humans engage in conflict and war and also employ methods for peace making and stability. Rituals, use of intermediaries, and compensation are various peace making techniques. One example of a peace making strategy is a compensation practice called wergild. A **wergild** is a regular payment made to the victim or to the victim's family for an injury rendered. Anthropologist Walter Goldschmidt points out that to instill peaceful behaviors, societies employ symbols of value and ennoblement which extol or promote attributes of "empathy, generosity, restraint of impulses, and the like—all of which are in the repertoire of human behavior."[53] When a particular society exalts these noble values—more than competition, aggression, and mistrust—there is a greater chance for peaceful settlement of conflict and fewer incidences of conflict, violence, and warfare.

Individuals possess contradictory tendencies for both cooperative and aggressive behaviors. Certain actions or circumstances can trigger aggressive behavior and set in motion a chain of events that creates conflict between individuals or groups. Even though negotiations attempt to resolve potentially disruptive conflict, these methods are not always successful and conflict ensues. Conflict between groups usually involves in-groups and out-groups. Aggression is mostly directed towards out-groups, while cooperation is more common among members of an in-group. In-group members often regard out-group members as wrong, the aggressors, morally or intellectually inferior, or not fully human. Antagonisms may escalate to the point that conflict turns into feuds, retribution, or warfare.

War is armed combat between groups that represent separate territorial contingents or political affinities. Although warfare is often thought to be an inevitable consequence of a bellicose human nature, systemic warfare is not universally practiced among contemporary foraging groups. Conflict is universal among humans, but warfare generally begins with chiefdom and state formation and the pressures of growing populations with their increased demand for resources. States organize and execute warfare. Causes of war are complex, with economic, political, ideological, religious, environmental and psychological explanations often cited. Those advocating the conflict persuade males to participate, and a great deal of societal indoctrination is employed to prepare young males for war. Most males comply with their culture's established values. If a society places emphasis on aggression and ferocity then warfare is more likely to occur.[54] Warfare is also likely when populations exceed the carrying capacity of their surroundings. Conflict over scarce resources ensues. If climate shifts occur that reduce the agricultural productivity of an area enough to cause malnourishment and starvation among a population, then conflict among rival groups to obtain basic necessities takes place.

According to one provocative interpretation, the roots of warfare can be traced to our ancestral legacy. Although dozens of theories concentrate on war as a means of achieving a tangible goal such as territory, spoils, wives, or revenge, anthropologist Robert Russell suggests that warfare may actually evolve and persist as a way to encourage bonding between competitive males, to redirect aggression outside the in-group, or to defuse other social problems. Leaders of power coalitions may arbitrarily define the enemy as a scapegoat. The identification of an external enemy is crucial to successful male bonding, and the enemy is almost always thought to be easy to overcome or bluff into defeat. Risks to the aggressors are perceived as minimal. At the conclusion of a successful war, the male power coalition forms strong social bonds. But some men are psychologically unable to return to society after combat, and instead redirect their aggression inward against society or exhibit self-destructive behaviors. While males are often attracted to risky exploits, the need for war is little understood by most females who see it as a terrible, wasteful, inefficient method for settling disputes between groups and as a threat to their and their children's survival. Perhaps, more than any other cultural function, warfare delineates the different goals and values held by males and females.[55]

Questions to Consider

1. In what ways does your society promote peaceful behavior? In what ways does your society promote warlike behavior? What behaviors are most promoted? Why?

HUMAN EXPRESSIONS: CULTURAL CURRENTS

Human expressions—worldview and ideology, spirituality and religion, communication, identity and belonging, and aesthetic expressions are part of our cultural currents.

Worldview and Beliefs

This sub-current encompasses a broad spectrum of elements including: experiences; a system of beliefs, values, norms, and ethical standards; feelings, emotions, and attitudes; and customs and traditions. Filtered through their worldview, humans make judgments of right and wrong, good and bad, and reality or fantasy. People often choose to believe what is pleasing, what we want to believe, and what we think we ought to believe rather than the reality of the situation.[56]

Attitudes are statements of preferences, likes, and dislikes, which are subjective reactions to experiences expressed in positive or negative terms. **Ethnocentrism** is an example of an attitude in which an individual imagines his/her own particular culture as superior. Societies foster ethnocentric attitudes that serve them well by creating feelings of group unity and cohesion. Ethnocentrism also is a way to affirm loyalty to one's own cultural ideals, and enhances one's sense of identity and belonging with other group members. A darker side of ethnocentrism is exhibited when barriers to understanding about other people's diverse customs and values are erected, which may contribute to conflict between the in-group and out-group.

Values, customs, and traditions vary cross-culturally. Distinguishing right from wrong, recognizing responsibility, keeping promises, expressing empathy, and coping with consequences are all part of a society's value system. Humans realize that they are responsible for their actions, and they have a capacity to make moral judgments and create moral orders. Diverse societies may have common customs and traditions, including: an ideal of etiquette and hospitality, routine greetings, customs of visiting kin, special times for feasts, daily routines, standards of sexual modesty such as not copulating or relieving oneself in public, and taboos on certain utterances and foods.[57]

Questions to Consider

1. Give examples of ethnocentric behaviors in your society.
2. Do you or your friends hold ethnocentric attitudes? What are they and why do people hold onto them?

Spirituality and Religion

Humans generally believe in something beyond the visible and palpable that is expressed in the form of spirituality. The essence of **spirituality** is to evoke a mysterious feeling of communion with a sacred realm. This is an attempt to explain aspects of the Universe that are beyond our control and comprehension. Spiritual rationalizations are devised to justify outcomes such as fortune and misfortune, disease and death, and chance happenings. Rituals and practices of divination are devised to heal the sick, control the weather, partake in rites of passage, and mourn the dead. Spiritual experiences have similarities across cultural and historical boundaries. When comparing these parallels, three forms of spiritual experiences can be categorized: theoretical or conceptual expression, practical functions, and sociological and psychological functions.[58]

Humans explore diverse paths in their aspiration to attain an awareness of the spiritual dimension. The chart shows the four possible paths in the search for spiritual insight.

Four Paths to Spiritual Insight

1. the path of science
2. path of religion and mythology
3. path of the spirit
4. path of psyche

First, the path of science follows a line of reasoning that uses cause and effect explanations, and proceeds in logical steps. It embraces a scientific method that begins with investigations, accumulates information, and tests conclusions. Second, the path of religion and mythology is based on traditions and beliefs that rely on explanations from the past. Although this path is based on traditional interpretations, it reads newer meanings into past explanations in order to make these meanings adaptable to a contemporary world. Third, in the path of the spirit, understanding is gained through personal experiences in which an individual is able to glimpse an invisible world hidden behind many veils. Along this path an invisible dimension is revealed through dreams, fantasies, and sudden insights. An invisible world is expressed through metaphor, myth, and ritual. The path of the psyche is beyond our everyday knowing process and lies in the mystical realm.[59]

Religion is a set of beliefs relating to supernatural powers and beings, with rituals designed to influence those beings and powers. It is a system through which people interpret the nonhuman realm as if it were human and seek to influence it through symbolic communication. Religion usually includes a moral code governing the conduct of human affairs. They spell out an ethical dimension by requiring adherents to observe certain rules and precepts as guidelines to follow. Religions fulfill various social and psychological functions important to humans. A religion's social functions enforce group norms and values, while providing moral sanctions to encourage the proper conduct of individuals. Religion also prescribes forms of social control, such as divine retribution, that laws alone cannot impose, which also helps reinforce notions of right and wrong. These functions maintain social solidarity and contribute to an individual's education and socialization process.

Religions provide certain psychological explanations that provide an orderly model of the Universe and formulate a definition of the unknowable in an understandable form. Religious belief also reduces individual fears and anxieties about uncontrollable events, such as death. In some cases, religion offers participants a way to transcend their arduous earthly existence, and offers an individual the possibility of attaining spiritual fulfillment in the form of ecstasy.[60]

Humans express their religious dimension in practical ways. A religious connection comes from participation in ceremonies or practices that bring a sense of personal transcendence, an altered state of consciousness, a wave of reassurance, security, closeness to fellow participants, and even ecstasy.[61] Religious rituals are a means through which humans interact with the mysterious sacred realm. In active religious ceremonies, the social bonds of a group are reinforced, tensions are relieved, events are celebrated, or consolation from a death is offered. Rites of passage and religious rituals mark important steps in an individual's life that includes the celebration of birth and marriage, and mourning at death.

Individuals who guide religious practices generally have personality traits that make them suited for contacting, influencing, and manipulating supernatural beings. Religious specialists undergo special training for their job. Religious specialists include shamans and priests or priestesses. **Shamans** have special spiritual gifts for healing and divination. **Priests** or **priestesses** are full-time religious practitioners believed to have supernatural powers bestowed on them by an organized religious group, and they perform rituals for the benefit of these religious groups. They are designated as able to mediate between a deity or deities and humans. They typically come from societies that have resources to support their full-time religious occupational status.[62]

Many humans attribute phenomena that cannot be controlled or understood to the realm of supernatural beings, which transcends the observable, natural world. These supernatural beings are interested in human affairs, and people appeal to them for assistance in difficult circumstances like drought, flood, or war. Supernatural beings can be categorized into three groups: animistic spirits, ancestral spirits, and gods/

goddesses. **Animism** is the belief that everything in nature—humans, animals, plants, ornaments, weapons, rocks, rivers, woods, and mountains—contains personified, animated, conscious spirits or souls. **Ancestral spirits** or souls of ancestors are active spirits from the past that influence present life and remain interested and involved in affairs of their descendants. They provide a sense of continuity with the past, present, and future. Gods/goddesses are seen as great and remote beings controlling the Universe.[63] A more complete description of supernatural spirits is explored in the five waves.

Folk religions and universal religions are different forms of spiritual expression.[64] Although more complete descriptions will be found in the discussion of each wave, a brief note comparing the two religious expressions informs the reader about the diverse kinds of spirituality and how they change historically. Participants in folk religion, which is practiced mainly during the Communal and Agricultural Waves, are bound within the unity of the community, and inextricably linked to the world encompassing them. In folk religions there is no concept of an isolated, individual self; each individual member is linked to the whole community. Each spirit is particular to the group and not universal. Various folk spirits animate the world and connect all into the web of life. A different human consciousness evolves with a shift to the Urban Wave. Tight-knit, community-centered folk religions no longer serve the needs of autonomous urban dwellers. The individual and community separate, with the individual seen as a detached entity. Between 800 and 500 BCE, often labeled the Axial Age, a shift occurs in some areas of Eurasia with the formation of universal religions. The historical parallels in this shift are unmistakable and include ideological changes in what are now Greece, China, India, Israel/Palestine, and Iran. An urban way of life tends to foster a detachment from the numinous communal world while a different connection to the spiritual world evolves. No longer are some individuals connected internally to their community, but linked to an external object, a place of veneration or a remote deity. A universal religion, unlike folk religions, joins individuals across boundaries of language, ethnicity, beliefs, and territory.

Questions to Consider

1. In what ways do you express (or not express) your religious connection?

Communication

Humans communicate both verbally and nonverbally. A universal form of nonverbal human communication is conveyed through facial expressions. Regardless of an individual's particular culture, a person's face shows a wide range of emotions—happiness, sadness, anger, fear, surprise, disgust, coyness, and contempt—which translates into a commonly understood language.[65] Body language is the oldest type of symbolic communication used by our species. Gestures, especially with arms and hands, are one such form of nonverbal human communication while humans listen, watch, and interpret body language in order to grasp intentions.

Humans possess a universal ability to learn, create, and speak symbolically. Our brains hold the capacity to speak at least one of over 5,000 known languages. Although symbols of communication are not genetically determined, the capacity to create and use symbols is inherited. Every human society has a spoken language, and normally our first language is learned with extraordinary ease.[66] Through a highly abstract verbal language, humans reflect upon their internal state, respond to the external world, and manipulate and communicate with fellow humans. A complex spoken language is a medium for communication. Language, according to sociologists Gerhard and Jean Lenski, is a basic tool with which humans are "able to think and plan, dream and remember, create and build, calculate, speculate, and moralize."[67] **Language** evolves primarily to foster social cohesion and not necessarily to communicate truth, beauty, or honesty; through language we are also able to deceive others and ourselves.[68]

Gossip is universal among humans and is an important type of verbal communication, manipulation, and social control. Gossip satisfies several human needs: it links individuals together in a group network, since one of the prerequisites for participation is to know the parties involved. Gossip also involves a story, and humans are drawn to a good story. An individual targeted by gossip is subject to criticism, ridicule, and ostracism by those participating and perpetuating the gossip. This informal means of social control is effective in regulating individual behavior, and enforcing group norms and values.

Written communication, invented in the Urban Wave, is a relatively recent development in human history. Writing becomes a necessary form of communication in large, complex, stratified societies in which face to face communication is no longer adequate. Writing is used primarily among the elites until mass education becomes prevalent during the Modern Wave.

Identity and Belonging

Individuals look to satisfy the need to belong to a group and seek affection and friendship (see Dimension 7 above for a more detailed description). People possess a cooperative nature that includes a capacity to share and reciprocate. In recent decades, a new form of personal identification has emerged called identity. **Identity** is an umbrella term used throughout the social sciences to describe an individual's comprehension of him/herself as a distinct, separate entity.

Religious Expressions in the Five Waves

The Wave	Religious Expression	Characteristics
Communal Agricultural	animistic beliefs	belief that everything in nature contains personified, animated, conscious spirits or souls, shamans spiritual leaders
Communal Agricultural	folk religions	spirit is particular to the group and not universal, shamans are spiritual leaders
Communal Agricultural Urban	ancestor worship	ancestors are active spirits from the past that influence present life and remain interested and involved in affairs of their descendants.
Communal Agricultural	goddess worship	the female goddess gives life to humans and gives food to people
Urban Modern Global	universal religions	between 800 and 500 BCE, Axial Age, in Eurasia the formation of universal religions
Modern Global	science as a religion	scientific reasoning and the scientific method, faith in science to provide answers
Modern Global	fundamentalism	rejection of aspects of modernity and attempt to return to principles of universal religions
Global	new age	connection to mystical elements of spirituality through rituals.

In the past people identified themselves in more narrow ways than today, such as a member of a tribe or clan. Today we have expanded our sense of identity to include what are called multiple identities. This new form of identification breaks down the understanding of the individual as a whole subject to a collection of various cultural identifiers that include age, gender, race, sexual orientation, class, occupation, level of education, marital status, geographic location, religious beliefs, and others. The combinations are endless. Some forms of identity we choose, such as marital status, religion, where we live, education, and religious beliefs, while others we are born with —gender, age, race, and sexual orientation (some say this is chosen).

Questions to Consider

1. How would you describe your identity? If you wish, share your identity with others.

Aesthetic Expression

Every society engages in a variety of aesthetic expressions reflecting recognition of beauty and affinity for nature. Art, music, poetry, literature, dance, and storytelling are aesthetic expressions that evoke pleasure for the artist as well as for those who enjoy the results. Art is a specialized kind of human behavior. The creative use of our imagination helps us to interpret, understand, and enjoy life, as well as to express life's pain, sorrow and grief. Art provides the means for imaginative play and thus helps sustain life. It is not just for elites but invites participation by other community members as well. In many societies the process of creating art is of greater importance than the final product itself.[69]

Humans have an emotional tendency to prefer certain kinds of natural settings—landscapes, lakes, rivers, cliffs, and savannas. Research on landscape preferences indicates that savanna-like environments are preferred to other environments. Known as the savanna hypothesis, proponents of this theory argue that this preference arises from our long evolutionary history on the savannas of east Africa. Linking us to our ancestral legacy, many landscape artists use features of the tropical savanna in their paintings.[70]

Music, visual arts, and verbal arts are variations of aesthetic expression. Music is perhaps the easiest art form to either perform alone or to participate in with others. The human voice is itself an instrument.

Verbal arts consist of three recurring forms: myth, legend, and tale. **Myths** have an explanatory function that typically provides a rationale for religious beliefs and practices. Myths depict an orderly Universe, describe appropriate behavior, express a group's ideology, show a group's place in nature, and reveal the limits and workings of the world. Diverse people express similar and recurring themes in myths.[71] **Legends** are semi-historical narratives that account for heroic deeds, movements of people, and local customs mixed with the supernatural or extraordinary. Legends usually serve to entertain, instruct, inspire, and bolster pride in a family, tribe, or nation. To a degree, in literate societies, myths have been displaced by history, although one historian astutely asserts that we now have "myth history" not history. Anthropologist William Haviland states, "Much of what passes for history consists of myths we develop to make ourselves feel better about who we are."[72]

Questions to Consider

1. What is your favorite form of aesthetic expression? Why?
2. One historian proclaims that we have "myth history" not history. What do you think that means?

Insights: Learning from the Past

COMMONALITIES: CONCLUDING INSIGHTS

This holistic world history is based on the interdependent psychological unity of all humans. Our cultural manifestations have biological roots, which people all over the world express in recurring patterns, or what I call currents. These currents of parallel developments form the foundation of this world history. Although all humans share a deep, psychological unity, they also have superficial cultural differences. Diversity is shaped by environmental factors, historical circumstances, change, and human choice. The five waves represent significant historical changes in our human history. During the last 40,000 years our human story increases in variety and scope as our physical circumstances stabilize and more complex cultural developments begin to influence our human path.

Paradoxically we experience both unity and diversity. Humans express unity in the commonalities that prevail during our 2.5 million-year human history. Yet we also recognize the diversity of our different cultures that we create and that create us.[73] We celebrate the wondrousness of both our commonality and diversity and are awe struck by the mysteriousness of the historical process that shapes our lives in the present day.

Questions to Consider

1. Do you think there is a deep psychological unity of all humans? Explain.

We turn next to the essence of this holistic world history: the five waves. The first wave to be discussed—the Communal Wave—spans the greatest duration of time in our human history and is currently the wave that is most threatened with extinction.

Chapter 4

People as Nomadic Foragers: The Communal Wave

"Snowflakes, leaves, humans, plants, raindrops, stars, molecules, microscopic entities all come in communities. The singular cannot in reality exist."

— Paula Gunn Allen, Native American poet

INTRODUCTION TO THE COMMUNAL WAVE

For 99 per cent of our human history—2.5 million years—we practiced a food foraging way of life that served us well. In other words, we spent most of our history in the Communal Wave. This holistic world history traces human history back to the emergence of the homo genus; a species native to grasslands that appeared between 2.5 and 2.7 million years ago, soon after global cooling turned much of the woodland to savanna. This era from 2.5 million years ago and ending with the origins of agriculture around 10,000 years ago is commonly referred to as the **Paleolithic** or Old Stone Age and the period from 40,000 years ago to 10,000 years ago is labeled the **Upper Paleolithic**. Our present universal human behaviors and instincts for coping and adapting to the world were shaped during this long, evolutionary history, which forms the foundation of how we see and live in the world today.

Although we have a long history as foragers, we will pick up the Communal Wave with the story of our human development from approximately 40,000 BP [1] (Before the Present) onward. People who practice a foraging way of life are also called hunters/gatherers or food collectors.[2] **Foraging** is where the primary subsistence method involves the direct procurement of edible plants and animals from the wild, without recourse to the domestication of either. Small mobile populations subsist on the resources available within their territory. They adapt to conditions as they find them, using what is already there. Not until about 10,000 to 12,000 years ago, when humans domesticated plants and animals, did another mode of living challenge the communal way of life. In this holistic world history, the Communal Wave spans a long developmental time frame from around 40,000 BP to foragers, albeit few, who still continue this way of life today.

Despite our long history as foragers, only a few foraging bands of people live this way today. In the early 1990s, estimates showed that approximately 250,000 people supported themselves primarily through hunting, fishing, and gathering wild plant foods.[3] Many anthropologists claim, and I agree, that no humans today live as "pure" foragers as they did over the last 40,000 years. Most have long since come into contact with more complex societies and have been influenced by this contact. To project their way of life today as representative of the distant past is therefore problematic. As a result I caution readers that this study of a wide spectrum of people over a long time expanse should not use modern foragers as exact models for those living in the Paleolithic past. Modern foragers are not "living fossils" existing unchanged in remote areas of the world.[4] Anthropologist Gary Ferraro suggests that it is also important to keep in mind that although modern foragers occupy remote habitats, they have had contact with non-foraging people. Today, foragers do not live in a pure, isolated world, nor is there evidence that foragers carry on an isolated existence once agricultural societies started to develop some 10,000 to 12,000 years ago. To the contrary, since the development of agriculture foragers have consistently interacted with neighboring groups.[5]

The MAP is not the TERRITORY

Nevertheless, commonalities can be found among people of the Communal Wave. Hence we can still make a judicious comparison between contemporary foragers and foragers of the past that illuminates common patterns.[6] Anthropologist Frank Marlow voices another cautionary note, "The special place of foragers in anthropology has been challenged by the revisionists on the grounds that contemporary foragers are not primary foragers, or that they have been oppressed by outsiders, or that they are a creation of our need to view others as simple and primitive, as living fossils. But if we are interested in the past, surely foragers are the best models we have if we hope to actually observe and measure behavior."[7] Thus, while being aware of these cautionary reminders, we will try to learn as much as possible from people in the Communal Wave.

Actually the life of foragers is and was quite variable, affected by numerous environmental factors, historical circumstances, and various human choices. Broad generalizations for understanding Communal Wave people over long stretches of time should not mask their underlying variability.

Various stereotypes both negative and positive describing foraging people have been reinforced in our society. Negative portrayals depict their lives in Hobbesian terms as "nasty, brutish, and short." Foragers are seen as constantly searching for food to support their undernourished bodies. They are often depicted as backward, primitive, uncouth, uncivilized, coarse, violent, and crude. Once they came in contact with a more "advanced" way of life, such as the life of farmers, they gratefully "broke through" to a preferable sedentary way of life with a "dependable" food supply. This negative observation of foraging people can be traced to the views prevalent in the West in late 19th century, which assumed that people who used simple technology must have led a grim life. This view was more of an ethnographic projection than an accurate account. Anthropologists now discredit this view but it still prevails among some of the general public.

More recently there have been more sentimental portrayals of foragers, idealizing them as leading a pure life, an idyllic and nonviolent existence in harmony with nature and untainted by corrupting modern influences. This view can be traced to the Enlightenment philosopher Jean-Jacques Rousseau, who in the 1700s referred to "primitive" people, as "noble savages." The entertainment industry has furthered this stereotype by portraying foragers or Native people "at one with nature." The popular 1990 film *Dances with Wolves* starring Kevin Costner comes to mind as an example. Even some anthropologists and academics have long thought of traditional people as peaceful and ecologically sensitive.

This view is also being challenged. Archaeologist Steven LeBlanc argues that attributing harmony and ecological balance to the lives of primitive peoples is essentially untrue. He believes such views have held sway because of the universal desire to believe that things were better in the past; that the past was unlike today.

To sanitize the past in this way, he continues, is to ignore important lessons from it, for the notion that indigenous people of the past lived in ecological harmony is disproved by the record. He finds that conflict, warfare and environmental exploitation have been an integral part of our human story from the beginning. Although he admits that many traditional people lived directly off the land and were more tied to the natural world than we are today, he warns "that being aware and worshipful of one's natural resources is a far cry from actually practicing ecological conservation." He contends that the idea of the noble savage has been embraced by some in the environmental movement and by some Native Americans because it implies that modern society has lost some of the magical insight that would enable us to live in ecological balance as people did in the past. He emphasizes that modern people today are inherently no less ecological than people in the past.[8] He warns us that we need to come to grips with the reality that we have always exploited our environment through population growth that eventually exceeds the carrying capacity of a particular locality. A lesson to be learned from this argument is that if we understand more fully why we expand beyond our means, then we can learn from this destructive behavior and subsequently forge a new direction in creating a more sustainable ethic.

Insights: Learning from the Past

Introduction to the Communal Wave

Are we innately exploitive? Does our species have the tendency to grow our population beyond the carrying capacity of the Earth without regard for future consequences? Contrary to LeBlanc's reasoning and research, many human societies of the past acted out concern for future generations and thought about leaving enough resources to sustain the next generations. Yet, as we definitely know, today many people throughout the world do not adhere to population control and non-exploitive environmental practices. Yet, the question remains: Are we innately exploitive? This question raises important insights into our human condition. If we holistically look at our human history, we can see that the way our society is organized and what it deems as valuable can influence how resources are treated. Ideas of the human condition can be placed on a continuum. Our modern society today is at one end of the continuum; looking back over our long human history we have arguably exploited the environment more than all previous societies. And comparatively, foraging people are at the other end of the spectrum and are/were the least exploitive. We can keep this continuum in mind as we learn more about foraging people and their way of life. We should take into consideration that we often project what we want the lives of foragers to be like—peaceful, ecologically balanced, worshipping nature, egalitarian, or warlike, crude, dull-witted—and how our hopes for and views of humanity influence these projections. Before we are either too critical or too idealistic we should consider the various kinds of foraging cultures that have existed. One label will not perfectly describe them all. It is more important to understand the role foraging cultures have played in our historical development and the impact of outside pressures on their way of life today.

Questions to Consider

1. Are we humans innately exploitive? What do you think?

EXPLOITATION CONTINUUM

COMMUNAL WAVE ◀ LESS EXPLOITIVE | MORE EXPLOITIVE ▶ GLOBAL WAVE

Change and Continuity

The approximate date of 40,000 BP marked a time of profound change in our human history. But like the changes from one wave to another, the transformation occurring at this time did not happen simultaneously around the world. By 33,000-24,000 BP, Neanderthals, a species of homo genus, had become extinct in Europe and modern humans were apparently the only hominid species dwelling on the planet.[9] Stone tool technologies were essentially static for almost 200,000 years but between 30,000 and 40,000 BP new sophisticated and stylish tool technologies burst onto the scene, while artistic expressions and trade connections exploded. Patterns of change were confusing at this time and it is unclear whether change was abrupt or gradual; apparently changes varied according to region. Anthropologist Roger Lewin argues that changes were quite abrupt in Europe but were more gradual in Africa and Asia.[10] But anthropologist John Gowlett maintains that changes in new technologies appeared in Western Europe around 34,000 BP, while similar technological changes actually occurred earlier—about 40,000 BP—in Eastern Europe, Middle East, and North Africa.[11]

Along with material developments were transformations in human consciousness. Consciousness is a feature of the mind that includes traits such as subjectivity, self-awareness, sentience, the capacity to perceive the relationship connecting oneself and one's environment, and the ability to reflect upon all of these. Although humans may always have been consciously aware of their environmental surroundings, evidence first appeared around this time showing that our species concretely expressed this environmental awareness. The twin developments of a larger human brain and an expanded cultural capacity interacted together in a system's reinforcing feedback loop stimulating further development. Artistic expression, construction of artifacts, sophisticated technology, and more efficient methods of social organization and cooperation proliferated among humans during the Upper Paleolithic era around 40,000 BP.

Humans thrived under a range of environmental conditions and created innovative and specialized technology best suited for their particular environment.[12] By 30,000 BP, human physical characteristics were essentially the same as those of people today; Paleolithic human's cranial capacity and elaborate speech patterns were equal to modern humans. The apparent widespread interbreeding among neighboring people during the Paleolithic era further stimulated expansion of our species.[13]

Although profound cultural changes marked the Upper Paleolithic era, foraging people experienced continuity as well. Variables like substantial population growth or climate change that interact to stimulate change were not intense enough

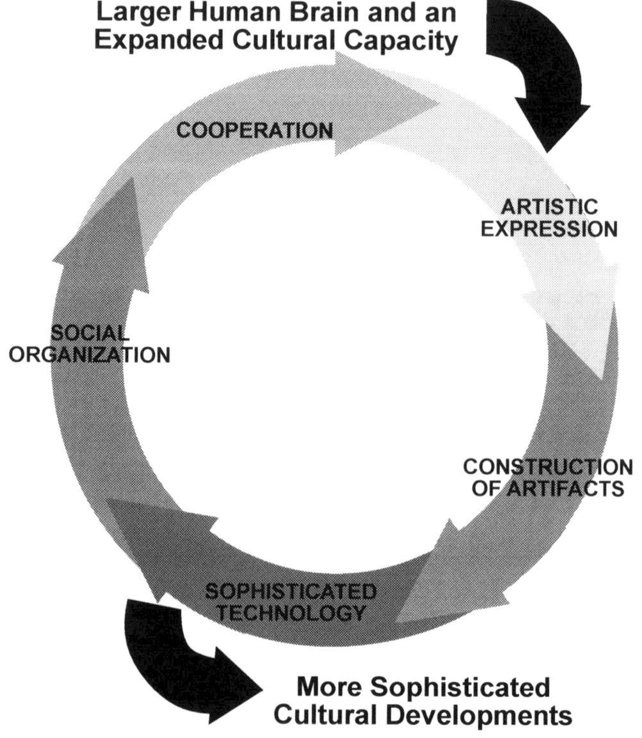

among our early ancestors to disrupt the foraging system.

A number of forager societies continue to exist today or at least until very recently. Among them are the !Kung in southwestern Africa, traditional Inuit groups, Australian Aborigines, the Piute and related groups in the Great Basin of Nevada and Utah in the United States, the Batek in Malaysia, the Hazda of East Africa, and the Mbuti of central Africa. These present-day foraging people, along with foragers of the past 40,000 years, despite their variability across time and space, share common characteristics; hence their inclusion in our discussion of the Communal Wave.

Three Indigenous Australians on Bathurst Island in 1939. Apparently, the island's population was isolated from modern society for 6000 years until the 18th century.

Insights: Learning from the Past

Change and Continuity

An examination of the Communal Wave gives us a broader context of our human history, a "big picture" perspective. History books typically start our story with the beginning of civilization: developments in Mesopotamia and slightly later in Egypt, then the Greeks and the Romans, the European Middles Ages and finally, its culmination in modern Europe. This traditional history of civilization leaves out a major chunk of our human past. Although these events are important in our history, they are merely a point in time on a long continuous history timeline that flows over millennia. Dividing history between prehistory and history (beginning of civilization and writing) artificially and arbitrarily divides our past. We have overly emphasized the Urban and Modern Waves in world history and that limits our perspective. To ignore the foraging way of life that our species experienced for most of our existence deprives us of a vital contrast with life today, and a comprehensive view of our detrimental shortcomings and stunning achievements.

As noted, humans around 40,000 BP were anatomically and mentally comparable to modern humans today. They had the brain capacity, although not the accumulated scientific knowledge, to design a way to fly a space ship to the moon. You might ask, "If they were so smart why did they continue to use simple tools and technology?" Knowledge, such as technological know-how, is learned and accumulates over time. Therefore, it would have been impossible for foraging people of the past to "choose" to "improve" their way of life. Often we who adhere to Western notions of progress will judge a forager's way of life as backward, and feel they should instead pursue progress in the area of technological and economic advancement. Technology cannot be learned in one generation but is passed on from one generation to the next. In essence, once foraging people encountered farmers or modern societies after 12,000 BP, many chose to maintain their particular way of life and resisted the influences of outsiders to the extent they were able.[14] Today we assume that change is preferable to continuity. But most Communal Wave people prefer continuity over change, since change involves risk and disorder, threatens stability, and does not necessarily bring happiness and well-being. Though they may resist change as much as they are able, foraging people through history have been forced to change either through outside pressures such as mandatory conversion, or have chosen to change by assimilating certain cultural elements into their altered society.

Questions to Consider

1. Why did people in the Communal Wave prefer continuity over change? What do you prefer: change or continuity? Why?

RELATIONSHIP WITH NATURE: ECOSYSTEM CURRENTS

Geography and Environment

We are all members of one species. Yet superficial characteristics evolve according to environmental and regional variations. When gene flow within a large population is restricted because of environmental or other circumstances, variations become specialized to the place. With this specialization, relatively isolated human communities develop unique adaptations to their environment, and these adaptations manifest as diverse races, languages, customs, traditions, and religious expressions. For example, physical characteristics—tall, short, dark and light skin, straight and curly hair—evolved in response to variations in climate, sunlight, and latitude. By 20,000 BP these physical changes reached their present state. For instance, Inuit populations of the northern climes have relatively short, thick bodies to conserve heat, and thick straight hair that protects their brains from the elements. Equatorial Africans have dark skin, a tall frame, and tight curly hair to guard against a hot tropical sun.[15]

Human Populations

The world human population grew relatively slowly until the exponential growth rates of the 20th century. Foraging women had on average four children who lived to adult status, although this was fewer than reproduction rates in other waves, except the Global Wave where population growth is slowing. In more environmentally plentiful regions, foraging populations rarely reached ten people per square mile. In environmentally sparse areas, populations seldom exceeded three people per square mile, and in less sustainable environments—mountain, desert, or tundra—population density dropped well below one person per square mile.[16] The steady but slow growth of forager populations is clearly evident in their expansion out of Africa and subsequent movement throughout the world, with population growth in the Americas and Australia being the most striking examples.

There is no indication that foraging populations in any region ever maintained zero population growth over the long run. Even though foragers did not live in "perfect" ecological balance with nature, many were acutely aware that an overtaxed local environment was usually followed by starvation, and some groups took precautions to minimize this occurrence. Because Communal Wave people, like people today and throughout history, were incapable of controlling population growth, at some point the number of people exceeded their resource supply or the carrying capacity of their local area and starvation and warfare ensued.[17] This scenario has repeated itself thousands of time in the past and is increasingly evident in parts of the world today.

Natural Populations

Part of this holistic history is to include species other than humans into our story. This section details the flora and fauna around the time that

A Sami (Lapp) family in Norway around 1900. Their subsistence is based on reindeer herding.

humans were developing in the Communal Wave. For more than one billion years, sheets of ice had been shuffling back and forth from the poles, sometimes actually linking up at the equator. Regular ice ages have recurred and lasted up to 100,000 years with intervening thaws averaging 12,000 to 28,000 years. The last glacier retreated 11,000 years ago. Under normal conditions, the next glacier scheduled to flatten our terrain is due any day now, although it is unlikely that it will arrive as planned. Humans have had a hand in postponing the frigid event because of our warming of the planet.[18] Let us go back about 11,000 years ago to see what the natural populations of the Earth looked like and what impact our human presence had on our planet at the time.

Around 11,000 BP with so much water sucked into frozen glaciers the oceans were 300 feet lower than today. Previously the Bering Sea lay buried under a half mile of ice, but around 11,000 BP the shallow sea opened up a land bridge 1,000 miles long that connected present day Siberia and Alaska. Humans were continuing their historic dispersal out of Africa and had traveled across the continental landmass of Asia to reach the farthest tip of Siberia. The intrepid travelers picked their way across the ice-free corridor, in places just 30 miles wide, while skirting around meltwater lakes. Without fanfare, they were apparently the first humans to arrive on the North American shores.[19]

Once humans had crossed the Bering Strait, they encountered an abundance of flora and fauna species. After all, humans were not the first species to occupy the Western hemisphere. This landscape, like the rest of the world, hosted a rich profusion of diverse plants and animals that lived alongside humans in a phantasmagorical display of fantastic beings. Scattered across the globe were hordes of deer with thick, tree-bough sized antlers, camel-like mammals with long trunks, furry rhinoceroses, enormous hairy elephants and even bigger sloths, wild horses of all sizes and stripes, panthers sporting seven-inch fangs, surprisingly tall cheetahs, and an array of wolves, bears, and lions that to us now would look like animals on steroids.[20] If so many diverse species proliferated around the ending of the last Ice Age, what happened to them all?

It looks as though about 13,000 years ago an extinction implosion occurred. The extinct species were not the small fur-bearing creatures such as mice, rats, shrews and marine mammals—they survived—but it was the lumbering mega-mammals which took a deadly wallop. Among the missing were legions of animal goliaths: giant armadillos, short-faced bears double the size of grizzlies and faster too, bear-sized beavers, wolves with a massive set of fangs, the famed ten ton wooly mammoth, mastodons, three genera of American horses, varieties of camels, antlered creatures including the stag moose, saber-toothed tigers, and the American cheetah. They, and many others, were gone.[21] But why? Of course, many interesting and controversial theories try to explain this sudden and dramatic extinction.

One theory suggests that as the climate grew milder, and the surrounding vegetation changed from treeless tundra to temperate deciduous trees, the giant mammals were unable to adapt to the warming climate and ultimately went extinct. A similar theory, often dubbed "over-chill," explains that a sudden temperature reversal just as the glaciers were melting plunged the world briefly back into the Ice Age. Caught off-guard, millions of defenseless animals unable to adapt met their tragic end. Another theory, cleverly called "over-ill," states that dispersing humans introduced ravaging pathogens that vulnerable animal species had no immunity to, thus triggering a far-reaching extinction.[22]

Paleoecologist Paul Martin offers an even more provocative theory called the "Blitzkreig" by detractors and supporters alike. He passionately explains that it was none other than our human ancestors who hunted large mammals to extinc-

The wooly mammoth disappeared from most of its range about 10,000 years ago.

tion. His hotly debated premise is that humans perpetrated the extinctions that killed off three-fourths of America's megafauna, a menagerie of animals far richer than Africa's today. Martin explains that as humans arrived on each new continent they encountered animals that had no in-born fear of their spear-throwing neighbors. These hunters were able to approach unsuspecting animals from a fairly safe distance and felled the mammoth creatures with their carefully-crafted, stone-tipped weapons with relative ease. The numbers dramatically decreased. That, says Martin, is why Africa has elephants and the Western hemisphere has none. The gigantic animals were the object of the hunt because they were the easiest to track, yielded the most food, and garnered the most prestige for hunters.[23]

Did our ancestors hunt species to extinction? Although I, and others, maintain that climate change contributed to the mass extinction of animal species, it makes sense that humans may have had a guilty hand in over-hunting species as well.

Questions to Consider?

1. What do you think: "Did our ancestors hunt species to extinction?" Defend your answer.

Human and Nature Interaction

People in the Communal Wave, compared to people in other waves, have treaded more lightly on the Earth. Generally, an intricate, reciprocal relationship connected foraging people and nature. Paleolithic humans utilized natural resources for survival needs, but still lived largely within the limits of their natural environment and depended upon the continued productivity of their local ecosystem. Foraging people moved on to another locale before food resources were depleted to the point of no recovery. Many foraging people received what nature had to offer and expressed gratitude and reverence for these gifts from nature. They devised ceremonies and rituals of gratitude to thank nature for the gifts offered and to acknowledge their dependence on nature. The gifts offered back to nature commemorated its bounty in the hope of insuring its continuance. Foraging people can generally be described as participators who were interdependent with nature and not dominators of nature.

Questions to Consider

1. Foraging people can generally be described as participators who were interdependent with nature and not dominators of nature. Do you agree with this statement? Why?
2. Do you think people in your particular nation are participators or dominators of nature? Explain.

Insights: Learning from the Past

Ecosystem Currents

What can be learned from the mass extinction of the past? Did humans contribute to the carnage or not? We need not contribute to another mass extinction of plant and animal species that would be far more devastating this time around. The lesson involves recognizing that we have a vast array of instincts and behaviors, some destructive and deadly, others creative and life-affirming. Yet much too often our deadly acquisitive and dominating instincts prevail, until something we never intended to harm is fatally extinguished. Recognizing this is one step; doing something about it is another. Like our ancestors, we are now at a critical crossroads of massive species extinction. Many people are working hard to prevent further extinctions from happening; hopefully, we can contribute to this notable effort.

An overriding question of our times is: How to share diminishing resources without resorting to violent domination or warfare? We can learn valuable lessons from foraging people in this regard. Their awareness and appreciation of nature's gifts connects them to the rhythms and cycles of nature. We can weave this respect and appreciation of nature into our thinking, actions, and being. We can get away from thinking of nature as separate from us and as a resource exclusively for our use. This way of thinking is a major shift for us to make, but it is imperative that we do so in the 21st century. Becoming more aware of nature's limits as well as its bounty is a lesson for our generation to contemplate and act upon.

Questions to Consider

1. I argue in this section that the first step in helping to avoid environmental destruction is to change our thinking from seeing nature as separate from us to recognizing that we are part of nature. What is your reaction to this statement?
2. What is your reaction to this whole insights section?

Easily moved Shoshoni tipis, circa 1900, western United States.

WAYS OF LIVING: TECHNO-ECONOMIC CURRENTS

Daily Life

Foraging people followed a nomadic or semi-nomadic way of life, and routinely moved their camp. Although they did not roam randomly from place to place, they typically never stayed much longer than perhaps a few weeks or so in one location. After this length of time the particular locale was stripped of food, or the trips away from camp in search of food became longer and longer. At some point the decision was made to move camp to a more plentiful area. The entire group moved at once. They restricted their movements to a fairly defined, familiar territory, often near a former campsite. Some foraging people even followed a regular circuit of visiting particular sites every year.

Foragers respected other groups' territory and generally did not inhabit a new terrain if others already occupied it. If a group invaded another's territory, conflict could ensue. Some felt a strong attachment to their frequently visited sites, and often lovingly expressed this attachment to the sacredness of place through song and legend.

The population of foraging groups alternated between large groups of 100 to 300 people for several months of the year, known as a public phase, to a longer period of separation into small local bands of 25-50 people, known as a private phase. When and where to move the band was a paramount decision, a resolution that usually required a consensus by the group. Shamans, hunters who were knowledgeable about potential game and gatherers who assessed food-gathering potential, all contributed to the band's decision about the optimum time to move to another location.[24]

Paleolithic people were resourceful regarding their food and clothing needs. Plant foods primarily comprised the bulk of Paleolithic people's diet in temperate zones, while those who lived in the northern climes during the Ice Age relied extensively on meat as their main food. Ice age Paleolithic hunters wielded their tool technology to hunt large grazing animals: musk, ox, woolly rhinoceros, mammoth, bison, bear, wild boar, reindeer, and the horse. Along with obtaining meat from animals, Paleolithic people tailored animal skins into protective clothing by utilizing their well-honed sewing skills. At a site in present-day Ukraine, archeologists recovered huge mammoth bones that were used as foundational building materials for huts, which were then draped with moss and grass for further protection from the elements. At the same site natural freezers or "lockers" were dug deep into the permafrost to store huge slabs of mammoth meat for later consumption.[25]

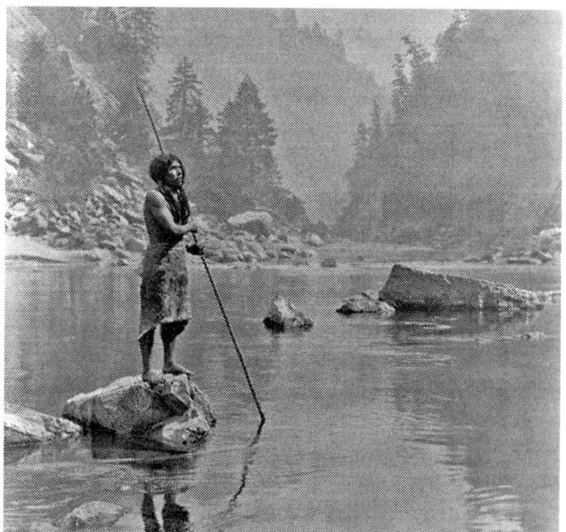

A Hupa man with his spear; a Native American tribe in northwestern California.

Foraging peoples' diet typically depended on locally available foods. Men did most of the hunting and butchered the meat at the site of a kill. Women processed and prepared the raw meat, and added gathered greens and spices for additional flavor. They also cooked gathered foods such as roots and seeds to make them more digestible and tasty. Women served cooked foods to other family members and to visitors who frequently joined with the group at mealtime.

Some foragers in the past carried out what were called **farm wilds**. This term meant that plants or animals in certain abundant regions were so dense that people were able to live in one place and intensely harvest the wild plants and animals on a regular basis, as if these foods were domesticated. Their lifestyles were similar to farmers, and some have called them sedentary collectors. The most famous of these "farmers of the wilds" or sedentary collector societies resided in the northwest coast of North America, where people relied on fishing and hunting marine mammals.[26]

Questions to Consider

1. Foraging people had to be self-sufficient in all of the needs of life. Are you self-sufficient today? Explain.

Economic System

People in the Communal Wave had a simple economic system: reciprocity. Since foraging people used simple technologies, practiced a nomadic way of life, and accumulated few possessions and goods, reciprocity best served their economic needs. **Reciprocity** is a system of exchange in which goods or services are passed from one individual or group to another as gifts without the need for payment. The partners in the reciprocal exchange take according to need and give back whenever and however they choose, with no set rules of time and quantity. Sharing is mutual and evenhanded. The reciprocal transaction is usually between kin or intimate associates and those engaged in the exchange do not place a specific value on the items to be exchanged, nor calculate whether an exchange is even or fair.[27] Reciprocity is the most basic economic mechanism to ensure that everyone within the local community has adequate provisions and all physical needs are met. Even those who cannot contribute products or services in return, such as the elderly and children, are provided for under the reciprocity system. If an individual or group fails to engage in exchange fairly, disapproval or exclusion is likely to occur. Reciprocity is recognized as a meaningful component of morality, rational action, and group life.

There are three forms of reciprocity: generalized, balanced, and negative. Generalized reciprocity is when gifts are given with no expectation of immediate exchange, and the giving person has a sense of obligation toward the welfare of others. An example is when goods and services are provided for children, or care is provided to the elderly. Balanced reciprocity is when goods are exchanged and a return gift is expected from the other party within a relatively short period of time. Balanced reciprocity is between those with no kinship relations or community ties and is commonly practiced among neighboring communities who produce specialized goods or control important resources.[28] The third form of reciprocity, negative reciprocity, occurs when one group or individual attempts to get more than it gives. Negative reciprocity can vary from simple greed to deceit, or even to outright theft. In this form of reciprocity a sense of duty to other participants is lowest and the desire for personal gain is greatest.[29]

The simple economy of foragers is called a **subsistence economy**. In this type of economy there are few specialized economic activities, and people consume what they produce. Each family basically produces enough for its own consumption or subsistence, and families turn out more or less the same number of goods. Little trade is conducted between groups since each is more than likely self-sufficient; there is no need for a market economic system. If exchange is conducted a **barter** system is often used, although money is not exchanged and some other token of value is used.

Spearhead from the Upper Paleolithic

The ecological impact of a foraging economy is light, especially when compared to modern society. Most contemporary foragers purposely do not over-utilize an area's resources since they know through experience that if an area is over used it does not provide enough resources in the future. Foragers live within nature's limits and generally respect those limits.

Technology

Humans in the Upper Paleolithic improved upon past technology and fashioned innovative new tools. Using their tool kits, which contained more than one hundred items, Paleolithic people manufactured a variety of delicately struck narrow blades into smaller and lighter tools. Men used tools such as blades to transform bone and antler into craft fishhooks, awls, harpoons, and needles with eyes. Points, knives, and scrapers were refined and added to a variety of gouging tools called burins. Women used string for sewing, fishing, gathering nets and containers and delicately woven baskets as well.[30]

Foragers devised a number of small-scale, personal, ingenious, multi-purpose, and portable tools for food foraging that was generally available to all families.[31] The principal subsistence tools used by remaining foraging societies today are digging sticks; spears, bows and arrows; fishing devices; traps; sandals from hide or cordage; and containers for storing, cooling, and transporting food, although food is generally not stored long. Some ingeniously use an ostrich egg shell as a canteen vessel holding precious water. A mother throws a resourceful sling bag made of animal skin across her shoulders to safely cradle her infant.

The individual skill and knowledge for using a particular tool is more important than the actual tool itself. While the tools are simple, the knowledge to use the tools is sophisticated. This knowledge has thoughtfully been passed from generation to generation, and is essential in the successful search for food and survival of the group.[32]

Questions to Consider

1. What does this statement mean to you: "While the tools are simple, the knowledge to use the tools is sophisticated?" Do you think this is true today?

Exchange and Trade

Foraging people decided on methods for the exchange and trade of valuable resources. Almost all exchanges were among kin or intimate acquaintances, for which the giving, taking, and using of goods had sentimental and special meaning. Trade among non-kin was based on the assumption that every individual tried to get the best deal from the transaction; therefore trading expeditions could prove hazardous. To remedy the harmful potential of non-kinship trade, members of distant groups frequently conducted a **silent trade**, a trading method that minimized possible conflict. In a silent trade, the two groups engaged in the trade placed their trading objects in a clearing and then the two groups retreated to their respective hiding places. According to arrangements made beforehand, the first group came out of its hiding place, inspected the objects, made an offer to exchange comparable objects or accepted the offer, and then retreated. The second group emerged to inspect the goods offered in exchange, and if satisfied took the objects and left; the exchange was completed. But if the exchange was not agreeable between the two parties, the goods were left untouched as a signal that the trade balance was not yet even or agreeable. This back and forth procedure continued until an agreement was reached or no trade was consummated.[33]

Patterns of Labor

Both gender and age differences demarcated labor tasks—called a **division of labor**—in foraging societies. Division according to age ensured sufficient time for skills to be learned and implemented by the young. Elders were highly respected members of foraging societies and a source for much appreciated wisdom, guidance, and experience. Dividing labor according to gender increased the chances for efficient productivity and the transmission of necessary skills to younger generations.[34]

Women wielded a simple digging stick to gather and process a diverse array of vegetable foods, roots, and nuts. Estimates vary, but on average most modern foragers obtain about 60 to 70 percent of their diet from plant food. Along with gathering food, women cooked most of the plants, carried water, cleaned the campsite area, and performed other household chores. Additionally, they bore children, nursed infants, cared for and transported children, and trained young girls to gather and identify foods and medicinal plants.[35] Women devised appropriate tools for storing, carrying, and processing foods, and for raising and transporting children. They tended to have duties that could easily be resumed after interruption, which usually meant interruptions due to child care responsibilities. Some women apparently hunted large animals, but their primary responsibility was to collect plant foods, fish with nets, and snare small animals.[36]

Men typically hunted large animals, butchered game, fished, collected honey, burned forests, and processed tough and hard materials from stone and wood. In general, men performed activities requiring more physical strength than women, such as bending strong bows, hurling spears, and wielding clubs. Men also performed duties that required rapid mobilization, high bursts of energy, frequent travel at some distance from home, and tasks that entailed high levels of risk and danger.[37] Boys underwent training for hunting that was similar to the training and skills needed in conflict situations, such as proficiency with weapons, maintaining physical stamina, and competency in tracking and scouting animals or humans.

Hazda men, in Africa, lighting a fire.

A question frequently asked about foraging people is why do women gather and men hunt? Hunting and gathering required different skills, training, and knowledge. Women's varied and complex tasks and responsibilities required sophisticated knowledge and skill for their successful performance, the same held true for male hunters. Hunters scanned the ground, horizon, trees, and other habitats for traces of large animals to track and hunt. Gatherers searched the ground for clues that led them to roots, plant foods, and the hiding places of small animals.[38] Women also carried children and food items in slings on their backs, which impeded their freedom to participate in hunting expeditions. Although both have the mental capacity to be trained for different skills, it would be an inefficient use of time or energy to do so. Different physical characteristics between females and males meant matching a to task to those who could physically perform it most efficiently. Foraging people did not necessarily regard one form of labor as superior to another, even though most foragers considered meat a more highly desired food than vegetables. Some researchers have concluded that traits for different hunting and gathering skills—scanning the horizon for game and detailing vegetation types—are genetically selected and passed on to succeeding generations. Over the generations these skills have evolved as specific to males and females.

Observations of contemporary foragers show that they spend less time "working" than agricultural or modern people. Work, in this context, denotes mental and physical labor involved in obtaining food and other necessities. It has often been assumed that foraging people were barely able to eke out a meager living from a hostile environment. Challenging this widespread stereotype, some anthropologists, including Marshall Sahlins, argue that contemporary foraging people do not have a difficult existence nor do they work very hard. The food quest is intermittent, leisure-time is abundant, and long naps are taken during the daytime. Sahlins estimates that the average length of time each person works per day in search of food and its preparation is four to five hours. He concludes: "Hunters keep banker's hours, notably less than modern industrial workers."[39] However, anthropologist Ferraro challenges the argument that foragers enjoyed an abundance of food and leisure time: "Today we are beginning to revise our view of food collectors as being clever 'lay ecologists' who live in an affluent society. Some studies indicate foraging groups spend as much time as seven or eight hours a day in subsistence pursuits, not the 12-19 hours per week that Richard Lee found."[40] Richard Lee, a noted anthropologist, conducted extensive studies of foraging people, most notably the !Kung, in the 1960s and 1970s. Although Ferraro makes a good point, I would argue that it is precisely because their environments are now so depleted and marginalized that foraging people today spend more time in subsistence strategies and trade than they did during the less environmentally stressed decades of the 1960s and 1970s when Lee and others conducted many of the studies.

Insights: Learning from the Past

Techno-Economic Currents

What we learn from foragers' use of technology can help us rethink our modern way of life. They used simple tools for their survival needs. Yet behind this simplicity is complex and sophisticated knowledge that is accumulated and honed over the generations to utilize these simple tools for their needs. The tools are simple but their knowledge is complex.

We often hear that foragers must be backward, why would they continue with their simple technology instead of making improvements that would result in more food and more material possessions to make life easier? Efficiency and improvement are values that modern people embrace in our technology-driven lives. Apparently foragers realize that their simple technology provides them with "enough" of their material wants. The use of complex technology does not result in more leisure time or social cohesion, something foragers highly value. They can show us that with increasing technology, workloads increase and leisure time decreases. Foragers in the Communal Wave work fewer hours than those in any of the other waves, while Americans in the Global Wave work longer than those in any other wave. Although I am certainly not a Luddite who wishes to ban technology, I do think we can learn an important lesson from their control of technology and a less stressful approach to life. Unlike today where the purveyors of technology in many ways dictate our way of life, foraging people used technology as a way to carry out their way of life as they saw fit. Complex technology did not interfere with what seemed to matter most to them: storytelling, conducting religious rituals, interacting with their children, and visiting with kin and visitors. Perhaps today we could rethink our use of technology to appropriate the leisure time that seems to elude us.

Questions to Consider

1. How does modern technology require us to work longer? How is the work different from that of foragers? Do you think that learning from foragers' use of technology can help us rethink our modern way of life?
2. What do foragers do with their leisure or "spare time?" What would you do if you had more leisure or spare time? What would you do with your spare time if you did not have access to any technology (TV, computer, cell phone, etc.)?

HUMAN NETWORKS: SOCIAL CURRENTS

Groups and Family

Foraging people were organized into bands, small kinship groups that usually numbered between 20 and 50 and rarely exceeded 100 people. In the past, when bands occupied areas of land with more abundant resources, a band's size could have been much larger, but not so large as to deplete their environment entirely. Bands consisted of families who camped together for periods ranging from a few days to several years. Families were more or less detachable units as families frequently moved from one band to another; hence band membership fluctuated. If a person had a serious disagreement with another person or a spouse, one option was to leave that band and join another. Also because of personal preferences or the desire to avoid conflict, a family could decide to move away from a particular band and join another.[41]

Kinship formed the basis of an interdependent social network. The group was of primary importance to foraging people and an individual did not think of her/himself as an autonomous individual. Foragers did not hold a concept of an individual identity separated from the group. The strong kinship ties among extended families encouraged and reinforced bonds of sharing. It was extremely risky for families to rely on just their own resources for survival since unforeseen circumstances, such as injury or illness, could result in starvation.[42] But through strong kinship ties, members shared the risks and rewards associated with a foraging way of life, while enhancing the chances for everyone's survival and well-being.

Inuit family 1930

Marriage reinforced a secure and stable social organization among foragers. Marriages typically allied members of different bands together. The parents of the future couple usually arranged first marriages, with a stable relationship for their children and potential grandchildren as a primary consideration. Premarital sex was commonly accepted for both males and females, and frequently a period of shifting partners and sexual experimentation took place before marriage. Marriage did not necessarily last a lifetime, and there could be several unions of short or long duration.

A marriage transaction between a husband and wife generally included: full obligation to each other's kin, joint custody of children, sharing the fruits of their labor, a common residence, and travel in the same band. Marriages were usually but not always exogamous. Through marriages outside their band, foraging people established a web of kinship ties and friendly relations with neighboring groups.[43] Whether the wife resided with the husband's family or vice versa depended upon whether the group followed **matrilineal** (through the mother) or **patrilineal** (through the father) descent. Extra-marital sexual relations did occur, and those who engaged in extra-marital affairs usually did so in secret to avoid disrupting the group or causing jealousy and anger for their mates. A potential source of conflict in foraging bands existed between men who had several wives and those who had none.

Foraging people loved their children but they also found it necessary to restrict their group's population to a manageable level in order to survive. Although foraging bands practiced population control, there was not zero population growth; their overall population numbers slowly increased. Children were typically spaced approximately four years apart. Extended breast-feeding, frequent aerobic exercise, and a diet high in protein and low in fat together reduced a foraging woman's fecundity.[44] If a woman became pregnant at what she considered an inopportune time and an infant posed a threat to the survival of an older sibling or to the ability of a mother to gather food, then the mother (it is unclear who actually made the decision) could decide to abort the unborn fetus or performed infanticide once the infant was born.[45]

Infanticide and, for some, abortion are "difficult practices" for us in modern society to accept or understand. Foraging people's practice of infanticide or abortion does not mean they are inhumane or heartless, but they have found from past experiences that too many children may hinder the survival of the group. For example, if a mother already nursed one child, she most likely could not give enough sustenance for two children, and both could suffer or die. Also, mothers who participated regularly in gathering food were unable to bear the burden of carrying two children over a long stretch of time and distance. Foraging women used special herbs to induce abortion and took contraceptive herbs derived from special medicinal plants as a means of birth control. Although these tactics may be abhorrent to some modern sensibilities, birth control and abortion served as forms of population control for foraging people that ensured the health and survival of mothers, children, and the group. Infanticide was common among all foragers for whom there is relevant information. Evidence for prehistoric infanticide existed from coastal foragers in South America to Africa, Asia, North America, and Australia.[46]

The elderly, both men and women, were respected by the group and influenced its affairs. The elderly served as storytellers, healers, political leaders, caregivers to children, and repositories of wisdom. Many elderly people exchanged services for food if they were too old or weak to forage.[47] A woman acted as a food gatherer well into old age, her extensive knowledge relied upon by the young. As a woman grew older she spent more time in camp where she helped care for and nurture children. Elderly men worked at sedentary tasks in camp, often related to hunting, and also cared for children. Both older men and women were storehouses of valued information, clever anecdotes, and group wisdom, and gratefully shared their good judgment with an appreciative group. The elderly frequently assumed the role of medicine man or woman, or shaman. A woman often gained extra status if she assumed the role of shaman during or after menopause, when her children were grown and her insights sharpened.

Under certain circumstances the band abandoned an elderly person, usually when he or she was unable to keep up with travel, make contributions to the group, or adequately care for him/herself. People of any age or sex who were too weak or injured could be left to fend for themselves, with the understanding that they would soon die.[48] Our modern values would deem this custom inhumane, but the group's inability to provide for too many indigent members forced them to place the well-being of the group over the individual's. Usually those considered "unproductive" readily understood and accepted

A woman shaman of Turkic Khakas ethnicity in Russia, 1908.

their situation; they willingly stayed behind and offered themselves freely to the spirits.

One interesting theory to explain how grandparents and the elderly contributed to cultural change and also population growth in the Upper Paleolithic is advanced by anthropologists Rachel Caspari and Sang-Hee Lee. They examined human teeth from an Upper Paleolithic site and found that beginning around 30,000 BP a sharp rise in the number of people over 30 years old occurred, a significant change since previous life expectancy had been typically 30 years or less. Since generations were calculated to have been around 15 years, they found a four-fold increase in the number of grandparents. Because grandparents carried out the essential function of taking care of, socializing, and educating grandchildren while adult members collected food and conducted other activities, the increased number of grandparents could help explain the increase in the creative expressions of culture in Upper Paleolithic societies. Women had more years for child-bearing, another consequence of increased longevity. Hence family size and populations increased. Caspari and Lee suggest that the cultural evolution as evidenced by new technology and art during the beginning of the Upper Paleolithic was a consequence of these demographic transformations.[49]

Questions to Consider

1. How are (were) the elderly treated by people in the Communal Wave?
2. How does your society/nation regard the elderly? What happens to the elderly in your society when they are no longer "productive" or "useful?"

Gender

For foraging people different roles for men and women helped to create social order, equilibrium, and a reflection of balance in the Universe. Another theory suggests that because women gave life, the task of taking life fell to men. If killing were part of a woman's responsibility, the balance between life giving and life taking would be egregiously violated. Women had the skills for hunting, but motherhood, gentleness, and forgiveness do not mix well with aggressive, competitive, and predatory behaviors.[50] The giving and taking of life were both imperative for the survival of any species, and humans were no exception. Foraging people recognized and created a balance between male and female roles, which gave them the necessary order and balance for their survival.

Another theory argues that women are more likely to achieve equality when environmental and other circumstances adequately provide for the physical well-being of the groups. During times of plentitude women attained a measure of economic autonomy and men appreciated and relied upon their countless contributions. Women's equality was frequently reflected in religious symbolism where fertility of the soil was extolled as a female attribute. In societies where there was reverence for fertility and women's economic contributions, they generally possessed equal, formal power and local authority.

Although men's and women's roles were separate, this did not necessarily mean that one dominated the other. Anthropologist Ernestine

Elderly !Kung woman. Photo by Isla K. Bardavid

Friedl defines **male dominance** as "a situation in which men have highly preferential access, although not always exclusive rights, to those activities to which the society accords the greatest value, and the exercise of which permits a measure of control over others."[51] When men dominate in a particular society they control what the society values. When a society values hunting and aggressive behaviors, men derive their power and authority from social and ritual mechanisms associated with hunting and aggressive activities. The rights and duties attached to hunting activities accord men formal power and authority at the local level, although this does not necessarily exclude women from the realm of power and authority.[52]

Friedl states that an important source of male power among foragers is control of a scarce, hard to acquire, nutrient: meat. She concludes, the "extent of male dominance increases directly with the proportion of meat supplied by individual men and small hunting parties."[53] Therefore, those foraging societies that have a higher proportion of meat in their diets are generally more male dominated. In societies where females significantly contribute gathered vegetable foods, there is generally more gender equality.

Prestige and Status

Foraging societies are generally considered to be egalitarian, meaning there is little differentiation between groups, either by age, sex, or kinship. According to anthropologist Robert Kelly, this term means everyone has "equal access to food, to the technology needed to acquire resources, and to the paths leading to prestige." Maintaining an egalitarian society required constant effort, and an intricate, balanced, sophisticated social system that ensured order and equal access to resources.[54] As mentioned earlier, equality between men and women was generally more the norm among foragers, and there was no social stratification between leaders and followers.

Although foraging people did not have status, some individuals probably possessed slightly more prestige than others. Prestige did not depend upon external qualities such as a title or family name. Both men and women were honored for personal qualities: spiritual powers, extraordinary skills in hunting or gathering, generosity, kindness, a sense of humor, and a flair for oratory and storytelling.[55] In some polygamous societies, men who had more than one wife might have additional prestige, which could result in conflict, especially if some men did not have wives. Age was generally the only or key prestige difference among foraging people with the elderly garnering a great deal of respect. Inheritance of prestige did not occur; positions were fluid and could change from generation to generation.

Different levels of skill existed among individuals, although these skills were not always acknowledged or praised. Most foraging societies discouraged individuals from incurring too much prestige, since group stability took precedence over individual recognition and potentiality. If certain individuals attained too much distinction or attention it could create jealousy and rivalry among group members and conflict could ensue.

Even though little differentiation in wealth, life style, and prestige existed in foraging societies, some individuals had reputations for generosity while some had reputations as freeloaders. A **freeloader** is a person who takes more from the group than s/he contributes. A group could usually tolerate a certain number of freeloaders, but a line had to be drawn. If freeloading escalated into an intolerable problem or over burdened a group, the freeloader could be subject to temporary banishment or in some cases physical violence was meted out.[56]

Foraging people saw the accumulation of material possessions as a burden. Since foragers did not accumulate luxury or surplus goods, differences of possession did not contribute to power and privilege. Foragers consciously chose what we would consider a low standard of living, with easily satisfied material wants. Sahlins states this concept simply: "The world's most primitive people have few possessions, but they are not poor." Poverty, therefore, is an invention of modern society, and he challenges the judgment of inferiority that is often attached to the term.[57]

Even though foraging people limited the accumulation of material possessions, individuals did own a few personal objects. Personal possessions—weapons, clothing, containers, ornaments, tools, jewelry and other personal effects—belonged to the owner and could not be borrowed without the owner's consent. The likelihood of theft was remote, since it was very difficult for the thief to remain anonymous in close-knit societies and no market existed for stolen goods. Reciprocity served as the prevailing mode of exchange, and if someone wanted to borrow another person's articles the owner usually obliged with permission. But if theft did occur, it likely led to conflict and possible expulsion of the guilty party from the group.[58]

Questions to Consider

1. How did foragers deal with freeloaders?
2. How does your nation/society deal with freeloaders? How does poverty relate to the idea of freeloading in the cultures you are acquainted with?

Socialization and Education

Socialization of the young in foraging societies was largely an informal process in which children learned through their play, and by observing and imitating their elders. Most young girls and boys had few major responsibilities other than being tutored in their future social and economic roles. The home base safely protected children and served as a place for learning. A formal initiation rite, which marked the transition from childhood to adulthood, frequently augmented the informal socialization process. These ceremonies signified that a girl had reached womanhood and that a boy had proven his courage and attained the privileges of manhood.[59]

Girls accompanied their mothers and adult women on gathering trips where they learned botanical knowledge needed for skilled identification of food and medicinal sources. They gradually built their physical strength as needed for packing large burdens, toting children, and ferreting out roots with digging sticks. Girls cared for young children at the camp when their mothers and fathers were out foraging for food. The onset of a girl's first menstrual period, menarche, signified an important event for her: she had reached physical maturity and was ready for marriage. The happy event was an occasion for a public ritual, in which a girl's sexual maturity and future economic contributions to the band were joyously celebrated.[60]

A boy's initiation rites could revolve around circumcision, notching out a scar, knocking out a tooth, or a first animal kill during a hunt. Boys were gradually admitted as apprentices to the hunt. However, they needed to attain competent hunting skills before venturing out with a

Hazda (Africa) man teaching archery skills.

hunting party, since one false move by a novice hunter could hinder the chances for a successful kill. Upon finally honing hunting skills and with the first major kill recorded, a boy received his honors at a ritualized ceremony. In this festive ceremony he proudly distributed meat from his kill to other group members, a commemorative act that validated his new role as a hunter and adult.[61]

The foraging band played a vital role in socializing other group members. The act of sharing, an important value, was deeply indoctrinated into young people at an early age, and reinforced throughout life. Sharing, a learned and reinforced behavior, built bonds of social responsibility, obligation, and generosity among foraging people, and involved an elaborate social network to ensure that these values continued for the benefit and survival of all group members.[62]

Questions to Consider

1. Why was sharing such an important socialized value among foraging people?
2. Is sharing an important value in your nation or society?

Insights: Learning from the Past

Social Currents

Forager's social values offer valuable insights for us to consider today. We often hear that humans are innately greedy and competitive, with their own self-interests paramount. Although I would agree that we do have these characteristics, our human behaviors and instincts are quite complex and varied. And as foragers have shown, we also have the capacity to share and act compassionately and cooperatively. Foragers, through the socialization process and because of the realities of their way of life, have fostered cooperative behaviors and placed a high value on them. Therefore, we can see that in our human history these values have been the most essential ones for extended periods of time.

One of my reasons for writing this holistic world history is to show that there is and has been a wide variety of values and attitudes that differ from our values today. Even though the values of individualism, accumulation, and self-interest are supreme in our society, this does not mean that they have always prevailed. Since these values are not intrinsic to our human condition, they can be changed. Changing today's values of cutthroat competition and selfish "me first" is possible. Although I am not advocating the suppression of recognizing individual potential and talents, positive qualities are within the gamut of human behaviors that can be called upon to contribute to a different worldview that also upholds the values of support, sharing and cooperation.

Another helpful lesson can be drawn from foraging people's concept of poverty. How a society assesses its standard of living reflects its particular values and beliefs. When a society places a high value on material possessions and accumulation of goods, then poverty, a negative or lowly condition, is associated with the lack of material possessions. Using these contemporary values, foraging societies have a low standard of living. Judging foraging people by modern society's standards is an example of ethnocentrism. We often assume that those who have few material possessions wish to acquire more; in other words, they wish to live like Americans, and increasingly like other affluent people around the world. But some do not identify possessions with wealth. Although many around the world today yearn for America's material abundance, when the glamorous facade is removed and the stark reality of the situation becomes apparent, many reconsider the magnetism of this consumer way of life.

Another lesson to be learned from foraging people is their respect and admiration for the elderly. The elderly served in leadership positions in all areas of life. American society today has reversed this, instead extolling youthful behaviors and lifestyles as exemplary, most often for economic gain. The elderly person is dismissed as "out of touch" with what is "really going on today" and rendered invisible. A society cannot survive without considering the wise council of its elders. I believe foraging people can teach us a great deal in this area.

> **Questions to Consider**
>
> 1. Do you agree or disagree with the following statement: "Since our values are not intrinsic to our human condition, they can be changed."

ESTABLISHING ORDER: POLITICAL CURRENTS

Political Systems

Foraging people had an informal, decentralized, participatory political and social organization called a band. A band, as described in the social currents section, is a small, simple, autonomous group of people found among food foragers and other nomadic societies. Since bands were small and members knew each other well, a formal, centralized political system was not needed. The decisions of the elders informally settled problems that arose. Along with social pressures such as gossip, derision, direct arbitration, and mediation, an emphasis was placed on achieving a solution considered fair by most of the involved parties and to alleviate in-group conflict. If compromise failed, the disgruntled individuals could leave the band and join a neighboring band.

Forms of Leadership

Leadership in foraging bands was informal, unofficial, and often temporary. Foraging societies usually did not have a single person as a leader but, to the extent that political leadership did exist in a band, a headperson or sometimes more than one headperson fulfilled the leadership role. Men served as leaders more often than women, but not exclusively. Informal discussions among the most influential and respected members of a band, usually the elderly, decided on choices that affected an entire group, while their decisions were usually made through consensus. Through group discussion leaders decided migration routes, arranged food distribution, and resolved interpersonal conflict. A group's small size and homogeneity made decision-making by consensus easier than in larger groups.[63] The quality of a headperson's advice and personality helped him/her to be selected as a leader. Often, a person came to the fore as a leader for a specific task or event and then gave up that leadership role when the task had been completed.

A headperson served as a leader as long as the group had confidence in his/her leadership abilities. Unlike kings, chiefs, presidents, or dictators, headpersons were relatively powerless figures incapable of enforcing obedience and had no guaranteed hold on their position. A headperson often had a frustrating position, because if a task needed to be done it usually fell to the headperson who ended up doing it or worked the hardest in guiding the task to completion.[64] Although a headperson provided minimal leadership, s/he usually had a charismatic personality and set an example of generosity for the group to emulate. Even though the leadership position carried no rewards or riches, occasionally a leader enjoyed slightly more prestige, and could even receive special gifts of food for his/her service.

Customs and Rules

The small size of foraging bands meant that all members knew each other personally and important decisions were made in a democratic manner. If everyone did not agree with a group's decision, dissenting members risked the social consequences of their disagreement or decided to break away from the group.[65] The group controlled the conduct of individual members through a complex system of mores, customs, norms, and sanctions that restricted individualistic, disruptive behavior. No formal political authorities—courts, police, or prisons—regulated or enforced individual behavior. However, an individual did not freely behave as s/he wished.

Foraging societies exerted three patterns of social control. First, among groups who held to the custom of blood revenge, an injured party punished the offender him/herself. Second, when an individual's irresponsible actions caused the entire band to suffer, s/he was punished through group pressure, such as ostracism or banishment from the group. Third, if a member violated an important custom or ritual, it was commonly believed that sanctions by spirits would mete out the needed restraint. All three methods were informal yet effective in keeping social control.[66]

Although individual foragers did not observe formal property ownership, they did decide who could gather plants and hunt game in a particular territory. A band collectively "owned" or occupied the land; individuals did not control it. Bands devised various methods for defining, maintaining, and protecting specific territory by allocating special tracts of land to individuals and planning ways to gain access to another's territory. Individuals had implicit access rights which, although not codified, applied to an agreed upon defined area.[67] A group's territorial rights were quite serious, and those outside the group asked permission to use and take resources within its area. Typically, a group granted permission to a visiting group, but they assumed that a return favor would be granted at some time in the future. A distinctive feature of the landscape such as a waterhole or special tree marked an area, while territorial boundaries remained vague and unfixed.[68]

Questions to Consider

1. What is meant by the statement: "A band collectively "owned" or occupied the land; individuals did not control it."
2. Are there any examples in your nation or society where there is collective or group ownership of land or other entities?

Migration and Interaction

In the Upper Paleolithic era, by approximately 40,000 BP, humans began to migrate beyond the African-Eurasian landmass to the Western hemisphere, Australia, and Japan. As we discussed earlier, humans trekked to the Americas across the Bering Strait land bridge that connects the northern reaches of Asia and America. This land bridge opened during the last glaciation period between 26,000 and 11,000 BP when low sea levels exposed navigable land. Paleolithic people followed the migration route of caribou and other animals across the land bridge, and then traveled southward to populate the two continents of the Western hemisphere. Dates for the arrival of migrating humans to the Americas vary widely with 10,000 to 15,000 BP as a likely average, but some estimates are much earlier.[69] Occupation of Australia and New Guinea appears to begin at least by 50,000 BP during a time of low sea levels, and by 30,000 to 20,000 BP humans even inhabited the southern part of Australia. The first Australians reached the continent sailing small boats of latched logs. Indigenous Australian aborigines adapted to the harshest environments and experienced few pressures to develop more complex societies or civilization.[70]

Conflict, War and Cooperation

In order to maintain cooperation and order and to deal with in-group conflict, foraging societies devised informal systems of authority. Not every form of conflict is warfare. For example, homicide and feuding aren't warfare but are considered conflict. When conflict broke out between two parties, an important method to dampen the clash was to temporarily isolate the disputing parties from their respective kin. It was important to separate the disputants from their kin because if their kin backed them in the controversy, the disputants could continue to press the issue that gave rise to the conflict. On the other hand, a disputant's kinship group could realize the consequences of entering the fray and exercise sound judgment by refraining from an emotional backlash. According to anthropologist Marvin Harris, "What matters is not so much who is morally right or wrong, or who is lying or telling the truth, the important thing is to mobilize public opinion on one side or the other decisively enough to prevent the outbreak of large scale feuding."[71]

A **feud** is hostility between kinship groups initiated by one group to avenge a wrong, usually the murder of one of its members by another group. Feuds occur between kinship groups who live in the same community, as well as between adjacent groups from different communities. A song competition, a public ritualized contest, served as one method for settling a conflict between individual disputants. Women frequently took part in deciding a method for conflict resolution and also sat in as part of the audience at contests where they voiced their opinion as to who "won" the particular competition.[72]

Another method of settling conflict is by retribution. **Retribution** is the redressing of a wrong committed by an individual or group that does not have a centralized governmental authority for the enforcement of its rules. In these cases, the responsibility for retribution falls to the person whose rights have been infringed upon. The violated person can use force to redress a perceived wrong, but force can only be used when other members of the community recognize that the violated party has a legitimate complaint that needs redressing. If retribution proves unsatisfactory to the violated party, or if neither party is satisfied with the outcome, a conflict can escalate into a feud. Some forms of retribution turn violent.[73]

Maasai Warriors (Eastern Africa) c. 1908-1916

Ritualized conflict or decentralized warfare took place in the Communal Wave. Although early foraging groups lived well below the carrying capacity of the Earth, localized shortages and exploitation of necessary resources occurred. Typically, conflict took place over the control of and access to scarce resources.[74] It is often assumed that foragers were peaceful people. However, anthropologist Ferraro challenges the common assumption that foragers lived an idyllic, nonviolent existence and argues that this view has likely been overstated. He maintains that foragers have been found fighting and raiding one another for food and revenge, and forcefully defend their prescribed territory.[75]

A comparison of conflict patterns among 42 contemporary foraging societies worldwide suggests that those who live near critical resources, such as watering holes or fertile land, typically engage in more group versus group conflict over control of these critical physical resources than those who live on more environmentally marginal lands.[76] LeBlanc concurs: "As resource richness declines, the ethnographic evidence for warfare also declines, until there is little evidence for warfare in extremely marginal areas. As expected, the wetter areas of the region were contested and fully populated."[77]

Questions to Consider

1. Why was it not so important to determine who was morally right or wrong in a conflict situation? Is this different from the way your nation administers justice?

Insights: Learning from the Past

Political Currents

The dialogue about whether foraging people lived peaceful or constantly engaged in warfare is relevant for us today. Many viewpoints on this subject use different supporting evidence that seem to hover around the extremes on a continuum. One side vigorously maintains that foragers were peaceful, while another side argues that they were inherently warlike, like those in the other waves. Some feminists have introduced interesting theories that many people during the Communal and Agricultural Waves were peaceful and worshipped the goddess with the feminine principle as prevalent (see the next section and chapter 5 as well). Other scholars have dismissed these theories as idealized visions of what feminists wish to see in the past, not what life was actually like. It is beyond the scope of this chapter to sort out all the evidence and come to a definitive conclusion, if there is one to be made. Suffice it to say that at least this topic can spark interesting conversation and research.

Once again, an important lesson from this section is that the availability of resources is an important variable in whether conflict between groups takes place. As our global resources diminish and our population continues to grow, this question of scarce resources will continue to be a defining issue in the future, as well as it is today. I think it is wise to look beyond conflicts that are often framed as ethnically or racially motivated, to see if the conflict over resources is the underlying reason.

Another valuable insight is to reconsider when the "first democracy" actually started. In our traditional history the Greeks claim that mantle, but once again when looking at the "big picture" of history, that claim does not hold up. Foragers actually can declare that they were the first working democracy. Democratic contributions by all members of the group, such as practiced by councils of elders, are all political strategies humans have apparently performed and experienced for thousands of years. Are we, as a species, inherently democratic? Foraging people seem to say yes!

Questions to Consider

1. What role did the scarcity of resources play in conflict? Does the scarcity of resources contribute to conflict today? Give examples.
2. Are we, as a species, inherently democratic? Explain.

HUMAN EXPRESSIONS: CULTURAL CURRENTS

Beliefs, Religion and Spirituality

Foraging people's spiritual beliefs reflected their particular way of life. A blurred division between self and others characterized their worldview; they saw themselves as united with nature and with the group, not standing apart from it. Rather than trying to change or dominate nature, foragers participated and interacted with nature. To them, their relationship with the Universe and nature, like all their social relationships, was morally significant.[78]

Contemporary foraging people had an animistic belief system. As described in chapter 3, animism is the belief that everything in nature contains personified, animated, conscious spirits

Some Inuit believed that the spirits of their ancestors could be seen in the northern lights.

or souls. Animistic spirits inhabited everything that could be seen in the world and constantly intervened in human affairs, sometimes helping and sometimes harming humans. Spirits were a diverse lot that could be awesome, terrifying, lovable, and even mischievous. For example, some foraging people believed that an animistic spirit caused an arrow to strike a deer, or a spirit to enter the body to heal a wound. People influenced these spirits through enacting proper rituals, sacrifices, and magic charms.

Foragers believed that the "Great Spirit" or "Power" revealed exceptional gifts to a shaman, who invoked his/her special powers to contact the spiritual world and to aid in healing. A shaman or medicine man/woman skillfully negotiated with the spirits. Dreams and trances paved the way for connecting with the spirits.[79] For instance, a shaman called upon the spirit powers to guide a successful hunt, protect a group against evil spirits, and ensure a group's well being. To exercise social control, a shaman sometimes conjured his/her special powers to punish someone who had violated a social custom or acted in a self-centered manner. The role of a shaman typically elicited respect, and s/he could be more influential than a headperson. A shaman had an important say in selecting a headperson, or s/he could serve as the headperson.[80]

Communication

Foraging people communicated orally, and did not have, or need to have, a written language. Talking about experiences and telling stories, usually around a campfire, entertained all and helped to form bonds of belonging among the group. Foraging people conversed with one another for many hours. A typical conversation might consist of a man describing a hunt, or a woman relaying something that happened while out gathering. Speakers gestured broadly, raised and lowered their voices, imitated sounds of animals and birds, exaggerated for effect, and included humorous anecdotes. Drama and excitement heightened a story's effect and much exaggeration and hyperbole accompanied the tale.[81] Not all people were proficient storytellers, and those who excelled could have more prestige than others. The elderly were often, but not always, master storytellers. Elders also served as repositories of customs and traditions, the source

Yup'ik shaman exorcising evil spirits from a sick boy. Nushagak (southwest), Alaska, 1890s.

for many stories. Legends depicted the origins of the world and the creation of a particular group, which were generally considered identical. Other popular stories told about the exploits of shamans of the past that often wove together explanations of group customs as well. Accompanied by music and dance, some stories turned into elaborate initiation rites.[82] People vividly recounted the primacy of their place in the cosmos, weaving a resplendent tale around a familiar tree, mountain, sky, stream, or animal.

Identity and Belonging

Foraging societies bound the individual into the collectivity and subordinated a separate self. Each person in the group had a positive and inseparable relationship with the community as a whole and the elementary unity of life. They did not fathom themselves as separate egos apart from the encompassing totality of the group or the Universe. The numinous world intricately connected participators into a dynamic web. Separation between good and evil did not exist, and neither were thought to be absolute, but equated to that which was valuable or harmful to a particular group. Each group had specific folk spirits unique to their own particular group.[83] For example, the Mbuti thought of themselves as children of the forest and were always aware not to disturb or displease the forest spirits.

> **Questions to Consider**
>
> 1. What does the following statement mean to you: "foraging societies bound the individual into the collectivity, and subordinated a separate self?" Do you do this in your particular culture? Explain.

Aesthetic Expression

The beginning of the Upper Paleolithic era represented a crucial shift in human consciousness and reflected the emergence of a more complex and highly structured cognitive system.[84] The emergence of modern languages was no doubt linked to this expanded cognition. Paleolithic people's art reflected a complex cognitive system. Their art included portable art as well as art in permanent settings such as rock shelters and caves. According to anthropologist Marjorie Eldredge artistic expression represented a sense of control over the natural world. "Being able to talk about, describe, to draw and paint a wild animal requires observation, thought, analysis, and even intimate experience. It requires knowledge, and knowledge is power."[85] It also signified a close connection and participation with nature.

Art of the Upper Paleolithic, primarily in Europe, can be divided into three categories: cave paintings, bone and stone objects, and goddess art. Displayed in the darkest recesses on cave walls, Paleolithic paintings are a spectacular art form. The artists painted with red pigments derived from iron oxide and the blue and green pigments extracted from plants. Paleolithic methods for applying pigments—fingers, a crayon type object, some sort of pad, or a paint

Hamatsa ritualist in British Columbia, Canada, 1914.

spitting technique—have recently been recreated and are considered practical ways of application.[86] The artistic representations on cave walls fall into three categories: first, abstract geometric patterns or signs that included dots, grids, spirals, chevrons, curves, zigzags, nested curves, and triangles; second, animal images that included bison, ibex, mammoth, big carnivores, rhinoceros, and the most common figure, the horse; and third, humans and non figurative designs such as a human/animal chimera.[87]

The significance of Paleolithic art has been the subject of a wide variety of interpretations. At one extreme, some early interpreters maintain that the art had no meaning and simply stood for doodlings, graffiti, play activity, or mindless decorations by hunters with little else to do. Others regard the art as merely for art's sake with no significant meaning. Another hypothesis describes the art as evoking hunting magic, and was part of a hunting ritual performed to ensure its success. A similar utilitarian viewpoint interprets the art as a means to summon fertility magic, in which animals were reproduced in hopes of guaranteeing food in the future. At the other end of the spectrum, recent interpretation suggests an intimate relationship between a shaman and his/her art. The artistic images are thought to be from the mind of a shaman/artist, who rendered these images while in a hallucinogenic state. The shaman/artist experienced three stages of hallucination, each one deeper and more complex than the other, and different images were expressed in each stage. In the first stage the shaman saw geometric forms, like the ones described above. In the second stage the shaman/artist depicted the images as real objects: the artist construed curves as hills in a landscape and portrayed chevrons as hunting weapons. What an individual saw in trance depended on his/her cultural experiences and circumstances. In the third stage, the artist experienced sensations from traversing in a vortex or rotating in a tunnel and then recreated these

Lascaux cave painting in southwestern France, estimated to be 17,000 years old.

fantastic scenes. One such image was a breathtaking human/animal chimera found in a cave in southwestern France. Known as the Sorcerer, the figure sported a large pair of antlers and appeared to be composed of body parts from many different animals.[88]

Artists carved portable bone and stone objects and engraved designs usually depicting animals, which served both utilitarian and non-utilitarian functions. Utilitarian art objects consisted of tools and weapons decorated with engravings of animal figures and carved from bone, ivory, antler, and limestone. Non-utilitarian art objects included pendants made of bone and ivory, and engravings of animal figures that represented bison, deer, horse, and bear.[89]

Female figures, a third art form found in Paleolithic Europe, are often referred to as Venus figurines. Large breasts, ample buttocks, and thick thighs typified these figurines that were either sculpted in clay or carved from soft stone or mammoth ivory. Other body parts such as arms, feet, and facial features are sketchy or absent. Often naked and usually obese, these female figures wore ornamental girdles or chest bands and possibly represented a mother goddess or fertility figure, since many of the objects appeared pregnant. The female art forms significantly outnumber the male art forms. The spectacular Venus of Willendorf, recovered in Austria, depicts a woman with a carefully arranged headdress or hair but no facial features, with her arms stretched across her ample breasts and her legs abruptly ending below the knees. Many of the Paleolithic figurines show marked similarities, which perhaps suggest a common meaning and interconnected social and religious traditions across Europe.[90]

Contemporary foraging people have various forms of aesthetic expression. Music is especially popular and often played at festivals or initiation rites, cheerfully performed on one or two different kinds of instruments and usually accompanied by joyful singers who repeat their lyrics and voice a few repeated words. Hopping or shuffling dance styles are enthusiastically performed by participants, who render lively up-and-down or side-to-side steps along with syncopated body movements.[91] Human participation in art, music, religion, and entertainment provides a strong foundation of traditions and social/cultural continuity.

A fragmentary ivory figurine from the Upper Paleolithic. It was discovered in a cave at Brassempouy, France in 1892. About 25,000 years old, it is one of the earliest known realistic representations of a human face.

Venus of Willendorf, 22,000 BCE, figures like these are collectively called Venus figurines.

Questions to Consider?

1. What is your favorite form of aesthetic expression carried out by foraging people?
2. How do researchers know about art forms such as storytelling and dance in societies with no written language?

Insights: Learning from the Past

Cultural Currents

An element in the cultural patterns that I think is an important lesson for us today is the inclusion of animism as the religious expression of foragers. The discussion of religion still remains a hot-button issue, and uncomfortable for many. Usually when discussing religions we highlight the universal religions (see Urban Wave) of Christianity, Buddhism, Islam, Judaism, and Hinduism. But the religious beliefs before the sweep of universal religions are rarely mentioned, or dismissed as "pagan" which often has a derogatory tone. I prefer the term animistic, which gives voice to the religious beliefs of many indigenous people throughout the world today and in the past.

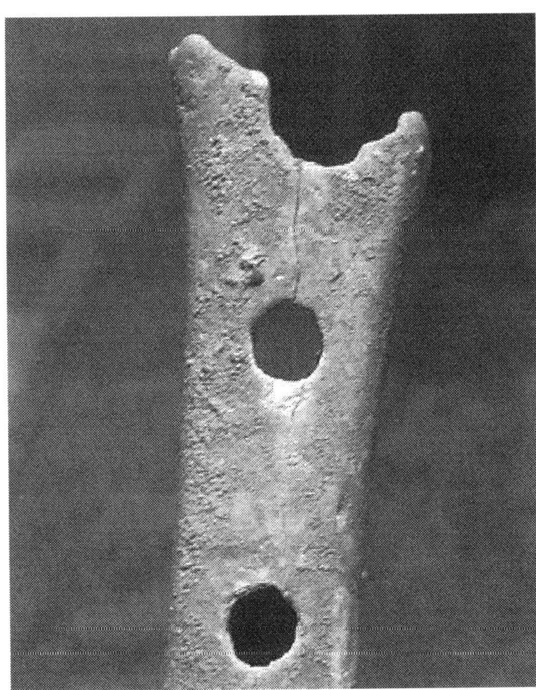

The Divje Babe flute, discovered in 1995 in Slovenia, claimed to be the world's oldest flute. A cave bear femur pierced with spaced holes, 43,000 years old.

Questions to Consider

1. Do you think it is important to study the animistic religious expression among foraging people? Why?

Foraging people constructed a way of life compatible with their nomadic practices: simple technology, group cohesion, consensus decision-making, animistic religious expression, and interdependence with nature. Although distinct differences among foraging people existed, they also shared many commonalities. The following case study of a contemporary foraging band, the !Kung, exemplifies one of the ways that foragers lived. The !Kung band has been selected because a substantial amount of research has been conducted and documented about their fascinating yet disappearing way of life.

THE !KUNG: NOMADIC FORAGERS OF THE KALAHARI DESERT

Probably the best known of contemporary hunting and gathering people are the San speaking !Kung or Ju/'hoansi people of southern Africa. They maintained their traditional foraging way of life into the 1960s. Since then they have been increasingly crowded into smaller territories where they are unable to sustain their population by foraging. In the 1990s, many of the San people settled near waterholes where they cultivated gardens or raised livestock. Today neighboring villagers significantly influence the !Kung's nomadic or semi-nomadic way of life with most of them living as poor subsistence farmers in Namibia in southwestern Africa. In 2002, the government of Botswana drove the foragers out of the Central Kalahari Desert because they continued to hunt in what was declared a game reserve. In 2004, a delegation of the displaced San went to Washington D.C., the World Bank, and the United Nations to plead for help.

They were hoping that world public opinion would force Botswana to allow them to return to what had been their homeland for the last 20,000 years. Few paid heed to their appeal.

The !Kung people thrived as food foragers into the 1960s and 1970s and held to many aspects of their traditional way of life. During that time anthropologists conducted a vast amount of research about their life. Anthropologist Richard Lee's research of a particular group of the !Kung people—the Zu/'hoasi of the Dobe area of the Botswaran—has proven particularly noteworthy. Since Lee's initial research in 1963-64, he and others have frequently returned for further fieldwork and have accumulated a detailed record of this foraging group. The following narrative about the !Kung is primarily from the 1960s and 1970s time period.

The !Kung belong to the Khoisan people, a large cluster of south Africans who include the San (Bushmen) hunters, the Khoekhoe herders, and the Damara herding people.[92] While some consider "Bushman" to be a pejorative term, it is what they call themselves today when speaking English.[93] The San are aboriginal inhabitants who once populated the whole of southern Africa. A 1650 population estimate calculated the number of San people to be between 150,000 and 300,00 In 1652 the Dutch arrived in the region and killed or enslaved nearly the entire San population by 1850. The !Kung today lead both a foraging and sedentary lifestyle and have a long history of contact with other peoples who share their land and trade goods.

!Kung man in the arid Kalahari Desert area of South Africa, commonly called the "Bush."
Photo by Isla K. Bardavid

Relationship with Nature: Ecosystem Currents

!Kung foragers studied by Lee and others, resided on the northern fringe of the Kalahari Desert. The !Kung experienced hot summers with a four to six month rainy season, and moderate to cool winters without rainfall. The environment significantly affected the !Kung's way of life. Food shortages often accompanied a scarcity of water during most seasons of the year. Although large game was scarce and hard to find, a variety of vegetation and plenty of small game were always available, especially in the rainy season.[94]

The current population of hunting and gathering !Kung is uncertain but there is a high probability that none still exist as the generation before them did.[95] At the turn of the 20th century, 60 percent of all !Kung groups were full-time hunters and gatherers but by 1976 that proportion had dropped to 5 percent. A mid-1950s population count estimated the number of !Kung to be around 50,000.[96] Although it is currently difficult to estimate the !Kung population at the turn of the 21st century, perhaps between 25,000 to 30,000 people still exist. The largest group are the Central !Kung with the Northern !Kung scattered across a larger land area.[97]

Questions to Consider

1. Why do contemporary foraging bands, such as the !Kung, live on environmentally marginal lands of the world? What hardships does this pose for them?

Ways of Living: Techno-Economic Currents

The !Kung had relatively simple technology and economy. For food foraging they primarily relied on a single tool, the digging stick, to root out tubers, bulbs, and burrowing mammals. Their major hunting tool kit consisted of the bow and arrow, spear, knife, and rope snares. With their carefully crafted bow and arrow the !Kung killed large antelope and giraffe, while they used a rope snare to trap small antelopes, carnivores, and birds. The bow and arrow appear to be easy to use, but looks are deceptive; it required persistence and skill for effective mastery. Men carried their hunting weapons in an easily accessible bag slung over their shoulders, although they clubbed some smaller animals to death. Men organized hunting trips about three days per week, and usually stayed in the field several hours and sometimes up to ten hours a day.[98] The !Kung were superb trackers and made uncanny deductions as to the trail of an animal from only the faintest marks. A tracker identified an individual by his/her footprints, skills honed over a lifetime of observing tens of thousands of findings. Trackers deduced an animal's species, sex, age, how fast it traveled, whether it journeyed alone or with other animals, its physical condition, the time of day it passed, and what it fed upon, all from its tracks and trail. A hunter carefully scrutinized this information before he pursued a particular trail.[99]

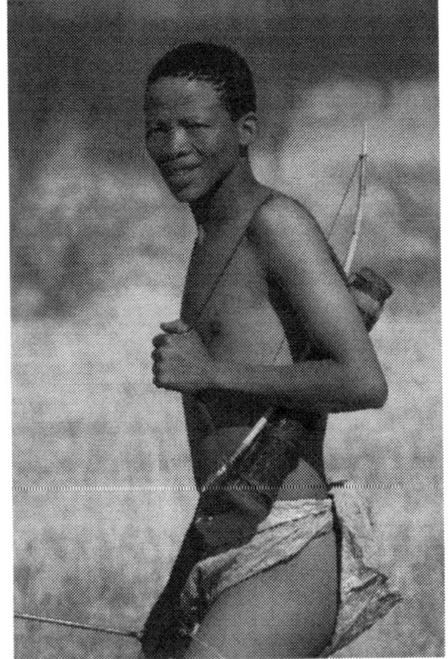
!Kung hunter with his bow and arrow in the Kalahari. Photo by Isla K. Bardavid

!Kung man displaying his simple hunting tools. Photo by Isla K. Bardavid

A simple digging stick was the food-gathering tool most likely used, but the knowledge about plant identification, growth, ripeness, and location was quite complex. It took women many years of intense study and practice to distinguish edible plant foods. The identification of edible plants took the utmost care, for a simple mistake could result in severe poisoning and possible death.

Women carried their gathered foods back to camp in multipurpose containers. The *kaross* served as the most utilitarian carrying device for women, as well as a dual-purpose sleeping blanket. Draped over the wearer's back, the *kaross* proved ideal for carrying heavy loads and held vegetables, water containers, firewood, or even a baby. Men fashioned the kaross for women from the hides of the kudu, gemsbok, wildebeest, or eland. Women used a baby sling, made of skin, to carry their young infants. Tied around her waist and slipped over a shoulder, a baby sling fit snugly inside the *kaross* and wedged against a woman's hip. Infants were allowed to nurse unimpeded. Soft grasses and other absorbent materials served as a "diaper" and lined this special baby carrier which women frequently cleaned and aired out.[100] An infant had constant access to stimulating cosmetic and decorative objects hanging from a mother's neck, and often amused him/herself for hours playing with these eye-catching objects.[101] Older, toilet-trained children sat directly in the *kaross* or were triumphantly perched on a man or woman's shoulders.

The !Kung spent about 20 hours a week gathering and hunting food. Vegetable food, not meat, formed the mainstay of their diet. Plant foods were abundant and predictable, while game animals were relatively scarce and more difficult to catch. The !Kung consumed over 100 different plants fit for human consumption: 14 types of fruits and nuts, 15 berries, 18 species of edible gum, 41 edible roots and bulbs, and 17 leafy greens, beans, melons, and other foods. They derived over 70 percent of their diet from vegetable foods and 30 percent came from meat.[102] The !Kung's daily per-capita calorie intake totaled 2,140 calories. About 1,975 calories per-capita were needed for a healthy diet, based on body weight, activity, and age-sex composition. The !Kung did not lead a life on the brink of starvation.[103]

The mongongo, a fruit/nut plentiful and available throughout the year, formed the core of the !Kung's diet. A highly nutritious food found near waterholes, the easily-collected mongongo rivaled only meat as their most desirable food. When a !Kung man was asked about his favorite foods, he replied: meat and mongongo for strength, honey for sweetness, and wild orange fruits for refreshment.[104]

Along with the mongongo, the Kung considered meat to be their most valued food. The killing of a large animal signified an occasion for celebratory feasting and festivities. Meat was barbequed round-the-clock in dugout pits, while people gathered from far and wide to partake in a delicious meal and enjoyed an occasion for friendship and socializing. Men properly distributed meat after a kill. Lee described the proper procedure: "Distribution is done with great care, according to a set of rules, arranging and rearranging the pieces for up to an hour so that each recipient will get the right portion. Appropriate distribution is remembered with pleasure for weeks afterwards, while improper meat distribution can be the cause of bitter wrangling among close relatives."[105]

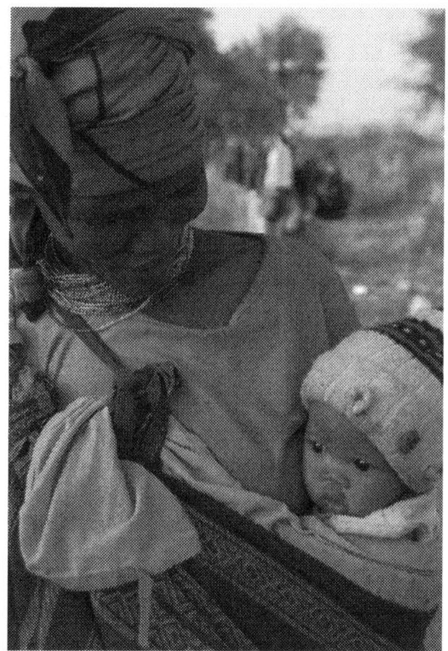
!Kung Mother with child in kaross. Photo by Isla K. Bardavid

Gathering vegetables was parceled into two types of activities: picking and digging. To extract tubers and bulbs necessitated a digging stick, essential during the dry season. Gathering provided a stable basis for subsistence, because plant foods yielded expected quantities with comparatively little effort. Gathering excursions lasted from one to several hours and took place almost every day. Gatherers consumed some of the food in the field, but most women toted back to camp their day's collection in some type of carrying device.[106]

The !Kung organized their village camps into five concentric circles, each with a different function. The camp's public space lay in the center of the circle, where children played, people gathered, and the evening's healing dances performed. The first circle from the center enclosed a ring of huts and hearths. Each woman built a circular hut under two meters in diameter and situated approximately three to five meters from her neighbor.[107] Domed roofs constructed from branches bunched together were perched atop the huts to form a steeple-like roof. A thick layer of grass loosely tied in place was laced together to form the hut's frame. A small entrance opened to one side. Used mainly to store personal belongings or to take naps, the hut was designated as the residence of the nuclear family.[108] The family's campfire rested towards the front of the hut, which served as a place for warmth and socializing, where food was cooked, and an area that the family settled in for the night. This campfire spot fostered a sense of security and belonging among the !Kung. Women dumped ashes from cooking and other refuse in the second ring. In the third ring, men butchered large animals and cooked them in the dugout cooking pits. The families assigned the fourth ring as an area for bodily elimination. Beyond the fifth ring, the perimeter of the camp, foraging took place.[109]

The !Kung divided labor according to gender and age. Gender labor differentiations meant women usually gathered food and men hunted. On gathering days a woman walked two to 12 miles round trip, and typically carried a 15 to 33 pound load on her back. !Kung women walked constantly. They often walked long distances to other campsites to visit neighbors, and then logged additional miles when the group moved to another campsite. A woman walked about 1,500 miles in a year, according to calculations, often carrying a child under four years old or heavy packs of food. A !Kung man hunted on average about 20 hours per week, or 2.7 days hunting. In one !Kung band Lee estimated that men provided 45 percent of the food and women contributed 55 percent. One man's hunting labor supported four to five people. Effective food collectors numbered about 60 percent of the band members, while the remaining people were either too young or old to contribute.[110]

!Kung Village. Photo by Isla K. Bardavid

The !Kung routinely conducted exchanges. The exchange of gifts helped to resolve or end conflict, and proved effective in maintaining amicable relations among group members. The *hxaro*, an ingenious system for circulating goods, also soothed social tensions. Lee explained *hxaro* as a "delayed form of nonequivalent gift exchange: I give you something today, and you give me something in return six months or a year from now." Returns did not have to be of precise equivalent value. The *hxaro* valued the good social relations that resulted from the gesture, rather than the economic worth of the goods. Anything could be used in an *hxaro*: dogs, pots, digging sticks, pipes, jewelry, arrows, spears, knives, beadwork, and ostrich-eggshell bead necklaces. Visitors employed an *hxaro* when calling upon relatives or neighbors. The number of goods accumulated by an individual did not determine wealth among the !Kung, but rather the frequency of exchange transactions.[111]

Human Networks: Social Currents

Kinship formed the basis of !Kung social organization. The kinship structure did not entail written laws but informal codes that provided order yet allowed for group flexibility. The camp served as the home base site of the band. Temporary camps could be moved when the band relocated. About 20 to 40 people camped together; the number and composition varied depending upon the local food resources, visitors, and those who decided to leave or join another band. Some !Kung split from a group because another area appeared more attractive and the vision of "greener pastures" enticed a family. The !Kung relished visiting other relatives or friends in different bands and sometimes a temporary visit to a different camp turned into a long-term residency. Residential shifts also occurred because of exogamous marriages, marriages outside the social group. Adjustments due to overall numbers, age, and sex ratios also changed group composition. Lee notes: "When a group's dependency ratio—the proportion of dependents per 100 able-bodied producers—gets too high or too low, steps may be taken to bring this ratio back into line."[112]

The search for marriage partners for girls and boys commenced soon after a child's birth. Parents generally arranged first marriages which involved a decade of gift exchange before the actual event. Typically, a boy's mother approached a girl's mother and proposed marriage. If a girl's family agreed to the marriage, a special gift sealed the occasion. Strict traditional constraints dictated whom a boy or girl could marry; [113] for instance, a form of incest taboo existed that prohibited a girl from marrying a man with her father's name, or a first or second cousin. All the prohibitions eliminated three-fourths of the band and their surrounding band's potential marriage partners. Of the remaining pool of potential mates, a girl's parents looked for a man who exhibited good hunting skills, did not have a reputation as a fighter, and came from a congenial family. To prove his hunting skills, a prospective groom might live with a bride's family for a certain period of time, sometimes up to a year. Traditionally, girls married between 12 and 16 years of age, and boys married between the ages of 18 and 25 The husband was customarily

!Kung socializing at their camp. Photo by Isla K. Bardavid

seven to fifteen years older at marriage than his wife.[114] Almost all !Kung married.

The !Kung were open about sexuality. Learning customary sexual behavior began at an early age as children slept under the same blanket as their parents. Anthropologist Marjorie Shostak concludes that "!Kung children [were] sexually aware at a very early age because of the relative openness and acceptance of adult sexuality." Plenty of opportunities existed in which children experimented with what they observed. Parents voiced their disapproval of such behavior, but little was done to prevent sexual experimentation, since they realized that as children they participated in the same behaviors. Children were naked until the age of seven or eight but upon reaching their early teen years they were expected to cover their genitals.[115] Homosexuality was not common but it did occur. A few same sex experiments took place among males, less among females. These same sex experiments were classified as bisexual. Lee notes, "Non participants in same sex relationships expressed attitudes of curiosity and bemusement toward them rather than embarrassment or hostility.[116]

The !Kung regarded marriage as an important social tradition. Many marriage ceremonies involved the mock forcible carrying of a girl from her parent's hut to a specially built marriage hut.

According to Lee, "!Kung marriages had some similarities to marriage-by-capture practices that were an ancient and controversial form of marriage in which a groom steals a bride."[117] Some marriages, especially by the elderly, did not have a ceremony but the couple was acknowledged as married simply by residing together. If an arranged first marriage displeased a young bride, she could show her unhappiness by kicking and screaming until, in some cases, the marriage was called off. Even if the protests subsided, a woman had asserted her independence. After a stormy period, the marriages that survived settled into stable, long-term relationships that could last 20 to 30 years. Almost half of all !Kung first marriages failed, but only 10 percent of the marriages that lasted five years or longer ended in divorce. When divorce did occur the wife customarily initiated it. Divorce, characterized by a high degree of cordiality, was a simple matter subject to mutual consent. In a marriage sample taken by Lee in 1968, 93 percent of the !Kung had monogamous marriages and 5 percent polygamous. Wives generally opposed polygamous marriages, while polyandry, more than one husband, was a much less common form of marriage.[118] Although data on marital fidelity and extramarital affairs was contradictory, Lee found that a majority of !Kung marriage partners remained faithful to one another, while a minority participated in extramarital affairs. No double standard existed among the !Kung; both husbands and wives took lovers. Those participating in affairs practiced discretion, because if detected their affair could trigger spousal sexual jealousy that might lead to conflict. Lee found that women expressed more sexual jealousy than men, and they might physically attack their husbands and/or rival lovers if provoked.[119]

!Kung loved children, and they played a central role in the life of the band. Women gave birth to their first child at an average age of 19.5 years. Anthropologist Melvin Konner describes the mother-infant bond as "close, of long duration, and characterized by great indulgence of infant demands while remaining low in restriction of infant operations." Infants remained in physical contact with mothers or other adults for a long period of time.[120] A mother breast-fed her child until about four or five years of age, or until she became pregnant again. She averaged 4.7 live births, a fertility level lower than other populations in the area. But the !Kung had about a 20 percent mortality rate for all children in their first year. Most !Kung families had up to four children spaced four years apart.[121] Like other foragers the !Kung took measures to ensure that a group was not over-burdened with the care of too many children, since a low fertility rate was an essential adaptive mechanism for the survival of the mother and band. In order to assure ideal population levels, a family practiced infanticide when they deemed it necessary. Infanticide most likely was performed when a child had birth defects, a child was a twin, one birth followed too closely on another, or a mother felt too old to produce milk for another baby. The number of infanticides among hunting and gathering bands varied significantly, but was considered a practical and moral means of population control.[122]

!Kung mother with child. Photo by Isla K. Bardavid

Integrating children into every aspect of !Kung life positively affected their cognitive development. In a study, Melvin Konner concluded that infants in the first six months of life were advanced compared to modern American infants in certain measures of cognitive development. He attributed cognitive stimulation and alertness to placing a baby in a vertical posture in a baby sling.[123] Infants graduated from a close relationship with their mother to an attachment with a multi-aged child group. The transition began at the end of the first year and ended several months after the birth of the next child or around 4 years old. Children had no formal training nor were they expected to follow specific rules. For example, there was no precise bedtime and children wandered among adults until they tired. In one !Kung band there were no exact duties for children until 10 to 15 years old.[124] A child spent most of his/her day with an assortment of people in the band. Although there were a limited number of playmates and few age mates, children appeared content with the play they created. Adults were keenly aware of where the children were during their playtime, and they almost always were within earshot or observation of an adult. The relationship between children and adults was easygoing and unselfconscious. Adults informally and unobtrusively supervised children, but they were by no means lax. Adults quickly stopped aggressive interactions, especially among children of unequal ages. Children preferred not to accompany adults on gathering or hunting trips, but rather stayed in camp to gossip, play, and interact with adults who remained in camp. Older children were responsible for certain tasks: at about 14 years of age, girls began to gather food, and boys started to hunt at the age of 16.[125]

A group of !Kung children. Photo by Isla K. Bardavid

The !Kung's social structure was egalitarian. Camps consisted of informal clusters of interacting people, including a variety of gender and age groups. Few physical or social barriers barred communication among band members, although the inside of a person's hut was considered private and access was restricted.[126] Even an individual who possessed certain admirable traits, such as prowess as a hunter, was not overtly recognized for his exceptional skill. For example, when a hunter returned from a successful hunt, he was not greeted with praise or adoration. Fellow band members often displayed indifference or negative reaction to the news of a triumphant kill by a skilled hunter, and this attitude continued during the butchering and distribution of meat. Many band members issued insults in an offhanded way and loudly expressed their disappointment that the hunter did not have more success in his endeavor. The following conversation exemplified the process of humbling a skillful hunter as told by Gaugo, an elder:

You mean you have dragged us all the way out here to make us cart home your pile of bones? Oh, if I had known it was this thin I wouldn't have come. People, to think I gave up a nice day in the shade for this. At home we may be hungry, but at least we have nice cool water to drink."[127]

The aim of the heavy joking and derision was a type of leveling mechanism that was intended to equalize social relations. Any potential arrogant behavior exhibited by an expert hunter was roundly silenced. The !Kung recognized that there could be a tendency toward arrogance by young men and took steps to combat it. Xai, a !Kung healer, explained:

"When a young man kills much meat, he comes to think of himself as a chief or a big man, and he thinks of the rest of us as his servants or inferiors. We can't accept this. We refuse one who boasts, for someday his pride will make him kill somebody. So we always speak of his meat as worthless. In this way we cool his heart and make him gentle."[128]

Insulting the meat was just one of many leveling mechanisms the !Kung people employed to maintain their sense of egalitarianism. Even though some hunters were more competent than others, the group derided their behavior to minimize the tendency toward self-praise and boastfulness. The practice of sharing arrows in hunting also reflected the egalitarian way of life. One !Kung custom allocated ownership of meat to the holder of the arrow used to kill an animal. Men circulated arrows in a trading network. A man said to another: "Give me an arrow, and if I kill something with it I will give the meat to you." Even if a kill was made weeks or months later with a borrowed arrow, the meat was still shared with the trading partner. If a man at another camp made a kill, dried meat was saved and distributed at a later time. Trading arrows strengthened the social bonds between men and helped reduce the considerable individual differences in hunting abilities to ensure group stability and continuity.[129]

Sharing was essential to the !Kung way of life. Each member of a band participated in a fragile collective that pooled all resources. The !Kung did not necessarily share out of nobility or because they were better people than others; in fact, they often complained about sharing. But the socialization process emphasized sharing. They shared because it worked for them and they were acutely aware that it was imperative that they all followed a sharing way of life for both the individual and the group to survive.[130]

Establishing Order: Political Currents

Most !Kung bands recognized particular leaders, most of whom were male. Leaders spoke out on issues and their advice was more carefully considered than that of other band members. Band leaders had no formal authority and could only persuade others to follow, not enforce their will.[131] Outside leaders who married into the group did not inherit their previous leadership position. Most bands found it beneficial to have designated leaders; for instance if a fight broke out a leader was instrumental in separating the disputing parties and negotiating a settlement. Much confusion and ill-will resulted if conflict was not resolved quickly and peacefully. Lee questioned a !Kung member about the existence of a headman or leader and he replied: "Of course we have headmen! In fact, we are all headmen. Each one of us is headman over himself!"[132]

The whole band, not individuals, "owned the land." Each water hole was used and, in effect, collectively owned, by a particular band. If a visiting band wanted to use the waterhole or resources surrounding the waterhole, they asked

Elderly !Kung women were often consulted for their wise counsel. Photo by Isla K. Bardavid

the group's permission to use their resources. The group rarely refused to grant permission. This permission was predicated on the understanding that a reciprocal exchange would be granted at some time in the future.[133]

Since there was no private ownership of property, except personal possessions, most conflict involved disagreements about sexual jealousies, infidelities, and marriage choices. The !Kung were scrappy fighters, and their fighting could turn violent. When a rare homicide occurred, it was usually instigated over an argument between two men over a woman.[134] Conflict among the !Kung occurred at three levels: talking, which included argumentative threats and verbal abuse, but no blows; fighting, which was an exchange of blows without the use of weapons; and deadly fighting, where poisoned arrows, spears, and clubs were wielded. When one killing took place it was often avenged by another. Nine people were killed in one known feud that lasted over a 20-year period. Once feuds were set in motion, they were difficult to end.[135] Although occasional flare-ups did happen and homicides occurred, generally the peaceful !Kung lived in relative harmony.

Human Expressions: Cultural Currents

The !Kung did not spend much time in abstract philosophical or spiritual discourse but were more concerned with such concrete everyday matters as life and death, and health and illness. They had a principal spirit and a trickster spirit. In some !Kung stories the principal spirit was portrayed as good and the lesser spirit as evil; in other stories the reverse was true. The !Kung had several origin stories. In one version, the beginning was a time when people and animals were not distinct but lived together in a single village led by an elephant. Spirits of the dead brought misfortune, and if death occurred before old age, either from serious illness or accident, the spirits of the dead were believed to be involved.[136]

The !Kung searched for and devised ways for a deep experiential resonance within the spiritual dimension. Anthropologist Richard Katz notes, this search "leads them to experience heightened states of consciousness that certainly could be called transcendent. Persons seek an ultimate level of being beyond their individual selves." To prepare for a trance state, participants engaged in an experiential educational process.[137] Some reluctantly entered a trance state and expressed fear of crossing the threshold of everyday life into an unknown state. Katz explains, "This education must also bring transcendence into ordinary life, and ordinary life into transcendence, if personal growth is to occur."[138] Approximately half of the adult men and one-third of the adult women prepared for experiencing *kia*, a trance state, a religious occasion in which healing occurred. Through the dance experience, an individual underwent an alteration in their consciousness. *Kia*, a harmonious or synergistic state, linked together the individual, cultural group, and spiritual world. To reach a *kia* state a participant joined in a dance. One dance called the Giraffe Dance, usually lasted from dusk to dawn and could be performed as often as once or twice a week. Participants gathered around a fire, danced blissfully, clapped hands, and worked themselves into a kia state in which they experienced an emotional cosmic connection. Along with an intense spiritual connection, a *kia* state served the group in a practical way by helping an individual or the group cope with illness and misfortune, while increasing social cohesion and solidarity. It also allowed an individual or group to release lingering hostilities they might harbor. Once participants reached a *kia* state, it could have a contagious effect on other members of the group, who might willingly partake in the experience as well.[139]

Kia is considered an altered state because an individual felt connected, uplifted with a sense of cosmic unity and harmony, more than s/he experienced in ordinary, everyday life. *Kia* triggered a very powerful and emotional physical state: the body trembled, breathing was heavy, physical fatigue set in, and fear was sometimes palpable. When in a state of *kia* an individual could perform cures, handled and walked on fire, claimed x-ray vision, and at times saw over great distances. *Kia* participation was part of a religious dimension that brought feelings of release and emancipation, liberation from pain and fear, and a feeling of death and rebirth. A *kia* state was a type of death where an individual gave up her/his separate identity and was reborn into the all-inclusive universal collective. However, participants also feared leaving their comfortable, ordinary state and being reborn, although many individuals accepted this unknown and set aside their fears in order to experience this state of mystery. A *kia* journey signified passage into and through the unknown.[140]

One healer described the *kia* state:

N/um is put into the body through the backbone. It boils in my belly and boils up to my head like beer. When the women start singing and I start dancing, at first I feel quite all right. Then in the middle, the medicine begins to rise from my stomach. After that I see all the people like very small birds, the whole place will be spinning around, and that is why we run around. The trees will be circling also. You feel your blood become very hot, just like blood boiling on a fire, and then you start healing."[142]

A !Kung method of social healing was based on the principle of *n/um*. *N/um* energy resided in the pit of the stomach and was activated during a kia state.[141] The !Kung believed the dancer's movements heated *n/um* energy to a boil, which then rose up the spinal cord and subsequently exploded in the brain. The dancers' felt enormous power and energy course through their body; their legs trembled, chest heaved, and throat dried. Strange visions flooded the participant's senses.

Both men and women aspired to become healers for their band, with almost half of the men and one-third of the women reaching their goal. It was not the province of the elite or few.

Cultural activities of the !Kung incorporated music and dance. Women performed one pleasing dance called the "Women's Drum Dance." In this weekly dance 8 to 12 women entered a trance state. Men, either spectators or playing a supporting role, beat complex rhythms on the long drum, a central symbol of the dance. The women danced in one place with short steps while rhythmically swaying from side to side. Once women were engaged in the dance, a *kia* state could be attained. The dancers felt intense trembling in the legs; they staggered, and often relied on other dancers to prop them up. After a few minutes a dancer could collapse into a *kia* state. It was said that when women danced, the medicine bubbled up in their chest and backbone, and then exploded in the cervical vertebrae. The spectators massaged the dancers to help soften the intensity of the experience. Women went through the same state of kia that men did in their Giraffe Dance.[143]

Every band had a number of storytellers who regaled captive audiences. Virtually all the elders

Elderly women were often master storytellers. Photo by Isla K. Bardavid

over the age of 45 told stories and eagerly did so. A younger or middle-aged storyteller was more rare and reticent. All band members enjoyed the time for storytelling, even though the tales tended to be bawdy, horrific, or centered on the ridiculous. Children were not barred from listening to stories but wandered in and out as their interest dictated. Younger adults listened attentively, often enraptured with the tale. Anthropologist Megan Biesele notes, "Storytelling [is] a natural outgrowth and perfection of verbal activities they have been practicing all their lives."[144]

Happy children. Photo by Isla K. Bardavid

Insights: Learning from the Past

The !Kung

An interesting quandary arises when studying foraging people such as the !Kung in world history. This quandary involves how their lives are portrayed: primitive and backward with few redeeming characteristics or idealized people living in constant reverence of nature. It is commonly assumed that since foraging people did not change much compared to the earth-shattering changes we experience today, they were primitive, backward, or undeveloped. This was not the case, as we can see with the !Kung. While their material comforts were limited, they apparently had leisure time and spent this time with family and fellow group members. They were in tune with a nurturing social life and deep spiritual connections, perhaps even more than those enjoyed today by modern humans who place a priority on pursuing economic and technological advancements with an emphasis on material comfort and accumulation. Before we evaluate others, we need to first examine the criteria that we use for our evaluations. If we evaluate the !Kung's technological advancement, we would come to the conclusion that they are underdeveloped. Yet if we evaluate the !Kung's social structures, we can see that they nurtured their children, respected the elderly and drew on their wisdom, and all members were included into the cocoon of the group. Perhaps evaluative criteria can tell us more about ourselves than others.

Questions to Consider

1. What criteria would you use to evaluate the !Kung's way of life?
2. What criteria would you use to evaluate your way of life?

Insights: Learning from the Past

THE COMMUNAL WAVE: CONCLUDING INSIGHTS

Studying the Communal Wave opens us to looking at our fellow humans across time and space in a more open-minded light and gives us a broader insight into historical change over time. I am not advocating a return to the foraging way of life as an ideal way to live, which is impossible anyway, nor do I see it as superior to our modern life. But by examining foraging societies in some depth, we can evaluate the values and beliefs that they hold and compare and contrast them with our own. As we reevaluate which of our values and attitudes promote environmental devastation and separated communities, the foraging way of life can offer a vivid portrayal of a different way that our species has lived for thousands of years. It can teach us some valuable lessons.

Foragers lived in a way that has been successful for over 99 percent of our human history. Yet this way of life is not lasting forever. For the first time in thousands of years, foragers are facing the extinction of their way of life. Foragers first encountered a different form of existence around 10,000 to 12,000 years ago when in many parts of the world some people gave way to village farming. The same destructive encounters happened with the spread of urbanization and modernization in our more recent history. But today's challenges are even more threatening. Soon we may be seeing people of the Communal Wave as we do the dinosaurs: living beings that existed in the past, but live no more.

Smiling !Kung child. Photo by Isla K. Bardavid

We continue with our look at the waves in this holistic history by turning to the next chapter: the Agricultural Wave.

ENDNOTES

1. B.P. denotes before the present. For example, 40,000 B.P. means 40,000 years ago. The Upper Paleolithic begins 40,000 B.P. through the beginning of the Neolithic that begins 10,000 B.P. I will dispense with the periods.
2. I will be using the term foraging when referring to both hunting and gathering people.
3. William A. Haviland, *Cultural Anthropology* (Fort Worth: Holt, Rinehart and Winston, 1990), p. 151.
4. Francis B. Musonda, "The Significance of Modern Hunter-Gatherers in the Study of Early Hominid Behavior," in *The Origins of Human Behavior*, ed. R. A. Foley (London: Unwin Hyman Ltd., 1991), p. 47-48.
5. Gary Ferraro, *Cultural Anthropology*: An Applied Perspective, (New York: Thomson Wadsworth, 2006), p. 161.
6. Margaret Ehrenberg, *Women in Prehistory* (Norman, OK: University of Oklahoma Press, 1989), p. 38. I am referring to the last 50 years or so when referring to contemporary foragers.
7. Frank Marlowe, "Why the Hazda are Still Hunters-Gatherers," in *Ethnicity, Hunter-Gatherers, and the "Other;" Association or Assimilation in Africa*, ed. Sue Kent (Washington D.C.: Smithsonian Institution Press,) p. 274-275.
8. Steven A. LeBlanc with Katherine E. Register, *Constant Battles: The Myth of the Peaceful, Noble Savage* (New York: St. Martin's Press, 2003), p. 13 and 19.
9. Richard Leakey, The *Origin of Humankind* (New York: Basic Books, 1994), p. 94.
10. Roger Lewin, *The Origin of Modern Humans* (New York: Scientific American Library, 1993), p. 115-6.
11. John A. J. Gowlett, *Ascent to Civilization: The Archaeology of Early Humans* (New York: McGraw Hill, 1993), p. 120-122.
12. Niles Eldredge, *Dominion* (New York: Henry Holt and Company, 1995), p. 55 and 88; and Haviland, *Cultural Anthropology*, p. 82.
13. Bernard G. Campbell, *Humankind Emerging* (Glenview, IL: Scott Foresman and Co., 1988), p. 433 and 449.
14. Haviland, *Cultural Anthropology*, p. 161-162; Kelly, *Foraging Spectrum*, p. 49 and 62-63; and Marshall Sahlins, *Stone Age Economics* (Chicago: Aldine and Atherton, Inc., 1972), p. 32-37.
15. Bernard G. Campbell, *Humankind Emerging* (Glenview, Illinois: Scott Foresman and Co., 1988), p. 449-450.
16. Gerhard Lenski and Jean Lenski, *Human Societies An Introduction to Macrosociology* (New York: McGraw-Hill, 1982), p. 112.
17. LeBlanc, *Constant Battles*, p. 76 and 126.
18. Alan Weisman, *The World Without Us* (New York: Thomas Dunne Books, 2007), p. 39.
19. Weisman, *World Without Us*, p. 49.
20. Weisman, *World Without Us*, p. 53.
21. Weisman, *World Without Us*, p. 56-57.
22. Weisman, *World Without Us*, p. 56 and 61.
23. Weisman, *World Without Us*, p. 56 and 61.
24. Ernestine Friedl, *Women and Men: An Anthropologist's View* (New York: Holt, Rinehart, and Winston, 1975), p. 13 and 29.
25. G. Siefried Kutter, *The Universe and Life: Origins and Evolution* (Boston: Jones and Bartlett Publishers, Inc., 1987), p. 541;

Eldredge, *Women in Prehistory*, p. 87; and Gowlett, *Ascent to Civilization*, p. 134-135
26. LeBlanc, *Constant Battles*, p. 104.
27. Marvin Harris, *Culture, People, Nature* (New York: Harper and Row Publishers, 1988), p. 301; and Friedl, *Women and Men*, p. 285.
28. Richard H. Crapo, *Cultural Anthropology: Understanding Ourselves and Others* (Guilford, CN: Dushkin Publishing, 1990), p. 76.
29. Marshall Sahlins, *Stone Age Economics* (Chicago: Aldine and Atherton, Inc., 1972), 194-196; and Crapo, *Cultural Anthropology*, p. 78.
30. Leakey, *Origin of Humankind*, p. 93; C. Loring Brace, *The Stages of Human Evolution* (Englewood Cliffs, NJ: Prentice Hall, 1991), p. 168-170; Haviland, *Cultural Anthropology*, p. 83; and Lewin, *Origin Modern Humans*, p. 120-121.
31. Allen Johnson and Timothy Earle, *The Evolution of Human Societies: From Foraging Group to Agrarian State* (Stanford: Stanford University Press, 1995), p. 29.
32. Crapo, *Cultural Anthropology*, p. 53; and Ehrenberg, *Women in Prehistory*, p. 48.
33. Harris, *People, Culture, Nature*, p. 285; and Crapo, *Cultural Anthropology*, p. 76.
34. Haviland, *Cultural Anthropology*, p. 188 -189.
35. Harris, *People, Culture, Nature*, p. 17.
36. Haviland, *Cultural Anthropology*, p. 64; Harris, *People, Culture, Nature*, p. 301; Friedl, *Women and Men*, p. 17; and Judith Brown, "Note on the Division of Labor by Sex," American Anthropologist No. 72 (1970), p. 1075-1076.
37. Haviland, *Cultural Anthropology*, p. 301; and Harris, *People, Culture, Nature*, p. 301.
38. Friedl, *Women and Men*, p. 16.
39. Sahlins, *Stone Age Economics*, p. 14-17.
40. Ferraro, *Cultural Anthropology*, p. 161.
41. Harris, *Culture, People, Nature*, p. 244; Haviland, *Cultural Anthropology*, p. 171; Friedl, *Women and Men*, p. 14; and Crapo, *Cultural Anthropology*, p. 54.
42. Lenski, *Human Societies*, p. 114-115.
43. Friedl, *Women and Men*, p. 23 and Lenski, *Human Societies*, p. 115.
44. Robert L. Kelly, *The Foraging Spectrum: Diversity in Hunter-Gatherer Lifeways* (Washington: Smithsonian Institution Press, 1995), p. 259.
45. Friedl, *Women and Men*, p. 26.
46. Lenski, *Human Societies*, p. 112-113; Ehrenberg, *Women in Prehistory*, p. 60-61, and LeBlanc, *Constant Battles*, p. 113.
47. Kelly, *Foraging Spectrum*, p. 180.
48. Friedl, *Women and Men*, p. 27-28.
49. Rachel Caspari and Sang-Hee Lee, "Old Age Becomes Common in Late Human Evolution," University of Michigan, 2004, as cited in *http://anthro.palomar.edu/subsistence/sub_2.htm*
50. Peggy Sanday, *Female Power and Male Dominance: On the Origins of Sexual Inequality* (Cambridge: Cambridge University Press, 1981), p. 89 and 90.
51. Friedl, *Women and Men*, p. 7.
52. Sanday, *Female Power*, p. 114.
53. Ernestine Friedl, *"Society and Sex Roles," in Anthropology: Contemporary Perspectives*, eds. Phillip Whitten and David Hunter (San Francisco: HarperCollins Publishers, 1990), p. 216-217.

54. Kelly, *Foraging Spectrum*, p. 296.
55. Lenski, *Human Societies*, p. 123.
56. Harris, *People, Culture, Nature*, p. 284-285.
57. Sahlins, Stone-Age Economics, p. 37.
58. Harris, *Culture, People, Nature*, p. 352 - 353.
59. Lenski, *Human Societies*, p. 125.
60. Friedl, *Women and Men*, p. 27.
61. Friedl, *Women and Men*, p. 27.
62. Kelly, *Foraging Spectrum*, p. 164-167.
63. Lenski, *Human Societies*, p. 119-120.
64. Harris, *People, Culture, Nature*, p. 356-357; and Haviland, *Cultural Anthropology*, p. 322-323.
65. Alexander Alland, Jr., *To Be Human: An Introduction to Anthropology* (New York: Alfred A. Knopf, 1980), p. 447.
66. Lenski, *Human Societies*, p. 120-121.
67. Kelly, *Foraging Spectrum*, p. 185.
68. Haviland, *Cultural Anthropology*, p. 194.
69. Alan Bilsborough, *Human Evolution* (London: Blackie Academic and Professional, 1992), p. 213.
70. John A. J. Gowlett, *Ascent to Civilization: The Archaeology of Early Humans* (New York: McGraw Hill, 1993), p. 139-140.
71. Harris, *People, Culture, Nature*, p. 353-354.
72. Friedl, *Women and Men*, p. 15; and Crapo, *Cultural Anthropology*, p. 100.
73. Crapo, *Cultural Anthropology*, p. 99.
74. LeBlanc, *Constant Battles*, p. 113.
75. Ferraro, *Cultural Anthropology*, p. 161.
76. William F. Allman, *The Stone Age Present* (New York: Simon and Schuster, 1994), p. 154 and p. 186-189.
77. LeBlanc, *Constant Battles*, p. 115.
78. A.F.C. Wallace, *Culture and Personality* (New York: Random House, 1970), p. 142.
79. Lenski, *Human Societies*, p. 123; Alland, *To Be Human*, p. 453; and Haviland *Cultural Anthropology*, p. 361-362.
80. Lenski, *Human Societies*, p. 124; and Haviland, *Cultural Anthropology*, p. 364.
81. Marjorie Shostak, "A Kung Woman's Memories of Childhood," *Kalahari Hunting and Gathering: Studies of the !Kung San and Their Neighbors* eds. Richard Lee and Irven DeVore (Cambridge: Harvard University Press, 1976), p. 249.
82. Lenski, *Human Societies*, p. 126-127.
83. Gustav Mensching, "Folk and Universal Religion," in *Readings on the Sociology of Religion*, eds. Thomas F. O'Dea and Janet K. O'Dea (Englewood Cliffs: Prentice Hall, 1073), p. 86.
84. Leakey, *Origin of Humankind*, p. 156; Lewin, *Origin Modern Humans*, p. 19; and Allman, Stone Age Present, p. 186-189.
85. Eldredge, *Women in Prehistory*, p. 91.
86. Paul G. Bahn and Jean Vertut, *Journey Through the Ice Age* (Berkeley: University of California Press, 1997), p. 114-118, 121, and 124.
87. Bahn, *Journey*, p. 142.
88. Leakey, *Origin of Humankind*, p. 111-112; and Bahn, *Journey*, p. 176-181.
89. Bahn, *Journey*, p. 84-103; Haviland, *Cultural Anthropology*, p. 84; and Leakey, *Origin of Humankind*, p. 105.
90. Ehrenberg, *Women in Prehistory*, p. 66-67 and 72; Bahn, *Journey*, p. 84-103; Haviland, *Cultural Anthropology*, p. 84; Leakey, *Origin of Humankind*, p. 105; and Marija Gimbutas, *The Language of*

the Goddess (San Francisco: Harper Collins Publisher, 1989), p. xv - xxi.

91. Harris, *Culture, People, Nature,* p. 496.
92. San is the Khoekhoe word for Bushmen or forager. Alan Barnard, *Hunters and Herders of Southern Africa: A Comparative Ethnography of the Khoisan Peoples* (Cambridge: Cambridge University Press, 1992), p. 3.
93. LeBlanc, *Constant Battles,* p. 107.
94. John Yellen and Richard B. Lee, "The Dobe-/Du/da Environment: Background to a Hunting and Gathering Way of Life," *Kalahari,* eds. Lee and DeVore, p. 42-44.
95. Nora Boustany, "The Bushmen's Advocate," *Washington Post,* (Dec. 18, 1995, D4), p. 1.
96. Richard B. Lee and Irven DeVore, *Kalahari Hunting and Gathering: Studies of the !Kung San and their Neighbors* (Cambridge: Harvard University Press, 1976), p. 8.
97. Barnard, *Hunters and Herders,* p. 39.
98. Jiro Tanaka, "Subsistence Ecology of Central Kalahari San," in *Kalahari,* eds. Lee and DeVore, p. 102.
99. Richard B. Lee, *The Dobe !Kung* (New York: Holt, Rinehart and Winston, 1984), p. 47.
100. Lee, *Dobe !Kung,* p. 37 and 39.
101. Melvin Konner, "Maternal Care, Infant Behavior and Development among the !Kung," in *Kalahari,* eds. Lee and DeVore, p. 222.
102. Lee, *Dobe !Kung,* p. 36-37 and 51.
103. Sahlins, *Stone Age Economics,* p. 23.
104. Lee, *Dobe !Kung,* p. 41-42.
105. Lee, *Dobe !Kung,* p. 45.
106. Tanaka, "Subsistence Ecology," in *Kalahari,* eds. Lee and DeVore, p. 101.
107. Lee, *Dobe !Kung,* p. 30.
108. Yellen, "Dobe Environment," in *Kalahari,* eds. Lee and DeVore, p. 67-68.
109. Lee, *Dobe !Kung,* p. 30-31.
110. Friedl, *Women and Men,* p. 17; Harris, *Culture, People, Nature,* p. 302; Lee, *Dobe !Kung,* p. 51; and Sahlins, *Stone Age Economics,* p. 21.
111. Lee, *Dobe !Kung,* p. 97-98 and 101.
112. Lee, *Dobe !Kung,* p. 57-60.
113. Lee, *Dobe !Kung,* p. 75.
114. Lee, *Dobe !Kung,* p. 76-77.
115. Shostak, "Childhood Memories," in *Kalahari,* eds. Lee and DeVore, p. 267.
116. Lee, *Dobe !Kung,* p. 85.
117. Lee, *Dobe !Kung,* p. 77.
118. Lee, *Dobe !Kung,* p. 70 and 79.
119. Lee, *Dobe !Kung,* p. 85-86.
120. Melvin Konner, "Maternal Care, Infant Behavior and Development among the !Kung," in *Kalahari,* eds. Lee and Devore, p. 220.
121. Howell, "Population," in Kalahari, eds. Lee and DeVore, p. 145; A.Stewart Truswell and John D.L. Hansen, "Medical Research among the !Kung," in *Kalahari,* eds. Lee and DeVore, p. 174; and Friedl, *Women and Men,* p. 17.
122. Howell, "Population," in *Kalahari,* eds. Lee and DeVore, p. 147.
123. Konner, "Maternal Care," in *Kalahari,* eds. Lee and DeVore, p. 245.
124. Konner, "Maternal Care," in *Kalahari,* eds. Lee and Devore, p. 220; and Truswell and Hansen, "Medical Research," in *Kalahari,* eds. Lee and DeVore, p. 175.
125. Patricia Draper, "Social and Economic Constraints on Child Life among the !Kung," in *Kalahari,* eds. Lee and DeVore, p. 202-211.
126. Draper, " Constraints," in *Kalahari,* eds. Lee and Devore, p. 202.
127. Lee, *Dobe !Kung,* p. 49.
128. Lee, *Dobe !Kung,* p. 49.

129. Lee, *Dobe !Kung*, p. 49-50.
130. Lee, *Dobe !Kung*, p. 55.
131. Harris, *Culture, People, Nature*, p. 356.
132. Lee, *Dobe !Kung*, p. 89.
133. Lee, *Dobe !Kung*, p. 87; and Harris, *Culture, People, Nature*, p. 352.
134. Lee, *Dobe !Kung*, p. 81.
135. Lee, *Dobe !Kung*, p. 92-95.
136. Lee, Dobe Kung, p. 106-107 and 109.
137. Richard Katz, "Education for Transcendence: !Kia-Healing with the Kalahari !Kung," in *Kalahari* eds. Lee and DeVore, p. 282.
138. Katz, "Education," in *Kalahari*, eds. Lee and Devore, p. 284.
139. Katz, "Education," in *Kalahari*, eds. Lee and Devore, p. 285.
140. Katz, "Education," in *Kalahari*, eds. Lee and Devore, p. 287, 290, and 300.
141. Katz, "Education," in *Kalahari*, eds. Lee and Devore, p. 286.
142. Lee, *Dobe !Kung*, p. 113.
143. Lee, *Dobe !Kung*, p. 114-115.
144. Megan Biesele, "Aspects of !Kung Folklore," in *Kalahari*, eds. Lee and DeVore, p. 306-308.144

Chapter 5

People as Village Farmers: The Agricultural Wave

"Think not forever of yourselves, O Chiefs, nor of your own generation. Think of continuing generations of our families, think of our grandchildren and of those yet unborn, whose faces are coming from beneath the ground."

— Peacemaker, founder of the Iroquois Confederacy (ca. 1000 AD)

INTRODUCTION TO THE AGRICULTURAL WAVE

Most of us don't have a clue about growing our own food. We take for granted the food ladled onto our dinner plates, or the ease with which we can grab something from the refrigerator or order at a fast food restaurant. Like most people in the developed world, Americans are far removed from the process of growing our own food or butchering our own meat. But this easy availability of food is a very recent phenomenon. As we saw in the previous chapter, for 99 percent of our human existence we lived as foragers, hunting or gathering our food. We have only grown our food for the last 10,000 to 12,000 years, a mere blip on the radar screen of our 2.5 million year human evolutionary history. What brought about this profound change from foraging to farming? Our investigation into this question begins as we journey into the Agricultural Wave. This journey will help us understand how humans changed from foraging for food to growing food and the profound way this shift impacted their way of life.

Our ancestors underwent a profound transition, a striking break from the past around 10,000 to 12,000 years ago (BP). At this time, two types of human development took place simultaneously. While most humans continued to live as foragers in small cooperative bands, others made the dramatic shift to a food producing strategy. This time period is often called the **Neolithic** or Stone Age, although I do not always use these terms since they are associated with a chronological framework rather than a developmental one. The development of farming took thousands of years. Initially, wild plants had to be selectively planted and harvested, a process anthropologists term **domestication**, in which genetic traits more useful for humans are selected and reproduced.

The process was also applied to certain animals that were domesticated for human use at this time. Between 12,000 and 7,000 BP, the process of domestication developed independently in certain core areas of the world, where agriculture originated, and then diffused to secondary areas to which agriculture gradually spread. The transition to agricultural production in secondary areas most likely took place sometime after 9,000 BP.

People in the Agricultural Wave practiced a food producing strategy technically called **horticulture** where food is grown using simple hand tools such as the hoe and digging stick, and without fertilization of the soil, crop rotation, and often without irrigation. However, I will use the more commonly referred to term, agriculture, instead

A Continuum: Human/Plant/Animal Interaction

PEOPLE COLLECTED FOOD AND LIVED WITHING NATURE'S LIMITS	PEOPLE COLLECTED AND DOMESTICATED FOOD	PEOPLE PRODUCED FOOD WITH LITTLE OR NO FOOD FORAGING

of horticulture, in this chapter. A transition to an agricultural, subsistence, food-producing system by some people around 10,000 to 12,000 BP was not a clean break or a sudden shift from food foraging, but a mix of strategies to a different way of life. These changes occurred within a continuum of human/plant/animal interaction. At one end of the continuum humans mainly collected food and continued to live closely within nature's limits; in the middle of the continuum people both collected and domesticated food; and at the other end of the continuum people intensively produced food with very little or no food foraging.[1] At different times and places in the Agricultural Wave humans around the globe were (are) at different points along this continuum.

Even today, some people continue to practice traditional methods of food production as their ancestors once did. I warned against viewing contemporary foraging societies as unchanged relics of the past; the same can be said of contemporary agricultural societies—they are not exact replicas of the past frozen in time. But they do have commonalities with earlier agricultural societies and I will highlight these commonalities in this chapter. Some anthropologists call these contemporary agricultural societies **modern folk societies**, composed of rural farmers who live in non-industrial societies but are dominated by the city and its culture, although marginal to both. In other words, these modern folk societies have similarities with both the Agricultural Wave and modern society, but don't neatly fit into either category. Besides simple agricultural methods found in the Agricultural Wave, farmers through history have practiced three other forms of agricultural production found in later waves. Plow agriculture was first practiced in the Urban Wave and utilized in later waves. Industrialized agriculture began in the Modern Wave and continues to dominate in the Global Wave. The fourth type of agriculture that is emerging in the Global Wave is a small but growing movement countering industrial agriculture and emphasizing local, sustainable, and organic farming on small, owner-operated or cooperatively-owned farms.

These four different forms of agriculture are briefly introduced here to indicate the continuity of the agricultural way of life in the Urban, Modern, and Global Waves and reinforce the concept that people who farm are developmentally, not chronologically, linked. The first form of agriculture is simple agriculture that will be discussed in depth in this chapter. The second form of agriculture, plow agriculture, was first used around 5,500 BP (3500 BCE) in some areas of the world that are explored in the Urban Wave. Plow agriculture is more labor and land intensive, has a higher degree of specialization, uses complex irrigation systems, applies technological improvements, and results in greater productivity than in simple agricultural production. In the Urban Wave, the agricultural workers or peasant farmers

Plowing rice paddies with water buffalo, in Indonesia, first developed in the Urban Wave.

Industrialized farming in the later Modern Wave.

continued to live in villages and retained many of the socio-cultural characteristics of Agricultural Wave people. Industrialized agriculture, the third form, relies more heavily on fossilized sources of energy rather than on human or animal labor. It also stresses monocrop production and uses heavy chemical inputs of fertilizer, herbicides, and pesticides to boost production. Industrialized agriculture, covered in the Modern Wave, is more productive than plow agriculture with fewer workers needed to turn out greater quantities of food. A local, organic, and sustainable agricultural movement in the Global Wave, the fourth form of agriculture, has evolved partly as an alternative to the harmful environmental effects of industrialized agriculture, as well as the depletion of productive soil and the low quality of food produced. A loose socio-cultural connection with earlier agricultural societies can be drawn to the agricultural movement in the Global Wave.

The reason for including the Agricultural Wave in this holistic world history is similar to the reasons for including the Communal Wave. The Agricultural Wave gives us a broader context of who we are and where we come from. One of my goals in this chapter is to paint a picture of how our agricultural way of life developed and the mechanisms necessary for its continuance. What changes occurred for people as they shifted to producing food and how did they fashion a way of life in harmony with agricultural production?

Also included in this chapter is a section on chiefdoms, societies composed of larger populations with more complex social and political structures, but still employing a simple agricultural food producing method. A final section examines Cahokia, a case study look at a chiefdom in North America.

Questions to Consider

1. What does the following concept mean to you: "people who farm are developmentally, not chronologically, linked?
2. Do you think the Agricultural Wave should be included in this holistic world history? Explain.

Change and Continuity

Evidence of agricultural production became apparent around 10,000 BP, but more subtle changes may go back twice as far. By 7,000 BP, farming villages, cultivated crops, domesticated animals, and other changes are seen in the archeological record in certain areas of Afro-Eurasia and the Western hemisphere.[2] From core areas in southwest Asia, east Asia, Mesoamerica, and the Andean area of South America, this technology apparently diffused later to secondary areas of southeast Asia, Africa, and northwestern tropical South America and outward. The Aegean region, Egypt and the Indus Valley probably received dif-

Organic, small-scale, agriculture in the village of Vincente Guerreo, Mexico.
Photo by Denise Ames

fused agricultural technology from the southwest Asia core, rather than discovering it independently.[3] The eastern and southwestern United States, Malaysia, Polynesia, and Europe were the third areas of agricultural domestication. However, some scholars now think that plants were domesticated independently in at least 10 core areas, including, in addition to southwest Asia, China, Mexico and Peru, places in Africa, southern India, and New Guinea. Some areas of the world remained external, or did not adopt agricultural strategies and continued in the Communal Wave.

An examination of all the centers of independent agricultural development is beyond the scope of this chapter; however, what follows is an examination of three core areas—southwest Asia, China, and Mesoamerica—with some reference to other regions reached by the new agricultural developments. Current research identifies southwest Asia, specifically the foothills of the Zagros Mountains on the Anatolian plateau in present day Turkey, as the first region to move to agricultural food production around 10,000 BP. Up until this time people in this region fed themselves by a combination of hunting, herding goats and sheep, and collecting a wide variety of edible wild plants. This pattern of subsistence supported a mixture of settlements with semi-sedentary, small villages of about 100 tightly knit people. As gathering became less important, wheat and barley—grains easily differentiated from their wild cousins—were increasingly cultivated. DNA molecules of einkorn, a type of wheat grown in arid areas, have been linked to a site in present-day southeast Turkey, indicating that the nutritious grain was first domesticated in this region. By 7,500 BP, agriculture surfaced as a major subsistence strategy in southwest Asia, commonly known as Mesopotamia (modern Iraq), the land between the Tigris and Euphrates Rivers.[4] Apparently, grains such einkorn and millet and domesticated animals such as the pig, goat, sheep, and cattle, originally domesticated in southwest Asia, were also found in Greece and the Balkans around 9,000 BP, leading researchers to conclude that the domestication process diffused to Europe.

Wheat first domesticated in southwest Asia, area now in Turkey.

Varying dates for the origins and spread of agriculture can be identified in Asia. About 9,000 BP, North China, an independent core area, experienced a shift to agricultural cultivation. Surprisingly, the elevated terraces and mounds along tributaries of the winding Yellow (Huang Ho) River served as the location for earliest habitation, not the fertile flood plain. Thick, rich **loess** soil—a wind-born soil made up of fine particles which was easy to work and high in mineral content—blanketed this semi-arid area. The first cultivated tall wild grasses, such as millet and dry-rice, sprouted from the fertile loess plains. Easily herded pigs, cattle, sheep and man's best friend, the dog, ranked as the first domesticated animals. Within a thousand years of the first evidence of agricultural activity, small villages dotted the rural landscape of north China.[5] Wet-field rice cultivation began in earnest in southeast Asia by about 5,000 BP, but new studies suggest that farming in southeast Asia and New Guinea, for example, took off independently as early as 9,000 BP. Wet rice agriculture spread to Korea, and to the Jomon people in southwest Japan by 2,000 BP.[6] In India the transition to agriculture apparently first took place in the east at the confluence of the Ganges and Yamuna Rivers in 9,100 BP.

In Mesoamerica, in the present-day states of Guatemala, Belize, parts of Honduras, El Salvador, and southern Mexico, the same independent plant domestication process took place about 9,000 BP, with villages and sedentary communities appearing on the scene about 4,000 BP. Most of the evidence of agricultural activity was found in the highland areas of Mexico, where the climate is dry enough to preserve plant remains. Populations in Mesoamerica depended upon a variety of plant foods, among them the ubiquitous beans, squash, and maize (corn). These three hardy, staple plants were among thirty varieties grown not only for food but also for dyes, medicines, and containers. Chili peppers, tomatoes, avocados, papaya, guava, five types of squash, gourds, and bean varieties rounded out the variety of nourishing crops raised in the region. The lack of suitable animals for domestication purposes—no sheep, goats, or cattle—hampered full-scale agricultural development. As a result, Mesoamericans hunted small game animals such as rabbit and deer and supplemented their diet with collected nuts and wild grasses. The original maize cobs were the size of a person's thumb, which resulted in low yields; higher-producing varieties were not perfected until about 4,000 BP. Since there was low agricultural productivity among cultivated crops, it was more efficient to gather food than grow crops. Even after 2,000 years of crop domestication, a typical Mesoamerican derived only about 25 percent of his/her diet from domesticated plants.[7] Despite its lack of high-yields, maize was carried north from the Mesoamerican highlands where it became a staple food for North American people like the mound cultures of Mississippi and Ohio River valleys and the Hopewell cultures in the upper Ohio valley, who planted grain crops around 2,000 BP. South American people along the present-day Peruvian coast first domesticated the potato and manioc, with squash, vegetables, beans, tobacco, and cotton appearing later.[8] Agriculture developed independently in the Andean highland region of South America as well.

Wet-field rice cultivation in northern Iran. Photo by Denise Ames

Red and green chili peppers grown in southern New Mexico, USA. Photo by Denise Ames

Africa had more varied agricultural production than other areas. In the Nile River of Egypt agriculture appeared to have started around 7,500 BP, influenced by developments in Southwest Asia. Although it appears that African agriculture evolved gradually around 7,000 BP, a scarcity of archaeological research and evidence collected from African sites makes conclusions difficult. New research shows the possibility of independent agricultural development in Africa from which agriculture subsequently dispersed. Development appears to take place in an east to west equatorial band of land that lies south of the Sahara desert. Researchers cannot detect a temporal sequence of events; instead a mosaic of cultures, crops, and farming practices seems to have existed.[9]

The Transition to Agriculture

A perplexing question about the transition to agriculture remains: Why did many humans change from a foraging to a food-producing, sedentary way of life? Many different theories are proposed, among them the theory of progress, the Oasis hypothesis, "hill flank" theory, "survival theory," "Marginal Zone" or "Edge" hypothesis, population theory, co-evolutionary theory, and social explanations for agricultural development. Let us examine these theories.

The theory of progress is embedded in deep cultural assumptions held by many people today who view human history as a record of steady progress or advancement over time. From this perspective, the shift to agriculture is commonly assumed to be the first significant technological advancement in the evolution of civilization. According to this theory humans made a so-called "breakthrough" or "leap" from a precarious and marginal existence as foragers, to a more secure and satisfying existence as farmers. This thinking reflects a deeply held bias that agricultural society is superior to foraging, and that foragers who welcomed agricultural "advancement" were culturally "ready," while those who remained foragers were stagnant, backward, and passive.[10] Obviously, this holistic world history approach rejects this explanation based on the "march of progress" and instead sees both beneficial and detrimental characteristics of the two modes of economic and social development.

In the first half of the 20th century supporters of the Oasis hypothesis found that around 10,000 BP, climates around the world and particularly in southwest Asia became more arid with higher temperatures. Because of these changes, vegetation grew only around limited water sources, where humans clustered and competed for lean resources. Proponents of this theory, considered to be overly deterministic by critics, held that as a matter of survival the only successful solution to increased food competition was for humans to domesticate both plants and animals.[11]

In the 1940s and 1950s proponents of a "hilly flank" theory contended that domestication began in southwest Asia around a zone of hills located near the Tigris-Euphrates river systems. Wild grasses, such as wheat and barley, naturally thrived on the hill area; people living in adjacent villages intentionally cultivated them. According to this theory agriculture was regarded as an "inevitable" process because over the years humans gradually acquired knowledge and familiarity with plant and animal resources. Once a sufficient level of knowledge was reached, a transition to agriculture "naturally" took place as more

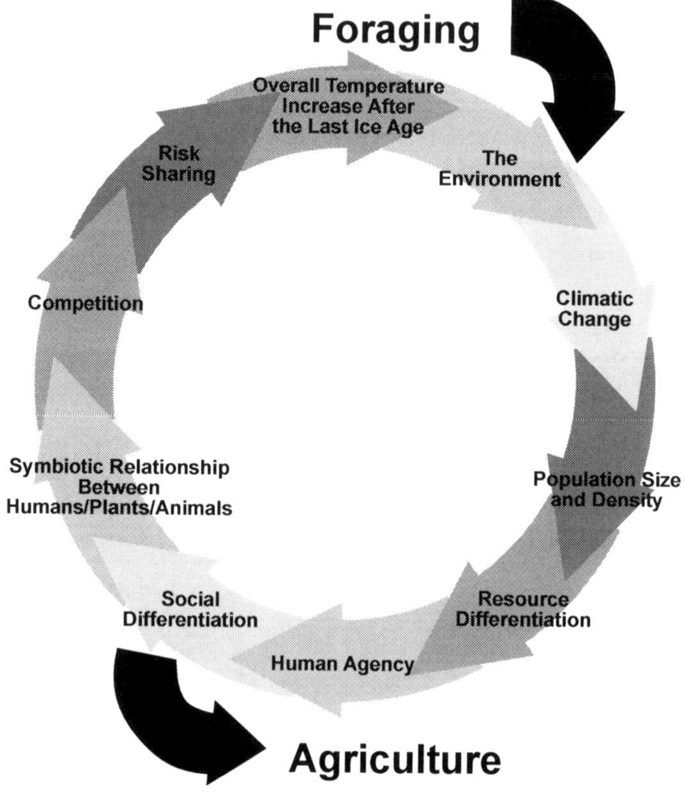

humans began to implement more of their newfound agricultural abilities. Although this theory has also lost credibility because of its cultural bias and assumption that the transition to agriculture was "natural," researchers do have evidence that early farming originated in the hilly flank area.[12]

Another theory challenges the "human progress" theory and instead argues that farming is a backbreaking, time consuming, and labor-intensive endeavor, and not a progressive step in human advancement. They contend that humans became farmers because of a disruption in the equilibrium between population increases and the amount of food acquired through food foraging. Foraging could no longer supply enough food for a growing population, thus humans at the time sought to solve this problem with the best solution available at the time: a sedentary way of life and the domestication of plants and animals. As a result of adopting this practical solution, food per acre of land increased and higher yields fed an increasing number of people.[13]

According to the "Marginal Zone" or "Edge" hypothesis, the effects of population pressures were felt most strongly in marginal, drier, less fertile areas that surround more productive central areas, where wild plants and herds of animals were more abundant. Agriculture, therefore, began in these marginal areas, where humans increased the productivity of land by deliberately planting grains.[14]

A theory based on population increase emphasizes resource shortages due to an increasing population as the primary cause for the development of agriculture. When mobile foraging populations adopted an agricultural, sedentary lifestyle women become more fertile and thus had more children. Consequently, the resulting population growth led to resource shortages for which there were four responses: to move, to split the group into smaller units, to attempt to curb the population, or to intensify food production.[15] Another option, not emphasized in this theory, is that those with a shortage of resources would raid others with resources.

One evolutionary approach based on Darwinian principles explores the relationship between natural selection and cultural change. According to this theory, domestication is a result of co-evolutionary interaction between humans, plants, and animals and is not influenced by cultural adaptations or human intentionality, nor is it a response to population increases or environmental change. According to David Rindos, co-evolution is an "evolutionary process in which the establishment of a symbiotic relationship between organisms increases the fitness of all involved."[16] Domestication relies on cooperation between humans/plants/animals, although the organisms do not necessarily recognize the advantages or disadvantages involved. As cooperation gradually occurs, it enhances populations of organisms who work together.[17] With cooperation, populations of both humans and domesticated plants and animals increase, but this increase is at the expense of other plants and animals that do not exist for human consumption and are forced to compete with the cooperating unit of domesticated species for resources. Although Rindos does not include human intentionality in his theory, some argue that animals and plants choose to be domesticated, since they prosper from mutual cooperative interaction with humans in which both species swell.[18]

Proponents of a human agency theory maintain that humans intentionally produce a surplus of food in order to hold periodic feasts. Competitive feasting between a few forceful rival leaders stimulates surplus food production, since one leader tries to outdo the other.[19]

Some researchers argue that social changes explain the origins of agriculture. They put forth the case that changes in the social, economic, and religious patterns in the early development of agriculture were more significant than were changes in subsistence; hence internal social relations were the main variable in the change to agricultural production, and not external events like climate and population growth.[20]

Another debate centers on whether the change from foraging to agriculture took place gradually or abruptly. For many years anthropologists favored the idea that the transition to food production occurred gradually. In the context of our 2.5 million year foraging history, the 5,000-year transition to agriculture, between 10,000 and 5,000 BP, happened in an astonishingly brief period of time. But, unlike today, the changes people experienced at the time were not so abrupt that those involved felt overwhelmed and disoriented by the social change.

Using a systems approach, several important variables explained in the theories outlined above as well as other factors together interact to bring about a transition to a different system. Although the single most important variable in this transition, if there is one, remains elusive, the consequences of these changes are substantial, including not only a new method of obtaining food but a more settled way of life, more complex forms of political organization, different social arrangements, technological innovations, and new cultural expressions.

Continuity accompanied change. Many human societies continued their food foraging existence until well into the 19th and 20th centuries while others continue to practice simple agriculture and live in small villages to this day. Most present day agriculturists live in areas such as New Guinea, the Pacific Islands, parts of South and Central America, and parts of central Africa, even though the climate, natural vegetation, and crops grown in these areas are different from what they were in early agriculture. Although caution should be taken against concluding that contemporary simple agriculturists are unchanged relics of the past, there are strikingly similar patterns among past and contemporary groups. Therefore, I have included characteristics of both farmers of the past and contemporary small village farmers in the five currents to follow.[21]

Questions to Consider

1. Do you think the invention of agriculture was an "inevitable" process? Explain.

Insights: Learning from the Past

Introduction to the Agricultural Wave

How agricultural people are represented in each of the four different waves is an example of the holistic approach used in this world history. This approach emphasizes the interaction of the past and present and the thread of continuity that runs through world history. One of the continuities is our relationship with and dependence upon nature to provide food for us. This connection with nature is largely ignored in conventional history. But what could be more vital to our species than food!

The way humans grow food and relate to nature is quite different in each of the five waves. In the Urban and Modern Waves humans become more removed from the act of growing food and disconnected with nature than in the Agricultural Wave. This disconnect has reached a low point today in the Global Wave, where some of the food we eat is not even food, but chemical concoctions that trick us into believing it is food. I want to emphasize this point in this insight section because modern people in the 21st century have lost touch with growing our own food and generally have no yearning to know where food comes from or how it magically lands on our plates. As an increasing affluent population demands a more varied diet and more meat, this demand puts pressure on existing food sources. It is important that we become more aware of where our food comes from, who is growing our food, and if food actually is food. Paradoxically, as the number of farmers decline around the world, our demand for food increases. How people through history have dealt with this vital activity is the subject of the rest of this chapter.

Questions to Consider

1. Do you think you or your society have lost touch with growing your own food and knowing what you eat? Explain.

RELATIONSHIP WITH NATURE: ECOSYSTEM CURRENTS

Geography and Environment

Before the Agricultural Wave began, important environmental changes started to sweep across the globe. During the last glacial age, when water was frozen into huge glaciers, the sea was about 120 meters lower than it is now. But about 12,000 BP, an inter-glacial period moderated the world's climate as ice sheets melted and rising sea levels inundated coastlines around the world. Large areas of continental shelves were flooded, including the land bridges connecting Siberia and Alaska, New Guinea and Australia, and Britain and Europe.[22] Milder climates enabled a profusion of hardwood forests to grow in previously frigid tundra regions of the north. Large herd animals migrated further northward, and game that had previously thrived became scarce in the southern and central regions of Eurasia and North America. Changing climate conditions and different food sources, along with extensive hunting by humans, drove the large game mammals—giant bison, oxen, elephants, woolly mammoth, giant cattle, and red deer—to extinction between 9,000 and 15,000 BP.[23] Those relying on these animals for their subsistence were forced to change their food procuring strategies to adapt to new environmental realities. A proliferation of abundant new plant foods, smaller game animals, and a plentiful supply of fish in lakes, rivers, and oceans assured humans of copious food sources. Our ancestors benefited from nature's plenty by improvising new and ingenious ways to hunt smaller animals, catch fish, and collect wild plant foods.

A reconstructed wooly mammoth, which became extinct between 9,000 and 15,000 BP.

Shepherd in Făgăraş Mountains, Romania.

Human Population

A general increase in human population took place, with higher population densities in some areas of the world and human migration into new found habitats. An estimated four million people inhabited the Earth by 10,000 BP, and by 7,000 BP the population totaled five million people. Agricultural societies in the past supported a population density of about ten people per square mile, compared to about one or two people per square mile in foraging societies. Farming villages ranged in size from small villages with a population of about 40 to 50 people to larger, more complex chiefdoms of several thousand.[24]

Populations in agricultural societies grew noticeably because of the advantageous climate and each acre of land that was farmed could support far more people than foraging for food. In fact, farming populations can be 10 to 50 times denser than foraging ones; as a result, farming affects the environment far more than foraging does. Farmers felled trees to make room for crops and domesticated animals grazed on hillsides. Early farmers' archaeological and historical records show that rapid population growth resulted in conflict, as farmers competed with each other over arable land. The wars over resources, if deadly enough, would frequently lead to subsequent population decline.[25]

Humans and Nature Interaction

With the development of agriculture, human impact on the environment increased. The domestication of plants and animals produced new interactions between humans and nature which eventually resulted in a reduction of biodiversity and destabilization of the Earth's complex ecosystem begun by foragers, if only minimally. Within agricultural areas, a simplified ecosystem containing a few crops and a limited number of animal species gradually replaced an interdependent and varied ecosystem. A symbiotic relationship existed among the new human/plant/animal domesticates, which gave them a competitive edge for their survival and multiplication. When humans and their co-domesticated plants and animals lived cooperatively they significantly increased their populations. Humans also acted as dispersal agents for various species of plants, and these domesticated plants become more common in the areas in which humans resided. But the consequences of this human/plant/animal advantage were the extinction of many plants and animals that were unable to compete with this newly dominant cooperative entity.[26] Hence, less biodiversity.

Slash and burn agriculture causes erosion.

With the development of agriculture, humans and their co-dependent domesticated plants and animals began to consciously divorce themselves from the surrounding natural ecosystem. Before agriculture humans experienced themselves as part of nature and dependent upon their local ecosystem. They were an integral component in a system of life and death, creation and extinction, within nature. Although an awe and respect for nature definitely remained after the transition to agriculture, humans invented a new ecology, one in which the resources that had previously supported millions of diverse species were increasingly channeled toward supporting just one species—humans.[27] We can clearly see the ramifications of this process today!

To make room for their preferred plant and animal species, farmers felled trees and burned vegetation to clear land for planting, denuded hillsides for pasture, and introduced foreign plants and animals into previously alien environments. For example, voracious domestic animals like goats stripped pastures of their grass cover, and soon overgrazed swatches of land. Torrential rains then eroded valuable topsoil and denuded hillsides, an occurrence that continues to plague hillsides today.

When populations—both human and other species—exceed the long-term sustainability of the environment, environmental degradation most likely results, and a population crash follows. With humans, when such a crash occurs it is often accompanied by intense warfare. If food shortages occur, humans will fight before they will starve, although the fighting may intensify the starvation. For example, in the prehistory of the Southwest United States, particularly the Chaco Canyon area of present day northwestern New Mexico, climate, population growth, and warfare were clearly linked. A shift toward a suitable climate for humans led to the population exploding to numbers far too large for the region to accommodate. When a drought occurred, it reduced the amount of food produced and malnourishment, disease, and starvation ensued. Warfare ripped through the region, reducing the level of human population to one more commensurate with the land's carrying capacity. According to archaeologist Steven LeBlanc, "This scenario, or ones very much like it, has probably played out hundreds of times the world over."[28]

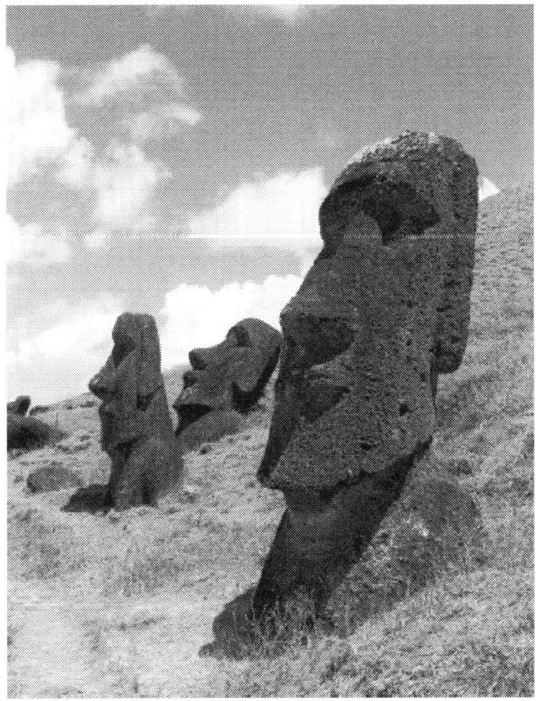

Easter Island in the Pacific Ocean. An environmental catastrophe similar to Chaco Canyon occurred here.

People living in the Agricultural Wave have often been portrayed as living peacefully and in harmony with nature, perhaps due to our longing for a romantic past when peace prevailed and environmental exploitation was nonexistent; but according to some researchers the reality may have been far different. LeBlanc offers another perspective; he argues that if any single family or even an entire village actually attempted to get into ecological balance by not overusing resources, nothing would stop its neighbors from doing just the opposite. To conserve Earth's resources requires strong leadership to ensure that all comply with the prevailing ethic. Lacking such leadership, effective conservation behaviors proved unenforceable. It did not pay for a farmer to be a conservationist, since his/her neighbor would probably not replicate his/her efforts. Early farmers constantly pressed their locale's carrying capacity to the limit. When resources were stressed, the archaeological evidence shows that farmers would often be beset by malnutrition-induced diseases and outright starvation, and as a result, LeBlanc continues, they would engage in warfare to obtain what they needed for survival. If warfare did ensue, it would certainly behoove the village being attacked to have a large enough population to resist the siege. Hence, with the advent of farming warfare became more common and deadlier than forager warfare.[29]

Although agriculture begins the process of ravaging nature that intensifies in later waves, the early farmers were acutely aware of their dependence on the forces of nature to produce their crops. This sacred interdependence with nature by farmers is ignored by LeBlanc and others. Their new lives as farmers connected them interdependently with nature's gifts, abundance, and an ever-renewing seasonal cycle. The seasonal sequence of spring birth, summer growth, autumn decline, and winter death entered the farmer's consciousness in profound spiritual and social ways. Their cultural expressions, explored below, reflected this deep regard for nature and its life-sustaining gifts. Understanding agriculture at a deep level, humans didn't simply take from nature and strive to dominate it, they also remembered their reciprocal interdependence with nature.[30]Although exploitation of the land did occur, farmers also recognized a deep-seated responsibility in knowing that the land must feed future generations as well as one's own. Both these destructive and constructive behaviors paradoxically co-existed with agricultural people.

Questions to Consider

1. Do you agree with the following statement: "Both destructive and constructive behaviors towards the environment paradoxically co-existed with agricultural people?" Why or why not?

Insights: Learning from the Past

Ecosystem Currents

Many ecologists and others believe that with the advent of agriculture human's domination of nature officially began. Although we see that foragers also manipulated their environment to get their needs met, it can be argued that they generally lived within the limits of nature. The relationship with nature changes with the Agricultural Wave. Forests are cleared with slash and burn techniques and surroundings are deforested of precious wood. Agriculturists also devise religious rituals that they believe will persuade nature to provide for their particular needs, offering gifts to the gods to provide adequate rainfall when and where they need it. Humans also thank nature for her gifts in these rituals, sometimes offering a sacrifice, either animal or sometimes human, to the gods. But, perhaps, nature can't be fooled, and continues its creative and destructive relationship with us, irrespective of our pleas or rituals.

An insight that I repeatedly refer to in this holistic world history is that warfare often results from competition over scarce resources. I believe this reason for warfare is ignored in traditional history that often attributes warfare to who shot first. Looking at conflict from a "scarce resources" perspective warns us that different approaches to solving conflict are needed. For example, population control is a better strategy for reducing populations clamoring for insufficient resources than the brutal slaughter of warfare. How to distribute scarce resources so that warfare will not ensue is a major challenge for all of us today and in the future.

WAYS OF LIVING: TECHNO-ECONOMIC CURRENTS

Daily Life

People in the Agricultural Wave lived in sedentary settlements with permanent housing structures, although the types of structures varied according to environmental conditions. In southwest Asia, for example, some dwellings rested on stone footings of cut blocks of limestone, surrounded by clay walls, and enclosed by a wooden framework. Storage bins were usually buried under the floor of a house to protect their contents from animal raids and unwanted theft.[31] In other hot climates such as southern China and Egypt, people constructed houses courtyard style, with rooms clustered around the edges of an open central courtyard. Animals were corralled in the courtyard, along with a cistern to collect precious rainwater. Flat roofs accommodated those who often wanted cooler sleeping conditions during the heat of summer. In the cold climates of northern Europe and northern China, people mostly built hearth houses: huts with one square or round room and a fire blazed on a stone hearth in the middle. Since chimneys were not invent-

Ancient apartment-style dwellings at the Taos Pueblo, New Mexico, USA.

ed until the 12th century CE, the smoke twirled through an opening in a thatched or shingled roof, which was slanted so that rain and snow would run off. Often animals and people resided in the huts together, providing warmth for each other. Some huts had two rooms, one for people and the other for animals. Animals like dogs and cats resided with their human housemates.

It is often assumed that when humans switched to cultivation of foods rather than foraging for foods, this ensured a more reliable and nutritious food supply; however, this was not always the case. Agriculture was typically based on the domestication of one of six plant species: wheat, barley, millet, rice, maize, or potatoes. Although they required hours of hard work to cultivate, these annuals had high yields, tolerated a variety of locations, and stored easily. Often, however, these plant species were not people's preferred foods. The average diet of a person living in the Agricultural Wave was actually less desirable and healthy than a forager's diet because of a lack of protein and variety. In some instances only one of these crops provided a village's major source of nutrition, such as wheat in the case in Egypt. The planting of single crops meant that deadly infestations could easily wipe out the village's only source of food, resulting in famine or food shortages.[32] Studies confirm that early farmers suffered a reduction in body size, and general enfeeblement; bending, thinning bones suggest disorders from rickets and tuberculosis. For example, excavated bones of Egyptian farmers show them to have arthritic toes and deformed, bent backs from squatting on their toes and stooping to grind grain.

Close contact with animals was the source of many previously unknown human diseases, such as small pox, chicken pox, and other infections that plagued humans. Closely packed villages with inadequate sanitary conditions were incubators for the spread of contagious diseases. Other health risks included intestinal parasites, contaminated water supplies, infections, infestations, and unchecked epidemics.[33]

Two common forms of farming in the Agricultural Wave were slash and burn and dry land gardening. Slash and burn agriculture was common in tropical forest environments or savannas. Men usually cleared the land of trees and cut away tangled underbrush that was left to dry and then burned off. Generally, women cultivated garden plots for several years until productivity declined and the soil's nutrients depleted. Farmers cleared and worked the land again once the fields had lain fallow for up to ten years or more. Ultimately the soil was again depleted of essential

Effects of slash and burn on primary forest can be devastating. Seen in this photo is a patch of forest in Namdapha National Park in Northeast India cleared for Jhum cultivation.

nutrients and at this time the villagers could relocate to another area and begin the process again. This soil-depleting system required large tracts of land, and population density remained relatively low compared to more intensive forms of agriculture.[34] Farmers practiced dry land gardening in areas where water for crops was insufficient. Although farmers did not construct complex irrigation networks, small canals channeled water from seasonal runoff and in drier periods they laboriously hand carried water to individual garden plots.[35]

The dog was probably the first animal domesticated during the Agricultural Wave. Human settlements attracted wolves, who scavenged for discarded garbage. Studies have shown that wolves fairly quickly evolved into domesticated dogs. Dogs, by nature social creatures, readily fit into human households. Although dogs were used as a source of food, they were more valuable for hunting, herding, warning of potential danger, and as pets. This dog and human co-domestication process was probably an accidental yet mutual compromise in which their close proximity bred tolerance, affection, and dependence.[36]

A pack llama. Since the Western hemisphere did not have domesticated pigs, cattle, sheep, goats, or horses until around 1500, the llama was used as a pack animal.

Surprisingly, only around 15 animal species have successfully been domesticated, with five of the most numerous—sheep, goats, horses, pigs, and cattle—populating the global landscape. These docile and even-tempered domesticated animals were easily bred in captivity, lived in herds with hierarchical social structures, and ate plants not readily digested by humans. This process of animal domestication enabled humans to tap an otherwise unusable food supply: grasses.[37] Farmers first domesticated sheep and goats about 10,000 BP, cattle slightly later, and pigs about 8,500 BP. Custom-built corrals held domesticated animals, and their reproduction was closely monitored and manipulated. Along with domesticated animals, the warm, shallow seas supplied abundant quantities of fish and shellfish that augmented the human diet.[38]

Questions to Consider

1. Were you surprised to learn that when humans switched to cultivation of foods it did not necessarily mean a more reliable and nutritious food supply than foraging? Why do you think it is always assumed that the cultivation of food was a step in human progress?

Economic Systems

In agricultural societies two types of economic systems co-existed: reciprocity and a redistribution system began to emerge. Reciprocal sharing by kinship groups, as we saw in foraging societies, was still common, especially in smaller village settings. But in a **redistribution** system members of the community contributed a certain percentage of the commodities produced to a common pool. From this common pool the contributed commodities, usually in the form of grain products, are then redistributed to certain members of the community. Redistribution requires an **intermediary** or third party who coordinates the contribution of goods and manages their distribution as well. A leader, who serves as an intermediary, directs the exchange of goods or services; s/he draws upon the pool of contributed goods to pay for his/her community services and is likely to be rewarded with power, wealth, and prestige. Although some officials siphon off a disproportionate share of the redistribution goods for their own or their kin's use, not all officials abuse their power.[39] This economic system usually develops after the domestication of plants and animals in the Agricultural Wave and continues in the Urban Wave. We even see redistribution in action today: our taxes are paid into a collective pool, the government coffers, which are then redistributed to enhance, hopefully, the collective well-being.

Questions to Consider

1. In what ways is your nation's economy a redistributive economy? Give examples.

Technology

Domestication of plants and animals and a sedentary way of life stimulated other technological innovations that revolved around agricultural production. New toolkits for harvesting domesticated grains contained knife-blades and sickles for cutting bunches of grain stems. Highly specialized flint **artisans** or craft people manufactured ax heads and other cutting tools to clear dense primeval forests. Artisans invented flat slabs of stone with indentations called **querns** for grinding harvested grains into flour. A shift from stone to metal tools occurred around 6,000 BP in some societies. Copper, the first metal humans learned how to work, was heated and hammered into various devices, and only later was it smelted and melted into molds. Along with use for agricultural production, metal artisans applied their skills to the invention of military technology in order to defend their territory from intruders and to invade new lands.[40]

Tools for grinding grain.

Agriculturists found that containers for storing surplus crops for future use were vital. A few baked clay products were known in the Paleolithic era, but not in notable quantities. Pottery vessels replaced carved stone bowls as containers about 9,000 BP in southwest Asia and Japan. Before the invention of the potter's wheel around 4,250 BP, women shaped pottery by hand, a technique that is still used in some societies today. Pottery vessels provided useful, durable, clean, and convenient storage for food and drink, did not decay, and were fireproof. Women used pottery to cook food over a fire or to bake food in a wood-fired oven. Pottery was invented independently in the Western hemisphere where it appeared about 4,000 BP. Since it was most useful in the domes-

Pottery vessel from the Acoma Pueblo, New Mexico, hand-coiled in the early 20th century.

tic sphere, women probably invented it and the firing process as well. Pottery was also a medium for artistic expression: painted designs adorned pottery vessels and clay was molded into eye-catching shapes and sizes.[41]

Textile crafts—weaving, stringing, sewing, and spinning—were performed mostly by women and flourished in agricultural societies. These crafts were readily incorporated into the female domestic sphere since they were easy to pick up after interruption, were reasonably child-safe, and could be done at home. Some of the earliest known woven baskets were made from wheat straw and found at Catal Huyuk in Anatolia (modern Turkey) around 8,500 BP.[42] String, a handy invention, was used to tie things up, and to catch, hold, bind, and carry items. Snares, fish lines, tether, leashes, carrying nets, handles, packages, and even skirts were fashioned from string. Though not worn for warmth, the string skirts are thought to indicate a female's readiness for childbearing, or perhaps simply that she was of childbearing age and in some sense available as a bride.[43]

Patterns of Labor

The division of labor was more specialized in the Agricultural Wave than among foragers. Labor still followed a **domestic mode of production**, in which the extended family was the primary unit of production. Families were relatively self-sufficient in providing all their basic needs, and carried out production tasks without much outside assistance. They basically lived at what is called a subsistence level. They had little incentive to produce a food surplus greater than what they needed throughout the year and therefore they had limited commercial exchange with one another. But political and economic leaders of the village knew that households needed to grow a greater surplus in order to compensate for those individuals who had a specialized trade and did not produce their own food or enough of their own food for their own consumption. These leaders pressured farmers to produce a food surplus and coerced individual households to enter into the flow of village commerce in order to perpetuate an economic system that produced more than a mere subsistence level for each household.[44] Villagers generally complied with the directive.

If a particular agricultural society could produce a surplus of food then certain members usually had some form of occupational specialization. The number of individuals and the variety of economic specialists in agricultural societies was linked to the quantity of food surplus that was produced. Pottery crafters, weavers, metal crafters, religious specialists, leaders, carpenters, brick-layers, and others provided items and services for their own villages and sometimes the excess goods or services were exchanged with other villages. On the other hand, some specialists labored at their specific economic specialty during times when they were not needed in the fields to plant or harvest crops.

Subsistence farming today in Zambia, Africa. Mostly women were (are) the farmers in the Agricultural Wave.

Labor responsibilities were frequently divided according to gender and age. Women had the primary duties of cultivating crops, preparing food, tending animals, caring for children, weaving, sewing, pottery making, and other domestic duties.[45] Men usually cleared the fields, tended and butchered animals, and hunted.

With the turn to agriculture, the workload for food producers increased; farmers had less leisure time than foragers. Human labor, not animal labor, provided the needed energy required for food production. They did not use plows, draft animals, soil fertilization, crop rotation, or complex irrigation networks but worked with common hand tools such as a digging stick and hoe. However, the workload for farmers in the Agricultural Wave was not as time-consuming as that of farmers who practiced plow agriculture in the Urban Wave.

Exchange and Trade

Exchange and trade took place between members of the village, with residents of nearby settlements, and with distant communities. An increase in occupational specialization and a surplus of material products meant that some communities had more of a particular item or service than they could use. Trade developed when one community wanted or needed a specialized product produced by another community. Most agricultural societies supplied all of their basic food needs, and traded with other communities' products such as surplus specialty foods, specialized craft items, or other nonessential items. Long-distance trade generally included luxury goods such as shell beads, obsidian, luxurious clothing, precious stones, fine cloth, and other rare objects. Pack animals like the donkey, mule, and camel or the llama in the Western hemisphere transported these goods along trade routes. Since long-distance trade was costly and risky, goods were limited to small, precious materials and finely crafted objects that commanded a high market price. Trading was conducted on a smaller scale than in the later waves.

Large celebratory feasts were also an occasion for trading valuable goods like pottery, baskets, clothing, tools, and other crafts. The medium of exchange for these goods varied but involved some direct barter, as well as the use of special purpose money like shells, beads, or brass rods. Some money had a specific value and could be exchanged for commodities like cattle, and pigs. A few traders did use, although rarely, all-purpose cash as we know it today for trade.[46]

Insights: Learning from the Past

Techno-Economic Currents

One of the points to consider in this techno-economic section is the question: Did humans progress with the transition to agricultural production? It is commonly assumed that they did progress, but I think the answer is more complex. One debate centers on whether the food supply was more dependable with farming than foraging. Although farmers did not need to go out to forage for food, grains were subject to disease, and poor harvests could result from droughts, floods, or other climate fluctuations. And as mentioned grains were not a food of first choice

Colorful trade in fabrics at a local bazaar in Thailand. Photo by Roger Harmon

and the overall diet of agriculturalists was not as nutritious as foragers' diet. Starvation and undernourishment were not solved with the advent of agriculture.

Another insight is the fact that women were the "first farmers." It has been assumed that men were always the farmers but the evidence does not support this conclusion. Farming was a natural transition for women, since their skills and knowledge as foragers helped them "invent" sedentary agriculture. It was a shock to Europeans when they first encountered women farming in the Western hemisphere in the 16th century and onward. They immediately thought that the men were lazy and inferior, a stereotype that persisted well into the 20th century. Women's role as economic providers also contributed to their egalitarian status in many small villages. They invented crucial early innovations such as pottery and weaving, as well. Along with their reproductive function, women gave life in the form of food, which translated into the religious symbolism of the goddess—the protectoress and the giver of life.

Questions to Consider

1. Do you think that humans progressed with the transition to agricultural production? Explain.
2. Were you surprised to find out that women were the "first farmers?"

HUMAN NETWORKS: SOCIAL CURRENTS

Groups

Social organization was ordered around what are often called tribes. The term has fostered considerable debate over how best to characterize them or whether the term should be used at all. However, since it is familiar and commonly used, I will also use the term tribe in this world history with the following definition. A **tribe** is a unit of sociopolitical organization—families, bands, clans, or lineage groups—who are united by ties of descent from a common ancestor, adhere to agreed upon customs and traditions, and are loyal to the same leader. A tribe shares the same language, lifestyle and territory. Family authority, and not tribal authority, typically rules in domestic matters, such as divorce, marriage, and punishment of family members. Tribal social organization cuts across kinship lines and provides a kind of social "glue" that helps keep the larger units within the community cooperating instead of competing. Such cooperation was necessary in order to build and maintain irrigation canals, raised fields, fortifications, and other cooperative enterprises.

Many contemporary agricultural societies have between 200 to 250 members and include up to 20 families. Kinship is the primary basis for organizing daily affairs, and the kinship group has influence over the lives of individual members. Each extended family has a council of leaders that handles daily problems and routine affairs. In larger agricultural societies there are also non-kinship associations drawn from the community that are based on age, religious or gender affiliation.[47]

Family

Upon reaching adult status most people in agricultural societies married, which meant an individual accepted the responsibilities associated with being a wife or husband. Marriage was mostly exogamous, outside the group. A woman routinely married a year or two after her first menstruation, and sometimes before. Her procreative function was considered a valuable asset for increasing the group's population, and a large family was avidly encouraged. A degree of sexual freedom was permitted before marriage for both males and females, and if a child was born before marriage the child could be assigned to the mother's kinship-group or adopted by another family. After marriage in patrilocal societies, a wife usually moved in with her husband's family and performed labor for his kin. In matrilocal societies, a husband moved in with his wife's family and performed assigned duties.[48]

Kinship groups often arranged marriages to cement an alliance with another group, or to acquire a source of labor. Couples usually had little say in their choice of spouses in their first marriage. Special marriage brokers, often elderly women, constantly assessed the pool of eligible marriage partners for the perfect match. People in the Agricultural Wave practiced polygyny, marriage with more than one wife, more so than foragers. This marriage form occurred where there was an increased emphasis on accumulation and distribution of wealth, with women considered valuable possessions.[49]

Extramarital affairs occurred but were usually considered a risky act. If a married man or woman engaged in an extra-marital affair, s/he could be punished or divorced. In some societies a husband beat his wife with varying degrees of severity if she was caught in an adulterous situation, while a wife scolded her husband or used force against him. The third party in the affair was treated differently depending on whether the offender was a man or woman. When the adulterer was a man, his behavior could be viewed as usurpation of a husband's right to exclusive sexual access to his wife, and the offender was required to pay compensation to the husband. If a married man had an affair with an unmarried woman, he could be subject to the wrath of her father and be forced to pay some form of compensation to her father. If a husband committed adultery, his wife was rarely able to exact a penalty from the offending woman. Sexual jealousy was apt to be intense in adulterous situations, and restrictions and penalties were implemented to limit such occurrences and their disruption to the group.[50]

Divorce was a permissible option for both wives and husbands, and rates appeared to be quite high. The main reason for divorce was a couple's inability to have children. In patrilineal societies it was usually assumed to be the woman's fault if the couple was barren, and the husband was entitled to divorce her on these grounds. If a woman wished to prevent a divorce, she could encourage her husband to take another wife, or another lover, in order for the union to bear a child. This child would normally be treated as a legitimate offspring, especially if a son. In patrilineal societies a woman could not divorce her husband because of childlessness, but a husband could divorce his wife if he was dissatisfied with her services. For example, divorce could be the outcome if he thought she was stingy with food, spent too much time visiting her relatives, neglected their children, committed flagrant adultery, spread gossip about him, or disobeyed him. In some matrilineal societies childlessness was not assumed to be a woman's fault, and she could divorce her husband. Divorce could also result if a husband was unable or unwilling to provide sufficient land for cultivating crops, or if he was inattentive to his wife's kin. A woman

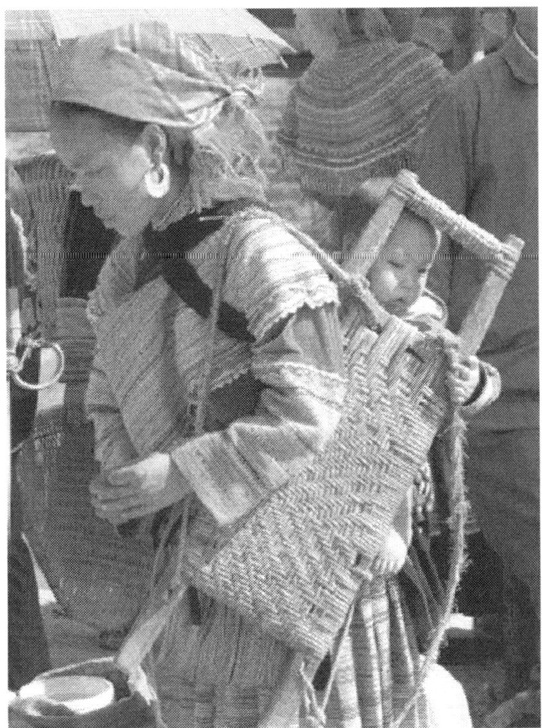

Mother and child in Vietnam. Photo by Roger Harmon

could divorce her husband for flagrant adultery or impotence. In matrilineal societies a woman's sexuality was not as strictly curtailed by her husband as in patrilineal societies. In both patrilineal and matrilineal societies, the welfare of the children deterred some parents from divorce, while remarriage was more frequent among divorcees who had no children. Generally, post-menopausal women chose not to remarry.[51]

Family size tended to increase with the Agricultural Wave. Women spent more time pregnant and caring for young infants than foraging women. Several factors contributed to the increase in family size: a woman walked less and used less energy than foraging women, thus increasing her chances for conception; infant mortality declined somewhat; the availability of cereals provided an alternative to breast-feeding; and more children were needed as farm workers.[52] Since children were needed as workers, infanticide was less frequent among agriculturists than foragers but it was still likely that twins or those born with defects were "exposed" to the elements, and left to die. Abortion was a woman's decision and could be chosen for many reasons. Abortion was an option when a mother was tending an infant and was unable to care for another child, or it could be employed as retaliation against a hostile husband. An unmarried woman could decide to have an abortion to conceal a pregnancy resulting from an affair. Or a woman who wished to postpone the end of her unrestricted sexual activity by the birth of a child could initiate an abortion. Some children whose parents were unable to care for them were adopted or given foster care, most commonly by relatives. Adopted children usually had the same rights as biological children. Not only parents but mature women, older children, and other relatives and neighbors also had responsibility for childcare.[53]

Men and women in their fifties and sixties with grown children were likely to retain social power and authority as long as they remained mentally active. The elderly performed rituals, mediated with spiritual forces, and served as political leaders. When conflict and cattle raising were important, elderly men, lacking clear political functions and regretting their loss of physical vigor, diligently attempted to keep up with athletic activities to prove their worthiness. Post-menopausal women who were already in charge of a household likely gained added authority and prestige by acquiring new spiritual powers from which their menstruation and motherhood responsibilities had previously barred them. Generally, elderly women acquired new roles more easily than elderly men, a reversal of their youthful situations.[54]

Gender

Men and women performed different roles in agricultural societies; women were usually responsible for the cultivation of crops, and men cleared and prepared the land for planting. Studies of 104 contemporary horticultural societies show that in 50 percent of these societies

Shaman from equatorial amazon rain forest.

women are exclusively responsible for agricultural production; in 33 percent, women and men share various tasks associated with agricultural production; and in 17 percent, men are wholly responsible for farming. Caution should be taken in concluding that these numbers were the same in the distant past. The study was conducted after decades, if not centuries, in which men have been indoctrinated to replace women as farmers; thus, the percentage of men engaged in cultivation is probably higher today than in the past.[55]

When women in patriarchal agricultural societies no longer contributed significantly to the daily production of food—a factor that was crucial in determining their social status—they become more subordinate and were more likely to be treated as property.[56]

Prestige and Status

Smaller agricultural societies were more egalitarian than larger agricultural societies. Individuals in small societies had more or less equal opportunity to obtain the necessities of life and gained the esteem of others. But substantial differences in prestige were not uncommon, with achieved status as important as ascribed status. In some agricultural societies, achieved status was bestowed upon political and religious leaders—those with military prowess, skill in oratory, and those who achieved material wealth in the form of pigs or cattle, or multiple wives; ascribed status was awarded to individuals based on age and lineage. Each society identified its own particular combination of characteristics as marks of status.[57]

The more complex and productive a society became, the more chances there were for economic and social differences to develop. With more occupational specialization and surplus production, some individuals controlled more wealth than others. Anthropologist T. Douglas Price contends that "the initial indications of status differentiation are associated with the beginnings of farming."[58] This greater inequality among individuals is connected to the accumulation of property and the inheritance of farmland. Those with more property and wealth achieve higher status and prestige. But compared to social differentiation in the Urban Wave, villagers in less complex agricultural societies had more egalitarian structures, and less emphasis was placed on status and hierarchical relationships.

Socialization and Education

Children's socialization was customarily organized around preparation for adult roles. If they were given any responsibilities, these were most likely to be related to their future labor roles. Men trained boys in male skills when they were around the age of five and not in the way or in danger. If men cleared land or engaged in conflict outside the village, small boys generally did not actively assist their fathers. But when men cultivated crops, children accompanied their fathers to the gardens. If raising cattle was important, a boy took cattle out to graze. Some small boys had no work responsibilities whatsoever.[59] When girls reached the age of five or six they began to care for infants, with or without much adult supervision. Both girls and boys fed infants and assisted in household tasks such as gathering wood, carrying water, or tending fires. Girls ordinarily helped out with cooking chores and aided their mothers and other women with their cultivation tasks—weeding, planting, and harvesting crops. If a mother left the village to engage in responsibilities outside the domestic sphere, such as trade, girls usually did not accompany her.

Clothing, body decorations, and ornaments worn by boys and girls normally had gender differentiating features. The age at which gender differentiation began varied, but by the age of five or six children wore particular articles or marks of some kind that demarcated their gender.[60]

Insights: Learning from the Past

Social Currents

An insight gleaned from this section is that less complex agricultural villages were communal and egalitarian. Women carried out the very important task of raising food, a status that accorded them equality in most agricultural villages. All members were involved in providing for the basic needs of the village. Labor was communal in nature, and work was broken by periods of leisure and social, celebratory gatherings. The village provided an atmosphere of stability and belonging for individuals. Individualism was not part of their value system. Instead individuals were immersed in a village structure that gave them a sense of identity and purpose. The group came before the individual, in contrast to the American value system today. The saying "it takes a village to raise a child" rings true in the community-focused structure of agricultural villages.

Questions to Consider

1. Do you think the saying "it takes a village to raise a child" rings true in agricultural villages? Does it "ring true" in your nation or community?

ESTABLISHING ORDER: POLITICAL CURRENTS

Political Systems and Leadership

The political organization of most agricultural societies was tribal. A tribe is decentralized, informal, with leadership roles held on a temporary basis. Authority was held by the family leaders of the local group, and by voluntary associations whose members were drawn from several families. When a situation such as warfare required consensus of several tribal groups, they joined together to address a particular problem; after the problem had been resolved, each group returned to its autonomous state. Voluntary associations often played a role in the defense of the tribal community.[61]

Leaders of agricultural societies had charismatic qualities acquired through their personal abilities and the reputation to convince others it was in their own self-interest to follow their lead. Leadership was more a matter of skill than inherited status, and a leader lacked the coercive power that may be derived from such status in other societies. Tribes did not have hereditary leaders but when a time of crisis occurred a strong leader emerged. Status among village leaders was generally achieved rather than ascribed, although both could be in play. Leaders were respected for their age, integrity, and wisdom. In more specialized and populous agricultural societies, political offices could be inherited and held within a particular family. Some village leaders were endowed with both religious and secular authority and imbued with a religious aura and sacredness.[62]

Customs, Rules and Laws

Like foraging societies, agricultural societies retained a basic, cooperative style of social and political organization. In less complex agricultural societies, with weak governmental authorities, other means of social control were needed to maintain a cooperative way of life. Religion was often used to maintain social control. For example, oaths were an administered ritualistic act that could be a powerful force in determining the guilt or innocence of an accused person. For fear of spiritual retaliation if a false oath was given, individual members strove to conform to social expectations. In more complex agricultural societies with more formalized rules and authoritative centralized institutions, the political representatives of these institutions exercised power. Specialized judges acted on behalf of these power structures to assert authority over parties in dispute and over those accused of violating the customs and rules.[63] They could exact punishments on those accused of infractions as they deemed appropriate.

Large kinship groups often owned land in the community. In foraging societies the band commonly owned the land, but in agricultural societies, land ownership patterns changed with the move toward a settled way of life. Farmers accumulated more possessions—stone cups, bowls, pottery, ornaments, storage containers, tools, and land—than nomadic foragers. With this acquisitiveness and accumulation of property, new rules were devised to protect ownership of these material possessions. Designated elders or officials of the group allocated plots of land from the group's holdings to nuclear families or extended family households. In some societies land use was regulated by a "lease," which could be provisional but was extended by officials to certain families who kept up designated obligations. In other societies a family or household gained access to land by merely clearing a new area, but after the land had been exhausted from farming the land reverted back to the larger collective group. Rules were devised to delineate inheritance procedures when property was transferred.[64]

For example, in Mexico today a small portion of the land continues to be owned collectively by small villages in the traditional pre-Spanish Indian land tenure system. The collective land, called the *ejido*, consists of cultivated land, pastureland, forests, and the legal site of the village. Although the land is owned communally, it is divided into separate individual holdings that can be passed down to the next generation with the proviso that the land cannot be individually sold.

Migration and Interaction

Interaction at this time was primarily between farming villagers and farmers and foragers. Many agriculturists migrated to productive agricultural lands to improve their farming operations. As human populations increased, more people vied for the best productive land, which often led to conflict and tension. It was not unusual for one family or group to clear land for planting, only to have another group claim ownership as well. Interaction between agricultural and foraging people or two agricultural groups could have at least two possible outcomes: the two groups could live in relatively harmonious interaction without undue influence by either group, or one group dominated the other, either through forced subjugation or by absorbing or assimilating the subordinate group into the dominate group's way of life. Although some foraging groups resisted influence from agricultural people, more often, in the course of thousands of years of interaction, farmers absorbed and dominated foraging people.

The world had not been populated by overwhelming numbers of foragers who evolved into farmers. Rather, descendants of farming groups expanded and took over much of the productive land in the world. A farming way of life could spread swiftly because they had larger numbers in their villages due to population growth. The more farmers encroached onto neighboring land, the more resources they gobbled up. Since there were more mouths to feed, more resources were needed, which led to more encroachment upon neighboring lands, like a system's reinforcing feedback loop. The replacement of foragers by farmers was rapid where anthropologists can measure it. It has been estimated that approxi-

Working ejido land in the village of Vincente Guerreo, Mexico. Photo by Denise Ames

mately one mile of new territory along the boundary between farmers and foragers may have been absorbed by farmers every year. The farmers enveloped foragers, especially women, into their societies as they expanded across the globe.[65]

Conflict, Cooperation and War

Although internal conflict was common among foraging and agricultural societies alike, as it is today, external conflict or warfare was more prevalent among complex, more centralized agricultural societies such as chiefdoms than it was among smaller agricultural societies. Conflict among agricultural people was expressed in the form of feuds, retribution, ambushes, raids, and organized warfare. Feuds and retribution have already been described in the Communal Wave chapter.

An **ambush** is a long-used military tactic in conflict still practiced today. Ambushers strike their enemies from concealed positions such as behind dense underbrush or hidden by hilltops. The purpose is to launch a surprise attack.

A **raid** is organized violence by one group against another to obtain an economic advantage. It is usually a repetitive and ongoing act motivated by economic gain. The goal is not to exterminate or even conquer the enemy permanently, but to accomplish the limited goal of seizing such goods as food, cattle, women, or other valuables. Where raiding is recurrent, the pillaged group is often regarded as a resource that must be left serviceable for future plundering.[66] Raiding was a common tactic employed by pastoral or nomadic people against agricultural people. Nomadic people who often had limited and unpredictable resources attacked agricultural people who held more plentiful and predictable resources. Classic forms of attack included the dawn raid and ambushing of an individual when s/he left the village unaccompanied. More elaborate types of warfare included pitched battles, massacres, war ceremonialism, alliances for making war, and contested no-man's lands.[67]Raids are further discussed in the Urban Wave chapter.

Feuding clans built defensive towers, Caucasus Mountains, Eastern Europe.

Groups protected and defended their land and crops from confiscation by others. The boundaries of a group's territory were critical areas of contestation, since many of the boundaries were not clearly demarcated and were subject to recurring interpretation and dispute. These boundary areas were sometimes called **no man's land**, a term for contested land that is not occupied or is under dispute between warring parties. The two parties did not occupy the land for fear that warfare would ensue. Agriculturists expanded geographically when their population growth overextended their capability to produce enough food locally. If they expanded into land that had already been prepared for cultivation, this act was likely to lead to conflict with their neighbors. The aggressive group found it easier to confiscate already cleared and cultivated land than prepare their own for production. Archaeological studies show that groups in such diverse places as New Zealand and Peru chose to fight over existing resources rather than create additional ones.[68]

Although warfare occurred in the past, some scholars such as archeologist Marija Gimbutas, argued that Neolithic villages in southeast Europe, what she referred to as Old Europe, were peaceful and practiced goddess worship. She states that these societies between 9,000 and 5,500 BP had long periods of peace with little evidence of ongoing and systematic warfare. She surmised that they were generally peaceful since there was little evidence of territorial aggression or lethal weapons found at their archaeological sites. Graves rarely contained weapons, and most communities had no walls for fortification or other defenses. Some had ditches and fences, but these seemed to be intended as protection against marauding animals rather than attacks by other people.[69]

Even though there were times when conflict apparently eased, it did not cease altogether according to the more extensive archaeological record. And there were times when it became especially virulent. These time spans seem to coincide with climate change, or the aftermath of rapid growth in population. According to LeBlanc, the fact that these correlations can be observed strongly implies that farmer warfare had real causes and was not sparked by revenge, the innate need of males to release pent-up aggression, or other such explanations unrelated to changes in climate, ecology, or population size.[70] In other words, scarce resources, population growth, and climate change seemed to be the major factors that caused violent conflict to arise among people in the Agricultural Wave as well as other waves.

When there was warfare, it was likely to be more deadly than forager conflict had been, resulting not only in higher fatalities but also in a constant—almost daily—threat of attack. Tribal-farmer warfare was more organized than that of foraging bands, although there was no military specialization in either. Every adult male, with few exceptions, was expected to fight. Few were exempted from the fray.[71]

One example of tribal warfare occurred on the island of New Guinea. The highlands of New Guinea were an extraordinary place, where population density was extremely high. In the 20th century, researchers found that warfare was endemic on the island, with formal battles, ambushes, and even occasional massacres going on almost continually. Fighting was nasty and deadly. Estimates found that 25 percent of the men and 5 percent of the women died from warfare in New Guinea. About 30 percent of all independent highland social groups became extinct each century because they were defeated in warfare by their attackers. These groups were either massacred or killed by attackers, or the survivors fled. The last place on Earth to have remained unaffected by modern society was not the most peaceful but one of the most warlike yet encountered.[72] Whether this exact scenario happened in the past is certainly unclear and debatable. Perhaps the scarce resources available on the island due to overpopulation contributed to the endemic warfare in the 20th century.

Another group, the Yanomamo, who are tribally organized farmers of the Amazonian rainforests on the border of Venezuela and Brazil in South America, had also been relatively isolated from modern society until approximately the 1960s. Descriptions of frequent, intense, and deadly warfare among this group are virtually identical to accounts from New Guinea.[73]

Kurulu Village War Chief, Baliem Valley, New Guinea.

Insights: Learning from the Past

Political Currents

There are three points to consider in the political currents section of the Agricultural Wave. One is the difference in political power between smaller agricultural societies and larger chiefdoms. In simpler agricultural societies, leadership was diffused and depended more upon the charismatic qualities of the leader than on the actual power or authority that s/he held. However, when villages increased in size and population, more power was concentrated in the leader. Therefore, from this scenario we can tentatively assert that for real democracy to take hold, decentralized political structures where power is diffuse and balanced are required. A second point to consider is that land, although still communally or family owned, started to become more associated with individual use and the concept of land ownership began to form. And third, periods of peace were interrupted by periods of warfare in direct relation to climatic conditions. When the climate was favorable to human needs and resources were plentiful, periods of peace usually prevailed. When less favorable conditions arose, the intensity and frequency of warfare increased. Therefore, high population density coupled with scarce resources due to climate shifts or soil depletion contributed to the frequency and intensity of warfare.

Questions to Consider

1. Of the three insights for the political current in the Agricultural Wave, which one to you is most significant?

HUMAN EXPRESSIONS: CULTURAL CURRENTS

Worldview and Religion

Agricultural societies had a decentralized, informal, yet complex religious life, with lavish ceremonial worship of gods and goddesses. Agriculturists imaginatively either devised or recognized spirits that personified the major forces of nature as they related to food production in order to sustain a rapport with the land that they depended on for their livelihood. Many agricultural people revered gods and goddesses of wind, rain, plants, human and animal fertility, land, peace and war. Gods and goddesses were not usually arranged in hierarchies, although they may be, as in India, for example, but rose in prominence and importance in relation to the occasion for which they were invoked. For example, rain deities were extremely important and called upon for assistance in time of drought.[74]

Folk religions and ancestral worship were both part of the religious milieu of agricultural people. Religious practices in the Agricultural Wave can be described as folk religions. **Folk religions** are religious customs, traditions, beliefs, superstitions, and rituals of a particular group, band, village, tribe, or ethnic group. The religion is transmitted from generation to generation in a specific culture. They are not organized or universal religions but particular to a group. Reverence for ancestral spirits was most passionate among societies that had strong kinship organizations. They were believed to parallel living humans in behaviors, appetites, emotions, and feelings. An ancestral link provided an enduring sense of continuity with the past, present, and future. Ancestral spirits were seen as retaining an active membership in the current happenings of that society, with the most recently departed generation holding influence over the actions of living individuals.[75]

People in agricultural societies formulated an ideology that motivated community members to produce food and then relinquish part of their harvest to the individual who had the vested authority to disperse that food in a redistribution effort. Political leaders or priests/priestesses sometimes had the power and authority to distribute collected grains.

Agriculturists performed elaborate rituals. Some of the specific purposes for the rituals included defending land from encroachment by others, protecting and growing crops, promoting human fertility and welfare, and asking for success in conflict situations. Generally speaking, men led the rituals in patrilineal societies and in matrilineal societies women were the leaders. Women conducted rites at the scene of childbirth, which men were usually barred from attending. Where midwifery was treated as a ritual specialty, women were, of course, the attending priestesses. Both men and women conducted rituals for infants and young children, such as naming ceremonies or the first haircut. Funeral rituals were significant for the community as a whole and were often the most elaborate of all rituals, especially when ancestor deities were of primary importance. If a prominent man or woman died, religious specialists, such as a priest or priestess, conducted these noteworthy ceremonies.[76] In complex agricultural societies where there was greater agricultural productivity, rituals were more elaborate and frequent, and priestly duties became full-time occupations.

Image of sitting goddess, Inanna, representing Mother Earth.

Gimbutas extensively studied the artifacts, mythology, and archeology in southeast Europe and southwest Asia during the early Agricultural Wave. She maintained that agricultural people of this era generally saw no separation between the secular and sacred; religion and life were indivisible. She argued that the religious aspects of Neolithic life have been generally ignored in past studies, thereby neglecting the totality of the culture. The essence of the Neolithic religion in this region, according to Gimbutas, was the sovereign mystery and creative power of the female, "the Great Mother Goddess, source of life that gave birth to all creation out of the holy darkness from her womb. A mother goddess was a metaphor for Nature herself, the cosmic giver and taker of life, ever able to renew herself within the eternal cycle of life, death, and rebirth."[77] This worship of the goddess affected all aspects of life in the villages.

Earth-based religions were deeply linked to agriculture. Farmers relied upon the productivity of the Earth for their survival, and their cultural expressions reflected this interdependence with nature. Symbols and images expressed a reverence and awe for the spiritual and physical fecundity of women and motherhood. Because children were much needed in agricultural societies as labor, these societies expressed the desire for children with images of pregnant women and women giving birth. One important image was that of the self-generating goddess, performing her basic functions as giver of life, wielder of death and regenerator.[78]

There were three main dimensions of the goddess in Neolithic Europe: mistress of nature, goddess of fertility, and goddess of perpetual life. The goddess as mistress of nature was manifested in the life-giving and life-destroying energies of nature. The goddess of death and regeneration personified the destructive and creative energies of nature. Her cosmic pattern was that of endlessly repeated cycles of birth, death, and rebirth, corresponding to the phases of the moon and the seasons of the year—spring, summer, fall, and winter. All life in nature proceeded from death, and death from life. Prehistoric mythologies expressed this interdependence and continuity linking life and death as the mystery at the core of all being. Secondly, the goddess of fertility or the pregnant goddess was a metaphor for the birth and renewal of plant life and the growth and death of vegetation. During the Neolithic era, an agricultural goddess was the progenitor and protector of the fruits of the harvest, especially grain and bread. And third, the goddess symbolized perpetual life. For example, some societies considered the snake, because it sheds its skin, a symbol of the regenerative vitality and continuity of life, the guarantor of life energy in the home, and the symbol of family and animal life. Bird and snake goddesses developed with agriculture and settled life and became protectors of the family and Earth.[79] They incarnated life energy and linked ancestors to a family's living members.

Conjoined image of three popular manifestations of the Hindu Divine Mother: Lakshmi (wealth/material fulfillment), Parvati (Power/love/spiritual fulfillment), and Saraswati (learning and arts/cultural fulfillment), left to right. Hinduism has folk religion roots.

During the Agricultural Wave, evidence of widespread ceremonial activity taking place in temples is found. Integrated into the goddess religions were rituals that commemorated the passing of seasons, the rise and decline of vegetative cycles, and the recognition of cosmological or astrological cycles. Temples were places dedicated to the rites of spiritual reverence; they served an important social function as well as a center for creative expression of religious feeling through the arts, interweaving religious symbols into everyday village life.[80]

A universal and institutionalized religion worshipping a single female goddess apparently did

Mother Goddess flanked by two lionesses - 6000 to 5500 BCE, Çatalhöyük, Turkey.

not exist during the Neolithic. But there is strong evidence of widespread worship of more than one goddess in the historical records of Anatolia in present-day Turkey along with many other locations around the world. Female figurines undoubtedly represented a series of manifestations of different goddesses.[81] Perhaps the close connection with nature experienced by people during the Agricultural Wave was reflected in tangible, visible ways by these various art objects.

Aesthetic Expression

Art, a symbolic form of communication, was abundant in agricultural societies, providing information about the way agricultural people experienced their everyday life. Thousands of goddess art objects have been recovered all over the world. In many of these objects, the essential features of the goddess are represented—vulva, breasts, buttocks, belly—all endowed with the miraculous, cyclical power of life.[82] Other symbols include chevrons, geometric designs, and series of dotted lines. A link existed between goddess representations, the large number of children in families, rising populations, and a close connection with nature. These cultural representations were almost always of women, and the women were usually corpulent; the ample figurines possibly symbolized the importance of reproduction and the importance of a successful harvest. They could also represent the bountifulness of the Earth pregnant with the fruits needed by humans for their subsistence. Some figures are sitting down, perhaps suggestive of a more sedentary and permanent way of life.

Folk festivals such as this one in Ecuador were common in agricultural villages. Photo by Roger Harmon

Insights: Learning from the Past

Cultural Currents

An insight to consider in the cultural currents in the Agricultural Wave is that humans continued to develop deep spiritual and religious traditions, often called folk religions, long before the beginning of universal religions such as Christianity. These folk religions continued in agricultural villages well after the spread of universal religions and are still practiced in some areas today. One aspect of the folk religions was their close association of nature with the feminine. In some areas this worldview and religion were goddess focused, celebrating the fecundity and fertility of nature. This awe and reverence for nature and the feminine is reflected in aesthetic expressions as well. The importance of the goddess continued for many thousands of years beginning in the Paleolithic until it was violently suppressed by universal religions in the Urban Wave and into the Modern Wave. Many consider the reverence for Mary, mother of Jesus, as a continuation of the concept of goddess worship. Apparently, unsuppressed sexual expression and lack of warfare were characteristic of the goddess worshiping societies. With the Urban Wave sexuality for women would be curtailed and warfare would become more institutionalized. The feminine influence that prevailed for a time would be suppressed by the masculine powers of dominance, authority, and repression during the Urban Wave. These patriarchal values continue to inform our society to this day.

Questions to Consider

1. Do you think the controversial research that shows the centrality of the goddess in many agricultural societies has any merit? Explain.

CHIEFDOMS

Chiefdoms are more complex, centrally organized, and densely populated agricultural societies in which social life is centered on tribal relationships. Chiefdoms exhibit certain technological, economic, social, political, and cultural features that distinguish them from simpler agricultural and urban societies. The population of chiefdoms could number 50,000 or more people, but not less than several thousand. Clusters of villages were likely to be unified under a district chief of higher rank than local village chiefs; hence, an entire chiefdom might consist of several hundred thousand people in various districts. The earliest chiefdoms were in the Middle East by 5000 BP and in the Western hemisphere by 4000 BP. Although modern chiefdoms have been subsumed into nation-states, they continue to exist today in parts of North and South America, Africa, Southeast Asia, Inner Asia, and some Pacific Islands. Samoa, a part of the Samoan Islands archipelago in the southern Pacific Ocean, is considered a classic chiefdom and still functions that way today.

Ways of Living: Techno-Economic Currents

Chiefdoms had a redistribution type of economic system in which families were required to contribute tribute to a common pool. From this common pool the chief, or a representative of the chief, redistributed these goods and services to those most in need, although a portion was given back to individuals when they participated in public efforts, like building an irrigation canal or temple. These centrally controlled resources were also used to support the occupational specialists, individuals who did not farm or fish but who were scribes, priests, generals, weavers, and bureaucrats. This use of tribute to reimburse specialists encouraged the diversification of social roles and the means to build massive public works projects.[83]

Redistribution was often conducted during a community feast or festival. The person in charge of redistribution had an important economic function in the community and was rewarded with power and prestige in direct proportion to his/her generosity. Sometimes the chief acted as the distributor and attained great personal or family wealth by siphoning surplus from the common tribute pool. At other times the level of gift-giving expectations exceeded what the chief received as compensation for his work, and his/her personal wealth could be drained.[84]

Chiefdoms had a high level of labor specialization that included crafts such as pottery-making, basket-making, weaving, woodcarving, carpentry, and religious or military occupations. The degree of specialization was not as diverse as in urban societies, but more than in simple agricultural societies. Families frequently perfected occupational specialties that were generally hereditary, and knowledge passed on through generations enabled these specialists to become highly skilled. Competent craft workers were sometimes subsidized with surplus from the redistribution center.[85] Some specialists used their skills in the construction of monumental architecture such as irrigation works, terracing of slopes, or temple-mounds.

Human Networks: Social Currents

Social relationships in chiefdoms were a combination of kinship and class-based relations, with most daily social life revolving around kinship ties. Families exercised domestic legal autonomy, overseeing marriages and divorces and enforcing laws dealing with theft and other petty crimes. In chiefdoms there was an increase in the size of residential groups, and no longer were the extended family groups able to be self-sufficient as they had been in less complex agricultural societies. Chiefdoms lacked the complex stratified social classes of urban societies but were not as egalitarian as foraging and simple agricultural societies had been. Kinship groups were ranked in a social hierarchy, with some families having greater social power and prestige than others. Political offices were usually inherited, and certain families of highest rank normally held the most influential political offices. Birth into these prestigious families conveyed special advantages not available to all social members.[86] The cultivators, with communal rights of ownership, still owned the land. This communal ownership changed in the Urban and Modern Waves where a landless peasant class worked for large landowners and was essentially chained to the land.

Establishing Order: Political Currents

As chiefdoms grew, strong leaders called chiefs emerged. The central authority of chiefs allowed them the power to exert control over the entire population as no form of government had done before. **Chiefs**, usually male, but not always, were political leaders with rank and authority. Chiefs had a variety of functions; they united the community, distributed land, recruited members into the military, promulgated war, taxed the populace, policed the local community, conducted judicial activities, controlled surplus goods, and recruited and directed a labor force for various projects. Chiefs could be called upon to adjudicate serious infractions of the law, like major thefts, insults to their chiefly dignity, or homicide. Chiefs judged the guilt or innocence of offenders and could exact penalties for certain offenses without negotiating with members of the offender's family. They mediated between quarreling parties with the goal of reinstating peaceful relations among village members. The chief's authority was independent of family authority, and the chief and officials exerted supremacy over non-kin. At the same time, however, the chief respected the right of families to exercise some autonomous legal authority in family situations.[87] A chief's leadership was irregular and he had no formal legal apparatus, police force, or army to back him up. He governed by the consent of those in secondary leadership positions, and not necessarily by coercion.

Each person in the elite class had a clearly determined place in the chiefly pecking order. This hierarchy was demonstrated by the order of service at feasts and ceremonies; those served first had the highest rank. The chief's office was typically hereditary, although the choice of his successor could be left to family members. In some cases the village as a whole was involved in choosing the new chief from a pool of pos-

An example of a chief, Geronimo (1829-1909), Apache chieftain for the Chiricahua tribe of the southwestern United States.

sible heirs. A chief could amass a great amount of personal wealth and pass this wealth to his heirs. The children of chiefs had greater access to food and other resources, and therefore chiefs tended to have more surviving children than ordinary villagers. This situation led invariably to more people of chiefly status than could actually become chief. As a result, constant competition and intrigue transpired among the heirs.

Deadly conflict between rival chiefs inevitably emerged in this highly competitive, contentious environment. It was not easy for a chief to live to a ripe old age. Many were defeated in war and lost their power—and usually their lives. By killing or capturing a chief, the conqueror took the losing leader's subjects and land. Because chiefdoms were precarious, allies were vital and it behooved every chief to recruit as many allies as possible. To enlist allies, a chief needed to appear strong, and one way of demonstrating strength was to look wealthy. The size and number of monumental buildings, the extravagance of a feast, the quality and uniqueness of gifts all served to prove a chief's strength to his potential allies or foes.[88] Despite the uncertainty of a chief's rule, there was never a shortage of people ready to take on the role of the most powerful chief.

Warfare was more common in chiefdoms than in less complex agricultural societies. Where social ranking of individual families was important, acquiring the prestige associated with military service was a common motivation for soldiers to participate in warfare. One of the main motives for warfare in chiefdoms was to achieve economic and political control over others.

The linkage between what the Earth can sustain, its carrying capacity, and warfare was strong among chiefdoms. For example, around 900 CE in the Southwestern part of present day United States, conflict among warring tribes that had gone on in the region for centuries ceased. For the next 250 years, there was little evidence of warfare anywhere in the Southwest. During this

Mesa Verde cliff dwellings, southwestern USA, this is a UNESCO World Heritage site.

interval a great population expansion occurred, with the population growing five-fold, according to most estimates. Impressive buildings such as those in Chaco Canyon in present-day New Mexico were constructed. This was a time of peace, prosperity, and artistic creativity. But the good times did not last. Beginning around 1150 CE and intensifying into the mid-to late 1200s, archaeological evidence shows a complete social and climate transformation; drought across the region and warfare became ubiquitous and intense. During this interval, virtually everyone in the Southwest moved into defensive villages. The famous Mesa Verde cliff dwellings are examples of defensive sites from this time period. Around 1250 the region's population began to decline markedly; apparently, during the severe drought, the large population exceeded the environment's carrying capacity. Entire areas were completely abandoned and considerable migration to outlying regions took place by 1300. The population of the Southwest withered to about one-fifth of its peak.[89]

Human Expressions: Cultural Currents

Chiefdoms were typically theocratic societies in which the chief was endowed with both religious and secular authority. The chief was most likely the religious leader, while other high-ranking officials were also considered sacred and could be full-time religious specialists. The chief was considered to be an awesome figure who possessed spiritual powers derived from ancestral traditions. The chief's authority was based in part on his/her ability to mediate with ancestral spirits of the past who had an aura of greatness and approached deity status. Since the reigning chief had a direct interest in his prosperity and continuity, the great deity of the chiefdom was usually an ancestor of the reigning chief. Members of the chiefdom thought of themselves as a single people who shared a common language, culture, and traditions. Religious affiliations frequently became institutionalized and were associated with permanent places of worship, such as elaborate temples administrated by a permanent, specialized priesthood, most likely headed by the chief.[90]

Insights: Learning from the Past

Chiefdoms

Humans experience a paradox with chiefdoms. They extract greater resources from the Earth to sustain a growing population, yet they balance this greater exploitation of nature with religious expressions that praise nature's bountifulness and fruits and pray for its continuance. They are deeply connected to nature's cycle of birth, death, and renewal and willingly sacrifice animals, plants, and even humans to appease the spirits that provide for them. Somehow this sacrifice is seen as a balance to the increasing extraction and exploitation of nature by agriculturists. Accompanying the increasing complexity of agricultural societies is the beginning of a separation of human consciousness from nature that widens in the Urban, Modern, and Global waves. Humans begin to test the limits of nature's boundaries.

Artist rendition of Cahokia present day southwestern Illinois, USA.

Questions to Consider

1. Do you think that humans experience a paradox with the development of chiefdoms? Explain.

CAHOKIA: A MISSISSIPPI RIVER SETTLEMENT

Today as you swiftly travel over the confluence of the Mississippi, Illinois, and Missouri rivers on a maze of conjoining concrete interstates and roads, you may find it hard to imagine that many years ago this land was home to the largest city in North America where thousands of people lived. In these fertile lowlands, known as the American Bottom, native Mississippian people developed a rich tapestry of life from 800 to 1300 CE. Cahokia, located eight miles east of present-day St. Louis, Missouri was the largest and most influential settlement north of Mexico. The Cahokian culture stretched across a vast area from the Gulf coast to the Great Lakes, and from the Atlantic coast to present-day Oklahoma in the United States.[91]

Inhabitants of Cahokia traced their line of descent to hunting and gathering Paleo-Indians who traversed the Bering Strait land bridge approximately 15,000 BP. An archaic culture evolved between 8000 BCE to 600 BCE in response to environmental changes and an altered food supply. Smaller game and new edible plants proliferated in milder climates and replaced extinct giant mammals such as the wooly mammoth of the Ice Age. Archaic people, who resided in temporary camps or seasonal villages, were responsible for a number of significant innovations including collecting edible plants, starting basic plant cultivation, hunting smaller game with new tools, and inventing food processing tools.

By 1000 BCE, a Woodland culture flowered throughout most of eastern North America and wound its way to the American Bottom land around 600 BCE. Over the next 1,400 years, to about 800 CE, native people of the American Bottom became ever more rooted to the land; populations rose, new technologies were invented, and by the end of the Woodland era the people produced a significant amount of their food through plant cultivation. During the Mississippian era, from 800 to 1400 CE, there was a greater dependence upon ample corn as a food staple, and the population correspondingly increased. Cultural activity and population peaked between 1000 and 1400 CE. At this time remarkable building projects were completed, trade expanded, farming intensified, and dozens of satellite settlements and smaller villages sprouted up around Cahokia.[92]

Striking cultural parallels between the societies of Cahokia and Mexico were evident. Flat-topped mounds, calendars, and ceramic styles diffused to Cahokia from Mexico. But most importantly, people from the American Bottom acquired knowledge from Mexico of how to grow corn that had originated there 4,000 years earlier.[93] Cahokia was a major cultural center for over 500 years, but by 1400 CE the culture had begun to decline and inhabitants dispersed to outlying areas. Over the years many of the impressive mounds have been lost to the bulldozer, plow, subdivisions, and roads. Today fewer than 80 mounds remain and 68 mounds are presently preserved within a frequently-visited 2,200-acre Cahokia Mounds State Historic Site in southwestern Illinois.

Relationship with Nature: Ecosystem Currents

The American Bottom is a fertile and expansive river flood plain that stretches over 70 miles along the Mississippi River from present day cities of Alton to Chester, Illinois in the Midwestern region of the United States. This area is up to 12 miles wide from the riverbanks, reaching east to the river bluffs. The flood plain is interlaced with creeks, sloughs, lakes, and marshes, and in the spring rich silt from the riverbeds renews nutrients essential for intensive farming. The climate during the Woodland era was similar to today, but from around 800 CE forward over the next 400 years the climate gradually warmed and became quite moist. These favorable conditions fostered a longer growing season than in previous centuries.[94] Also a wealth of natural resources surrounded the Cahokia settlement. White-tailed deer supplied the primary source of meat and skin, while other animal life such as raccoon, turkey, squirrel, wolf, gray fox, black bear, possum, and bobcat, stalked the woodlands. Bountiful fish and other aquatic life—geese, ducks, and migrating birds—served as food for human consumption. Vast prairies stretched north of Cahokia, and these grasses availed as a source for building materials. Immense forests of oaks and hickories furnished excellent hardwoods for well-built canoes, fires, tool making, and sturdy buildings. Ample mineral deposits of granite, sandstone, limestone, and chert were mined and manufactured into tools.[95]

Cahokia reached its population zenith of approximately 20,000 people around 1150 CE. At this time Cahokia surpassed London in population, and it was not until 1800 CE that a city in the area of the present-day state of Illinois exceeded Cahokia in its 1150 CE population count. But around 1200 CE the Cahokia region began its decline. Natural resources were exhausted, and by 1400 CE the formerly vibrant region was virtually empty.[96]

Four types of Mississippian communities in North America were organized according to degrees of complexity. A first type of community was politically complex and densely populated with the capital serving as a political, religious, commercial, and artistic center. Lively neighborhoods, central plazas, mounds and temples graced these communities. In Mississippian history only Cahokia was characteristic of this first type of community. A second type of community was a regional center, where the population could reach into the thousands. Features of this type of community included an impressive plaza, a temple, and several mounds. A third type was a village of several hundred people situated on a body of water such as a lake or stream. Homes flanked a small plaza and usually one mound was evident. Populations swelled seasonally when the village became a processing center for food resources grown or hunted nearby. A fourth type of community was a small hamlet, village, or farmstead that consisted of a few structures surrounding a courtyard. These hamlets were typically clustered around larger communities.[97]

An example of the second type of community was a satellite settlement located on the east side of the Mississippi River in what is now East St. Louis, Illinois. This community consisted of perhaps as many as 45 earthen mounds and small wooden buildings; at the center of the site stood an unusual elliptical enclosure called Cemetery Mound. This building could have been the site of fertility rituals or purification rites, or it could have served as a place for ceremonies to commemorate seasonal renewal and the cosmic cycles of the planets and stars. Constructive and destructive forces were evident at the East St. Louis site as residents abandoned this satellite community by the end of the 12th century, just prior to the decline of Cahokia. The desertion of the 12th century community parallels the current decline of East St. Louis, which now stands as a wasteland of worn-out factories and vacant lots.[98]

Cahokians overextended the environmental limits of the region, causing massive destruction of natural resources and the collapse and abandonment of the settlement. Probably thousands of campfires burned night and day filling the sky with smoke. Harvesting of trees for building and fuel eventually depleted forests and disturbed wildlife for miles around. Overuse by Cahokians, combined with the demand for wood and other resources by people from nearby communities, caused forests and animal resources to be adversely affected. Deforestation upset the ecological balance leading to soil erosion, deforested slopes,

Artist rendition of community life in Cahokia.

clogged streams and silted lakes, and increased flooding of valuable farmland.[99] Cahokians dispersed from the area and created new but less complex settlements elsewhere. Life continued but in a different locale and in less complex societies.

Ways of Living: Techno-Economic Currents

Cahokia based its economy on wide-scale agriculture. Cahokians needed corn, the main cultivated crop, in considerable amounts on a daily basis. Along with several varieties of corn, squash, pumpkins, and sunflowers were grown, and pecans, hickory nuts, blackberries, tubers—such as Jerusalem artichokes—and day lilies were regularly gathered. Leaves and shoots served as ingredients for salads, and were dried for use as refreshing teas and seasonings. Sunflower seeds were roasted, mashed into butter, or boiled to extract the nutritious oil. No animals were domesticated, but hunting and fishing provided needed protein sources from meat. A typical diet consisted of venison—roasted, dried in strips, or mixed with nuts and berries—and corn served in a variety of tasty dishes. Another common dish, vegetable stew, was a savory mixture of squash, nuts and pumpkin, seasoned with salt, animal fat, herbs, and bits of meat.

Like other agricultural people around the world, Cahokians suffered health problems related to nutrition. Their diet—too high in carbohydrates and too low in protein—was nutritionally unbalanced, causing malnourishment and chronic illness including iron deficiency anemia, arrested growth, arthritis, endemic syphilis, and tuberculosis. During lean winter months some even died from starvation. Disease, coupled with a high infant mortality rate, resulted in an average life expectancy of 35 to 40 years. Villager's teeth were worn and prematurely decayed from bits of stone that had been ground into the cornmeal. Other health problems resulted from smoke pollution, cramped living spaces, proximity of human waste, and even urban stress.[100]

The daily life of Cahokians changed with the four seasons. In the summer, neighborhoods bustled with outdoor activity, children played games, women ground corn, and those engaged in hunting, fishing, and farming would come and go. Villagers engaged in a flurry of construction projects and commercial activities. In the autumn, villagers focused on preparing for winter: building projects and repairs were completed, crops were gathered and stored, and meat and fish were preserved. In the dead of winter Cahokians worked and lived mostly indoors, with an emphasis on completing indoor tasks. The spring brought a renewed commotion of activity as the fields were made ready for spring planting, and winter reserves of meat and fish were replenished.[101]

Most Cahokian households were grouped according to kinship affiliation. Individual dwellings were small, rectangular, one-family pole-and-thatch structures with grass mats covering the walls. Residents built their living quarters around a communal plaza. Small circular sweat lodges, community meeting halls, granaries and storage buildings, and menstruation huts were other structures commonly found in the Cahokian village.[102]

Cahokians ably manufactured a wide range of tools using local natural resources. Artisans made a vast number of tools from the mineral chert, a form of flint commonly found in and around limestone beds in Illinois and Missouri. They worked it into a number of commonly used tools—knives, drills, picks, spuds, maces, axes, and projectile points. Chert was formed into specialized hoes for more efficient soil cultivation than simple digging sticks. Sandstone, abrasive like sandpaper, was altered into files to shape, grind, and polish other objects. Granite, found in the Missouri Ozarks and local glacial deposits, was transformed into axes, chunkey stones, and tools for pounding and grinding seeds, nuts, and grains. Galena, ochre, and hematite from southeastern Missouri were ground into paint pigments. Wild game, a source of meat, also provided materials for copious other products: needles were made from catfish spines; turtle shells were tooled into bowls, rattles, combs, and ornaments; animal fat was boiled into soothing ointments; and talons, bones, and feathers of falcons, hawks, and turkeys were fashioned into tools, necklaces, capes, garments, ceremonial headdresses, hair ornaments, and other decorative finery. Snake rattles and bear claws were considered to be powerful symbolic fetishes. The skins of bear, rabbit, deer, raccoon, and opossum were fabricated into bags, blankets, robes, and other practical clothing. Animal hooves were an essential ingredient in medicine and glue, while rattles and sinew served as bindings.[103]

Large quantities of pottery have been recovered at the Cahokia site. Pottery was made from rich clay dug along stream banks. It was dried, and a tempering or strengthening agent, such as crushed mussel shell or limestone, was added. Water was stirred into the mixture, which was then kneaded and formed into a lump. Rolled ropes of clay were built up in a series of snake-like shapes, which were then placed over a shallow bowl base to form a basic frame. Each successive coil was blended and smoothed until a vessel was gradually formed. Potters decorated their crafts by incising fine engraved details on the surface before firing took place. Pottery—pans, bowls, plates, beakers, bottles, and jars—was mainly used for such practical purposes as food preparation, serving, and storage.[104]

Cahokia crafters manufactured important raw materials such as wood and shells into usable objects. Freshwater and marine mollusk shells were crafted into items ranging from common implements to ornaments and burial goods. Thousands of shells, most of them beads, have been recovered. Mussels or fresh water clamshells were more utilitarian than ornamental and were used for everyday objects like scrapers, spoons, and hoes—which were pierced and then securely lashed to wooden handles. Wood, used in stockades, buildings, and countless campfires, was also carved into tools, weapons, handles, baskets, bowls, bows and arrows, and canoes; wood was also an important ingredient in oils, dyes, and foodstuffs. Dugout canoes were chiseled from thick logs of poplar, oak, tulip, and cottonwood. Canoe makers hollowed out these massive logs, which weighed up to 2,000 pounds, by alternately burning, scraping, and chopping a cavity into the log. A finished canoe varied in length from 12 to 70 feet long.

Plants supplied a variety of fiber items; stalks and leaves from tall prairie grasses were lashed together into thatch for houses, temples, and other buildings, and also woven into fine baskets and long-lasting fabrics. Inner bark from the cedar trees and cattails were interlaced into floor mats, sewn into mats covering walls, roofs, and doorways, and twisted into cordage and bowstrings. Animal fur and silky fibers were spun into durable fabrics.[105]

The 120 ceremonial mounds, a spectacular feature of Cahokia, punctuated the village landscape. Spread over a five square mile area, these earthen structures were the largest prehistoric monuments in the Western hemisphere. Most were platform mounds with rectangular, flat tops

Cahokia pottery.

that supported massive ceremonial temples as well as conspicuous homes for the elite. In these ceremonial temples, priests and chiefs performed religious rituals and conducted key administrative duties. Mound engineers applied scientific principles to these technological marvels to assure proper drainage and structural integrity. The mounds were enlarged several times from 900 to 1200 CE.

Monk's Mound hovered over the center of a site on the northern edge of the 40-acre Grand Plaza. The mound covered 14 acres at its base and ascended in four terraces to a staggering height of 100 feet. It took an estimated 19 million man-hours of labor to excavate, carry, and deposit over 22 million cubic feet of earth for this enormous project. Workers laboriously transferred earth from nearby borrow pits to the construction site in woven baskets carried on their backs. Atop Monk's Mound sat a 104 foot long and 48 foot wide wooden building painstakingly decorated with wooden animal figures. From this majestic mound, leaders performed sacred ceremonies, consulted with the spiritual world, or set up housekeeping in these splendid mound buildings. Bones of deceased chiefs were buried in Monk's Mound, a customary tradition among historical tribes in the Southeast part of North America.[106]

Reconstructed Woodhenge in Cahokia.

Monks Mound in Cahokia.

The ruling elite lived on a 200-acre Sacred Precinct that also served as a burial place. Surrounding the Sacred Precinct was a log stockade that reached up to ten or twelve feet tall. This monumental construction project incurred a tremendous cost of time, labor, and materials; an estimated 20,000 logs were used each time the wall was rebuilt. Perhaps the construction of the stockade inadvertently contributed to the decline of Cahokia, since its demands for wood were staggering and further caused depletion of the valuable resource.[107]

Cahokia supported a solar observatory: Woodhenge. It was recently named after the famous archaeological site in England, Stonehenge, which it resembles. Twelve posts laid out at regular circular intervals near the mound made five precise circles that stretched 240 to 480 feet in diameter. The posts could possibly have been used to calculate the position of the sun as the seasons changed; to mark important dates such as harvest festivals, lunar cycles, moon and star alignments, equinoxes and solstices; to place certain mounds and other landmarks; or for farmers to forecast the best planting time.[108]

Cahokia was located at the center of an extensive trade network that linked distant people via the Mississippi River and other waterways. Elite members imported and owned rare, precious, and exotic shells of saltwater animals from the Gulf of Mexico. Archaeologists found Cahokian pottery and hoes at sites ranging from northern Minnesota, eastern Kansas and Oklahoma, lower Ohio River Valley, Arkansas, to Mississippi. Im ported goods found at the sites included copper from Lake Superior, mica from southern Appalachian Mountains, shells from the Atlantic and Gulf coasts, and galena, ocher, hematite, chert, fluorite, and quartz from the Midwest.[109]

Human Networks: Social Currents

Cahokia had a complex community organization centered on kinship ties, marriage bonds, and other alliances. The family served as the basis of neighborhood and community organization with members of several generations living in clusters of family dwellings. Each individual contributed according to gender, age, and status with his/her social status, gender, age, and kinship affiliation generally shaping each person's specific role in life. Small neighborhoods of families were fairly self-sufficient with each having their own facilities for sweat lodges, meetinghouses, granaries, menstrual huts, and artisans.[110]

A four-tiered socio-political hierarchical system structured Cahokian's life. At the top of the hierarchy was the supreme power, the chief. The chief was believed to have divine affiliation, which further consolidated his power and control over food surpluses. With the chief in the elite class were his close relatives and other associates who generally lived in detached areas from the general population. At the second level were the chief's advisors or sub-chiefs who exercised authority over heads of family clans. They designed and supervised agricultural and building projects. The third level was composed of community leaders who were the heads of family clans and had control over many of the daily functions of the family. And at the fourth level, and by far the largest group, were the commoners who toiled in the fields, constructed large monuments, and manufactured goods needed to support their own daily needs, society at large, and the demanding lifestyle of the elite class.[111] The elites erected the stockade apparently as a barrier to ensure social isolation and exclusiveness for their class while limiting access by the commoners.

Women and men had different gender roles. Women's responsibilities and duties centered on the domestic sphere: child rearing, crop cultivation, the gathering of plants, processing of animal skins, and pottery-making. Men constructed monumental buildings, hunted, and made tools needed for the hunt. Both were personally

Artist rendition of community life in Cahokia.

involved in socializing the youth into their designated social roles.[112]

Establishing Order: Political Currents

A theocratic chief who claimed divine power governed Cahokians. The chief, called the "great Sun," sat atop a well-defined social order and was thought to be brother of the sun. The chief directed urban planning, designated areas for special use, mobilized work forces for vast building projects, and oversaw a complex trade network.[113]

Evidence of the existence of warfare is largely circumstantial. For example, the stockade erected around the Sacred Precinct had been rebuilt three times in a 100-year period, although it is not conclusive whether the reconstruction was due to enemy attacks or general deterioration. The stockade appears to have been constructed for defensive purposes with built-in platforms from which warriors launched arrows at would be attackers. The wall may also have been erected to provide a social barrier for isolating and protecting the Sacred Precinct. During time of war, commoners may have been admitted to this otherwise restricted area.[114]

Human Expressions: Cultural Currents

Cahokians had a shared system of integral beliefs, which gave meaning and purpose to their lives and explained the grand scheme of existence. Although Cahokians did not have a written language, interpretation of their worldview was extracted from archeological artifacts. They recognized a natural order in the Universe, and attempted to live in harmony with it. They saw the world as composed of opposing forces—dark and light, order and anarchy, good, which is rewarded, and evil, punished. The nonmaterial world was imagined to have three levels: the light Upper World was seen to be steady and predictable; the dark Lower World, unstable and chaotic; and This World, where people struggle to balance perfection and utter confusion. The swift falcon and powerful eagle symbolized the Upper World. Icons of the Lower World were frogs, fish, lizards, and snakes, with the beaver, owl, and cougar characteristic of both worlds. The red cedar—which is resistant to disease and decay, has an evergreen quality, a deep red color, and a lasting fragrance—was sacred and symbolized a long, fulfilling life.[115]

From the evidence found in caves, it is likely that Cahokians believed in an afterlife. They buried their dead with lavish trappings and honored them with elaborate rituals. Those with high status had the most ornate graves; one example, Mound 72, is 140 feet long, 70 feet wide, and six feet high. This mound, supporting ceremonial activity from 950 to 1050 CE, was built over three smaller mounds that enveloped surface burials and a series of burial pits. Mound 72 holds a spectacular array of grave goods and the remains of 300 people. The dead were borne to graves on litters or wrapped in mats or blankets. Others were tossed into grave pits, which signified a lower status. The person with the highest

Engraved beaker, Cahokia.

status in Mound 72 was the obvious leader, a 40-year-old man laid upon a bird-shaped platform sprinkled with nearly 20,000 marine shell beads. Around him were buried six young men and women, perhaps retainers or relatives who appear to have been sacrificed. Piled atop the six bodies were caches of mica, rolled sheets of copper, 15 chunkey stones, 800 perfect flint projectiles points, and beads made from Gulf shells. Another grave held skeletons of four men without heads or hands, their arms overlapped across their chest. This may represent a ritual sacrifice of vassals or retainers who accompanied their leader to his death. Although how and why people were sacrificed remains a mystery, the beliefs may have been similar to those of 17th and 18th century Natchez Indians who volunteered to be sacrificed upon their leader's death in order to raise his/her own status or the family's status. In another nearby pit the remains of 53 young, sacrificed women, between the ages of 15 and 25 years old, were neatly arranged in two rows and buried three deep.[116]

Cahokians expressed their artistic talents in a variety of forms. Many of the motifs decorating art objects and pottery symbolized life, fertility, strength, and the order of the Universe. Many beads and other objects carved from mica, bauxite, and various rocks and minerals depicted animal and human figures. These objects were used for rituals and then buried with people of high status. From these artistic objects, evidence of elaborate hairstyles, lively fashions, exquisite clothing, tattooing, and body painting were found. Tattooing was common for both men and women, with faces and even an entire body painted with geometric patterns.

Cahokians enjoyed music, song, and dance at festivals. Musicians created sounds with rattles, whistles, and flute-like instruments. Songs consisted of lyrics and chants, sung responsively and accompanied by repetitive monotone melodies. Dancing was basic and symbolic. For example, weaving lines of people mimicked a snake in a fertility dance ritual. Although the stockade generally excluded commoners, apparently the

Birdman Tablet, Cahokia.

Mother and child, Cahokia.

general population was admitted to this area for special ceremonial occasions or market days.[117]

Games were a community pastime for Cahokians. They regularly engaged in all-consuming games of chance and skill. Shell guessing games, gambling with dice, and attempting to catch hollow bones on tips of pointed tethered sticks were just a few of the many games regularly played. Hoop and pole was a popular stick ball game similar to lacrosse. But the premier sport was chunkey, a contest in which two players threw the javelin at a rolling, concave stone and attempted to mark the place where it would come to a stop. Chunkey engaged the entire community. Even the youngest Cahokians played with miniature chunkey stones, and some leaders were even buried with puck-like objects. They took their sports very seriously, and betting on chunkey was a common leisure activity. Sometimes matches continued throughout the day, and heavy gamblers could lose all their worldly possessions by making a wrong bet.[118]

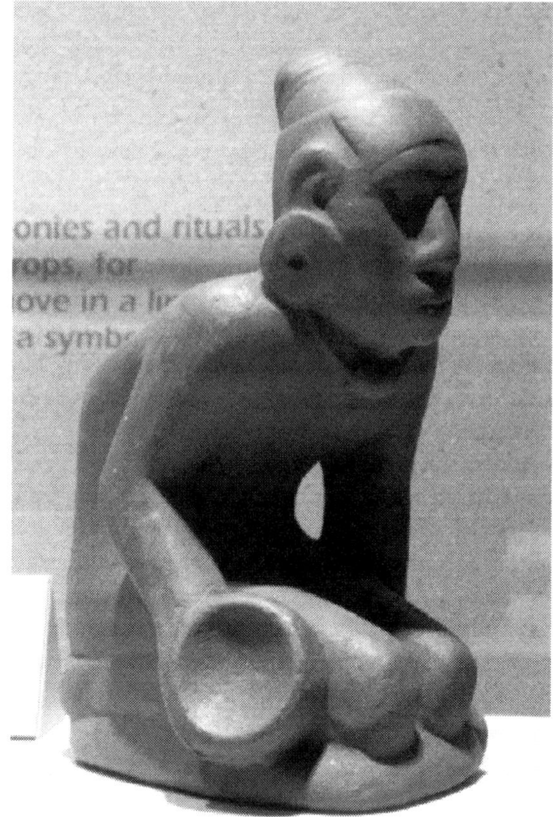

Chunkey Player, flint clay figurine.

Insights: Learning from the Past

Cahokia

Cahokia's decline as a vibrant, creative society is not completely understood. Excavations have not yielded signs of an epidemic, invasion, or natural disaster; thus a catastrophic occurrence cannot account for the demise of an entire society. Using our systems approach, perhaps a convergence of a number of factors combined to usher in the destruction of the society. Around 1250 CE a shift in weather patterns brought a cooler, drier climate and more frequent droughts. Earlier and later frosts led to a shorter growing season, while more crop failures and reduced crop yields accompanied the spread of contagious diseases along with pervasive malnourishment and starvation. An unrelenting exploitation of land, forests, and animal habitats contributed to environmental collapse. The area reached its environmental limits around 1250 CE and thereafter was unable to sustain its sizable population. As food and other natural resources became scarce, economic disruption and social unrest destabilized the society. The battle over scarce resources may have led to wars between Cahokia and its neighbors. Eventually Cahokia's centralized political power, economic wealth, and social network eroded as groups became more autonomous and scattered.[119] It appears that Cahokia's inhabitants dispersed into smaller groups and established smaller communities and new ways of life outside the previous environs.

Cahokia experienced the creative energy of a complex, sophisticated society, and also the destructive energy of decline, erosion and collapse. But the cycle did not end at the point of decline.

As the population dispersed, new societies were constructed and the process began anew, in this case in a different form.

Questions to Consider

1. Is there a chance that your nation could decline like Cahokia's? What might be some of the contributing factors?

Insights: Learning from the Past

THE AGRICULTURAL WAVE: CONCLUDING INSIGHTS

There are many valuable insights to be learned from the Agricultural Wave, and several have already been touched upon in the preceding sections. But I would like to expand upon a theme already mentioned in the earlier part of this chapter: our modern disconnect with the food we eat. For all but a tiny fraction of our human existence, we humans have lived close to nature, producing food for our local, immediate consumption. This has changed drastically in the last 50 years or so, and I believe this disconnect has dire consequences. Using our systems approach, there are several interconnected consequences resulting from this profound detachment. One, farming as an occupation does not garner much recognition or status. Very few young people proudly proclaim that they want to be a farmer when they grow up. Why has such an important occupation been degraded over the past generation? Perhaps, the struggle to "achieve a better life" propelled children and grandchildren of farmers off the land and into the city. They had first-hand memories or had heard stories of their parents or grandparents working hard physically and mentally seven days a week. Jobs in the city were supposed to be better, easier and have higher status. We can see the same mindset at work in China today, as millions of peasant farmers flock to the cities to "have a better life." But who is going to grow our food?

This leads us to the second consequence. For decades in the United States, industrial agriculture has stepped to the plate to grow our food on large industrialized farming operations using lots of irrigation and plenty of chemical fertilizers and pesticides, and raising animals—laced with antibiotics—inhumanely in large-scale feed lots. Yet, this farming approach has resulted in calamitous environmental and health repercussions. Because of the depletion of underground water reservoirs and worn-out soils from chemical overuse, this form of industrial agriculture is unsustainable and cannot continue.

A third consequence is that the crops grown in the United States—mainly corn, soy beans, and wheat—have been processed into low-cost, low-nutrition "foods" that have contributed to an epidemic of obesity and health-related illnesses associated with a "Western" diet. Our ancestors never would have understood this paradox—overfed but undernourished people! We are growing food, but it is not keeping us healthy, at least in the U.S.; instead, it is making us sick. Therefore, our industrial agricultural system is on the road to collapse, going the way of extinction that we repeatedly see in world history.

What will replace it? It is beyond the scope of this short insight section to address this question, but suffice it to say that we can learn from the people of the Agricultural Wave. Agriculture was/is intricately connected to their daily lives—their religious rituals, social celebrations, their patterns of work, and so on. We modern folk, on the other hand, have disconnected ourselves from growing our own food. Perhaps, for our own well-being, we might reconsider and connect ourselves, once again, to what we grow.

Questions to Consider

1. What is your reaction to the message in the concluding insight section?

In the next chapter we find that some villages around the world grew in population and complexity to the point that a transition to a different way of life, a new wave, developed: the Urban Wave.

ENDNOTES

1. Naomi F. Miller, "The Origins of Plant Cultivation in the Near East" in *The Origins of Agriculture: An International Perspective*, eds. C. Wesley Cowan and Patty Jo Watson (Washington D.C.: Smithsonian Institution Press, 1992), p. 39.
2. John A. J. Gowlett, *Ascent to Civilization: The Archaeology of Early Humans* (New York: McGraw Hill, Inc. 1993), p. 156. It is common to see the distinction Old World (Europe, Africa, Asia) and New World (Western hemisphere or North and South America) used. I prefer to use the terms Western hemisphere and Afro/Eurasia. Actually the "worlds" are the same age, and the terms "old" and "new" are terminology used in traditional world history.
3. Richard S. MacNeish, *The Origins of Agriculture and Settled Life* (Norman, OK: University of Oklahoma Press, 1991), p. 20-21.
4. Clive Ponting, *A Green History of the World* (New York: Penguin Books, 1991), p. 45; Alexander Alland Jr. *To Be Human: An Introduction to Anthropology* (New York: Alfred A. Knopf, 1980), p. 250-251; Robert P. Clark, *The Global Imperative: An Interpretive History of the Spread of Humankind* (Boulder: Westview Press, 1997), p. 37; and Economist staff writer, "The Origins of Agriculture: Bringing Home the Harvest," *Economist* (Nov. 15, 1997), p. 88-89.
5. Alland, *To Be Human*, p. 251; Ponting, *Green History*, p. 49; Gary W. Crawford, "Prehistoric Plant Domestication in East Asia," in *Origin of Agriculture*, eds. Cowan and Watson, chapter 7 or chapter 2; and Jack R. Harland, "Indigenous

African Agriculture," in *Origins of Agriculture*, eds. Cowan and Watson, p. 146.

6. Gary W. Crawford, "Plant Domestication in East Asia," in *Origins of Agriculture* eds. Cowan and Watson, p. 7, or chapter 2.
7. Ponting, *Green History*, p. 51.
8. Emily McClung de Tapia, "The Origin of Agriculture in Mesoamerica and Central America," *In Origins of Agriculture*, eds. Cowan and Watson; and Deborah Pearsall, "The Origins of Plant Cultivation in South America," in *Origin of Agriculture*, eds. Cowan and Watson, chapters 8 and 9.
9. Harland, "Indigenous African Agriculture," in *Origins of Agriculture*, eds. Cowan and Watson, p. 69 and 143.
10. I. J. Thorpe, *The Origins of Agriculture in Europe* (London: Routledge, 1996), p. 1; and William A. Haviland, *Cultural Anthropology* (Fort Worth: Holt, Rinehart and Winston, 1990), p. 225.
11. V. Gordon Childe is the main proponent of this theory. Anne Birgitte Gebauer and T. Douglas Price, "Foragers to Farmers: An Introduction," in *Transitions to Agriculture in Prehistory* eds. Anne Birgitte Gebauer and Douglas T. Price, (Madison: Prehistory Press, 1992), p. 1-2.
12. Robert J. Braidwood is the primary proponent of this theory. Robert J. Braidwood, "The Agricultural Revolution," in Dennis Sherman, et.al., *World Civilizations: Sources, Images, and Interpretations* (New York: McGraw-Hill, Inc., 1994), p. 20-22; Thorpe, *Origins Agriculture in Europe*, p. 2; Alland, *To Be Human*, p. 247; and Gebauer and Price, "Foragers to Farmers," in *Transition to Agriculture*, eds. Gebauer and Pride, p. 2.
13. Lewis Binford is the main proponent of this theory. Gebauer and Price, "Foragers to Farmers," in *Transition to Agriculture*, eds. Gebauer and Pride, p. 2; Thorpe, *Origins Agriculture in Europe*, p. 3; and Robert J. Wenke, *Patterns in Prehistory* (New York: Oxford University Press, 1984), p. 189-191.
14. Kent Flannery is the main proponent of this theory. Gebauer and Price, "Foragers to Farmers," in *Transition to Agriculture*, eds. Gebauer and Pride p. 2-3; and Alland, *To Be Human*, p. 248.
15. Marvin Harris is the main proponent of this theory. Thorpe, *Origins Agriculture in Europe*, p. 4.
16. David Rindos, *The Origins of Agriculture: An Evolutionary Perspective* (Orlando: Academic Press, 1984), p. xiv and 99.
17. Rindos, *Origins of Agriculture*, p. 100.
18. Steve Budiansky, *The Covenant of the Wild* (New York: William Morrow and Company, Inc., 1992).
19. Thorpe, *Origins Agriculture in Europe*, p. 1; Gebauer and Price, "Foragers to Farmers," in *Transition to Agriculture*, eds. Gebauer and Pride, p. 3.
20. T. Douglas Price, "Social Inequality at the Origins of Agriculture," in *Foundations of Social Inequality*, eds. T. Douglas Price and Gary M. Feinman, (New York: Plenum Press, 1995), p. 138, 144 and 146.
21. Margaret Ehrenberg, *Women in Prehistory* (Norman, OK: University of Oklahoma Press, 1989), p. 81; and Gerhard Lenski and Jean Lenski, *Human Societies: An Introduction to Macrosociology* (New York: McGraw-Hill, 1982), p. 155.
22. John A. J. Gowlett, *Ascent to Civilization: The Archaeology of Early Humans* (New York: McGraw Hill, Inc., 1993), p. 154.

23. Haviland, *Cultural Anthropology*, p. 194; and Lenski, *Human Societies*, p. 135.
24. Fagan, *World Prehistory*, p. 123; Ponting, *Green History*, p. 37; Lester J.Bilsky, *Historical Ecology: Essays on Environmental and Social Change* (Port Washington, NY: National University Press, 1980), p. 39; and Crapo, *Cultural Anthropology*, p. 284.
25. LeBlanc, *Constant Battles*, p. 134.
26. Wenke, *Patterns in Prehistory*, p. 156; Robert P. Clark, *The Global Imperative: An Interpretive History of the Spread of Humankind* (Boulder: Westview Press, 1997), p. 44-45; and Rindos, *Origins of Agriculture*, p. 139.
27. Niles Eldredge, Niles, *Dominion*, (New York: Henry Holt and Company, 1995), p. 103; and Colin Trudge, *The Time Before History: 5 Million Years of Human Impact* (New York: Scribner, 1996), p. 278-279.
28. Steven A. LeBlanc with Katherine E. Register, *Constant Battles: The Myth of the Peaceful, Noble Savage*, (New York: St. Martin's Press, 2003), p. 149.
29. LeBlanc, *Constant Battles*, p. 156.
30. Brian Swimme and Thomas Berry, *The Universe Story* (San Francisco: Harper Collins, 1992), p. 168; and Marija Gimbutas, *The Language of the Goddess* (San Francisco: Harper Collins, 1989), p. xiii.
31. Ehrenberg, *Women in Prehistory*, p. 86; and Fagan, *World Prehistory*, p. 123.
32. Wenke, *Patterns in Prehistory*, p.156 and 160; and Haviland, *Cultural Anthropology*, p. 209.
33. Trudge, *Time Before History*, p. 266-267; Clark, *Global Imperative*, p. 47; Haviland, *Cultural Anthropology*, p. 224; and William H. McNeill, *Plagues and People* (Garden City, NY: Anchor Press/Doubleday, 1976), p. 37.
34. Ernestine Friedl, *Women and Men: An Anthropologist's View* (New York: Holt, Rinehart, and Winston, 1975), p. 47 and 53-54; and Crapo, *Cultural Anthropology*, p. 60.
35. Crapo, *Cultural Anthropology*, p. 60.
36. Alland, *To Be Human*, p. 241.
37. Clark, *Global Imperative*, p. 44.
38. Ponting, *Green History*, p. 44; Trudge, *Time Before History*, p. 270; Bernard G. Campbell, *Humankind Emerging* (Glenview, Illinois: Scott Foresman and Co., 1988), p. 469.
39. Sahlins, *Stone Age Economics*, 187-190; and Crapo, *Cultural Anthropology*, 79.
40. Lenski, *Human Societies*, p. 140, 143, and 145; Crapo, *Cultural Anthropology*, p. 59; Ehrenberg, *Women in Prehistory*, p. 87; and Clark, *Global Imperative*, p. 45.
41. Gowlett, *Ascent to Civilization*, p. 164-165; and Ehrenberg, *Women in Prehistory*, p. 88.
42. Elizabeth Wayland Barber, *Women's Work: The First 20,000 Years* (New York: W.W. Norton & Company, 1994), p. 30 and 96; and Clark, *Global Imperative*, p. 46.
43. Barber, *Women's Work*, p. 44 and 59.
44. Clark, *Global Imperative*, p. 49; and Crapo, *Cultural Anthropology*, p. 285.
45. Crapo, *Cultural Anthropology*, p. 74.
46. Friedl, *Women and Men*, p. 49; and Gowlett, *Ascent to Civilization*, p. 177.
47. Crapo, *Cultural Anthropology*, p. 284-285.
48. Friedl, *Women and Men*, p. 87 and 89.
49. Friedl, *Women and Men*, p. 52 and 87.
50. Friedl, *Women and Men*, p. 92-93.
51. Friedl, *Women and Men*, p. 87 and 94-95.
52. Ehrenberg, *Women and Prehistory*, p. 89 and 105-106; and Friedl, *Women and Men*, p. 48.

53. Friedl, *Women and Men*, p. 91-92.
54. Friedl, *Women and Men*, p. 85.
55. Ehrenberg, *Women and Prehistory*, p. 81.
56. Ehrenberg, *Women and Prehistory*, p. 105-106; Friedl, *Women and Men*, p. 96.
57. Crapo, *Cultural Anthropology*, p. 285; and Lenski, *Human Societies*, p. 156
58. T. Douglas Price, "Social Inequality," in *Foundations*, eds. Price and Feinman, p. 130; and Crapo, *Cultural Anthropology*, p. 83.
59. Friedl, *Women and Men*, p. 60 and 82.
60. Friedl, *Women and Men*, p. 83-84.
61. Haviland, *Cultural Anthropology*, p. 324; and Crapo, *Cultural Anthropology*, p. 91 and 285.
62. Ruth Whitehouse and John Wilkins, *The Making of Civilization* (New York: Alfred A. Knopf, 1986), p. 90; Crapo, *Cultural Anthropology*, p. 285 and 92; and Haviland, *Cultural Anthropology*, p. 324.
63. Crapo, *Cultural Anthropology*, p. 98.
64. Whitehouse and Wilkins, *Making of Civilizations*, p. 112; and Friedl, *Women and Men*, p. 50 and 64.
65. LeBlanc, *Constant Battles*, p. 143-144.
66. Crapo, *Cultural Anthropology*, p. 100.
67. LeBlanc, *Constant Battles*, p. 147.
68. LeBlanc, *Constant Battles*, p. 147.
69. Lenski, *Human Societies*, p. 41; Swimme and Berry, *Universe Story*, p. 175; Marija Gimbutas, *The Civilization of the Goddess* (SanFrancisco: Harper Collins Press, 1991), p. 48; and Riane Eisler, *The Chalice and the Blade: Our History, Our Future* (San Francisco: Harper Collins, 1989), p. 13.
70. LeBlanc, *Constant Battles*, p. 155.
71. LeBlanc, *Constant Battles*, p. 155-156.
72. LeBlanc, *Constant Battles*, p. 151.
73. LeBlanc, *Constant Battles*, p. 151.
74. Crapo, *Cultural Anthropology*, p. 285.
75. Haviland, *Cultural Anthropology*, p. 360-361; and Crapo, *Cultural Anthropology*, p. 215.
76. Friedl, Women and Men, p. 52, 75-76, and 79.
77. Gimbutas, *Civilization*, p. 222 and x; and Eisler, *Chalice and Blade*, p. 23.
78. Gimbutas, *Civilization*, p. x; and Swimme and Berry, *Universe Story*, p. 175.
79. Gimbutas, *Civilization*, p. 42, 228, 236, and 243.
80. Haviland, *Cultural Anthropology*, p. 221; and Gimbutas, *Civilization*, p. 9 and 326.
81. Ehrenberg, *Women in Prehistory*, p. 73.
82. Eisler, *Chalice and Blade*, p. 17; and Gimbutas, *Civilization*, p. vii and 243
83. LeBlanc, *Constant Battles*, p. 159
84. Whitehouse and Wilkins, *Making of Civilization*, p. 52; and Crapo, *Cultural Anthropology*, p. 92 and 287.
85. Elman R. Service, *Primitive Social Organization: An Evolutionary Perspective* (New York: Random House, 1965), p. 148.
86. Whitehouse and Wilkins, *Making of Civilization*, p. 53; Crapo, *Cultural Anthropology*, p. 92 and 287-288; and Service, *Social Organization*, p. 149 and 164-165.
87. Whitehouse and Wilkins, *Making Civilization*, p. 90; Haviland, *Cultural Anthropology*, p. 328; Service, *Social Organization*, p. 94 and 97; and Crapo, *Cultural Anthropology*, p. 92 and 287.
88. LeBlanc, *Constant Battles*, p. 160 and 161.
89. LeBlanc, *Constant Battles*, p. 147-148.
90. Haviland, *Cultural Anthropology*, p. 360-361; and Service, *Social Organization*, p. 171.

91. William R. Iseminger, "Mighty Cahokia," in *Archeology* Vol. 49, No. 3 (May/June, 1996), p. 32; and Robert Silverberg, *The Mound Builders* (Athens: Ohio University Press, 1967), p. 235.
92. Iseminger, "Cahokia," *Archeology*, p. 32-33; and Claudia Gellman Mink, *Cahokia: City of the Sun* (Collinsville, IL: Cahokia Mounds Museum Society, 1992), p. 12, and 16-17.
93. Iseminger, "Cahokia," *Archeology*, p. 32; and Mink, *Cahokia*, p. 3.
94. Mink, *Cahokia*, p. 9; and Iseminger, "Cahokia," *Archeology*, p. 32.
95. Mink, *Cahokia*, p. 9.
96. Mink, *Cahokia*, p. 4; and Iseminger, "Cahokia," *Archeology*, p. 32. Population estimates between 1050 and 1150 C.E. range from 8,000 to 40,000, with 20,000 an average.
97. Mink, *Cahokia*, p. 19-20.
98. John E. Kelly, "East St. Louis Yields a Satellite Settlement," *Archeology* Vol. 49, No. 3 (May/June, 1996), p. 38.
99. Mink, *Cahokia*, p. 56-57; and Iseminger, "Cahokia," *Archaeology*, p. 37.
100. Mink, *Cahokia*, p. 46-47 and 67.
101. Mink, *Cahokia*, p. 38-39 and 45.
102. Iseminger, "Cahokia," *Archeology*, p. 35.
103. Mink, *Cahokia*, p. 53-54, and 57
104. Mink, *Cahokia*, p. 54-55.
105. Mink, *Cahokia*, p. 55-57.
106. Mink, *Cahokia*, p. 24-25; and Iseminger, "Cahokia," *Archeology*, p. 33.
107. Iseminger, "Cahokia," *Archeology*, p. 32 and 37.
108. Silverberg, *Mound Builders*, p. 257; Mink, *Cahokia*, p. 33; and Iseminger, "Cahokia," *Archeology*, p. 35.
109. Mink, *Cahokia*, p. 9; and Iseminger, "Cahokia," *Archeology*, p. 33.
110. Mink, *Cahokia*, p. 38 and 45.
111. Mink, *Cahokia*, p. 44.
112. Mink, *Cahokia*, p. 45.
113. Mink, *Cahokia*, p. 21.
114. Iseminger, "Cahokia," *Archeology*, p. 37.
115. Mink, *Cahokia*, p. 49.
116. Mink, *Cahokia*, p. 50; and Iseminger, "Cahokia," *Archeology*, p. 34-35.
117. Mink, *Cahokia*, p. 47 and 54; and Iseminger, "Cahokia," *Archeology*, p. 37.
118. Mink, *Cahokia*, p. 48.
119. Mink, *Cahokia*, p. 67; and Iseminger, "Cahokia," *Archeology*, p. 37.

Chapter 6

People Create Civilizations: The Urban Wave

"Civilization is a stream with banks. The stream is sometimes filled with blood from people killing, stealing, shouting and doing the things historians usually record, while on the banks, unnoticed, people build homes, make love, raise children, sing songs, write poetry and even whittle statues. The story of civilization is what happened on the banks."

— Will Durant, *The History of Civilization*

AN INTRODUCTION TO THE URBAN WAVE

The Urban Wave marks a significant turning point in our history: urbanization and civilization co-evolve. Briefly stated, **civilization** designates a loose configuration of peoples who share a common culture or political rule and usually form urban centers in which large populations live. Civilizations are not static entities but living societies that shift over time, have fluid boundaries, and interact with other societies to exchange ideas, goods, and people. The word civilization comes from the Latin word meaning city; therefore the terms civilization and urban society will be used interchangeably in this chapter. The transition to the Urban Wave marks momentous changes in the way societies are organized. Urban societies mark a distinct break from agricultural and foraging societies. The diagram on the next page shows some of the characteristics of urban societies.[1]

The transition to urban living did not radiate out smoothly from one single location, but developed independently in numerous autonomous zones around the world. This transition first occurred around 3500 BCE in Mesopotamia in the Middle East; slightly later in Egypt along the Nile River Valley; in the Indus River valley of India around 2500 BCE; in the Huang Ho (Yellow) River valley of China about 2200 BCE; on the Greek peninsula around 2000 BCE; and among the Olmecs in Mesoamerica around 1000 BCE.[2]

The Urban Wave covers a large period of time and encompasses diverse peoples and environments. Nevertheless, despite the unique characteristics of each individual civilization, the process of urbanization has similar underlying characteristics wherever it occurs, as evidenced by the similar ways in which urban societies in the Western and Eastern hemispheres develop. Since this vast period of time in world history cannot be covered in-depth in this chapter, after this introduction the focus in Part I will be to call attention to the commonalities of the era, in Part II an overview of pastoral societies, and in Part III a brief description of the historical eras and major civilizations of the period.

Change and Continuity

During the beginning of the Urban Wave, only a minority of people actually lived in the city, but the city acted as the center of change and power, gradually extending its influence to surrounding areas. The point of origin of an urban society, where early urban development takes place, is called the **core** in this world history. An urban core is a city, or city-state at the center of its larger surrounding area called the **periphery**. The city dominates its surrounding periphery regions by extracting raw materials, agricultural produce, and forced labor from these areas to provide for the urban inhabitants' many needs ranging from necessities to luxuries. The city's rulers protect both areas from external threat and maintain internal law and order by legalized force.

Core urban areas experienced significant change, but in the periphery, local people experienced both change and continuity. Peasant farmers were drawn into the web of urban development by supplying part of their crop as tribute or tax payments to the ruling urban elites. This surplus crop was then sold to urban dwellers who no longer grew their own food. Peasant workloads intensified as they were required to produce more economic surplus to cover their tribute payments while growing enough food to provide for their families and sell or barter a portion at the local market. Peasants were also routinely called upon or forced by rulers to contribute labor—**corvee labor**—for the construction of monumental projects built by the state. However, kinship relations, family patterns, social rituals, and religious expression continued relatively unchanged in the peasant's daily life, more akin to the social organization in the Agricultural Wave.

Some areas remained beyond the periphery; not incorporated into the web of core/periphery urban interaction, they were considered **external** to that relationship and continued as foragers, horticultural villagers, chiefdoms, or pastoral societies. They carried on their lives relatively unaffected by changes radiating from urban centers.

How the Urban Wave developed has perplexed anthropologists, historians and others for decades. Single cause explanations do not adequately explain why this profound and intricate transformation occurs. Several such theories are outlined below. As we shall see, a systems approach, which describes the interaction of relevant variables, offers the most comprehensive explanation for this complex development.[3]

The "hydraulic hypothesis," an early theory proposed by Karl Wittfogel, suggested that urban societies arose in arid environments and depended upon small-scale irrigation systems in order to grow crops. Construction of these irrigation networks increased in complexity as time progressed from a system of small dikes and canals to larger and more sophisticated irrigation networks. Planning, constructing, maintaining, and protecting these complex irrigation networks

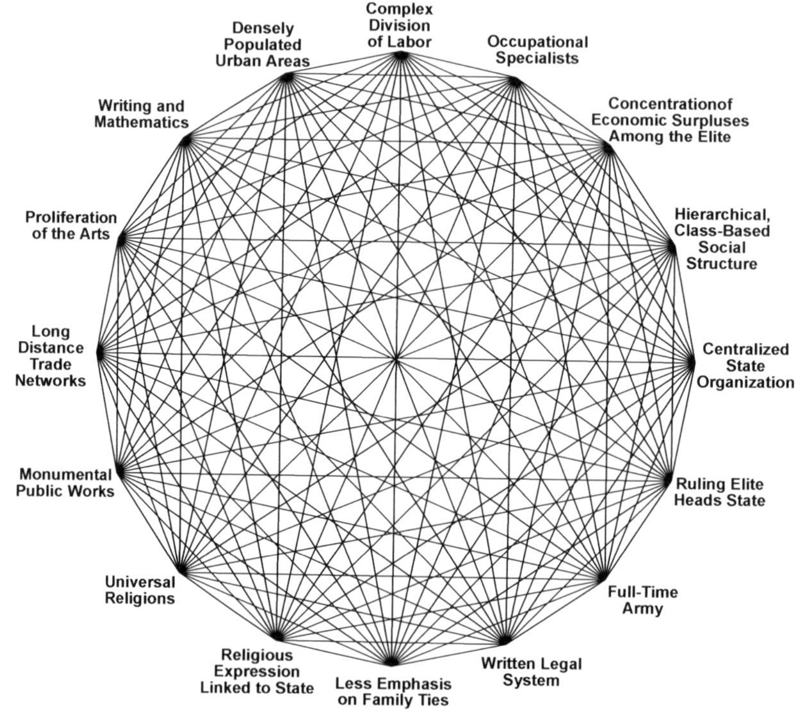

were necessary for their proper functioning. Organization on such a large scale called for some form of central political authority to direct it, hence large-scale governments formed to manage the irrigation and flood control projects. This formal, centralized political organization, according to Wittfogel, was the most important step in the formation of urban civilizations.[4]

Another theory cites population growth as the prime cause for the emergence of urban societies. Construction of irrigation networks and intensification of agriculture was a response to population growth. Like the theory that population pressure caused the development of agriculture, this theory asserts that populations have a natural tendency to expand unless restrained by a limited food supply, disease, or natural predators. As rapid population expansion occurred, new economic and social organizations took shape to accommodate the growth. Though, population growth alone, according to critics of this theory, was not enough to spark the emergence of civilization.[5]

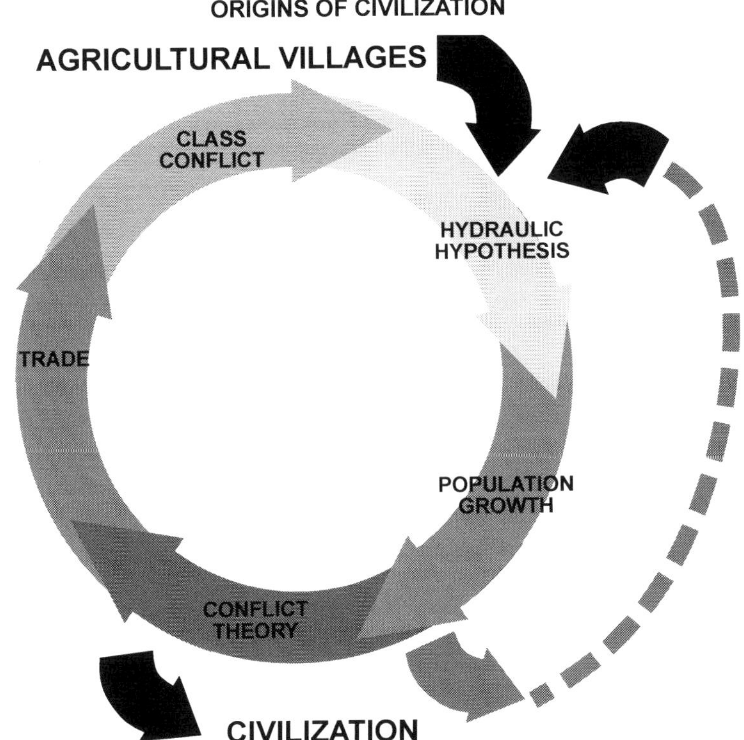

Related to the population growth theory is the "conflict theory" that maintains that civilizations developed where geographical barriers—mountains, deserts, seas, or neighboring populations—hemmed in populations. When population pressures reached a certain point and populations could not expand, they competed with each other for scarce resources. This competition led internally to social stratification in which powerful elite controlled scarce resources. The elite exacted tribute or taxes from the non-elite majority and thus became a powerful centralized political authority. Competition for scarce resources also led to external warfare and conquest. Warfare and conquest required an elaborate centralized political organization to obtain a steady supply of scarce resources by force. Leaders organizing warfare seized permanent authority by eliminating competitors and eventually formed an established elite class of powerful military officials. Militarily dominant states expanded at the expense of their less dominant neighbors who lacked centralized political and military organization. The less powerful states were thus dominated by their more powerful conquerors.[6]

Another theory attributes local and long-distance trade as the primary stimulus for the development of urban societies. Trade required a centrally organized state to control the appropriation, transport, protection, and distribution of raw materials and other goods. Also, money, which was now needed as the medium for exchange, required a central authority to establish its value for the orderly transfer of goods. In some cases, this centrally organized state controlled the production of specialty crafts, especially luxury goods.[7]

Marxist theorists postulate that class conflict or the maintenance of hierarchical status by elites over commoners is a primary cause of urbanization. They maintain that changes in social institutions preceded changes in technology, subsistence patterns, trade, and population increases. Hence, from this point of view, changes in social organization and class conflict were the key to the urbanization of societies.[8]

The search for one theory to explain urban development and a transition to the Urban Wave is unnecessary, if not impossible. All of the interacting variables in the above theories when synthesized together help explain this complex urbanization process. From a holistic perspective, the urbanization process ushered in deep structural changes that eventually reinforced each other enough to generate change to an urban way of life.

Questions to Consider

1. Which of the civilization origination theories described above seems most plausible to you? Why?

Insights: Learning from the Past

The Urban Wave

The term "civilization" has multiple and often confusing meanings. I will be using the term to describe an urban way of life and the characteristics that make it unique. However, the term civilization is also used in a way to connote a mode of living that is somehow superior or preferable to that of communal or agricultural people, or even of nomadic people. Typically, people living outside urban societies are referred to as barbarian or primitive, implying they are inferior to those living in urban societies. However, this holistic approach dispenses with this evaluation and instead looks at various groups as developing in concert with their particular environmental, experiential, and historic circumstances.

Another insight is that world-wide developments in the Urban Wave serve to remind us of our human commonalities. Everywhere, urban developments follow the same basic patterns. Since no apparent hemispheric interaction took place, this similarity between civilizations emerging in separate hemispheres is a testament to our creative human commonalities, as well as our dark side that results in the subjugation of others, environmental damage, and inhumane cruelty. Regardless of location, people behave much the same way.

Questions to Consider

1. What does the term civilization mean to you?

PART I: CURRENTS IN THE URBAN WAVE

RELATIONSHIP WITH NATURE: ECOSYSTEM CURRENTS

Environment

More intensive agricultural production during the Urban Wave placed greater strain on the environment. Some areas, such as the temperate forest ecosystem of northern and western Europe, withstood agricultural intensification reasonably well, while others, like Mesopotamia, with its fragile ecosystem and high population density, were adversely affected within a thousand years after urbanization. One problem in Mesopotamia was deforestation, where forests supplying wood for heating, cooking, and construction were cleared and the natural protective cover of soil was lost to erosion. Overgrazing by sheep, cattle, and goats reduced vegetation in many areas to low scrub plants. Soil erosion scarred deforested land. Immense quantities of silt from denuded hillsides engorged rivers and blocked watercourses. Deltas and marshes fanned out at the mouths of choked rivers.[9]

Many early urban societies were unable to sustain intensive agriculture over a long period of time because of their inability to balance feeding a growing population with the environmental carrying capacity of the land. Even though some societies grew crops successfully in the short term, some, such as in Mesopotamia and the Mayans, ultimately, created disaster in the long run by over-stretching their environmental limits. In many societies food production dropped as it became more difficult to support a large number of inhabitants. Elites continued to retain their proportion of declining crop production by collecting tribute payments, which meant a reduction in the share left for the commoners. The peasants responded to this inequity by revolt or other forms of resistance. In the case of the Mayans, for example, the effect of environmental degradation was the dramatic collapse of their civilization. In Mesopotamia, salinization turned large areas of formerly productive farmland into desert. As evidenced in the Communal and Agricultural Waves, pressing the environmental limits contributes to the collapse of civilizations throughout our human history.

Questions to Consider

1. Describe the environment of the area called Mesopotamia today? What impact does the environment have on the people today?

Human Populations

Urban centers had dense populations. Population increased even though death rates from war, disease, accident, and famine were high as well. Several Mesopotamian cities, like Sumer, passed the 100,000 mark shortly after urbanization. Urban commoners had little incentive to limit the size of their families, since large families, especially those with many sons, were a valuable source of cheap labor and a form of old-age insurance for parents. Religions also advocated large families, which were considered a favorable sign from a deity. It was also assumed that large families helped to perpetuate ancestor worship.[10]

Population growth during the Urban Wave remained low compared to today's exponential rates, but growth was substantial when compared to the past. Not until 300 years ago did the world's population increase by more than 0.1 percent a year, one-twentieth the current rate.[11]

Human and Nature Interaction

The awe, respect, and reverence for nature that was characteristic of agricultural people began to dissolve during the Urban Wave. Nature was increasingly regarded as a commodity, a provider of natural resources for material development, and a source for fuel and food for both humans and animals. Urban dwellers around 1500 CE had all but lost the mystical bond that had existed between humans and the natural world.[12] Now humans looked upon nature as a force to be

Estimated Population Totals for the Urban Wave

TIME PERIOD	POPULATION
10,000-5,000 BCE	4 million
3,000 BCE	14 million
2,000 BCE	27 million
1,000 BCE	50 million
Year 0	100 million
200 CE	200 million
400 CE	220 million
500 CE	190 million
1000 CE	265 million
1200--1300 CE	360 million
1400 CE	350 million
1500 CE	400 million

tamed, dominated, controlled, and harnessed to suit their own needs.

For example, as early as 2700 BCE, the Egyptians recorded the logging of the famed cedars of Lebanon, known for their legendary fragrance and beauty. Loggers felled the coveted trees, then their timber was delivered downstream to nearby coastal ports such as the present-day Lebanese cities of Sidon, Byblos, and Tyre, and then on to destinations across the Mediterranean Sea. The Egyptians craved the magnificent cedars for construction of their vast sailing fleets, funerary equipment, and fine furniture. Written records show that cedars were sold to King Solomon of Israel who built his famous temple in Jerusalem in the 10th century BCE from their wood. With the removal of the cedar forest, the denuded hillsides succumbed to overgrazing by flocks of sheep and goats, and erosion peeled off the protective layer of soil to expose the rocky foundation underneath. Fertile lands became desert. Only small groves of the celebrated cedars exist today in a protected national park in Lebanon.

Another example of environmental destruction occurred among the classic Mayan cities of the Yucatan peninsula in Central America. The Mayan populations peaked around the year 800 CE, after which the worst drought in 7,000 years devastated a previously thriving civilization. Prior to the drought, while the population was increasing, the area of usable farmland was decreasing from the effects of deforestation and hillside erosion. According to the archaeological record, coinciding with the collapse of the classic Mayan civilization was a period of intense and frequent warfare between inhabitants over land, as overpopulation became excessive and productive land became scarce.[13]

Cedars of Lebanon. Photo by Denise Ames

Insights: Learning from the Past

Ecosystem Currents

The awe and respect for nature felt by many foraging and agricultural people was supplanted by urban dwellers' demand for nature's bounty. The result in certain areas of the world was that the environment was overtaxed to the point of collapse, a harbinger of more environmental destruction to take place in the future. This stretching of nature's limits to accommodate humans is a re-occurring theme found in our human history, intensifying with the Urban Wave, expanding with the Modern Wave and exploding with the Global Wave.

Questions to Consider

1. What is your reaction to the statement: "This stretching of nature's limits to accommodate humans is a reoccurring theme found in our human history?" Do you agree or disagree?

Techno-Economic Currents

The vast majority of urban residents were commoners. Only a fraction of urban dwellers were of the elite class, but both groups were able to access at least some urban services such as recreational facilities, sports grounds, assembly halls, distribution and administrative buildings, water systems, public baths, drains, sewers, and internal roads.[14] Urban sanitation was very rudimentary. Contagious diseases spread quickly in tight living conditions with some diseases reaching epidemic proportions, wiping out thousands and even millions of people. The mortality rate from childhood diseases was quite high. In general, living conditions for urban commoners were less healthy and secure than for foragers, horticulturists, and peasant farmers.

The daily life of peasant farmers was quite varied. Their diet could be adequate in the summer, fall, and into the winter, but they often experienced food shortages in the spring when stored food supplies were lean. When compared to the diet of struggling urban commoners, they at least had access to food. For example, the typical diet of a European peasant farmer during this time consisted of a hunk of bread, cheese, soup or pottage, ale, and occasional meat. They slept on straw-covered earthen floors, with a table and stools as the only furniture, and cooking utensils as the few, meager household possessions.[15] The life of the Chinese peasantry was one of hard work on small plots of land that was most likely owned by aristocratic landowners. Typically, the peasants had to pay about one-tenth of their crop as a rent payment to the owner of the land and they subsisted on the rest.

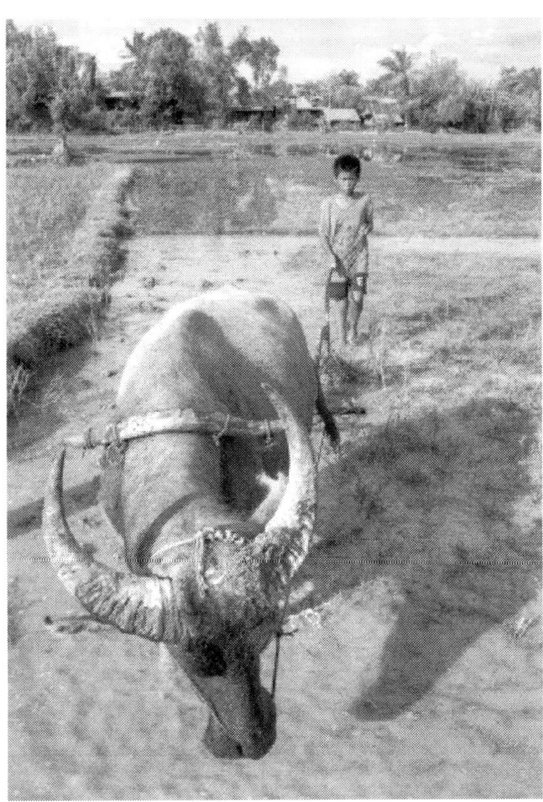

Child plowing in Laos.

Economic Systems

During the Urban Wave two types of economic systems coexisted simultaneously: redistribution and the market economy. The redistribution system was the most common, operating much as it had during the Agricultural Wave. A rural-based agricultural sector and a city-based commercial sector were two complementary but unequal components of the urban system. The political elite extracted wealth in the form of tribute from the peasant's agricultural surplus, and to a lesser extent from trade and manufacturing, while the landed elite extracted rent payments, sometimes excessive, from peasants who farmed their land. The urban commercial economy depended upon the ability of the rural economy to produce an agricultural surplus to feed urban populations. Besides agricultural products, raw materials such as timber also flowed from surrounding villages to larger towns and cities. Although the land providing these raw materials was usually owned by wealthy landowners, the goods were produced by the labor of serfs, slaves, or landless peasants. This economic surplus from the countryside supported commercial activity and the cities.

Tribute, a form of taxation collected from the peasants, took the form of rents, interest on debts, compulsory labor service (corvee), tithes, fines, and obligatory gifts to the elite. The basic philosophy of the elite class was to tax peasants to the limit of their ability to pay. Any surplus left after the peasants met their subsistence needs for the year and paid their tribute to the state was traded with others at newly formed local market centers. For example, in Europe metal tools, salts, and farm delicacies such as eggs, cheese, and butter were items commonly traded. If the tribute was not excessive and peasants were able to have enough food to last the year and some left over for trade, the system was likely to remain stable and orderly. Even though there was an increase in food production during the Urban Wave, widespread malnutrition and starvation often resulted from inequitable distribution of food resources. The ruling elite comprised one to two percent of the urban population, but it appropriated one-half of the total resources.[16]

In the **market economy**, the second type of economic system in the Urban Wave, production and distribution were based on direct buying and selling according to laws of supply and demand. Exchanges were carried out between strangers who placed little value on mutual obligation, unlike reciprocal exchange. Each person was responsible for his/her own transaction, while the profit motive and self-interest, rather than goodwill and generosity, were the guiding principles. In a market system, economic activities were divorced from social and family life; obligation and kinship ties were generally not a factor in exchange.[17] Some historians claim that a market economy originated in 5th century BCE Athens, while others disagree and argue for an earlier or later date. Participants engaged in long-distance trade were more apt to use money and the market system for the exchange of goods. In general, markets appeared to have more influence in decentralized political societies, where powerful rulers had less influence over the merchants.

The plow in ancient Egypt.

Merchants established themselves as intermediaries in the exchange of goods and services and extracted a portion of the profits or surplus of an exchange as payment for their services. Although merchants provided a useful service in the exchange of goods, elites did not accept them as social equals. Elites were wary of merchants, since merchants extracted a portion of the wealth from a transaction that would otherwise belong to them. Merchants also diminished the elites' power by appropriating control of trade and production of goods from them. The elites often sought the merchants' economic services for loans, while at the same time limiting their economic activity.[18] Merchants in many societies did not gain a foothold as a prestigious class until the Modern Wave. Some societies, such as China and Japan, disdained merchants and severely curtailed their activity, while in Arab societies no stigma was associated with merchant activity. In Europe the church attempted to stifle merchant activity by declaring the charging of usury or interest as a sin. Since the accumulation of wealth by merchants was alarming to powerful elites, the market economy was usually conducted by foreigners or traveling merchants.

Questions to Consider

1. What do you think were the repercussions on the merchants and market economy since they were usually curtailed by the elites? Do you think this was a good idea or bad?

Technology

The horticultural method of crop production did not meet the insatiable appetites of growing urban populations. **Plow agriculture**, a more intensive form of agriculture, replaced horticulture as the dominant method of food production in areas surrounding urban centers. The plow was invented in Egypt and Mesopotamia around 3000 BCE. The technology for early wooden plows spread from North Africa through Europe and into Asia, but it did not extend to sub-Saharan Africa or the Western hemisphere, nor was it independently developed at these locations. Many Chinese farmers, on the other hand, intensively cultivated small plots of land until about 400 BCE, and had no need for the cumbersome plow. The shift from horticulture to plow agriculture meant that weeds were more effectively controlled, soil fertility was enhanced, fields were systematically under cultivation, and productivity increased, unless, of course, a weather crisis such as a drought occurred. Accompanying the invention of plow agriculture was the utilization of draft animal labor; construction of extensive dikes, canals and reservoirs for irrigation purposes; terraced lands; propagation of new plant and animal varieties; diversified crops; and increased crop yields.[19]

The construction of monumental architecture—Indian temples, China's great wall and bridges, Egyptian pyramids, Buddhist temples, Muslim mosques, Mayan and Aztec temples, and European cathedrals—was long-lasting, visible evidence of urban societies' technological achievements. These large, elaborate, impressive public buildings and monuments offered homage to the power, authority, and sacredness of the elite. Temples, in societies organized as theocracies, were the most common buildings found in urban centers. Palaces and castles were large, elaborately decorated royal residences, usually perched atop hilltops for all to see, while protecting residents from attack. Other monumental buildings included administrative centers; public entertainment places, such as ball courts, theaters, and amphitheaters; civic buildings such as market-places, public baths, council chambers, and law courts; statues and figurines commemorating the elite; royal tombs holding rich grave items; and commemorative monuments such as statues, stele (tall slabs erected for funerary or commemorative purposes), obelisks, arches, and columns. The buildings were exactingly constructed with the intention of immortalizing those honored. These structures utilized standardized modular units such as fired mud-bricks or stone cut precisely to size in order to construct these elaborate buildings without mortar; their flawless fit and sheer mass held these buildings together for eons of time.[20]

Other technological advances included the new alloy of copper, tin, and bronze to be forged into ornaments, weapons, and tools. The Hittites, a nomadic tribe in the Middle East, were the first to refine the technique for smelting iron around 1500 BCE. Iron-smelting technology diffused unevenly across the Africa/Eurasian continents and advanced the versatility and destructive capability of military weaponry. Other military

Water wheel used for irrigation in Hama, Syria. Photo by Denise Ames

The Great Pyramid of Giza, Egypt, built c. 2560 BCE.

Ball court at Monte Alban, Oaxaca, Mexico.
Photo by Denise Ames

innovations included the crossbow, gunpowder, and catapult. With the discovery of horseback riding came the invention of horseshoes, stirrups, and a workable harness. Other notable inventions included porcelain making, printing, iron casting, sailing vessels, wheelbarrows, water-powered mills, windmills, the clock, spinning wheels, mining equipment, and food preservation techniques. People adopted these inventions at different times across the globe.[21]

One of the most important discoveries of the Urban Wave was the invention of the wheel, which is often considered to be the most important technological invention of all human history. The wheel first appeared in the city of Ur in Mesopotamia around 3500 BCE in the form of the potter's wheel, while its first use for transportation was on Mesopotamian chariots around 3200 BCE. A wheel with spokes first appeared in Egypt around 2000 BCE and Europe invented the wheel, apparently independently from outside contact, around 1400 BCE. Human portage continued to serve as a means for hauling goods, but more efficient wheeled carts drawn by pack animals—donkeys, mules, camels, oxen, and horses—transported goods across long distances. Many early civilizations were located on rivers or near water, because water transport was the most efficient and easiest method for conveying large numbers of both people and goods.[22] Wheel transportation was of no use in the Western hemisphere because there were no pack animals except the llama, although makers of Incan toys replicated the wheel.

After a flourish of technological innovations with the beginning of the Urban Wave, the rate of technological innovations slowed and a period of technological continuity ensued. The state forced slaves, serfs, and those incurred for debt bondage to work on agricultural plantations or for monumental building projects. Urban elites far too often abused subordinate slave and corvee labor. The elite class hindered technological innovation, since they found it easier to extract economic surplus from peasants or slaves than to take the financial risk of further technological innovation. Peasants also lost the incentive to innovate, for greater agricultural production meant the elite

Roman Ballista

Depiction of a Sumerian wheel in the Standard of Ur around 2500 BCE.

class extracted more of their surplus in tribute while they received few benefits. Elites, who were far removed from the actual work of farming, also did not provide any stimulus towards innovation. In general, elites tend to be conservative, as we will see in later waves as well, preferring to continue the system that has benefited them and perceiving change as a usurpation of or threat to their wealth and authority. Therefore, they continued to use technological inventions that had served them well for hundreds of years.[23]

Questions to Consider

1. After an initial flurry of technological innovation, a period of continuity ensued. Why didn't elites encourage technological innovations? Why didn't peasants invent technological innovations?

Exchange and Trade

Extensive trade routes began to cross the world. Centralized governmental authority helped to organize trade, moving goods from their place of origin to locations where they could be sold. State bureaucratic administrators selected storage facilities, checked quality, and controlled personnel and price. These redistribution specialists had a prestigious position that carried with it a certain authority and the financial reward of exacting a profit from the transaction, often locating at advantageous trade centers or where several trade routes intersected. The Middle East became a crucial trade nexus.[24] The state controlled trade in luxury, high-status goods. Small luxury items were ideal for trading over long distances, which was too expensive for less valuable and bulky items. Luxury trade items consisted of small, precious gemstones, especially the highly prized lapis lazuli, silk, spices, and fine swords. Price for these luxury items was set by the elite consumers and not subject to the supply and demand forces in a market economy. In addition to luxury, long-distance trade, local trade continued to be conducted at a market center not far from where the products were produced. Self-reliant farmers traded their surplus agricultural products or specialty craft items.

Grains served as the medium of exchange in early urban societies. For example, barley was the medium of exchange in Mesopotamia, while wheat provided the same function in Egypt. Wages, rents, tribute, and various obligations were paid in specific quantities of grains. But grains were not ideal as a medium of exchange, since they were perishable and bulky to transport. Later, various metals, particularly highly-prized silver, gold, and copper, emerged as handy options for exchangeable coinage. **Money**—a standard medium of value that itself is not consumed—was in the form of metal currency. It was first introduced in China around 1000 BCE, while silver coinage in the Middle East—that later spread to Greece and Rome—appeared around 500 BCE. Initially metals circulated in the form of crude bars and only later did a full-fledged money system surface, with the state assuming accountability for production and regulation of currencies.[25]

Ancient Greek coin.

Patterns of Labor

Since urban dwellers did not produce food, they took up numerous unskilled and skilled occupations, becoming silversmiths, sculptors, potters, tanners, engravers, butchers, carpenters, spinners, bakers, stone masons, glassmakers, jewelers, architects, and engineers. In each field, new artisan specialties emerged; in the clothing industry, for example, occupational specialists included wool combers, silk spinners, girdle makers, weavers, and headdress makers. Non-artisan specialists—merchants, civil servants, tutors, priests, soldiers, teachers, lawyers, doctors, and astronomers—also proliferated. Slaves toiled on monumental building projects, served the elite, and were forcibly impressed into the military.[26]

With the invention of the plow, more arduous work requirements were required. Agriculture that relied on the plow and irrigation systems was economically more productive than horticultural methods but also more labor intensive. Farmers worked harder to meet the food needs of a larger urban population. They had far less leisure time than their horticulturalist counterparts, because the demands of feeding livestock and maintaining crop schedules were relentless. Instead of a seamless, integrated part of every day life, farming became "work," an activity separate from the rest of life, which took up increasing hours per day.

Two types of goods were produced: those for elite consumption and products for everyday use. The elites commissioned special artisans to craft expensive luxury objects for their own personal use. Making these unique pieces required more exacting skills, and orders showed little regard for time requirements. Among the prized luxury objects were bronze crafts; fine gemstones; cotton, silk, and wool textiles; and Chinese lacquer and porcelain pieces. By contrast, commoners consumed products that were of standard quality, rapidly produced, and more or less identical. For example, in the fourth millennium BCE, the potter's wheel sped up pottery production resulting in greater output. Also, a mold method , instead of the more time-consuming hand-made, coil method, sped up pottery production. Metal and glass industries churned out such utilitarian tools as axes, knives, coins, and glassware.[27]

In European towns and smaller cities during the Middle Ages (500 to 1500 CE), merchants and artisans in the same specialty begin to organize into guilds. **Guilds** functioned as mutual aid associations that protected their members' interests by restricting competition, regulating apprenticeships, and establishing uniform prices and quality. Guilds prevented, with some success, the disruptive forces of a market economy by tightly and mutually regulating their economic system for the benefit of themselves and their customers. Some of the different guilds included bakers, cobblers, blacksmiths, textile makers, bankers, and others.

Questions to Consider

1. Do you think guilds should be incorporated into our economic system today? What would be the benefits? Drawbacks?

Insights: Learning from the Past

Techno-Economic Currents

Who benefited from greater agricultural productivity during the Urban Wave? With plow agriculture and other innovations came longer hours for the peasant farmer, who gained little from his increased productivity. The elites siphoned off this economic productivity in the form of tribute payments they used to build monumental architecture and other projects to enhance their wealth and prestige. It can be said that the peasant farmers in rural areas in effect subsidized elites and urban dwellers. Today in the United States we are encountering the same

The Great Wall of China, under the Qin dynasty - 3,500,000 people died constructing the wall, 70% of the Chinese population.

phenomenon; where are the results of greater productivity in the workplace ending up? The top 10 percent of the workforce has profited handsomely from increases in labor productivity, but the average worker has less to show for his/her efforts than his/her actual productivity would indicate.

Yet, paradoxically, the increases in agricultural productivity allowed for some workers to be released from farm labor obligations and they were able to practice craft specialization. The truly remarkable work of ancient artisans and engineers is still fully appreciated today, despite our centuries-long technological advancements. Urban monuments like the pyramids, European cathedrals, Muslim mosques, and the Great Wall of China stir a sense of awe and wonder as we marvel at the human capacity for ingenuity and creativity. Yet the admiration for the extraordinary craftsmanship and durability of these ancient monuments, at least for me, is tempered by the fact that many thousands of laborers and slaves were forced to construct these testaments to rulers and that human misery and suffering were built into these spectacular works as well.

Modern re-creation of chariot races in the Roman Coliseum.

Questions to Consider

1. What were the repercussions of greater agricultural productivity during the Urban Wave? Who benefitted? Who did not?
2. How does this increase in labor productivity relate to what is going on today in the U.S. and other parts of the world?

HUMAN NETWORKS: SOCIAL CURRENTS

Groups and Family

Kinship ties continued to form the glue holding together extended families among urban dwellers and peasant villagers alike; both groups had large families. Parents, usually with the aid of a local marriage broker, arranged marriages for their children. Sometimes the couple did not meet until the ceremony. In urban societies the purpose of marriage was not necessarily sexual or psychological compatibility; instead the economic and status implications of the match were paramount. Some marriages were outright economic transactions. Husbands paid the brides' parents a bride price, or the parents provided a dowry for their daughter.[28] A **dowry** was the money, goods, or estate that a wife brought to her husband in marriage. To the poor, these dowry transactions were a financial hardship, especially if the family had many daughters.

Most marriages in urban societies were monogamous, although polygamy was common among wealthy, powerful men. In some societies, sequestering of women was frequent, especially by men with political power who hoarded large numbers of wives or concubines. A large portion of surviving legal documentation from the Urban Wave deals with marriage, divorce, dowries, and inheritance. This evidence shows that a sexual double standard was common, with adultery by the wife almost always a more serious offense than adultery by the husband. Adultery was defined in terms of the marital status of the woman, and whether the man was married was largely irrelevant.[29] According to anthropologists Margo Wilson and Martin Daly, "Adultery is often treated explicitly as a property violation. The victim is the husband who may be entitled to damages, to violent revenge, or to divorce with refund of bride-price." Adultery may be criminalized as well. They continued, "Another legal status of adultery is its provisions as grounds for divorce, which is nearly universal in the case of an adulterous wife but much rarer in the opposite direction."[30]

Peasant families needed numerous children to serve as workers for labor-intensive agricultural production, and the overall number of children in families increased. Urban dwellers commonly practiced female infanticide, since girls were generally considered a financial burden if dowry payments were required for marriage. The state coveted an abundant supply of male citizens to staff its armies and provide corvee labor, while females were thought to be more or less expendable. Even though family size increased during the Urban Wave, women continued to employ abortion and herbal remedies as birth control measures.[31]

Gender

One of the most notable and long-lasting developments during the Urban Wave was the creation and institutionalization of patriarchy. **Patriarchy** is the term that describes the dominance of males in a society where they occupy the positions of power and authority. Patriarchy is a historic, not a biological, creation. Women had been the primary producers in early agricultural societies but with the introduction of the plow, men largely displaced women as the main food producers. With that displacement, women's status declined. The backbreaking labor of wielding the plow was more physically demanding than handling the digging stick in horticulture, and, therefore, women and children were excluded from this work. Distinctions arose during this time between women's "inside" domestic work and men's public, "outside" work, with women's roles viewed as less important than men's roles. These developments contributed to a decrease in women's status during the Urban Wave and the proliferation of patriarchal attitudes and institutions.[32]

Male dominance was also the rule in the patriarchal organization of the urban family. Typically, the eldest male was head of the family with this title passed on to his eldest son. Generally, a wife was not viewed as an equal partner in the marriage but as her husband's property. Any property she may have brought to the marriage became her husband's exclusive property after marriage. Submission, deference, and obedience were demanded of women and considered to be their prime virtues. The patriarchal family reflected hierarchical authoritarian patterns and the importance of property ownership, both ubiquitous values in urban societies.[33] In that regard, patriarchy was similar to slavery.

Another theory that explains the development of patriarchy suggests that men wished to pass on private property to their children and therefore demanded that there be no doubt about the paternity of their sons. During the Communal and Agricultural Waves, paternity of children was generally not an issue because property ownership was unknown and sexuality was generally not vigilantly regulated. But urban elite men, who owned property, stood to gain the most by imposing these patriarchal standards as the model for the rest of society to follow. Therefore, they demanded chastity in women.

To ensure their children would be biological heirs of their lineage, elite leaders of patriarchal societies went to great lengths to contain female sexual activity. The higher the social status of a woman the more likely she would be sequestered and controlled by force or through social mores and rules. When the sexual regulation of women, especially elite women, became more entrenched, the virginity of respectable daughters became a financial asset and mark of status for a family. Maintaining a female's virginity turned out to be an important family endeavor. Restraints of female sexuality included chastity belts, castration of men who served as harem guards, and clitoridectomy. Female genital mutilations ranged from partial to complete clitoridectomy, to the removal of most of the external genitalia. These practices were designed to destroy the sexual interest of females and thus give them fewer reasons to escape from their confined situation.[34]

Unlike female sexuality, male sexuality was not strictly curtailed. Because of the restriction of female sexuality and the reduction of women to property, the emergence of commercial prostitution arose during the Urban Wave. Prostitution, unheard of in the Communal and Agricultural Waves, was labeled a "social necessity" for meeting the sexual needs of men. As prostitution became more common in urban societies, guidelines were established to clearly distinguish between respectable wives and concubines and non-respectable women or prostitutes. One solution in some societies was for women who sexually served one man and were under his protection—either as a wife or concubine—was for her to wear a veil that served as a sign of respectability. Women not under one man's protection and sexual control were designated as public women and did not wear a veil.[35] Veiling, chaperoning, purdah, and incarceration of women were practiced in patriarchal societies. Purdah literally means curtain and is the practice of preventing women from being seen by men. Usually only women of reproductive age were confined and controlled with pre-pubertal and postmenopausal women enjoying more freedom than women of childbearing age.[36]

A cruel but effective example of curtailing a woman's freedom of movement—foot binding—was practiced in China for 1,000 years from the 10th into the 20th century. Purportedly started by an elite man who found the small "lotus" feet of a woman attractive, this practice had the ulterior motive of restricting women's movement and subordinating them. Young Chinese girls of wealthy households, as early as six and sometimes younger, wore tightly wrapped bandages bound around their feet. The bandages prevented their feet from growing normally and instead over the years morphed into deformed stubs of about 4-6 inches. The misshapen "lotus" foot—deemed desirable by men—consigned females to pain and infections for their entire lives. They hobbled about in specially designed platform shoes that accentuated their seductive "lotus gait." This brutal display of patriarchal control entitled a man who had authority and wealth to dispense with a woman's labor and restrict her freedom of movement. Although foot binding proved more prevalent among elite women, some peasants adopted this custom as well.

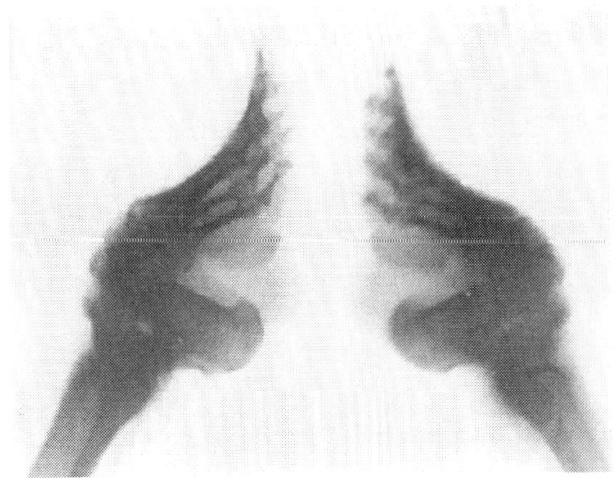

An x-ray of bound feet in China.

Occupations for women varied according to social status. For all women, regardless of class, marriage was the most prevalent occupation. Elite women were largely confined to the domestic sphere. They managed the household with the help of slaves or domestic servants. Some elite women, on very rare occasions, received a literary education and became priestesses or political leaders. Women were responsible for making clothes, spinning and weaving and food preparation with these domestic skills taught at home. Female slaves and commoners held various occupations—domestic service, textile manufacturing, food preparation, midwifery and childcare, wet nurses, and occasionally doctors. Women singers, dancers, and actresses performed for male audiences. Although a few wealthy prostitutes were from the elite class and patronized high-ranking men, most prostitutes were slaves or members of the urban poor.[37]

Questions to Consider

1. Do you agree with the following statement: "patriarchy is a historic creation, not a biological one?" Why?

Prestige and Status

Urban dwellers formed a class-based social system. The social life of the villages was largely egalitarian, but in urban centers a sharp differentiation formed according to occupation, rank, status, wealth, and class. In urban societies, where populations could reach into the millions, kinship ties proved inadequate to provide the diverse skills and knowledge for administration of political and economic affairs. Along with social stratification, social tension intensified among the following groups: elites and commoners; a "high and low" culture; an urban minority and a peasant majority; commoners and serfs or slaves; and the conquered and the conquerors.[38] From Mesopotamia to Mesoamerica a similar pattern of social stratification was found in urban centers.

With the dominance and spread of large empires such as the Persian, Roman, and Chinese, many states included a vast number of diverse ethnic groups. Those who emerged as the elite class in these far flung empires were usually the conquerors that seized power and then cemented alliances with the prevailing elite ethnic group. These indigenous elites were able to continue their privileged status but their members were now subservient to the conquering empire. Through this subjugation, the conquering empire consolidated its political, economic, military, and social power of the region it claimed. Social tensions often erupted into rebellions and revolts by oppressed groups, but the elites, with the back up of the military that they usually controlled, were almost always able to brutally quash most uprisings.

During the Urban Wave the elite developed as a separate class, numbering between three to five percent of the overall population. Their ranks included priests, ruling authorities, wealthy traders, artists, scribes, intellectuals, landowners, bureaucrats, and military leaders. Priests and religious leaders frequently dispensed advice when societies were faced with difficult decisions, serving as arbitrators in disputes between individuals or groups, while some achieved positions of political leadership. The literary skills associated with the invention of writing required extensive training, time to devote to study, and the financial means to pay for training. This created a social cleavage between elites who learned to write and commoners who did not. Elites abhorred physical work except warfare; hence a social stigma was attached to those involved in manual labor. Elites turned to educational subjects that interested them: philosophy, art, literature, history, science, and administrative techniques.[39]

Peasants comprised the vast majority of the population. Peasants rented a swatch of land from a landowner; in return they turned over to their landowner and their ruler a portion of the crops produced. Some peasants acquired their own land and were able to keep their own produce after paying tribute to the ruler. Although a peasant's life seemed bleak from today's perspective, it was punctuated with different communal activities: house raisings, harvest festivals, religious celebrations, weddings, and other community affairs, which occupied a great deal of time and added joy to an otherwise hard life.[40] Peasants in northern climates "laid about" during the winter months when labor demands diminished. But wet rice peasant farmers in southeast Asia worked the longest amount of time during the year compared to other peasant farmers and among some of the harshest conditions. The economic condition of the peasantry varied considerably with the weather. If weather conditions were favorable a good crop was harvested, and when there was enough extra for the family after paying tribute, life could be quite pleasant.

Besides peasants and the elite, other groups of differing social status lived in urban centers. Socially sandwiched between the elite and peasants were artisans, skilled workers such as building engineers, teachers, and merchants, with some merchants attaining great wealth. Low status urban dwellers made up the majority of people living in cities. The working conditions for urban unskilled laborers were often horrendous; injuries were common, and their work life was short. When they lost their youthful strength and vigor, they most likely became beggars or thieves on city streets. Beggars comprised perhaps one-tenth to one-third of an urban population.[41] Unskilled women workers were likely to turn to one of the few labor alternatives for them: prostitution. Others were domestic servants with long hours and little pay. Life for them was likewise short and oppressive.

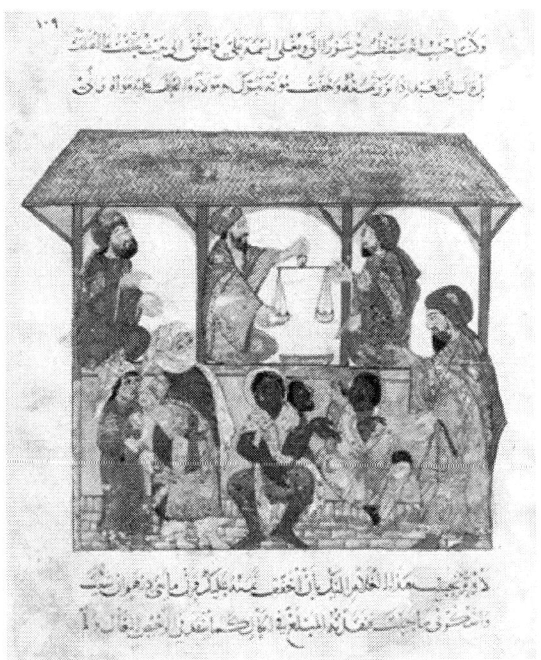

Slave market in Yemen, slavery was practiced by Islamic people and others.

Slavery developed during the Urban Wave. With hierarchical social structures, warfare, property ownership, and the demand for more workers, slavery became an entrenched institution. Slaves were the lowest of all on the social status ladder. Those captured and not slaughtered by conquerors during warfare were forced into slavery; others were born into slavery. Once enslaved, they served as laborers on monumental construction projects, such as the pyramids in Egypt. Slaves toiled as household servants, labored on state-owned farms, and served as soldiers in the military, among many other tasks. Women slaves were household servants, prostitutes or low-level concubines.

Peasants, commoners, and slaves generally tolerated their exploitation by the elite due to a combination of coercion, psychological manipulation, and direct military force or the threat of it. Subjugated people were convinced by elites that the status quo was not only desirable but also divinely ordained. Spiritual or religious justification for caste systems was upheld by the Egyptian pharaohs, the Hindu caste system, Aristotle's elitist philosophy, the Roman and Chinese Empires, and Russian czars; all incorporated mechanisms that extolled the authority and virtue of the ruling elite. When the ruling elite overstepped its authority, revolts and uprisings by suppressed people disrupted social stability, although very rarely did they successfully eliminate elite rule or change the system.

In stratified societies individuals with higher social status exercised real power and authority over individuals of lower status; this power was displayed in the political, social, and economic arenas. Anthropologist Morton Fried maintains that in urban society there were two forms of access to strategic resources: one was privileged and unimpeded, while individuals of low status were coerced into actions that benefited the elite social group by paying them dues, rents, or taxes in labor.[42] Historians traditionally study elites, which is often called high culture, since information about them is derived from documents they wrote themselves. Anthropologists study commoners, which are known as low culture, whose traditions are passed on orally.[43]

Socialization and Education

Formal education was mainly for elite males. Writing, mathematics, astronomy, languages, and philosophy formed the nucleus of this institutionalized training. Writing required intensive and expensive education not only for learning the script but to be indoctrinated into the worldview associated with writing. Candidates selected for literacy training were typically the sons, not daughters, of the elite. A cycle of elite male control ensured their unbroken power, especially since commoners and women were routinely excluded from formal education. However, a few male commoners of extraordinary ability were occasionally able to enter the educated ranks. For example, a few exceptional male commoners who passed the Chinese civil service exam were able to attain a state bureaucratic position typically reserved for the elite. In medieval Europe, young peasant boys with religious promise were admitted to monasteries to study and attain posts as priests or other church officials.

Insights: Learning from the Past

Social Currents

Some critics proclaim that women have always been "second-class citizens" or there has always been slavery. The above section proves this is not true. The Urban Wave has the distinction of ushering new social values of dominance and hierarchies as ways to organize society. Dominance extended into multiple realms. Patriarchal dominance became the way women were treated in most urban societies. Class-based hierarchies replaced egalitarian kinship-based social networks. Nature was dominated as resources were extracted. Land was divided into hierarchical allotments for property owners who maintained their wealth through enforced laws of property ownership and military might. People were enslaved through wars and then regarded as property to be owned by others. All these developments were legally sanctified. Children were objects, treated as little workers or as a sign of wealth and status. Patriarchal, class-based hierarchies and slavery are all historical creations developed during the Urban Wave and not innate to the human species. To recognize the factors that contributed to the rise of these forms of dominance can help us more systematically dismantle the forms of oppression that still linger in our modern society.

Questions to Consider

1. How would you respond to the statement "women have always been "second-class citizens"?
2. How would you respond to the statement "there has always been slavery"?

ESTABLISHING ORDER: POLITICAL CURRENTS

Political Systems

A formal, centralized government that controlled a wide spectrum of unrelated kinship groups characterized most notable urban societies. **Centralized governments** have strong, concentrated, formal authority situated in a centralized location where they wield considerable power, with a strong military and bureaucracy to back them up. However, some societies during the Urban Wave had **decentralized governments** in which power was diffused and precarious, with a weak military behind it. As is often the case in the past and now, secondary groups such as the nobility or warlords rivaled decentralized governments in the wielding of authority. European feudal monarchs and their vassals in the Middle Ages come to mind as examples of decentralized governments.

The political structures discussed in the Urban Wave are city-states, states, kingdoms, a republic, and empires. Sometimes the label **kingdom** is used to describe regions under a king's control (although you never see the term "queendom" even when there's a queen). Sometimes the terms culture, civilization, and society are loosely and vaguely referred to as representing a political entity. Precise terminology for political entities during the Urban Wave is difficult, since definitions vary and usage is not standardized. I do not use the term nation in the Urban Wave, but designate a nation as a type of political organization only in the Modern and Global Waves.

City-states consist of an independent large city that has sovereignty over contiguous territory and serves as the center of the region's political, economic, and cultural life. Urban Wave city-states were geographically restricted in area to an urban center and the adjoining territory that they ruled. A few examples of such city-states included the Phoenician cities of Tyre and Sidon, early Athens and Sparta in ancient Greece, medieval Italian city states such as Venice, Florence, and Milan, and ancient Zimbabwe (now a nation) and Timbuktu in Africa.

Timbuktu, 1853, the city gained wealth from the Trans-Saharan caravan route.

As the size and complexity of an urban society increased, a new form of governmental structure called states emerged. States are regionally organized societies with populations that reach into the hundreds of thousands or millions. They have a formal administrative bureaucracy that assist in carrying out state functions. As expansion into new territories outside urban centers took place, governmental officials were strategically placed throughout the state to administer its affairs. The state's bureaucratic employees collected and recorded tribute payments, administered local affairs, and monitored military operations. To further ensure control, state officials often created their own state religion to give legitimacy to state rule through the use of rituals and ceremonies that commemorated the state and its quasi-religious leader.[44] A few of the many examples of states in the Urban Wave were China, (later to

Nubian pyramids, Meroe, in present-day Sudan. Two of these pyramids are reconstructed.

become an empire), Songhay and Nubia in Africa, Tuscany in Italy, and Thracia (also known as Macedonia) near present day Greece.

Empires were states that expanded beyond their city or provincial boundaries to encompass expansive territories to control diverse peoples politically, militarily, or economically. The above description of states also applies to empires. Usually geographically approximate territories were conquered by a centralized state military and annexed to the empire's center both politically and economically. The empire's core region siphoned wealth usually in the form of food and mineral resources from the conquered territories to the empire's center in an unequal relationship. The unpaid labor from slaves or others that was used to extract these resources was just one form of wealth that was accumulated in the core. Slaves were captured in warfare and put to work in mines or on plantations owned by the empire or elite associated with the empire. An empire was made up of diverse groups of people without a common language, customs, religion, or history, but held together by means of military force and economic exploitation. The Assyrian, Persia, Roman, Arab, Gupta, Incan, Aztec, Hellenistic, Mongol and many others are all examples of empires in the Urban Wave.

Czar (Tsar) Stefan Uroš IV Dušan of Serbia, ruled 1345-1371 CE.

A less frequent political form in the Urban Wave was a republic. A **republic** is not led by a hereditary monarch; instead, the people or at least some of the people have some impact on the governmental policies. Often power was divided among the members of a small ruling elite who battled each other for dominance. An example of an early republic was Rome, before it became an empire.

> **Questions to Consider**
>
> 1. What difficulties arise with applying specific terminology to political entities? Do you have a solution to this problem? Explain.
> 2. Do you think the concept "it is the map, not the territory" might relate to this problem?

Forms of Leadership

As urban societies grew larger and encompassed a larger and more diverse population, the intimate, informal leadership practiced during the Communal and Agricultural Waves proved inadequate. Instead what emerged was a supreme authority that ruled over a defined territory, recognized a power that made decisions in matters of government, enforced such decisions, and maintained order.[45] The crucial ingredient in leadership was the capacity to exercise coercive authority and not just the persuasive type of power held by leaders in other waves.

The leaders—monarch, king, emperor, pharaoh, consul, czar, (tsar), khan or dictator—were almost always men. Leadership positions were customarily inherited, with the heir usually the eldest son of the ruler, who was groomed for the position. A war commander sometimes established leadership during wartime and through skillful maneuvering extended his authority to non-military matters. Some military leaders were able to gain the confidence of elites and carried their leadership positions into peacetime. War, territorial expansion, and conquest enhanced the popularity and influence of military leaders who were able to gain the support of commoners by promising reform, land, or other benefits. When military leaders acquired more power than the elites, the elites became wary of those who did not support their interests.[46] For example, the heralded military commander Julius Caesar met his brutal death in 44 BCE as a result of defying the elite Senators of the Roman Republic.

Urban leaders exercised direct authority over their territory through intermediaries who acted on their behalf and enforced the government's rule. There were two kinds of intermediaries: those who directly advised, controlled access to resources, and carried out the leader's orders; and those at a local level who transmitted and implemented decisions on the leader's behalf. The functions of leaders and intermediaries entailed defending against external enemies, running public services, collecting tribute, organizing corvee labor, and securing order.[47]

Rules and Laws

During the Urban Wave a formal, codified legal system was established in written form that formalized the relationship between individual and state. The legal system, composed of a society's socially accepted customs and rules (or those most likely favored by the elites), became clearly articulated and standardized over the centuries into detailed, written legal codes. Inscribed in stone, the Code of Hammurabi from Babylonia dated to the early second millennium BCE.[48] These codes, legal documents, law texts, court records, and legal transactions were designed to set general standards of justice and enforced strict forms of behavior. Members' rights as well as their obligations to the state were encoded into law, not informally sanctioned by oral custom as in the Communal and Agricultural Waves.

A class of land-owning elites did not exist during the Communal and Agricultural Waves; instead, the families who communally farmed the land shared most of it. In urban societies the concentration of wealth and power shifted to a class of elite nobles, aristocrats, and high religious officials who seized vacant or communally-owned land, legalized their ownership of the land, and foisted control over a dependent, landless peasantry. They obtained their land through struggle, conflict, war and sometimes, outright thievery. Land ownership served as the elites' primary source of wealth, power and control well into the Modern Wave.

Along with urban dwellers' obligations—taxes, service, and military duty—they received certain benefits. They were able to utilize such state-organized structures as irrigation networks, dikes, and canals; roads and bridges; city fortifications and

Prologue to the code of Hammurabi on a clay tablet in the Louvre museum in Paris, France.

the protection of a standing army; state-provided entertainment; and a system of justice if applicable. By contrast, the rural peasantry was required to make tribute payments to the state, but any benefits they may possibly have derived from the services provided by the state were clearly outweighed by their unequal financial obligations. The elite class surely benefited from the system, as they were able to extract as much wealth as possible from the labor of both the peasants and urban commoners.

Questions to Consider

1. What was the effect of the new formal, codified legal system in the Urban Wave? In what ways is it like our system today?

Migration and Interaction

During the Urban Wave more interaction took place among people living in diverse and remote areas than in the other two waves. When one society that is economically, militarily, or politically more powerful than another interacts with a less powerful society, the most powerful system tends to dominate. Historian Dave Kaplan defines this tendency as the **Law of Cultural Dominance** in which the cultural system that more effectively exploits a given territory will tend to spread into the territory at the expense of the less effective systems.[49] Interactions between diverse societies mutually affect each other, but usually the dominant society is more likely to alter the subordinate society. Although there are exceptions to this theory, usually those societies with greater technological control expand at the expense of technologically less complex societies. This process is apparent during the Urban Wave and continues in the Modern and Global Waves. Once urban societies developed, they tended to spread, engulf, and overwhelm non-urban peoples. This process took several forms: non-urban people peacefully assimilated urban society's values and way of life; non-urban people violently resisted changes; or a combination of resistance and assimilation resulted.[50]

Early urban societies were relatively isolated, as interaction, other than trade, was limited. It was not until some urban societies fanned out into empires that cultural interaction increased. In empires, diverse populations were incorporated under a centralized government ruling from a central, capital city and dominating local governments. This process of expansion by empires weakened the autonomy of many agricultural and tribal societies that were assimilated or conquered by urban societies. Urban people's knowledge of other societies increased as interaction widened, while older ethnic customs, traditions, and values began to be undermined by urban values and customs.

Questions to Consider

1. Do you think the Law of Cultural Dominance continues today in your nation? In the world? In what ways?

Conflict, Cooperation and War

Warfare became increasingly common in the Urban Wave. During the Communal and Agricultural Waves there was no standing army, no professional warrior class, and no resources for prolonged fighting. Ad hoc leaders emerged as needed. Men who engaged in the brief, limited, but often deadly skirmishes with neighbors were the participants in the struggle. The situation changed as agricultural societies became more complex and grew, and pastoral societies expanded. Evidence of the increase in warfare consists of the increased number of weapons—battle-axes and daggers—buried in adult male graves. Less land suitable for cultivation, growing populations, more wealth to control, resources needed by the core, and advances by pastoral groups who depended on raiding for survival, all contributed to an increase in organized warfare.[51]

As urban societies became more centralized, the manner in which they waged war became more sophisticated and lethal. Urban societies with more centrally organized political institutions had more complex military organizations, more efficient weapons and tactics, and more deaths in their skirmishes than societies with less political centralization. Some urban societies who were engaged in empire building maintained highly trained, professional armies for expanding and maintaining their conquered territories. Professional armies were maintained through taxes or tribute collected by a centrally organized state bureaucratic tax collection branch. The central government raised full-time professional standing armies by mandatory conscription or through recruitment. The deaths, hardships, and suffering experienced through military service were glorified with images of duty, honor, and noble sacrifice for a greater cause. Military conscription usually applied to most adult males, although property-owning deferments released certain classes, mostly the elite, from military duty. [52]

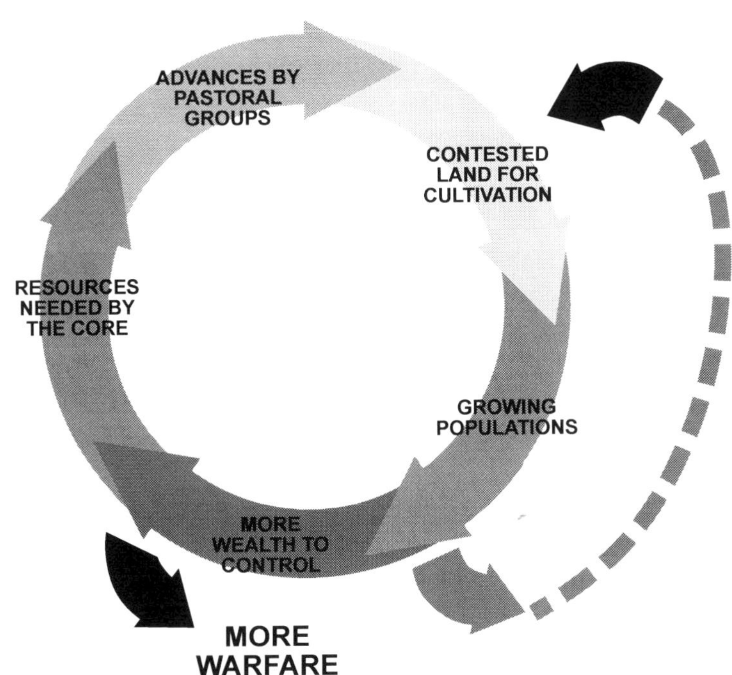

Urban societies employed large-scale warfare for offensive and defensive purposes. Offensive warfare was linked to developing craft industries that were in constant need of raw materials for production. These raw materials were not always available in their immediate locale but could be obtained either through trade or by conquering areas where these materials existed. Urban armies also offensively conquered specific territories they regarded as buffer zones that provided a defensive barrier for the protected territories against attacks by nomadic people or by other urban societies. The resource-rich river valleys of the Nile, Tigris-Euphrates, Indus, and Yellow were prime targets for attack by resource-poor nomads who inhabited the deserts and steppe regions.

Throughout the Urban Wave, pastoral nomads and urban dwellers battled over resources in a tense, push-pull relationship. Urban societies pushed nomads back from their urban zone and then nomads broke through and raided urban societies again. This push-pull tension incessantly continued throughout the Urban Wave with neither side gaining the upper hand for long. For example, the Mongols repeated attacks along China's northern border led the Chinese to undertake the construction of the Great Wall in the 5th century BCE to halt nomadic raids.

An urban military force was used to quash internal conflict that ignited when commoners and slaves rebelled against the state or their owners. Commoners and slaves revolted when they felt that economic hardship and tribute payments were unbearable, or when natural disasters occurred and the state was unable or unwilling to respond to their needs effectively. Even though elites maintained an elaborate mechanism to prevent rebellions, outbreaks did periodically spring up.[53] Nevertheless, when rebellions did break out they were brutally and efficiently subdued.

One famed slave uprising was led by Spartacus, a Roman gladiator-slave, who unsuccessfully led a rebellion against the Roman Republic in 70 BCE. Perhaps as many as 120,000 slaves joined in the mutiny with 6,600 captured followers crucified on crosses along the Apian Way to Rome. On orders from Roman generals, the bodies remained hanging from the crosses for years or perhaps decades as a grisly visible reminder of what awaited slaves who contemplated rebellion.

Warfare was a way for power coalitions to consolidate their power. In societies where warfare was highly valued, men devoted considerable time and energy to participating in military exercises. They formed a prestigious class of professional soldiers who were publicly rewarded with special distinctions and privileges given to them by the rulers. Along with duty, honor, and allegiance as motivators for service, soldiers were also coerced to participate in the military. If allies were needed in time of warfare, the elites' extended kinship relationships were called upon to form temporary wartime alliances. Marriage was frequently used to cement such alliances, and women were mere pawns in these agreements. Men, the principal fighters and defenders in war, accounted for the vast majority of deaths.[54]

Greek Soldiers, a part of a Hoplite phalanx military formation. (l) slinger, (m) soldier with shield and curtain, (r) spearthrower.

Often warfare sparked technological innovations that were later utilized by the domestic sector. For example, the invention of iron was used for weaponry and also forged into an iron-tipped plow. The invention of sophisticated bronze and later iron military technology shifted the balance of military power to those states that manufactured and used these resources. But this technological advantage was temporary, as the technology for weapon-making spread to the enemy who utilized the inventions for their own benefit.

Warfare was usually cyclic, especially for societies with well-defined, permanent military groups. Cycles of war and peace defined Urban Wave history; wars marked out time in history books where one war followed another. And sometimes, paradoxically, a "golden age" followed war.[55] An example is the Roman Republic's civil war was followed by the *Pax Romana* (period of peace) in the Roman Empire. Although the Roman Empire was brutal in its suppression of those who agitated against its authority, simultaneously a flowering of literature, architecture, and poetry flourished.

Questions to Consider

1. Do you think that your nation uses the same offensive and defensive purposes/reasons for large-scale warfare as urban societies did? Explain.

Insights: Learning from the Past

Political Currents

A valuable insight from the political currents in the Urban Wave regards the destructive tendencies of large empires. Who benefits from the formation of empires? The relative few that govern the empire are able to extract resources from the periphery that support their lavish life style, while the vast majority who are under imperial control are coerced and manipulated into serving imperial interests and expansion. Historical movies and books often glorify warfare and the nobility of those fighting for a worthy "cause." However, the brutal reality is quite different. As repeatedly evident in history, empires reward a relative few with power, wealth, and control, while the vast majority of the people are subject to impoverishment, pillaging, and suppression.

Questions to Consider

1. Who do you think benefited from the formation of empires? Who did not benefit?

HUMAN EXPRESSIONS: CULTURAL CURRENTS

Worldviews and Beliefs

A transformation of human consciousness or spiritual vision took place from about 800 to 300 BCE in the Urban Wave. In the Communal and Agricultural Waves, humans were enfolded into the rhythm of the natural world while in urban societies people were cut off from this envelopment and suffered a sense of tragedy or loss of innocence from this fissure. Group-centered consciousness characteristic of the Communal and Agricultural Waves shifted to an individual consciousness and a more differentiated self. In agricultural societies entrenched customs, traditions, and strict social controls by family and groups had hindered the formation of a separate, individualized personality, while in urban societies the new focus on the individual self led to a breakdown of the group psyche and separation from traditional group or village life. Caste, state, and individual replaced the group as a source of identity.[56] Entrancing sights, sounds and sensations of urban life enticed the individual who was also filled with ambivalence as the atmosphere was threatening and alienating as well. Varying degrees of individual centered versus group behavior distinguished different civilizations, with Eastern societies, in general, emphasizing the primacy of the group, while Western societies favored individualism.

Religion and Spirituality

One form of religious expression in the early Urban Wave, known as **state religion**, was intended to reinforce the primacy of the state, king, elite, reigning priesthood, and class hierarchies; they employed various tactics to achieve this goal. One such strategy was to hold religious celebrations with communal feasts, festivals, and repetitive rituals that glorified the state's priorities and values. Monumental ceremonial buildings, temples, tombs—elevated in the central part of the city—were clear visual reminders of the state's religion and power. Religious buildings were built with long-lasting materials like marble that did not deteriorate and gave an outward show of permanency designed to embody the eternal. Expensive, elaborate finishing materials and finely crafted accents decorated the buildings to convey an image of splendor and wealth. The gigantic scale and spatial setting of these buildings dwarfed the individual and reduced his/her personal significance in relation to the grandeur of the state. Instead of individuals participating in ceremonies, as they did in bands and villages, they were now separated from religious participation and relegated to observer status. Remote priests conducted the ceremonies, often in a secretive manner or with special sessions reserved only for the elite. Religious buildings were open to the public, but the inner sanctuaries were generally closed to all but the elite. For example, the Greek gods, such as Zeus, resided on Mount Olympus and reigned aloof, disengaged, and contemptuous of ordinary human affairs.[57] One aspect of a state religious ideology was that it persuaded farmers to turn over part of their surplus crop as tribute payment to the ruler, or face retribution from a vengeful deity if they did not comply.

Commoners and peasants blended state religion with their folk religions and had recourse to a wide range of minor deities, cults, and magic for practical assistance with daily life. Family or domestic spirits continued to be worshipped as ancestors or as agricultural deities. Some deities were responsible for aspects of daily life such as the weather or protection of a craft skill. Deities from a variety of traditions reflected the arbitrary, capricious, and unpredictable aspects of everyday life that included violent storms, plagues, wars, and the whims of leaders.[58]

A strong mutually beneficial tie between priests and the political elite evolved. Political leaders were generous to religious elites who owned large tracts of land and granted them special tax exemptions. Religious institutions, on the other hand, legitimized actions by the elite and conveyed their supremacy to their flock in return for the elite's generous financial support. As some early civilizations became more secular, they developed a growing differentiation between secular and religious functions in state bureaucracies. When this happened one set of bureaucrats controlled utilitarian affairs and another organized religious activities.[59]

During the Communal and Agricultural Waves religious expression centered around the worship of nature, the life-giving creator mother, and a pantheon of gods and goddesses, while in the Urban Wave there was a shift away from the mystic force of female energy symbolized by the importance of goddesses and nature. In an urban setting, a mixture of many ethnic groups from diverse areas meant that the folk religion and deities of a particular village were insignificant, unwelcome, or misunderstood by someone from a different ethnic group or village. In the early Urban Wave in some core areas of Eurasia, there was a process of blending folk and state religions into universal religions or worldviews.[60] With

The god Marduk and his dragon from a Babylonian cylinder seal.

this transition, goddesses were systematically demoted to a secondary status, often murdered by a powerful storm and sky god who then ascended in significance. The female-centered traditions emphasizing the cycles of life and death and the centrality of nature were methodically whittled away and displaced by the sun-moon dualism that extended the cosmic system of polar opposites.[61] The god-king of early urban state religions, such as in Egypt, began to diminish in importance as well, while religious leaders who embraced a following greater than just the state political apparatus began to gain significance.

The Babylonian creation epic *Enuma Elish* written about 1200 BCE, is an example of how the god replaced the goddess. The story is about the mother goddess Tiamat, who generates creation as part of herself, and her subsequent dismemberment by a god who makes creation as something separate from himself. The goddess no longer brings forth heaven and earth; instead heaven and earth are made from her carcass by a god—the sky, wind and sun god, Marduk. This mythic act coincides with the culmination of Sumero-Babylonian civilization, and with its increasing emphasis on war and conquest.[62]

> **Questions to Consider**
>
> 1. In the Urban Wave there was a shift away from the mystic force of female energy symbolized by the importance of goddesses and nature to male gods and a demotion of nature. Why do you think this happened? In your opinion, was this a beneficial change? Explain

Universal Religions

Universal religions brought attention to the issues of spirituality, the afterlife, and a sweeping divine force. The religions shared a capacity to extend beyond their local culture to embrace diverse people with a common set of beliefs and rituals. A move away from the earlier multiplicity of nature spirits and deities toward a concentration of a single spiritual force or overriding divinity occurred. Although there were many compromises and blending of diverse beliefs, universal religions competed with and often displaced, sometimes forcibly, traditions of animism, ancestor worship, and goddesses. Where different religions existed simultaneously, violent conflict, mistrust, and mutual contempt were evident, with the universal religions often forcibly stamping out indigenous religions. Usually a blending of folk religions and universal religions occurred, as in the case of indigenous people in the Americas who blended the imposed Catholic religion with their native religions. Although commoners launched more resistance to the imposition of universal religions than the elites, eventually they and the elites embraced the shift to universal religions.

This shift from state religions and the displacement of goddesses is followed by the emergence of **universal religions** or ideologies in core urban areas. Religious and philosophical thought shifted during a changing social-cultural atmosphere: the transition to greater urbanization. Urban individuals searched for a different kind of immortality, salvation, and spiritual dimension that explained, imagined, and met the cosmopolitan spiritual needs of individuals as they constructed a way of life in urban cities or in vast empires.[63] Universal religions appealed to different classes of individuals and reconfigured these diverse groups into a broader and more expansive collectivity. They offered an explanation for how the world came to be, how it worked, and the place of the individual in that world.

This crucial shift to universal religions is identified, according to philosopher Karl Jaspers, as the **Axial Age**, a watershed episode occupying the centuries between 800 and 200 BCE in Eurasia. A secondary phase, which built on the Axial Age foundation, occurred later with the universal religions of Christianity in the 1st century CE and Islam in the 6th century CE. Jasper argued that during the Axial Age "the spiritual foundations of humanity were laid simultaneously and independently… the foundations upon which humanity still subsists today."[64] These new religious concepts introduced a timeless, stable, predictable, and (presumably) just universal order.[65] During this time major spiritual and intellectual developments and key thinkers had a profound influence on future philosophy and religion. Although universal religions did not develop in the Western hemisphere, in the four core urban regions of Eurasia—the Middle East, Ancient Greece, India, and China—each experienced similar developments. The axial age religious leaders and followers were carriers of a new cultural and social order: Jewish prophets and priests, Greek philosophers, Chinese literary figures, Hindu

Brahmins, Buddhist monks, Christian disciples, and Islamic caliphs.

The following is a brief summary of the major universal religions/worldviews that continue to be influential today.

Middle East

In Persia, around the 8th century BCE a new religion took shape that would influence other religions of Western civilization: **Zoroastrianism**. It started from the teachings of a prophet named Zoroaster and a compilation of texts based on his teachings called the ***Avestas***. The thrust of the religion is that there is only one god to be worshipped: *Ahura Mazda*. The god of darkness, *Ahriman*, should not be worshipped. This religion calls attention to the cosmic struggle between these gods of good and evil. Historians have found that Zoroastrianism had a significant influence on Judaism, Christianity, and Islam.

Ancient Israeli prophets transitioned from a folk, tribal religion to a more universalistic outlook around the 8th century BCE. The roots of the Israeli tribal religion can be traced back to Abraham around 1900 BCE, and the covenant or promise that the creator god, **Yahweh**, made with Abraham to sustain his descendants in the land of Canaan. Sometime around 1200 BCE Moses introduced a moral code of conduct for the tribes of Israel called the **Ten Commandments**. The covenant, the Ten Commandments, and the Torah, the Jewish holy writings, formed the foundation for the universal religion of **Judaism** that reinforced the idea that the Israelites are accountable for their actions. The prophets proclaimed there was only one male god who ruled the entire world according to socially just principles, and therefore, systematically impeded worship of the goddess. They also introduced the idea of equality for all people, because according to their beliefs, all human beings had infinite worth and dignity. All of these ideas became a key part of Western civilization's ethical, intellectual, and cultural foundation.

Zoroastrianism bird man adorning a temple in Yazd, Iran. Photo by Denise Ames

Zoroastrian symbol of world peace, Iran. Photo by Denise Ames

Ancient Greece

The ancient Greeks created new ways of thinking based on humanism and rationalism, expounding upon the supremacy of logical thought while diminishing the importance of the traditional gods. **Humanism** affirms the dignity and worth of all people, while **rationalism** is the doctrine that knowledge comes from reason without the aid of the senses and that humans and the universe are understandable, predictable, and behave according to determined laws. The new discipline of philosophy was largely developed by three of the most notable **Greek philosophers**: Socrates (470-399 BCE), Plato (427-347 BCE) and Aristotle (384-322 BCE). All three had a profound influence on Western philosophy and helped to form the foundations of Western civilization. **Socrates** studied human behavior, ethics, and the field of logic. He was famous for his ability to argue and challenge ideas through questioning that became known as the Socratic method. His questioning focused on the search for truth—absolute truth, not relative truth. **Plato**, a student of Socrates, examined the politics of the Greek city-states, whose ideal ruler, he thought, should be a philosopher-king. He stressed the importance of ideals and ultimate truths. **Aristotle**, a student of Plato, was more interested in the meaning of life than politics and produced over 200 different written volumes. He was also a master of logic and argued, logically and rationally, for the concept of a single god. Later scholars who drew on Aristotle's many intellectual writings called him simply "the master."

India

In India, **Hinduism** built upon the spiritual and contemplative compilations of the Vedic folk traditions of the earlier Aryan religion around 800 BCE. The Aryans were polytheistic and believed in several gods including Agni, the god of fire; Indra, god of thunder and war, and Usha, goddess of the dawn or rebirth. These gods controlled the natural forces. Some religious discontents began

Abraham, considered the father of Christians, Jews, and Muslims—monotheistic religions. An angel prevents Abraham's sacrifice of Isaac.

Bust of Socrates, a leading Greek philosopher.

Indra, king of gods, in Hinduism; also god of thunder, war, and weather.

to collect their religious beliefs in writings called the **Upanishads**, ancient Sanskrit scriptures of India. These writings transformed Hinduism into a universal religion by advancing the idea that there is one eternal spirit called Brahma, yet many manifestations or expressions of the one spirit. To become one with the eternal spirit a person's soul needs to be pure. If a person dies before the soul is purified, reincarnation takes place. Into what living thing or caste one is reincarnated depends upon a person's karma in his/her previous life. **Karma** is the Hindu belief that actions performed in one stage of a person's life determine the next stage of one's existence. Through self-denial such as fasting and meditations like yoga, a person can be released from reincarnation (*moksha*). Hindus also try to practice non-violence toward all living things, ***ahimsa***.

Buddhism, an offshoot of Hinduism, started with the birth of Siddhartha Gautama (563-483), later called the Buddha, in northern India. He was born into a wealthy family and married a beautiful wife who gave birth to a son. After he became disenchanted with the suffering that he witnessed in his surrounding village, he left his family and wealth to wander throughout India for seven years looking for the meaning of life and a way to end all suffering. At the end of this period, he learned about the meaning of life and began to share this message with a group of followers who called him the Buddha, "the Awakened One," since he had attained enlightenment. Buddha taught that there were **Four Noble Truths**: first, all people suffer; second, people suffer because of their desires; third, they can end their suffering by eliminating desires; and fourth, to eliminate those desires, the Eightfold Path should be followed.

THE EIGHTFOLD PATH

1. right view, or knowing the truth
2. right intention, or resisting evil
3. right speech, or saying nothing to hurt others
4. right action, or respecting life
5. right livelihood, or working for the good of others
6. right effort, or freeing the mind from evil
7. right mindfulness, or controlling thoughts
8. right concentration, or practicing meditation.

A statue of the Buddha from Sarnath, 4th century CE.

By following this path a person can ultimately reach **nirvana**, a state of freedom from the cycle of reincarnation. Later Buddhism split into two sects: the Theravada sect regards Buddha as a great teacher and the Mahayana sect worships Buddha as a god. Probably because of the Buddha's rejection of the caste system in India, the religion did not fare well there, but it did expand throughout most of Southeast Asia, China, Korea, and Japan.

About the same time as the Buddha, **Jainism** also took root in India. **Mahavira**, who lived 549 to 477 BCE, taught that all life has a soul, so all life is sacred and should not be destroyed. One must be a vegetarian and disavow material possessions in a form of self-denial. To liberate oneself, Mahavira taught the necessity of right faith, right knowledge, and right conduct. Although small in number, the Jains' belief in the sanctity of all life and non-violence influenced 20th century leaders Mahatma Gandhi and Martin Luther King Jr.

THE JAINS FIVE VOWS OF RIGHT CONDUCT

1. non-violence, not to cause harm to any living being
2. truthfulness, to speak the harmless truth only
3. non-stealing, not to take anything not properly given
4. chastity, not to indulge in sensual pleasure
5. non-attachment, complete detachment from people, places, and material things

China

Confucius (551-470 BCE) established a social and moral philosophy for China that highlighted familial piety and the correctness of social relationships. He worked as a government official during the chaotic time of the decline of the Zhou dynasty and saw first-hand how a state should and should not work. He felt that order and hierarchy should be of primary importance, and the well-being of the group supersedes that of the individual. Good government was the re-

Painting of Mahavira.

sponsibility of the ruler, and being good subjects was the responsibility of the people. Everyone must perform the duty of his or her position for society to work effectively. His influence continues today in China and parts of Southeast Asia.

Lao Tzu or "Old Master," perhaps a Chinese contemporary of Confucius, is considered the founder of **Daoism** (Taoism). Like Confucianism, Daoism appeared in response to the turbulent times of the Zhou Dynasty and is considered the

The yin/yang symbol.

complementary opposite of Confucianism. Lao Tzu's ideas, recorded by his followers in the ***Dao De Jing***, believed that people attained happiness and wisdom by seeking the *dao*, or mystical path, in all things. The yin and yang symbols represent the Daoist theory of harmony that can be found in following nature. The yin is the cool, dark, feminine, and the submissive side of people, in contrast to the yang that is the warm, light, masculine, and the aggressive side of people. All people have both elements, and harmony is obtained when people have balanced both. The four jewels of Daoism are humility, compassion, moderation and the right relationship of humans to nature. Daoism spread quickly throughout China and later had a strong cultural influence on Japan and Korea.

Christianity and Islam

Christianity and Islam developed later in the secondary phase of the Axial Age. **Jesus**, (born 6 BCE) whose teachings are the basis of **Christianity**, was born in Nazareth in present day Israel, and was a carpenter by trade. Although little of Jesus' life can be found in historical records, his disciples provided many details of his life and teachings in the four gospels that make up the New Testament of the Bible, the Christians' holy book. Jesus preached for a period of about three years, during which time he spread a new message to the Jewish people. It was not a message about the importance of Jewish law, but the importance of transforming the inner person. He preached about the power of love and compassion; the greatest commandment to him was to love your neighbor as yourself. He proclaimed the poor were the salt of the earth. After Jesus was crucified on the cross, **Paul of Tarsus** was instrumental in spreading Christianity's message to gentiles, or non-Jews, and helped make Christianity a universal religion. Christianity's missionary zeal spread to Europe and parts of Africa and the Middle East.

Muhammad (born 570 CE), the messenger of Islam, (which means, submission), taught that there is only one God, Allah. The foundation of **Islam** is the **Qur'an**, (sometimes spelled Koran) the Muslim holy book that was revealed to Muhammad by the angel Gabriel over a 22-year

Prophet Muhammad at the Ka'ba, according to tradition, the face of Muhammad is not shown.

6th-century mosaic of Jesus at Basilica of Sant'Apollinare Nuovo in Ravenna, Italy. Though depictions of Jesus are culturally important, no undisputed record of what Jesus looked like is known to exist.

period. The **Five Pillars of Islam** found in the Qur'an represent the core of the practices that each member of the faith must follow.

FIVE PILLARS OF ISLAM

1. faith, recited as "There is no God but Allah; Muhammad is His prophet."
2. pray five times daily facing Mecca
3. almsgiving, or giving to the poor
4. fasting during the holy month of Ramadan
5. undertaking, if possible, a pilgrimage to Mecca, or *hajj*, once during one's lifetime

In the sixth and seventh centuries CE, the Islamic faithful converted populations from north Africa, the Middle, East, northwest India, and Central Asia to parts of China and southeast Asia, assuring Islam's stance as a universal religion.

Questions to Consider

1. Which of the universal religions mentioned do you find most interesting? Why?

European Christian scribe, Bibles were hand-written.

Communication

A shift from local, face-to-face relationships that were common in smaller communities to remote, less personal relationships was characteristic of communication in urban societies. Oral conversation was no longer the only form of communication; writing became another communication medium. **Writing** enables language to be stored and transmitted through time and space. With writing, the length and complexity of communication expands, and wisdom is conveyed increasingly in written, rather than oral, form, which is available only to those who read.[66] The early writing systems of late 3000 BCE were not a sudden invention but an evolution based on ancient traditions of symbol systems. Writing apparently began as a means of recording a temple's business activities in ancient Sumer. It spread in the Eastern hemisphere and was independently invented in the Western hemisphere during the Urban Wave.

The development of writing ushered in a change of consciousness, from a non-rational, non-linear all encompassing spirituality to ways of knowing based on human inquiry, rational thought, and segmented logical analysis. With this new me-

Maya glyph for Day 10 of the Tzolkin calendar.

dium of communication, a society was able to record data, tax more efficiently, develop complex law codes, create written literature, and appeal to a more individualized consciousness. Writing differed markedly from oral traditions in which the storyteller conveyed his/her rendition of a legend from the ancestors of the past, to individual authors who were generally unknown. With writing, an individual writer put his (most writers were men) mark on written material that permanently left his personal memorials in an unchanging form for generations. With writing, the state was now more effectively able to influence urban dweller's attitudes, beliefs, and values by creating an external state organization that was more uniformly managed by the state bureaucracy. Writing was also used by the state's bureaucratic system to count, classify, summarize, plan, and record ownership, which further legitimized and perpetuated property ownership. Since most people couldn't read, priests used written liturgical ritual texts to standardize religious functions, thereby acquiring more legitimate authority and power.[67]

Questions to Consider?

1. What is your reaction to the statement: "The development of writing ushered in a change of consciousness, from a non-rational, non-linear all encompassing spirituality to ways of knowing based on human inquiry, rational thought, and segmented logical analysis?" Do you agree or disagree with this statement? In what ways do you think this shift was expressed (or not expressed)?

Aesthetic Expression

Frequent festivals, holidays, celebrations, and religious observances tempered hard manual labor for commoners. Kin and neighbors joined together to enjoy weddings and religious festivals with singing and dancing as the basic forms of

This ancient wall painting (c. 1994-1781 BCE) appears to depict jugglers. It was found in the 15th tomb of the Karyssa I area, Egypt. The fact that jugglers are represented in a tomb suggests religious significance: Round things were used to represent large solar objects, birth, and death.

entertainment, while alcoholic beverages added to the merriment. Gambling, dice games, and contests entertained participants, and courtship, lovemaking, gossip, and storytelling continued to be pleasurable activities. Recreation frequently turned raucous and crude and sometimes was brutal and violent. In some of the games, the losers lost their lives, while in others games the winners were killed as a ritualistic form of sacrifice. Leisure activities for the elite included the above, as well as falconry, jousting, chess, and archery. The rise of professional entertainers—actors, minstrels, jesters, clowns, acrobats, jugglers, and geisha—catered to the elite's entertainment whims.[68]

With great pride and expertise the artisans of the Urban Wave created works of lasting magnificence. The construction of thousands of cathedrals, churches, mosques, pagodas, temples, and palaces still stand today as impressive reminders of superb urban craftsmanship and appreciation for eternal beauty. Achievements in literature, poetry, music, and theater proliferated as well.[69]

Insights: Learning from the Past

Cultural Currents

Writing has had a profound impact on the way humans think and see the world. Writing is done in a linear, progressive fashion in which ideas follow in a logical successive order. Therefore, the writing practice trains human thought into thinking in a logical, rational, and chronological manner. This way of thinking differed from the undifferentiated, inseparable, nonsequential type of thought process practiced among non-urban peoples. Writing must be learned, which is a time-consuming extravagance that can take years to accomplish. Thus, it was a luxury that only the elite had the wherewithal to master. The written word did not pass away with the writer, but persisted for centuries; examples are the Ten Commandments and Hammurabi's Code, which were etched in stone. Thus, officials who could write codified laws and religious traditions into more permanent forms which, though subject to different interpretations, did not change. The text became a hedge against failing memory and more important than the lived experiences of the old religions.

A second insight is the concept of individualism which was sown in the Urban Wave. The Axial Age religions gave expression to this new individual consciousness. It is a testament to the durability and relevance of the universal religions and worldviews that developed during the Axial Age that they have continued for centuries to speak to the religious, philosophical, emotional, and intellectual needs of individuals across the ages.

Questions to Consider

1. Why do you think the universal religions have been such durable institutions and continued for thousands of years?

Insights: Learning from the Past

Part I The Urban Wave: Concluding Insights

One is the favorite number of the Urban Wave. With the Urban Wave there is a move from the diversity of the Communal and Agricultural Waves to singularity: displacement of polytheistic religions with monotheistic religions, from a variety of crops grown to mono-crop production, from group consciousness to individual consciousness, from community to the individual, from many bands and villages to one empire dominating many people, from multiple chiefs and headpersons to one ruler, from communal land ownership to one individual owning vast tracts of land, from many experiencing and participating in religion to one religious leader or founder, from equality of many to domination by elite men, from many oral stories to one written moral or law code. The list goes on, but the trend is clear.

Questions to Consider

1. Do you agree the number "one" is reflected in changes in the Urban Wave? Explain.

PART II
PASTORAL SOCIETIES

PASTORAL SOCIETIES

Urban societies do not develop in isolation, but in relationship with pastoral societies. This relationship is beneficial and destructive for both. Pastoral nomadism is a significant historical development that took place around the same time as the development of ancient urban societies. One theory holds that pastoralism developed as an offshoot of the Neolithic domestication process, and by 1500 BCE had widely dispersed or developed independently in environmentally compatible areas of the world. Based on this the-

A yurt in front of the Gurvan Saikhan Mountains. Today, approximately 30% of Mongolia's 3 million people are nomadic or semi-nomadic.

ory, pastoralism is included in the Urban Wave because its development falls within the Eurasian urban chronological time frame, and pastoral and urban societies interacted in significant ways both peaceful and violent. History often treats pastoral nomads superficially, portraying them solely as violent barbarian intruders who disrupted civilized societies. However, this simplistic good and bad dichotomy belies the complex interaction between the two different societies, and in this holistic approach, we try not to judge one society as superior to the other.

Pastoralism is a food procurement strategy based on animal domestication and found in environments where agriculture is insufficient to support a sedentary population. During the Paleolithic era, hunting was an important strategy in areas that did not have sufficient edible vegetation, but by 5000 BCE pastoralism began to replace hunting in some areas of the world. Some estimates show an earlier development of pastoralism around 8500-6500 BCE in the area of present day Syria and Jordan. Their herds of animals—reindeer, cattle, horses, sheep, goats, and camels—provided pastoralists with meat, milk, hair, and wool as well as transportation. Pastoralism is a way of making a living, and a way of life. Diverse forms of pastoralism range from fully nomadic societies to partially sedentary, agricultural societies.[70]

Change and Continuity

Life in pastoral societies includes a mix of change and continuity. Those who argue that societies undergo continuous linear change are perplexed by the relative continuity of pastoral societies, especially compared to urban societies that experienced more rapid cultural change. But pastoral societies were not locked into rigid stagnation; they evolved and changed in concert with environmental conditions and through interaction with sedentary societies.

Like village farmers and foragers, nomads today are rapidly dwindling in number. Their way of life today is not the same as it was in the past. Because of encroaching modern influences, pressure from the state to change their way of life, and climate changes, nomadic life is giving way to a modern and sedentary existence. Some estimates show that 30 to 40 million people are considered pastoralists, although this number includes hunters and gathers as well. A few of the pastoral tribes that still exist today include the Kurds of southern Turkey and northern Iran, Bakhtiari of Iran, Kushis of Afghanistan, Maasai of Kenya and Tanzania (although mostly settled now), Bedouin Arabs in the Saudi Arabia region, Urkmens of Turkmenistan, and Nuer of southern Sudan.

Why did nomadic pastoral societies develop? One early theory holds that pastoralism started before the development of agriculture and evolved from hunting large herbivorous mammals. With the extinction of large game animals at the end of the Ice Age during the Paleolithic era, people living in dry steppe regions devised new food procurement strategies. Nomadic hunters followed herds of animals that they eventually domesticated; the reindeer's domestication is as an example of this process. According to another theory, population increases caused agricultural societies to exert pressure on their neighbors, which pushed them onto the marginal areas of the steppes and deserts where animal herding was the only alternative form of subsistence. From 5000 BCE onwards, or perhaps as early as 8500 BCE, population growth and the domestication of animals combined to create a pastoral way of life.[71]

A well-researched theory by anthropologist Anatoly Khazanov maintains that pastoralism developed in the Neolithic with the emergence of food-producing societies. Two forms of economic activity proliferated during the Neolithic: cultivation of crops and animal husbandry. According to Khazanov, only groups who led a relatively sedentary way of life and had food surpluses were able to domesticate animals. Food producing economies diffused from various Neolithic centers by migration and the sharing of food-producing techniques. Agricultural societies adapted to diverse habitats while domesticating new species of plants and animals. In arid zones, the domestication process environmentally favored pastoralism over agriculture. But Khazanov warns, "Nomadism itself was never anywhere absolutely predetermined; everywhere it developed it had its own preconditions, stimuli and motivating and inhibiting factors."[72] Pastoralism developed independently in some areas, and then diffused into other areas that had comparable ecological habitats. Thus, the process of pastoral nomadism did not occur simultaneously in all regions of the world but evolved in different times and places over several thousand years. Whatever the length of time it took for the pastoral process to take place, it emerged as a result of adaptation to a natural, rather than to a cultural/social environment.

A man herding goats in Tunisia.

Questions to Consider

1. What is your reaction to the way pastoralists are traditionally treated in world history?

Relationship with Nature: Ecosystem Currents

Climate changes around 1500 BCE ushered in drier conditions. According to archaeological evidence and written sources, this period of drier conditions coincided with the intensification of pastoral nomadism. Khazanov states that, "It would appear that the dry climate was the final stimulus for pastoralists to abandon agriculture once and for all and become fully nomadic."[73] For example, in Africa the desiccation of the Sahara increased about 1500 BCE. As the Sahara became drier, the nomadic populations ventured to the south and east of the desert as they adapted to changing environmental conditions.[74]

The steppe region of Eurasia was (and still is) the largest area of pastoral nomadism. Its arid climate and seasonal fluctuations in temperature had a powerful effect on its social development from prehistory to the present. The area's flat expanses pose no major barriers to impede human interaction. After the third millennium BCE this steppe region became drier than before and pastoralists had no choice but to adapt to the drier environmental conditions.[75]

Most pastoralists lived in environments that were too dry or grassy for agriculture and had lower than average population densities. These less densely populated areas were found mostly in arctic, subarctic, desert, mountain, savanna, and steppe regions. Since these marginal agricultural areas were not conducive to growing crops, animals became an essential food resource. Different environments hosted different types of animals. Since semi-arid and arid lands were unable to support large herds of animals, pastoralists frequently let their herds overgraze the pastures. These practices destroyed fragile environments, which helped turn them into deserts.[76]

> **Questions to Consider?**
>
> 1. Once again we see the effect of environmental change on humans. What was the effect of drying climate conditions on pastoralist people?

Ways of Living: Techno-Economic Currents

Pastoralists devised three ways of dealing with scarce resources: animal domestication, trade, and raiding.[77] The first two ways are examined in this section, and the third way, raiding, is considered in the discussion of social and political currents.

Pastoralists led a nomadic or semi-nomadic way of life where home consisted of seasonal, transient settlements. To feed their domesticated herds, pastoral tribes followed cyclical, traditional migration routes that usually required several years to complete. Animal husbandry served as their major food and material resource, with environmental conditions influencing which animals were raised. Such items as milk and milk products, meat, and blood were staple ingredients in a pastoralist's diet. The diets of almost all nomads included some vegetable foods, although in differing quantities and procured by different means.

A campment of the Bakhtiari people, Chaharmahal and Bakhtiari province, Iran.

Animal domestication necessitated three preconditions: a good knowledge of the behavior of domesticated animals, a relatively sedentary way of life, and a surplus of agricultural products to use as fodder. According to some studies, the shift to pastoralism occurred as nomads obtained from agriculturists the necessary knowledge to raise already domesticated animals.[78]

Pastoralists traded or bartered as a way of compensating for their lack of economic resources. They had an advantage in trade by owning and knowing the habits of their transport animals—the camel, horse, donkey, and oxen. Trade goods were first transported by donkey and later by camel, which was domesticated in Arabia in the third millennium BCE. Camels mainly served as pack transport animals on the Eurasian steppes and were not used for riding. Animal-driven, wheeled transport was first used in Western Asia no later than the third millennium BCE. At first nomads harnessed oxen as transport animals, but these cumbersome animals were eventually displaced by the more agile horse.[79]

Long distance trade linked urban core areas of Afro-Eurasia with the pastoral periphery, connecting them into an interdependent economic system. The nomad traders had superb knowledge of huge swaths of terrain that helped them skillfully traverse long distance trade routes through dangerous territory. They developed superb military skills that aided them in protecting their expensive trade goods from seizure by marauding looters.[80] Although pastoralists were infamous for their raids, they actually obtained goods and services more frequently through peaceful exchange.

Most nomadic people traded regularly with local peasants and town dwellers for grains and vegetables and bartered their animals and animal products for silk clothing, iron tools, and weapons. Horses were a particularly valuable trading item in China, India, and western Asia, since cavalries in these regions used horses in warfare. By the third and second millennium BCE, overland trade routes were well established. The fabled Silk Road crisscrossed from western China through the mountains and steppes of central Asia to the lucrative urban centers of Mesopotamia, Rome, and Western Europe. Pastoral nomads played a critical role in establishing and expanding these trade routes. Not only did they supply animal transport but they also stocked caravans. At times they also transported goods and conducted trade, but trade operations were controlled by specialized merchants who resided either in urban centers or trading centers along the Silk Road. These trade routes were of vital economic importance in the Urban Wave until they were supplanted by shipping networks and later by railroad transport in the Modern Wave.[81]

Pastoralists owned pasture and water supplies communally, while separate individuals or a family owned their herds. They considered ownership of livestock an indisputable individual right, but in practice a majority of nomadic societies supplemented ownership with acts of reciprocity and sometimes redistribution. When there was greater social equality, there was more emphasis placed on acts of reciprocity. When there was great social inequality, pastoralists practiced redistribution—the reallocation of livestock and pastoral products. Redistribution also functioned as a form of collective mutual aid and insurance.[82]

Since accumulation of material possessions was limited by the demands of a nomadic life style, large herds of animals constituted the wealth of pastoralists. Nomads often overproduced livestock to display their prosperity and pride, and as a way to guarantee against future famine. Although it was in the greater community's long-term interest to limit their herd size to prevent overgrazing and environmental destruction, it was not in an individual's best interest. Even if pastoralists were aware of the consequences of overgrazing, and few were, they did not limit herd size; to do so would have jeopardized their own personal survival for the benefit of a group that most likely would not follow their example.[83]

Questions to Consider

1. Why didn't pastoralists limit their herd size to preserve the environment? Do you think that people are doing basically the same thing today? Explain.

Human Networks: Social Currents

There are three social groups in nomadic societies: the family, the primary kinship group or camping group, and the community.

Nomadic families were small and usually included only two generations of adults. Most consisted of husband, wife, and their unmarried sons and daughters. Polygamy did exist in pastoral societies; for example, in East Africa a small percentage of the families practiced polygyny, where the husband had more than one wife.

A primary kinship group consisted of closely related families, often called the **camping group**.

Kazakh nomad family in the steppes of the Russian Empire, ca. 1910.

Although camping groups were less permanent than nuclear families, they typically pastured all or part of the year together and lent support to each other. Camping groups ranged in number from ten to over 100 individuals. Each family maintained some autonomy within a primary kinship group by managing its own household and keeping its own livestock.[84]

Communities were frequently based on ties of kinship and common descent. Individuals linked by kinship ties made up the core of the nomadic community. Within these communities, labor sharing and other forms of mutual aid were regularly practiced. But resources were shared in proportion to the level of individual participation in the nomadic unit. In groups where membership fluctuated and members did not necessarily live or move permanently together, there was usually only limited sharing. Typically, groups that were more permanently connected and less mobile were likely to share more. Whether a community moved together or separately was dependent upon the seasons of their region, the size of herds, productivity of pastures, and the state of water resources.[85]

Pastoral societies were primarily patriarchal with men controlling valued herds, trading with outside people, conducting warfare, and directing their family's activities. Inheritance was patrilineal. For example, today, two-thirds of pastoralists are patrilineal, with fewer than 10 percent matrilineal. Marriage patterns varied among pastoralists, but generally young girls married an older husband and resided in his household. Polygyny was common among men who possessed sufficient wealth and prestige to support more than one wife. A woman's position in the household depended upon her ability to produce healthy children, preferably sons. Pastoralists primarily viewed marriage as an alliance between families and clans. They quite likely treated brides as property, especially when husbands and fathers haggled over the exchange of dowry payments in the form of cattle, camels, or horses. Women's domestic tasks included breaking and establishing camp, cooking, sewing, and caring for children. Occasionally women gained prestige and power, but rarely.[86]

Ideally nomadic communities strove to maintain property equality among their members in order to foster a system of cooperation and mutual aid. However, some families owned more livestock than others. If a sharp decline in the material circumstances of a family occurred, they were considered to be unsatisfactory partners in the community. Three possible responses occurred: leveling mechanisms were enacted that equalized property differentiation; wealthy families exploited impoverished families; or impoverished families became dependent upon wealthy families. For instance, nomads in need of work pastured livestock and did other work for wealthier relatives or neighbors.[87] Social differentiation arose not only out of economic inequality, but political distinctions as well. But those who held high political status still needed the support of many community members to ensure their own power, and communal agreement was required in order to carry out the necessary functions for their community's survival.

Socialization in pastoral societies emphasized behaviors and attitudes such as obedience, deference to authority figures, and a competitive and socially dominant role for male warriors.[88] Although there was no formal educational system, these traits were reinforced at a very early age.

Questions to Consider

1. Why did patriarchy become so ingrained in pastoral societies? Do you have any of these conditions in your nation that would warrant patriarchal attitudes?

Establishing Order: Political Currents

Chiefs were the leaders in nomadic societies. Nomadic chiefdoms were generally politically weak and unstable, and had a temporary form of decentralized leadership. Those who became chiefs, invariably men, performed certain political functions: they allocated key resources such as pasture and water; established and regularized routes of pastoral migration; organized defensive operations; oversaw livestock ownership and pasture disputes; and negotiated group conflict.[89]

Nomadic political organizations fluctuated between a weak, decentralized political unit and an integrated, centralized political unit, depending upon a tribe's relationship with other sedentary and nomadic societies.[90] In times of crisis, such as war, a strong leader brought together large encampments of tens of thousands of neighboring clans and camping groups to form a complex alliance system. Ties of kinship bound these networks together into large tribal groups that merged into formidable armies. The famed Mongol, Genghis Khan, cemented alliances in the 13th century CE and formed one of the largest and most fearsome armies in all of world history. Tribes consolidated disparate groups by tracing their origins back to a fictional common ancestor who served as a unifying and inspirational symbol or a legendary hero in a historic battle in which their united tribe triumphed.[91]

Genghis Khan, Mongolian warrior.

A nomadic community's subsistence economy fostered aggressive behavior among its male members. Environmental challenges like increasing aridity often meant that nomadic people had to obtain resources from outside their immediate area. Thus, aggressive behavior by nomadic people was a necessary adaptation strategy, enabling them to go outside their group to obtain those resources crucial for their survival.

When pastoralists were unable or unwilling to trade for goods, they engaged in raiding neighboring settled communities that possessed coveted surplus resources. Pastoralists usually launched raids during a time of natural calamity, such as drought, when resources were even more limited than usual. Cattle-herding societies were often subjected to raids since vulnerable herds were fairly easy to steal and were considered a valuable asset. Herders lived in perpetual readiness to defend against such theft. The same qualities that gave pastoralists an advantage as traders also benefited them as raiders. They stealthily carried out raids with little warning and then quickly dispersed.[92] However, it did not behoove a pastoral society to deplete the resources of their neighbors, since they would no longer be a gainful source for future raids. A raiding subsistence strategy was an adaptation that pastoral people developed to compensate for their scarce resources.

Key to nomadic people's raiding ability and military success was their mobility. The domestication of the horse began in present-day Ukraine and areas further east around 4000 BCE. Animals such as the horse and camel gave pastoralists the advantage over their vulnerable, less-mobile, sedentary neighbors. Riding enabled nomads to swiftly and effectively loot cattle and steal horses in raids. With the horse, pastoralists were able to cut traveling time by a factor of five or more, shredding the territorial defenses of villages and cities. Inner Eurasia, in particular, is a vast, flat land with no natural barriers to impede military conquest. It was home to many fierce nomadic people such as the Mongols. The horse also served as a valuable commodity for trade, especially in China and Assyria, where they were imported for military use.[93] Along with the horse, nomads benefited from iron technology, which gave them military advantages.

By 3000 BCE warlike migrations by pastoral societies from the Eurasian steppes swept into southeastern Europe and northern parts of south Asia with pastoral people leaving their cultural imprint upon sedentary communities. An example of this nomadic invasion was the conquest by the Indo European Aryans of indigenous people of northern India, around 1500 BCE. The nomads' recurrent invasions into urban societies profoundly shaped world history between 1000 BCE and 1500 CE.

Human Expressions: Cultural Currents

Pastoral societies in the past typically displayed a war-like, aggressive, patriarchal worldview. The pastoralists' history of feuds, warfare, forced migrations, and struggle for survival in scarcity-prone environments has prompted anthropologists to label these societies **courage cultures**. Physically strong males bound to each other through ties of kinship and personal loyalty dominated these societies. A premium was placed on personal honor, physical courage, and heroic deeds.[94] Physical strength, endurance, and the ability to withstand hardship were required to control large animals and to ride horses; these attributes in turn influenced pastoral society's customs, values, and beliefs. Anthropologist Walter Goldschmidt states, "The pressures of pastoralism encourage aggression and a willingness to resort to physical violence; a limited willingness to empathize with the sufferings of others and limited warmth in personal relationships; a high regard for the ability to suffer hardship and pain; limited interest in hard and monotonous labor; a strong sense of machismo; and high levels of anxiety about self, status, and the future." Pastoralists had an ethos of pride in their way of life, a readiness to engage in battle, strong personal commitments, and flexibility in reacting to changing needs. Their rituals and religious beliefs reinforced these characteristics.[95]

The worldview of pastoral people reflected their constant struggle with the natural elements and sedentary societies. Male deities, who were depicted as warriors, mirrored their war-like behavior. Pastoralists described the hunter, warrior, and thunder deities as fighting an evil adversary,

A Maasai herdsman grazing his cattle, Africa.

Traditional Maasai jumping dance.

the deity of death and the underworld. Other religious symbols—the sun and horse—reflected their close association with these important objects in their everyday lives. The importance of weapons and tools to males is evidenced by the burial of these objects with them in their graves. Archeologist Marija Gimbutas maintains that the male pantheon of one pastoral society, the Indo-Europeans, manifested the "social ideals, laws, and political aims of the ethnic units to which they appertained."[96] In this culture in the lower Volga basin, the Indo-Europeans placed preeminence upon the horse and armaments such as the bow and arrow, spear and dagger. The cultural expressions of pastoral societies generally reflected a warrior mentality and patriarchal form of social organization.[97]

Questions to Consider

1. Some feminist scholars, such as Marija Gimbutas mentioned above, argue that the Indo European Aryans conquest of eastern Europe instilled patriarchal attitudes onto formerly peace-loving, female-centered societies. This theory is controversial but some feminist scholars strongly support it. What do you think? Do additional research if it interests you.

Insights: Learning from the Past

Pastoral Societies

Numerous and repeated pastoralist invasions disrupted urban societies and contributed to their collapse when their internal political and economic structures were weak and they were unable to defend their cities. Recurrent waves of nomadic invasions altered urban societies even though the nomadic conquerors were eventually assimilated into urban societies. The Aryans in India in 1500 BCE, Arabs in the Middle East beginning in the 7th century CE, and the Mongols in the 13th and 14th centuries were among the nomadic groups that acquired elite status in the societies they conquered. These cyclical interactions between pastoral and urban societies altered, transformed, and sometimes led to the collapse of one or the other.

PART III
HISTORY OF CIVILIZATIONS

This holistic approach to world history is designed around the concept of five waves that describe human development through time. Because of its vast scope, the Urban Wave is probably the most complex and difficult to categorize and communicate. Therefore, this section includes within the human development approach, a traditional, chronological, historical approach in helping to sort out the vast number of civilizations—urban centers, dynasties, kingdoms, states, and empires—that proliferated from 3500 BCE onward. I have added this overview to help clarify the complexity of the period and to highlight several major themes of this vast but important era in our world history. In this section civilizations are divided into three chronological and historical eras.

Three Eras of Civilization

1. ancient civilizations
   (3500 BCE to 1000 BCE)
2. classical civilizations
   (1000 BCE to 500 CE)
3. post-classical civilizations
   (500 CE to 1500 CE [98])

ANCIENT CIVILIZATIONS

The ancient civilizations (3500 BCE to 1000 BCE) are considered core areas of development during this time because their characteristics dominated other lifestyles, influenced neighboring cultures, absorbed and homogenized diverse groups of people, and continued to shape civilizations long after their centers collapsed. The formation of ancient urban civilization began to take shape over a 2500-year period until widespread invasions by nomadic pastoralists signaled their collapse or regrouping by 1000 BCE. This date marked a definable break between the initial phase of ancient civilizations and the next phase. Although ancient civilizations dotted the globe by 1000 BCE, the process of civilization development had not spread to most areas of the world. But these civilizations were beginning to actively reduce local village autonomy through military conquest and trade expansion. Even though civilization was expanding during this period, most of the world's inhabitants continued to live as foragers, horticultural villagers, pastoral nomads, or in chiefdoms outside the cities and were unaffected by the development of civilizations.

The demarcation of the period from 3500 BCE to 1000 BCE, commonly known as the Bronze Age, reflects the emphasis placed by anthropologists and historians on the development of technology. Although stone tools continued to be used, this technology receded in the Middle East and was largely displaced by metalworking. Knowledge of metalworking developed independently in diverse areas and fanned out to other areas of the world as societies adapted metal hoes and tools to work the ground more efficiently than was possible with stone and wood tools.

Rather than emanating uniformly from one dominant center, ancient civilizations sporadically radiated outward from diverse centers. Because interaction among ancient centers was intermittent and superficial, each civilization developed its own unique, cultural identity. For instance, in Egypt and Mesopotamia, civilizations in close historical and geographic proximity, institutions and cultural forms developed independently, with different approaches to religious expression, art forms, social structures, technological innovations and political organization. Despite their variability, in this era we can visibly see the common ways in which civilizations developed, as well as the diversity of forms that were created.

Five major ancient civilizations developed during this historical era. Although they were all densely populated, together they contained only

Five Ancient Civilization Centers

CIVILIZATION	RIVER	BEGINNING DATE
Mesopotamia	Tigris-Euphrates	3500 BCE
Egypt	Nile	3000 BCE
northwestern India	Indus	2600 BCE
northern China	Huang He (Yellow)	2000 BCE
Olmec in Meso America	along Gulf of Mexico	1200 BCE

An oracle bone during the Shang Dynasty. A diviner asks the Shang king if there would be misfortune over the next ten days; the king replied that he had consulted the ancestor Xiaojia in a worship ceremony.

gation projects and drained flood waters in fertile river valleys.

With a varied topography made up of mountains, plateaus, and deserts, China has only 12 percent arable land. To feed its large population on limited arable land has been a continuous struggle throughout its long history. The farming village and the family were the basic social unit of ancient Chinese life. Along with gender and hierarchical differentiation within the Chinese family, there was social differentiation among the Chinese: usually elite families owned land and peasants toiled as farmers.

Olmec

Beginning around 1200 BCE and continuing to about 400 BCE, **Olmec** culture developed in the hot and swampy lowlands along the coast of the Gulf of Mexico in present day Mexico.[99] Although it developed somewhat later than the river valley civilizations of the Eastern hemisphere, the Olmec is included in this section because it provided a foundation for the emergence of other civilizations in the Western hemisphere. Also, the similar ways in which ancient civilizations develop, despite lack of interaction, is striking. Like Egypt, the Olmec had no known large cities, and populations lived mostly in small farming settlements surrounded by major ceremonial centers. The civilization was known for obsidian and jade art objects, a differentiated social structure, elite-control, and extensive trading networks. It was possible that the Olmec people invented writing and techniques for recording dates on stone calendars, which has long been attributed to the Mayans.[100] A similar early urban society, the Chavin, developed in the northern Andes region of present-day Peru from 900 to 200 BCE. They extended their influence to other civilizations along the coast, and provided a cultural foundation for the later Incas. From all indications, the two centers in the Western hemisphere developed in isolation from developments in the Eastern hemisphere.

Insights: Learning from the Past

Ancient Civilizations

You probably noticed that there is not an ancient civilization that developed in Europe. Yet, our history books often trace Western civilization's roots to Mesopotamia. But, does Mesopotamia actually qualify as a foundation for Western civilization? Some may argue that Mesopotamia was the home of the Judeo-Christian heritage; but the origin of these two religions is not until the classical era. It is easy to trace the development of Chinese institutions and culture from its ancient

Olmec head in stone, over 9 feet tall, Mesoamerica.

roots, but more of a stretch to link ancient Mesopotamia and modern Europe. Are there durable institutions from Mesopotamia that are recycled into Western institutions and culture? This is a question that I do not have an answer for but I think is worth considering.

Questions to Consider

1. What do you think, should we trace Western culture's roots to Mesopotamia? If so why, if not, why not?

CLASSICAL CIVILIZATIONS

Classical civilizations, which developed between 1000 BCE and 500 CE, built upon earlier ancient civilizations, although their geographical setting expanded beyond the former centers. With the emergence of classical civilizations, the pace of change significantly accelerated in the core areas. These civilizations are labeled classical because of their significant cultural traditions that greatly influenced later generations and served as models for subsequent developments in new civilizations. Classical civilizations in India, China, the Mediterranean (Greece and Rome), Central America (Maya) and Persia expanded outward to become powerful empires until their decline around 500 CE. Nomadic invasions, like the ones that ushered in the beginning of the classical era, also signaled their waning. Classical civilizations established values, ideologies, belief systems, religions, and institutions that continue to influence society today.

Major spiritual and intellectual shifts have been identified in six classical regions of the world.

Six Classical Regions of the Urban Wave

1. India
2. China
3. Persia
4. Greece
5. Rome
6. Maya

Five Themes in Classical Civilizations

1. Formation of large cities. Among the numerous notable urban centers were Alexandria in Egypt, Rome in Italy, Xian/Changan in China, Athens in Greece, Pataliputra in India, Persepolis in Iran (Persia) and Tikal and Palenque in Central America and Teotihuacan in Mexico.
2. Human migrations. Some people within the dominant ethnic groups moved from urban centers to the outlying conquered areas. They carried their beliefs, language, customs, technologies, and traditions with them. During periods of imperial expansion, a huge inflow of prisoners of war and migrant workers reconfigured the ethnic composition of many civilizations.
3. Technological innovations. The classical era is known as the Iron Age in the Eastern hemisphere. There, iron replaced bronze, as the preferred metal, making it possible to create new tools like the iron plow and weaponry like swords. Iron is easier to produce than bronze and the specialized work of ironsmiths became a new occupation.
4. Long-distance trade expanded. Long-distance trade expanded over land and sea routes. For example, trade crossed the Mediterranean Sea first with the Phoenicians, then the Greeks, and later the Roman Empire. Trade between civilizations extended outward. For instance, the Silk Road linked the Mediterranean region and China for the first time. Caravans traversed the vast Sahara of northern Africa and a maritime trade network stretched across the Indian Ocean.
5. Axial Age. During the first millennium BCE, between 800 BCE and 200 BCE, the spiritual and philosophic foundations of the modern world were articulated on the Eurasian continent. This was the time when universal religions and ideologies incorporated diverse people under a common religious or ideological umbrella.

Once again, for brevity's sake, the following are concise case studies of six classical civilizations.

India

From the Aryan invasion of the Dravidian people around 1500 BCE until the fall of the Gupta Empire in the 600s CE there was a shift of urban centers from the Indus to the Ganges River valley. The Aryans cleared the dense forests of the northern Indian plains, developed Sanskrit writing, and introduced the iron plow. The population was a mix of light skinned Aryans and dark-skinned Dravidians. The color difference between the Aryans and Dravidians was apparently an important factor in the development of a social differentiating **caste system**. In this five tier caste system, the first three castes were the highest and composed of Aryans—priests or *brahmins*, warriors or *kshatriya*, and merchants or *vaisya*. The Dravidians comprised the lower two castes—the commoners or *sudra*, and the lowest caste, the untouchables. The caste system continues to exist today in varying degrees in India. Association in a particular caste is inherited, and intermarriage or even sharing a meal with those outside one's caste is strictly forbidden.

Hinduism, a blend of the religious beliefs of the Aryan and Dravidian cultures, is central to the history of India. Belief in reincarnation, performance of extensive rituals and ceremonies, the worship of many deities, and the belief of one unity beyond all diversity are part of Hindu thought.

Two important political empires in classical India were the Mauryan (324-183 BCE) and Gupta (320-600s CE). Under these empires, India unified politically, which was unusual since there was a historic tendency towards political fragmentation because regional states were powerful and the Indian subcontinent enormous in size. One of the most notable rulers of the Mauryan Empire was **King Asoka** (r. 273-232 BCE), who is considered to be one of India's greatest rulers. He conquered many territories, but after one particular brutal battle, he became a pacifist and turned his concerns to human suffering, a long-lasting tradition in Indian culture. The Gupta leaders' political authority began to decline in the 5th century CE followed by nomadic invasions during the 6th century. The invaders penetrated into central India and destroyed the weakened empire. Though the Guptas' days of glory came to an end, the classical traditions of Hindusim and the caste system survived. India did not generate a system of unifying social beliefs like Confucianism, or a durable institution like the Chinese bureaucracy that recovered after invasion and chaos, but Hinduism and the deeply entrenched village structure served as unifying factors in the face of political fragmentation and decentralization.

China

Classical Chinese society expanded during the reign of two vital dynasties: the Zhou (1172-221 BCE) and the Han (202 BCE-221 CE). During the Zhou dynasty, Confucius forged a system of thought in which government was not limited to those of noble birth but open to all men of merit. This ideal developed into an efficient bureaucracy in which workers were selected through a civil service examination. The Han dynasty, comparable in power and lasting influence to the Roman Empire, conducted long-distance trade with Rome along the ancient Silk Road. China continued to be primarily an agricultural society, with the family as the social and economic unit. The economy centered on the **well-field system**, in which peasants worked lands owned by their landlord but also cultivated their own small plots.

During the classical era, Chinese civilization formed durable social institutions. For example, Confucian pragmatic philosophy devised a social and moral order for Chinese society. In this order filial piety was the cornerstone of a hierarchical system in which all family members subordinated their needs and desires to other members in what was called the **five relationships**: the individual subject was subordinate to the emperor, the family to its male head, the son to the father, the younger brother to the elder brother, and always, females to males. Confucius did not speculate about metaphysical questions but was concerned with human behavior, which he assumed to be relational like the universe. Proper behavior revolved around the concept of duty. It was the individual's responsibility to subordinate his/her own individual interests and aspirations whenever required by any of the five relationships. An intense work ethic defined individual responsibility. Confucian philosophy also encouraged a sense of compassion, empathy for others, and an element of tolerance. This system has continued for over 4,000 years, even through dynastic collapses, reconfigurations, nomadic invasions, and, many would argue, even under communism.

Daoism, complementary to pragmatic Confucianism, held that it is best to act in harmony with the universe and flow with nature's course. The Daoists embraced a spontaneous and more individualistic attitude than the Confucians, and provided a framework that incorporated popular spiritual and animistic beliefs.

The Grand Canal of China is the world's oldest and longest canal. Construction began in 486 BCE and continued onward. The canal is 1,795 km (1,114 miles) long with 24 locks and some 60 bridges. This is the Jiangnan section of the canal.

Classical China is known for its monumental building projects. Among those still in use today are such large-scale water control projects as dams and canals. The renowned Great Wall was built to block nomadic invasions along the northern frontier, and rulers expanded it even after the classical era.

The Han dynasty, like the Roman Empire, collapsed during a period of confusion, social unrest, intellectual decline, and a weak economy. The Chinese imperial court became mired in intrigue and civil war. Many peasants lost their farms as large landlords seized control of peasant land. Nomads broke through the northern frontier and overturned the emperor. Chaos ensued as regional rulers and weak dynasties rose and fell. During this period of chaos, Buddhism spread from India along the fabled Silk Road, one of the few times when China imported a major belief system from outside its borders. China revived politically near the end of the 6th century, rebuilt its classical institutions, and by 618 CE the Tang dynasty ushered in a new period of rich Chinese history (covered in next section). Such firmly entrenched institutions as the imperial bureaucracy, Confucian social system, well-field agricultural economy, Daoism, and Buddhism were retained and enhanced. Unlike other civilizations that have collapsed, China did not reinvent its civilization but continued its social, cultural, economic, and political systems relatively intact.

Persia

The Persian people migrated from central Asia into present-day Iran around 2000 BCE. Under the leadership of **Cyrus** (r. 559-530 BCE), Persian tribes were united and overthrew the existing monarch. Over the course of three decades, Cyrus redrew the map of western Asia as his armies conquered most of the Middle East by 525 BCE. After Cyrus' death, his son Cambyses

(r. 530-522 BCE) conquered Egypt. When Cambyses died, Darius I (r. 522-486 BCE) seized the throne, crushing challengers with skill and ruthlessness. He extended Persian control eastward to the Indus Valley and westward into Europe. His empire grew into the largest the world had yet seen and encompassed myriad ethnic groups. To manage the vast empire more effectively, Darius I placed each of the empire's twenty provinces under a Persian *satrap*, or governor, which mirrored the royal court except on a smaller scale. King Darius built the magnificent ceremonial capital Persepolis, in present-day Iran, that was completed by his son Xerxes (485-465 BCE). The palaces, audience halls, treasury buildings, and barracks were built on an artificial platform elevated for effect. Also constructed was the Royal Road which spanned 1,500 miles and aided communication across the vast empire. The empire slipped into decline beginning with King Xerxes and his failed attempt to conquer the Greek city-states in 480 BCE.

The religion of Zoroastrianism, already described, was practiced by the Persians. They also drew on pre-Zoroastrian moral and metaphysical concepts. They venerated water, which they kept pure, as well as the beauties of nature, and fire, which burned continuously at altars. Upon death, Zoroastrians exposed corpses to carrion-eating birds and the elements to avoid sullying

Ruins of Persepolis in Iran, built by Darius I and completed by his son Xerxes I. Photo by Denise Ames

Painting, Cyrus (559-530 BCE) liberated the Hebrew exiles to resettle and rebuild Jerusalem, earning him an honored place in Judaism.

the earth. Mithra, a sun deity, retained divine status despite the focus on one god. The Islamic conquest in the 7th century CE triggered the faith's decline in Iran. Only tiny communities survive there today.

Greece

From 800 BCE onward Greece became a core area of the Mediterranean region. **Homer**, the author of the Greek classics the *Iliad* and *Odyssey*, lived in the 8th century BCE and extolled what are known as the Homeric principles in his epic poems—self-assertion, courage, craftiness, and joy in material gain. These values were passed on through oral tradition and became deeply embedded in Greek, Roman, and later Western thought. Meekness, patience, and submission played no role in Homer's catalog of virtues.

Classical Greek civilization flourished between 600 and 300 BCE. From the ancient Greeks, Western civilization derived its model of democracy, however limited, and citizen participation in community affairs. Actually, the political model resembled more of an oligarchy than democracy, since real power and control was held by only a handful of elite men. Also derived from the Greek political and philosophical traditions was the belief that men can discover "good law" by using their own rational thought, and not relying on the willful and spiteful deities for help in devising laws. Through their political institutions and artistic expression, the Greeks recognized the value of the individual, in direct contrast to Confucian ideas. The famed Greek philosophers—Socrates, Aristotle, and Plato—developed critical, rational thought, and glorified individual achievement.

Hellenistic civilization, a hybrid of elements composed of classical Greek and west Asian influences, was located on territory conquered by Alexander of Macedonia (usually referred to as the "great") around 330 BCE. Greek language, architecture, traditions, and ideals were disseminated from Greece and Egypt to Asia as far as the borders of India. Greek traditions were most influential among the Greek ruling elite, while the commoners generally continued their local traditions. After Alexander's death, his conquered territories were divided into four monarchies, which ultimately collapsed politically.

Alexander fighting the Persian king Darius III. From Alexander Mosaic, Pompeii, Naples, Italy.

Rome began to take shape around the time classical Greek and subsequently Hellenistic civilization began to decline. Rome did not supplant Greece, as is commonly thought, but the two civilizations existed simultaneously for a number of years before Rome reached ascendancy.

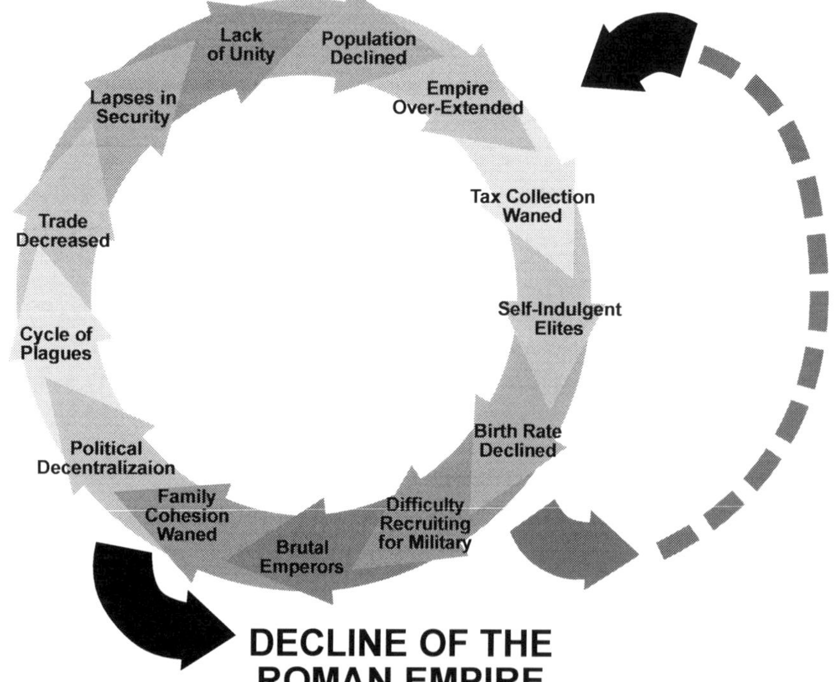

Rome

In the first millennium BCE, the city of Rome was established on the Italian peninsula. Rome expanded from a small community to forge a republic in 509 BCE that conquered all of Italy, and then incorporated the Mediterranean world into its realm. A practical people, Romans extended citizenship to conquered peoples, forming an integrated civilization. The republic, unable to govern such far-flung territories, gave way to an empire

The Roman Coliseum, as it now stands, the Coliseum is an iconic symbol of Imperial Rome. Capable of seating 50,000 spectators. Completed in 80 and used for entertainment such as gladiatorial contests. Thousands died a tortuous death, including Christians, in the Coliseum.

amidst violent upheavals in 31 BCE. The first emperor, **Augustus Caesar** (r. 27 BCE-14 CE), laid the social, economic, military, and political foundation for the **Roman Empire**. Although Rome liberally borrowed Greek culture and ideas, its main contributions to Western society were in government, law, engineering, and imperialism. Roman law, political institutions, engineering skills, and the Latin language spread throughout the empire.

In the third century CE, the Roman Empire nearly collapsed when population levels declined, difficulties in recruiting soldiers arose, brutal and arbitrary emperors ruled, and tax collection waned. A cycle of plagues and a spiral of steadily worsening conditions triggered the decline. Rome's elites became increasingly self-indulgent in sensual pleasures, with the result that family cohesion and birth rates declined dramatically. Greater decentralization of political and economic authority gave rise to a landlord system that foreshadowed the feudal manorial system of the European Middle Ages. Political decentralization weakened the hold of emperors and stifled trade. All of these systemic factors contributed to the decline and eventual collapse in 476 CE of the western portion of the Roman Empire.

Rome's collapse disrupted the political unity of Mediterranean lands. Unlike China, Greece and Rome did not produce durable political and bureaucratic traditions strong enough to withstand a period of chaos and disintegration. Even though the Mediterranean world accepted a common religion, Christianity, it generated only limited political unity.

Maya

Although the Mayan civilization developed slightly later than the other classical civilizations and did not produce one of the universal religions or worldviews, it deserves inclusion in this category because of its cultural achievements, such as writing and mathematics, its architectural accomplishments, and its long-lasting influence in the Western hemisphere. The **Maya** replaced the collapsed Olmec civilization and occupied an extensive area of Central America. The classical period of the civilization dates from 250 CE to 900 CE, but continued in a weakened state until the Spanish arrived around 1500. At its apex, it was one of the most densely populated and culturally dynamic civilizations in the world.

The Mayans cultural achievements included a fully developed and only known written language of the Western hemisphere, the Mayan calendar, and mathematics. They wrote using individual signs or glyphs that could be combined to form any words or concepts in the Mayan language. Over 850 characters made up the system of hieroglyphs that was used to record everything they thought worth documenting: astronomy, dynastic lineage, history, and religious practices. The Mayans carved their information into preserved stone slabs and scholars have been able to successfully decipher the hieroglyphs. The highly complex Mayan calendar reflected their interest in time and the cosmos, with each day marked by three complicated separate dating systems. Their calendar was accurate to within a second. Their sophisticated system of mathematics, which was needed to construct the calendar, incorporated the concept of zero and place value. It is considered to be more advanced than European mathematics of the period.

The underpinning of Mayan culture was a complex set of religious beliefs that included the worship of serpent gods, jaguar deities, and a fascination with the cosmos. The Mayan cosmos consisted of three layers: the earthly arena of human existence came between the heavens and a dark underworld. A sacred tree rose through the layers, its roots in the underworld and its branches in the heavens. The temple precincts of Mayan cities physically represented this cosmology: the pyramids as sacred mountains climbing to the heavens while their entrances were gateways to the underworld.

Although the Maya shared a single culture, they were never unified politically. Instead, rival kingdoms led by hereditary rulers, competed for regional dominance. This resulted in intense and frequent warfare among rival city-states. The torture and sacrifice of captured enemies was infused with an elaborate ritual conducted at temples. Towering pyramids linked the all-powerful kings to the authority of gods.

At its population peak, Mayan civilization may have reached 14 million, the largest of any state outside Asia at that time. Intensive forms of agriculture were used to support this vast population. Swamps were drained and elevated fields were built to grow maize. Crops were irrigated and hillsides terraced for optimal productivity. Every household planted a garden for its own use, and forests were managed for deer hunting.

Mayan ruins at Palenque in Central America.

Political and economic collapse befell many major Mayan urban centers between 800 and 900, although a small number survived for centuries. Apparently, collapse was due to climate changes, soil depletion, decline in agricultural productivity, and over population. This in turn might have caused social conflict and warfare as desperate elites sought additional agricultural land through conquest. Most likely, the decline was accompanied by pestilence and disease. By the time Europeans arrived, Mayans had scattered to surrounding areas and resumed practices characterized by a decentralized, agricultural, small village way of life. However, their descendants maintained the cultural and religious expressions of their ancestors, as they continue to do even today.

Insights: Learning from the Past

Classical Civilizations

The long-lasting achievements of the classical era are a testament to the era's sweeping impact on our world today. The universal religious and worldview foundations exemplify the flow of continuity that spans thousands of years and still resonant with our contemporary world. The universal truths that underlie each of the universal world religious (worldview) traditions speak to the commonalities that we humans share, despite the long passages of time and space.

Questions to Consider

1. What do you consider the 3 most important and most long-lasting achievements of the classical era?

POST-CLASSICAL CIVILIZATIONS

The post-classical civilizations spanned 1,000 years, 500 to 1500 (we will dispense with the CE designation from this point forward). By around 500, the nomadic invasions from central Asia spelled the decline of the major classical civilizations: first the collapse of the Han Dynasty in China in 220 and the succeeding Jin Dynasty in 420; the collapse of the Roman Empire and the end of Mediterranean political unity in 476; and finally the Gupta Empire in India in 550. After the period of classical decline, additional core areas of civilization were in formation and faced the task of reviving and reworking key institutions of the classical era.

There is no agreed upon or widely accepted label for this millennium. The term "post-classical" is perhaps the least awkward of a number of alternatives. The term "Middle Ages" or "medieval period" is often given to the era between the classical and modern periods in Europe, but European history is not altogether typical of other world societies of the period, and it is best to avoid Eurocentric periodization in this holistic approach. Civilizations diffused far beyond the classical civilizations, and budding centers emerged in northern and western Europe, Japan, sub-Saharan Africa, most of the Americas, Polynesia, and southeast Asia. Invasions, which seriously disrupted the political rule of civilizations, marked both the beginning and end of the post-classical era in some areas, as they did in the previous era.

The following four key themes in the textbox on the following page distinguish post-classical civilizations. The next section uses a regional approach to give an overview of the most notable civilizations, empires, and societies of the post-classical era.

Post-classical civilizations are grouped according to geographical regions. Some individual civilizations are briefly described in each of these regional groupings.

Post-Classical Geographical Regions:

1. the Middle East
2. Africa
3. Western hemisphere
4. China
5. Asia (other than China)
6. Byzantine Empire and Russia
7. Europe

The Middle East

Islam, the most recent of the universal religions, exploded onto the scene during the early part of the post-classical era. After the death of Muhammad, messenger of Islam, in 632, the rule of the Islamic state, which consisted of the Arabian Peninsula, passed to men called caliphs. The first caliph, meaning successor, was Abu Bakr, a long-time friend of Muhammad's. Followers called Abu-Bakr and his two successors the "Rightly Guided Caliphs." During their rule, the Islamic state expanded from the Arabian Peninsula to the rest of the Middle East, northern Africa, and Persia. After the death of the three caliphs in 656, a quarrel over who would succeed led to a clash that involved Muhammad's cousin and son-in-law Ali, who was married to Fatimah, Muhammad's favorite daughter. After several years of struggle, another leader named Muawiyah, un-

POST-CLASSICAL CIVILIZATION THEMES

1. **Influence of the Arabs and Islam.** During the classical period three major Eastern hemisphere civilizations—Mediterranean, China, and India—were basically equal, but in the post-classical era there was a reshuffling of the balance of power and the emergence of a new world leader in Afro-Eurasia: the Arabs.
2. **Towards the development of a world trade network.** An increasing level of economic exchange and hemispheric interaction took place between the civilizations of Asia, Europe, and parts of Africa in the Eastern hemisphere and expanded trade in the Western hemisphere. The Silk Road crossed Central Asia and connected Mesopotamia with Persia and China. The trans-Saharan caravan trade linked northern Africa, the Middle East, West Africa, and sub-Saharan Africa. Indian merchant activity extended over maritime routes along the coastal lands of the Indian Ocean. Trade networks connected Central America with northern societies, including the Anasazi and Cahokia. Luxury goods still constituted the main goods traded, but the volume expanded, the geographical scope widened, and the economic impact increased.
3. **Institutionalization and spread of universal religions.** In the classical era, the Axial Age burst forth, but during the post-classical era these universal religions spread from their point of origin across much of the Eastern hemisphere. Because of political confusion and social unrest after the collapse of the classical empires, many people were willing to change their basic belief structures and sought new religious meaning, while others were forcibly converted. This process was already in motion during the late classical era, and defined itself more fully in the post-classical era. The spread of individual universal religions is explored in the description of specific regions below.
4. **Expansion of civilization to secondary regions of the world.** Societies that took on characteristics of the Urban Wave expanded to parts of the world hitherto untouched by these developments. Their expansion, and new interactions between them, created more dynamic connections among core areas than in the classical period.

related to Muhammad, claimed that he was the new caliph and established leadership. A majority of Muslims accepted his rule, and they became the **Sunni** branch of Islam (currently about 80 percent of all Muslims are Sunni). Those who did not accept Muawiyah's leadership because he was not related to Muhammad believed that Ali was the rightful successor and they became known as the **Shiites** or Party of Ali.

The Umayyad dynasty (660-750), founded by Muawiyah, spread Islam through faith and conquest to Spain, northern and eastern Africa, the Middle East, and Persia. It became the sixth largest empire in history and ruled about 30 percent of the world's people at the time. The dynasty moved its capital from Mecca to Damascus. Muslim forces attempted to conquer more of Europe but were stopped by the army of Charles Martel at the historic Battle of Tours (France) in 732. They also battered the borders of the Byzantine Empire but did not defeat the empire. The Umayyad rulers preferred to be religiously tolerant and accepting of other religions; those who were not Muslim in Umayyad controlled lands were allowed to keep their legal systems and worship as they pleased.

Those disenchanted with Umayyad rule allied themselves with the Abbasid family, whose ancestors had been cousins of Muhammad, and overthrew the dynasty in 750. The new rulers moved the capital to Baghdad, which became a thriving, cosmopolitan center of Islamic culture. During the Abbasid dynasty (750-1258), especially during the rule of Harun al-Rashid (786-809), Islamic culture experienced its Golden Age (of Islam). Art, literature, the sciences, and philosophy all flourished. Calligraphy, the art of elegant handwriting, developed in response to the need for religious decoration, since Islamic dictates did not permit the depiction of human images. Also, elaborate, repeating geometric designs that echoed the forms of plants and animals, called the art of arabesque, colorfully decorated the walls of mosques. Luckily, imminent Arabic scholars preserved and translated many classic works of antiquity, including the Greek heritage, into Arabic. Public lending libraries that housed books of antiquity and scholarship were opened during the era. Public hospitals, psychiatric hospitals, observatories, and educational and research institutions thrived. Avicenna (980-1037), regarded as the father of modern medicine, studied physiology and contagious disease, advocated quarantine, and conducted clinical work. Arab philosophers sought to combine the teachings of the Qur'an and those of Greek philosophers, Aristotle in particular. Ibn Khaldun (1332-1406), often called the father of all of the social sciences, examined history scientifically by looking for a cause and effect relationship in events. In literature, Muslim writers produced many influential works, including the *Rubaiyat* by Omar Khayyam and the classic *A Thousand and One Arabian Nights*. The dramatic fall of the last Arab caliphate occurred in 1258 with the brutal Mongol conquest and their sacking of Baghdad.

Dome of the Rock built by the Umayyad dynasty in Jerusalem on the Temple Mount, completed in 691-692.

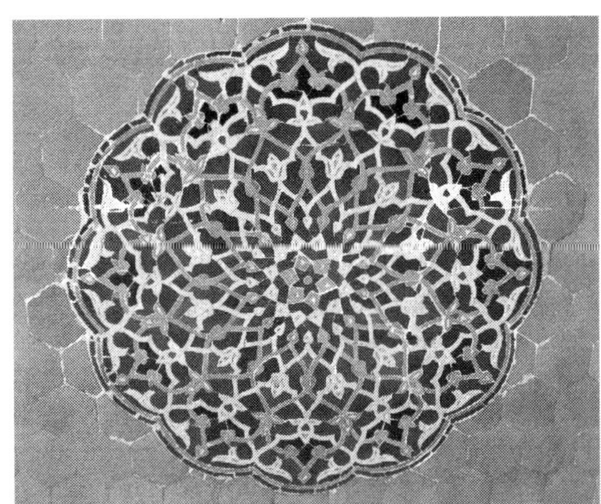

Art of arabesque, tile work wall of mosque, Yazd, Iran. Photo by Denise Ames

The Arab Empire, which was the leading civilization of the era, had expansionist aspirations and the ability to influence other civilizations. Arab commerce encompassed vast trade networks along the coast of east Africa, across the Sahara desert, and over the Indian Ocean to the western Pacific. The Arabs implanted their language, religion, and cultural values upon these vast areas. International trade created fertile conditions for conversions to Islam. Missionaries reached out to convert non-Arabs to Islam through a combination of zeal and political and economic strength.

Africa

Bantu, meaning "people" in many Bantu languages, includes over 400 ethnic groups living across sub-Saharan Africa. People in these ethnic groups share a common language family, the

Coin of the Almoravids, Sevilla, Spain, 1116.

Bantu languages, which include a diverse array of languages, much like the varied Indo-European languages. After the year 1000, Bantu people of Africa migrated eastward and southward, settling in small villages and bringing iron implements and new techniques of food production to sub-Saharan Africa. Interestingly, the Bantu villages traced their ancestry through the mother, making their culture matrilineal. Religious beliefs during this time centered on the worship of a single supreme god who created the universe. Many believed that the spirits of the dead dwelled among the villagers and served as guides for the living. People of the Bantu migration created cultural traditions, such as sculpted masks and figures, to represent the spirits of the dead in the village. They performed music for religious ceremonies and also to accompany everyday work, using a variety of instruments including drums, harps, flutes, and horns. They also passed on from generation to generation a remarkable oral literary tradition. Three notable regional trading kingdoms—among them Ghana, Mali, and Songhay—developed along the fertile banks of the Niger River.

The prosperous kingdom of **Ghana** (750-1076) flourished in West Africa as a result of commerce and trade. For the first time, resources of the region—gold, ivory, and salt—were transported by camel to the Middle East, north Africa, and Europe in exchange for manufactured goods. The kingdom grew rich from the trans-Saharan trade and led to the development of several trading centers, including the key city of Saleh. By 1059 population growth had resulted in a density that was seriously overtaxing the environment. Also the Sahara was expanding southward, threatening food supplies. The trading centers proved too attractive to outside groups, particularly the Almoravids, a Muslim group who invaded from North Africa. Finally these attacks ended the kingdom, and in 1076 the faithful converted much of the population to Islam.

The kingdom of **Mali** (1235-1600) occupied the region of grassland and mixed savanna between the Sahara and the tropical forest. Like the kingdom of Ghana, it depended on trade for its wealth. Its economic prosperity was garnered in part from heavy taxes imposed on the merchants who transported the valuable trade commodities of gold, salt, and slaves across the Sahara. The largest city of the kingdom, Timbuktu, near the edge of the Sahara, emerged as the center of cultural and political activity. One of the most notable kings or "mansas" was Mansa Musa, who

Mansa Musa depicted holding a gold nugget from the 1375 Catalan Atlas.

is famous for his pilgrimage or hajj to Mecca in 1324. A caravan of 60,000 men accompanied the king, including 12,000 slaves all clad in brocade and fine silk, and 80 to 100 camels all laden with 80 to 100 pounds of gold each. Mansa Musa triumphantly rode on horseback and 500 slaves preceded him, each carrying a four pound staff of solid gold. After his rule, the kingdom began a slow decline, and by 1450 it was divided up into many different small states.

Songhay, the kingdom which bore the name of its leading ethnic group, rose to power after the decline of Mali. Gao, the capital city, had existed since the 11th century. Songhay was able to gain control of the lucrative salt and gold trade. Sadly, the decline of the kingdom started when it reached the apex of its power and influence in the late 15th century. By 1529, a Moroccan army overthrew the last king, ending Songhay's reign in West Africa.

A series of small East African coastal city-states—Mombassa, Kilwa, Malindi, Sofala, and Mogadishu—became influential cosmopolitan, commercial entities that flourished at varying times after the Arab conquest in the 7th and 8th centuries. During the 1300s, these cities reached the height of their power and influence, trading in slaves, gold, ivory, animal skins, amber, and other luxury goods. Their extensive trade networks connected east Africa, central Africa, the Middle East, and south Asia. Many Arabs and Africans intermarried, with large numbers of the population weaving their indigenous religions into their newly found religion, Islam. The syncretism of languages and cultures of these multi-ethnic cities is called **Swahili**, a Bantu term meaning "mixed." The Swahili language continues to serve as a common form of communication among black and Arab east Africans. Another commercial urban and trade center, Great Zimbabwe (900-1400), prospered in southern Africa.

The Tomb of Askia, in Gao, Mali, is believed to be the burial place of Askia Mohammad I, one of the Songhai Empire's most prolific emperors. It was built at the end of the 15th century and is designated as a UNESCO World Heritage site.

Western Hemisphere

The Western hemisphere had its own vibrant urban societies before European conquest around 1500. People of the Western hemisphere developed urban societies apart from any apparent contact with the Eastern hemisphere. Several civilizations were noteworthy at this time, but just two are included in this section: Aztec and Incas.

The nomadic **Aztec** people invaded and conquered the remains of the short-lived Toltec civilization in central Mexico around 1300, and for 200 years these militaristic people suppressed their neighbors. Although their origins are not altogether clear, apparently the Aztecs were part of a nomadic group referred to as the *Mexica*. They founded their major city, Tenochtitlan, on a

Model of the temple district of Tenochtitlan, capital of the Aztec Empire.

marshy island in the middle of Lake Texcoco, site of present day Mexico City. From there they built a complex city with over 5,000 buildings and a population surpassing 500,000. Temples stood at the center of the city perched upon a complex irrigation and drainage system. As the Aztecs conquered Central America, they developed a tribute system that ensured their short-term dominance. Those conquered were forced to pay tribute, surrender lands, and perform military service.

The Aztec religion took many forms. One included a variety of festivals and ceremonies with feasting, dancing, penance, and human sacrifice. Human sacrifice held a special place in the Aztec religion. According to the Aztecs, sacrifice was based on the belief that the sun god, Huitzilopochtli, needed strength for fighting the forces of darkness and cold with warmth and light, which was derived from human life in the form of the heart and blood. So the Aztecs had to continually perform human sacrifice to help fight the forces of darkness. When the Spanish arrived, with their sophisticated weaponry and deadly contagious diseases, they allied themselves with the Aztec's

Huitzilopochtli, as depicted in the Codex Telleriano-Remensis, was the Aztec sun-god, in which sacrifices were made.

numerous enemies to mastermind the overthrow of Aztec rule.

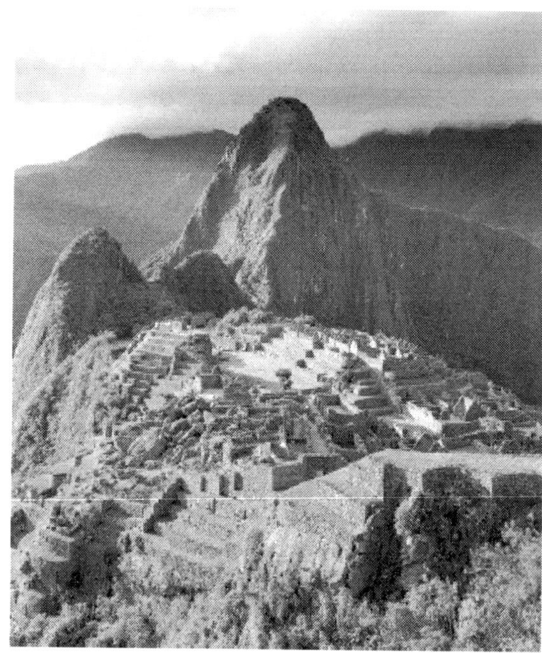

Machu Picchu, sacred site of the Inca Empire.

The **Incas** evolved from the region of Cuzco in the Andes Mountains of present-day Peru and consolidated their powerbase around 1200. The Incas built a vigorous state that grew as it absorbed surrounding communities. By 1442 the Incas had defeated and conquered all of the surrounding neighbors to create a large and powerful state that extended from present day Columbia to the tip of South America with a population numbering around 12 million. A civil war broke out between two brothers vying for succession to the throne in 1527. This left the empire vulnerable to invasion by the Spanish *conquistador* Francisco Pizarro in 1532. The Spanish found willing allies who helped them overthrow the Incan government centered in Cuzco.

China

China built upon its ancient and classical civilizations to develop even more glorious dynasties in the post-classical era. After the collapse of the

Han dynasty in 200 CE, China suffered from more than 300 years of civil war, chaos, discord, and dynastic instability. The short-lived Sui dynasty (581-618) reunified and brought stability to China in less than 40 years, calling its new capital Chang'an. To facilitate north-south communications and transportation with the growing populations of the south, the dynasty constructed the 1,100 mile Grand Canal, linking the Yellow River with the Yangtze River. In 618, the powerful Li family ended Sui rule and created the **Tang dynasty** (618-907). The Tang dynasty expanded westward and south, even incorporating Tibet into their dynastic realm. They also restored the civil service examinations, which had been out of use since the Han dynasty, to administer these new far-flung regions more efficiently. Tang emperors took on the unenviable task of breaking up the powerful landed aristocracy and redistributing land to the peasant population. Turkish-speaking nomadic people from central Asia overthrew the Tang dynasty in 907. However, the nomadic people ruled briefly, as the Song dynasty (960-1279) wrested their power away. The dynasty lost control of Tibet and the nomadic people continued to pester the borders, forcing the Song to move the capital from Chang'an to Hangzhou in the southern region. When the harassment on the northern border continued, the Song rulers made the fateful decision of inviting the nomadic warriors, the up and coming Mongols, to protect them. The Mongols overthrew the Song dynasty in 1279 and created the Yuan dynasty (1279-1368). The Ming (1369-1644) followed the Yuan dynasty but will be covered in the Modern Wave.

For a 700-year period from the Sui to the end of the Song dynasty, China experienced a period of cultural achievement considered by some to be a Golden Age. The restoration of civil service exams provided able bureaucrats that made for a large and efficient government. With a stable government, trade flourished. Trade on the Silk Road revived. Traders transported exports of silk, tea, and porcelain westward in exchange for exotic woods and precious stones. Technological inventions included steel and the manufacture of quality swords, while gunpowder was used in explosives and fire works. A new class emerged called the scholar-gentry, producing the civil servants and bureaucrats that became the Chinese elites. However, the Golden Age did not change the status of women who continued to be of the lowest status, and poor families often sold their daughters to wealthy villagers for menial labor.

Chinese literature and art reached their zenith during the Golden Age. The invention of block printing made it possible for the production of many works of literature; poetry was especially popular. The most admired poets were Li Bo, who wrote about nature, and Duo Fo who penned poems to highlight social inequalities and the poor. Daoist religious philosophy inspired artists to paint landscapes. If humans were depicted in the paintings they were mere small figures, to illustrate their insignificance compared to nature. More Buddhist monasteries and Daoist religious shrines were built throughout China. Even though Tang emperors saw both religious traditions as a threat to their rule and confiscated their land and destroyed many of their temples, they did not completely stamp out Buddhism or Daoism.

Wall scroll painted by Ma Lin in 1246. Ink on silk, notice the small human figure.

Asian Civilizations

Japan is a mountainous island country close to the Asian continent but its history is mainly one of isolation from other peoples and cultures. Japanese history in the post-classical era picks up with the Nara and Heian Period (710-1185) that is marked by a decentralized political system called feudalism. Feudalism in Japan and Europe is similar at this time. The aristocrats held power, since the government was weak and unable to do so. The aristocrats hired warriors called ***samurai*** to protect the people and their lands. They followed a code of conduct called the "way of the warrior," to guide their actions. At the end of the 12th century, a centralized Japanese government around the city of Kamakura (1192-1333) formed. But the real power rested in the hands of the ***shogun***, a commanding military authority that ruled by the sword. Mongols, who were ruling China at the time, demanded tribute from the Japanese but they refused. This defiance angered the Mongols who launched an invasion by sea, the first in 1174, in which 600 ships carrying 23,000 troops set sail for Japan. The Japanese fought bravely against a superior force and were able to finally repel the Mongols, with the help of an opportune typhoon, in 1281 that wrecked havoc on the Mongol fleet. The Kamakura Shogunate fell in 1333, after which local aristocrats, called *daimyo*, and samurais rose again to prominence during the 14th and 15th centuries. Civil war between daimyo rivalries lasted until 1477. The capital, Kyoto, was destroyed and depopulated, with the whole island engulfed in constant warfare.

Connections to nature through religion, art, and farming distinguished life in post-classical Japan. Farming was the main occupation, with wet rice the staple crop. Two religious practices—Shintoism and Buddhism—were the most popular. **Shinto**, or the "sacred way," started as the worship of spirits, living in trees, rivers, and mountains, and then later included ancestor worship. Eventually, Shinto became a state religion; the emperor was considered divine and the state sacred. In the 6th century Buddhism arrived in Japan from China. The Zen sect of Buddhism became the most popular. Although Japan adopted Buddhism, it continued to practice its native Shinto religion as well. In Japan, literature was a female vocation. The *Tale of Genji*, written around 1000, is still a popular tale of the era. Nature influenced art and architecture, with balance and harmony as recurring themes. Landscape gardens turned nature into a simple but beautiful work of art.

Japanese samurai warriors around 1860s.

In India, the Gupta Empire that had unified the country during the classical era declined after 550 and gave way to kingdoms and dynasties that held control of regions but did not unite all of India. The **Delhi Sultanate** (1206-1526) refers to the many Muslim dynasties that ruled in India over that time period. The **sultans**, a title pertaining to certain Muslim rulers, did not owe allegiance to other Muslim rulers in the region, but they did base their laws on the Qur'an and s***haria***, the body of Islamic religious law. They allowed non-Muslims to practice their religion, albeit if they paid a head tax. The Sultanate, at least temporarily, insulated the subcontinent from the potential devastation of the Mongol invasion in the 13th century. A cultural renaissance—the Indo-Muslim fusion—led to enduring contributions in architecture, music literature, and religion. The sacking of Delhi in 1398 by Timur (Tamerlane), a descendant of Genghis Khan, fractured the Sultanate rule and laid the groundwork for the later establishment of a Muslim Mongol-Turkic regime in India, the Mughals, in the 16th century.

Southeast Asia includes diverse geography and cultures; hence, separate regional kingdoms developed during the post-classical era. China initially conquered and ruled the people of Vietnam, like Korea, around 111 BCE. Even though the Vietnamese had assimilated Chinese cultural influences for almost 1,000 years, they finally drove them out in 939 and gained their independence. However, the new government of Vietnam adopted the model of Chinese central government and Confucianism as the state religion. By 1600 Vietnam was considered a powerful state in Southeast Asia. During the 9th century a kingdom called Angkor emerged to dominate the Khmer people in the area of present-day Cambodia. The kingdom was renamed the **Khmer Empire** in 802 and ruled until 1432. During the 11th and 12th centuries the Thai people created the kingdom of Thailand or Siam. They adopted Buddhism as the state religion and adopted the political principles of neighboring India. By the 11th century the Burmese created their first state—the kingdom of Pagan. Like Thailand, this kingdom was influenced by China and India. The Burmese adopted Buddhism and the political principles from India. The arrival of the Mongolian invaders during the 13th century accelerated Burma's decline. From the Malay Peninsula, four unique states emerged during the 8th century and by the 15th century Islam became an important cultural influence in the region.

Nomadic invaders from central Asia sliced through much of Asia and Eastern Europe to establish a far-flung **Mongol Empire** (1206-1405). Around the Gobi Desert and steppes of central Asia, the Mongols lived as nomadic tribes in a hard-scrabble environment. Through skill and cunning, Temujin, who took the name of Genghis Khan "meaning ruler of all," created a series of tribal alliances that united the eastern and western Mongolian kingdoms into one formidable military might. The Mongols were natural warriors. Raised on horseback, they were expert marksmen with the short bow, able to accurately hit a target of up to 400 yards while on horseback. At times they would ride for days on end, and even slept on their horses—they were actually bandaged to their horses so they did not fall. Genghis Khan used a terrorizing policy of revenge if his attacks were met with opposition. Whole towns that resisted Mongolian offensives were destroyed, the men, women, and children slaughtered and tortured. After establishing his empire, Genghis Khan founded a capital city at Karakorum. His grandsons—Batu, Hulegu, and Kublai—continued to conquer and plunder well into the 13th century. Batu and the Golden Horde invaded Russia and reduced the city of Kiev to rubble. Hulegu plundered the Abbasid territories and destroyed Baghdad. Kublai advanced into China, attacking the powerful Song dynasty from 1235 to 1271. He established the Yuan dynasty and located the capital city at Tatu, present-day Beijing.

With the help of their mounted archers, as depicted here, the Mongols conquered most of Eurasia.

The Pax Mongolia renewed trade and commerce. Disruptions sped up the decline of the old order in Asia and Eastern Europe as budding new empires emerged. As a consequence of Mongol rule, Eurasian empires had varying degrees of political unification and centralized authority. Many of them developed a viable military built around a horse-mounted cavalry, indigenous religious systems, relative peace and prosperity, social stability and longevity, an agriculture-based tax system, and powerful elites who discouraged large-scale commerce by an entrepreneurial class. In the wake of the Mongol's iron-fisted domination, a prelude to the modern period of world history got underway.

A former Orthodox basilica, later a mosque, now a museum in Istanbul, Turkey. From the date of its dedication in 360 until 1453, it served as the Hagia Sophia Cathedral of Constantinople. It was a mosque from 1453 until 1934, when it was opened as a museum.

Byzantine Empire and Russia

When the Roman Empire collapsed in 476, its territories were divided into two zones: the Byzantine Empire and North Africa in the east and Italy, Spain, and points north in the west. The **Byzantine Empire** had been divided administratively in 395 from the western portion and continued as a political entity until its collapse in 1453. Historians invented the term Byzantine—even though it was never used during the time of the empire, but it has been commonly used since the 19th century. Its capital and cultural center was the city of Constantinople (present-day Istanbul), built by the Emperor Constantine. The city sets astride the narrow Bosporus Strait overlooking the Black Sea, technically located in Europe but strategically only 12 miles away from the continent of Asia, a unique position of straddling two worlds—the West and East. Despite being founded on Roman traditions, the empire stressed the Greek heritage and language, as well as Persian influences. The size of the empire shrank and expanded over its 1000 year history, experiencing constant threats and invasions by attackers.

The most notable Byzantine emperor was Justinian (r. 527-565). Along with military victories over the Persians, he reinitiated the Roman legal tradition by compiling the laws of the Roman Empire into the **Body of Civil Law**, which remained a legal standard in Europe well into the 19th century. He also oversaw additions to the Hagia Sophia, the splendid Christian church with magnificent art and architecture.

Christianity was the official religion of the empire, and there was no separation between church and state. A schism in Christianity in 1054 permanently divided the **Eastern Orthodox Church** from the Roman Catholic Church in the West. The decline of Byzantium occurred over an extended period of time. European armies of the Fourth Crusade (1202-1204) struck a heavy blow to its vitality, when crusading knights sacked Constantinople. It never recovered its former glory and limped along until it fell to the invading army of the Ottoman Turks in 1453.

The **Slavic people** who settled in Russia were a branch that originally came from the steppes of Asia north of the Black Sea. Eastern Slavic people encountered different Viking groups out of Scandinavia from 800 to 1100, who soon came to dominate them. The Viking invaders were called Rus, from which the name Russia comes. The Vikings founded the principality of Kiev at the beginning of the 10th century and it developed into

The Baptism of Saint Prince Vladimir in 989. He brought Christianity to Russia. Painting by Viktor Vasnetsov (1890).

a collection of city-states. The Byzantine Empire sent missionaries to Russia to convert the Slavs to Eastern Orthodox Christianity. They were successful. In 989 Prince Vladimir himself converted to Christianity and later his people followed his example. Thus, Eastern Orthodox Christianity became the official religion of Kiev, although traditional religions continued to be a vital force in people's everyday lives. With the development of a strong governmental system and the addition of the cohesive force of Christianity, Kiev enjoyed a golden age during the 10th and 11th centuries. But as the Byzantine Empire declined, so did Kiev, and in 1240 Mongol invaders brutally conquered the area. Moscow alone remained free of Mongol rule as a result of cooperating with the invading armies. By 1350 Moscow thrived as the most powerful city-state in the region, and by 1380 the Muscovites were able to overthrow the yoke of Mongol rule. Ivan III, known as Ivan the Great, pushed the last of the Mongols from Russian territories in 1480. Ivan had married Sophia, niece of the last Byzantine emperor; thereafter, rulers of Russia took the title of Czar, meaning "Caesar," in reference to their loose connection to Roman tradition.

Europe

Western Europe became an unlikely core area in the Modern Wave beginning in 1500, since it remained on the margins of world history during the post-classical era, especially during the earlier period. In European history the post-classical era is most often referred to as the Middle Ages, however, it is called the post-classical era in this world history. Rome's collapse in 476 shattered political unity in the west, and the once centralized Roman authority gave way to regional kingdoms governed by Germanic people who came from northern Europe and settled former Roman lands. The area was subject to repeated nomadic invasions and internal political squabbling and posturing. The **Roman Catholic Church**, the western Christian church, was the only vital force in this European "dark age," just as Buddhism was in China during a similarly chaotic period.

The region was composed of small, competing, unstable, decentralized political units with little political unity, loosely connected by the authority of the Catholic Church. Politically, warring feudal kings and land-owning lords replaced Roman imperial authority. A system called feudalism emerged, similar to the kind found in Japan. **Feudalism** is a system of obligations that bound the lord with his subjects. In theory, the king owned all or most of the land and gave it to his leading nobles in return for their loyalty and military service. The nobles, in turn, held land that peasants, called serfs, were allowed to farm. The serfs in return gave the nobles a portion of the food they produced and also labored on the noble's land, the nobles provided protection for the serfs from outside attacks. **Serfs** under feudalism were peasant farmers who were bound to the land and subject to the owner of the land. Militarily, the centralized, well-oiled armies of the Roman Empire gave way to local feudal knights, who defended their local enclaves from aggressive neighbors or who themselves launched offensive attacks against neighbors. Occasionally, the knights were called upon to fulfill their military obligations for service to the feudal monarchs or church, as was the case in the Crusades.

Instead of the highly centralized Roman imperial economy, a self-sufficient, local, domestic economy called **manoralism** developed. Cities shrank, and trade almost disappeared. Not until around 1100 did European city guilds spark a more flourishing commercial, urban economy. Merchants slowly began to fill an economic gap not covered by the local, domestic economy or guild system, even though the merchants remained on the economic margins until around 1500. Since the European nobility was decentralized and local, the monarchs and church looked to the merchant class for loans, which in turn gave merchants increasing power and wealth. Socially, peasants and serfs comprised the vast majority of the European population, with a small elite noble class at the top of the social ladder, and a very small merchant class.

A German knight in armor plate.

As European cities grew in the later post-classical era, the merchants in Western Europe grabbed chances to engage in entrepreneurial activities that added to their accumulation of wealth. Technologically, a relatively sparse European population and loose political controls spurred entrepreneurial individuals to invent labor-saving devices to compensate for the dearth of manual labor resulting from the devastating Black Death (the Plague) in the 13th and 14th centuries. Manual laborers in Europe were thus able to achieve a higher status than their counterparts in Asian imperial societies. Culturally, the state religion of the Roman Empire gave way to a universal religion, Christianity. By the time of the collapse of the Roman Empire, the Catholic Church had emerged as a unifying, official religious institution of Europe—supported by monarchs, aristocrats, and peasants alike.

Insights: Learning from the Past

Post-Classical Civilizations

The post-classical era ended as it began, with powerful nomadic invasions sweeping across the globe. By 1400, after Mongol unity ended, Asia began to decentralize into a series of realignments and new empires: the collapse of the Byzantine Empire officially occurred in 1453 and the Arab caliphate collapsed as well, both followed by the Turk formation of the Ottoman Empire. Russia began its imperialistic expansion to the east and the first Western European explorations of the Western hemisphere commenced.

I have used a holistic method for studying world history because I believe it is a good method for looking at the "big picture" of world history and gleaning valuable insights from our past that we may use today. However, in Part III I used a more traditional, regional, chronological approach to world history in the study of individual civilizations. I think this method is useful for conveying information and helping to place world events in a chronological time frame. It is wise to use many approaches to world history so that we can learn as much about the past as possible.

Questions to Consider

1. Which approach do you like the best: historical, regional (chronological) or development? Why?

Insights: Learning from the Past

THE URBAN WAVE: CONCLUDING INSIGHTS

The Urban Wave involves complex changes for millions of people experiencing the transformation to urban centers and empires. Along with remarkable human creativity, technological innovations, religious insights and cultural developments comes a destructive aspect as well. The quest for human domination and conquest becomes an aspiration for countless leaders and their followers, as they seek to impose their will and authority over others. The empire is the trademark of the Urban Wave. Many people are no longer part of a close-knit village or band community but members of a more individualistic, impersonal urban system. People undergo a further separation from the group and nature. A move from group identity to individual consciousness is reflected in the belief systems of universal religions, helping individuals make sense of their urban way of life. People become more individualistic and separate as they congregate in larger and more densely populated urban environments.

Questions to Consider

1. Do you think the creative (constructive) aspects of the Urban Wave outweigh the destructive aspects or vice versa? Why?

Many of the vital civilizations described above continued after the artificial ending date of the post-classical era around 1500 CE, the watershed date for the beginning of the Modern Wave. These civilizations wielded a great deal of power, prosperity, and influence in their local regions and remained viable, influential political units and culturally vibrant societies even into the 19th and 20th centuries.[101] But the date does mark the emergence of a vital new core region of development on the world scene, which has enormous influence during the Modern Wave: Western Europe, the subject we turn to next.

ENDNOTES

2. Some of these characteristics are from V. Gordon Childe, "The Urban Revolution," in *The Rise and Fall of Civilizations*, eds. Jeremy A. Sabloff and C.C. Lamberg-Karlovsky (Menlo Park, CA: Cummings Publishing Company, 1974), p. 10-13; Charles Redman, *The Rise of Civilization: From Early Farmers to Urban Society in the Ancient Near East* (San Francisco: W.H. Freeman and Company, 1978), p. 4-5; and Ruth Whitehouse and John Wilkins, *The Making of Civilization* (New York: Alfred A. Knopf, 1986), p. 10-11.
3. Whitehouse and Wilkins, *Making Civilization*, p. 40-41.
4. Allen W. Johnson and Timothy Earle, *The Evolution of Human Societies: From Foraging Group to Agrarian State* (Stanford: Stanford University Press, 1987), p. 247.
5. Karl A. Wittfogel, *Oriental Despotism: A Comparative Study of Total Power* (New Haven: Yale University Press, 1957), p. 3; Whitehouse and Wilkins, *Making Civilization*, p. 37; and William A. Haviland, *Cultural Anthropology* (Fort Worth: Holt, Rinehart and Winston, Inc., 1988), p. 246-247.
6. Whitehouse and Wilkins, *Making Civilization*, p. 38.
7. Haviland, *Cultural Anthropology*. p. 247; Whitehouse and Wilkins, *Making Civilization*, p. 38; and Richley H. Crapo, *Cultural Anthropology: Understanding Ourselves and Others* (Guilford, CN: Dushkin Publishing Group, 1990), p. 93.
8. Whitehouse and Wilkins, *Making Civilization*, p. 38.
9. Robert M. Adams, *The Evolution of Urban Society: Early Mesopotamia and Prehispanic Mexico* (Chicago: Aldine Publishing Company, 1996), p. 12.
10. Clive Ponting, *A Green History of the World: The Environment and the Collapse of Great Civilizations* (New York: Penguin Books, 1991), p. 68 and 75.
11. Gerhard Lenski and Jean Lenski, *Human Societies: An Introduction to Macrosociology* (New York: McGraw-Hill Book Company, 1982), p. 173 and 183.
12. Ponting, *Green History*, p. 90 and 92.
13. Brian Swimme and Thomas Berry, *The Universe Story* (San Francisco: Harper Publishers, 1992), p. 199.
14. Jared Diamond, "The Last Americans: Environmental Collapse and the End of Civilization," *Harper's Magazine*, (June, 2003).
15. Whitehouse and Wilkins, *Making Civilization*, p. 146.
16. Lenski, *Human Societies*, p. 191-193.
17. L.S. Stavrianos, *Lifelines From Our Past: A New World History* (New York: Pantheon Books, 1989), p. 71-72; and Lenski, *Human Societies*, p. 188-190.
18. Crapo, *Cultural Anthropology*, p. 290; and Whitehouse and Wilkins, *Making Civilization*, p. 111-113.
19. Lenski, *Human Societies*, p. 196-197.
20. Johnson, *Evolution Human Societies*, p. 247; Whitehouse and Wilkins, *Making Civilization*, p. 42-43; Lenski, *Human Societies*, p. 171; and William H. McNeill, *A History of the Human Community, Volume I* (Englewood Cliffs, NJ: Prentice-Hall, Inc., 1987), p. 172.
21. Lenski, *Human Societies*, p. 171; Whitehouse and Wilkins, *Making Civilization*, p. 98-101 and 144; and McNeill, *Human Community, Vol.I*, p. 172.
22. Lenski, *Human Societies*, p. 142-146, and 180-182; and Swimme and Berry, *Universe Story*, p. 184.

23. Whitehouse and Wilkins, *Making Civilization*, p. 148-149.
24. Lenski, *Human Societies*, p. 170 and 190; and L.S. Stavrianos, *Lifelines*, p. 71-72 and p. 91.
25. Whitehouse and Wilkins, *Making Civilization*, p. 51 and 108.
26. Lenski, *Human Societies*, p. 176.
27. Brian M. Fagan, *People of the Earth: An Introduction to World Prehistory* (Glenview, IL: Scott, Foresman and Company, 1989), p. 238-239; Whitehouse and Wilkins, *Making Civilization*, p. 156-157; and Lenski, *Human Societies*, p. 187.
28. Whitehouse and Wilkins, *Making Civilization*, p. 106 and 150.
29. Lenski, *Human Societies*, p. 208; and Whitehouse and Wilkins, *Making Civilization*, p. 164.
30. Lenski, *Human Societies*, p. 208.
31. Margo Wilson and Martin Daly, "The Man Who Mistook His Wife for Chattel," in *The Adapted Mind: Evolutionary Psychology and the Generation of Culture*, eds. Jerome Barkow, Leda Cosmides, and John Tooby (New York: Oxford University Press, 1992), p. 301 and 310.
32. Whitehouse and Wilkins, *Making Civilization*, p. 164; and Lenski, Human Societies, p. 208.
33. Stavrianos, *Lifelines*, p. 68.
34. Gerda Lerner, *The Creation of Patriarchy* (New York: Oxford University Press, 1986), p. 212-213; and Lenski, *Human Societies*, p. 208.
35. Wilson and Daly, "Wife for Chattel," in *Adapted Mind*, p. 302; and Stavrianos, *Lifelines*, p. 69-70.
36. Lerner, *Creation of Patriarchy*, p. 133-135.
37. Wilson and Daly, "Wife for Chattel," in *Adapted Mind*, p. 301.
38. Whitehouse and Wilkins, *Making Civilization*, p. 166.
39. Simon Roberts, *Order and Dispute: An Introduction to Legal Anthropology* (Oxford: Penguin Books, 1979) p. 139; Whitehouse and Wilkins, *Making Civilization*, p. 91; Johan Goudsbloom, E.L. Jones, and Stephen Mennell, *Human History and Social Process* (Exeter, England: University of Exeter Press, 1989), p. 80; and Alexander Alland, Jr. *To Be Human: An Introduction to Anthropology* (New York: Alfred A. Knopf, 1980), p. 263.
40. Goudsbloom, Jones, and Stephen, *Human History*, p. 80; Lenski, *Human Societies*, p. 177; and Whitehouse and Wilkins, *Making Civilization*, p. 91.
41. Lenski, *Human Societies*, p. 177; and Stavrianos, *Lifelines*, p. 56.
42. Lenski, *Human Societies*, p. 198.
43. Morton H. Fried, "On the Evolution of Social Stratification and the State," in *The Rise and Fall of Civilizations* eds. Jeremy Sabloff and C.C. Lamberg-Karlovsky (Menlo Park, CA: Cummings Publishing Company, 1974), p. 33.
44. Stavrianos, *Lifelines*, p. 2; and Swimme and Berry, *Universe Story*, p. 200.
45. Johnson and Earle, *Evolution of Human Societies*, p. 246; and Elman R. Service, *Origins of the State and Civilization: The Process of Cultural Evolution*, (New York: W.W. Norton and Co., Inc., 1975), p. 15.
46. Roberts, *Order and Dispute*, p. 138.
47. Lenski, *Human Societies*, p. 198-199; and Whitehouse and Wilkins, *Making Civilization*, p. 91.
48. Roberts, *Order and Dispute*, p. 138.
49. Roberts, *Order and Dispute*, p. 139; and Lenski, *Human Societies*, p. 176.

50. David Kaplan, in *Evolution and Culture* eds. M.D. Sahlins and E.R. Service (Ann Arbor, MI: University of Michigan Press, 1960), p. 69-92. Quoted in Crapo, *Cultural Anthropology*, p. 276.
51. Crapo, *Cultural Anthropology*, p. 276. Also see William McNeill, *A World History* (New York: Oxford University Press, 1979), chapter two.
52. Lenski, *Human Societies*, p. 141.
53. Crapo, *Cultural Anthropology*, p. 100; Stavrianos, *Lifelines*, p. 82; Lenski, *Human Societies*, p. 174; and Keith F. Otterbein, *The Evolution of War: A Cross-Cultural Study* (New York: Hraf Press, 1970), p. 105 and 107-108.
54. Stavrianos, *Lifelines*, p. 82-86; and Crapo, *Cultural Anthropology*, p. 106.
55. Lenski, *Human Societies*, p. 145-146; Crapo, *Cultural Anthropology*, p. 100; and Ernestine Friedl, *Women and Men: An Anthropologist's View* (New York: Holt, Rinehart, and Winston, 1975), p. 51 and 60.
56. Robert Jay Russell, *The Lemur's Legacy: The Evolution of Power, Sex, and Love* (New York: Putnam Books, 1993), p. 193-194.
57. Kevin Reilly, *The West and the World: A History of Civilization Volume I* (New York: Harper Collins Publishers, 1989), p. 111.
58. Whitehouse and Wilkins, *Making Civilization*, p. 122-123.
59. Whitehouse and Wilkins, *Making Civilization*, p. 122-124; and William A. Green, "Periodization in European and World History," *Journal of World History* Vol. 3, No. 1 (1992), p. 42-43.
60. Whitehouse and Wilkins, *Making Civilization*, p. 95
61. Gustav Mensching, "Folk and Universal Religion," in *Readings on the Sociology of Religion*, eds. Thomas F. O"Dea and Janet K. Odea (Englewood Cliffs: Prentice Hall, 1073), p. 86-89.
62. Swimme and Berry, *Universe Story*, p. 183 and 185; Lerner, *Creation of Patriarchy*, p. 151 and 180; and Rosalind Miles, *The Women's History of the World* (New York: Harper & Row Publishers, 1989), p. 59.
63. Anne Baring and Jules Cashford, *The Myth of the Goddess* (London: Arkana Books, Penguin, 1991), p. 273 and 278
64. S.N. Eisenstadt. *The Origins and Diversity of Axial Age Civilizations* (Albany, New York: State University of New York Press, 1986., Eisenstadt, *Axial Age*, p. 19.
65. Karl Jaspers, *Way to Wisdom: An Introduction to Philosophy* (New Haven: Yale University Press, 1951), p. 99-100.
66. Mensching, "Folk and Universal Religion," *Readings*, p. 89; Green, "Periodization," *Journal World History*, p. 42-43; and Eisenstadt, *Axial Age Civilizations*, p. 4 and 8.
67. Whitehouse and Wilkins, *Making Civilization*, p. 128-130.
68. Whitehouse and Wilkins, *Making Civilization*, p. 128-132.
69. Lenski, *Human Societies*, p. 208.
70. Lenski, *Human Societies*, p. 209.
71. Anatoly M. Khazanov, *Nomads and the Outside World* (Madison, Wisconsin: The University of Wisconsin Press, 1983), p. xxxiii, xli, xlii, and 4; and Crapo, *Cultural Anthropology*, p. 285.
72. Khazanov, *Nomads*, p. xxxiii, 85-86, and 89; and David Christian, "Inner Eurasia as a Unit of World History," *Journal of World History* Vol. 5, No. 2 (1994), p. 190.
73. Khazanov, *Nomads*, p. 89-90.
74. Khazanov, *Nomads*, p. 95.
75. Khazanov, *Nomads*, p. 107.

76. Christian, "Inner Asia," *Journal World History*, p. 176-179.
77. Crapo, *Cultural Anthropology*, p. 62-63 and 286; Haviland, *Cultural Anthropology*, p. 226; and Victor Barnouw, *Anthropology: A General Introduction* (Homewood, IL: The Dorsey Press, 1979), p. 151.
78. Christian, "Inner Asia," *Journal World History*, p. 191.
79. Crapo, *Cultural Anthropology*, p. 62; Barnouw, *Anthropology*, p. 151; and Khazanov, *Nomads*, p. xi and 39.
80. Khazanov, *Nomads*, p. 48-49 and 93.
81. Crapo, *Cultural Anthropology*, p. 63; and Christian, "Inner Asia," *Journal World History*, p. 184.
82. Stearns, Adas, and Schwartz, *World Civilizations*, p. 85-86.
83. Khazanov, *Nomads*, p. 154.
84. Khazanov, *Nomads*, p. xii, 76 and 123; and Crapo, *Cultural Anthropology*, p. 63.
85. Khazanov, *Nomads*, p. 128; and Christian, "Inner Asia," *Journal World History*, p. 195.
86. Khazanov, *Nomads*, p. 126-128, 130-131, 133, and 135.
87. Peter Stearns, Michael Adas, and Stuart B Schwartz, *World Civilizations: The Global Experience* (New York: Harper Collins Publishers, 1996), p. 81.
88. Khazanov, *Nomads*, p. 153.
89. Crapo, *Cultural Anthropology*, p. 63; Khazanov, *Nomads*, p. 73; and Reilly, *West and World*, p. 34.
90. Khazanov, *Nomads*, p. 148.
91. Khazanov, *Nomads*, p. 134 and 151.
92. Stearns, Adas, and Schwartz, *World Civilizations*, p. 80.
93. Crapo, *Cultural Anthropology*, p. 63; Christian, Inner Asia," *Journal World History*, p. 184 and 197; and Margaret Ehrenberg, *Women in Prehistory* (Norman, OK: University of Oklahoma Press, 1989), p. 105.
94. Marija Gimbutas, *The Civilization of the Goddess* (San Francisco: Harper Collins Press, 1991), p. 354; Khazanov, *Nomads*, p. 101; and Christian, "Inner Asia," *Nomads*, p. 178, 193-194.
95. Stearns, Adas, and Schwartz, *World Civilizations*, p. 80.
96. Walter Goldschmidt, "A General Model for Pastoral Social Systems," in *L'equipe ecikigique et anthropologique des societes pastorales* (Cambridge, 1979), p. 20-21. Quoted in Christian, "Inner Asia," *Journal World History*, p. 192-193.
97. Gimbutas, *Civilization*, p. 398-400; and Marija Gimbutas, *The Language of the Goddess*, (San Francisco: Harper Collins Press, 1989), p. xiii.
98. Gimbutas, *Language*, p. xx; and Riane Eisler, *The Chalice and the Blade: Our History, Our Future* (San Francisco: Harper Collins Press, 1988), p. 45.
99. Factual information for this section has been gathered primarily from the following general world history textbooks: Reilly, *West and World*; Stearns Adas, and Schwartz, *World Civilizations*; William J. Duiker, Jackson J. Spielvogel, *World History, Volume I to 1800* (Minneapolis/St. Paul: West Publishing Company, 1994); Philip J. Adler, *World Civilizations* (Minneapolis/St. Paul: West Publishing Company, 1996); Peter N. Stearns, *World History: Patterns of Change and Continuity* (New York: Harper Collins Publishers, 1995); John P. McKay, Bennett D. Hill, and John Buckler, *A History of World Societies Volume I* (Boston: Houghton Mifflin Company, 1996). Although the information has been gathered from secondary sources, the configuration is my own.

100. Whitehouse and Wilkins, *Making Civilization*, p. 30. Different dates are used for the development of the Olmec civilization. Some use later dates such as 800 to 400 BCE
101. Whitehouse and Wilkins, *Making Civilization*, p. 30.
102. Edward L. Farmer, "Civilization as a Unit of World History: Eurasia and Europe's Place in It," *The History Teacher* Vol. 18, No. 3 (1985), p. 358.

Chapter 7

People Multiply and Dominate the Globe: The Modern Wave

"To build may have to be the slow and laborious task of years. To destroy can be the thoughtless act of a single day."

— Sir Winston Churchill

INTRODUCTION TO THE MODERN WAVE

Around 1500, a fourth profound transformation in our world history occurred with the beginning of the Modern Wave. The 1500 date is a compelling watershed date that marks when modern developments began in Western Europe and then unevenly diffused to other areas of the world. The Modern Wave brought deep and interconnected changes: political, with the development of liberalism; economic, with the spread of capitalism; technological, with the scientific and industrial revolutions; social, with the rise of the middle and working classes; and cultural, with a new emphasis on scientific, rational thinking and the consequent weakening of the authority of the Catholic Church.

The Modern Wave signifies the systematic development and diffusion of new political, cultural, economic, technological, environmental, and social ideas in Western Europe and ultimately across the globe. However, the process of modernization was not uniform even within Western Europe, and less so beyond; instead, modern ideas were assimilated to varying degrees ranging from eager acceptance to forceful resistance. The modern story has many dimensions: the conventional story of the "march of progress" which has been so ingrained in us as one of linear, forward progression must be seen in its context to include the destruction of traditional cultures, widespread deterioration of the environment, alarming population growth, and devastating world wars. We can learn many valuable lessons about our world today from examining the history of the Modern Wave.

The concept of the core and the periphery, introduced in the Urban Wave, which describes the unequal relationship of the urban center to its surrounding regions, has particular application during the Modern Wave. Core areas are where intense and extensive modern changes in technology, military, society, politics, culture, and especially the economy take place. Here is where wealth generation and accumulation are concentrated and also where rules for the system are devised and enforced. Periphery regions are drawn into a dependent interaction with core regions; commercial wealth is extracted from the periphery in the form of cheap raw materials produced with cheap labor—or, more recently, manufactured goods produced with cheap labor. The wealth from this transaction is siphoned to core areas where it is concentrated or used to generate more wealth. External areas are those that have not been incorporated into the core-

and-periphery world system; they remain outside modern developments. Core and periphery areas are not fixed but shift over time. The story of the Modern Wave is how the vast majority of the world is ultimately brought into this modern world economic system.

While 1500 marks the beginning of significant modern changes taking hold in Western Europe, the rest of the world was still external to modern developments and retained its Urban, Agricultural, or Communal ways. Except for the Western hemisphere and parts of Western Africa, it would not be until the 19th century that Western Europe's dominance around the world would be significantly felt. Before looking at the development of the Modern Wave, let us first briefly examine world political entities from 1500 forward into the 19th century and Europe around 1500.

The World After 1500

In West Asia, the Ottoman Turks in 1453 captured the once powerful Byzantine Empire's capital at Constantinople and established the Ottoman Empire. They spread Islam throughout the empire and ruled from their capital, Istanbul, the former Constantinople, until they were defeated,

Mehmed II enters Constantinople in 1453, conquest of the Byzantine Empire by the Ottoman Turks, painting by Fausto Zonaro

Naghsh-i Jahan Square, Isfahan, Iran.

along with their German allies, at the conclusion of World War I in 1918. At this point, much of the empire except Turkey was broken up into mandates under the guardianship of the French and British.

The **Safavid dynasty** (1501-1722) united Iran into a magnificent empire, the first since the Sassanian Empire that ended in 651CE. The Safavids established the societal and territorial foundations for the modern state of Iran; Shi'a Islam became the official religion, and it spread throughout the region. The stunning capital city of Isfahan was built during the reign of Shah Abba and became the center of flourishing Persian arts and culture.

As the post-classical era came to a close around 1500, Africa was generally in a state of decline, especially compared to the heights of civilization it had attained during the preceding centuries. This decline was due to a combination of internal quarrels, conquest by outsiders, and environmental factors. Until about 1850, Arabs and Moors remained the major external influence in sub-Saharan Africa. When Europeans arrived on the African coast in the 16th and 17th centuries, they witnessed cities teetering on the brink of collapse. Early Portuguese traders arrived at the time of African decline and had the misguided impression that Africans were subservient, backward, and lacking civilization. Later traders—the Dutch, English, and other Europeans—shared their racist attitudes, which can be attributed partly to the circumstances of African decline they witnessed.[1]

In south Asia, the **Mughal Empire** (1526-1739) unified small kingdoms in India. Mughal, the Persian word for Mongol, generally refers to the Central Asians who claimed descent from the Mongol warriors of Genghis Khan. The rulers of the empire brought the Muslim religion to India. Babur (r.1526-1530) founded the Mughal Empire, and his armies slowly conquered the subcontinent. He ruled with an iron hand but also loved learning and culture. His grandson, Akbar, came to the throne at the age of 14 and expanded the empire. Although a Muslim himself, Akbar tolerated other religious traditions and continued the love of learning practiced by his grandfather. But by 1739, the weakened empire succumbed to British rule.

The Chinese **Ming dynasty** (1368-1644) proved stable for close to 300 years. The dynasty strengthened the Great Wall to the north to ensure that the Mongols would not return to rule again. They created a highly efficient bureaucracy, using the civil service exam to fill bureaucratic positions. The Ming even devised a national school system to help recruit able students for a career in the bureaucracy. They completed the Grand Canal that provided shipment of agricultural products from north to south. At the time, the Chinese surpassed Europeans in their capacity to launch naval expeditions. Chinese voyager Zheng He commanded seven naval expeditions of 28,000 men and 62 ships between 1405 and 1433. However, the Ming emperor suddenly and inexplicably recalled the Chinese expedition to Africa during the 15th century; instead, China concentrated on internal affairs and turned its back on external matters like world exploration. The Manchu people from Manchuria overthrew the Ming dynasty and ruled as the **Qing dynasty** (1644-1911). Like the Yuan (Mongol) dynasty

Akbar, widely considered the greatest of the Mughal emperors (1556-1605).

A display at the Ibn Battuta mall in Dubai purports to compare the size of ships used by Zheng He and Christopher Columbus.

before them, the Manchu ruled as outsiders but did adopt many Chinese customs and culture.

In 1603 **Tokugawa** Ieyasu became the leading political power in Japan and took the title shogun. Successors to Tokugawa continued in power until 1868. During this time, called the period of "Great Peace," the shoguns politically unified Japan and eliminated feudalism. Trade and industry flourished, the economy prospered, and culture thrived. At first Portuguese traders who landed in Japan in 1543 were welcomed. Jesuit missionaries arrived in 1549 and by end of the 16th century thousands of Japanese had converted to Catholicism. However, the Japanese Catholics became intolerant, which prompted officials to oust all Jesuit missionaries from the island. Finally, all European merchants were expelled from Japan except for a small Dutch community in Nagasaki.

In Eastern Europe and central Asia the Russian Empire (1480-1917), after ridding itself of the Mongolian yoke, flexed its muscles by aggressively expanding eastward. It was the second largest empire the world had ever seen, second only to the earlier Mongol Empire. Czars ruled as absolute monarchs. Great disparity in wealth separated peasants, who mostly labored as serfs on estates, from the wealthy landowners.

Questions to Consider

1. What characteristics of the societies mentioned above would lead you to consider them as part of the Urban Wave?

Europe Around 1500

Europe's emergence as the leader of the Modern Wave can be traced back before 1500. At the beginning of the Modern Wave, Western Europe had an unfavorable balance of trade with Asia, and entrepreneurs strove anxiously to sell more goods to the eastern regions in order to equalize trade flow. The material poverty of Western Europeans around 1500, compared to the richer East, helped stimulate merchants to seek wealth by engaging in sea trade along the coastal areas outside Europe. In their sea-faring adventures, they added to their technological skills by drawing on the long-standing technology and knowledge the Arabs and Chinese pioneered in building and navigating ocean-going fleets. Europeans continually encountered societies more wealthy and powerful than they were. But unlike the ambitious Europeans, the more prosperous elites of the Arab and Asian empires were content with their wealth and stability and saw no need to actively pursue risky sea trade. It was the Europeans, lacking fewer options than more established regions, who assumed the risks of sea trade in order to seek a more equitable economic footing with their more affluent neighbors to the East.[2]

The development of a core area in Western Europe involved a number of interacting factors that can be described as a feedback loop system. These factors can be placed into two categories: material and measurable factors, and factors derived from culture and worldview. On the material side, Western Europe by 1500 was on the way to becoming a technologically sophisticated society. Western skills in shipbuilding, navigation, and high-quality weaponry catapulted the West into a world leadership position in these areas. Technological and military innovations enabled Western Europe to explore, exploit, and conquer the Western hemisphere. The material riches from the continents, especially silver, added to European coffers and provided surplus capital to spend and invest, spurring even more economic growth in a spiral of expansion.

Non-material factors included the influence of the Italian Renaissance, the Protestant Reformation, and the emergence of new scientific, rational, and secular ways of thinking. The Renaissance sparked an adventurous spirit in which monarchies competed with each other to acquire overseas colonies. The Protestant Reformation

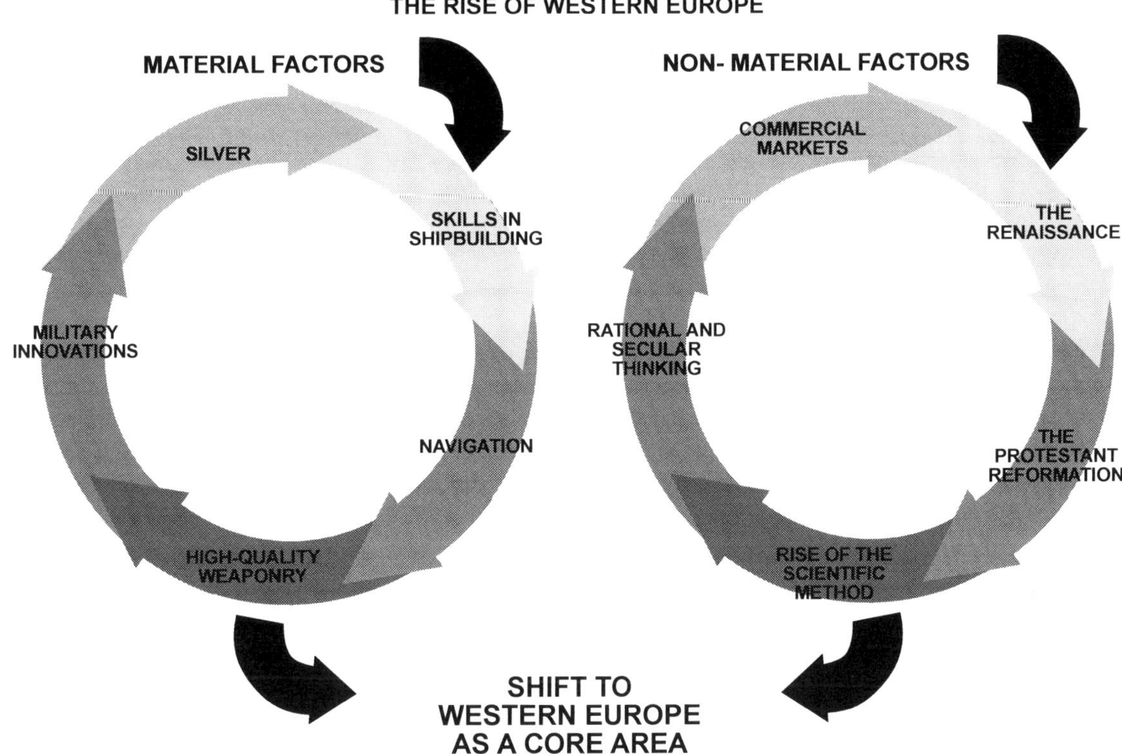

shredded the singular authority of the Catholic Church and loosened its control. These factors contributed to flourishing creativity, innovation, and competition in areas ranging from the arts to the economy. Along with the subsequent Catholic Reformation, Christian missionaries raced to spread their message of Christianity either peacefully or by force to the non-Christian world. Trade followed the cross, as it would repeatedly, to bring new lands into the Christian fold and the thriving commercial market place. Scientific, rational, secular ways of thinking that also challenged the Catholic Church were instrumental in fostering new ideologies that complemented economic expansion and exploitation.

To understand the Modern Wave more clearly, the rest of this chapter after the insight section is organized into three eras.

Three Eras in the Modern Wave

- early modern era 1500-1750
- the modern industrial era 1750-1900
- the 20th century 1900-2000

This chapter does not purport to give an all-encompassing historical account of people and events in this 500 year modern era but instead highlights significant themes according to the five currents and sub-currents to give a more holistic account of the interdependent variables that interacted to form the complex and dynamic Modern Wave. The world beyond Western Europe, as described briefly above, continued to flourish. But the modern era is such a significant development in world history that the non-Western world is, unfortunately, relegated to the sidelines in this chapter because of length. The principal attention will be directed to developments in Western Europe and later the United States, with the non-European world mentioned in relation to the West. Although some may claim this is Eurocentric, I claim that the modern era—both its destructive and creative forces—cannot be overlooked. Around 1500 modernity did not yet influence the entire world, but the process was getting underway.

Insights: Learning from the Past

Introduction to the Modern Wave

As is evident from the brief description of the world around 1500, most of the world continued to hold characteristics of the other waves previously discussed: the Urban Wave with flourishing empires, dynasties, states, or nomadic pastoralists; the Agricultural Wave with village farmers and chiefdoms; or the Communal Wave with bands of foragers. Although Western Europe begins its ascendancy on the world stage around 1500 ushering in the Modern Wave, an important insight to consider is that modern attitudes, beliefs, and policies did not significantly influence most regions of the world until the 19th century. One of the hallmarks of this holistic approach to world history is its recognition of the developmental simultaneity that characterizes our human history. At any particular point in time, human societies around the world are at differing developmental junctures—some are foragers, some are farmers, some live in urban city-states or empires, even as in the Modern Wave, some are developing modern ways of life. This is particularly evident in the Modern Wave, perhaps more so than any other wave, when clashes among people at different junctures led to conflict and both positive and negative interaction.

Questions to Consider

1. Do you think directing attention to Western Europe's modern development is the best approach to use in this chapter? Do you have other suggestions?

EARLY MODERN ERA (1500-1750)

Relationship with Nature: Ecosystem Currents

A constant theme in the Modern Wave is the more systematic and extensive human effort to dominate and tame nature for material benefit. The philosophy of domination and exploitation intensified with the advancement of scientific ideas that developed in the early modern era. Scientific thinkers, like Sir Issac Newton, depicted the world as a giant machine, in which nature existed to be controlled, classified, investigated, and divided up by humans. The Protestant religion intensified the Catholic view that nature should be subdued and dominated by humans.[3] Unlike the animistic religions of the Communal and Agricultural Waves, European religious traditions thought of humans as divinely created and thus above the plane of nature and other animals. Therefore, humans had the right, ordained by God, to control nature as they saw fit.

Utilizing this scientific and religious justification for the subjugation of nature, the rise of commercial capitalism further exploited nature for human material wants by reducing it to a monetary commodity. For example, beaver and other fur-bearing animals in North America were trapped to near extinction in the mid-17th century in order to provide hats and coats for a rising middle class consumer market. Nature was drawn into the capitalist web as an economic product assigned a specific value according to laws of supply and demand. A scientific, capitalist modern worldview displaced the awe and respect for nature held by people in the Communal and Agricultural Waves.

A reconstructed dodo bird, which has been extinct since the mid-to-late 17th century. Standing about one meter tall, its extinction was directly attributable to human activity.

Ways of Living: Techno-Economic Currents

Economic Systems

The formulation of the capitalist economic system characterized, and perhaps defined, the Modern Wave. **Capitalism** is defined here as an economic system in which private parties make their goods and services available on a free market and seek to make a profit on their activities. Private parties, either individuals or companies, own the means of production—land, machinery, tools, equipment, buildings, workshops, and raw materials. Private parties decide what to produce. The center of the system is the market in which business people compete, and the forces of supply and demand determine the prices received for goods and services. Businesses may realize profits from their endeavors, reinvest the profits gained, or suffer losses. Although capitalism is sometimes referred to as a market economy, I distinguish between the two in this world history. The market economy operates according to capitalist principles but is smaller in scale and mostly locally based. It had existed largely on the fringe of urban economies for centuries before 1500. Even in Europe after the rise of cities after 1200, the market economy operated only on the margins of European economic activity, curbed by city guilds whenever they saw a threat to their regulated, organized economy. The market economy in the Urban Wave did not exert undue influence on the political, cultural, or social currents at the time. Capitalism, on the other hand, would become much more influential in shaping the other currents in the Modern Wave and, therefore, had a greater impact on all developments in the West and subsequently around the world.

A capitalist economy is a multi-dimensional system that has diverse ways of functioning; there is no one standard version of capitalism. In other words, capitalism as an economic system can operate with minimal government regulation or with government heavily guiding and regulating the process. Under capitalism, the elites can devise laws and regulations that favor them in accumulating wealth or, on the other hand, laws and regulations can require that wealth be distributed to greater numbers of people in an equitable way. Thus, capitalism takes on different forms during the Modern and Global Waves. In the Modern Wave, the expansion and intensification of capitalism has a profound impact on the organization of society, the environment, technology, and political process. In other words, capitalism as an economic system extends its economic web into all dimensions of modern life.

During the early modern era, the main ingredient in capitalist wealth creation was the development of **primary industries**—mining, agriculture, forestry, trapping animals, and fishing—that changed natural resources into primary products. The manufacturing industries that amass, package, clean or process the raw materials close to the primary producers are generally considered part of this sector as well, especially if the raw material is unsuitable for sale in its raw form or difficult to transport long distances. For example, in boiling houses attached to sugar cane plantations, the raw cane was boiled into raw sugar for easier transport to markets in Europe. Production and trade in these primary industries, along with an increase in commercial agricultural productivity, became the most dynamic sectors of the European economy and spurred wealth creation. Thus, capitalism in the early modern era has often been called **commercial capitalism**.

Capitalism burst onto the world stage around 1500 largely because Europe incorporated the riches from the Western hemisphere into its economic orb. At this time, one of the particular versions of capitalism called mercantilism emerged. **Mercantilism** was based on the economic relationship between a European country, called the "mother country," and the colonies that it had established throughout the Western hemisphere and beyond. The colonial rulers strove to maintain a favorable balance of trade for themselves by importing cheap raw materials from their colonies and in turn exporting back to their colonies the more profitable manufactured goods that they produced. With this economic policy, Western European commercial cities were the core areas of economic development, and the colonies were the periphery. Many European colonial governments like the British and the Dutch encouraged mercantilism through legislation that made it legal and profitable to monopolize as much manufacturing as possible in the mother country.

The famed Potosi silver mines in Bolivia. Shows the first image of the mines in Europe in 1553.

Mercantilism was dependent upon a form of control called **colonialism**: the extension of a powerful country's control over a dependent, weaker country, territory, or people. Colonizers generally dominate the resources, labor, and markets of their colonial territory, and may also impose religious, socio-cultural, and linguistic structures on the native populations and intervene in their political affairs. The periphery, or colonies, supplied the natural resources to the colonial rulers: silver from Mexico, Bolivia, and Peru; furs and skins from North America and Siberia; sugar from the West Indies and Brazil; tobacco and cotton from the American South; coffee and rubber from Southeast Asia; and jute from India. Low-paid native laborers, indentured servants, or slaves extracted the raw materials. For example, the former Spanish colonial city of Potosi in Bolivia, purportedly the highest city in the world, lies in the shadows of the fabled "mountain of silver." To extract the prized ore, the Spanish from 1540 to 1640 forced local indigenous men to labor in the mines for weeks on end, some never seeing the light of day. Indigenous miners died by the thousands due to exhaustion, horrible working conditions, and mercury poisoning from the mining method. The Spanish eventually replaced indigenous workers with slaves from Africa, who were called "human mules," since they replaced mules who could not survive the horrible conditions.

Wealth accumulated in the core areas from this legalized commercial process. Money poured into Western European treasuries, and profits were reinvested in other enterprises, as was the case in England, but not in Spain. Most of the Spanish wealth found its way into royal hands, who chose to spend their newfound wealth on wars of expansion and extravagant luxury goods.

The additional infusion of money into the European economic system eventually flowed to British bankers and investors or to private Western European shippers, financiers, merchants, and manufacturers.[4] This transfer of wealth was a significant development that spelled the eventual decline of Spain from core status and the rise of Britain to that station.

Agrarian changes also spurred the growth of commercial capitalism. For centuries in Europe, peasants practiced an **open field system**, a form of agricultural organization in which they farmed large tracks of land for elite landlords. Peasant farmers produced food for their own subsistence needs and paid a required amount of the surplus as tribute to the landowner. In this system, efficiency and productivity were largely secondary, with the tribute payment to the landowner and the subsistence needs of the peasants as primary. But the open field system began to give way to farming according to capitalist principles with the **enclosure** process, where efficiency and productivity became primary. Farms, as well as shared areas called "the commons," were first enclosed or converted to privately owned plots marked with clear boundaries and specific private ownership. This privatization and commodification process first took off in England in the early modern era where it was enthusiastically embraced by landowners who benefited from this move to a capitalist economy. Although uprooted peasant farmers vainly protested their plight, since they were the ones who lost the land they had farmed for centuries, their welfare was largely ignored in this strictly financial process.

Scientific methods to increase crop yields were applied to newly enclosed fields that were now capable of producing two crops yearly, while one-third lay fallow. Many landowners found these new agricultural methods generated sizable profits in expanding domestic markets, hence the enfolding of agriculture into the commercial economy. With these agricultural innovations, increased productivity, and favorable climate conditions, demographic growth ballooned. Europe in the 18th century continued to be predominately agricultural, but the function of this key sector changed from the general production of foodstuffs for the local population to a profitable business enterprise.

Questions to Consider

1. The expansion of capitalism ushered in what changes in European society? Do you think these changes were beneficial or detrimental? Explain

Exchange and Trade

By 1400, Europe's unfavorable balance of trade with Asia verged on an economic crisis. Europeans imported valuable spices, silk, sugar, perfume, and jewels from the East, while they exported less valuable wool, tin, and copper. Faced with a need for new markets, Europeans embarked on a frenzied activity of shipbuilding, utilizing their refined knowledge of the compass, map-making skills, and shipbuilding techniques, some borrowed from Chinese inventions. After the Ming dynasty of China called back Zheng He's expedition, world exploration fell by default to the risk-taking Europeans, and by 1500, they seriously set out to explore the sea in a frenzied pursuit of trade and profit.

Stone fences, such as this one in Glean Llchd, UK, define property boundaries.

Portugal and Spain forged the way to finding new trade routes and lands, but Britain, France, and the Netherlands impatiently snapped at their heels as they sought to overtake the leaders. The voyages of such well-known explorers as Vasco de Gama, Ferdinand Magellan, Christopher Columbus, and others ushered in the age of European exploration. Even though Indian and Arab ships had been trading on the seas for centuries and continued to do so, by the 18th century they were muscled aside as European vessels dominated the world's sea-lanes. But Europe's sea power was limited, and other than the Americas, European exploration until the 1800s was largely confined to island outposts, scattered port cities, and coastal areas.[5]

With invigorated European exploration, the trade network shifted from Arab merchants concentrated along the Mediterranean Sea to northwestern European merchants centered on the Atlantic Ocean. Europeans overtook Muslim and Hindu traders' chief trade routes, which were largely relegated to regional specialties. Spices and tropical products formerly carried in Arab ships now traveled via European vessels; in return, European manufactured textile goods flowed to ports in Africa and Asia. For example, the **Triangle Trade** in the 18th century developed between Africa, Europe, and the Americas. European ships carried guns, knives, metal-ware, manufactured items, beads, colored cloth, and liquor to the West African coast to be exchanged with African chieftains who dealt in captured slaves. The captured slaves shipped to the Americas were exchanged for raw materials such as sugar, tobacco, furs, precious metals, and raw cotton that were in turn transported to Europe to be made into finished goods that were either shipped back to the colonies or to Africa to begin the trading network again.[6] The slave trade generated exorbitant profits.

Slavery was a common practice in the Urban Wave with Africans, along with others, forced into the system through debt bondage, by outright capture as prisoners of war, or by inherited status. Originally controlled by Arab traders, African slaves passed northward to the Middle East through the states of Ghana and Mali long before Europeans engaged in the Atlantic slave trade. During the Urban Wave and the early modern era, African and Muslim societies, like European societies later, did not consider slavery to be morally reprehensible.[7] But with the Modern Wave and the increasing expansion of the capitalist economic system, the buying and selling of slaves expanded and intensified.

Along with their European counterparts, West African elites engaged in the slave trade to gain an economic advantage for themselves by trading captured slaves for firearms and other manufactured items from Europe. The African slave traders used their additional firepower to raid neighboring tribes and villages to capture even more slaves for trade and profit. Slaving sparked conflict between local tribes as deadly competi-

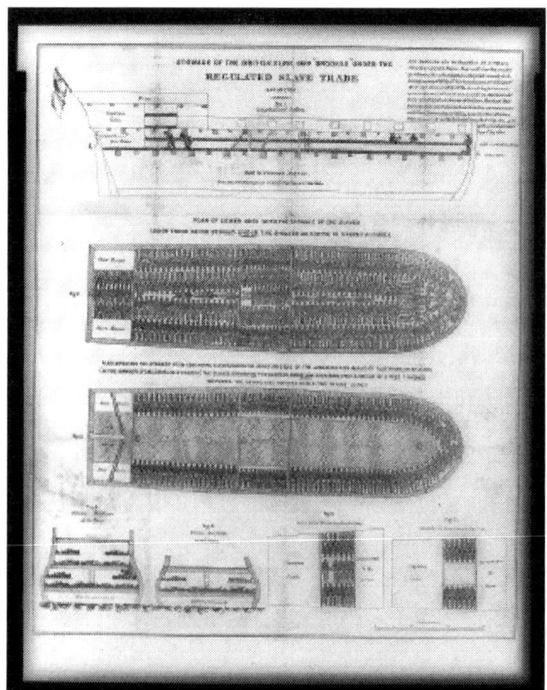

Stowage of African slaves on a British slave ship.

tion increased. African slavers sold their human commodities to eager European buyers at port cities along the Atlantic seaboard who, in turn, transported their human cargo to slave dealers in the Western hemisphere. Misery, starvation, or early death awaited many of the captured victims; estimates show that on average, 25 percent of the slaves apprehended and transported to the Western hemisphere in what was known as the Middle Passage suffered an agonizing death.[8]

The long-term effects of the slave trade on the population of Africa are subject to intense debate. Estimates indicate that about ten million humans were exported from Africa to the Western hemisphere between the years 1650 and 1870, and another 3.5 million were forcibly transported from Africa to the Near East and the Mediterranean region in the same period. The African population remained stagnant for about 150 years (1650-1800), before rising again after the end of the slave trade. The slave trade also had a destructive effect by disrupting and contributing to the collapse of previously stable and prosperous African village societies. I suggest using a systems approach to examine the slave trade. All the actors in the process—both African and European traders and slave buyers—were intricately connected in this lucrative line of work to make a profit with little regard for the ethical considerations. The slave trade also pitted Africans against each other as they competed for captured slaves in the ghastly era of enslavement and genocide.

The origins of cartels or corporations can be traced to the 16th century when English and Dutch merchants formed **joint stock companies**. European monarchies granted royal charters to joint-stock companies for trade with their colonies. One advantage of joint stock companies was that now one individual was not required to raise all the capital for entrepreneurial activities and, therefore, investors could pool their capital to lessen their possible losses from risky ventures. This form of organization was more advantageous for risky ventures where large investments were essential and a large pool of investors was needed for capitalization.[9] On the other hand, the main

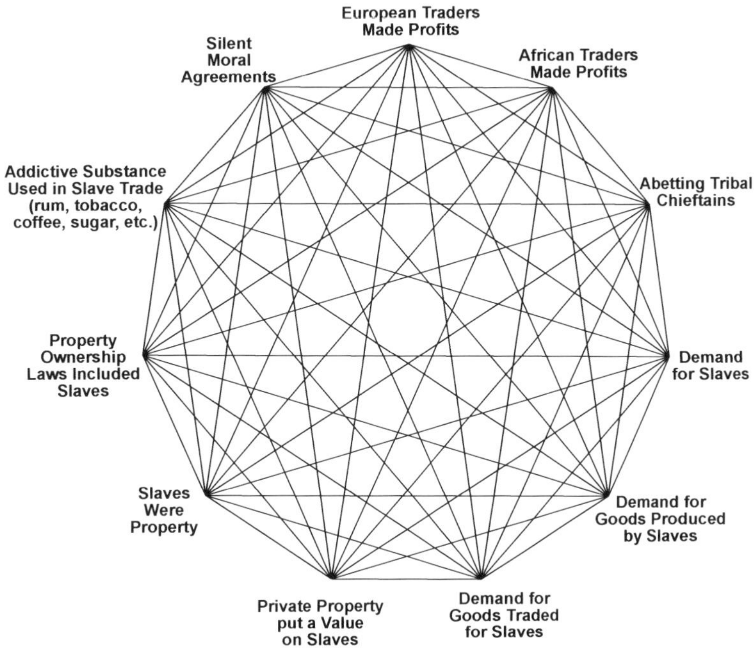

objective of joint stock companies, the forerunners of the modern corporation, was to make a handsome profit for their shareholders with little regard for the social, environmental, or moral consequences of their actions. The most famous or infamous joint stock company falls to the British East India Company, chartered in 1600 by Queen Elizabeth I. The company obtained monopoly trading privileges with India that were expanded into virtual rule of the sub-continent until its dissolution in 1858.

Questions to Consider

1. What is the connection between slavery and capitalism?

Human Networks: Social Currents

Family

During the 15th and 16th centuries, perhaps even earlier, Western European family patterns began to shift to a "European-style" family that differed from other societies around the world. The extended, three-generational family was a rarity in western and central Europe by 1700, and instead, a **nuclear-family** household—a form of family that consisted only of married persons and their children—was more the norm. Although elites continued to marry at a younger age, studies have shown that the average marriage age in the 17th and 18th centuries was around 27 or older, while a substantial minority never married. Late marriage ensured that the couple and their children were self-sufficient and self-reliant and not a burden on the community. It also tended to reduce birth rates with usually just three or four children surviving infancy. Having fewer children living to adulthood protected property against repeated divisions among numerous children. This system of late marriage required considerable individual self and social control and family supervision. Laws and community controls also curbed impetuous physical attractions. For example, local officials granted permission for couples to marry. But poor couples were not automatically granted permission to marry, since local officials believed that poor couples were irresponsible and their children would end up being landless paupers. This pattern helped society maintain some kind of balance between the number of people and the available economic resources.[10] As a result of this and other customs, the European population did not become dense as in China.

Monopolistic activity by the British East India Company triggered the Boston Tea Party in 1773.

Social Status

Commercial economic expansion generated an increase in wealth, although this wealth was not evenly distributed among all. Farmers and some peasants had a valuable asset if they owned land, but most landless peasants continued to live a subsistence existence. Merchants and entrepreneurs who engaged in commerce amassed wealth according to the profitability of their ventures. The formation of a larger middle class—skilled craftsmen, merchants, landed peasants, professionals, and shopkeepers—accompanied commercial expansion. An expanding and affluent middle class purchased a wide array of consumer items that became available in the marketplace as a result of expanded trade.

A rising class of newly rich merchants gained influence, respect, and wealth as they challenged the political, economic, and social dominance of the landed aristocracy. The landed aristocracy continued to hold considerable power and prestige, but as a class began to show signs of decline as inflation gradually eroded its main source of wealth: land. Even though the new rich amassed great wealth, the landed elites slighted them for not gaining their prestige through inherited aristocratic ancestry. Some marriage alliances were conveniently arranged between the new wealthy entrepreneurs, who sought aristocratic prestige, and the cash-strapped landed aristocracy who needed additional finances. This tidy arrangement continued well into the 19th and 20th centuries.

Establishing Order: Political Currents

Political Systems

The key political change in early modern Europe was the growth, power, and efficiency of the sovereign state. A vigorous period of state building and the creation of strong, independent, sovereign monarchies got underway. Developments such as the Renaissance, the Reformation's breakdown of Christian unity, and the Enlightenment influenced this political movement. In the latter part of the post-classical era of Europe, but more intensely in the early modern era, political power and control shifted from the Church and decentralized feudal units to centralized states. The **Treaty of Westphalia** in 1648 that concluded the Thirty Years' War (1618-1648) was actually a series of treaties which signaled the primacy of the sovereign state as the acknowledged form of political organization. The treaties resulted from the first modern diplomatic congress, thereby initiating a new political order in Europe, based upon the concept of a sovereign state governed by a sovereign.

A state has legitimacy, assumes moral authority, claims its right to exist, commands sovereignty, and encompasses territory within defined boundaries. By the early modern era, the Catholic Church's centuries-long religious uniformity and political dominance tipped in favor of more secular state political organizations where populations were divided into separate independent and rival states. Unlike empires in which ethnically diverse populations lived under an emperor's political and military umbrella, states were more homogenous, with a shared official language, customs and beliefs, and invented or reconstructed a common history. In order to maintain control and stability, the state's dominant ethnic group usually imposed its language, traditions, religion, and values upon minority ethnic groups, sometimes with much resistance from the oppressed groups. Supporters of the state system considered cultural homogeneity the ideal, although it was not always realized.

Frontpiece of the Leviathan, by Thomas Hobbes. He argued that absolute monarchy was a necessity to curb the natural state of chaos among humans.

Two Western political forms of organization evolved as options for the newly emerging states: absolute monarchy and liberalism. Political theorists Niccolo Machiavelli and Thomas Hobbes, along with the nobility and Catholic Church supported an **absolute monarchy**. With their pessimistic view of human nature, they firmly believed society's natural state was that of chaos and anarchy. A strong government with an authoritative monarch was imperative to restrain the naturally aggressive impulses of humans. If rebellions against political control occurred, they needed to be crushed swiftly and without mercy. Machiavelli's divine right school of thought held that the king's power was derived directly from God, and the king was conveniently accountable only to God, not to the people. The French king Louis XIV, who identified himself as the Sun King, exemplified the concept of the divine right of kings. During the 17th century the French monarchy defeated a decentralizing, feudal political force led by the nobility, and instead instituted a highly centralized absolute monarchy. Louis XIV built sumptuous palaces, streamlined military administration, increased tax revenues, and shifted the allegiance of the nobles from their decentralized local power base to one of deferential loyalty to the king. This form of absolutism was replicated in several states, particularly the Hapsburg monarchy in central Europe, and in Russia the all-powerful tsars ruled into the early 20th century. Some monarchs embraced modest reforms and euphemistically called themselves enlightened monarchs.[11]

Liberalism, an alternative to absolutism, evolved during the 17th and 18th centuries in Britain and the Netherlands. The English political philosopher, John Locke (1632-1704), helped to

King Louis XIV (1638–1715) of France known as the Sun King, exemplified absolutism. Painting by Hyacinthe Rigaud (1701).

John Locke, English political philosopher, wrote about liberalism.

formulate Enlightenment principles based on the premise that all men possess certain natural rights due to their innate ability to reason. The state acted as protector of the individual's basic rights of life, liberty, and property; at the same time, an independent Parliamentary branch would control and limit the monarch's powers. Locke stressed the importance of religious liberty in government and society, laying the foundation for the principle of separation of church and state. These ideas formed the basis of the modern, liberal Western political tradition that has continued, with modifications, into the Global Wave.

Liberalism drew on the parliamentary model from the English medieval tradition. This tradition is traced to the famous Magna Carta of 1215, a document that stated a separate assembly of landed aristocracy would check the king's power. In England, the **Glorious Revolution** of 1688-1689 established the principle that Parliament, not the monarch, had supreme power. Except in Ireland, the Glorious Revolution was a bloodless revolution that had significant political consequences. The most concrete result was the adoption of the Bill of Rights by Parliament in 1689, spelling out some of the rights and powers granted to Parliament. For example, the monarch could not suspend laws, levy taxes, or raise an army without parliamentary consent. England became a **constitutional monarchy**, in which the monarchy was limited by the laws of a written constitution. This was a momentous move toward full parliamentary government, although it was not a fully democratic revolution.[12] While parliamentary rule was popular among members of the middle and newly rich classes who owned property and wished to protect their newfound wealth with the help of laws passed by a supportive parliament, commoners were basically excluded from the political process.

Both centralized monarchies and parliaments required sophisticated bureaucracies in order to govern efficiently. Western monarchs drew upon bureaucratic principles similar to those developed in China during the Urban Wave. Many bureaucrats were drawn from the educated middle class and provided a check on the power of monarchs, clergy, and aristocrats. Bureaucrats also administered provincial districts, managed court systems, supervised construction of roads and public works, and oversaw tax collection.[13]

Questions to Consider

1. Which political form do you consider to be the best—liberalism or absolute monarchy? Explain.

Migration and Interaction

With explorations and an increase in trade, interaction among people living in distant locations became more prevalent. The period marked new contact between Western Europeans and the people of the Western hemisphere and other regions; this interaction took the form of colonialism. Portugal and Spain blazed the way in planting colonies in South and Central America and the southwestern part of North America, and explored or established posts on the coasts of Africa, the Middle East, India, and East Asia. During the latter half of the 16th century the British colonized Ireland, but it was not until the 17th century that Britain, France, and Netherlands successfully established overseas colonies outside Europe. Those three countries claimed colonies primarily in North America. Spanish and Portuguese subjugation of the southern part of the Western hemisphere exemplified a recurrent pattern of colonial conquest and exploitation. Spanish *conquistadores* rapidly and brutally seized parts of the Western hemisphere in the 16th century and for the next 300 years, most of this region was administered by Spanish or Portuguese colonial systems imposed upon indigenous peoples and reflecting the conquering nation's values, including the Roman Catholic religion and hierarchical structures of governance. Nobles, church elites, and bureaucratic officials dominated the Latin colonial administration which concentrated on extracting profits from their commercial ventures, subjugating native peoples, and maintaining the status quo. While Catholic missionaries exuberantly converted indigenous people to the official colonial church, the region became a unique blend of different cultures: indigenous people, African slaves, and Spanish/Portuguese. The colonial experience, in what came to be known as Latin America, was quite different from that of North America, which adopted northwestern European values and primarily English institutions.

The exchange between the Western hemisphere and Europe is sometimes referred to as the **Columbian Exchange**. This was an exchange of plants, animals, goods, and diseases that followed Columbus' contact with the Americas. New agricultural products such as potatoes, corn, tobacco, coffee, squash, and tomatoes were introduced from the Americas to Europe, while wheat production was brought to the Americas from Europe. Europe introduced animals such as the horse, sheep, cattle, and goats to the Americas, while the Americas sent the turkey, llama, and squirrel to Europe. Diseases were also exchanged with the Europeans spreading smallpox, influenza, scarlet fever, measles, and typhus among the indigenous people, and, arguably, syphilis reached Europe from the Americas. Gold and silver flowed to Europe from the mines in America to provide a foundation of wealth for their expanding commercial network.

Questions to Consider

1. What were the beneficial aspects of the Columbian Exchange? Detrimental? Which one do you think was most important? Explain.

Human Expressions: Cultural Currents

Four significant cultural movements defined the early modern era: the Renaissance, the Protestant Reformation, the Scientific Revolution, and the Enlightenment.

The **Renaissance**, meaning rebirth, extended roughly from the 14th to the 17th centuries in Europe. It began as a cultural movement among an educated elite class in the prosperous northern Italian city-states of Florence, Genoa, and Milan. Mainly an urban phenomenon, the Renaissance involved both socio-economic changes and artistic and cultural innovations. The Renaissance espoused the values of individualism, humanism, secularism and human progress, encouraged the revival of classical Greek and Roman traditions, and extolled the advancement of knowledge. Renaissance ideas fostered pride in human potential and the uniqueness of the individual. Because the individual was considered the center of intellectual and artistic endeavors, the primacy of individualism became a principal value that distinguished the modern era. Some individuals shifted their spiritual and otherworldly dimension advocated by the Catholic Church to a growing

Western hemisphere native plants. Clockwise, from top left: 1. Maize 2. Tomato 3. Potato 4. Vanilla 5. Rubber tree 6. Cacao 7. Tobacco

Eastern hemisphere native plants. Clockwise, from top left: 1. Citrus 2. Apple 3. Banana 4. Mango 5. Onion 6. Coffee 7. Wheat 8. Rice

emphasis on secular, worldly, rational affairs. Renaissance thinkers viewed the here-and-now as a critical factor in actions and thought, rather than merely a transitory stage to either eternal bliss or damnation. For many, "man was the measure of all things," not the church. As an artistic movement, the Renaissance arts represented secular and religious motifs, with the nobility of the individual, pride in human accomplishments, and religious devotion as a recurring theme.[14] The Renaissance spurred new thinking in economic and political life. Merchants improved banking procedures and pursued profit as a justifiable human endeavor; thus, they ignored the decrees outlawing usury promulgated by the Catholic Church. Trade and exploration flourished. In the political realm, many thinkers questioned the role of the Church in politics and advocated more secular rule.

The Protestant Reformation, a second major cultural development, grew partially out of the Renaissance's questioning of Catholic authority and unity as well as criticism of the egregious behavior of church officials over the years. In 1517 a German monk, Martin Luther, protested the Catholic Church's policy and set in motion a critical challenge to their centuries-old authority, resulting eventually in Protestants breaking away from the Catholic Church. Gaining momentum and spreading widely in northern Europe, Protestantism ruptured Christian unity of the past as new groups objected to Catholic authority. The disruptions did not occur peacefully. The Thirty Years' War from 1618-1648 was fought partly in response to religious differences, as well as competition among rival and powerful state monarchies.

Martin Luther initiated the Protestant Reformation.

A connection between Protestantism, individualism, and the rise of capitalism is clear. Protestantism is considered by some to be more politically flexible than Catholicism, since Catholicism held to a patriarchal and hierarchical organization headed by an all-powerful pope and enforced traditional standards of orthodoxy. On the other hand, the newness of Protestantism meant it lacked entrenched traditions and was more open to a change in attitudes. Therefore, Protestantism, although it was also patriarchal, tended to be more readily adaptable to the novel political ideas of liberalism and constitutionalism, and especially the economic ideas of capitalism. Protestantism particularly appealed to artisans, small merchants, and middle class entrepreneurs who firmly believed that God had planted in them a divine respect for the principle of private property.[15] Protestant preachers and church members promoted an industrious work ethic that was thought to be for the common good, while their values and attitudes—rationality, frugality, hard work, accumulation, competitiveness, individualism, efficiency, and delay of gratification—provided a convenient theological rationalization and justification for those engaged in a newly emerging capitalist economic system. Unlike the traditional values of the Catholic Church during the post-classical era, Protestants freely pursued wealth, consumed material goods, and reinvested profits in enterprises without guilt imposed or objections raised by their churches.[16] They regarded wealth as a well-deserved divine sign from God, a reward for their virtue. Many condemned and abhorred pleasure, diversion, immediate gratification, and the "wasting" of valuable time. Internalization of these values was channeled into a work ethic that endorsed hard work, efficiency, dominance of nature, and productivity, all key attitudes of the modern era.[17] These Protestant attitudes continue to be important values, even at the turn of the 21st century.

The third major cultural development during the 16th and 17th centuries was a proliferation of scientific ideas known as the **Scientific Revolution**. The shift away from the absolute authority of the Church opened the door for scientific thinkers to eventually thrive. They created a new method for examining phenomena—the **scientific method**. Through careful observation and systematic experimentation based on those observations, scientists evaluated theories regarding the nature of reality. Thinkers interpreted experiments using mathematical measurements as the chief evaluating tool for arriving at new conclusions and knowledge.[18] Along with scientific discoveries came the notion that human knowledge was expanding, and that reason, not faith, was the key to understanding how the world operated. The source of human knowledge changed among scientists from a divinely sanctioned and authoritarian worldview to one that was scientific, secular, and based upon natural law.[19] Although they were deeply religious men, Nicolas Copernicus, Galileo Galilei, Rene Descartes, Francis Bacon, and Sir Issac Newton led the way in formulating this scientific worldview. It soon became the dominant worldview in the West, and later, as the West extended its influence throughout the world, the scientific mode of thinking took precedence over the magical, superstitious or religious description of perceivable phenomena. The development of science further enhanced the West's worldwide power and dominance.

Scientific knowledge made possible the technological innovations of the 17th and 18th centuries that laid the foundation for later industrial development. Scientific writers like Francis Bacon in England forecasted that scientific discoveries would lead to technological improvements that would make life easier and more rewarding. Scientific knowledge sparked widespread interest in technical experiments and applications for utilitarian purposes. Clever tinkerers, self-taught mechanics, and engineers used a trial-by-error method of innovation and a willingness to experiment with inventions that transformed society at all levels. A vast redirecting of Europe's intellectual outlook followed these revolutionary scientific findings.[20] Science also contributed to the philosophy that nature could be rationally understood and controlled, which further alienated humans from nature, with disastrous repercussions in the later Modern Wave.

A fourth cultural movement took place in the 18th century among educated elites: the **Enlightenment**. Centered in France, 18th century Enlightenment ***philosophes*** reasoned that scientific methods drawn from the natural sciences also applied to the social and intellectual sciences. Two key ingredients—optimism and rationality—distinguished Enlightenment thinking. Optimism is the belief that change is possible for all of society. Rationalism refers to the assumption that humans and the universe are understandable, predictable, and follow determined laws.[21] To Enlightenment thinkers, these basic rational laws could be applied to human social and physical behaviors, with the assumption that general human progress was indeed possible.

Enlightenment secular ideas discredited the influences of nature, religion, and superstition and instead emphasized human power to dominate nature and the human ability to create its own moral code in accordance with rational, scientific principles. For example, John Locke applied the new methods of science and reason to the humanities and philosophy. A contemporary and friend of Newton's, he founded empiricism—the belief that sensory experience through observations and experiments is the only source of human knowledge. The French *philosophe*, Jean Jacque Rousseau believed that children could improve through education, and criminals could be rehabilitated into useful members of society if educated properly and treated humanely. The French *philosophe,* Voltaire, wrote about injustice and inequality and the dignity of all humans. The Enlightenment *philosophes* popularized scientific ideas that encouraged numerous modern ideas: secularism, liberalism, socialism, humanism, reform movements, a rationalistic scientific approach, and the doctrine of laissez-faire economics.[22] Enlightenment thinkers reinforced the ideas of rational manipulation of the environment and mastery over nature. Not everyone at this time advocated for Enlightenment ideals, but it was a popular movement woven into the Western worldview.

Questions to Consider

1. Of the four important cultural developments during the Early Modern Era, which one do you think was most important? Explain.

Insights: Learning from the Past

The Early Modern Era

One insight to consider in this section is the term "new world" that is often used to refer to the Western hemisphere or the term "discovery" used to describe European contact with the Western hemisphere. Both terms are couched in the Eurocentric attitude that history is told from the European perspective. Indeed, from the European perspective, the Western hemisphere was a "new world" and they discovered it. But from the perspective of native people residing in the Western hemisphere the Europeans were the "new people" who made contact, or actually just stumbled upon, their land. Deconstructing, or turning the tables and looking at the flip side of an issue, often brings a different perspective and a clue to our attitudes and beliefs, in other words, to our worldview.

Another insight to consider in this early modern era section is how and why different attitudes and values developed to form a Western worldview and what has been the impact of these values on the world today. We have traditionally looked at the major changes in the early modern era—the Scientific Revolution, the Reformation, capitalism, free trade, liberalism and parliamentary rule—in a positive light as major "breakthroughs." However, in this holistic approach, I think it is wise to look at the flip side of these admirable achievements and deconstruct the term "breakthrough" as well. Along with the advance in scientific understanding came the notion to separate nature into an object of classification and dissection. When studying capitalism, which has been celebrated as a breakthrough from the "backward" feudal economy and the guilds, we have ignored the repercussions of its implementation upon the unfortunate ones who have not benefitted from it. Many garnered great wealth and status, but far more people were cast aside as causalities of the winner-take-all system. Trade and exchange boomed. But exchange also included the transmission of deadly diseases that ravaged the Western hemisphere in an unintentional genocide that eliminated about 90 percent of the native population and decimated untold numbers of traditional societies. Trade also flourished, but trade included the transport of human cargo, as millions suffered in a cold-blooded slave system that exposed the raw, dark side of our humanity.

The term "breakthrough" is also problematic. It is used here to indicate a welcomed phenomenon from the stagnation of the past, one that produces a better way of life for people. But once again, the context of the breakthrough is left unexamined. It is assumed that the breakthrough was beneficial. Using a systems perspective, we look at all angles of the breakthrough to understand the benefits and drawbacks as well.

As we turn today to face the overwhelming issue of our time—the widespread environmental devastation of our planet—I think it is important to examine the roots of this destruction. Our dire environmental state of affairs did not suddenly spring up overnight but is steeped in the attitudes and belief structures that uphold notions of unprecedented economic growth, material abundance, and the philosophical and religious justification for the exploitation and disregard for nature and other people. Along with the stunning achievements outlined above, paradoxically, we also see attitudes of conquest and exploitation take shape and intensify in the early modern era. Taking some time to examine the historic roots of this Western worldview is essential for understanding the deep structural changes required for averting environmental catastrophe in the 21st century and reassessing both the positive and negative aspects of the modern worldview. On a positive note, we will see this re-evaluation of the modern worldview is increasingly taking place, and solutions to alleviate the environmental distress on our planet, are being offered.

Questions to Consider

1. Do you think the term "new world" is problematic? "Breakthrough." Explain.
2. How do the "roots" of the Western worldview contribute to our environmental problems today? Do you think there is any merit in this argument?

We next turn to the modern industrial era, where industrialization sparks even more profound changes for Europe and the world.

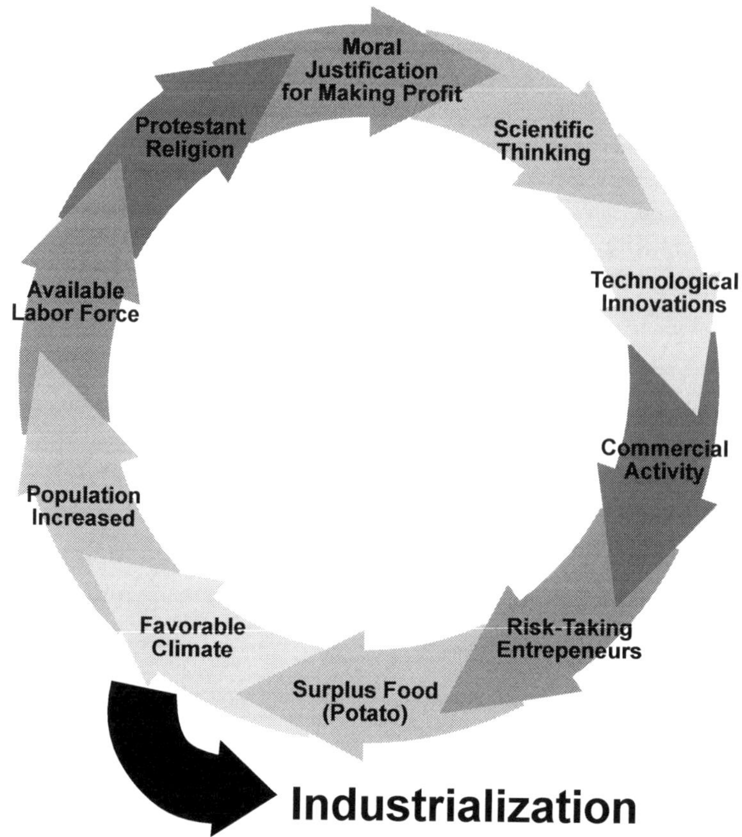

THE MODERN INDUSTRIAL ERA (1750-1900)

A historical transformation with far-reaching consequences occurred about the middle to late 18th century in England: industrialization. **Industrialization** is the process of change from an economy based on home production of goods to one based on large-scale, mechanized factory production with a wage-based labor force. The industrialization process, which moved rapidly from England to neighboring countries, is often referred to as the **Industrial Revolution**, which, along with a change in technology, resulted in vast political, economic, social, and cultural implications. This transformation marks one of the turning points in world history, when humans fundamentally change the ways in which they live. It is a change of such magnitude that it represents a major discontinuity in the course of our human history.[23]

Change and Continuity

Interacting factors combined to create the complex development of industrial transformation in the West. Instead of dwelling on one or several factors as the cause of industrialization, a systems approach can be employed to describe how a number of factors, interacting in a feedback loop system, generated the change.[24] Some of these factors have been more fully explained in the previous section but are reintroduced here along with the industrial development that occurred in this era.

Scientific ideas taking root provided a technical foundation for industrialization and generated widespread interest in technical experiments. Scientific theory supported the belief that nature could rationally be understood and controlled. Industrialization was preceded by and built upon intense commercial activity, the most dynamic sector of the European economy in the early modern era, which generated the necessary capital to finance industrialization in the 18th and 19th centuries. Northwestern Europe had an experienced entrepreneurial class, a group of risk-takers who had already acquired expertise in investing, managing, financing, and organizing commercial activity. Moderate summers and adequate rainfall meant better growing conditions that resulted in surplus agricultural production. Two important American crops—the potato and maize—added to the diets of swelling European populations. As a result of population increases, a sizable work force for employment in the newly emerging factories was available. The new Protestant religion and later the Catholic Church provided an ethical and moral justification for the rise of capitalism. Manufacturing technology became more sophisticated as scientific ideas spread and a confidence in mastering the forces of nature gained momentum. Successive innovations occurred once the industrial process was underway, and inventions in one field triggered inventions in others in a spiral of expansion, innovation, and economic growth.

Industrialization in Great Britain

Britain led the way in industrialization. Along with its ample supplies of coal and iron ore, the fuel of industrialization, several developments interacted around 1750 to spark the process. Although industrialization diffused and adapted differently in other areas of the world, there were some common features that may best be understood by taking a look at the process in Britain.

In the 15th century, Britain had been on the periphery of the world economy but by the latter half of the 16th century, its economy began to surge. Financed by silver from colonization of the Western hemisphere, joint stock companies began to form by pooling capital resources and establishing centralized management to direct operations. The companies conducted potentially profitable long-distance trade where risks and capital requirements were too high for a single individual to assume. The British Parliament issued charters for monopolistic trading companies to the Moscovy Company (1555), the Levant (Turkey) Company (1583), and the British East India Company (1600). Experienced British traders and entrepreneurs, aided by supportive political legislation, insisted on using mercantilist principles to arrange the delivery of raw materials from their colonies to feed their profitable commercial endeavors. The English National Bank, established in 1603 as a credit and finance institution, issued loans at the lowest interest rates of any in the world. The British stock market became the world's largest and most flexible, with investment capital sufficient to underwrite and sustain growing industrialization. London served as the center of world trade, displacing the Dutch in market dominance, and becoming the headquarters for the transfer of raw materials and manufactured products.[25]

Before industrialization, most urban artisans in Britain and Western Europe belonged to guilds, which protected their members' working conditions by limiting new technology and preserving wage rates and prices. Guilds stabilized the economy and ensured an adequate standard of living for their members but, on the other side, they inhibited labor mobility, creativity, and innovation. Expanding capitalism displaced the centuries-old guild system, one of its earliest victims. With legislation and economic pressures, the British Parliament squeezed out the guilds by the 18th century. English factory owners employed formerly independent, skilled workers as low-waged, unskilled wage earners. Although this provided the factory employers with a large labor pool of cheap labor, it meant a lower standard of living for the former independent guild members.[26]

The enclosure or privatization of agricultural land made farming a more efficient and profit-driven operation. But it also destroyed the existing rural social order that had carried on relatively unchanged for centuries. The changeover took place when British landlords pried land away from small farmers with the blessings of the Enclosure Acts. There were over 4,000 Enclosure Acts passed by a business-friendly Parliament from 1750-1850. Fields were enclosed, pastures fenced, and unused lands converted to agricultural production. An early form of privatization, villages that had been surrounded by open fields were now surrounded by a new agricultural landscape in which walls, fences, and hedges divided compact, consolidated, and enclosed fields. Carried out at the expense of small peasant farmers who were forced from the land, the enclosure movement ran its course by the 1840s with a majority of common fields and so-called wastelands turned into private lands. Large estates worked by wage laborers now dominated the rural British landscape. With a smaller percentage of farm laborers needed in the countryside and the overall population skyrocketing, a stream of unemployed farmers migrated to find work in the rapidly industrializing cities.[27]

In the British countryside before the 18th century, cottage industries, or a putting out system produced textiles. Before this time, master textile artisans had used time-worn methods in their guild workshops to produce quality finished linen and woolen goods. In a capitalist putting out system a merchant bought raw materials, most commonly wool and flax at that time and "put them out" or sent them to rural workers who spun the raw materials into yarn and then wove it into cloth on simple looms. The merchants collected the finished products from the textile workers, paid them according to a piecework wage, and then sold the cloth for a profit. This system was called a **cottage industry** because spinners and weavers worked in their own cottages where families—women, men, and children—all worked to supplement their family's agricultural income. The work was done in the rural countryside to bypass the regulations of the city's guilds, which frowned on this capitalist enterprise that skirted their regulations on competition and price. By the second half of the 18th century, cotton cloth was so popular that the traditional cottage industry method of production was no longer able to supply the mounting demand.[28]

Industrialization in Britain first took place in the cotton textile industry. The linen and woolen industries were already well established by the time of industrialization, but cotton emerged as a new and highly preferred material that was more suitable for innovation in the burgeoning clothing industry than either of the other materials. Through legislation, the government aided the infant British textile industry by imposing tariffs to protect the domestic industry from cheaper and higher quality imports from India. **Tariffs**, an import tax, made India's imported textiles more expensive than Britain's domestic cotton goods. Consumers chose the protected and cheaper domestic product; thus, the British textile industry flourished.

Industrialization in Britain can be linked to the insatiable demand for cotton that contributed to the tumultuous conflict over slavery and the Civil War (1861-1865) in the United States. High consumer demand for the popular cotton textiles spurred a rush of new technological innovations to process cotton more rapidly. For example, an American named Eli Whitney invented the cotton gin in 1793, which quickly separated seeds from the raw cotton, a process that was previously performed by slaves in a time consuming manner. With this invention, the American South responded to increasing demand for raw cotton by growing more of the valuable raw material. The capitalist trade network and British textile production were intricately connected to the growth of large cotton plantations in the American South: slaves toiled longer hours to produce more cotton, cotton farming expanded into new U.S. territories, more slaves were needed as farm laborers, and the price of land, slaves, and cotton skyrocketed as demand for cotton swelled.

A cotton gin on display at the Eli Whitney Museum.

A carder carding white alpaca wool.

British textile entrepreneurs responded to the mounting demand for their product by creating a new method for producing greater quantities of their product: the factory system. Before the 18th century, a guild member or cottage workers produced textiles at, what we would consider today a leisurely pace. But a very different work environment existed in the newly constituted factories; numerous workers, sometimes hundreds, gathered under one roof, were paid a standard wage, divided tasks into individual parts, and worked under the close supervision of the owner or manager. The small guild owners had to compete, eventually unsuccessfully, with this more cost effective production process. Although the factory produced products were lower in price than guild products, workers merely performed routine and repetitive tasks in an impersonal, mass-

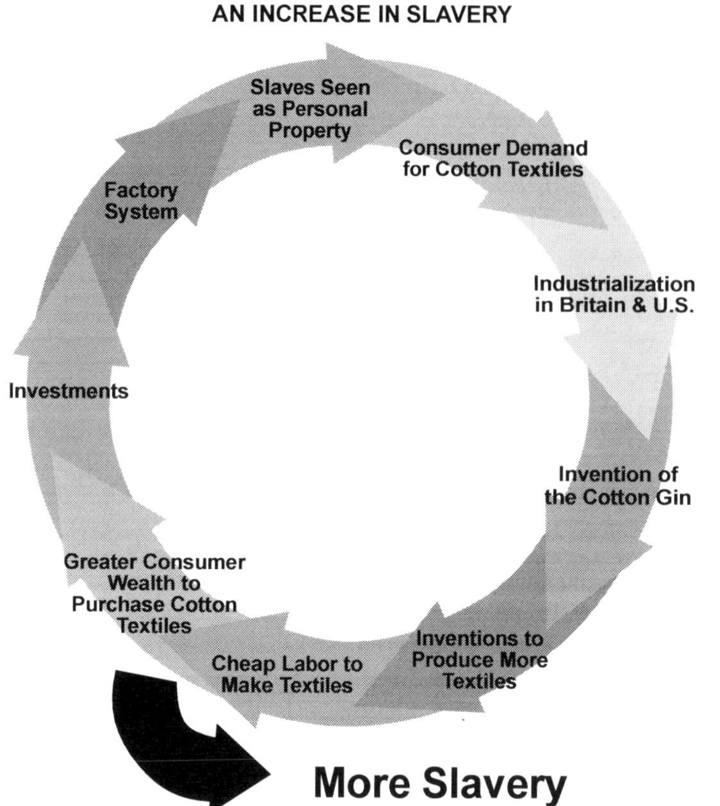

Even cotton planters in the American South organized slave labor into gangs of workers that replicated the mass-production factory system in Britain, performing repetitive tasks at a relentless pace closely supervised by an ever-watchful overseer.

The prosperity of the modern middle and entrepreneurial upper classes rose rapidly. In Britain, Parliament showed its support for the development of a domestic market economy by passing laws that eliminated internal tariffs and tolls and financed infrastructure like new turnpikes, canals, and ocean harbors which facilitated the movement of goods. The philosophy of the Parliament was to financially assist and encourage businesses by passing laws that made the formation of new companies relatively easy and affordable. This political support rewarded the Parliament's expanding and wealthy constituency: the capitalist middle and upper classes.

production environment, most often under horrendous working conditions.

The factory method of production was economically successful, as individual productivity increased substantially, but at the expense of worker autonomy and creativity. The more relaxed work styles typical in home production and small farming, and the varied work of the guilds were abandoned for robotic, impersonal, and dangerous work in assembly-line factories. Transition from cottage industries to a factory system was not immediate. Many of the early and small factories were located in cities, unlike the cottage industries that were located in the countryside. With the increase in the numbers of workers, factory organization shifted to an emphasis on greater specialization and subdivision of tasks resulting in a tremendous increase in total factory output. By 1851, three-fifths of those employed in cotton manufacture worked in factory mills.[29]

Questions to Consider

1. What do you think was the most important change in Britain as a result of the shift to a capitalist economic system? Explain.

Relationship with Nature: Ecosystem Currents

In 18th century Europe, a more moderate climate fostered growing conditions more suitable to agricultural production, which, combined with agricultural innovations, helped boost output; thus, more food became available and population increased. The 17th century phenomenon known as the "Little Ice Age," in which cooler temperatures and more rainfall prevailed, came to an end during the 18th century. A temporary lull in major plagues, especially the virtual disappearance of the bubonic plague, meant lower death rates. All of these factors contributed to a general population explosion. The estimated European population was 120 million in 1700, 140 million in 1750, and 190 million in 1790. The British population quadrupled in the 18th century, while the British and French populations doubled between 1750 and 1800.

World Population

350 million in 1400

545 million in 1600

610 million in 1700

one billion in 1825[30]

Economic utility governed the relationship between humans and nature in industrial societies. Under industrial capitalism, nature's bounty was given economic value and assigned a specific price. The market value of fertile farmland was relative to the number of crops it could produce. This economic thinking meant that nature was not seen as a sacred source of beauty, awe, inspiration and reverence but as a supplier of resources, an economic commodity. Although probably unintentionally, Westerners tampered with the world's ecosystem by introducing new species into colonial areas and by over-hunting, overgrazing, and deforesting vast areas, which reduced, altered or exterminated fellow species. **Monoculture**, growing just one crop, increasingly displaced subsistence farming, with its diversity of heirloom varieties, in the colonial periphery areas; monoculture was harmful to the environment. Plantation owners understandably preferred lucrative market crops highly desired by the insatiable market economy—cotton, sugar, coffee, tobacco, cocoa, and others—and grew these almost to the exclusion of subsistence crops in some areas. But along with destroying traditional, local ways of agricultural production, this type of monoculture depleted the soil of nutrients, devastated biodiversity, and reduced farmers to a dependency status in the world market economy. Later in the Modern Wave, farmers turned to toxic chemical fertilizers so that their spent soils could continue to churn out commercial crops for far-away consumers.

An Alberta, Canada fur trader in 1890.

Natural Populations

Both the diversity and breadth of wildlife drastically diminished in every part of the world that Europeans colonized. Beginning in the 16th century, trappers killed fur-bearing animals in North America and Siberia to supply furs for unquenchable fashion appetites and as warm, protective outer garments for European consumers. By the late 19th century, the population of fur-bearing animals drastically declined, with near-extinction of many species that once flourished. By 1840, for example, beaver trapping in North America sputtered as the species dramatically declined to the point of obliteration. As beaver prices rose and supplies fell, trappers switched to other furs; they shipped 500,000 muskrat skins to England in 1842 and exported 137,000 marten in the early 1850s. Over-trapping eventually exhausted supplies of these animal furs as well.[31]

North American bison herds once numbered around 40 million in North America before Americans intentionally began their extermination rampage in the 1830s. Bison provided food, clothing, and shelter for Native Americans, whom American settlers wished to eliminate in order to claim their land. By the end of the 19th century, the mass slaughter drove the bison herds to the point of near extinction and contributed to the acquiescence and reduction of Native American populations.

The passenger pigeon is another striking example of the mass extinction of a species. The exact number of passenger pigeons in North America at the time of European arrival is unknown, but the best guess is about five billion. Estimates conclude that it was the most abundant bird on Earth. Flocks of pigeons stretched to 300 miles long, darkening the skies as they took hours to pass by. The dusky blue, rose-breasted species, whose meat was considered a delicacy, ate unimaginable quantities of acorns, beechnuts, and blueberries. Cutting their food supply by shearing forests from the eastern plains of the United States to plant crops contributed to their mass extinction. After about 1850, with the eastern woodlands converted to farms, pigeons roosted in the few remaining trees where they were easily picked off by hunters, who, with a spray of shotgun pellets, could fell a dozen in one blast. Stuffed into railroad boxcars for transport, millions of pigeons wound up on the dinner plates of city dwellers in Boston and New York. When people realized their numbers had been decimated, it set off a mad frenzy by hunters to kill those remaining few. By 1900, it was all over. The species was unable to survive contact with human predators. The last known survivor died unceremoniously in captivity in a Cincinnati zoo in 1914.[32]

With the process of commercialization, industrialization, and capitalism, these few examples were repeated untold times as the altered relationship between humans and nature took a destructive turn in the modern industrial era.

The now extinct Passenger Pigeon.

Questions to Consider

1. Did an expansion of capitalism contribute to increasing environmental destruction in the modern era? Explain.

Ways of Living: Techno-Economic Currents

In Western Europe, farmers were able to provide an abundance of food for most classes in the late 18th and 19th centuries. As more land was cultivated, yields per acre increased, healthier and more livestock was raised, and a more suitable climate led to greater agricultural production. Vegetables from the Western hemisphere, such as the potato and maize, added variety to the European diet and contributed to a more diverse food supply. The versatile potato had several advantages over traditional European grains: it had higher caloric value than grains produced on comparable plots of land, and it could be grown in less fertile soil. Although agricultural productivity increased, the percentage of English workers in agriculture declined steadily from about 36 percent at the beginning of the 19th century to less than 10 percent at the end of the 19th century. Entrepreneurs found that more efficient agricultural methods and crop rotation practices reaped profits equal to industrial manufacturing. Holland in the late 1700s drained swampland for agricultural land and introduced nitrogen-fixing crops that enabled fields to be cultivated every year instead of lying fallow every third year to regain fertility.[33] Innovators applied new agricultural ideas through a trial-by-error method, to increase productivity and profits.

Economic Systems

Along with the primary industries—commerce, trade, and agriculture—the capitalistic economic system extended its tentacles into a new area of wealth creation with the development of **secondary industries**—manufacturing and construction—which converted raw materials into finished, usable products using greater inputs of energy. Many of the policies and institutions of commercial capitalism continued into the early modern industrial era, but they were expanded significantly and intensified. For capitalism to take hold, certain conditions are necessary.

Conditions for Capitalism

- private ownership
- private profits
- commodification of resources
- availability of capital
- large and willing workforce
- market forces of supply and demand
- reliable and easy access to necessary raw materials
- business-friendly legislation passed by government
- rationale that justifies profit-making
- government-provided large infrastructure

Profits from commercial enterprises poured into Western Europe. As more capital accumulated, enterprises plowed profits back into businesses that generated even more income if successful, making a profit for owners and investors.

A new form of capitalism, as opposed to mercantilism, was introduced in this era. Englishman Adam Smith outlined a free trade economy in his seminal book the *Wealth of Nations* in 1776. He argued that the economy is governed by natural laws, especially the law of **supply and demand**. In classical economic theory, the relation between these two factors determines the price of a commodity. This relationship is thought to be the driving force in a free market. As demand for an item increases, prices rise. When manufacturers respond to the price increase by producing a larger supply of that item, this increases competition and drives the price down.[34] In a **free-market economy**, competition will force producers to manufacture goods more efficiently so that they can sell quality, lower cost goods. Government laws and regulations that interfere with the natural laws of a self-governing economy—or, as

Adam Smith, author of The Wealth of Nations, which rejected mercantilism.

Smith called it, the "invisible hand of the marketplace"—should be repealed. Smith, therefore, disagreed with the mercantilists' regulations on trade and protective tariffs. Smith believed that tariffs should not protect home industries from competition from exporting countries, but the home industries should be left to freely compete in the marketplace. Later the term ***laissez-faire* economics** has been applied to the principles of free trade advocated by Adam Smith.

Under capitalism, many joint stock companies, small family businesses, and guilds gave way to the modern corporation. **Corporations**, a legalized form of economic organization, extended their operations globally in order to gain cheap or hard-to-find raw materials and more markets. Commercial expansion required additional capital for investments in factories, ports, warehouses, and transportation networks. Considerable investment funds were raised for corporate formation through an expanding stock market, partnerships, financial institutions, speculation, and government programs. A national banking system established in Britain, the United States, and other countries regulated currencies and provided capital for further corporate enterprises. The bank's role in early industrial growth should not be overly emphasized, since bankers often considered loans to industrial enterprises as too risky.[35] Instead of corporations, often the national governments took the greater financial risks and were responsible for infrastructure, building large, expensive capital improvements such as railroads, canals, harbors, roads, and dams.

A new class of entrepreneurs ably and willingly calculated risks, raised capital, and adapted new ideas and technology for profit. Although they came from varied backgrounds and rags-to-riches stories were not unknown, in fact most industrialists came from an artisan or manufacturing background. A common characteristic of entrepreneurs was their ability to recognize potential new technology, to seize opportunities for making a profit, and to adopt personal habits and beliefs that rationalized and justified their acquisitive, aggressive behaviors. A close symbiotic relationship existed between political leaders and entrepreneurs. Political leaders relied on entrepreneurs to provide a stable economic foundation for the nation; in return entrepreneurs were rewarded with laws and policies that promoted a secure economic environment with limited risks for their financial undertakings.[36] Entrepreneurs needed a fairly steady economic atmosphere where they agreed upon rules for operation to ensure their profitability and continuity.

Economic productivity characterized industrial societies. Enterprises reinvested the surplus wealth accumulated from increased economic productivity and redistributed it to a wider population, although certainly not everyone. Greater economic surplus for the few translated into more money for them, permitting a more widespread and lavish standard of living. An increase in capital-intensive forms of production like machines, factories, transportation networks, and communication enterprises resulted in greater economic productivity.[37] An industrious, and in many cases exploited, work force labored long hours in capital-intensive industries for relatively low wages; while the productivity gains from low wage labor were diverted to the factory owning elite. It would not be until later into the 20th century that labor would be able to divert more of the productivity from their labor into their own pockets.

The local, domestic economy was giving way to the capitalist economy in the modern industrial era. Economic alternatives to the private, free market capitalist system—communism and socialism—were debated during this time, although they both still had industrialization as the main form of wealth creation. Karl Marx proposed a communist alternative to capitalism in the short book, the *Communist Manifesto* in 1848. To explain the relationship of capitalism

AN ECONOMIC CONTINUUM

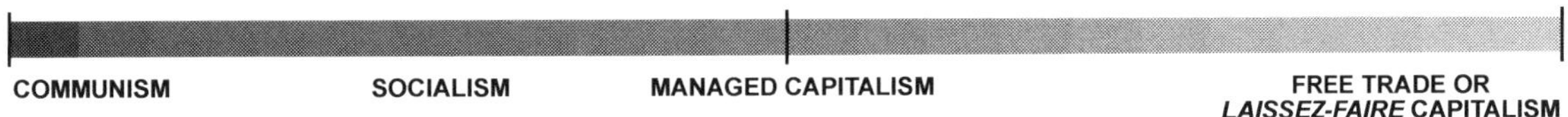

and communism, we can place the two concepts on a continuum. At one end are capitalist societies, including societies in which private individuals or corporations, and not the government, own the means of production. Wage and profits earned from the capitalist system are used to buy goods and services from the market place with prices determined by supply and demand. The capitalist system rewards those who capture productivity, efficiency, initiative, and creativity, while those unable or unwilling to participate in the market place are left to their own means. At the other end of the continuum are **communist** or command economies in which there is more emphasis on government planning by state officials than in capitalist societies and less response to supply and demand pressures. Workers in state enterprises have little risk of unemployment, and labor unions have more influence than in capitalist societies. The ostensible purpose of a socialist or communist system is to eradicate abject poverty, reduce the degree of economic inequality, both inherent in capitalist societies, and provide a comfortable safety net for those unable to participate in the workplace. **Socialism** denotes the combination of some large state-owned enterprises with private capitalism.

All the different economic theories rejected the domestic economy and instead embraced industrialization as the preferred method for production of goods and services, but they advocated different systems of ownership and distribution. In the modern industrial era Britain, the most advanced economy, would be located on the free market or laissez-faire capitalism end of the continuum. The United States, following more of a mercantilist or regulated system with high tariffs that protected their domestic industries, would fall somewhere in the middle of the continuum. State-owned communist/socialist societies would be on the left end of the continuum, although they technically did not develop until the 20th century.

The industrial capitalist economy produced a dizzying range of manufactured goods and some services. Starting in this era there were mechanized transportation networks, such as railroads, harbors, and roads; telecommunication systems, such as the telegraph and telephone; military equipment such as huge naval squadrons; the chemical industry; energy production that included petroleum and coal-fired electricity; industrial equipment, machines that made machines; the steel industry; and the construction industry that employed engineers, architects and construction workers. Although the manufacturing industry dominated during this era, the infant service industry provided education, medical care, consumer retail services such as large department stores, entertainment, organized sports, leisure activities, publishing, and the news.

During the 19th century, the colonies of the European powers in Africa, Southeast Asia, and elsewhere were incorporated into the periphery status of the capitalist economic system. For example, small farmers in the periphery and plantation owners alike grew **cash crops** such as coffee, tea, fruits, tobacco, cotton, and sugar that were sold on the world market. Small farmers in the periphery increasingly relied on growing cash crops for the market economy, almost to the exclusion of subsistence crops in some areas, for income to purchase necessities as they were enfolded in the world market economy. The price small farmers received for their cash crop on the world market depended on supply and demand but were usually low since overproduction by large plantations kept the supply high and prices low. In addition, colonial authorities imposed taxes on small farmlands that had to be paid in cash, further enveloping the farmer into the capitalist economic web. This reduced small farmers to a dependency status. Because of recurring taxes and low prices for cash crops, many small farmers in the colonies were unable to make a living and sold their farms to large landowners eager to expand their holdings. As a result of the transition to market based agriculture, farmers in the colonies suffered the same consequences as their small farmer counterparts in Europe.

Questions to Consider

1. What are strengths and weaknesses of both capitalism and communism/socialism? What economic system do you prefer?

A loom from the 1890s with a dobby head.

Technology

The spread and increase of scientific ideas and research of the late 18th and the 19th centuries triggered a spiral of technological innovations and inventions. A sampling of the many English inventors and inventions included the flying shuttle, John Kay; the water frame, Richard Arkwright; the spinning jenny, James Hargreave; the spinning mule, Samuel Crompton; and the power loom, Edmund Cartwright. James Watt responded to the demand for plentiful and reliable power by inventing the steam engine. These inventions revolved around the mushrooming cotton textile industry. New cotton machines and steam engines required a greater supply of iron and coal, which stimulated mining and government financed infrastructure improvements in transportation facilities—canals, roads, railroad lines, and steamships.[38]

New mechanical inventions reduced the time to complete certain tasks with increased efficiency. For example, in the 18th century, hand spinners in India required 50,000 hours to prepare 100 pounds of cotton for spinning. By 1825, British workers with the aid of mechanical innovations processed 100 pounds of cotton in 135 hours. With the cotton gin, a worker could separate 50 pounds of cotton from the seeds in the same amount of time a hand laborer could separate only one pound. This advance assured a plentiful supply of cheap raw cotton for ravenous British and American textile mills.

But technological inventions also had a downside. Even though technological inventions increased efficiency and productivity, paradoxically these advances meant that people worked longer hours than previously. New inventions required new tasks that took additional time to learn and master. Contrary to what is often assumed, more sophisticated technology does not reduce human working hours; they increase.

Questions to Consider

1. Were you surprised to learn about the above statement: "Contrary to what is often assumed, more sophisticated technology increases human working hours." Do your own experiences support or refute the statement?

Trade and Exchange

An expanding consumer market for manufactured goods and services accompanied industrialization. Intra-European trade dominated total trade figures, but overseas trade boomed as well. France, Netherlands, and Britain increased their control of international commerce in the 19th century, while Portugal and Spain languished. Western Europeans acquired mineral and agricultural products from periphery areas; from Eastern Europe came grain, furs, and timber; from America, precious metals, sugar, tobacco, and cotton; from India and Southeast Asia, spices, tea, and gold. Core areas sold value-added manufactured goods such as fine furniture, textiles, guns, and metal goods to their internal market and to the periphery areas. Many business people in the middle and upper classes in Western Europe and the United States were able to generate a profit from trade and exchange, and along with their expanding domestic market, steadily accumulated wealth. The slave trade between Europe, the Americas, and Africa sadly proved to be another source of immense profit for traders. Core areas of industrial development drew disproportionately on world resources from periphery regions to concentrate wealth and power in Western Europe, and later the United States.[39]

Patterns of Labor

A profound change in labor patterns accompanied industrialization. With industrialization many workers moved from primary industries—farming, fishing, and mining—which produced raw materials, into secondary industries—mills and factories—that processed the raw materials into manufactured goods. Tertiary or **service industries**—education, health care, police, fire protection, social services, government, retail trade, clerical work, and others—employed more workers later in the industrial modern era. A by-product of industrialization was the decline in the proportion of workers who were self-employed, as workers increasingly found themselves employed by factories.[40]

Men, women and children entered the ranks of an emerging industrial work force. A large work force was on hand for factory employment due to a growing population, the dislocation of peasant farmers as a result of the enclosure movement, and the displacement of cottage industry workers. Workers faced limited options for earning their livelihood as they made their way into newly forming factories where their unskilled wage labor was in high demand. Factory workers arguably received slightly higher wages than agricultural laborers, domestic servants, or workers in the cottage industry but also became more dependent upon others for employment. Many rural women lost income from their cottage industries when spinning was mechanized and moved to factories. Artisans' standard of living declined, as the higher cost of their handcrafted items could not compete with lower cost, mass-produced, machine-made goods. For example, linen weavers in Scotland experienced extensive unemployment and the eventual disintegration of their craft in favor of cheaper, machine-loomed linens. One of those displaced men was the father of Andrew Carnegie, who would go on to become one of the world's richest men and a leader in the mass production of steel.

A massive migration took place during the later 19th century as displaced workers moved to seek employment from the countryside to cities and even across continents. Huge numbers of people from Europe and other nations sought work in the factories in the United States or other countries in the Western hemisphere. Escaping starvation, unemployment, and displacement, approximately 12 million people left their homelands in Europe to immigrate to the United States from 1870 to 1900. Peasants and artisans uprooted from their traditional occupations were forced to cope with the shock of starting a new livelihood in a factory town while living in crowded, unsanitary tenements and experiencing profound disruptions to their traditional family life.[41] Alcoholism, domestic violence, and rising desertion rates all accompanied these wrenching social disruptions.

Deplorable conditions and low wages generally marked the debasing experience of most industrial workers. Although the standard of living for the industrial working class improved minimally by fits and starts from 1750 to 1850 in Western Europe, the wages of the lowest paid workers improved only slightly in comparison to higher middle class incomes derived from salaries, rents, interest on investments, and profit from business. A significant change in the distribution of income and wealth occurred. Historian Rondo Cameron notes, "The inequality of the distribution of income and wealth, which was already great in the pre-industrial economy, became even greater in the early stages of industrialization."[42] Early industrialization was built upon the backs of exploited cheap labor and the poor.

By the end of the 19th century, small groups of workers, disgruntled with their miserable working conditions and low wages, banded together to form unions, like the Knights of Labor in the United States, which formed in 1869 to demand better wages, reduced hours, and improved working conditions. Working-class organizations, friendly societies, trade unions, and cooperatives lobbied politicians for reforms such as higher wages, accident insurance, unemployment benefits, reduced working hours, medical insurance, regulation of child labor, and improved working

Shows the densely populated and polluted environments created in the new industrial cities, Over London by Rail, Gustave Doré c. 1870.

conditions.[43] The elite business class countered labor's demands by encouraging immigration and internal rural migration to guarantee an ample labor supply, thereby keeping wages low. The government did not regulate the boom and bust cycle inherent in unfettered capitalism. Workers did gain slightly better wages and an improvement in their working conditions, but they did not make real progress until the 20th century.

Insights: Learning from the Past

Techno-Economic Currents

Economist Joseph Schumpeter aptly calls capitalism a process of **creative destruction**. Competition under capitalism brings about bursts of technological and institutional creativity and increased productivity, creating a more comfortable standard of living for some. But technological innovations and economic expansion also demolish traditional institutions, and those who do not follow the capitalist precepts of "profit or perish" lose out. Capitalism destroys foraging and farming societies, their traditional cultures, stability in the periphery regions, and the ecosystem itself. World historian Lefton Stavrianos explains, "The particular combination of creativity and destruction that capitalism has generated provides the foundation both for the extraordinary achievements and the appalling setbacks of recent centuries, for the unprecedented promise and peril of our own time."[44]

Questions to Consider

1. Economist Joseph Schumpeter calls capitalism a process of creative destruction. What do you think outweighs the other, the creative factors or the destructive factors?

Human Networks: Social Currents

Family

Family patterns changed dramatically in the modern industrial era. By the late 18th and 19th centuries, the ideas expounded by 18th century Enlightenment thinkers began to filter into middle class family practices. In many middle class homes in the 19th century a small nuclear family became the expected norm. The economic role of the middle class family shifted from one centered on production to one focused primarily on consumption of material goods. Along with consumption, the family's role included reproduction, socializing children, fulfilling psychic and emotional needs of adults and children, instilling societal values, providing affection to all family members, guiding the personality development of children, and encouraging and guiding school and career decisions for children.[45] Although this shift did not necessarily apply to the working class, peasants, or the elite, we can see changes beginning in the ideal European-style family; the nuclear family decreased in size, children were accorded greater affection, incidence of divorce increased, women became more independent, and the family no longer was the center of economic activity.

During the modern industrial era, middle class marriages shifted from an economic or political alliance arranged by parents or a marriage broker to a system based on individual choice undertaken for personal reasons. Individual choice, sexual and psychological attraction, affection, and personal satisfaction became important criteria in selecting a spouse, and more emotional interaction between middle class men and women was encouraged. Marriage was carried out primarily to fulfill personal desires for home and children and to enhance personal happiness. Monogamy, the normative marriage form in the West, expressed democratic, egalitarian ideals in reaction to inequalities and hierarchies often found in polygamous marital systems. Western Europeans socially and legally disapproved of polygamy.[46]

The middle class family encouraged affection. The importance of love as an ingredient in family life became an important Western value. The family served as a pleasurable nurturing center that provided an emotional bond among individuals and a reliable, comfortable refuge from outside strife. With fewer children, childrearing practices among the middle class began to change. Parents increasingly treated children with love and respect. This practice coincided with Enlightenment beliefs, especially advocated by Jean Jacques Rousseau and others, which assumed children could improve and become responsible adults through humane and supportive treatment. Harsh discipline as a means of dealing with childhood transgressions declined, although it certainly was not eliminated. Instead, it was believed that children should be afforded certain rights and protective services, and the tradition in which children were obliged to accept arbitrary parental directives decreased. Middle class parents spanked children less and drew them more closely into the family orbit of affection. The old European practice of swaddling—wrapping infants tightly in cloth to prevent movement—began to disappear. Adult supervision increasingly replaced physically restraining children.[47]

The lives of working class children differed from those of middle class children. In the Urban Wave and early modern era, peasant and artisan families functioned as a work unit with the home serving as a place of work as well as a residence. Members of the family, including children, shared in the work, which consisted of some form of production, usually farming. Working class families in the industrial modern era still adhered to the attitude that children were productive workers, and they were expected to supplement the family's income. On the other hand, middle class reformers, appalled by working conditions for children, strove to remove children from the workplace. They cited moral considerations and helped pass legislation making child labor illegal. Under middle class pressures, the government passed laws requiring compulsory school attendance. Certain institutions also hastened the decline of children as producers; factory mechanization reduced the need for child labor and labor unions called for restricting child labor, correctly charging that child labor lowered the wage scale for adults.[48]

Parents experienced a decline in their traditional authority, especially the father's role as authoritative head of the family. Although the father's influence did not fade away completely, this subtle decline of traditional family authority and male preeminence were linked to a lessening of family members' reliance upon each other for mutual benefit and even survival. Instead, family dependency shifted towards more reliance on the outside marketplace as a source of necessities and income. In middle class families, the fathers, some mothers, and children spent at least parts of the day outside the home, which meant that at least a partial transfer of family influence shifted to other institutions, such as schools or the workplace, that began to take over some of the family's traditional functions.[49]

Questions to Consider

1. Do you think the shift to a nuclear family was more democratic? Explain.

Gender

Women's roles, both middle class and working class, changed with industrialization in the early 19th century. With industrialization, many former farming women shifted their toil from a family-based domestic economy to a new factory-based, capitalist wage economy. Employers considered these working class women to be a cheaper, more docile work force than men, since they were less likely to organize and participate in unions and thus were exploited accordingly. An increase in the demand for female domestic servants expanded as a swelling middle and elite class had money to spare for household help.[50] Along with factory and domestic work, working class women maintained their traditional responsibilities of household chores and care of children, sometimes renting an extra room to boarders or taking in laundry for extra income.

Middle class women during the 19th century performed different roles than working class women. Middle class women generally did not labor as wage earners but discharged more family-centered duties and responsibilities. Men usually earned the wages, while women managed households, cared for children, and oversaw their children's education and socialization. Women no longer produced goods used in everyday life, but consumed the newly mass-produced goods and services. Catering to the middle class female consumer, new department stores such as the *Le Bon Marche* in Paris and Marshall Fields in Chi-

Le Bon Marche, Paris, France, sometimes regarded as the first department store in the world.

cago attractively displayed and sold consumer goods and services. Lower middle class and single women worked at jobs such as sales clerks at these new retail outlets or as secretaries in businesses and governmental offices. The ideal middle class wife provided a nourishing, protective environment "inside" the home for her husband, while he engaged in a competitive, commercial, "outside" world. The social norms directed women to participate in a non-competitive, passive domestic sphere, while men competed in an active, aggressive public sphere. Women prepared elaborate meals at home and presided over mealtime ceremonies and conversation; this pattern continued as a Western ideal until very recently.[51]

Elite women managed households, usually with domestic help, and performed social duties commensurate with their class. Families often arranged marriage for upper class women, sometimes to ally themselves with the newly rich business class, while they offered an elite royal heritage. Even though elite women luxuriated in a lavish material standard of living, conventions confined them to very limited roles, education, perspectives, and proscribed activities.

The availability and reliability of birth control for women increased in the late 19th century. Improved birth control technology, such as the vulcanization of rubber in 1844, led to the invention and distribution of condoms. Middle class women utilized birth control more than working class women and had a corresponding reduction in their family size. Working class women and men continued to rely on numerous children as an economic asset and as a symbol of fertility and status.

The **feminist movement** emerged in Europe and in the United States in the 19th century. Mary Wollstonecraft, one of the early feminist writers, in her ground-breaking book, *A Vindication of the Rights of Woman,* argued in 1792 that women were not naturally inferior to men but merely lacked proper education. She championed women's education and supported children's rights. By 1870 in Great Britain, women won the right to own property, gained access to universities and fought for political rights. The Seneca Falls Convention, organized by Elizabeth Cady Stanton and Lucretia Mott in New York in 1848, launched the feminist movement in the United States. Women and their (few) male supporters gathered to rally for their suffrage rights and other legal reforms, such as the right to own property.

Questions to Consider

1. In what ways did middle class women's roles reflect the economic system? Is this different than women's roles today?

Social Status

Important shifts in social status occurred in industrial societies during the 19th century, while in some respects the hierarchical social structure characteristic of the Urban Wave continued. Slaves and serfs occupied the bottom of the social hierarchy. On agricultural plantations in the southern United States, in the Caribbean, and in Brazil, slavery was organized as an assembly-line system of labor, brutally squeezing every ounce of productivity from the workers. Serfs in Eastern Europe experienced a "second serfdom" as the Western European markets needed their labor to produce foodstuffs, such as wheat. Wealthy landowners essentially chained serfs to the land, who were unable to leave their servitude until their bondage contract legally ended. Landowners formed an elite, propertied, conservative class bent on retaining these profitable institutions at all costs, even to the point of Civil War in the United States over the slavery question. Although Russia officially abolished serfdom in 1861, and the U.S. ended slavery in 1863 with the Emancipation Proclamation issued by President Abraham Lincoln, former serfs and slaves continued to furnish cheap labor as tenant farmers or poor peasants for the production of essential raw materials for industrial capitalism.

A new social group, the proletariat, an industrial working class, emerged with industrialization. Unlike slaves and serfs, the working class labored for wages in newly formed factories. With their wages the working class bought food, rent, and consumer products, with prices determined by the market forces of supply and demand. A wage system, in which labor was transformed into a commodity with a particular monetary value, was a vital component of the capitalist economic system. This differed from the tribute system where peasants paid rents with a share of their agricultural produce and engaged in little monetary exchange. Because of the abundant supply of unskilled labor, early industrial workers earned low wages and were subject to grievous working conditions in the factories. The market in the unregulated capitalist system fluctuated in a "boom and bust" cycle, causing misery for many in the working class. In "boom" cycles of economic upturns, wages responded to supply and demand and work was plentiful, but in "bust" cycles of economic recession or depression, lay-offs were prevalent, wages fell and workers were mostly left to their own devices to survive.

An enlarged, prosperous middle class emerged in modern industrial societies. Middle class members consisted of merchants, professionals, educators, shopkeepers, managers, and highly skilled artisans. Industrial factories mass-produced goods consumed by the middle class and the elite. The middle class profited from and helped to shape a capitalist economic system and democratic ideology that supported capitalist economic principles. They advocated political representation, initiated reforms, and instilled and reinforced their values to ensure the success and continuation of the existing system that benefited their class. Middle class values and attitudes—hard work, frugality, temperance, efficiency, proper manners, productivity, and strict Christian morality—became the normative values for modern society in the 19th and well into the 20th centuries, although these values were not necessarily shared by the working class or elite.

Land ownership, the traditional source of wealth and status, continued to define the elite class in the modern industrial era; however, the land-owning aristocrats now had to share their elite status with a wealthy, entrepreneurial class. This group of elites—landed aristocrats, industrialists, bankers, merchants, and government leaders—constituted about five percent of the population in the second half of the 1800s but controlled over 40 percent of the wealth. The new entrepreneurial elite acquired considerable wealth with the expansion of capitalism and the formation of profitable business enterprises. However, they were not members of the landed aristocracy and did not have a long lineage of noble ancestors; hence, the established land-owning aristocracy often snubbed the newly rich. Some of the land owning wealthy were able to retain their riches, but the passage of income tax laws, inflation, and other measures in the early 20th century cut into some of their holdings.

At times during this era, tension over the goals, views, and policies of the middle class, the landed aristocratic elite, business elite, working class, and peasant farmers simmered below the surface and on occasion could turn violent.

Socialization and Education

In the 19th century, modern families surrendered a greater share of responsibility for education, socialization, and supervision of children to other institutions and facilities such as schools and religious institutions. A new role for children emerged—student. The growing need for a better-educated work force meant children remained financially dependent upon their parents for a longer period of time as they completed prescribed schooling. Educational institutions expanded to house students during the long, protracted period between childhood and adulthood.[52] With children congregated in schools, peer groups become a new socializing influence. Some Western countries, such as the United States, instituted education for all, or almost all, as idealized by Enlightenment thinkers. Political leaders decided that education helped inform citizens, who then could be trusted to vote and defend the interests of the nation. With these benefits in mind, governments financed primary schools, and legislation required compulsory education for children, at least from the ages of six to twelve. As a result, literacy rates rose dramatically.

Mass education's primary role was to educate youth for work in assembly-line factories and to instill national pride. Schools divided children into separate classrooms according to their age. In assembly-line fashion, schools often bolted desks to the floor and arranged them into straight, tidy rows. Teachers ruled the class as the unquestioned supreme authority and meted out corporal punishment to those who did not comply. The curriculum consisted mainly of well-established facts that students learned through rote memorization and repetitive drill. Punctuality, neatness, and obedience were enforced as the main virtues of a good student. Public schools emulated the German military model, with teaching methods designed to replicate the assembly-line factory system as the proper way to prepare students for future factory work. This system of mass-produced, military-style education remained the model well into the 20th century and survives even today in many schools.

Questions to Consider

1. In what ways do you think education in the 19th century is different than education today? Similar.

Establishing Order: Political Currents

Political Systems

New political institutions and various political ideologies—liberalism, nationalism, socialism, and conservatism—shaped modern political currents during this era. These ideologies did not always peacefully coexist; tensions and disruptions between conflicting ideologies unleashed violent revolutions and political changes in this dynamic era.

Political liberalism continued to evolve from its roots in the early modern era. Liberals vied with conservatives for implementing political policy and power during the early part of the modern industrial era. They embraced institutions derived from Enlightenment ideals: representational government, constitutions, individual and property rights, human progress and rationality, and political self-determination. Liberalism challenged the grip of the **conservatives**—monarchs, landowning aristocracy, military elites, and church leaders—who had an interest in policies that supported tradition, stability, and obedience to political authority and organized religion. They were generally hostile toward revolution, liberal reform, individual rights and representative government. Conservatives had a vested interest in maintaining the existing non-democratic system and did not want to see their power and control eroded by reforms and by an expanding middle class.

The growth and acceptance of liberalism was linked to the development of industrialization and capitalism. A necessary ingredient in the development of capitalism is respect for and legalization of individual private property rights, a central tenet of liberalism. Instilled in the citizenry is the idea that property rights, laws instituted to protect property owners, are sacred, beyond question and override the rights of the community.

As economic prosperity increased and capitalism became more entrenched, challenges to traditional monarchies grew and the adoption of liberal forms of government became more widespread. Often the term **democracy** is used to describe the political changes occurring, but the term is deceiving since it is perceived to be a form of government in which all citizens have equal rights and power. In the context of the modern industrial era, democracy is a representative system in which the adult population is permitted at intervals to choose among a limited number of candidates for public office. Although access to high political office is not restricted to a small, hereditary aristocratic class, a small number of political elite jockey for power and privately decide most policies. The political elites in this era consisted of political professionals, civil servants, news media owners, landed aristocrats, businessmen, military leaders, and special interest groups. Occasionally, exceptional individuals without elite ties were able to make a political mark; Abraham Lincoln, for example, came from a very poor and humble background but despite the odds was elected president in the U.S. in 1860.

The nation-state emerged in the modern industrial era as a place of belonging and identity similar to the band in the Communal Wave, the village in the Agricultural Wave, and the city and empire in the Urban Wave. A nation-state is a social, cultural, and political community with defined national boundaries and usually a shared common identity and origin, with a sense of history and ancestry that extends across past, present, and future generations. Those determined to legally reside in nations are called citizens. Historian Benedict Anderson calls a nation an "imagined community," that is, a political entity that, unlike the state or empires, is the creation of the collective imagination.[53] Nations affix symbolic forms of identification and rituals to unify individuals into a national community: a flag, pledging an oath of allegiance, ritual holidays, an inspirational national history, celebrations, ceremonies, parades, a national anthem or other patriotic songs. Military service and even dying in service to one's country is ennobled. All of these symbols validate the legitimacy of a nation and a citizen's affiliation with it.

Accompanying the emergence of the nation-state, the powerful political doctrine of nationalism burst onto the scene in the modern industrial era. **Nationalism** is the political movement that holds that a nation has the right to form an independent political community based on a common destiny, identity, and shared history. Most nationalists believe the nation should have defined borders that should be defended at any cost. Nationalism is closely associated with patriotism, which elicits a passionate response and loyal fervor from its citizens. Nationalism emerged in the American and later French Revolutions and gained momentum as disruptions caused by industrialization unleashed new loyalties. Nationalism evoked an emotional allegiance to the nation and gave a sense of identity to citizens that had been previously reserved for religious affiliation, loyalty to a monarch, or ties to a local village. National achievements in technology, athletics, colonial acquisitions, and particularly military power inspired national pride and passion.

Questions to Consider

1. Do you have nationalism in your country? In what ways is it expressed? Is it used for some purpose by the government? Explain.

Conflict and War

During the modern industrial era, a series of political revolutions of varying magnitude took place. The ideals of the Enlightenment inspired these revolutions, and, with varying degrees of success, the revolutionary leaders sought to implement a liberal political form in the newly created nation-states. Along with the Glorious Revolution in Britain in 1689, already mentioned in the early modern era, political revolutions took place in United States, France, and several colonies formed nations in Latin American.

The **American Revolution** pitted the independent-minded American colonies against their British colonial masters in 1776. Enlightenment political ideas that advocated for a republican form of government, a decentralized federal system, and limited male suffrage inspired this modern revolution for political independence. After winning a battlefield victory against the British in 1781, the colonists drafted the Articles of Confederation that served as the framework for their first attempt at government. In 1787, a more centralized government, the U.S. Constitution, still in place today, replaced the decentralized Articles of Confederation that had not proven strong enough to respond effectively to domestic disturbances. The 1787 constitution provided for a separation of powers between the three branches of government: judicial, legislative, and executive. In 1789, ten amendments, known as the Bill of Rights were added to the Constitution to guarantee such freedoms as religion, press, speech, petition, and assembly. Initially these rights did not include African Americans, women, or non-property owners, but over the years they were eventually extended to all Americans.

The siege of Yorktown ended with the surrender of the British army, paving the way for the end of the American Revolutionary War and the establishment of the United States as an independent nation.

The **French Revolution** in 1789 took many unusual twists and turns as its 26 years of tumultuous events finally reached a conclusion in 1815. Inspired by the American Revolution and influenced by Enlightenment ideals, the French Revolution arose amidst an outdated social structure, rising commercialization, destabilization resulting from population growth, an inefficient monarchy, and a large tax burden from a series of wars that fell disproportionately on the middle class and peasants. In the first stage, the revolution aspired to the moderate aims of a written constitution and limits to the monarch's authority. However, the revolution took a more radical and bloody turn with the rise of ruthless authoritarian leaders like Robespierre. When revolutionary leaders beheaded by guillotine the monarchs—King Louis XVI and his wife Marie Antoinette—shockwaves coursed throughout Europe. In response to the growing unrest in France, a coalition of states declared war on the nation in 1793. A reprieve from the violence took place with the formation of the Directory that lasted until the brash young general, Napoleon Bonaparte, staged a successful military *coup d'etat* in 1799. With Napoleon firmly in charge, the military spread liberal ideals throughout Europe. One of the notable acts carried out by Napoleon was the creation of the Napoleonic Code that codified the laws of equality and religious tolerance, abolished serfdom and feudalism, and legalized property rights; sadly, however, he took the rights of property ownership from women and reaffirmed their inferiority. Napoleon ultimately met defeat at the Battle of Waterloo in 1815. Although the monarchy was reinstated, the liberal tide had turned, and a return to the conservative order of the past was not to be.

Revolutions followed in some of the colonies of the Western hemisphere. With Napoleonic France fighting against most of Europe, a revolution took place in one of her colonies in 1804. Over 100,000 slaves, led by Toussaint Louverture, declared their freedom from France and the first independent state of Latin America, Haiti, came into existence. Mexico revolted against Spain in 1821 and followed the path to nationhood. Numerous other Latin American nations also declared their independence in the early 1800s. Although most of these countries wrote liberal constitutions similar to that of the United States or liberal nations in Europe, large landowners had become very prosperous growing export crops such as coffee and kept voting rights strictly curtailed in order to retain their political and economic power. Latin American elites used this strategy of political and economic repression, which continued well into the 20th century and even continues today.

The signers of the Congress of Vienna in 1815 negotiated an end to the Napoleonic wars and aimed to return Europe to conservative principles. With minor interruptions, peace prevailed in Europe for the next hundred years. Conservatives dominated Europe for the period 1815 to 1848, and attempted, with some success, to quell the revolutionary fervor and nationalistic impulses that had been unleashed by the French Revolution. However, revolutions broke out throughout Europe in 1848 that challenged the conservative policies of the early 19th century. Both the middle and working classes wanted liberal reform, but their aspirations were in direct conflict. Revolutionary participants advocated on behalf of urban workers, displaced and alienated by the upheavals of early industrialization, which frightened the property-owning middle class. The revolutions of 1848 did not result in profound change but did result in a more weakened aristocracy, the abolishment of the remnants of feudalism in Western Europe, wider male suffrage, benefits for the middle class, and the beginnings of what would become a gradual implementation of a welfare state benefiting the urban working class.

Napoleon Bonaparte Crossing the Alps (1800).

Toussaint L'Ouverture, leader of the Haitian Revolution.

The interval of 1848-1871 saw the spread of what became known as "flexible conservatism." In 1871, both Italy and Germany became unified nations, and the Civil War in the United States concluded with the reunification of the union in 1865. The German state was considered conservative, even though the Germans passed a progressive package of worker reforms under Otto von Bismarck in the late 19th century. However, nationhood would come later for the ethnic groups of the Habsburg's Austrian-Hungarian Empire, and the ultra conservative Ottoman and Russian empires. These empires opposed liberalism and strove to retain the institutions of the absolute monarchy and aristocratic control.[54]

From 1873-1914, the West embarked on a form of aggressive intervention in the non-Western world: imperialism. This period of imperialism is often referred to as "new imperialism," which differentiates it from colonialism in the early modern era. The term **imperialism** describes political and economic control by a greater power over a less powerful territory or country. During this imperialist era, much territory in Asia, the Pacific islands, the Middle East, and sub-Saharan Africa was the object of an extensive land-grab by the more powerful nations of Europe—particularly Great Britain, France, Netherlands, Belgium, Russia, and Germany—and the United States and Japan.

From a systems perspective, several interconnected factors contributed to the burst of imperial expansion. Westerners commonly assumed that a nation must expand its territory and power in order to retain respect among its peers. If a nation stood idly by as others joined in territorial seizure, then its prestige, economy, and power base suffered. Secondly, nations were intent on military expansion. A proliferation of oceangoing steamships in the 1860s carried huge cargoes long distances, and these steamships needed bases for refueling. Controlling key foreign harbors as refueling stations enhanced a nation's military control over a far-flung colonial empire. Third, industrial output in the last half of the 19th century exceeded consumer demand, and stagnation ensued. Industrialized nations were frantic to secure new consumer markets to peddle their excess products in the periphery areas and obtain cheap raw materials for their insatiable industrial machines. Fourth, many misguided, but well-meaning people firmly believed that Western culture, European people,

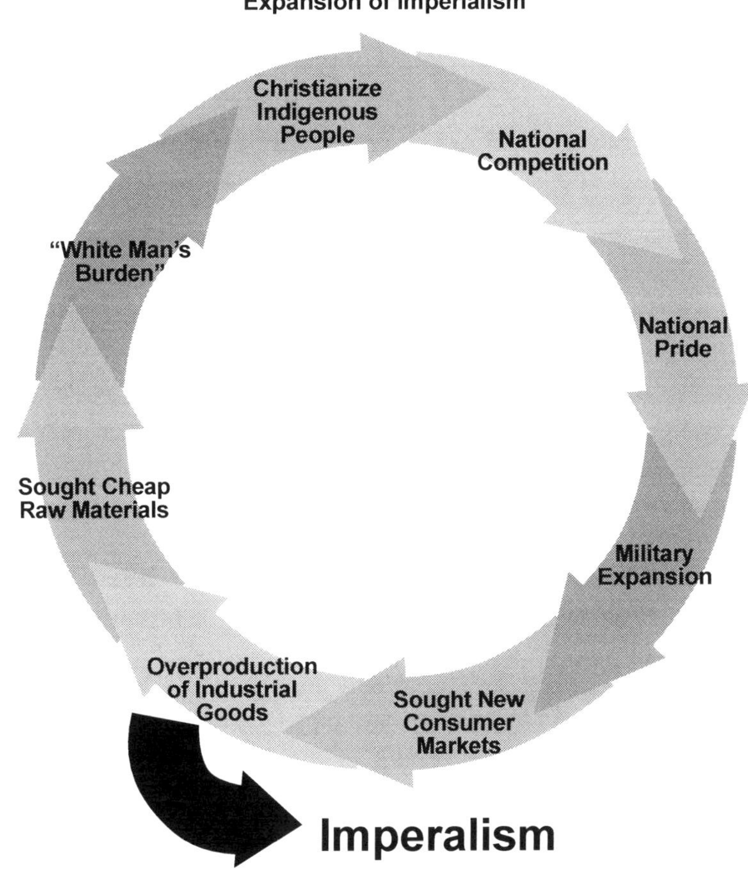

American Progress by John Gast, 1872. It is an allegorical representation of the modernization of the new west. Here Columbia, intended as a personification of the U.S., leads civilization westward with American settlers, stringing telegraph wire as she travels; she holds a school book. The different economic activities of the pioneers are highlighted and, especially, the changing forms of transportation. The Native Americans flee her advance.

and Christianity were superior to non-Western culture, people, and religion, and thought it was their duty to "civilize the heathens." The philosophy of the **white man's burden**, satirized by Rudyard Kipling's poem of the same name, placed responsibility on Christians and Europeans to "civilize" those considered unfortunate enough to be non-Western. A combination of these factors provided an impetus and justification for core Western nations to brutally colonize periphery non-Western areas.[55]

Even though each region had its own reaction to colonization, their experiences had much in common: colonial powers brutally interacted with their colonies but contributed to modern developments as well; tensions existed between a colony's traditional culture and Western/modern culture; a Western consumer-driven way of life seduced many colonists; Western law, liberalism, and culture appealed to many colonists; and others violently resisted the West's domination.[56] Although Westerners did not colonize the entire world during this era, the next section is an overview of the regions—Americas, India, Southeast Asia, Africa, India, and China—that succumbed to the "new imperialism" in the late 19th and early 20th centuries.

Questions to Consider

1. Why do you think that war was the only answer, in this era, to change? Can you think of other ways in which change could have been accommodated without war?

Migration and Interaction

Americas

As we discussed in our consideration of the Early Modern Era, Europeans first subjected the Western hemisphere to colonization. Many of these former colonies had declared independence during the 19th century and embarked upon developing their own modern nations.

The most powerful former colony, the United States, immediately embarked upon its own form of imperialistic expansion, majestically called **Manifest Destiny**. The new nation expanded westward, gobbling land and destroying native peoples who resisted their encroachment. In reaction to native resistance, the U.S. government attempted assimilation programs, such as "Indian schools," herded native people unto reservations, destroyed buffalo, a key subsistence resource

Native American pupils at the Carlisle Indian School in Pennsylvania, c. 1900. An attempt to assimilate and "civilize" indigenous peoples.

for the Plains Indians, and fought violent wars to eliminate native resistance. These acts "opened up" the western lands to American settlers who marched onward to the Pacific Ocean. A contrived war with Mexico in 1848 added another huge swath of territory in the American southwest and California to the expanding nation. The U.S. annexed Hawaii in 1898 and subjugated native Hawaiians, another act of imperialism. While American missionaries embarked on converting native Hawaiians to Christianity, commercial enterprises followed the cross. Resistance from native Hawaiians to the intrusion grew so intense that the Marines were sent in to suppress the uprising and overthrew the native rulers. Hawaii's native culture and traditions were systematically, although not entirely, dismantled.

Even though much of Latin America gained political independence from Portugal and Spain between 1804 and 1830, Latin America then became an economic periphery to Britain in the late 19th century and to the United States in the 20th. Raw materials—beef, coffee, bananas, wheat, copper, nitrates, and guano—were exchanged at or below free market prices for manufactured goods from European and American factories. Latin America had little industry of its own and remained largely an agrarian area controlled by large landowners and foreign corporations. Politically, the region alternated between independent, liberal republics and military dictatorships. The peasants continued to live in poverty and were unable to dislodge the landowning elite, the Catholic Church, or foreign corporations from their entrenched power base. Spanish speaking Latin Americans abolished slavery in 1855 and Portuguese-speaking Brazil in 1888.[57] Unlike in the United States, there was widespread intermingling among indigenous people, slaves, and Europeans to form a racial and ethnic mixture.

Gandhi on the Salt March, 1930. It was a campaign of nonviolent protest against the British salt monopoly in colonial India.

India

British power in India increased with the decline of Mughal rule in the mid 19th century. The British government issued a charter to the British East India Company, which commenced trade with India in the 1600s and hired Indian soldiers to protect their interests in the region. The British consolidated their power in India with military victories over their colonial rival, France, in 1763. In the 18th century, Britain robbed India of her treasures—jewels, and precious metals—while tariff restrictions stifled imports of India's superior textiles into Britain. In 1857, Indian distrust of the British erupted in the Great Rebellion, but the British army crushed the revolt. From that point onward, the British government took over direct control of India from the British East India Company, with Queen Victoria given the title Empress of India in 1876.

In the 19th century, the British intensified their role as guardians of India, pushing modernization measures, educating India's intellectuals in British universities, and instituting Western political structures. The British implemented their legal and educational systems and built an infrastructure that included railroads, telegraphs, and a postal service. Although a second language after Hindi, English became the language of the educated people throughout India. The Indian National Congress in 1885 advocated for Indian nationalism, with the goal of sharing in the governance of India. However, the nationalist movement did not pick up steam until the 20th century when two nationalist leaders, both recipients of a British education, Mohandas Gandhi (1869-1948) and Jawaharlal Nehru (1889-1964) both turned against their colonial benefactors and pushed for India's independence.[58]

Southeast Asia

By 1900, the imperialist powers of Britain, France, Netherlands, and United States dominated a majority of Southeast Asia. The British gained control of the port of Singapore, now an independent nation, in 1819. They followed with command of the kingdom of Burma. France promoted Christian missionaries in Vietnam and then forced the state to accept French protection. In 1884, French armies made Vietnam an official French **protectorate**, a state or nation that is dominated or controlled by a much stronger state or nation. From Vietnam, France extended its control over the regions of Cambodia and Laos, territories that were united in 1900 into the Union of French Indochina. With their victory in the Spanish-American War in 1898, the U.S. acquired the former Spanish colony of the Philippines. However, the Filipino population did not appreciate this turn of events and launched what has come to be known as the Philippine-American War. The resistance army, led by Emilio Aquinaldo, fought against U.S. occupation until 1902, ultimately losing the conflict. The Filipino population suffered enormously with an estimate of 250,000 to 1,000,000 civilian and military deaths. In 1602, the Dutch (Netherlands) had established the Dutch East India Company (VOC) to trade for the valuable spices within the region that is the modern-day nation of Indonesia. The company went bankrupt in 1800, and the Dutch established the Dutch East Indies as a nationalized colony.

A group of Filipino combatants are photographed just as they lay down their weapons prior to their surrender in the Philippine-American War (1899-1902).

Africa

After the mid-19th century, Europeans moved into Africa and divided the continent into colonial possessions, in keeping with the spirit of the new imperialism. But Africa was not an empty land; the Ottoman Empire controlled the Nile valley, and elsewhere on the vast continent, stalwart states and village life existed when Europeans arrived. Compared to the Americas, European contact with the African continent was relatively late. One of the reasons for the delay was the prevalence of deadly African diseases, to which many Africans were immune but which ravaged the susceptible Europeans who penetrated the interior of the continent. Fevers and infections wiped out many European invaders and settlers until medical advances provided vaccinations and treatment.[59] Between 1880 and 1914, at the height of imperialism, a **scramble for Africa** ensued. European nations met at the infamous Berlin conference in 1885 to carve out their territorial claims upon defenseless Africans. Europeans haphazardly drew colonial borders with no attention to boundaries established by native customs, tribal affiliation, or economic relations. Upon the completion of the "scramble," about 175 million Africans were subject to colonial control.

European colonial rulers undertook the self-serving task of training African leaders to locally enforce their colonial rule and to help them exploit Africa's vast natural resources for their benefit. Except for occasional local uprisings like the Zulu wars in South Africa, resistance

Cetshwayo kaMpande (1826-1884) was the king of the Zulu Kingdom from 1872 to 1879 and their leader during the Anglo-Zulu War (1879).

to European rule was weak, since Europeans held a significant edge in military weaponry and economic enticements. Many African elites submitted to or assimilated the values and customs of their colonial rulers, especially in the English and French colonies. But in the Belgian, Italian, Portuguese, and German colonies, where the colonial rulers did not incorporate Africans into political positions, tribal leaders generally chose to withdraw as far as possible from European contact.[60]

Administrators, merchants, and missionaries were in direct contact with their colonial subjects, and it was arguably the missionaries who had the most effect on the daily lives of Africans. Missionaries taught basic education, even though the curriculum was inferior and heavily biased in promoting and extolling European culture and the values of the modern worldview. The spread of Christian missionaries condemned the worship of tribal deities, and Western medicine weakened the shaman's work.[61]

By the 20th century Europeans had virtually demolished traditional African divisions of land, commercial contacts, and cultural relations. Equally random national boundaries later replaced the arbitrary colonial boundaries during the widespread de-colonization movement that followed World War II. Although almost all Africans continued to live in villages and followed traditional ways in the 19th century, subtle changes altered traditional customs. Tension between Western and traditional African culture generally created confusion, conflict, anxiety, resistance, and humiliation for the native people.

In western Africa in 1821, the British Gold Coast, today the nation of Ghana, was formed. The British seized privately held lands from native people and took over the claims of other European nations to the area. Instead of exporting slaves as in the early 1800s, exports from the region in the later 1800s included gold, diamonds, ivory, cocoa, timber, peanuts, oil, and hides. The British also established a protectorate over Nigeria, while the French, not wanting to be left out, established itself in 1900 in the region called French West Africa. Germany set up colonies in Togo, Cameroon, and German Southwest Africa.

The British were the first to gain territories in north Africa. Egypt became an independent state in 1805, and completed the massive project of digging the Suez Canal. The British were intricately involved in Egyptian affairs, purchasing a share of the canal and loaning Egypt huge sums

The Suez Canal at Ismailia, Egypt, c. 1860. The Ismailia segment was completed in November 1862.

of money for building its infrastructure, which effectively helped the British more than the Egyptians. The British even put down an Egyptian revolt against their influence in the region in 1881. In 1898, the British seized the Sudan, located south of Egypt, and by 1915, the British considered Egypt a protectorate. The French extended their imperialist reach into Algeria, Tunisia, and Morocco, while Italy, in 1912, took over the territory of Tripoli, which became the Italian colony of Libya.

Central Africa also came under the influence of imperialist Europe. The Englishman David Livingstone explored the area, and later in the 1870s, Henry Stanley sailed the Congo River. King Leopold II of Belgium wanted a colony and laid claim to the vast region. Leopold brutally exploited the Congolese people for their riches, notably rubber. It is estimated that approximately 10 million Congolese died as a result of Belgium's gruesome quest to obtain rubber and other riches from what became Leopold's personal colony.[62]

In east Africa, the competition for colonies heated up between the British and the Germans. The Berlin Conference in 1884 settled a possible conflict between the two and recognized both their territorial claims, while Portugal received Mozambique. In typical fashion, no Africans were present.

The first European settlers in south Africa were the Dutch, and by 1865 over 200,000 settlers known as the Boers had planted stakes in the area. In the negotiations after the Napoleonic wars, the British received control of the region, and the British encouraged settlers to immigrate to the Cape Colony. In response, the Boers fled north in the "Great Trek," forcing native tribes in the region, among them the Zulus, onto reservations. The Zulus had a strong military tradition and forcibly resisted the invasion but were no match for the combined efforts of the Boers and British. Next, the British and Boers faced off for control of the region in the Boer War, with the British winning and establishing the independent Union of South Africa in 1910. A system of **apartheid**, a legal and institutional segregation of blacks and whites, lasted until the end of the 20th century.

Congolese laborers who failed to meet rubber collection quotas imposed by the Belgians were often punished by having their hands cut off. About 10 million Congolese died during Belgian imperialism.

At the end of the 19th century, various European nations imperially ruled most of Africa. Only Liberia and Ethiopia remained independent states.

China

European powers also subjected China to their influence. Among the most humiliating stories in colonial history, and there were many, were the two **Opium Wars** (1839-1942 and 1856-1860) between Britain and China. In the first half of the 19th century, the British were engaged in an unfavorable balance of triangular trade with China and India, in which the British shipped manufactured goods to India, Indian cotton to China, and Chinese tea, porcelain, silk, and other luxuries to Britain. But the British imported considerably more from the Chinese than they exported to them. The British corrected this imbalance of trade by selling China a product from India that the Chinese were unable to resist: opium. Even though Chinese officials had outlawed

A Chinese opium house, photograph, c. 1900.

the highly addictive drug, the British launched the Opium War in order to force Chinese authorities to legalize opium sales for trade with the British. The Chinese forcibly resisted this immoral intervention but were unable to turn back a technologically superior British military and finally succumbed to British encroachment. The terms of the treaty ending the war forced the Chinese to pay crushing war reparations, and they also reluctantly conceded several port cities to the victorious British, including Hong Kong.

In the later 19th century, imperial European nations—Great Britain, France, Russia, Germany, and Japan—"carved up" China into spheres of influence. Mounting Chinese resistance to colonial arrogance was demonstrated in several anti-colonial rebellions including the Taiping Rebellion (1850-1864) and the Boxer Rebellion in 1900. Increasing popular unrest added to the woes of an already severely weakened Chinese Qing (Manchu) dynasty, resulting in their eventual abdication of dynastic power in 1911.

Japan

Japan avoided invasion by a colonial power and in the 20th century became one itself. Japan abandoned its isolationist stance in 1853 when the American Commodore Perry negotiated the opening of Japanese ports. The feudal Tokugawa system ended, which led to the restoration of the Meiji emperor in 1868. Japanese leaders were intent on modernizing their society along Western lines. They proved the success of their modernization efforts with the military defeat of Russia in the brief, but nonetheless significant, Russo-Japanese War in 1904-1905. For the first time in the Modern Wave, an Asian state defeated a European nation, an event that stunned Europeans.

Middle East

Although the diminished Ottoman Empire limped along until it dissolved at the end of World War I in 1918, its leaders were marginally successful in imposing modernization from the top down in some regions. For example, Turkey developed a Western-type army and introduced Western inspired schools, press, and political structures in the 19th century. Not all Muslims embraced modernization, however, and some continue to see it as incompatible with their religious law and moral code. Other countries in

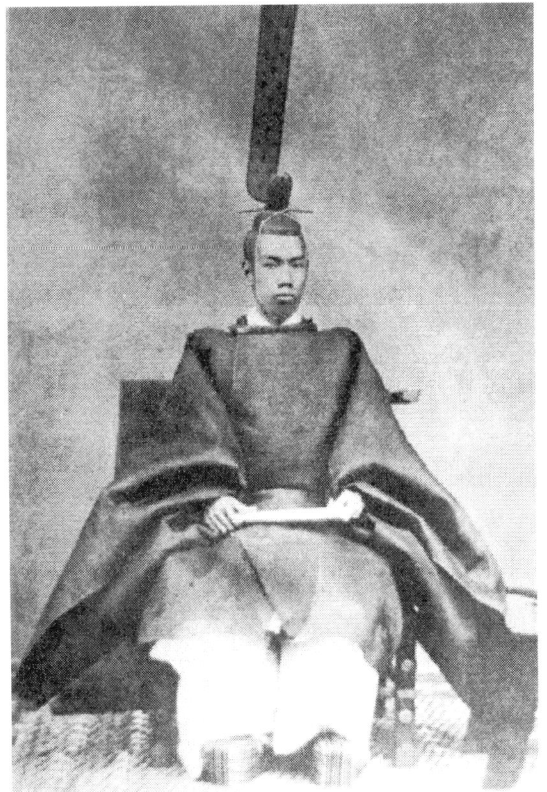

The young Meiji emperor, Japan, 1872.

the Middle East will be covered more in the 20th century section.

Questions to Consider

1. Some critics argue that Western imperialism has benefitted non-Western people by bringing Western ideas, democratic forms of government, a capitalist economy, and modern infrastructure to their societies. What do you think?

Human Expressions: Cultural Currents

Ideologies

A number of new ideologies or secular faiths competed with traditional religion as new belief systems for Westerners: liberalism, individualism, socialism, communism, nationalism, science, consumerism, racism, and a faith in technology as the solution to all human problems.

The Enlightenment's tradition of rationalism and liberalism, as noted in the early modern era, continued into the 19th century. However, a small but influential number of Romantic poets and authors of the early 19th century, such as Wordsworth and Coleridge, rejected as stifling the enthronement of reason advocated by the Enlightenment philosophes and instead eloquently expressed passion, intuition, and love for the beauty of nature. In liberalism, there was a special emphasis placed on the worth and dignity of the individual. **Individualism** fits in well with a prevailing Newtonian mechanistic worldview, in which the observer or individual stands apart and distinctive from the object of analysis, and mind and body are considered separate. Individualism also corresponds with a democratic ideology that promotes individual rights at the expense of community or group rights; emphasis is on rights rather than on responsibilities. Rights include freedom for individuals to pursue their potential, the pursuit of personal happiness, unlimited economic opportunity, and ownership of private property. The importance of individual rights is linked to capitalism, and the importance of private property is a sacred pillar of capitalist success. The ethos of individualism is a dominant theme in capitalism, with its drive for perpetual expansion, its emphasis on personal initiative and its call for a supposedly independent and free work force.[63]

Karl Marx wrote about and supported communism or socialism, introduced earlier. He used a historical approach to explain change. He observed that there is a conflict between the owners of property and production and the workers who wish to have more control. He argued that in the 18th and 19th centuries, the middle class wrested primary control of the means of production from the landed aristocracy and that the working class will inevitably overthrow the middle class and control the means of production. At this ideal moment, the state withers away and each individual will receive goods according to his/her need. The 19th century socialist movement was closely identified with communism and the writings of Karl Marx.

The shift from the primacy of theology to the importance of scientific thinking had begun with the emergence of scientific ideas during the 17th century. This movement gained force with scientific developments in the second half of the 19th century. The work of **Charles Darwin**, who applied Newton's mechanistic explanations to his theory of evolution, ranked as an important contributor to 19th century thought. Darwin's theory postulated material causation as the explanation for how life formed and evolved over time. Natural selection was the key. Organisms that survived developed certain advantageous adaptations in response to the struggle for survival in which weaker organisms died. The traits that enabled them to survive were passed on to successive generations. Evolutionary theory eliminated the role of a creator in the formation of life, clashing with traditional religious beliefs. Darwin's theory gained credence among many modern thinkers and served to weaken the hold of traditional religion on intellectual life. Darwin, Marx, and other social theorists connected scientific inquiry with the idea of progress and helped to shape the modern worldview.[64]

In modern culture, a split between rationalists/scientists and non-rationalists/artists was expressed in different ways. By the late 19th century many scientists and social scientists associated with universities pursued scientific reasoning as the ideal form of inquiry. In contrast, the artistic vision in the 19th century, beginning with the Romantics in the middle of the 18th century, saw emotion and feeling rather than reason as the essence of humanity. Romantics defied literal representation and interpretation and accentuated non-rational aspects of nature and human nature. Their creations were not widely popular in their day. In contrast to academics, artists worked outside institutional organizations.[65] This fundamental split between the two groups has had dire results for holistic thinking. The split between reason and feeling has been a characteristic of Western thinking since the Greeks. This dualism has proven to be problematic, prompting contemporary calls for more holistic thinking to resolve the separation that has sprung from existential duality.

An 1871 caricature following publication of The Descent of Man was typical of many showing Darwin with an ape body, identifying him in popular culture as the leading author of evolutionary theory.

Insights: Learning from the Past

The Modern Industrial Era

With the expansion of capitalism, new things were systematically turned into commodities. One was time. Since the adage "time is money" aptly applied to labor in the modern industrial era, great efforts were made to squeeze as much productivity from the work force as possible. The wealth earned as a result of productive labor was channeled into more enterprises that created more wealth and prosperity for some people, particularly the property owning class in the Western world.

Industrialization brought about many far-reaching changes that are connected to each other; profound and rapid changes occurred in each of the five currents. Migrations displaced massive numbers of people as they moved from rural to urban centers and from one nation to another. With industrialization, two new social classes evolved: the middle class and the working class. The working class experienced major discontinuities as they adjusted, sometimes fitfully, to an urban life of squalor and uncertainty. Lawmakers passed laws that favored private property and the accumulation of wealth, which benefitted those who owned the means of production. Laws did not favor the working class. The environment was increasingly ravaged as smoke from coal-burning furnaces spewed into the air, shrouding cities in a thick, deadly haze. The rising middle class's demand for consumer items sparked new businesses to provide for their increasing consumer desires. Industrialization needed cheap raw materials and markets to perpetuate the expansionist economic process, which led to imperialist policies. The skilled artisans and guilds gave way to mass-production of goods in factory settings. Medical advances meant people lived longer, leading to an increasing population. Mass education became an ideal for many nations to emulate. Expanded suffrage meant more men were able to vote. Sanitation in cities improved, which meant fewer deadly diseases.

It's impossible to survey the modern industrial era without noting its astounding advancements in the sciences, technology, trade, medical breakthroughs, expansion of democracy, move to mass education, and a more comfortable standard of living for many. Yet, accompanying the astonishing successes have been shocking atrocities carried out in the name of "helping others;" which in reality has been a thin veil covering the greed, brutality, and arrogance of Western imperialism. The subjugation of the non-Western world into the world economic system has resulted in untold millions of deaths, uprooted and obliterated many traditional cultures, and exploited the environment for resources to fuel industrialization. The neo-imperialist invasion of the world by the Western nations has served as an attempt to homogenize the globe into Western values, attitudes, and political and economic structures. Resultant tensions led to increasing conflicts and, in the 20th century, to a new development in warfare: global conflict.

Questions to Consider

1. Using our theme of destructive and creative forces, do you think the creative aspects of industrialization outweighed the destructive aspects? Explain.

THE MODERN TWENTIETH CENTURY WORLD

The 20th century poses particular problems for historical analysis. Although the mountains of information and dramatic events make it difficult to identify overarching themes, one dominant theme does emerge from this era—challenges. Challenges occur on several fronts: challenges to the Earth to support billions of people, challenges to free-market capitalism, challenges to traditional social structures, challenges to traditional Victorian moral values, challenges to political liberalism, challenges to Western imperialism, and challenges to Newtonian science. Reactions to the challenges posed in the 20th century are not uniform but are met in different ways in different regions of the world.[66]

Relationship with Nature: Ecosystem Currents

During the 20th century, unprecedented population growth occurred. World population nearly tripled in the first three quarters of the century. After taking several million years for the human population to top the billion mark in 1825, it took only 100 years to add a second billion by 1930. An additional one billion people were added in just 35 years, from 1925-1960, raising the total to three billion people. By 1975, after only 15 years, world population jumped to four billion people. And only 12 years later, from 1975-1987, population escalated to five billion people.[67] In the millennium year of 2000, the world's population escalated to an astonishing 6 billion people. Several interconnected factors contributed to this astronomical rise in population: birth rates rose, devastating plagues abated, medical advances slowed death rates, and the climate was conducive to agricultural production that fed more people. Despite two horrific world wars, massive population growth triggered rapid urbanization throughout the world as people migrated across national boundaries and from the countryside to urban centers. The rapid rise in the number of people helped to account for frequent and violent unrest in the 20th century.

Ways of Living: Techno-Economic Currents

During the 20th century, industrialization spread into the far reaches of the world, including Eastern Europe, the Pacific Rim, China, Southeast Asia, India, and parts of Latin America. Japan's rapid industrialization, combined with continued economic growth in the U.S. and Western Europe, characterized economic developments during the first three decades of the 20th century. The Soviet Union instituted a communist economic system and embarked on hasty industrialization after its revolution in 1917.

Along with the primary industries—mining, agriculture, trapping, fishing, and forestry—and the industrialized secondary industries—manufacturing and construction—another form of wealth creation expanded in the 20th century: tertiary or service industries. Services are intangible goods that are provided to businesses and final consumers. Services may involve the transport, distribution and sale of goods from producer to consumer. Goods may be transformed in the process of providing a service, as happens in the restaurant industry. However, the focus is on serving the customer rather than transforming physical goods. Examples of services may include retail, insurance, government, tourism, banking, education, public utilities, entertainment, legal, medical, accounting, and social services. Sociologists Gerhard and Jean Lenski note, "As industrialization proceeds, the initial rapid growth in secondary industries slows down considerably, and tertiary industries become the chief growth sector of the economy."[68]

In the 20th century, there were three basic economic models for modern nations to choose from: capitalism, communism, and socialism. Within capitalism itself there were two models, free-market/laissez-faire capitalism and managed/regulated/state capitalism. Unfettered, laissez-faire capitalism, as advanced by Adam Smith in the late 18th century, limited government intervention in the economy and eschewed tariffs as barriers to free trade. The British practiced this form of capitalism from around the middle of the 19th century until the outbreak of World War I in 1914. In contrast, the U.S. protected its domestic industries with high tariffs, which restricted outside competition, especially from the British, and continued this practice even after World War II into the 1970s, when its industrial might was the envy of the world. In **managed or regulated capitalism**, the government closely regulates the financial sector to prevent wild financial speculation and insures transparency of the system. Tariffs protect manufacturing jobs in the home country; therefore, wages and prices are set according to supply and demand at the national level rather than global level. For the most part, education, health care, the military, utilities and prisons are government run and paid for through taxes, and the state sometimes owns companies such as airlines and transportation networks or closely regulates them. Private enterprise exists but is carefully regulated, with tax brackets for the wealthiest individuals hovering as high as 90 percent. Corporations also pay a larger share of their profits in taxes than in the laissez-faire model. Labor unions have a powerful say in wages and other benefits. There is a more equal distribution of wealth with managed capitalism, while wealth tends to concentrate in the hands of the elite and corporations in laissez-faire capitalism. The U.S. and other nations such as Great Britain switched from managed capitalism to the laissez faire capitalism economic model in the 1980s.

After its formation in 1917, the Soviet Union championed a communist or command economy. After World War II many developing industrial nations and Europe chose managed capitalism or a mixed economy of some socialism and capitalism, where some state-owned enterprises, usually large public services such as electricity, coexisted with free markets. Many countries, such as Cuba, China, Vietnam, and others incorporated communist economic principles.

Western capitalist nations seriously challenged the primacy of laissez-faire capitalism during the Great Depression in the 1930s. The depression hit Germany particularly hard, since heavy war reparation payments levied by the victors after World War I burdened their economy. At the height of the depression, the U.S. experienced unemployment rates as high as 25 percent, and the future of capitalism was in doubt. Analysis of the causes and repercussions of the Great Depression is shaped by one's economic persuasion. Marxists, on the left, argue that the Depression was the most severe in a series of periodic economic crises that can be expected to emanate from an unregulated and immoral capitalist system. Conservative free-market believers, on the right, regard the Depression as a temporary setback characteristic of capitalism; government interventions enacted as the "New Deal" smacked of socialism and should be abandoned. Whatever the explanation, the great suffering inflicted by the Great Depression has been seen as instrumental to the rise of fascism in Europe, which led to the outbreak of World War II.

With the crippling effects of the Great Depression affecting Western nations, many economists advocated that governments should take a more active and responsible role in planning national economies. To these economists, government intervention would soften the "boom and bust" cycles of unfettered capitalism characteristic of the 19th century. The British economist **John Maynard Keynes** (1883-1946) expounded this line of reasoning and argued that the government must accept more responsibility for regulating capitalist economies. He advocated regulation through a number of controls: running government surpluses or deficits when necessary; creating public works projects for the unemployed during economic downturns; adjusting the flow of money and credit; and raising or lowering interest rates. The purpose of these interventions was to make capitalism work better through government planning. The U.S. implemented and accepted Keynes' ideas during the Depression, but more widespread adoption of his ideas by Western nations took place after World War II. For example, during the Depression President Franklin Roosevelt initiated the New Deal to help stimulate the U.S. economy. Although these programs eased the situation for many working people, the New Deal did not officially end the depression. World War II, with its tremendous government spending and astronomically high tax rates on the wealthy, brought an end to the Great Depression.

Crowd at New York's American Union Bank during a bank run early in the Great Depression.

Keynesian economic theories prevailed in the West, in varying degrees, until challenged in the 1980s by a revival of free-market, neo-liberal capitalist theories. Milton Friedman (1912-2006) at the University of Chicago, known as the "Chicago School" of economics, and other neo liberal economists advanced these theories. U.S. President Ronald Reagan and Prime Minister Margaret Thatcher of Britain championed these ideas and spearheaded their implementation. Under their administrations, government planning still played a role in the economy, but their policies enthusiastically revived laissez-faire, free market theory and practice that is sometimes referred to as neoliberalism. In many "third world" countries—Indonesia, Chile, Bolivia, Argentina, Brazil, Poland, and others—local economies were either manipulated into accepting or voluntarily agreed to implement free-market principles in which elites and corporations prospered mightily, but the average person suffered a declining living standard.

Most economic interaction between Western and non-Western societies continued to be a core/periphery relationship in the 20th century. Western nations competed with each other, often violently, for colonies, markets, national prestige, and raw materials for their factories. Economically, periphery regions exported raw materials produced by cheap labor to core nations, which, in turn, sold manufactured items to periphery regions for a handsome profit. After World War II, many periphery nations set out to develop their own manufacturing industries with general levels of success, following a managed capitalism economic policy. But the managed form of capitalism has been challenged by the U.S. and others in the late 20th century, while the U.S. served as the beacon of neoliberalism during this period and applied more pressure for periphery nations to convert to their preferred economic model.

Questions to Consider

1. What economic system seems best to you? Explain

Human Networks: Social Currents

Modernization challenged traditional social structures on many fronts during the 20th century. The power and wealth of landowning aristocrats declined as wealthy capitalist entrepreneurs and their families increased their power and wealth. As agricultural production shifted to a capitalist economy, the rural peasantry class declined in the West with more farmers from rural areas moving to cities and joining the ranks of a growing urban working class. In more industrially developed capitalist societies, especially after World War II, through the efforts of unions and favorable government policy, an increase in real wages, benefits, and an improved standard of living meant the urban working class had been economically incorporated into the middle class; many also accepted middle class values and aspirations, such as home ownership and higher education.

Named for Queen Victoria of Britain who reigned from 1837 to 1902, the traditional normative values, called Victorian values, of the 19th century—a cohesive nuclear family, religious affiliation, and strict codes of moral behavior—frayed in the 20th century. One of the traditional Victorian values was the strict regulation of sexual behavior. Psychologist Sigmund Freud (1856-1939) concluded through case studies of his patients that the social mores of the Victorian era abnormally repressed sexual desires and caused neuroses. Along with these insights, the development of birth control loosened Victorian conventions regarding sexual behavior for both women and men. In the 1960s and 1970s, a "**sexual revolution**," broke the remaining sexual barriers wide open in the U.S. and Western Europe. Later in the 20th century, female sexuality, homosexuality, and sexual activity outside marriage became more socially acceptable but were vigorously rejected by religious social conservatives.

Women's equality and what advocates called the women's liberation movement was an important trend in the 20th century. For centuries, women had been largely defined by their reproductive capacity and confined to the domestic sphere. Now women applied Enlightenment ideas of equality and individual rights to their own situation. As more contraceptives became available, the biological constraints on women's choices were lifted. A woman's sexual expression no longer meant more children. As women gained control over their reproductive functions, birth rates declined dramatically, especially among middle class Western women. By the late 20th century, women had begun to enter the economic and political sphere. Women's paid labor spurred the economy as their purchasing power grew with their contribution to family income as producers. By the late 20th century, men and women were both consumers and producers.

Questions to Consider

1. Do you think the changes women experienced in the 20th century were beneficial or detrimental to them?

Establishing Order: Political Currents

Political Systems

Political change was a common theme in the 20th century. By the 1990s, most nations had a different political system than they had had in 1900. Even governments that retained their political system, such as the United States, had redefined the role of government from the 1930s onward. Governments played an increasing role in the economic and social realm. In the U.S., presidential powers and authority grew significantly for the executive branch of government. Democratic nations expanded universal suffrage with most European nations granting adult males the vote between 1870 and 1912. Although the United States instituted universal male suffrage earlier, it still retained discriminatory racial restrictions against African Americans in many states until the 1960s. After a long struggle, women's suffrage was implemented in the United States in 1920 and other Western nations at varying dates in the 20th century, most after World War I or II. Those non-Western nations that gained independence and followed liberal traditions granted suffrage to men and women as well.

Conflict and War

At the turn of the 20th century, Westerners were confident that stability, peace, and progress would continue indefinitely into the future. In order to maintain this stability, an intricate system of entangling alliances upheld a precarious balance of power in Europe. The system was designed to ensure peace but ultimately failed. Instead of cooperation, an intense competition among nations involved rivalries over colonial possessions, commercial interests, and national pride. With the intensification of nationalism, each nation boasted its superiority. Tensions mounted as war seemed imminent. The devastating two world wars of the 20th century can be viewed as an intermittent war from 1914 to 1945 with a 10-year depression sandwiched in between, rather like a second European Thirty Years War (the first was 1618-1648).

World War I, or the Great War as it was called at the time, broke out in June 1914 when a Serbian nationalist assassinated Archduke Francis Ferdinand of Austrian which sparked the powder keg of entangling alliances. Each side confidently marched off to war with the unshaken belief that they would be victorious by the onset of winter. But the reality of the war sobered participants. Makers of modern military technology had devised creative new ways of inflicting death and destruction, such as poisonous gas, the machine

Feminist suffrage parade in New York City, May 6, 1912. Women gained the right to vote in the U.S. in 1920.

gun, and barbed wire, demonstrating that technology had a dark, demonic side as well. The terrible onslaught stalemated in the dreary trenches of northern France for four bloody years with both sides suffering millions of causalities. The scale tipped in favor of the Allied forces with the entrance of the United States in April, 1917. On the 11th hour of the 11th day of the 11th month, 1918, the Great War ended with a casualty figure totaling over ten million. The optimistic war "to make the world safe for democracy," to use U.S. President Woodrow Wilson's phrase, had turned into a ghastly, modern nightmare.

The victors negotiated a peace treaty to end the war at the Versailles Palace in Paris, France. Woodrow Wilson optimistically drew up a plan known as the **Fourteen Points** for post-war order. One of the points was the right to self-determination, which meant that people of a given territory could freely determine their political status and how they will be governed, without undue outside influence from another country. For example, the Ottoman and Austro-Hungarian Empires were divided into sovereign nations or mandates that were closely supervised by the victorious imperial powers of Britain and France. Identifying the precise territory and ethnic group or groups that would comprise the new nations proved to be problematic. Wilson's points of self-determination encouraged former European

Demonstration against the Treaty of Versaillesin front of the Reichstag building in Berlin, Germany.

colonies to form their own nations, ostensibly free of colonial rule. However, most colonies had to wait until the end of World War II to assert their national independence.

Wilson's 14th point outlined his ambitious idea for a League of Nations. Its purported purpose was to guarantee political independence and territorial integrity for large and small nations and to reconcile potential conflicts in the hopes of preventing future wars. The U.S. Senate failed to ratify the Versailles Treaty and refused to join the organization, severely hampering the success of the fledgling world organization. France and Britain lost momentum as world leaders following World War I, and the U.S., already the world's most powerful economy, rejected stepping into the vacated leadership role in world affairs. Noble aims aside, the Versailles Treaty actually contributed to further conflict. According to the treaty, Germany was blamed for the war and endured national humiliation and economic hardship when forced to pay exorbitant war reparations to the victors, Britain and France. The seeds for future conflict were sown.

The power balance among nations began to shift in the 1930s as the Soviet Union, Japan, and a resurgent Germany asserted their industrial strength and military might. These nations challenged Western liberalism by embracing a new form of state organization, totalitarianism. Totalitarian governments imposed total state control over the public and private life of a society. In this atmosphere, there is unquestioning obedience to governmental authority, and individual subordination is a matter of faith. State control was carried to the extreme in four totalitarian experiments: Soviet Russia, Fascist Italy and Japan, and Nazi Germany.

The humiliating defeat of Germany in World War I profoundly embarrassed Germans and devastated national morale. Saddled with the burdensome war reparations and a ruined economy, millions of Germans lost their trust in a liberal democratic form of government and free market form of capitalism. With the onset of the world depression, Germans turned to the charismatic leader of the **Nazi** Party in 1933, Adolph Hitler. Much of Nazi ideology, borrowed from Benito Mussolini who consolidated power in Italy after 1922, rejected and assaulted reason, democracy, individualism, and liberalism. Rearmament increased German prosperity and boosted national pride by the mid-1930s. A majority of Germans were satisfied with Hitler's leadership, despite his frequent anti-Semitic ranting and aggressive maneuvers to conquer Europe.

The **Soviet Union**, the world's first communist nation lurched into existence in 1917. During World War I, Russia, ruled by the autocratic and inept Tsar Nicolas II, was woefully ill-equipped for modern warfare and promptly lost over two million soldiers by 1916. In the spring of 1917, the communists' cry for "Peace, Bread, and Land" spread among a receptive and weary peasantry and workers who were experiencing deplorable living conditions and mass starvation at home. Along with incompetent and antiquated military and political leadership, crop shortages and severe weather added to the Russians' misery. These chaotic conditions created an undertow of tension that stirred unrest among many Russians clamoring for political change. Taking advantage of the volatile situation was the charismatic Vladimir Lenin, the first organizer of the Communist party and the leader of the Bolshevik revolution in 1917. After Lenin's death, Josef Stalin maneuvered himself into a leadership role and imposed a ruthless dictatorship. Through a series of Five Year Plans, Communist leaders rapidly industrialized and organized peasants into collective agriculture communes. Through the 1930s under Stalin's brutal command, the Communist party eliminated an estimated 15 million peasants, who opposed collectivization of their privately owned lands and other resisters. Although Soviet policies improved mass education and medical care and instituted industrialization, the populace paid a high price for these limited reforms.

Two fascist leaders: Benito Mussolini of Italy and Adolf Hitler of Germany in 1940.

Germany, losing its colonies after World War I, was intent on uniting German speaking peoples of Europe into a Third Reich that would last a thousand years. After incorporating Sudetenland, Austria, Czechoslovakia, and other regions into his orb, Hitler invaded Poland on September 1, 1939, the act that led to the outbreak of World War II. The major powers involved were the Allied nations of Great Britain, Soviet Union, France, and United States against the major Axis powers of Germany, Japan, and Italy. The war pitted the hostile European nations, other industrialized nations such as the U.S., colonies of the combatants, and other countries such as China

Painting of the 1917 Bolshevik Revolution, painter Boris Kustodiev, 1920.

(who suffered horribly in the war) into a global conflict of a magnitude that the world had never experienced.

The causes of **World War II** are varied and complex. Looking at the causes from a systems perspective, several are important. Competition was the key word of the 19th century and well into the 20th century. Nations that supported diverse modern political ideologies—liberalism, fascism, and communism— competed with each other to flaunt their preferred political outlook. Communist and democratic nations—the Soviet Union, Britain, France, and U.S.—were forced into an unlikely alliance against those nations supporting fascism: Germany, Italy, and Japan. Competition also existed among Western imperial powers. The established imperial powers of Britain, France, and U.S. had a stable of colonies, protectorates, or dependent nations already under their economic or political umbrella. Japan, Italy, and Germany, since it had been stripped of its colonies after World War I, raced to "catch up" with their more established competitors. They did so brutally. Another competition was over military might and world leadership in the post-war years. The dropping of the atomic bomb on the Japanese cities of Nagasaki and Hiroshima in 1945 signaled that the U.S. had won that particular contest. The atomic bomb was the final act of violence in a war that was witness to unspeakable atrocities. Over 60 million civilians and combatants alike died in the global war.

Atomic bomb mushroom clouds over Hiroshima (left) and Nagasaki (right), August 6 and 9, 1945.

The **Cold War** (1945-1989) between the Soviet Union and the United States was a story of confrontation between two contrasting ideologies that were both a product of the modern worldview. Unlike World War II, there was not direct conflict between the two super-powers and the Cold War did not escalate into an unlimited, total war; instead, conflict was conducted in proxy wars in many regions around the world including Korea, Guatemala, Vietnam, Afghanistan, Nicaragua, Cuba, Cambodia, and Chile. After World II, the colonies of the West demanded independence from colonial rulers and faced the question of what kind of political and economic system to adopt in their particular nation. Both the U.S. and the Soviet Union tried to impose, sometimes forcibly, their particular ideology onto former colonies.

The sophisticated military technology that each nation accumulated in a show of power and prestige was capable of destroying the world multiple times. Both nations selfishly placed all humans in peril with the continual looming threat of an all-out nuclear war. Each side fortunately understood the risks of an unlimited war and refrained from initiating a nuclear holocaust. In one saving grace, the Cold War was a war of economic, not human, attrition, measured not in the number of lives lost, but in the number of dollars spent. Both sides squandered trillions of dollars on military armaments, missiles, troops, and military research, which rapidly became obsolete as one rival nation or the other discovered new and deadlier innovations in a fruitless competition for the latest in expensive weapon technology. In a game of one-upsmanship, each side struggled for military superiority as each nation tried to outdo the other. In the final outcome, a more efficient capitalist economy outspent the crumbling Soviet economy as the pressures of economic stagnation and bloated bureaucracies combined to signal the collapse and dismemberment of the Soviet nation and control of its satellites in Eastern Europe. The last gasp of the bellicose Cold War finally ended in 1989-1991.

Migration and Interaction

The guiding political principle of the 20th century was the movement toward the formation of self-governing nation-states throughout the world, although the process in accomplishing this global goal was uneven and often fraught with violence. The political interaction between leading Western nations and their colonies, protectorates, mandates, or their economic dependencies was largely an unequal relationship. These powerful nations who had given birth to the idea of nationhood in many cases thwarted the less powerful countries from forming their own independent, self-governing nations. In one sense, the ideals of self-determination and the organization of the world into individual, sovereign nations outlined by Wilson's Fourteen Points at the conclusion of World War I had been realized at the end of the 20th century.

The Middle East experienced the force of Westernization and modernization, but traditional, tribal peoples in the region often resisted these new ways. At the conclusion of World War I, according to provisions in the League of Nations, much of the defeated Ottoman Empire was divided into mandates under the administration of the victorious French and British. The British administered the mandates for Iraq, Palestine (part would become the nation of Israel in 1948) and Transjordan (includes the nation of Jordan today). The French administered a mandate for Syria that was divided into the nations of Syria and Lebanon. Turkey formed an independent republic in 1923 under the leadership of Mustafa Kemal Ataturk, who adopted a Western parliamentary system, modern military, and secularization. Reza Shah Pahlavi, a former army commander, reigned in Iran from 1925 to 1941 and his son, Muhammad Reza Shah, ruled

Protesters against the U.S. and the Shah and in support of Ayatollah Khomeini in Tehran, Iran 1979.

Iran with an iron fist until 1979. The election of Mohammed Mosaddeq as Prime Minister from 1951-1953 briefly challenged the Shah's rule, as he opposed foreign influence in Iran and started to nationalize the oil industry. This move countered British and American interests, and under the direction of the American Central Intelligence Agency (CIA) a *coup d'etat* removed Mosaddeq from power. Later, Islamic fundamentalists under the leadership of *ayatollah* Khomeini deposed the autocratic regime of the Shah in a 1979 televised coup and established the Islamic Republic of Iran that rules according to what they consider traditional Islamic values.

Jewish people had longed for a homeland since the 19th century. They turned to their ancient homeland of Palestine as the site for their desired nation. Immigration to the region in the early 20th century increased and became particularly desperate during the **holocaust** in Germany. However, the Palestinian people resented the influx of Jews buying land, and resistance turned violent in the 1930s. After the war, many Westerners sympathized with the Jewish quest for a permanent homeland in Palestine because of the extermination of six million Jews by Hitler during World War II. The Israelis proudly raised their flag of independence in 1948. However, the Palestinians deeply resented their displacement from their native soil and organized resistance movements, sometimes violent, to regain their traditional homeland. Arabs throughout the region deeply resented the interference of the West in establishing the state of Israel and the displacement of thousands of indigenous Palestinians. But attempts at cooperative Arab internationalism and military efforts to overthrow the state of Israel have repeatedly failed.

In Eastern Europe after World War I, the Austria-Hungarian Empire was divided into nations composed of various, often hostile, ethnic groups. World War II drew these fledgling nations into the violence and after the war the Soviet Union forced many of them into becoming part of the communist Warsaw bloc of Soviet satellites. After the fall of communism in the early 1990s, the nations were freed from Soviet influence and remain independent today.

Western political ideas and organization appealed to many former colonies. Political tensions proliferated as these former colonies asserted their political independence and determined their political, economic, and social structures. They became pawns in the tense standoff between the Soviet Union and the United States, which each promoted their particular ideology by using military force, bribery, deception, and ideological arguments to gain political favor.

Fervent nationalism, anti-imperialism, and revolutionary movements engulfed Asia after 1945. **Vietnam** sought political independence from the French after the war, only to be thwarted in their nationalist aspirations. They successfully defeated the French in 1954, only to have the Americans replace their former colonial ruler. Communist supporters, led by Ho Chi Minh, battled the Americans until they were finally forced to flee in a humiliating exit in 1975. China in 1949 adopted a communist form of government after a violent social and political revolution. Led by Mao Zedong, the social revolution overthrew the landed aristocracy, disrupted the Confucian social order, and established agricultural communes. The West essentially isolated China after its adoption of communism and did not reopen relations until 1972. Relations between the West and China warmed after Mao's death in 1976, accompanied by a relaxation of command eco-

German concentration camp, Lager Nordhausen, 1945. Six million Jews were killed by the Nazis.

The mass departure of Vietnamese refugees from Communist-controlled Vietnam, many by boat, following the Vietnam War during the late 1970s.

nomic principles under the leadership of Deng Xiaoping. Thereafter, China followed communist political policies but embraced some capitalist economic principles.

India wrenched its political independence from Britain in 1947. It was fast becoming the world's largest democracy but resembled a monarchy by inheriting the British parliamentary system. Leadership began with Jawaharlal Nehru, who ruled until 1964; his daughter Indira Gandhi governed as prime minister from 1966 to 1977, and her son Rajiv Gandhi presided from 1984 until his assassination in 1991. Tremendous violence and social upheaval marred India's road to nationhood. In 1947, the northwestern part of India, which was predominately Muslim, separated from primarily Hindu India to become Pakistan. The civil war that broke out between the two nations reshuffled over 20 million people according to religious preference. In 1971, the eastern portion of Pakistan formed the independent nation of Bangladesh.

The United States occupied Japan after its humiliating defeat in World War II. It willingly adopted an American style democratic constitution with gender equality and radical land reform as outlined in its post-war reconstruction. Stripped of its military but aided by the fact that the lack of a military budget did not drain funds, Japan embarked upon a remarkable economic expansion and industrialization of its devastated industries.

Since 1945, Africans formed nations out of former colonies. Some nations attained independence relatively peacefully, including Ghana, Nigeria, and Senegal. Others were embroiled in bloody conflict: Kenya, Zaire, Angola, Mozambique, and Zimbabwe. But Africa faced many trials, perhaps more so than any other region, in its efforts to modernize; national borders established by colonial nations had little regard for ethnic or geographic boundaries; tribal leaders had little experience with Western political organization, birthrates were high and the population rapidly grew, rapid urbanization occurred, and racism was official apartheid in some nations. The Cold War conflict wracked some African nations and they were manipulated as pawns by the Soviet Union and the United States. In the post-World War II years, through bribery and deceptive schemes, the West systematically siphoned off Africa's rich natural resources. On the positive side, many Africans continued to hold to traditional tribal customs and village life as a source of stability and hope under the onslaught of modernization, poverty, corruption, disease, and the West's exploitive economic policies.

Latin America experienced turmoil in establishing stable democratic nations in the 20th century as well. The Spanish tradition of hierarchical, autocratic, and bureaucratic government, with a strong role for the church and military, was still in place after 1945. Some Latin American nations attempted to establish democratic or communist governments, nationalizing foreign corporations, toppling the landed aristocracy, and redistributing land to the hapless peasantry, but few survived. However, pro-Soviet Fidel Castro in a successful revolution overthrew the pro-United States Cuban dictator, Fulgencio Batista, in 1957. The U.S. retaliated to this usurpation of its power in the Western hemisphere by imposing a trade embargo against Cuba after the Bay of Pigs fiasco in 1961. During the Cuban Missile Crisis in 1962, a near-confrontation between the two super-powers was averted at the last minute when the Soviet Union agreed to remove its missiles from Cuba and the U.S. agreed to remove its missiles from Turkey. In Chile, the democratic election in 1970 of the socialist-leaning Salvador Allende met with opposition from the U.S. government, multinational corporations, wealthy Chileans, and the military. Another brutal CIA-led military coup orchestrated the overthrow of Allende in 1973 and replaced him with the U.S.-friendly but brutal dictator, August Pinochet.

American economist Milton Friedman guided the institution of neo-liberal market reforms that re-structured the economy for the benefit of large foreign corporations and the wealthy. Frequent revolutions also occurred on the right in the form of military coups, often covertly supported by the United States, which imposed corrupt and brutal dictatorships in several Central American countries, among them Samoza, who ruled in Nicaragua from 1936 to the 1979.

Questions to Consider

1. After time has passed, do you think the Cold War was a real threat to the U.S. by the Soviet Union (or a threat to the Soviet Union by the U.S.), or merely a government-manufactured enemy to keep the citizenry fearful and compliant? Explain.

Human Expressions: Cultural Currents

Identity and Belonging

The rise of mass culture characterized 20th century society. Traditionally, the family, tribe, village, and church served as the source of identity and belonging. These groups provided security, protection, reaffirmation, and loyalty for the individual. With the spread of modernization, individualism, population growth, and the accompanying disruption of traditions, individuals were left to seek a new sense of community and identity as an anchor in a rapidly changing world. Even though many Westerners embraced the ideal of individual freedom, they attached themselves to mass culture as a source of identity. Three types of mass identification in the 20th century were nationalism, totalitarianism, and corporatism.

Nationalist ideas of the 19th century intensified as a powerful emotional force in the 20th century West, eventually spreading around the world. Along with the rituals and symbols of national allegiance, the image of soldiers who nobly sacrificed themselves on the battlefield for the cause of their nation was a powerful message.

A second form of mass society in the 20th century was the totalitarian state. The collapse of traditional societies and the failure of liberalism, democracy, individualism, and capitalism during the depression of the 1930s drove individuals, especially in Italy and Germany, into a desperate search for a new form of community. Adolph Hitler and Benito Mussolini created a fascist community to coalesce the disaffected German and Italian people, complete with identifiable enemies to blame for all societal ills. Using manipulation and emotional mass appeals, like corporate propaganda, they strove to subordinate and sacrifice the individual for the greater national community. The values and beliefs of totalitarian regimes included a rejection of liberalism, democracy, and individualism, constant warfare and struggle, and sacrifice of the individual self to the higher purpose of the nation. Unlike in corporate cultures, though, these totalitarian states forcibly coerced their citizenry to participate, and those who did not comply met with death or horrible imprisonment.

The corporation is a third type of mass identification, especially significant in capitalist societies after World War II and continuing presently (see the Global Wave). Corporations increased in size as capitalism expanded and corporate business spread throughout the world. Western individuals employed by corporations or aspiring to be employed by them identify with a spreading corporate culture and corporate values—efficiency, productivity, hierarchal structures, bottom line profits, competition, and rational organization—become part of an individual's values and attitudes. An individual employed as an assembly line worker becomes a cog in the mechanical process of mass-producing goods, while the corporation's white-collar workers exercise more power as they move up in the financial, managerial, and marketing ranks. The modern educational system educates students to become efficient members of the corporate world and to internalize its values. To manipulate, convince, and mold individual personalities and values into a corporate culture is the purpose of advertising, marketing, and public relations industries, owned and operated by corporations. Through these industries, the corporate culture is largely successful in creating a consumer ethic that regards consumption, accumulation, and display of material goods as desirable. This indoctrination is necessary for the continuation and expansion of the corporate, capitalist system. Corporations do not just distort the liberal concept of individualism by fostering the illusion that freedom means individual consumer choice; actually, corporations scorn individual freedom and profit from an individual's dependence and subordination as corporate employees and compliant, insatiable consumers. For following and identifying with a corporate culture, compliant individuals are rewarded with a comfortable standard of living, relative security, and association with like-minded individuals who participate in the same process. Individuals, particularly in the United States, sanction the corporate culture and willingly support its values, attitudes, beliefs, and way of life. Although the corporate culture is deeply entrenched, individuals still have the choice not to participate in this form of mass society.

Questions to Consider

1. Do you think your educational system is an institution that reinforces mass identification and the values of mass society? Explain.

Ideology and Aesthetic Expression

New ideas emerged in the arts, sciences, social sciences, and philosophy in the 20th century that either expanded upon ideas of the 19th century or rejected them completely to see things anew. This brief overview only examines a few of the many different fields that experienced change.

One academic field that experienced significant transformations in the 20th century was physics. Early 20th century physicists challenged the objective modern worldview and the mechanistic order outlined by Newton. Newtonian laws of certainty were found to be inapplicable in dealing with subatomic particles; probability was all that could be determined. Furthermore, the status of the observer was found to alter the process being observed.

The most influential scientist of the 20th century, **Albert Einstein**, postulated his theory of relativity in 1905. His famous formula $e=mc^2$ established that matter and energy were interchangeable; not polar opposites, as had been thought, but two forms of the same pervasive substratum of existence—one becomes the other. Einstein's findings shattered Newtonian certainties and introduced the element of uncertainty, time and space were relative to the viewpoint of the observer and only the speed of light was constant for all frames of reference in the Universe.

Albert Einstein, 1921. He was awarded the Nobel Prize for Physics the same year.

He theorized that space and time were also not separate entities but formed a continuous whole. Measurement of this so-called fourth dimension—space-time—depended as much on the observer as on the subjects of the measurement themselves.[69]

Physicist Max Planck proposed that the energy released by atomic particles did not flow smoothly but jumped in discontinuous spurts or quanta, leading to the formulation of quantum theory. Scientists also concluded that both wave and particle theories, although seemingly contradictory, coexisted logically—hence Werner Heisenberg's theory of complementarity. He found in his principle of indeterminacy or uncertainty in 1927 that instead of Newton's dependable, rational laws, there seemed to be only tendencies and probabilities; scientists would never attain more than probable knowledge, and certainty was impossible. The "uncertainty principle" of modern physics challenged the Newtonian world machine and substituted probability for absolutes.

Equally unsettling as advances in physics were developments in psychology that disputed established 19th century Victorian concepts of morals and values and challenged Enlightenment rationalism as well. According to psychologist Sigmund Freud (1856-1939), human behavior was basically irrational; the primitive unconscious was driven by sexual aggression and pleasure seeking desires, which the conscious mind suppressed according to the accepted mores of the period. Human behavior was a delicate, unpredictable, tension-laden compromise between instinctual drives and the controls of reason and moral values. He viewed humans as a closed system driven by two forces, self-preservation and sexual drive.

Early 20th century novelists used a stream-of-consciousness technique to explore the psyche. Virginia Woolf's novel, *Jacob's Room* (1922), consisted of a series of internal monologues, in which ideas and emotions from different time periods randomly bubbled up. James Joyce abandoned conventional grammar in his novel, *Ulysses* (1922), in favor of a bewildering confusion of language intended to mirror modern life, a colossal riddle waiting to be unraveled. In his famous poem, *The Waste Land* (1922), T. S. Eliot depicted a world of growing desolation and despair.

Artists of different schools in the early 20th century desired to know and depict an unseen, inner world of feeling and imagination, expressing an obscure psychological view of reality as well as evoking powerful emotions. Vincent van Gogh painted the vision of his mind's eye in *The Starry Night* (1889) with blazing trees and exploding stars all swirling together in one great rhythmic cosmic dance. Pablo Picasso founded the cubist movement, which emphasized a complex geometry of zigzagging lines and abstract sharply angled planes. And Wassily Kandinsky turned away from nature and emphasized form and color to represent mood and emotion instead of depicting objects.

Jazz, a musical expression coming from the African American experience, diverged sharply from the classical music tradition. Played by bands, in contrast to the traditional symphony orchestra, jazz improvised, and the lead performer often spontaneously invented and varied both melody and rhythm in non-standard repetitions. Similarly, modern dance broke from tradition. Whereas formal, classical ballet was performed on an elevated stage at some distance from the audience, modern dance, freed from the conventions of ballet, conveyed deep individual emotions and passion. In jazz clubs and cabarets, dancers energetically merged into the emotional ecstasy of the music and did not act as detached, remote performers or observers.

Post-modernism, a skeptical philosophical and cultural movement in the 20th century, disdained predetermined patterns and displayed an affinity for the fragmented, fractured, unfinished, disharmonious, serendipitous, conflicting, and random. Sequences could not be imposed, since discontinuity was the norm. Philosophical idealism was rejected in favor of functionality, while the object of study was how the object functions in and of itself. Post-modernists asked how things worked. They rejected absolute polarities. For example, 19th century thinkers assumed the polarity of male and female, object and subject; however, post-modernists claimed that polarities were not absolute and separate but integrated with one another and interactive. Post-modernists openly accepted sexuality and embraced homosexuality, androgyny and bisexuality.[70] It was also sympathetic to feminism. Scholars of the 19th century believed that social science, philosophy, literature, and art should be readily accessible to a general educated audience; instead, post-modernists espoused complexity and difficulty, and spoke to a narrow, highly professional, educated audience. To participate in post-modern thought required a great deal of learning, sophistication, and intense application.[71] A distinct break developed between "high and low" cultures. Critics of post-modernism found there was a tendency toward pessimism and despair. A common post-modernist image was a bleak, depressed urban landscape with themes of alienation and fragmentation. The trends of post-modernism tended to pull society apart, rather than unify society around common ground or a common purpose.

Questions to Consider

1. Do you see the 20th century themes of uncertainty, relativity, and irrationality at play in your own life? Explain.

Insights: Learning from the Past

The Twentieth Century

A theme in this modern 20th century section is challenge. The challenge of astronomical population increases was met with a response of a corresponding increase in agricultural production called the Green Revolution. In the 1960s and 1970s, scientific principles in the form of increased use of chemicals in food production spurred a dramatic boost in agricultural output. Enough food was produced to feed the world, but distribution remained a problem. The challenge of environmental pollution was met with technological and political fixes. For example, political legislation in the U.S. such as the Clean Air and Water Act in the 1970s cleaned up air and water pollution. The challenge to liberalism by fascist nations was met with an all out war, which defeated fascism in a clear military decision in 1945. Following the end of World War II, Soviet-style communism posed another challenge to liberalism and capitalism and was met with a war of economic attrition that resulted in the dramatic and agonizing collapse of communism in 1989-1991. The challenge to the horrific violence during World War II was met with the organization of peace movements. The challenge to managed capitalism and socialism that flourished from 1930 to 1980s was met with a resurgence of corporate power and neo-liberal economic principles. The challenge to Victorian social values, behaviors, and the traditional middle class family was met with a post-war sexual revolution, a woman's liberation movement, and a homosexual rights movement. The challenge to the "white man's burden" of white racial superiority was met with a post-war civil rights movement and decolonization actions throughout the world. All of these challenges occurred in the 20th century, and their responses are still being felt.

Questions to Consider

1. Of all the movements listed above, which one do you think was (is) most important? Why?

Insights: Learning from the Past

THE MODERN WAVE: CONCLUDING INSIGHTS

The Modern Wave has wrought tremendous changes upon the world. At the end of the 20th century, the world was quite different than it was at the beginning of the Modern Wave. The theme of destructive and creative energies can be applied to these changes. Destruction includes extinction of native ecosystems in many parts of the world, obliteration of traditional cultures and societies, death of millions in violent wars using modern technological warfare, diminution of the central authority of religion, and fraying of complex social systems and extended families. Creative aspects of the Modern Wave include technological innovations that have made possible a more comfortable material standard of living and longer life for millions, formation of governments that protect human rights and individual freedom, liberation of women and more control over their reproductive choices, and a cultural forum in which creativity flourishes. But the creative and destructive aspects of the Modern Wave pose a paradox. Greater creativity, rapid change, and individual freedom also include social disruption, alienation, fragmentation, and demolition of traditions that have lasted for thousands of years. All are part of the Modern Wave.

The 20th century's unresolved challenges and repercussions continue to reverberate in the Global Wave that we turn to next.

ENDNOTES

1. Philip J. Adler, *World Civilizations* (Minneapolis/St. Paul: West Publishing, 1996), p. 220-229.
2. Edward L. Farmer, "Civilization as a Unit of World History: Eurasia and Europe's Place in It," *The History Teacher* Vol. 18, No. 3 (1985), p. 360-361.
3. Clive Ponting, *A Green History of the World* (New York: Penguin Books, 1991), p. 140-148.
4. Philip J. Adler, *World Civilizations* (Minneapolis/St. Paul: West Publishing, 1996), p. 554-555.
5. Peter N. Stearns, *World History: Patterns of Change and Continuity* (New York: Harper Collins Publishers, 1995), p. 311.
6. Stearns, *World History*, p. 297.
7. Adler, *World Civilizations*, p. 225.
8. Adler, *World Civilizations*, p. 541-542.
9. Gerhard and Jean Lenski, *Human Societies: An Introduction to Macrosociology* (New York: McGraw-Hill, 1992), p. 294; and L.S. Stavrainos, *Lifelines from Our Past: A New World History* (New York: Pantheon Books, 1989), p. 102.
10. John McKay, Bennett Hill, and John Buckler, *A History of World Societies* (Boston Houghton Mifflin Company, 1996), p. 629-633.
11. Stearns, *World History*, p. 284-285.
12. Adler, *World Civilizations*, p. 376.
13. Stearns, *World History*, p. 286-287.
14. Adler, *World Civilizations*, p. 322-324; and Stearns, *World History*, p. 290.
15. Christopher Hill, *Change and Continuity in Seventeenth Century England* (London: Weidenfeld and Nicholson, 1974), p. 94-95.
16. Hill, *Seventeenth Century England*, p. 85 and 99.
17. David S. Landes, *The Unbound Prometheus: Technological Change and Industrial Development in Western Europe from 1750 to the Present* (Cambridge: University Press, 1969), p. 22-24.
18. Adler, *World Civilizations*, p. 396.
19. Loring H. White, "A Technological Model of Global History," *The History Teacher* Vol. 20, No. 4 (1987), p. 510-511.
20. Rondo Cameron, *A Concise History of the World: From the Paleolithic Times to the Present* (New York: Oxford University Press, 1993), p. 167; and Peter N. Stearns, *The Industrial Revolution in World History* (Boulder: Westview Press, 1993), p. 35.
21. Adler, *World Civilizations*, p. 400.
22. Stearns, *World History*, p. 273 and 295; and Adler, *World Civilizations*, p. 400-401.
23. Landes, *Unbound Prometheus*, p. 1.
24. These factors are not listed in order of importance. See Stearns, *Industrial Revolution*.
25. Adler, *World Civilizations*, p. 451; and Robert E. Meacham, Alan T. Wood, Richard W. Hull, Edward M. Burns, *World Civilizations: Their History and Their Culture* Volume II (New York: W.W. Norton & Company, 1997), p. 229.
26. Stearns, *Industrial Revolution*, p. 38.
27. Cameron, *Economic History*, p. 168-169; Deborah Valenze, *The First Industrial Woman* (New York: Oxford University Press, 1995), p. 34; and Adler, *World Civilizations*, p. 451.
28. William J. Duiker and Jackson J. Spielvogel, *World History Volume I to 1800* (Minneapolis/St. Paul: West Publishing Company, 1994), p. 718-719.
29. Stearns, *Industrial Revolution*, p. 6.

30. Stearns, *Industrial Revolution*, p. 18; and Ponting, *Green History*, p. 240.
31. Ponting, *Green History*, p. 181-182.
32. Weisman, Alan. *The World Without Us*. New York: Thomas Dunne Books, 2007, p. 192 and Ponting, *Green History*, p. 165 and p. 168-171.
33. Stearns, *Industrial Revolution*, p. 18 and Cameron, *Economic History*, p. 167-168.
34. Dictionary.com, supply and demand, *http://dictionary.reference.com/browse/supply+and+demand*
35. Adler, *World Civilizations*, p. 449; and Stearns, *Industrial Revolution*, p. 34-35.
36. Stearns, *Industrial Revolution*, p. 2-3 and 35
37. Lenski, *Human Societies*, p. 281, 283-285.
38. Lenski, *Human Societies*, p. 267-268; and Stavrianos, *Lifelines*, p. 114.
39. Stearns, *Industrial Revolution*, p. 36.
40. Lenski, *Human Societies*, p. 285-286.
41. Cameron, *Economic History*, p. 189-190; Stearns, *Industrial Revolution*, p. 27; and Stavrianos, *Lifelines*, p. 125.
42. Cameron, *Economic History*, p. 190.
43. Stavrianos, *Lifelines*, p. 125-126.
44. Stavrianos, *Lifelines*, p. 90.
45. Lenski, *Human Societies*, p. 341.
46. Lenski, *Human Societies*, p. 342-344.
47. Stearns, *World History*, p. 300.
48. Stearns, *World History*, p. 299-300.
49. Lenski, *Human Societies*, p. 342-344.
50. Valenze, *Industrial Woman*, p. 155-180.
51. Stearns, *World History*, p. 299.
52. Lenski, *Human Societies*, p. 278, 342-344, and 351.
53. Benedict Anderson, *Imagined Communities: Reflections on the Origin and Spread of Nationalism* (London: Verso, 1991), p. 5-7.
54. Stearns, *World History*, p. 408-409.
55. Adler, *World Civilizations*, p. 499.
56. Kevin Reilly, *The West and the World: A History of Civilization* Volume 2 (New York: HarperCollins Publishers, 1989), p. 135.
57. Reilly, *West and World*, p. 135-137.
58. Reilly, *West and World*, p. 139-141.
59. Adler, *World Civilizations*, p. 540-541.
60. Adler, *World Civilizations*, p. 546-547.
61. Adler, *World Civilizations*, p. 549-551.
62. Adam Hochschild, *King Leopold's Ghost: A Story of Greed, Terror, and Heroism in Colonial Africa* (New York: Houghton Mifflin, 1999).
63. Valenze *Industrial Woman*, p. 184-185.
64. Stearns, *World History*, p. 412; and Adler, *World Civilizations*, p. 583.
65. Stearns, *World History*, p. 412-413.
66. Factual information for this section is garnered from several of the following sources: Reilly, *West and the World*; Stearns, *World History*; Adler, *World Civilizations*; Stavrianos, *Lifelines*; Ralph, Lerner, Meacham, Wood, Hull, and Burns, *World Civilizations*; and Stearns, *Industrial Revolution.*
67. Ponting, *Green History*, p. 240
68. Lenski, *Human Societies*, p. 285.
69. Adler, *World Civilizations*, p. 585.
70. Norman F. Kantor, *The American Century: Varieties of Culture in Modern Times* (New York: HarperCollins Publishers, 1997), p. 43-50.
71. Kantor, *American Century*, p. 43-50.

Chapter 8

People Creating a Future: The Global Wave

A Hopi prophecy speaks of two roads humanity can choose between ... that of the Two-Hearted People who only think with their heads—creating chaos and ultimately their own destruction or that of the One-Hearted People whose heads are united with their hearts in making choices—leading to a sustainable Earth for many generations to come. The Hopi say now is the time to make that choice.

INTRODUCTION TO THE GLOBAL WAVE

Ours is a time of great unrest. Hurricane-gale forces are disrupting our lives, making us feel uneasy and uncertain about the future and how we can adequately prepare for it. Yet it is also a time of promise. Simultaneously, thousands of visionary groups and organizations around the world are working to find solutions to critical issues facing us, so that we may create a more life-affirming, sustainable, and peaceful future. As the Hopi proverb above affirms, we as humans have choices to make, and the time is now to make these choices.

We are all living through a unique period of human history, a fifth turning—what I call the Global Wave—that is transforming our human story at the beginning of this new millennium. As we have seen, deep transformations are not new in history; such watershed moments have disrupted and changed the flow of events before. Today rapid technological, economic, social, cultural, environmental and political changes are profoundly altering familiar patterns of the past. Periods of discontinuity like this alter the balance of continuity and create change. Now, once again, is a time of fundamental change.

Rapid changes in almost every aspect of our lives characterize the Global Wave. Individual reactions to these new conditions vary according to one's particular perspective, history, geographic location, traditions, experiences, and worldview. Nor have these changes coalesced into entrenched social, cultural, political or economic formations. One thing that does seem to be certain in the Global Wave: the shape of the future is still very much in flux. Let's first look at 15 features describing the Global Wave.

15 Features of the Global Wave

1. **Integration** connects humans across the globe more so than at any time in the past. Instantaneous high-speed communication devices and sophisticated digital technologies are revolutionizing our relations with each other by dissolving former barriers of time and distance and providing new links between people. The Internet, television, high-speed travel, cell phones, social media networks and other forms of sophisticated telecommunication devices connect people around the world.

2. **Global Capitalism** is the dominant (but not the only) economic system in the world, with almost all nations pulled into its economic web. National and local economies, regulated and protected by national and local governments, have been largely subsumed into a globalized economy where mul-

tinational corporations and large state enterprises make the rules and conduct global business. Yet, different versions of capitalism—neoliberal (laissez-faire), managed, and state capitalism—exist. Since the 1980s, neoliberal capitalism, led by the U.S. has held sway, but since 2000 well-funded state capitalist enterprises backed by strong national governments, as practiced in China, have gained momentum.

3. **Environmental Pressures** and the health of the planet are a primary concern for global citizens regardless of national identity. This is a global issue that knows no national boundaries; viable solutions have to be made at a cooperative international level. We have already exceeded sustainability levels identified in the 1980s; dramatic changes must be made soon to avert disastrous consequences.

4. **Nations** continue as workable political organizations but are no longer the only defining political entity. They share sovereignty, in varying degrees, with other world organizations such as the United Nations (UN) and World Trade Organization (WTO); regional organizations such as the African Union (AU) and European Union (EU); regional trade alliances like the North American Free Trade Association (NAFTA); and non-governmental agencies such as Amnesty International and Greenpeace.

5. **English Language** is the language of business, commerce and education, and the unofficial language of global interaction. A common language acts as a unifying factor and English is increasingly that universal language. The world's elites speak English in part because of the influence of the British in the 19th century and the supremacy of the U.S. in the 20th century.

6. **Consumer Culture** is a dominant ideology and generates global economic wealth. A vast entertainment and advertising industry has perpetuated and glamorized consumerism as a form of status and as a symbol of global identity. It promotes products as necessities that define individual identity.

7. **Democracy** is the preferred political philosophy of the West and implemented by about half of the world. But authoritarian governments, such as in Saudi Arabia, Russia, and China, are resisting democracy while prospering economically.

8. **Human Rights** are heralded as a universal, cultural value system. Implemented by about half of the world, equality and justice for women, children, non-elites and minorities, along with racial equality and protection from hate crimes, are becoming common moral, ethical standards to guide nations.

9. **Population Growth** has skyrocketed in the 20th and 21st centuries. The current human population and its consumption levels severely strain the carrying capacity of the Earth. Will our Earth be able to sustain 9 to 12 billion people, a number projected to occur around 2050?

10. **Globalized Conflict** is much different from warfare between relatively equal nations and alliances in the Modern Wave. Conflict has become unpredictable, asymmetric, random, irrational, and volatile and can be sparked by different factors including ethnic strife and environmental problems. Conflict called terrorism, which involves civilians, has escalated in the Global Wave.

11. **Social Inequality** has dramatically increased between rich and poor nations and within nations.

12. **Technological Marvels** have exploded since the 1990s. Technology's positive effects have brought people closer together; on the downside, it has been unrealistically dubbed the solution for all social ills.

13. **Global Citizenship** identity highlights the interdependence, commonalities and differences among people of the world. Global citizens interact across geographical and political boundaries.

14. **Compression of Space and Time** reduces the constraints of geographical location and time differences through technological marvels. The speed of social activity alters the traditional notions of space and time, while also working to undermine the former importance of local and national boundaries.

15. **Recognition of Systems** means there is an increasing awareness that formerly autonomous events, actors, and institutions are now recognized as linked together into an interdependent system. No longer do separate and isolated solutions to problems work.

Our reaction to these 15 features of the Global Ware varies according to our worldview: indigenous, modern, fundamentalist, globalized, or transformative. The globalized and transformative worldviews, introduced in chapter 1, are further elaborated upon in this chapter.

RELATIONSHIP WITH NATURE: ECOSYSTEM CURRENTS

In the Global Wave one of nature's species—ours—has exceeded the limits of sustainability, threatening future generations with possible extinction. This dire prospect reminds me of a story about goats.

> **The Earth is an Island**
>
> *During the days of sailing ships, sailors would leave goats on islands to guarantee that on their return trips they would have an abundance of fresh meat. But with no natural predators, the goats bred faster than the sailors could eat them. Lacking natural or self-imposed limits, the goats ultimately devoured all the island's vegetation and over-taxed the environment to such a degree that native species could no longer survive. The multiplying population of goats in due course starved to death. The lessons of this tale are applicable to today. Our "island" the Earth has suffered the consequences of our goat-like instincts to consume everything in sight without regard for the future. With no natural predators or self-imposed limits, we are in peril of suffering the same fate.*

The interdependent environmental issues we face in the Global Wave are immense and urgent. Population growth and the demand for a rising standard of living by more people mean that the environment is under increasing stress. Although climate change has received the most attention in the last few years, other issues are also vitally important: desertification, deforestation, shortages of fresh water, rising sea levels, soil depletion, population escalation, extinction of wild plants and animals, air and water pollution, and the Earth's carrying capacity. These environmental dangers pose a threat to all people across the world. I try to walk a fine line between sounding too alarmist and presenting a scenario so pessimistic that you are reduced to a depressive stupor of inaction, or being overly optimistic and suggesting that all we need to do is change our light bulbs and climate change will be solved. These issues won't go away and will take collective effort and persistence. Let's take a look at the five eco-system sub-currents that can help us apply systems thinking to these issues: geography, environment, human populations, natural populations, and human and nature interaction.

Geography and Environment

Desertification

Advancing deserts and expanding sea levels are squeezing our global community. These forces are significantly altering the physical geography of our planet. Expanding deserts, **desertification**, result from deforesting land and overstocking and overgrazing grasslands. The problem is worldwide, but it is especially acute in China, where the loss of productive land is occurring at an accelerating rate. From 1950 to 1975 an average of 600 square miles of China succumbed to the desert each year, but by 2000 over 1,400 square miles were yielding to desert encroachment annually. Massive forest rings around the city of Beijing are the government's attempt to keep the prowling deserts at bay. Chinese officials report that since the 1960s residents deserted over 24,000 villages in northern and western China as drifting sand silently buried their settlements. In the 1990s, the Gobi Desert grew by 20,240 square miles, an area half the size of the U.S. state of Pennsylvania. With the advancing Gobi within sights of Beijing, China's leaders are realizing the gravity of the situation.[1]

The Sahara Desert in North Africa is wreaking mayhem on people's lives. It is pushing the people of Morocco, Tunisia, and Algeria northward toward the Mediterranean Sea. In countries like Senegal and Mauritania in the west, to Sudan, Ethiopia, and Somalia in the east, the demands

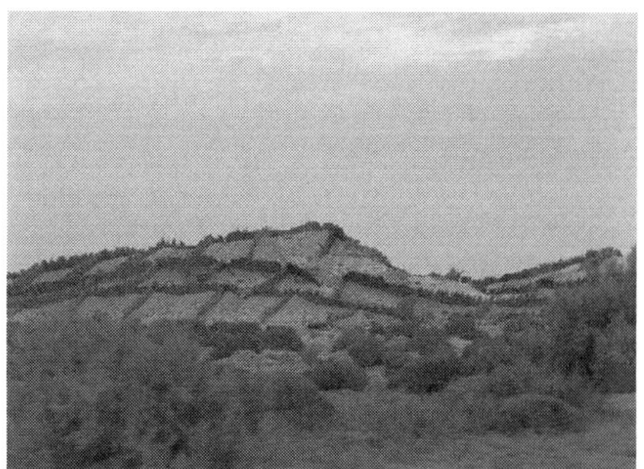

Anti-sand shields protect agricultural plots in north Sahara, Tunisia.

of growing numbers of people and animals, along with the effects of climate change, are switching arable land to desert at an alarming rate. Nigeria is surrendering 1,355 square miles to desertification each year. Its human population swelled from 33 million in 1950 to 174 million in 2015, and likewise its livestock numbers grew from 6 million to 66 million. Desertification is compressing Nigeria's population into an ever-smaller marginal area of land.

In Mexico about 70 percent of its land is vulnerable to desertification. Cropland degradation forces some 700,000 to 900,000 Mexicans off the land each year. Most flee from the arid and semi-arid regions of Mexico, where the desertification process yearly impairs 1,000 square miles and causes the abandonment of another 400 square miles of farmland. Desperate former farmers direct their search for jobs to nearby cities or immigrate, either legally or illegally, to the United States.[2]

Deforestation

A wide belt of forests holding immense diversity and significance to Earth's ecosystem stretches out from the equator. But this is changing. Large-scale forest clearance is dramatically altering tropical rainforests. Loggers are systematically reducing these ancient forests at the rate of about 100 acres per minute as they harvest timber and clear the natural landscape to make room for farms and pasture. More than half the loss of the world's natural forest has occurred since 1950. If the clearing rate stays constant, the unprotected primary forest will be gone in 90 years. The tropics suffered most of the loss.[3] Although tropical forests cover only about 7 percent of the Earth's dry land, they harbor an estimated half of all its species. Many species can be found in only small areas; their specialization makes them especially vulnerable to extinction. Forests also take in and hold a great stock of carbon which helps balance the stock of carbon dioxide in the atmosphere, reducing the greenhouse effect and climate change.

The reasons for tropical forest loss include multinational timber and paper companies seeking higher sales; governments increasing timber exports to pay external debts; ranchers and farmers converting forest to agricultural or grazing land for profit; and landless people scrambling for firewood or growing food on a patch of land. A single old-growth tree can be worth $10,000 or more, which poses enormous temptations for those harvesting it. Another problem with deforestation of tropical areas is that tropical soils appear fertile but are actually very thin and poor in nutrients. When exposed to the tropic's high temperatures and torrential rains, the underlying rock weathers rapidly, and over time this process leaches most of the minerals from the soil. Nearly all the nutrient composition of a tropical forest is in the living plants and the decomposing debris on the forest floor. When farmers deforest an area for cultivation, as in the Agricultural Wave, they cut down or burn trees and vegetation—slash-and-burn agriculture—to create a fertilizing deposit of ash for

Jungle burned for agriculture, Brazil.

the crops. But after a few harvests, the forest loses its nutrient reservoir, and flooding and erosion further deplete the soil of nutrients. The farmer abandons the site and moves to another location to start the destructive process once again.

Water evaporates from soils and vegetation, condenses into clouds, and falls again as rain in a perpetual cycle. Up to 30 percent of the rain in tropical forests has been recycled into the atmosphere. When humans scalp vegetation cover from the Earth's surface, solar energy is reflected from the ground rather than absorbed by trees; hence, temperatures rise, soils dry, and dust accumulates in the atmosphere, hindering rain cloud formation. Pockets of disastrous drought are the result. Replacing tropical forests with pasture and crops creates a drier, hotter climate in the tropics and disrupts rainfall patterns far outside the tropics, reaching as far as China, northern Mexico, and the south-central U.S.[4]

Forests take in great stores of carbon dioxide, helping to balance the stock of it in the atmosphere and ameliorating the greenhouse effect. In the Amazon alone, scientists estimate that trees hold more carbon than 10 years' worth of human-produced greenhouse gases. And when people strip the forest, usually with fire, carbon stored in the wood returns to the atmosphere, exacerbating the greenhouse effect and climate change. The soil of cleared forests becomes a source of carbon emissions instead of carbon sequestering.

People have been deforesting the Earth for thousands of years, but recently this has been done to meet global demands, not just local and national needs. Because of swelling populations, the single biggest direct cause of tropical deforestation is the conversion of forests to cropland and pasture for growing crops or raising livestock to meet the daily needs of burgeoning populations and selling for export. Commercial logging also takes its divvy from the forest. In Indonesia, for example, the conversion of tropical forest to commercial palm tree plantations to produce bio-fuels for export is a major cause of deforestation on the islands of Borneo and Sumatra.[5] The policies of the national government encourage economic development, such as road building and forest clearing, with tax breaks for related businesses, agricultural subsidies for farmers, and tax concessions for timber companies. The accumulated foreign debt of developing countries also means that they are often forced to sell off their natural resources on the world market in order to repay their loans to institutions such as the World Bank. These valuable lumber products are in high demand in developed countries, where most of their forests have already been cut.

Fresh Water

Most people still think of water as abundant and renewable. It isn't. The amount of fresh water available is finite, and the world is quickly running out of it. The limited supply of fresh water is a grave and volatile environmental issue. Only 2 percent of the Earth's water is fresh, fit for human consumption, and two-thirds of this amount is trapped in ice caps, glaciers, and underground aquifers too deep or remote to tap. Only 0.01 percent (one-hundredth of one percent) of the planet's water is accessible for human use. If the entire world's water was contained in 26 gallons (100 liters) then what is readily available to us would amount to one-half teaspoon![6] While the world's population explodes, the fresh water supply necessary for life is diminishing in many vulnerable areas. A 2015 UN report warns that the world will have only 60 percent of the water it needs in 2040 unless countries dramatically change their use of this vital resource.[7]

Compounding the fresh water shortfall is the fact that per capita water consumption is rising twice as fast as the world's population. A 2015 World Water report says that about 748 million people worldwide have poor access to clean drinking water, cautioning that economic growth alone is not the solution—and could make the situation worse.[8] Wasteful sanitation systems, particularly in core nations, have encouraged people to use far more water than necessary. Yet even with this increase in personal water use, households and municipalities account for only

Irrigation in Punjab, Pakistan.

10 percent of water use. Industry claims 20-25 percent of the world's fresh water supplies, and its demands are increasing. Many of the world's fastest growing industries are water intensive.[9]

Irrigation is the real water hog, claiming 65 percent to 70 percent of all the water used by humans. It takes some 500 gallons a day to produce the daily food each one of us consumes. Water-intensive commercial farming, employing wasteful practices, snatches increasing amounts of irrigation water. Generally taxpayers subsidize water use, while farming operations don't pay the real costs. This creates a strong disincentive for farmers to employ more conservation practices and to install, for example, more water-saving drip irrigation systems.[10]

Greater water usage accompanies rising standards of living, and our food choices reflect this. Diets of the affluent usually comprise less grain and more meat, and animal products require more water than grain. For example, it takes 518 gallons of water to produce a pound of chicken, pork clocks in at 718 gallons per pound, and beef guzzles the most water at 1,847 gallons per pound! Eggs need 395 gallons of water to produce one pound of plant based protein. For dairy products, cheese and butter take 381 gallons of water per pound and 665 gallons per pound respectively, more water than milk which consumes 122 gallons per pound. Tea necessitates less water to grow and process than coffee: tea uses 108 gallons of water to produce a gallon of brewed tea compared to coffee that requires almost 10 times as much—1,056 gallons of water per gallon of brewed coffee. Pasta needs 222 gallons of water to produce a pound, but rice isn't too far away, requiring 299 gallons of water per pound of processed rice. Bread from wheat takes 193 gallons per pound and barley consumes 237 gallons per pound. Nuts require lots of water to grow, with almonds and cashews swallowing 1,929 gallons and 1,704 gallons respectively.[11] With an increase in more Western style meat diets by more affluent Chinese and Indians this increase in water usage is unsustainable.

Irrigation for food production, which heavily depends on aquifers, is depleting them at an unprecedented rate. Over 70 percent of China's food is produced with irrigation. Water tables on the fertile North China Plain dropped more than 12 feet in a recent three-year period, and half of China's urban areas experience water shortages. India, with a population of over 1.3 billion, uses irrigation to produce 50 percent of its food, and the rate of groundwater withdrawal is twice that of the recharge rate, a deficit higher than any other country.[12] The U.S. produces 20 percent of its food with irrigation and is witnessing falling water tables as well. The enormous Ogallala Aquifer providing ground water throughout most of the Great Plains and in the American Southwest is dropping precipitously. Ominous droughts in the American Southwest have put greater demand on the region's rivers—the Colorado and Rio Grande—providing water for much of the Southwest.

California (U.S.) has been experiencing a punishing drought since 2011 that has necessitated the state to enact unprecedented measures in 2015 to reduce water consumption. The governor's order mandates a 25 percent overall reduction in water use throughout the state. This order is forcing a reconsideration of whether the aspiration of unconstrained growth that has for so long been the state's driving engine has finally run up against the limits of nature. This disconnect between growth and nature can be seen in places like Palm Springs, in the middle of the desert, where daily per capita water use is 201 gallons—more than double the state average.[13]

Climate change and pollution are making it difficult for middle and periphery countries to provide their own food. Africa has 9 percent of the planet's water resources but uses only 3.8 percent because of distribution problems. Many of its water sources are also dwindling, such as Lake Victoria (Victoria Nyanza).[14] In central Asia, Iran, a country of 80 million people, is facing an acute shortage of water, especially in the agriculturally rich Chenaran Plain in the northeastern part. Vulnerable Iran must now import more wheat than Japan, the world's leading wheat importer in the recent past.[15]

Historically, water shortages have been local, but in an increasingly globalized world, water scarcity crosses national boundaries. Countries facing water shortages need to accommodate the water requirements of cities, industry, and agriculture. They often do this by diverting water to their cities and then importing grain to offset the loss in agriculture production. Since a ton of grain equals 1,000 tons of water, importing grain is an efficient way to import water. But this precarious scenario depends on other countries, mainly the U.S., to continue to export plentiful grain at cheap prices and to extract their diminishing reserves of fresh water. Also, the use of grain for ethanol production drives up grain prices and adds to already strained food budgets for the poor.

Climate Change

Climate change is a change in average weather conditions. The cause may be volcanic eruptions, variations in the sun's intensity, or very slow changes in ocean circulation that occur over long time periods. But humans also cause climates to change by releasing greenhouse gases and aerosols into the atmosphere. We often hear the popular term **global warming**, which refers to any change in the global average surface temperature. However, the world will not warm uniformly, even though the term implies that it will; some areas warm more than others, such as the North and South poles. Some areas will even become cooler. This author uses the term climate change.

Triggering climate changes are **greenhouse gases**. These gases are a natural system that regulates

A petrochemical refinery in Grangemouth, Scotland, UK.

the temperature on Earth, just as glass in a greenhouse keeps heat in. Sunlight passes through the atmosphere to warm our Earth, and the warmed Earth emits heat energy back to the atmosphere, thus keeping the Earth's energy budget in balance. As this energy radiates upward, it is mostly absorbed by clouds and greenhouses gases in the lower atmosphere. Next, a process of absorption and re-emission is repeated until finally the energy escapes from the atmosphere to space. Because of the increase in greenhouse gases in the atmosphere, much of the energy is recycled downward, causing surface temperatures to become warmer than in the past. This natural process is the greenhouse effect.

The Earth's climate has gone through countless cycles of warming and cooling in its long history. However, over the past 10,000 years the amount of greenhouse gases in the atmosphere has been relatively stable. But around 1800, the concentrations began to increase due to industrialization, rising populations, and changing land use. This change has resulted in excessive greenhouse gases that have turned from life enhancing to life threatening.

A major human contribution to greenhouse gases is the release of carbon dioxide from the burning of fossil fuels, which has increased astronomically during the 200-plus years of industrialization. For example, current coal consumption has jumped to 100 times more than it was in 1800, and current oil consumption escalated more than 200 fold in the 20th century. Deforestation, as mentioned, also contributes to climate change, since fewer plants and trees absorb carbon dioxide during photosynthesis. The second major component of greenhouse gases is methane. The increasing number of rice paddy fields to feed Asia's growing population release volumes of methane gas from decaying vegetation. Methane from animal waste is also injected into the atmosphere from domesticated animals raised for meat consumption. Chlorofluorocarbons (CFCs), a third source of greenhouse gases, were formerly used as refrigerants and cleaning solvents but have been banned because of their effects on the ozone layer.

An international scientific consensus has emerged that our world is getting warmer and humans are significantly contributing to the warming. Scientists predict that hotter temperatures and higher sea levels will continue for centuries no matter how much is done now to control pollution. It is virtually impossible to blame just natural forces.[16] Many skeptics and disbelievers are changing their position, since the scientific evidence is irrefutable. Sea levels have risen and climatic zones are shifting. The 1980s, 1990s, and 2000s were the warmest decades on record. The 10 warmest years in global meteorological history have all happened in the past 15 years.[17]

Climate change is more than a warming trend; increasing temperatures will lead to changes in wind patterns, the amount and type of precipitation, and types and frequency of severe weather events. These climate changes will have far-reaching and unpredictable environmental, social and economic consequences. The U.S. has 5 percent of the world's population but accounts for nearly 25 percent of global greenhouse emissions. It is crucial that the U.S. participates and actively provides leadership in efforts to address climate change and protect the livability of our planet for future generations.

Polar bears depend on diminishing sea ice as a platform for hunting seals.

Sea Levels

The melting of the polar ice caps is a result of planetary warming, which is raising sea levels and adding increasing levels of radiation into the atmosphere. The atmosphere's protective ozone shield is becoming depleted at an astonishing rate of about one percent per year through holes hovering over the poles. With this rise in levels of ultraviolet radiation, the number of skin cancer cases each year goes up as well. During the 20th century sea levels rose by 6 inches, but during the 21st century seas may rise by 4 to 35 inches. Since 2001, record-breaking high temperatures have accelerated ice melting. If the Greenland ice sheet, a mile-thick in some places, melted entirely, sea levels would climb by 23 feet or 7 meters. Because of the slow inertia—long response time for parts of the climate system—we are already committed to a sea-level rise of approximately 2.3 meters for each degree of temperature rise within the next 2,000 years. A one-meter rise would deluge many rice-growing deltas and floodplains of Thailand, Viet Nam, China, Indonesia, and India. Forecasts predict that a one-meter rise in sea level would displace 30 million Bangladeshis. London, Bangkok, Shanghai, New York, and

Washington D. C., along with hundreds of other cities would be at least partially inundated by water.[18]

Soil Depletion

Soil depletion, another pressing environmental issue, occurs when the nutrients contributing to soil fertility are removed and not replaced. Estimates show that up to 40 percent of the world's agricultural land is seriously degraded.[19] For example, fruits and vegetables grown decades ago in the U.S. were much richer in vitamins and minerals than the varieties today. The main culprit in this nutritional trend is soil depletion. Modern intensive agricultural methods have stripped increasing amounts of nutrients from the soil which grows the food we eat.[20]

Soil depletion has occurred as a result of erosion, reduction in soil fertility, and desertification. One analysis of global soil depletion estimates that, depending on the region, topsoil is currently being lost 16 to 300 times faster than it can be replaced. The UN Environment Program suggests that over the past 1,000 years humans have turned more than the total area farmed today into wasteland. Between 1950 and 2000, world grain production has more than tripled. But during the past few decades the rate of grain production has slowed until it has fallen below the population growth rate. Per capita grain production peaked in 1985, and it has been slowly falling ever since. Although there is presumably enough food, at least in theory, to adequately feed everyone, the 2008 food riots in poor countries such as Haiti, Egypt, and Bangladesh point to the difficulty of providing food for everyone.[21] Some valuable grain supplies have been diverted to ethanol production, but grain production cannot supply enough ethanol to meet the gasoline needs of motorists and enough food for the world's poor at the same time.

The methods of commercial agriculture that have produced abundance in the past are unsustainable and show signs of exhaustion in many areas of the world. Efforts to conserve and enhance worn out soil using methods that have been successful for centuries are underway. Terracing, composting, cover-cropping, polyculture (as opposed to monoculture), crop rotation, and contour plowing are methods that famers can employ without synthetic fertilizers and pesticides. These methods of farming are not primitive or inefficient but actually produce crop yields equivalent to conventional methods; they also improve soil fertility and have few environmental side effects. For example, currently thousands of farmers in India are reverting to traditional farming methods as the consequences of modern agriculture have begun to negatively impact the region's food and water supply, and the health of its people.[22]

Farmers have successfully implemented these methods in Vincente Guerrero, a small Mexican village in the state of Tlaxaca that I visited in the summer of 2007 with the Food First organization. The village's farming community had been ravaged by drought, soil depletion, North American Free Trade Agreement (NAFTA) policies, and migration. Yet this small village is staging a dramatic comeback. Farmers are intent on becoming sustainable and organic in their local food production. Through terracing, crop rotation, organic methods, and lots of hard work, the soils are slowly recovering. These dedicated efforts signal a sign of hope that soil depletion can be reversed, and small agricultural villages can continue to be sustainable throughout the world.

Reclaimed terraced land on a farm in Vincente Guerrero in Tlaxaca, Mexico. Photo by Denise Ames

Carrying Capacity

Earth's resources are being devoured faster than they can be replaced by her most rapacious species, us! We have overshot our Earth's carrying capacity, which means we are taking from the Earth more than it can replace through natural systems. **Overshoot** means to go too far, to go beyond limits accidentally or on purpose, without intention and without consideration for the consequences. A useful tool for understanding this concept is the "**ecological footprint**," which calculates the amount of land required to supply needed resources (grain, food, water, wood, urban land, etc.) and the land required to absorb the resulting wastes (carbon dioxide, pollutants). Our footprint has become as large as Bigfoot's!

Since the late 1980s, humans have been using more of the planet's resources each year than can be regenerated in that year. In other words, the ecological footprint of our global society has overshot the Earth's capacity to provide.[23] Some experts conclude that we are about 20 percent above the Earth's carrying capacity; others maintain that in 2003, it was 25 percent larger than the planet's carrying capacity, while some dire estimates project that it will be an astonishing 100 percent by 2050. In other words, by 2050 humans will demand twice the number of resources than the planet can provide.[24] While this imbalance can continue for a while, overshooting will ultimately lead to liquidation of the planet's ecological assets and the depletion of Earth's resources unless we halt this devastating trajectory.

Some estimates calculate that the Earth has the carrying capacity for 4 to 5 billion people, yet there are over 7 billion of us! How many people can the Earth sustain? It depends. If everyone lived like an American, our Earth would be able to support only about 2.5 billion people. One reason is that each American's heavy meat diet consumes 1,760 pounds of grain annually, mainly because grains are more inefficiently fed to farm animals than consumed directly. The U.S. consumes far more grain than India, where each person annually consumes about 440 pounds. If everyone else in the world ate the same amount as

Global Footprint Network

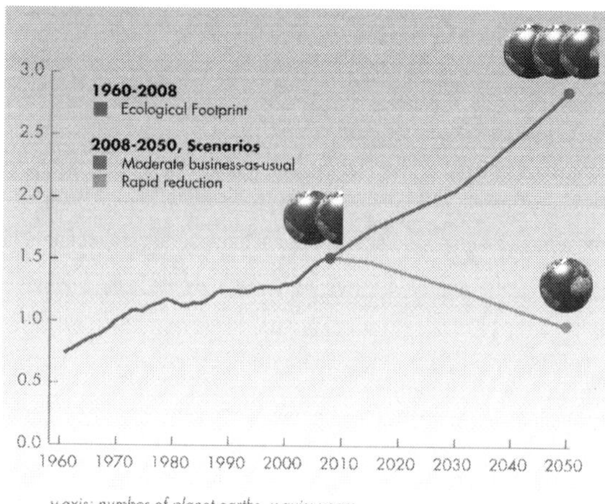

y-axis: number of planet earths, x-axis: years

the people of India, the world's grain production could support about 10 billion people.[25]

Our use of the world's resources has reached such a level that it can only be sustained on a planet 25 percent larger. In the early stages of overshoot, which is where we are now, the signals from the environment are not yet strong enough to force an end to growth and the overuse of resources. In systems thinking terms, it is a **delay in feedback**. In other words, the stresses on the Earth have not sent strong enough signals to force us to shrink our ecological footprint. Overshoot is possible because there are accumulated resource stocks that can be drawn down. For example, you can spend more money each month than you earn, at least for a while, if you have saved funds in a bank account. You can remove timber from a forest at a rate exceeding its annual growth rate as long as you start with a standing stock of trees that has grown and accumulated over many decades. The larger the initial stock, the higher and longer the overshoot. If a society takes its signals from the available stocks of resources rather than from their rates of replenishment, it will overshoot. This is what we are doing to Earth's resources. Any population, economy, or environmental system that has feedback delays and slow responses to the signals of overshoot and yet keeps on growing is literally out of control. If a society constantly tries to accelerate its growth, eventually it will overshoot.[26] No matter how fabulous its technologies, no matter how efficient its economy, no matter how wise its leaders, it can't ignore the natural consequences forever.

A period of overshoot does not necessarily lead to collapse. But it does require fast and determined action in order to avoid collapse. We must protect the resource base quickly and reduce the drains on it sharply. We must lower excessive pollution levels, and cut back emission rates. It is necessary to reduce both population growth and living standards to lower humanity's collective ecological footprint. If the size of the human footprint is a serious problem then the issue of population growth needs to be addressed. It is an emotionally charged bombshell of a topic that takes into account issues of ethics, morality, equity and practicality. The good news: there is waste and inefficiency in the global economy, and tremendous potential exists for reducing our footprint while still, perhaps, maintaining our quality of life.[27]

Human Population

For most of humans' 2.5 million years of history, the population was less than one quarter million. Yet, currently it has surpassed the 7+ billion mark and is still climbing. Approximately 80 million people are added to the world's total number every year. In fact, population time clocks tick away the number of peoplc added to our planet every few seconds![28] The overall growth rate hit a peak of about 2 percent in the late 1960s, and the good news is that it has recently fallen to 1.3 percent. A United Nations forecast says that world population will rise to 9.2 billion by 2050. This, however, depends on fertility in periphery countries dropping from 2.75 children per woman in the five year time period 2005-2010 to 2.05 in the time period 2045-2050. If, on the other hand, fertility remains at 2000-2005 levels, world population in 2050 will reach 12 billion. The increase in population will take place mostly in periphery nations. The population in core nations is expected to remain unchanged at 1.2 billion and would decline except for migration from periphery countries that averages around 2.3 million annually.[29] An increase in the elderly will continue. Between 2005 and 2050, half the increase in the population will be among people 60 and over, whereas the populations under 15 will decline slightly. In the core nations, the population of those 60 and over is expected to nearly double, while those under 60 will decrease.[30]

The U.S. population currently stands at 321 million; it is projected to reach 400 million by 2043 and will climb to 420 million by mid-century. The U.S. grows by 1.8 million people each year or 0.6 percent; about 8,000 more people are added every day. Another person joins the nation every 11 seconds! This contrasts with Europe and Japan where populations are either stable or declining slightly.[31]

In 2015, China ranks as the most populous nation in the world with 1.4 billion people, but India is closing in with 1.3 billion people. The U.S. ranks third. If taken as a whole, the 27-member European Union (EU) would rank third with a population of 507 million. Ranked fourth in population after the U.S. is Indonesia with a population of 249 million and Brazil, with 200 million people, stands at fifth. Rounding out the top ten are Pakistan, Bangladesh, Nigeria, Russia, and Japan. Aside from nations, some of the fastest growing areas around the world are cities, or more aptly described as megacities.

There are several reasons for the stunning population increases in the last two centuries, especially

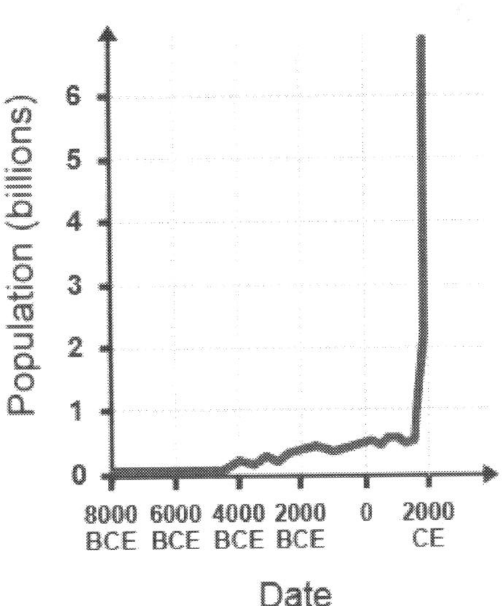

Human Population Growth

the last half of the 20th century. One reason has been the shift to carbon-based fuels. The burning of coal, gas, and oil has produced energy to fuel the large scale machinery that mass produces agricultural products to feed a mushrooming population. Other contributing factors—clean water, sewage treatment, antibiotics, and medical breakthroughs—have resulted in lower mortality rates and increased life-expectancy. Paradoxically, the creative forces that have made it possible for many of us to live longer and healthier lives have the destructive flip side of increasing our capacity to multiply and consume more resources, placing our planet in peril. The present rates of population growth are unsustainable.

Natural Populations

Another environmental challenge is the ongoing loss of biodiversity through species extinction. Although extinction is a natural process—the basis of evolution is the appearance of some species and the disappearance of others—this extinction is different: humans are almost wholly responsible. Fifty percent of the plants and animals on Earth—cattle, hogs, chickens, corn, soybeans, wheat, rice—are for human use. Since many resources are directed to these species, this puts considerable stress on the survivability of species not contributing to human consumption, as well as the world's ecosystem.[32]

An alarming extinction of species is what Elizabeth Kolbert calls the **sixth extinction**, following upon the five previous known extinctions in the Ordovican, Devonian, Permian, Triassic and Cretaceous periods.[33] Some experts estimate the rapid loss of species to be between 100 and 1,000 times higher than what is called the background or expected natural extinction rate. However, some studies suggest this estimate may be too conservative; current extinction rates could be as high as 1,000 to 11,000 times the background extinction rates. Habitat loss and degradation affect 86 percent of all threatened birds, 86 percent of threatened mammals, and 88 percent of threatened amphibians.[34]

Why should we care? Although the moral and ethical dimensions of contributing to the obliteration of our fellow species are important, there are also practical reasons to be concerned. Living organisms keep the planet habitable. Plants and bacteria carry out photosynthesis, which produces oxygen, while trees absorb carbon dioxide, which helps combat climate change. This complex, interdependent process is necessary for the natural food chain to produce enough for human consumption. The monetary value of goods and services carried out by natural ecosystems is estimated to be about $33 trillion per year, nearly twice the global production resulting from human activities. But the monetary value means little if we create a world that is uninhabitable for us and other species.[35]

Insights: Learning from the Past

Ecosystem Currents

One's particular worldview shapes how we see these dire environmental issues. Those holding a globalized worldview place an economic value on natural resources based upon current market values and do not take into account their disappearing supplies. They believe that natural resources should be utilized for economic production, while environmental restrictions limit economic growth and result in job loss. Even though China and the U.S. are the world's largest consumers of natural resources and pollution emitters, many Americans fear that instituting environmental limits will trigger a decline in our standard of living and threaten their livelihoods. Many people think of immediate financial considerations instead of the long-term consequences of our current environmental practices.

Those holding a transformative worldview treat the environment not just as an economic commodity but feel that the Earth must be healthy to sustain humans and our fellow species. This view represents a shift in attitude that has been gaining momentum throughout the world. Events such as the first Earth Day in 1970, the Rio Environmental Conference in 1992, the Kyoto Treaty in 2001, the Copenhagen Climate Conference in

2009, and the United Nations Climate Change Conference in 2015 address the importance of a safe, healthy environment for sustainable human life. A growing number of people think it is of utmost importance to save the planet from environmental ravages.

Some ecologists suggest replacing the current economic measurement method—**Gross Domestic Product** (GDP), that merely measure's national spending without regard to economic, environmental, or social well-being—with a **Genuine Progress Indicator** (GPI). The GPI, created by the organization Redefining Progress in 1995, measures the general economic and social well-being of all citizens. For example, if a business is responsible for an oil spill, the costs associated with the clean-up contribute to an increase in GDP, since the clean-up costs actually grow the economy according to this measurement. But GDP ignores environmental damage that has a negative long-lasting cost and impact. In calculating the GPI, the costs of the oil spill would be subtracted from the total, since it damages the environment over the long-term. When using GPI calculations, the U.S. economy has been stagnant since 1970.[36]

A growing number of ecologists see the Earth as an interconnected organism that awakens our sacred relationship with nature and positively supports our psychic well-being. This shift of consciousness revives an ancient mystical accord with nature that has sustained humans for millions of years. A Modern Wave mechanistic view of life has contributed to a destructive relationship with the Earth. Some people feel that a more benign connection would improve human health and mental well-being, as well as prevent the extinction of many endangered species that add to the diversity of life.

After reading and reflecting upon this brief summary of the dire state of our environment, many of you may feel a sense of depression and hopelessness. I felt the same way as I researched and wrote this summary. But depression and hopelessness are the easy way out. Even though we are overshooting our Earth's carrying capacity, it is not too late to make changes. Our human capacity for thinking long-term, globally, and holistically does not have precedence, yet it is not beyond our capabilities. We can change, and we must do so. Adjusting our thinking to view the long-term consequences of our actions is paramount. Growth needs to be reconsidered as the mantra of our society; instead, practicing and acting within the limits of our Earth's capacity holds the key to our future well-being and survival.

Siberian tigress and cub in captivity. They are a critically endangered subspecies; three subspecies are already extinct.

This overview shows how these environmental issues interact and affect us all. Much of the environmental destruction is due to human actions, but on the bright side we can also modify and temper our actions and policies. There are many organizations advocating specific ways to be actively engaged in preventing environmental suicide. Through individual and collective actions we can turn around these devastating trends or we risk being overwhelmed by them. Hopefully, we will be empowered to act in constructive ways to prevent further environmental devastation and usher in positive changes.

Questions to Consider

1. Some critics say that there is no (or little) connection between consumerism and environmental problems. What do you think?

WAYS OF LIVING: TECHNO-ECONOMIC CURRENTS

Economic Systems: The Global Economy

The "Golden Age," from about 1947-1973, was a time when the global economy—managed capitalism, socialism, and communism—generally prospered throughout the world. During this heyday, the U.S., in particular, experienced high growth, low unemployment, and low inflation; the real wages of the middle and working classes rose and prosperity was more equally distributed than ever before or since. Although profits for the business class grew, too, the working and middle class prospered more. However, this world-wide prosperity was coming to an abrupt end.

The global economy, particularly the U.S., experienced convulsions of calamitous proportions in the 1970s. High oil prices, the removal of the Bretton Woods agreement that tied the dollar to gold, U.S. government spending on the war in Vietnam, a decline in labor productivity relative to wages, and other factors all contributed to an economic crisis. A phenomenon known as **stagflation** saw high inflation coupled with stagnant economic growth. According to Keynesian policies, to bring the economy out of a downturn government spending would stimulate the economy, consumer demand would increase, and the downturn would end. But in the 1970s, this did not happen. Instead, more government spending only contributed to inflation. When the government addressed inflation by cutting back government spending, unemployment rose. Managed capitalism championed by Keynes since the 1930s appeared to no longer work. Why? Even though business profited during the golden age, those in business were eager to gain more profits for themselves and do away with what they regarded as a "stranglehold" of "cumbersome" regulations. Therefore, they took the lead in promoting an economic system that benefitted them the most.

The 1970s and early 1980s looked like the 1930s. Different interest groups fought over their preferred path to structuring national and global economic policies. There were the nationalists and globalists, free market advocates and those who wanted to continue managed capitalism, those on the political right and those on the left. There were leftists who promoted socialism and rightists who wanted less government and more corporate influence. Their political positions polarized. When the dust settled, it was the political right, the free-market and deregulation advocates, who emerged as the group who had garnered political and popular support. It wasn't an over-night victory; they had been working on their agenda throughout the 1970s and even before, but the victory was decisive and has shaped the economic and political landscape to the present day.

Conservative business and political leaders pushed for a change in the way the global economy operated. It was not an overthrow of the economic system, as in a military coup, but an all-out effort to change the global economy in a way that would enhance their businesses profitability and expansion. The response to the crisis of the 1970s was three-fold: neoliberal restructuring, economic globalization, and support for the financial sector. This section will look at these three factors as well as explain four related concepts: state capitalism, core and periphery, the rise of consumerism, and devotion to economic growth.

Neoliberalism: A Version of Capitalism

Neoliberalism, a version of capitalism, has prevailed in the U.S. since the early 1980s. Although the concept is the same, it is also known as free market capitalism, free trade capitalism, supply-side economics, laissez-faire capitalism, classical capitalism, corporate capitalism, market fundamentalism, or an Anglo-American version of capitalism. I will use the term neoliberalism because it is more commonly used around the world, yet outside academic circles it is somewhat unfamiliar in the U.S. Neo in neoliberalism means new, since it is a newer version of the classical economic system found in the 19th and early 20th centuries pioneered by Britain. A brief definition of **neoliberalism** is the modern politico-economic theory favoring free trade, privatization, minimal government intervention in business operations, and reduced public expenditure for social services and programs.[37] After the fall of communism in the early 1990s, neoliberalism reigned as the dominant economic system in the world until state capitalism emerged as a potent rival in the 2000s. Neoliberals give several reasons why they support it: self-interest motivates humans, competitive behavior is more rational than cooperation, materialism is a measure of progress, markets allocate resources most efficiently, governments should only provide infrastructure and enforce property laws and contracts, economic growth reduces global poverty, and inequality results from failing to integrate fast enough into the world economy.

Western countries in the 1980s, particularly the U.S., pushed a turn from managed capitalism to neoliberal policies. Two world leaders enthusiastically supported the neoliberal agenda—Margaret Thatcher, prime minister of United Kingdom (UK) and Ronald Reagan, president of the U.S. They were convinced that the principles of neoliberalism were best for their countries and the world.

As part of the neoliberal restructuring agenda,

U.S. President Ronald Reagan spearheaded neoliberalism.

the U.S. pressured managed capitalist, communist, or socialist nations to privatize industries and sell them to private enterprises. The privatization of the state owned coal industry in Great Britain in the 1980s, spearheaded by Thatcher amidst great labor resistance, exemplifies this process. After governments sell off their income-generating, state-owned assets to private multi-national corporations, the customers of these services have been gouged by exorbitant prices, impacting the poor, while the profits are siphoned to elite owners and investors. For example, in Cochabamba, Bolivia, the privatization of the municipal water supply in 1997 led to increased prices for customers. Persistent protests by the residents of Cochabamba in 2000 finally culminated in ending the privatization debacle. Carlos Slim Helu, the world's second richest person in 2015, owns many enterprises. One of his most lucrative is Telemex, which was Mexico's profitable state-owned telephone company. The U.S. pressured the government to sell Telemex to a private enterprise as part of its global push for neoliberal restructuring in the 1980s. Carlos Slim Helu purchased 50 percent of the stock in Telemex in 1990 and amassed a fortune.[39] Privatization has had mixed results for customers and workers, but it has brought immense profits to those buying up state enterprises, usually at bargain-basement prices, and contributed to the concentration of wealth in the hands of a very few well-connected

Ten Principles of Neoliberalism[38]

1. **free trade, remove protective tariffs**
2. **deregulation, remove government oversight of business**
3. **tax cuts for wealthy who invest in business**
4. **wealth "trickles down" from the wealthy to poor**
5. **government support for infrastructure and subsidies**
6. **privatization of publicly-held industry, services, etc.**
7. **economic growth is the way to prosperity**
8. **rapid commodification of every aspect of life**
9. **elimination of unions**
10. **dissemination around the world.**

business people.

Neoliberals favor **multinational corporations** (MNCs), with services in at least two countries, as a form of ownership of capital in the global economy. State capitalists favor ownership of capital by state enterprises in which governments have close control. MNCs have maneuvered to gain access and authority over the international rule-making institutions like the World Bank, World Trade Organization (WTO) and International Monetary Fund (IMF). The World Bank loans money to nations to build large infrastructure projects, the WTO governs the rules of global trade, and the IMF fosters global monetary cooperation. The rules of all three of these institutions favor Western countries and MNCs. Because rules made by these institutions take precedence over national laws, national enterprises are obliged to comply with them or risk economic ruin. Thus, these global institutions have generally usurped oversight of corporations from national governments.

State Capitalism and Other Versions of Capitalism

The U.S., UK, and others advanced neoliberalism as the preferred version from the 1980s onward. In the 1990s, after the collapse of communism in the Soviet Union and Eastern Europe, it appeared that the neoliberal model was becoming a global favorite. Even China and Russia appeared to be adopting neoliberal policies, although they had disastrous results in Russia. But in the 2000s, another version of capitalism—state capitalism—emerged as an attractive alternative to neoliberalism in many countries.

The power of the state is back in the form of state capitalism in which government officials direct markets to create wealth as they see fit. This economic system is not merely the re-emergence of socialist central planning in a 21st century package, but it is a form of state engineered capitalism particular to each government that practices it. Economist Ian Bremmer defines **state capitalism** as "a system in which the state plays the role of leading economic actor and uses markets primarily for political gain." State capitalist governments believe that public wealth, public investment and public enterprise offer the surest path toward political stability and economic development.[40]

State capitalist governments micromanage entire sectors of their economies to promote national interests and to protect their domestic political standing. The royal family of Saudi Arabia, for example, invests the kingdom's massive oil wealth for lucrative returns. The Chinese government sends state-owned firms abroad in search of long-term access to oil, gas, metals, and minerals.[41] China continues to have a communist form of government with many state-owned enterprises, while also following an export-oriented form of capitalism in which the government supports industries that export products to other countries. It is similar to the principles of mercantilism found in the early modern era.

Japan, South Korea, Taiwan, and Singapore also follow this approach in varying degrees. After the break-up of the Soviet Union, the new nation of Russia privatized its natural gas and oil industries and the owners formed one of the largest corporations in the world: Gazprom. Exemplifying the close connection between government and corporations Demitry Medvedev, president of Russia 2008-2012, served as Gazprom's former Chairman of the Board of Directors.

Since 2000, the governments of several state capitalist countries have worked to ensure that valuable national assets remain in state hands and that governments maintain enough influence within their domestic economies to preserve their survival. For example, they have used state-owned energy companies to accumulate wealth or to secure access to the long-term supplies of oil and gas needed to fuel further growth. They have created **sovereign wealth funds**—state-owned investment funds composed of financial assets such as stocks, bonds, property, precious metals or other financial instruments—that invest globally using these pools of excess capital. Among the world's leading state capitalist countries are China, with ties to the Chinese Communist Party; Saudi Arabia, with ties to the Saudi royal family; and Russia, with ties to those associated with the powerful current President Vladimir Putin.[42]

Over the past several years, lists of the world's largest companies published by business magazines such as *Forbes* and *Fortune* have begun to feature state-owned companies. Between 2004 and the start of 2008, 117 state-owned and public companies from Brazil, Russia, India, and China (BRIC countries) appeared for the first time on the *Forbes* Global 2000 list of the world's largest companies, measured by sales, profits, assets, and market value. A total of 239 U.S., Japanese, British, and German companies fell off the list; their market values dropped from 70 percent to 50 percent over those four years. The market value of the BRIC-based companies rose from 4 percent to 16 percent. The corporate failures and government bailouts of 2008-2009 accelerated the trend. *Bloomberg News*, a business news agency, reported in early 2009 that three of the world's four largest banks by market capitalization were state-owned Chinese firms—Industrial and Commercial Bank of China (ICBC), China Construction, and Bank of China. The 2009 *Forbes* Global 2000 listed ICBC, China Mobile, and Petro China among the world's five largest companies by market value. Energy giants like China National Petroleum Corporation, Petro China, Sinopec, Brazil's Petrobras, Mexico's Pemex, and Russia's Rosneft and Gazprom, and Saudi Arabia's Aramco are among the world's richest companies.[43]

Petrobas, Brazil's national oil industry.

State capitalism is a powerful economic system. The middle and periphery countries have not been standing idly by as the core countries maintain their traditional global economic control through institutions such as the World Bank, IMF, and WTO. For example, in 2013, China proposed a government-supported bank, the Asian Infrastructure Investment Bank (AIIB), to compete with the World Bank and IMF—the U.S-led Western model. The bank will lend cash for infrastructure and development projects across Asia. Member nations will make individual contributions to the bank's resource pool, helping back those projects. However, since 1966 the U.S. and Japan have led the Asian Development Bank, which essentially serves the same purpose. Some see the AIIB as a move by China to increase its economic influence in the region, although the U.S. government helped to fuel the creation of China's new economic tool.

In 2010, the U.S. Congress failed to pass reforms proposed by the Obama administration to the IMF—the global financial union of 188 member nations. The reforms would reduce U.S. power within the IMF which holds 16.74 percent of the votes and veto power—giving more voice to member nations such as Brazil, Russia India, China, and South Africa (BRICS countries). Despite the reforms, the U.S. would ultimately retain its dominant status and veto power. But of the 188 countries in the IMF, the U.S. is the only world economy that hasn't signed on because Congress refuses to pass the bill. The IMF has actually threatened to completely bypass the U.S. and proceed with reforms, undermining U.S. authority. In the meantime, China—whose say in the IMF is currently dwarfed by smaller economies like the UK, France, Germany and Japan—appears to resent being marginalized. Enter the AIIB. Through it, China gains more influence and power. Initially, China and India will have significant voting rights, and all Asian member countries will have over 50 percent of the total voting rights. China will also command a leading role in the New Development Bank, an institution similar to the IMF that the BRICS countries will spearhead. Through these new institutions and the bank's investment of $40 billion into a Silk Road infrastructure project, China will be able to increasingly flex its economic muscle without the restrictions placed on it by the IMF and World Bank. Many EU nations, under U.S. protest, have joined the AIIB.[44]

Many nations differ in their national and cultural interpretations of how their economy should operate. Some nations with long histories of trade wish to maintain their traditional market economy that differs from neoliberal and state capitalism. For example, in Iran the *bazaaris* or merchants that sell goods at the *souk* or marketplace, have followed this market economy tradition for centuries. If Iran would "open up" to competitive, global capitalism, the *bazaaris* and *souks* would give way to big box chain stores that would offer more "choices" of consumer items but would ultimately drive the *bazaaris* out of business. Currently, Iranian politicians favor the *bazaaris* but that is likely to change. The Iranian economy has stagnated and unemployment from the 2000s onward has ranged from 11 to 16 percent.[45]

Questions to Consider

1. Which version of capitalism would benefit you the most? Explain.

Economic Globalization

A second response to the economic crisis of the 1970s was the push towards economic globalization. **Economic globalization** refers to the increasing expansion of capitalism around the world, integrating non-capitalist economies into a world economic system. Even though countries may have different versions of capitalism, they still participate in the world economy. With economic globalization, trade, investment, business, capital, financial flows, production, management, markets, labor movement (although somewhat restricted), information, competition, and technology are carried out across local and national boundaries, subsuming many national and local economies into one integrated economic system. There is also a growing concentration of wealth and influence in multi-national corporations, huge financial institutions, and state-run enterprises. With economic globalization has come the absorption or systematic destruction of centuries-old local/domestic economies around the world.

Economic globalization differs from industrial capitalism of the 19th and 20th centuries. While industrial capitalism flourished in a world marketplace, factories were located in communities where workers lived, churning out great quantities of goods for consumers in local and national markets. Global trade and exchange were secondary, while local and national trade was primary. Although elements of industrial capitalism and local businesses continue today, megalithic, global corporations and state-run enterprises operate across local and national boundaries and increasingly dominate the global economy.

Certain factors are necessary for economic globalization to function. These factors are organized into 10 puzzle pieces that when pieced together make up an economic globalization puzzle. All of the puzzle pieces make up the full picture of economic globalization. Although I will not be able to cover all the pieces of the puzzle in great depth (see *The Global Economy: Connecting the Roots of a Holistic System*), they are highlighted in different sections throughout this chapter.

Nations are persuaded, some say duped, into conforming to the rules of economic globalization with the threat that if they do not participate in the global marketplace they will be left behind in economic development. The metaphor of the train leaving the station is often cleverly used to describe this phenomenon. If your nation is not on the economic globalization train, then you will be left behind at the station. Therefore, you must jump on board the globalization express for the fast ride to economic riches.

The Financial Sector

The **financial sector** encompasses a broad range of organizations that deal with the management of money. Among these organizations are banks

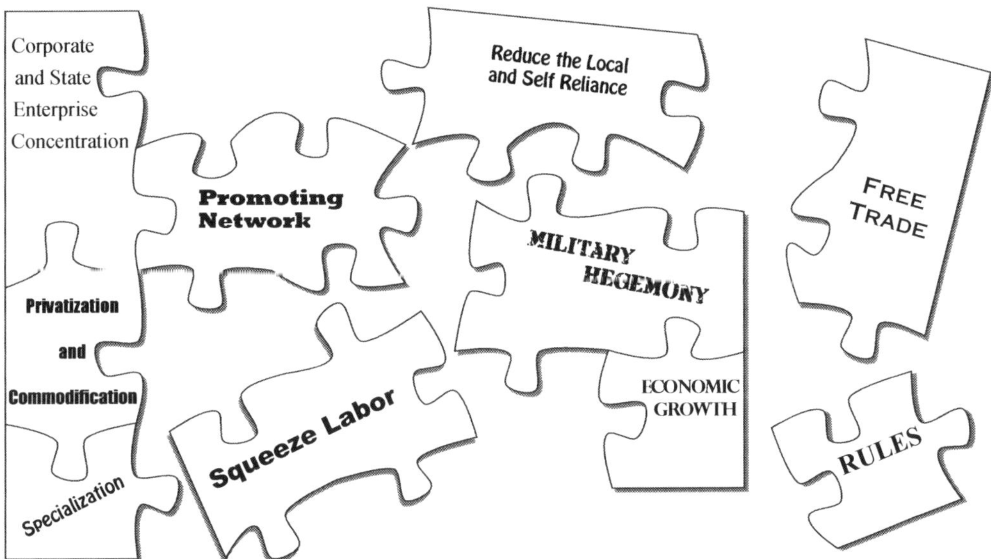

The Economic Globalization Puzzle

(commercial and investment), credit card companies, insurance companies, consumer finance companies, stock brokerages, investment funds, foreign exchange services, real estate, and some government sponsored enterprises. These businesses have been around for many years, and since the 1930s, the U.S. government has closely regulated the industry, because their excesses contributed to the Great Depression. The financial sector had remained regulated until the 1980s.

Financialization took off after the crisis of the 1970s because of technological advancements that made it easier and more efficient to devise financial products and because of the deregulation of the industry. As a result, there was a rash of sophisticated speculative financial products like derivatives that escaped governmental monitoring and regulation. The trading in speculative financial products was little more than gambling; hence, the name "casino economy." In fact, speculative finance boiled down to an effort to squeeze more "value" out of already created value, instead of creating new value.[46] During this time, instability has rocked the financial sector, skipping from one crisis to another. The government has had a hand in rescuing the financial sector with "bail-out" packages funded by taxpayers that shield them from having to face the problems of their industry. As a result there is an increased bifurcation between the hyperactive financial economy, known as Wall Street, and the stagnant real economy, known as Main Street. This is not an accidental development; the financial sector exploded precisely to make up for the stagnation owing to overproduction of the real economy.[47]

Questions to Consider

1. What impact has the growth of the financial sector had on your life?

Core and Periphery

In discussing the global economy, it is readily apparent that economic discrepancies are evident among individual nations and within individual nations as well. Unequal wealth distribution and ownership of resources has characterized most of world history since the beginning of the Urban Wave 5,000 years ago; the Global Wave is no exception. Several different terms describe this reality; the question is which ones to use. After World War II the terms first, second, and third world were used; the first world was the U.S. and Western Europe, the second world made up the Soviet Union and its satellites, and the remaining nations were lumped into the third world category. As you can imagine, this ranking was offensive to those in the third world category. Now terms such as developed and developing, or even less-developed nations are commonly used. Sometimes industrialized or non-industrialized describe the concept. Also used are the more neutral but geographically inaccurate terms "the global South" or "the global North," but once again the meaning is the same: the South is poor and the North rich. But it gets confusing when referring to a country like Australia that is in the south but really is in the "global North." Are you confused? To simplify this, I am using the imperfect but flexible terms core and periphery that I explained in earlier chapters. A core and periphery model helps explain the asymmetrical levels of participation and development by different nations, regions, and people in the global economy.

All these labels, including the core and periphery, say that the worth of a nation is based on its economic development. When this criterion is used for evaluation, a nation's poverty or wealth becomes an implied value judgment of its success. Using this system of evaluation, the North, first world, developed, core, or industrialized nations are superior to the periphery, the South, non-industrialized, third world, or developing nations. It further implies that the periphery must emulate and adopt the economic policies of the core nations lest they be "left behind." It would be more indicative of a nation's well-being to consider its environmental policy or social relations as factors in evaluation, or perhaps a happiness index. In a happiness survey, Denmark ranked first, Switzerland came in second, Austria third, and Iceland and the Bahamas rounded out the top five "happily developed" nations. The United States, which ranked 23rd on the survey, would be "developing happiness"![48]

Core areas continue to be the centers of wealth creation, management, experimentation, and concentration. They usually have an industrial past, sophisticated technology, a well-educated workforce, sacrosanct private property laws, and an entrenched ideology that emphasizes the value of wealth. The major core nations include the U.S., the world's largest economy (by most indicators), China, individual nations in the European Union (EU), Japan, Canada, Australia, China (parts), and smaller nations such as South Korea, Taiwan and Singapore.

Other nations and people live on the periphery of global developments, separated from core regions by a wide economic gap. The periphery nations supply core areas with cheap or relatively cheap raw materials such as oil, mineral resources, agricultural products, and timber, which have increased in price as supplies diminish. Many people in the periphery labor for minimum wages to extract, grow, and manufacture raw materials into finished goods that are shipped to core areas as affordable consumer items. Many also eke out a living through growing cash crops for global consumption. But not all nations fall neatly into the core or periphery camps. The bulk of the world's nations, such as the BRICS, fall somewhere in-between the core and periphery status and have characteristics of both. They have middle status or are called developing. Today about 80 percent of the current world population either lives in periphery or middle areas or occupies periphery status in core nations.

The periphery areas are poorer than core and middle areas, but elites and non-elites reside in both. In the periphery countries, the elites are large land and mine owners, business entrepreneurs, government officials, and other professionals. Usually their numbers are small with an undersized middle class, while non-elites make

Street child in Bangladesh.

up the vast majority of the periphery population. Elites also reside in core countries with tax policies, superb educations and laws that favor their retention and accumulation of wealth. Core nations usually host a larger middle class than periphery nations. Favorable tax policies, laws to support home ownership, outlays for education, and other legislation help prop up middle class economic status in core nations. A significant percentage of periphery-status people live in core nations as well. For example, in the U.S. the periphery population or the underclass is 25 percent of the population. They are unemployed or labor for minimum wages at low-skilled jobs, lack health insurance, do not own homes, live in blighted neighborhoods and are increasingly pushed to the margins of society. This group also includes children and undocumented workers from other countries.

There are various reasons for the periphery status of certain nations and regions. Some core nations encouraged or coerced leaders of periphery nations into following the path to "modernize" their countries. Periphery nations attempted to join wealthy nations in a share of the economic abundance that modernization promised to bring. Many periphery nations borrowed heavily from the World Bank and other financial institutions for infrastructure construction with the implicit understanding that this would lead them on a path to higher living standards and improved economic status. But now many periphery countries have discovered that it is much harder to reap benefits from the global marketplace than they originally thought. The deck, they have found, is stacked against them. Many of the reasons for failure are found in the structure of the global economy: it needs dependent periphery nations for the core to prosper. The core nations are able to profit from cheap labor and obtain cheap resources for their benefit. Other reasons for failure are inept leadership and corruption among the leaders of periphery nations. Also, they lack sophisticated technology, are paid low commodity prices for their raw materials, are prone to more disease, and are mired in debt. The economic realities in the periphery and the economic policies of the core nations ensure that the economy in the Global Wave is not equitable for all participants.

The core and periphery concept is happening within the U.S., China and other nations. Core areas within the U.S., for example, are large cities where information workers add value to goods and services, such as accounting procedures, insurance, marketing and advertising, or political lobbying for favored treatment. For instance, athletic shoes may be manufactured for as little as \$5.00 (US) in Chinese factories and then shipped to the U.S. where value, such as advertising by a well-known sports figure, is added to each shoe. The shoes then command a much higher retail price, perhaps over \$100. Also, financial firms create products that are packaged into units, traded on the stock exchange, and sold as investments to institutions such as pension funds around the world. Under the current system, the "value" added to these services is circuitously paid out in high salaries, bonuses and benefits to those who control the process, such as Chief Executive Officers (CEO), boards of directors, high-level managers or celebrity endorsers.

Those who add information or wealth to the cheaply produced goods and services or devise financial instruments are the ones who create, generate, and control the whole process of wealth concentration and distribution in the global economy. These information workers are members of the upper middle class, or the world's elite. Hence, the wealth creation of the elite class has shifted from manufacturing goods to adding information to goods manufactured elsewhere or creating financial instruments such as hedge funds, mutual funds, derivatives, credit default swaps, or mortgage services. The upper 20 percent of Americans consume a disproportionate percentage of the world's resources, siphoning wealth from periphery regions and from their own workers and fellow citizens in order to enrich themselves. All but the top 20 percent of Americans have witnessed stagnant and declining wages since the 1980s.

Pockets of periphery-status people in core nations lag behind core-status people and reside on the margins of economic development and political participation. For example, within the U.S. approximately 50 percent of Americans are non-elite and about 25 percent are members of the underclass, many of them children. One periphery pocket is in rural areas that supply raw materials and cheap labor for the global economy. Ravaged inner cities are another periphery area dotting the urban landscape in the U.S. Inner city residents who do find jobs are usually unskilled service workers or low-wage manufacturing employees toiling for minimum wages that barely provide for basic needs, let alone health care. To add to their troubles, many workers must commute long distances outside of their blighted neighborhoods to service jobs in more affluent parts of the city. Having to rely on public transportation or an unreliable car, the costs of commuting add to work-related expenses and worries. Housing woes also plague many low-wage workers. Unable to afford to purchase a home, they often live in sub-standard housing with high rents. Compared to their wealthy fellow citizens, the poor endure inferior education, fewer governmental services, higher crime rates, sub-standard transportation services, limited choices of healthy foods, and work at mind-numbing, dead end jobs, such as at fast-food corporate franchises like McDonald's.

An issue in the Global Wave, reminiscent of the enormous inequality in Urban Wave cities, is the unprecedented growth of mega-cities, such as Mexico City in Mexico, San Paulo in Brazil, Mumbai in India, and Cairo in Egypt. They have grown enormously as a result of population growth and because of lapsed government support for the agricultural sector, a flood of poor farmers has left their villages for jobs in the cities. Once in the cities, they face extreme poverty, few job opportunities, horrendous living conditions, crime, and hopelessness. The villages, once vibrant and full of life, are left decimated; only the elderly, children, and a handful of women stay behind. This shift from village life to urban squalor is occurring for millions around the world.

Slums in Indonesia.

One of the reasons that periphery regions and people are becoming poorer is that it is more difficult for local businesses to survive. The presence in a neighborhood of a goliath retailer like Wal-Mart forces smaller businesses to close shop because they cannot compete with its primary appeal: lower prices. This means that profits, instead of circulating in the local community where they might be re-invested locally, are transferred to the pockets of corporate giants. This scenario has contributed to the economic decline of many local economies, destabilizing local communities that have long provided a sense of stability, identity, and meaning for Americans and people around the world.

The core nations have traditionally built up the following six advantages that favor them in the global economy. By controlling these six advantages, core nations are able to shape the world economy to favor large multi-national corpora-

Advantages for Core Nations[49]

1. **Technological advantages**
2. **Disproportionate influence on World Bank, WTO, IMF**
3. **Access to natural resources and markets**
4. **Media and communication monopolies**
5. **Control of national and international policies**
6. **Military advantage**

tions, in the U.S. case, or preferential state industries, in China's case. But shifting core areas are not new in world history. Middle and periphery countries have noted these advantages and have taken steps to reverse their dependency status. Currently China is maneuvering, such as with the Asian Infrastructure Investment Bank, to swing these six advantages in its favor.

> **Questions to Consider**
>
> 1. In what ways do you see the core and periphery concept played out in your life?

Consumer Capitalism

Capitalism needs constant new sources of wealth creation to expand and grow. Manufacturing was the leading sector of the American economy in the post-war years, but since the 1980s, the expansion of consumerism has been the underpinning of wealth creation in the U.S. and global economy. For example, private consumption expenditures make up about 70 percent of U.S. GDP. **Consumerism**, first named in the 1960s is a social and economic order that is based on the systematic creation and fostering of a desire to purchase goods or services in ever greater amounts. It is similar to **materialism**, an approach to life and social well-being that elevates the material conditions of life over the spiritual and social dimensions. A consumer society acquires goods and services not only to satisfy common needs but also to secure identity and meaning. Consumption is powerfully shaped by forces such as advertising, cultural norms, social pressures, and psychological associations.[50] Sociologist Madeline Levine criticized what she saw as a change in American culture in the post-war years—"a shift away from values of community, spirituality, and integrity, and toward competition, materialism and disconnection."[51]

Economic globalization has profited from a consumer ethos. Many critics call consumerism the new religion of the world, worshipping at the altar of the shopping mall or the on-line retailer, performing the ritual of purchasing dazzling products

Racy Audi sportscar at the Xian, China airport. Photo by Denise Ames

that are beyond what makes for a comfortable life. On a 2011 trip to China with fellow educators, I was dismayed to see the proliferation of late model cars in the cities of Beijing and Shanghai. I was dismayed because the smog hung so thick in the cities that it stung my eyes and hindered my far-off vision. I found out that consumerism is rampant in the two largest cities in China. The most desired consumer purchase is a late model car, preferably one with high status, such as the racy Audi sports car displayed at the airport in Xian.

Capitalism has been immensely successful at producing goods and services for about 20 percent of the world's population that can afford these products. They have more than enough goods for a comfortable life, yet the other 80 percent of the world's population do not. This is one of the many paradoxes of capitalism. It is supremely efficient at producing goods and services but is not proficient at distributing these goods and services to those in real need. In fact, capitalism has been too successful in producing goods and services. Thus, producers have become inventive in seeking ways to induce consumers to buy more—more than they need. Enter the advertising industry. The single goal of this industry is to create gimmicks and enticements to convince consumers to purchase more and more.

The advertising industry finds ways to stimulate new consumer needs and desires, creating a malaise whose only remedy is to buy. The traditional values of the Protestant ethic that have shaped the American value system since the country's founding include thrift, hard work and its rewards, long-term planning, rational behavior, stability, and adherence to rules and laws. The dilemma for advertisers is that a person with these values does not impulsively consume. The advertising industry figured out that it needed to change individual behaviors and values, and it launched a brazen campaign to change Americans' entrenched Protestant and patriotic values. The industry sought to transform the rational, logical, steadfast behaviors of mature adults into what journalist Benjamin Barber calls "infantilizing adult behaviors." The advertising industry encourages behaviors that are impulsive, irrational, self-centered, and reckless—in other words, infantile. Billions of dollars later, its sizable investment has paid off.[52]

The advertising industry is not content to just transform adult behaviors but seeks to change children's and teens' behaviors as well. Since children are young and have not fully developed rational, mature behaviors that we normally associate with adults, their impulsive, impetuous behaviors are perfect for consumption but need to be focused into desiring more profitable adult products. Advertisers, intent on luring even pre-consumer children as young as toddlers to identify with their brands, strive to embed early brand identification for the rest of their consuming lifetime. Teens, flush with cash from part-time jobs or indulgent parents, are prime advertising targets. With their impulsivity and need to vie for peer status, they must have the latest products, which adults typically bought in the past. They feverishly buy high end goods such as cars, technological gadgets, or a closet-busting wardrobe of the latest hip fashions.

Adults holding to a consumerist ethic are pawns to the advertising industry. The demands of the mobile global economy have severed their ties to the traditional community; instead, their sense of belonging and identity have shifted to brands of consumer products. As Barber explains, "Consumerism has attached itself to a novel identity politics in which business itself plays a role in forging identities conducive to buying and selling. Identity has become reflective of 'lifestyles' that are closely associated with commercial brands and the products they label, as well as with attitudes and behaviors linked to where we shop, how we buy, and what we eat, wear, and consume.[53] The brands selected by an individual or family indicate their particular income, class, and place. These branded identities are superficial veneers replacing traditional ethnic, cultural, and national identity. Although it appears that we freely choose these identities, in reality they are reflective of the permeation of the ubiquitous commercial culture into every aspect of our lives. Advertisers happily promote this brand identification among consumers because it cuts across national and ethnic boundaries to mold a true globalization of identity.

The omnipresent impact of advertising on consumers actually homogenizes taste and narrows rather than expands variety and choices. Perhaps this would all be fine if the consumption of goods and services made us happier and healthier and resulted in loving relationships, something that advertising implicitly and explicitly promises. But we are not happier, and we are certainly not healthier. In fact, impulsive consumption often leave us more depressed and unsatisfied. Of course, this is exactly what advertisers have planned all along, since that unquenched desire is the catalyst for the consumption of more goods in an endless cycle of trying to achieve the pleasures that advertising assures us they will provide and that we innately crave. Fortunately, even though the consumer society may appear to be all-embracing, it is not totalitarian. Unlike citizens living under totalitarian regimes, we do have the choice to reject or participate in the consumerist society.

Questions to Consider

1. Do you think there is too much emphasis on consumerism in your life? In your country?

Economic Growth

Nature knows when things should stop growing. I love to watch my spring flowers grow. My children grew up to be responsible adults. There are lots of ways in which we use the word grow. Growth's factual definition is to spring up and develop to maturity. Thus, growth has some concept of maturity or sufficiency. In other words, development continues, but growth gives way to a steady-state balance in nature in which the rate of inputs is equal to the rate of outputs so the composition of the system is unchanging in time. For example, a bath would be in balance if water flowing into the tub from the tap then escaped down the drain at the same rate. The total amount of water in the bath does not change, despite being in a constant state of flux.

Through much of human history, having more comforts and surplus food has made human lives easier. As populations have grown, so have the economies that housed, fed, clothed and kept them. Unlimited growth made sense decades ago when the human population of the world was relatively low, and natural resources for human consumption appeared to be endless. In this "empty world" money and human labor were the limiting factors, while natural resources were abundant. In this context, there was no need to worry too much about environmental destruction and social disruptions, since they were assumed to be relatively small and ultimately solvable. It made sense to focus on growth of the economy as a primary means to improve human living standards.[54] But growth cannot continue indefinitely.

Economic growth is the process by which wealth increases over time as the economy adds new market value to goods and services. Environmental economist James Speth notes that growth is an essential component of capitalism, which must expand constantly to generate new wealth. Growth is inherent in capitalism; the two are inseparable. Its drive to accumulate and its built-in tendency to expand distinguish capitalism from other economic systems. Innovative activity—which in other types of economies is optional—becomes mandatory under capitalism, a life-and-death matter for businesses. Through history, the creation of new technology proceeded at an even-handed pace, often requiring decades or even centuries to develop, under capitalism time speeds up because, quite simply, time is money. The capitalist economy is a machine whose primary output is economic growth.[55] The noted economist Paul Samuelson wrote the conundrum in 1967: "A growing nation is the greatest Ponzi game ever contrived."[56]

The Western economy faithfully follows economic growth. The reasons are partly to do with policy habits and political posturing, and also because our economic system is set up in such a way that it has become addicted to growth. Watch any newscast or read any news report about the economy and I wager that they will mention the word growth. Economists constantly watch growth's movements, measure it to the decimal place, praise or criticize it, and judge it as weak or healthy. Even I hope to grow my nonprofit organization—the Center for Global Awareness—and sell lots of educational books. In our daily lives we assume that growth is good. Promoting growth—achieving ever-greater economic wealth and prosperity—may be the most widely shared and forceful cause in the world today. Industrial societies regard growth as their "secular religion."[57]

The pursuit of economic growth has been part of capitalism since its beginnings over 500 years ago. Yet, the specific policy of economic growth has a rather short history, and it has especially come to be a central feature of U.S. economic policy since the end of World War II. The Council of Economic Advisors recommended in a 1949 report that growth should be elevated from an economic goal to a new organizing principle for the economy. The report distinguished "the new primary principle of growth ...from the decidedly secondary aim of economic stability."[58] Not all signed on to the new policy. Republican President Eisenhower questioned the wisdom of promoting economic growth over economic stability. But Democratic candidate John Kennedy, who championed the cause of economic growth in his 1960 campaign, severely chastised him for his views. On the economic growth band-wagon were big business and organized labor, both of which saw growth as an opportunity to further their own interests. Growth policies won the day and continue to be a central principle in economic policy for both parties.[59]

Economic growth meant that Americans would consume and produce more consumer goods, earn more wages in factories and businesses, and spend this surplus on more consumer goods. Americans were eager to shed the austerity and hardship of the depression years and embark upon a new way of life based on plentitude and a seemingly endless supply of comforts. Economic growth and consumer spending went hand and hand. Also, the Gross Domestic Product (GDP) could scientifically measure growth. The GDP is an official measure of a country's overall economic output. It is the market value of all final goods and services made within the borders of a country in a year. Since Americans have an abiding faith in numbers, they widely considered the GDP to be an accurate measurement of a country's living standards. When the GDP is up, it is assumed the country's living standard improves. A recession describes the absence of growth. Depressions are prolonged recessions. The joining of a consistent scientific number with rising living standards became entrenched in American and later global thinking.

While it seemed reasonable at the time to measure the economy in marketed goods and services and to measure the success of an economy by the GDP, the world has changed dramatically and rapidly in the last 60 years. We now live in a world relatively full of humans and the infrastructure that we built. In this new world, human populations and labor supply are enormous, while the natural resources to support human life are limited. There is a dawning recognition that the growth model eagerly adopted by modern countries is no longer working; the model is geared towards a time in the past that differs from the reality of today.[60] All this is happening at the expense of our natural world, which is being battered by the demand to produce more products

Deepwater Horizon oil spill, the clean-up of the BP spill added to GDP.

for human consumption and absorb its wastes.

There are limitations to growth. Perhaps a new measurement of economic well-being and a rethinking of economic growth is needed. Yet, the commitment to growth is so deeply engrained in our way of thinking that to question it is regarded as an affront to capitalism. My purpose in raising this issue is to examine and question the over-reliance on economic growth in our society and not to advocate for the overthrow of capitalism. The fact is that a growing economy tells us nothing about the quality of economic activity that is happening within it. For example, when British Petroleum's (BP) oil leak spewed crude oil into the Gulf of Mexico in 2010, it actually contributed to an increase in the GDP! The number of dollars spent on cleaning up after disasters such as Hurricane Katrina in New Orleans in 2005, Love Canal in New York in 1978, or the flooding in Texas in 2015 all contributed to an increase in GDP. Those in the logging industry contribute to an increase in the GDP by cutting trees for lumber products, but if the trees cut are old-growth forests that take centuries to replace, it is actually harmful to the general well-being. Growth in GDP doesn't specify if the activity is good or bad. Spending on prisons, pollution and disasters pushes up GDP just as surely as spending on schools, hospitals and parks.

Individuals support growth policies because they accept the commonly-held notion that growth will give them and the next generation a better standard of living. Governments seek growth as a remedy for just about every imaginable problem. Economists believe growth to be essential for full employment, upward mobility, and technical achievements. Politicians encourage growth because it expands the economic pie, and they can postpone hard choices.[61] Growth, development, progress, advancement, gain, success, improvement, and prosperity are deeply embedded modern assumptions that are cause for celebration. Systems thinkers refer to these qualities as structural reasons for the continuation of growth.

Mainstream economics is frozen in its one-eyed obsession with growth. But growth has a surprising drawback. The industrial world has come to expect its mature economies to grow by a certain percentage, usually 3 percent a year. This expectation evolved out of several centuries of experience with capital creating more capital. At this 3 per cent growth rate, the economy will double in just over 23 years. The recent growth rate of up to 10 per cent in a few economies, such as China, will double the size of those economies in less than 7 years. This astonishing rate of growth is unsustainable.[62]

Economic growth, as it is presently structured, will not abolish poverty. Actually, current modes of growth perpetuate poverty and amplify the gap between rich and poor. In 1998, more than 45 percent of the world's people survived on incomes averaging $2 a day or less. That means there were many more poor people than 8 years earlier, despite astounding income gains. The 14-fold boost in world industrial output since 1930 has made some people very wealthy, but it has not ended poverty. Another 14-fold increase (even if that were possible within earthly limits) would not end poverty. In the current system, economic growth generally takes place in the already rich countries and flows disproportionately to the richest people within those countries.[63] Growth is not the primary ingredient in the recipe to end poverty.

The concept of growth is understood differently when using a systems approach. As evident, growth can solve some problems but creates others. The earth is finite. Growth of anything physical, including the human population and its cars, houses and factories, cannot continue forever. There are limits to the rate at which humans can extract resources (crops, timber, fresh water, fish, etc.) and discharge wastes (greenhouse gases, toxic substances, and polluted water) without exceeding the carrying capacity of the Earth. As is readily apparent, the human economy cannot maintain present flows at their current rates for very much longer. The good news is that we can reduce our ecological footprint by lowering population rates, altering consumption, and implementing more resource-efficient technologies.

The challenge for those who take a holistic view of the converging crises of climate change, global poverty and inequality is how to confront the dogmatic belief that humanity's prosperity is dependent on the growth of GDP. But even a cursory analysis of economic growth reveals its shortcomings: growth pursued at all costs is ecologically unsustainable, socially unjust, and unnecessary.[64]

Questions to Consider

1. Does your country want to continually grow the economy? What are the dangers to this way of thinking? What are the benefits? Why do people worry that it will be a disaster if the economy doesn't grow?

Information Technology

In the industrial era, the main ingredients in industrial economic production—land, labor, and capital—were organized around the uniform, mass-production of goods in rigid, hierarchical industries. In a global economy, information is a new ingredient added to the economic mix of land, labor, and capital. **Information** is specific data or particular services applied to a product, service, or activity that adds monetary value. Some examples of value-added information are services from advertisers, marketers, accountants, insurance, financiers, lawyers, efficiency experts, risk analysts, and computer applications. The purpose of adding information is to maximize productivity, profitability, efficiency, and attract recognition to a product or service in an intensely competitive world.[65] Information in the globalized economy is not just applied for societal well-being, but for the maximum profit of private interests.

A **sharing economy** takes a variety of forms, often leveraging information technology to enable individuals, corporations, non-profits and government with information to efficiently distribute, share and reuse the excess capacity in goods and services. This sharing economy succeeds because of a depressed labor market, in which many people supplement their income by commodifying their property and labor in different ways. People join the sharing economy because they may have lost a full-time job, including a few cases where the pricing structure of the sharing economy may have made their old jobs less profitable, such as full-time taxi drivers who may have switched to be Uber drivers. The Uber transportation company develops, markets and operates the Uber mobile app, which allows consumers to submit a trip request that links to the network of Uber drivers. Uber is displacing traditional economy taxi drivers and companies with mostly part-time workers who use their own car to transport people for extra income. The real economic benefit goes to the privately owned Uber Corporation and its shareholders, currently worth $50 billion, which takes in a big slice of the profits.[66]

Information is a commodity. **Commodification** is the process of turning something with little or no economic value into a product or service that has a specific value or a higher monetary value. An example of the commodification process is weddings. Several decades ago, most weddings were low budget affairs with the reception held in a church basement, resplendent with cake and punch, mints if you were lucky. Today many weddings are extravagant affairs that even necessitate a wedding planner. Costs skyrocket into the tens of thousands of dollars range.

In core nations, the service and information sectors are displacing the manufacturing sector. Economic information has come to the center of the wealth-producing process. Economies that have greater complexity and productivity typically have a greater information component. The question is, to what end is this information applied. If information is applied to products or services for the sole purpose of enticing more people to buy more products they don't need, then information may be seen as detrimental. An example is the 2008 financial crisis when information was applied to financial products that were so complex that no one could calculate their actual worth. When confidence eroded in these intricate and opaque financial products, the market for them crashed, leaving vulnerable financial institutions exposed and taxpayers footing the bill for a bailout. But if information is used to reduce environmental degradation or makes energy more efficient, then it is useful to society.

Questions to Consider

1. What do you think are positive ways in which information may be used? Destructive ways?

Exchange and Trade

The ideological heart of economic globalization is free trade. Although trade increased globally in the Modern Wave, it was mainly between nations. Most countries conducted trade through **bilateral trade** deals, which were one-on-one, country-to-country agreements. In the Global Wave trade has expanded beyond local and national boundaries to encompass the globe and global institutions are governing the trade agreements. There is a concerted effort by those who support economic globalization to require national governments to eliminate regulations, laws, or tariffs that restrict trade across national borders. Free traders established a global institution in 1995—the World Trade Organization—that regulates trade between participating countries and provides a framework for negotiating and formalizing trade agreements as well as a dispute resolution process enforcing their adherence to WTO rules. Headquartered in Geneva Switzerland, the WTO currently has 161 member states.

The WTO is a very powerful organization. In fact, many of its rules override national rules. For example, in September 1997, a WTO panel ruled that the European Union (EU) was giving preferential access to bananas produced by its former colonies in the Caribbean under the Lome treaty negotiated in 1975. The U.S., which does not produce any bananas, had brought a lawsuit against the EU on behalf of the U.S.-based Chiquita Corporation. Chiquita produces bananas in Latin America on huge plantations employing low-wage farm laborers. In the Caribbean, banana producers tended to be small-scale farmers who owned and worked their own land (an average of three acres), often incurring higher production costs. The U.S. and EU bandied threats and sanctions between them, nearly setting off a trade war. The EU eventually capitulated and said that it would comply with the WTO rules and not give preferential treatment to Caribbean producers. The small scale farmers would thus have to compete with large-scale corporate plantations.

When we think of free trade we usually think of goods imported and exported across national boundaries so that consumers can enjoy inexpensive clothes made in China, savor specialty cheese from France, pump cheap gasoline into our cars from Saudi Arabia, communicate on gadgets made in South Korea, and take pleasure in movies from Hollywood. The goal of free trade is noble—global integration through trade in order to achieve a higher standard of living for all. However, there is a debate about whether free trade policy is best for labor and for individual countries as a whole.

The 1941 Stolper-Samuelson theorem explains the impact of economic globalization on trade as well as labor. They showed that owners of abundant resources gain from trade, while those with scarce resources lose. For example, those with capital are able to invest in products that return a high value in trade. Those without capital suffer. To see this relationship, consider a resource like oil. In a country rich in oil, oil is cheap, and opening up to trade is good for oil producers because it allows them to sell oil to foreigners. In a country poor in oil, where oil is expensive, opening to trade is bad for oil producers because it leads to oil imports that push the domestic price of oil down. Even if the resource in question is more general—land, labor, capital and information—the logic holds; protection helps owners of a nationally scarce resource; trade helps owners of a nationally abundant resource.[67]

Samuelson pointed to the drastic change in mean U.S. incomes and in inequalities among different classes and suggested that this may be the consequence of free trade. The outsourcing of jobs to foreign countries is tantamount to importing labor from those countries into the U.S., with similar consequences of depressing wages. The ability to import consumer items at a low cost is a poor consolation to the jobless. Economists examining long-range data find that the globalization of the American economy has helped to freeze or lower middle-class incomes, further widening the gap between the very rich and the middle class. While America's rich are enjoying the fruits of globalization, America's middle and working classes are swallowing the bitter pill of economic globalization.[68]

Patterns of Labor

The Western progressive agenda of the last 150 years has made great strides in improving working conditions and increasing wages for the working and middle classes, while at the same time requiring elites to contribute their fair share of taxes to the economic pie. Three interacting developments are currently eroding the foundations of the middle class and the gains made by labor in the Modern Wave: technological innovations, neoliberal policies, and economic globalization. We looked at technological innovations above; neoliberal policies and economic globalization are examined in this section.

Neoliberalism and Labor

With the shift to neoliberalism from managed capitalism around 1980, there have been markedly different economic priorities, actions, and policies regarding labor. Neoliberalism's impact on labor, in this brief section, primarily focuses on developments in the U.S. but apply to labor conditions throughout the world. Neoliberals aim is to create low unemployment. They argue that unemployment exists primarily because labor markets do not follow the free movements of supply and demand. They claim that in a free market unemployment would clear itself with falling wages. When trade unions or minimum wage laws prevent wages from falling, unemployment continues. Thus, neoliberals strive to abolish unions and repeal minimum wage laws to achieve low unemployment rates. Hardship and poverty, they argue, are unfortunate but necessary in the short term if the market is to operate freely and bring about long-term prosperity. In addition, when wages are lower, they believe increased incentives to work should be enacted. Lowering income taxes would in effect increase workers' disposable income, which they see as an important way to incentivize work.

Full employment prevailed during the post-war golden age of capitalism. The year 1953 marked the height of union strength when 32.5 percent of the U.S. labor force was unionized. That ended with the crisis in the 1970s when the Federal Reserve's policies turned to taming inflation, which led to a decrease in wages and greater unemployment. But companies continued to trim wages even after inflation ended. The real wages of American workers, adjusted for inflation, rose in 1993, but they had fallen 15 percent below their 1978 levels.[69] By the late 1980s, the power of the labor movement had been waning for years, and corporations had adopted an increasingly aggressive negative stance toward labor This was due in part to increasing automation, increasing productivity per worker, and the outsourcing of manufacturing jobs to low-wage countries.[70]

Neoliberal policies attacking unions and enacting laws directing more money to the elite have resulted in workers' wages not keeping up with rising productivity levels. In principle, wages rise with productivity. **Labor productivity** is the amount a worker produces in a unit of time, usually per hour. But whether wages actually rise with productivity in practice depends on the relative bargaining power of workers and their employers. Economist James Cypher has carefully analyzed labor productivity data. He found that "in 2009, stock owners, bankers, brokers, hedge-fund managers, highly paid corporate executives, corporations, and mid-ranking managers pocketed—as

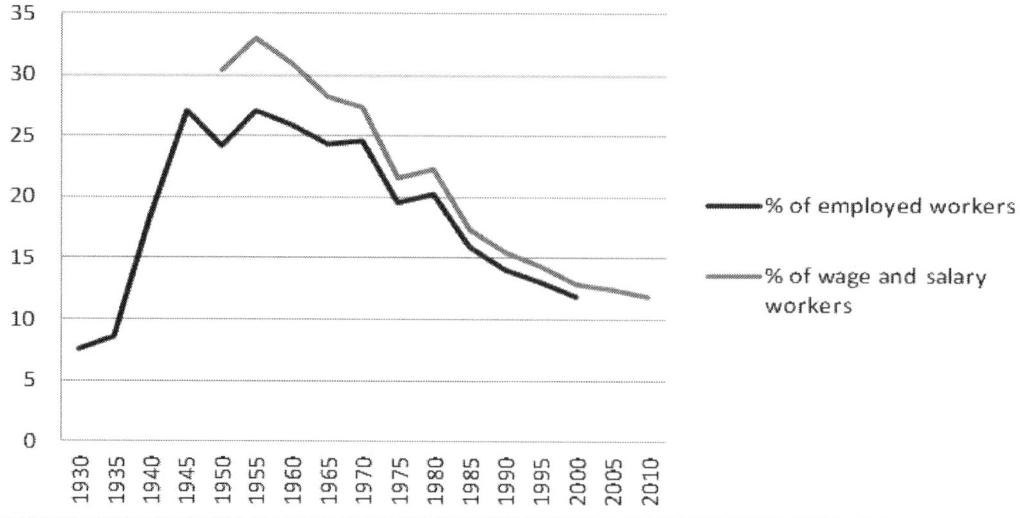

Union Membership in the United States

either income, benefits, or perks such as corporate jets—an estimated $1.91 trillion that over the past 40 years ago would have collectively gone to non-supervisory and production workers in the form of higher wages and benefits. These are the 88 million workers in the private sector who are closely tied to production processes but not responsible for the supervision, planning, or direction of other workers." If workers had received the value of their annual productivity increases, as they had been prior to the early 1970s, they would have earned an average of $35.98 per hour in compensation in 2009 instead of the $23.14 they actually received. The difference is $12.84. On an annual basis each worker lost an average of $22,701. From 1972 through 2009, neoliberal policies transferred productivity gains from non-supervisory workers to managers and owners. This upward redistribution of $1.91 trillion has taken various forms—bonuses, excessive salaries, large stock options, padded consulting fees, outsized compensation to boards of directors, expensive conferences, lavish offices, large staffs, private dining rooms, and generous retirement agreements.[71]

The total increase in the wages paid to all 124 million non-supervisory workers was less than $200 million in six years—a raise of $1.60 per worker—not per hour but a grand total of $1.60 in higher wages per worker over nearly six years. Compare this $200 million for workers to the $38 billion paid in bonuses by the top five Wall Street financial firms during the same period. For example, during the 1990s, the reported pay of senior corporate executives increased almost five-fold. If workers' median pay had grown at the same rate as CEO's compensation, their pay would be over $200,000 a year![72]

Labor and Economic Globalization

The 1941 Stolper-Samuelson theorem also explains labor trends accompanying the spread of economic globalization, as well as trade. It basically says that the effect of trade between a core nation and a periphery nation is that the wages for the unskilled labor force in the core nation will be lower because they are competing globally with unskilled workers in a periphery nation. This theorem is currently being played out in the U.S. and other core countries. Economist Thomas Palley states that since the 1980s, two and a half billion people in China, India, Eastern Europe and the former Soviet Union have discarded economic isolationism and joined the global economy. When the global economy added these workers, wages fell across the board. When a core, capital-abundant country (such as the U.S.) trades with a labor-abundant country (such as China), wages in the core country fall and corporate profits go up. The theorem's economic logic is simple. Free trade is tantamount to a massive increase in the core country's labor supply, since the products made by periphery country workers can now be imported. Additionally, demand for workers in the core country falls as the corporations shift labor-intensive production to the periphery country. The net result is an increase in the labor supply and a decrease in labor demand in the core country; thus wages fall.[73]

Is the theorem actually depicting what is really happening in our global economy? Palley notes, "Now, this shift is coming together in the form of a 'super-sized' Stolper-Samuelson effect, and has depressing consequences for American workers."[74] Adding two and a half billion people from low-wage countries to the global labor market is an unprecedented event in world history.

Samuelson questioned the benefits of economic globalization for labor. With the emergence of China, India and Eastern Europe, the dam of isolation holding back two and a half billion workers from the global economic workforce has been removed. If two swimming pools are joined, the water level will eventually equalize. A threat to labor is competition. Manufacturing workers in core countries are already competing with technological innovations and also labor from periphery countries, with dire consequences for manufacturing workers in the core countries. Samuelson claimed "that since U.S. labor has lost its old monopoly on American advanced know-how and capital, free trade could indeed lower the share of wages in the U.S. GDP and increase overall inequality."[75]

Outsourcing is an imprecise term but involves the contracting out of a business function to an external provider, usually to a low-wage country. One of the reasons for the rapid decline in manufacturing jobs in core countries is the outsourcing of jobs to low-wage periphery countries, such as China, Mexico, Indonesia, India, and Vietnam. For example, many Mexican farmers left their villages to seek employment in Mexico's *maquilladores*, which were factory cities built along the border with the U.S. in the 1980s and 1990s. One of these cities, Juarez, Mexico, employed thousands of Mexican workers in factories that churned out television sets to auto parts that were mostly shipped to the U.S. However, many of these factories have closed down in order to seek even lower-wage workers in China or Vietnam. Juarez is now left with high unemployment and a staggering crime rate. The same is happening to professional and higher-paid knowledge workers in core countries with similar effects. Outsourcing is not just the province of the manufacturing sector. Predictions are that from software to banking, insurance, pharmaceuticals, and engineering, between 13 and 50 percent of jobs could be sent offshore. Therefore, in core countries most of the new jobs are in domestic services and low-paying retail work.[76]

Maquiladora in Mexico.

Insights: Learning from the Past

Techno-Economic Currents

A number of viable alternatives to the concentration of wealth in a globalized economy are evolving. One alternative is the redevelopment of the once flourishing local or domestic economy. Local community members, government officials, and business owners can alleviate the wealth depletion of the local economy by returning to "economic self-determination." This return to local capitalism reduces dependency on multinational corporations, while creating wealth-accumulating enterprises at the local level. Local economies can produce, market, and process many of their own products for local or regional consumption, reducing transportation and middleman costs. **Local capitalism** can bring local economies into harmony with the surrounding ecosystem, foster cooperation within the community, and substitute more personalized local products for more expensive imported and often sub-standard goods. In order for such a change to occur, the real effort must come from the local community that can better utilize available resources in imaginative ways and provide more economical and high quality food, clothing, shelter, transportation, and energy. A transfer of economic interests and activities from urban, core centers to the local community can reduce dependency on the core and revive local economic vibrancy.[77] A number of communities scattered throughout the world are working to incrementally achieve this goal. A revitalization of the local economy does not mean isolation and a complete rejection of the global capitalist economy, but incorporating both the global and the local economy. For example, the Green City Growers in Cleveland, Ohio is a worker-owned hydroponic greenhouse that supplies fresh produce to retailers and wholesalers in the Cleveland area.

Questions to Consider

1. What can be done in your own community to revive the local economy?

HUMAN NETWORKS: SOCIAL CURRENTS

In the Global Wave, social currents are still taking shape as the world adjusts to economic and other changes. Indeed, social structures are usually the last current to change as these systems tend to hold on to many of the familiar values, attitudes, and traditions of the past. This section will access changes in a core nation, primarily the U.S. and other global developments.

Groups and Institutions

I have organized global social groups in the Global Wave into two categories: those holding values-based beliefs and those prioritizing economic development. Values-based social groups are further divided, irrespective of income, into three subgroups: fundamentalist/religious, globalized and transformative. Groups according to income level are further divided into income percentiles (see Status section).

Fundamentalist social groups usually have strong religious convictions. All major religious denominations have religious fundamentalist branches. In the U.S., the religious fundamentalists are usually Christian and believe in **traditional family values**; they are generally against abortion and same sex marriage, favor prayer in the schools, promote strict moral limits, advocate abstinence before marriage, and question scientific evolution. Their income levels can vary widely, but social and cultural views bind this group together more than income. They tend to be politically and socially conservative.

The globalized social group, which is global in scope, comprises upper-income people who partake of a conspicuous consumer life-style with well-appointed homes or apartments and newer model cars. This group of people drive the consumer economy, attend universities, and determine life-style trends. Generally they believe in multi-culturalism and tend to be socially liberal but politically conservative. They are well educated, culturally sophisticated, and have experienced world travel.

The transformative social group, also global in scope, is generally well educated, socially active, religiously liberal, and accepting of alternative life-styles. They question the prevailing materialistic/consumer ideology and tend to be politically liberal, support racial and ethnic diversity, accept multiculturalism, and promote religious toleration. Some stress the importance of community rights and see their diminishment as a result of an over-emphasis on individual rights.

No matter which group people identify with the disruptions, rapid changes, and upheaval of a global economy threaten many individuals across the globe. Turbulent changes in work, life style, and habits cause a segment of the population to be fearful of the future and to respond in reactionary ways. Social discord surfaces as the disconnected spout a multiplicity of ideologies and explanations. Some see the main reason for this discord as neither political nor economic, but existential. People need roots and participation in a community, while the global economy advances a more disconnected, alienating, individualistic, and competitive way of life. As many people become more disconnected from their local communities, they long for a geographic, linguistic, religious, or cultural community which they can be part of and understand.[78]

The Family

Diverse families characterize the Global Wave. Western middle class and elite families are smaller than in the past and have fewer responsibilities as they grant more authority to other social institutions for what previously were traditional familial responsibilities. For example, families entrust a child's care to such institutions as day care centers and schools that provide services for children from birth to their twenties. Families turn the care of the elderly over to institutions as well, with retirement homes, nursing care facilities, and home health care providers offering services that historically fell to the family. The traditional American family configuration so idealized in the 1950s—a mother, father, and children—continues to be the standard to emulate in the U.S. But the 1950s standard is not the norm and instead,

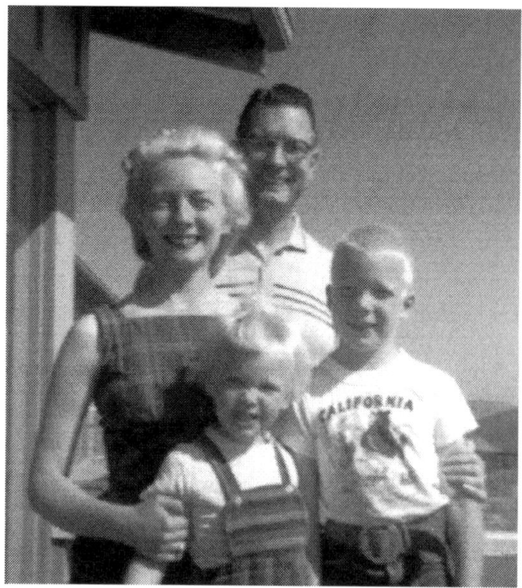

The nuclear family of the 1950s was, and still is in many cases, considered the ideal. Today many different types of families exist.

family make–up has shifted to flexible households consisting of extended and blended families, single parent households, single households (particularly women), homosexual partners and families, domestic partners, unrelated individuals forming families, and communal families.

Increasingly, in some countries the workplace is more central to social life than the family. Adult family members, and increasingly teens, are spending more time at work or school or going to and from work, than in the home. Many critics contend that the workplace has evolved into a substitute family. Generally, both men and women spend more time at work than with their families, resulting in personal workplace relationships. While the workplace offers rewards, acceptance, and recognition that are often missing in family relationships, it can also be shattering to an individual if his/her workplace ceases operation or if s/he is terminated from a job, as is happening with growing frequency in the Global Wave. Some critics argue that work consumes so much family energy and time that in many cases family life is an empty shell. Instead of creating their own viable family life with all the accompanying trials and tribulations, many individuals turn to television, computers, and social media as a fantasy replacement for family life. As a substitute family, the workplace fails to provide the stability, continuity, and acceptance that a healthy family traditionally furnishes. With growing temporary employment stints, job uncertainty, and telecommuting the workplace is not a source of stability and security needed by individuals; thus, many people feel more insecure and experience growing uncertainty, anxiety, alienation, and fragmentation.

Questions to Consider

1. Is the family still important in today's society? Is it important to you?

Gender

Gender relations differ according to worldviews as well. For those following a modern, globalized, and transformative worldview gender relations have changed significantly in the last 100 years and continue to evolve. Since the turn of the 20th century, political equality has been extended to women in many countries following modern values. Women have been able to gain (in varying degrees in different countries) the right to vote, an education, liberal divorce laws, equality in career opportunities, political representation, a rejection of a double sexual standard, available birth control, abortion rights, equality before the law, and other protections. Among core nations, middle class and elite women have decreased their fertility rates and if having children, many are postponing child-bearing until their 30s. As more women enter the workplace, more childcare is transferred to institutionalized day care and schools.

Many countries and societies following a fundamentalist worldview have not granted women equality and instead have imposed traditional restrictions on women's freedom or created new restrictions. Each country is a mixture of often contradictory rules and regulations regarding women. For example, in Iran women are legally conscribed to a modest dress code but may actively participate in education and careers. In

Saudi Arabia, women are restricted from driving but enjoy other modern conveniences. In India, women are legally protected from discrimination but the ancient practice of sati, in which widows are burned alive on their husband's funeral pyre, continues in many rural villages. Even though traditional practices may treat women unequally, imposing modern views of women on traditional cultures is a delicate negotiation that is bound to cause hostilities on both sides.

Since around the 1990s, **LBGT movements**, a term that did not exist before 1990, have been achieving human rights for lesbian, bisexual, gay, transgender and transsexual people around the world. The LGBT social movement advocates for the equalized acceptance of LGBT people in society. Although there is not an overarching central organization that represents all LGBT people and their interests, many organizations are active worldwide. Today these movements include political activism and cultural activity, including lobbying, street marches, social groups, media, art, and research. The 1990s saw a rapid push of the transgender movement, and it continues today.

Prestige and Status

The increasing social gap between haves and have-nots is worldwide. Social arrangements systematically reward the privileged with the power and resources to acquire even more privilege. Examples of elite privilege include tax loopholes, greater access to capital, superior education, political access, and low or no inheritance taxes. Class is an important factor in determining access to information. Elite and middle class families furnish their children with computers, Internet service, and other learning opportunities that poor children cannot afford or do not have access to, exacerbating the technology and social divide. In systems terms, these structures are called reinforcing feedback loops that reward and keep rewarding the successful with the means to maintain their wealth and power. These arrangements tend to be prevalent in any society that does not consciously apply counterbalancing structures to level the playing field, such as anti-discrimination laws, progressive tax rates, exemplary universal education, universal health care, a social safety net, inheritance taxes, and the separation of policy-making from the influence of money.[79]

Poverty-perpetuating structures arise from the fact that it is easier for rich populations to save, invest, and multiply their capital than it is for the poor. Rich countries have built up a large stock of capital that multiplies itself but in poor countries with large populations, capital growth has a hard time keeping up with population growth. Excess capital that might have been reinvested is more likely to be channeled to schools, hospitals and the subsistence needs of a growing population. Thus, the economy grows slowly. When women

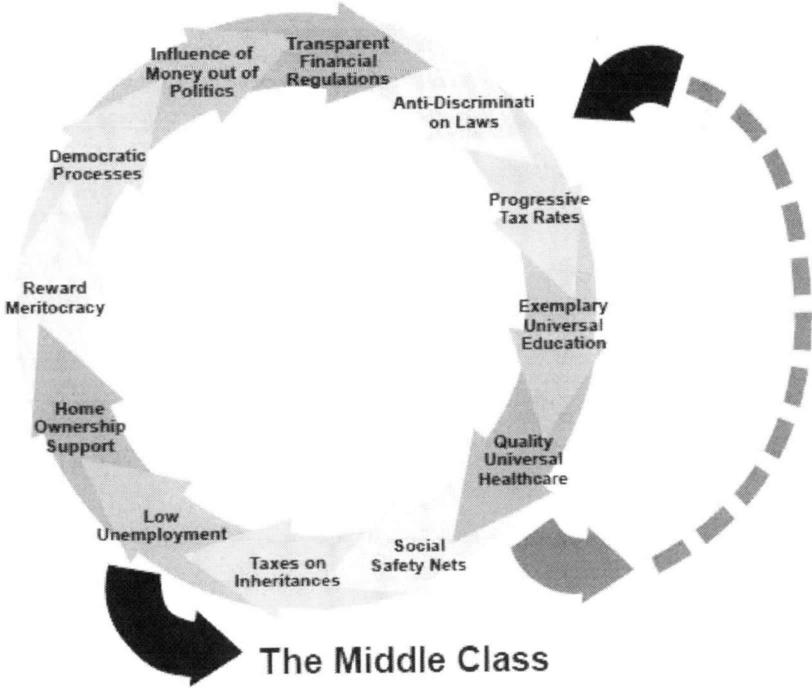

see no attractive educational or economic alternatives to childbearing, then children become one of the few forms of security available; therefore, populations grow larger without growing richer.[80]

Economic globalization has resulted in a change from a class structure that was formerly nation-based to one that is now globally-based. The American economy has been in the midst of a sea change, shifting from industry to services and information technology and integrating itself far more tightly into a single, global market for goods, labor, and capital. China, India, and other middle countries have emerged as economic competitors, capable of producing large volumes of high-value, low-priced goods and services. This transformation has been underway since the 1980s, but the pace of change has quickened since 2000 and even more so since the 2008 financial crisis.[81] The hollowing out of the American middle class has taken place amidst a surge in the formation of a middle class in Brazil, Russia, India, China, and South Africa (BRICS), and other countries. Since the economy is global in scope, the class structure is as well. Although the U.S. government and charity programs subsidize the very poor somewhat for food, shelter, and health care, their counterparts in the BRICS have limited safety nets.

The extreme gap between the global rich and poor is due in part to economic globalization, although technology contributes to growing inequality as well. Economist Joseph Stiglitz states, "There is growing inequality in most countries of the world, and globalization is one of the factors that has contributed to this global pattern."[82] Economist Nouriel Roubini adds, "Globalization and innovation are not without risk. Take the daunting challenge of adding billions of people to the global labor supply. Globalization has also been associated with growing inequalities of income and wealth in advanced economies and emerging-market economies alike."[83]

Next, we examine prestige and status among the world's elite, middle class, and poor.

1. The World's Elite

You might think the world's most expensive home would belong to the Bill Gates' family; after all, he has topped the list of the world's richest people for many years and lives in the U.S., the world's richest country. No need to fear, Gates does have a very large home. Yet, the Gates family home pales in comparison to the world's most expensive home which is in India—with a never-before-seen $1 billion price tag. Mukesh Ambani, India's richest man, owns the 27-floor, 570-foot-tall home located in Mumbai, India, one of the most unequal cities in the world. The home features such amenities as a health club with a gym and dance studio, at least one swimming pool, a 50-seat movie theater, a ballroom, three helipads and an underground parking lot that holds 160 vehicles.[84]

Gates and Ambani are among the elites of the world, both billionaires and symbolic of the growing gap between rich and poor. While Gates is more well-known as founder of Microsoft, Ambani is an Indian entrepreneur, and managing director of Reliance Industries, the largest private sector enterprise in India and a Fortune 500 company. In a world where the 400 highest income earners from the U.S. earn as much money annually as the total population of 20 African countries, inequality seems out of bounds.[85] At the very top of the wealth pyramid, there are over 1,000 billionaires globally, of which 245 are in Asia Pacific, 230 are in Europe and 500 are in North America. Moving down the wealth pyramid, there are 80,000 ultra-wealthy individuals worth over $50 million each. Added into this wealthy summit are another 24 million adults with worth between $1 million and $50 million—800,000 live in China, 170,000 live in India, and over four million are in the rest of the Asia Pacific. Below this, more than 330 million individuals have average wealth per adult of $100,000 to $1 million. The world's richest 1 percent—adults who have at least $588,000 to call their own—hold 43 percent of the world's wealth.

No other nation holds as much total wealth as the United States. With only 5.2 percent of the world's population, the U.S. boasts 23 percent of the world's adults worth at least $100,000 and an even greater proportion—41 percent—of the world's millionaires. Switzerland and Norway have emerged as the richest nations in the world in terms of average wealth per adult, which stands at $372,692 and $326,530 respectively. They are followed by third-place Australia with average wealth per adult of $320,909 and Singapore at $255,488. Figures for Australia and Singapore have both doubled in the last decade.[86]

Many of America's business elites appear removed from the continuing travails of many in the U.S. workforce: the globalized world in which they increasingly live and work is thriving. An American CEO who runs one of the world's largest hedge funds said his firm's investment committee often discusses the question of who wins and who loses in today's economy. In a recent internal debate, he said, one of his senior colleagues had argued that the hollowing-out of the American middle class didn't really matter. "His point was," the CEO recalled, "that if the transformation of the world economy lifts four people in China and India out of poverty and into the middle class, and meanwhile one American drops out of the middle class, that's not such a bad trade." A Taiwanese-born, 30-something entrepreneur of a U.S. internet company was also not sympathetic to the complaints of the American middle class. He stated, "We demand a higher paycheck than the rest of the world, so if you're going to demand 10 times the paycheck, you need to deliver 10 times the value. It sounds harsh, but maybe people in the middle class need to decide to take a pay cut."[87] For the super-elite, a sense of meritocratic achievement can inspire high self-regard, and that self-regard—especially when compounded by their isolation among like-minded peers—can lead to obliviousness and indifference to the distress of others.

2. The World's Middle Class

The world's middle class is essentially a tale between two groups: one is the old middle class of the core nations, and the other is a new middle class of the middle and periphery countries. The old middle class is seeing the erosion of their established standards of a middle class way of life, and the new middle class is developing its own standards. The prospects for both of them are tied to economic globalization.

The American middle class made real headway during the golden age of 1948-1973. The wealthy made strides as well, but the middle and working classes gained the most. It was a time when the working class also gained income and were able to attain a middle class standard of living. Although partially a result of America's unique status after the war, it was also a result of a set of governmental policies enacted to support the growth and prosperity of an expanding middle class. During the post-war years, governmental policy was firmly in the middle class camp.

The American Middle Class Way of Life

job security, retirement pensions, disposable income, home ownership, two cars, free highway transportation, free, quality public education in grades k-12, low-cost higher education, the chance for upward mobility, leisure time, low-cost medical care, low-cost material comforts, cultural stimulations, honest institutions, personal security, safe and low-cost food, low taxes, array of social services

For core nations, the middle class way of life has changed since the 1980s, with the double-edged onslaught of three developments that favor the wealthy: technological innovations, neoliberalism and economic globalization. The wealthy have designed the rules of neoliberalism and economic globalization to benefit them; they encourage competition among countries for business, which drives down taxes on corporations, weakens health and environmental protections, and undermines labor rights, such as collective bargaining.[88] On the other hand, policies that favor the middle class—higher income tax rates on the wealthy, ample funding for education, low-interest loans for education, research and development that encourages job creation, a fair inheritance tax rate, tax deductions for home ownership, a safety net for economic hardships, and pensions for retirement—have all been eroding since 1980.[89]

Governmental policies in Europe favor the middle class, although this is eroding in some countries. Denmark, Finland, Netherlands and Slovenia rank as the most equal countries, while Greece, UK, and Spain were among the most unequal. Canada follows the European model, with the typical Canadian family in 2010 worth $94,700, double the $47,771 U.S. median net worth. Studies have found that once nations are industrialized, more equal societies almost always do better in terms of health, well-being and social cohesion. Large income inequalities within societies erode its social fabric and quality of life.[90]

The global middle class consists of one billion individuals situated in the middle segment of the wealth pyramid. They have average wealth per adult of $10,000 to $100,000 and own one-sixth of global wealth. Almost 60 percent or 587 million individuals in the middle segment are located in Asia Pacific, the fastest-growing economies of the world. The middle class of this region is expected to replace the indebted U.S. middle class households as the global growth locomotive.[91]

The middle class expanded in Asia Pacific countries and shrunk in many core and other periphery countries mostly because countries simply stopped making things and started buying them from the Asian Pacific countries. Since 2000, the U.S. has lost over 3 million manufacturing jobs; Brazil has lost 2 million since 1998, and South Africa has lost nearly 1 million. In the past, Argentina assembled televisions; now it purchases most of them from abroad. Mozambique in Africa packaged its cashew crop 30 years ago; today the country ships its raw nuts overseas for others to bottle and can. Zambians made their own clothes in the 1980s; now they sort through bundles of clothes shipped from the U.S. and Europe. The Hunters Point neighborhood in San Francisco, California (US) manufactured the ships that delivered American-made goods to the world; now the ships docked in the Bay Area's ports are mostly from East Asia, unloading foreign-made products for U.S. consumers.[92]

The Middle Class in China. Photo by Denise Ames

3. The World's Poor

Global social and economic inequalities exist at astounding levels. The world's poor make up at least 80 percent of humanity and live on less than $10 a day, which does not include those living on less than $10 a day from core nations.[93] Data from the IMF finds the earnings of the richest 10 percent of the global population is 117 times higher than the poorest 10 percent. This is a considerable increase since 1980, when the earnings of the richest 10 percent was around 79 times greater than the poorest 10 percent.[94]

At the other end of the global economic spectrum are parked three billion people—more than two thirds of the world's adults—whose wealth averages less than $10,000. About 1.1 billion of them have a net worth of less than $1,000 and of that number 307 million are in India. Half the world's people who are 20 and older hold under $4,000 in net worth (subtract debts from assets). They have less than 2 percent of global wealth. There are now 1.3 billion people who live on the equivalent of less than $1 per day.[95]

Income inequality in Latin America has increased in the 2000s. For example, its per capita income increased by 82 percent between 1960 and 1980 and only by 13 percent from 1990 to 2005. The richest10 percent of the Latin population earns 48 percent of the region's total income, while the poorest 10 percent earns only 1.6 percent. In 2010, the Inter Press Service reported that 10 of the 15 most unequal countries in the world are in Latin America: Bolivia, followed by Haiti, Brazil, Ecuador, and Chile, which is tied in fifth place with Colombia, Guatemala, Honduras, Panama and Paraguay.[96]

What is the reason for this rising inequality? Critics such as Jon Jeter forcefully argue that "the global economy has ripped a hole through the earth, city by city, block by block, house by house. Globalization has widened inequality, corrupted politicians, estranged neighbors from one another, unraveled families, rerouted rivers, emptied ports of ships, and flooded streets with protesters. It has created poverty where it did not exist and deepened poverty for women, people of color, and indigenous people."[97] For example, global institutions have blindly prescribed policies favoring economic globalization to periphery countries. One policy is that opening markets to foreign investment will improve exports and contribute to economic growth. If loans are incurred, the prescription is to cut back on social spending, such as health and education, as a way to pay back loans and debts. Periphery nations lose their ability to develop their own policies, and local businesses end up competing with well-established multinationals. World income has increased by nearly $1 trillion since 1990, while sub-Saharan Africa's per capita income has fallen by 20 percent in that same time. Black South Africa vanquished apartheid only to confront unemployment rates approaching 40 percent and whole city blocks plunged into darkness because no one can afford the rising costs of electricity charged by privatized utility companies.[98]

The persistent gap between rich and poor, both within and between countries, is a crisis. Supporters of economic globalization firmly maintain that it is the only path leading to global poverty reduction, while the causes of enduring inequality are to be located principally in the failure of countries to integrate fast enough into the world economy. They argue that more, rather than less, globalization is the principal remedy for eradicating global poverty. The way that economic globalization works to end poverty is to increase economic growth, which will result in wealth trickling down to the poor. Many sincerely believe that the pursuit of growth will end world poverty. They cite the number of middle class Chinese and Indians as testimony to the growth strategy for ending poverty.

Despite the evidence, supporters of growth argue that it is still the best way to secure a prosperous future for the 3 billion people who continue to live on less than $2.50 a day. The fact that decades of economic growth have not made a significant dent in global poverty is enough evidence that the proceeds of growth are not sufficiently "trickling down" to those most in need. In fact, any trickle there may have been is rapidly drying up despite any increases in the size of the economic pie; in the 1980s, 2.2 percent of global growth went to the poor, compared to only 0.6 percent in the 1990s. The consequence of this skewed distribution of growth is, unsurprisingly, that the world is increasingly unequal, with the richest 10 percent having accumulated 3,000 times more wealth than the poorest 10 percent.[99]

The following fact further questions economic growth as a solution in reducing world poverty. A single dollar of poverty reduction took $166 of additional global production and consumption, with all its associated environmental impacts. It creates the paradox that ever smaller amounts of poverty reduction amongst the poorest people of the world require ever larger amounts of consumption by the richest people.[100] In other words, the world's richest

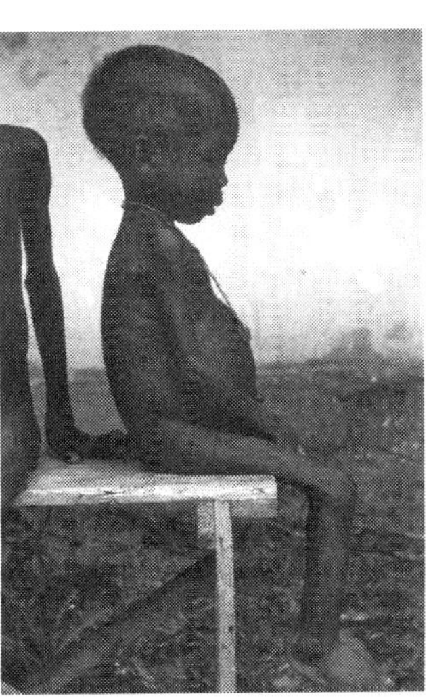

Starving girl in Africa.

people cannot reduce world poverty by just consuming more!

Questions to Consider

1. Has the growing gap between the haves and have nots had an impact on your life? Explain.

Socialization and Education

Educational institutions play a significant role in socializing young people. They inculcate children with the worldview of their culture, and educate children to become workers in the future economic system. Schools act as caretakers for children as parents head off to the workplace outside the home. In the 1800s and 1900s, public education was the primary educational institution for the vast majority of American children. However, neoliberals are now working to privatize public education, and have done so with varying degrees of success in the U.S. Today's pressing social problems make the work of public education even more difficult for educators and students alike.

Public educational institutions promote secular, conformist attitudes which different groups criticize. On the one hand, fundamentalists insist that state-supported schools should provide time for compulsory prayer, teach traditional family values, and present religious explanations for evolution and other scientific theories that include a divine presence. Some members of the transformative community challenge the mind-numbing conformity, rigid rules and excessive testing of some public schools and believe that home schooling, progressive charter schools, independent schools, or more flexible public schools can best teach creativity, encourage expressions of individuality, and provide a holistic approach to the curricula. Many elite children attend private schools where rigorous academic standards prepare students for highly selective, top quality colleges and universities and entrance into elite careers. Non-elites attend public schools, which can vary from dismal to exemplary. Although many public schools provide a high quality education, others, especially in poverty enclaves, merely teach rudimentary skills, offering little hope that the many of the nation's young people will be able to succeed in the future.

Questions to Consider

1. Do you think education is the way to "success" in the global economy? Define what you mean by success. Are there any drawbacks associated with receiving an education?

Insights: Learning from the Past

Social Currents

The negative and positive effects of social changes in the 20th century and early 21st century are playing out in the Global Wave. Although strides have been made in gender and minority group equality, our society is fraying at the edges because of social fragmentation and alienation.

The social structures that are in place in the U.S. today widen the income gap, perpetuate poverty, alienate individuals and families, foster rampant individualism, and encourage the growth of a consumer society at great cost to the environment and individual well-being. These seemingly intractable problems, when looked at from a holistic perspective, can be addressed more effectively. We are constantly blaming groups or individuals as "causing" these problems: politicians blame teachers for not educating students satisfactorily, teachers blame parents for not providing a good foundation for education, liberals blame television and social media for "dumbing-down" students, advertisers say just be "cool" and all is well. Yet the whole system is out of balance. The values and beliefs of the modern worldview govern our social system. Our society drives us to pursue individual rewards, pleasures, and recognition. The family, community, and commons are devalued, rendered subservient to the individual. Children are trucked to day-care centers so that parents can earn money in the market-place that takes them away from the home and their children. Even when there is enough leisure time for family or community enjoyment, it frequently revolves around the marketplace providing opportunities for enjoyment. The adage "it takes a village to raise a child" has been replaced by "it takes a day care to raise a child."

The social currents in the Communal and Agricultural Waves can provide valuable insights into societal readjustments. Historically, the band, group, family, village, clan, and tribe have provided mechanisms for human belonging. Humans have a universal, innate sense of wanting to belong to something bigger than just themselves. It is in our deep collective unconscious to live in connection with each other; it has only been recently that we have deviated from this norm. Instead, since the Urban and Modern Waves, there has been a shift from community to the individual. This has intensified since the end of World War II and further intensified since the 1980s, when the ideal of the individual has reigned supreme. Now rampant individualism has reached the crisis point. Social disengagement and alienation are expressed in the upsurge in the use of anti-depressant drugs, the rash of teen suicides, and an untold number of broken families. We have become untethered to our innate human need—the need to belong.

For individual well-being, our social currents need to change to a more equitable, nourishing, and sustainable way of life. The good news is that many people recognize this is an urgent issue and are remaking social institutions to foster more community spirit and rethinking the self-serving individualism that permeates the values and attitudes of many parts of American and world society. For example, many religious institutions are once again encouraging their places of worship to provide a setting for social interaction and support for their members and others in the community. Changing parts of the system can trigger changes in the whole system. It is a huge challenge, but once awareness is reached, change can come about. Perhaps once again we can claim that it takes a village to raise a child.

Questions to Consider

1. What does the saying "it takes a village to raise a child" mean to you?

ESTABLISHING ORDER: POLITICAL CURRENTS

Political Systems

In the Global Wave, political systems are undergoing significant change. In the Modern Wave, the nation-state arrangement organized political functions. Although that continues to be the case in the Global Wave, other political configurations are emerging to challenge or complement the sovereignty of the nation state. The organization, structure, and services that governments provide for their citizenry are changing markedly because of the shift by many nations from managed capitalism and socialism to neoliberalism and state capitalism. With more wealth concentrated in the hands of the elite, politicians have increasingly supported policies that favor the wealthy. Although the political organization in the U.S. is a republic with democratically elected representatives, increasingly we see that democracy is divided into two contending segments that I call elite democracy and participatory democracy.

Elite and Participatory Democracy

In **elite democracy** elites manipulate the democratic process for their own self-interest and control. They exert their influence by channeling huge sums of campaign donations to buy the allegiance of supportive politicians. The way the election process in the U.S. is structured, for example, politicians desperately need large sums of money to mount expensive campaigns for offices ranging from city council to president. Money pours into advertising mediums where the candidate's carefully honed message is portrayed as good for the public but in reality serves the interest of the elites who provide the large campaign donations. The politicians then promote the elites' particular self-serving agenda, such as privatization of community-owned assets, a consumer driven ethic, economic growth without regard for the environment, and military power to exert dominance throughout the world.

In contrast to elite democracy, **participatory democracy** attempts to check the abuses of corporate economic and political power with regulatory legislation and careful oversight of the whole political process. Increasingly, citizen groups play a "watchdog" role over giant corporations in an effort to curb their financial excesses and detrimental policies. Participatory democracy is at work at the local and state level where efforts appear the strongest to take back democracy.

Questions to Consider

1. Do you see evidence of elite or participatory democracy in your life?

Global Organizations

During the 20th century, world political institutions evolved that reflected a more interdependent world. One of the first such institutions, the League of Nations established after World War I in 1920, failed to prevent the outbreak of World War II, although its successor, the United Nations (UN), has proven to be a more successful organization and has a peacekeeping wing to enforce its objectives. International political entities in the Global Wave include world, regional, non-governmental organizations (NGOs), and citizen-diplomat groups. World institutions and organizations are gaining more authority and legitimacy as they complement the nation-state. International organizations, such as the UN and the International Court, are charged with the overwhelming task of helping to stamp out terrorism, regulate arms, monitor human rights, prevent disease and hunger, and protect the environment. The WTO, World Bank, and IMF, as mentioned earlier, are global institutions charged with governing the global economy.

The United Nations headquarters New York City, USA.

Non-governmental organizations (NGOs) are privately created organizations with an international scope, unaffiliated with a particular nation. According to political scientist Farouk Mawlawi, NGOs are "private, voluntary, non-profit organizations whose members combine their skills, means and energies in the service of shared ideals and objectives."[101] NGOs transcend narrow national interests in dealing with issues affecting the world and include such well-known world organizations as the Red Cross, Amnesty International, Greenpeace, Doctors' Without Borders, and Human Rights Watch.

Regional political organizations complement national governments in the Global Wave. A regional organization like the North Atlantic Treaty Organization (NATO) has taken on new objectives along with its primary Cold War goal of protecting Western Europe. The Organization of American States (OAS), established in 1948 with 21 members, is the oldest regional organization of states. The European Union (EU), a regional organization of currently 27 member nations, has achieved a cooperative economy, has its own currency, the euro, and has removed tariff barriers for easier trade. Formed in 2001, the African Union has 54 members on the African continent. One of its objectives is the promotion and protection of human rights, such as the right of a group to freely dispose of its natural resources in the exclusive interest of its members. In 1945, Egypt, Jordan, Iraq, Lebanon, Syria and Saudi Arabia signed the Pact of the Arab League States and created the League of Arab States with 22 members in 2011. The League of Arab States is separate from the Organization of the Islamic Conference, which was the second largest inter-governmental organization in 2011, with 57 member states, just below the UN in membership. The Association of Southeast Asian Nations (ASEAN) has 10 members and was formed in 1967.

World Leaders

Even though the United States is sharing world leadership with transnational organizations, it continues its 20th century role as undisputed world leader in the economic, cultural, technological, military, and political realm. Some contend that the United States is taking an autocratic role in world affairs and acting more like an empire than a republic. The U.S. calls for the expansion of democratic institutions and free markets to authoritarian counties around the world. But often in contradiction to these stated ideals, the U.S. has thwarted the democratic decisions of the people when they do not conform to America's "national interests." The U.S. announces human rights as a central tenet of its foreign policy, but it does not always practice this ideal. For example, the U.S. is critical of China's human rights record but is also dependent on its purchases of U.S. treasury bills to finance its substantial debt. Therefore, it is often silent about crucial Chinese human rights abuses because of its monetary predicament. The U.S. calls democracy a "natural" political complement to its preferred economically globalized world economy. But, once again, democracy and capitalism are often in tension with each other. In some cases, as in the invasion of Iraq in 2003, the U.S. acted as the self-appointed world police. The U.S. defied a resolution passed by the UN condemning its plan to invade Iraq in 2003. Instead, along with a sparse "coalition of the willing," it barreled ahead into war. In 2015, after failing to "turn" Afghanistan into a democracy, the U.S. has also continued with a limited troop presence in the country and the domestic situation is chaotic.

Despite U.S. aggression and meddling in many parts of the world, America's democratic ideals and open society are still widely respected. Although realized in a variety of forms, many nations emulate its political and economic institutions. Today, 118 nations—containing over 55 percent of the world's population—govern with some form of democratic organization, an accomplishment that the U.S. had a hand in attaining.

Cooperation, Conflict, and War

A high level of economic interdependence deters conflict, particularly among democratic governments. Adherents to this idea believe that citizens will see the benefits of peace and the drawbacks of war, and work towards stable democratic political institutions. Generally, democracies do not fight each other. But, according to political scientist Robert Jervis, economic interchange alone will not insure peace and stability. He states, "To many people values are more important than wealth."[102] Despite democracy, perhaps the most serious cause of conflict today, and one likely to become the dominant cause in the future, is competition over scarce resources like water, food, fuel, land, and other basic necessities.

Tribalism often creates discord in the Global Wave. Tribalism, a political philosophy discussed in the Agricultural Wave, is composed of ethnic groups who share a common ideology, history, language, traditions, and religion. Tribes may not accept the political philosophy of a multi-cultural, multi-ethnic nation; some strive to establish nations based on their own exclusive ethnicity. This occurred in some of the nations carved from

Reasons for Conflict

1. **scarce resources**
2. **religious differences and perspectives**
3. **ethnic hatred**
4. **conflicting worldviews**
5. **territorial expansion**
6. **core exploiting periphery**
7. **rapid social disruption**
8. **prestige and power rivalry**
9. **economic competition**
10. **hostile nationalism**
11. **territorial disputes**

the collapsed Soviet Union and its satellites in Eastern Europe. Instead of forming multi-ethnic nations, a small number of ethnic groups, such as the Serbs in the 1990s, attempted to form an "ethnically pure" nation. As the dominant ethnic group in Bosnia, the Serbs sought to exterminate and exclude Muslims (a religious, not ethnic group) from Bosnia to realize their goal of an ethnically pure Serbia. They engaged in ethnic cleansing, a euphemism for mass murder of innocent peoples that were not part of their dominant ethnic group.

Terrorism is a critical issue in the Global Wave. Terrorism has many definitions; Dr. Jeffrey Record tabulated over 100 definitions of the term.[103] However, the UN definition may be the most helpful, even though it is a bit vague. **Terrorism** is any act "intended to cause death or serious bodily harm to civilians or non-combatants with the purpose of intimidating a population or compelling a government or an international organization to do or abstain from doing any act." The U.S. Department of Defense offers a somewhat different definition: "The calculated use of unlawful violence or threat of unlawful violence to inculcate fear; intended to coerce or to intimidate governments or societies in the pursuit of goals that are generally political, religious, or ideological." It is interesting to note that only the UN definition identifies civilians as targets, although both definitions agree that terrorism involves violence and the threat of violence. However, violence such as war, organized crime, assault, or riots is not considered terrorism. Where the line is drawn between terrorism and other acts of violence often varies according to one's perspective.

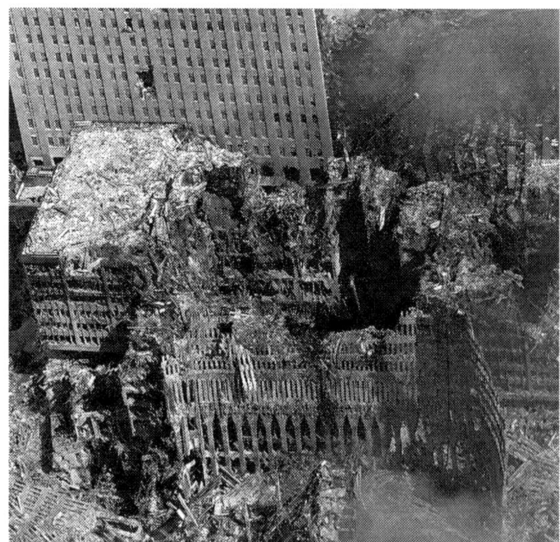

The 9/11 terrorists attacks in New York City.

Terrorism is designed to have a psychological impact and instill fear among witnesses. Terrorists often attack national symbols, such as the 2001 attacks on the World Trade Center in New York City and the Pentagon in Washington D.C, to show their power and boldness. Terrorist acts are a political tactic. Unlike letter writing or peaceful protests, terrorist acts are usually born of desperation; terrorists feel they have no other means to effect the change they desire, which is often so urgent that civilian deaths are seen as justified for the cause. Terrorists target civilians not because they are a specific threat but because they are "symbols" of the views that the terrorists violently disagree with. The anguish wrought from civilian attacks achieves the goal of instilling fear, acting out revenge, and getting their message out to a wider audience. Terrorist acts are illegitimate because governments do not sanction them, although some governments sponsor terrorist acts, classified as **state terrorism**. This may be confusing, since what one state may regard as defensive actions, another may categorize as state terrorism. Among the many nations accused of state terrorism include Libya, Iran, Syria, Israel, China, Russia, and the U.S.

Terrorism is a form of **asymmetric warfare** that is between nations or groups that are uneven in their economic, political, and military power. Terrorist attacks usually occur where there is unresolved political conflict, such as the unsettled Palestinian and Israeli conflict. Historical examples of when terrorism takes place include secession by a territory to form a new sovereign state, such as the attempt by Chiapas to separate from Mexico; dominance of a territory by an outside group, such as the occupation of Chechnya by the Russians; imposition of a particular form of government, as in Indonesia's rule of East Timor

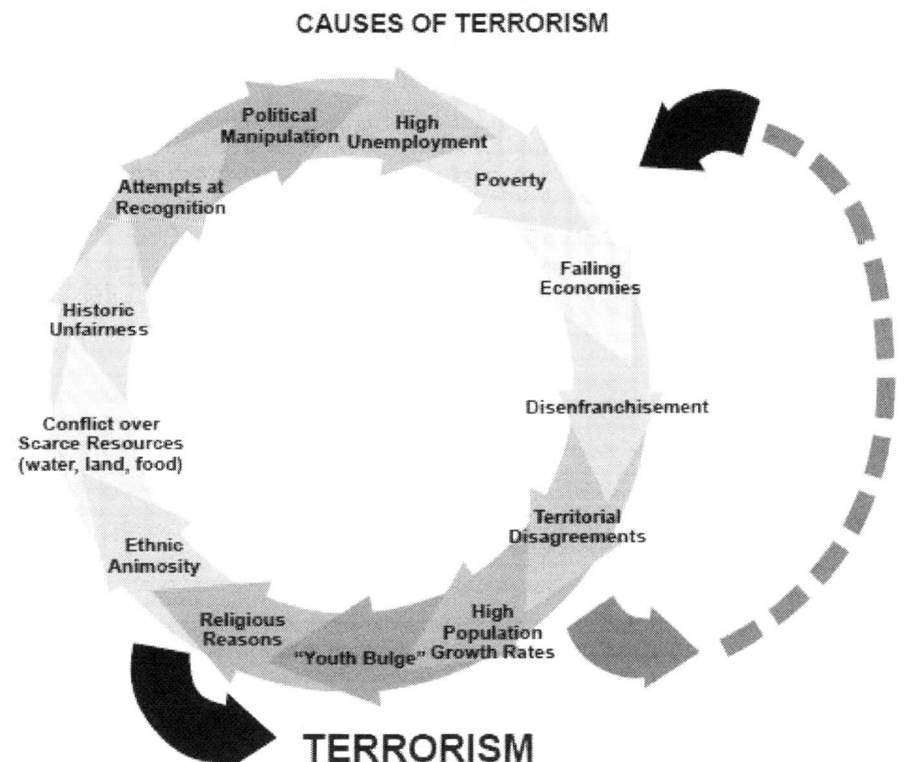

until it gained independence; and opposition to a domestic government or occupying army, such as the U.S. military presence in Iraq and Afghanistan.

> **Questions to Consider**
>
> 1. What do you think is the greatest threat in your country today? Explain.

HUMAN EXPRESSIONS: CULTURAL CURRENTS

Cultural currents reflect rapid economic and technological changes. When we look at these changes from a holistic perspective, the economy and technology have been the two driving variables in catalyzing gut-wrenching changes in the Global Wave that are simultaneously felt around the world.

Communication

Accompanying the sophistication and expansion of computer technology in the Global Wave is the availability of an overwhelming amount of information. Technological and economic developments have outpaced our cultural and social responses, often leaving us confused about how to make sense of this overwhelming influx of information. Intense debates rage among diverse religious, civic, environmental, and other concerned groups about the future; some are problematic as the dialogue descends into acts of incivility. Others see the debates as a reaction to complex changes and anxiety brought about by rapid technological and economic developments and future uncertainty.

One key change in communication is the deemphasizing of face-to-face, interpersonal communication. Technological devices—smart cell phones, texting, email, Twitter, Facebook, and on-line courses—erase the boundaries of time and space that had previously slowed and restricted communication by fostering instant communication with anyone in the world. These forms of communication connect people removed from their social and physical environment, but also separate interactions from the social spaces in which people physically exist. In this way, technological forms of communication contribute to the annihilation of the public space which had connected people with one another. For example, a huge trend in education is on-line or distance learning courses, in which students do not attend a traditional classroom but complete the subject material on the computer through an on-line program. The direct, inter-personal exchange between students and instructor is eliminated and displaced by on-line communication.[104] Our attention is no longer directed only to those within the confines of our physical space but beyond it. We are isolated islands in the public sphere, separated from others through our technological wonders.

> **Questions to Consider**
>
> 1. What do you think about the quality of conversation/discussion that social networks encourage? Have we lost anything in interpersonal communication?

Identity and Belonging

Our sense of identity and belonging depends a great deal on our particular worldview. **Identity** describes an individual's understanding of him or herself as a distinct separate entity. An individual identifies with a particular ethnicity, nation, gender, worldview, among others. Fundamentalists derive their sense of identity and belonging from their family, their religion, and the cultural values upheld by the group. Patriotism and a deep national identification connect people holding a modern worldview and they would sacrifice themselves to preserve the "freedoms" or values of their cherished nation. Those adhering to a transformative worldview, as described more fully below, believe in a local and global identity or "glocal." Those holding a globalized worldview have a sense of identity and belonging connected with consumer brands and lifestyle identification.

Aesthetic Expression

Aesthetic expression also varies according to an individual's particular worldview. I will primarily describe aesthetic developments in the transformative and globalized worldviews.

Art, music, entertainment, and literature in a globalized worldview often follow a commercial bent. Mass produced shows featuring a renowned celebrity can command premium prices for star-packed spectacles. Entertainment can range from celebrity singers to Broadway musicals and plays, comedians, musicians, and stage acts. All have in common a hefty price that globalized viewers are willing to pay. Dazzling sets and astonishing effects provide manufactured excitement. In the art world, sophisticated buyers with fistfuls of cash are intent upon purchasing authentic and unique art pieces that distinguish them as connoisseurs of fine art. Many are collectors of one of a kind memorabilia ranging from old movie posters to out-of-print books, rare coins, Superman comics, or antique furniture. Undoubtedly the collections bring pleasure to the collectors, but collecting still involves commodification of items and attaching monetary value to the items. Critics of the commercialized entertainment industry maintain that there is no interaction between the performer and the audience. Instead the audience merely observes the performance and responds through admiring applause. The entertainer then packs up the show to present the exact same performance in another locale in a franchise-like duplication of artistic services. The result is a "McDonaldization" of the entertainment industry.

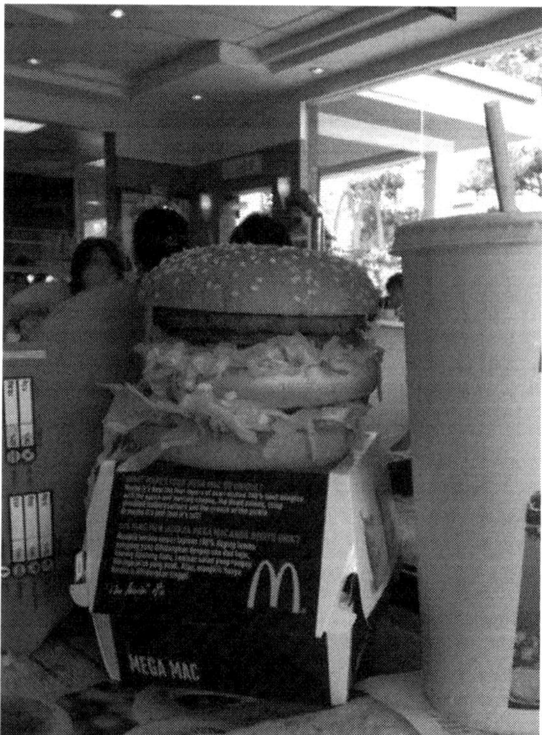

McDonaldization (bigger) of McDonalds' burger, coke, and fries in Malaysia.

Aesthetic expression in a transformative worldview differs from the globalized worldview. In many instances, the distance between the observer/observed or entertainer/entertained is reduced or eliminated. A person does not go to a concert and sit passively as the observer but may participate in the musical production. Or a dancer might participate in the dancing. The professional qualities that make certain artists celebrities are blurred and the boundaries between the performer and audience fall away. A small, neighborhood performance-theater featured audience participation as they followed sing-a-long tunes reminiscent of the 1960s "Sing-a-Long with Mitch" television show. The audience was the performer. Another example is the self-publishing book industry, which has recently skyrocketed. The big publishing houses no longer dictate what will be available to the book-buying public. Instead, individual authors can "self-publish" their own books, freed of restrictions imposed by corporate publishing entities.

Questions to Consider

1. What are the more positive aspects of technology? Do the web, blogging, Facebook, YouTube, and Twitter democratize information? Explain.

Religion/Spirituality

Religious and spiritual connections have changed in the Global Wave. Once again, our worldview shapes this choice. For example, fundamentalism has surged during the past several decades. Social commentator Mary Clark states, "A too rapid rate of change can alienate people and destroy social cohesion. This is why violent ideological revolutions so often fall back into the old social patterns they supposedly displaced."[105] Many people encounter considerable uncertainty and insecurity in their lives, from precarious jobs, expensive health care, and disappearing pensions to displacement of family location and community fragmentation. Fundamentalism represents a return to certainty, traditional values, exact morals, religious certitude, and a strong family connection that gives stability and meaning to one's life.

There is a growing awareness of the common moral foundations of different universal religions—Christianity, Judaism, Islam, Hinduism, Buddhism, Daoism, Confucianism, and others. For example, religious scholars such as Karen Armstrong, say that compassion is a common theme in all universal religions. Along with the universal religions, there is a revival of pagan rituals and goddess worship, an embrace of New Age spirituality, a renewal of Earth-based spirituality, such as found in indigenous traditions, and a devotion to the mystical traditions of universal religions, such as Sufism in Islam. Some critics argue that religion means more to people at the beginning of the 21st century than in the 1970s.[106]

Even though there are many people in the U.S. who claim a religious affiliation, many critics still contend that a spiritual malaise permeates American society. This spiritual malaise may have to do with the absorption of many religious leaders and their flocks into the consumer ethos. Although the values and attitudes of consumerism are anathema to most religious values, somehow the internal contradiction seems to go unnoticed at best or purposely ignored at worst. For example, many preachers, including the bestselling author Joel Osteen, preach and write about the "prosperity gospel." It also resonates at some Evangelical Protestant churches in South Korea. The teaching is basically that if a person deeply holds religious beliefs, material prosperity will unfold. If prosperity does not materialize, then perhaps something is wrong with the individual's devotion to God. This doctrine holds that financial prosperity and success in business and personal life are external evidence of God's favor. The failure of many religious leaders to speak out about the destructive and pervasive consumer society that is poised to take religion asunder is disheartening. Religious justification of the rampant greed and selfishness of a society awash in the consumer ethos does not bode well for the moral reputation of religious leaders.

Worldview/Beliefs

Five different worldviews shape the attitudes and beliefs of millions of Americans. Below are further remarks on the globalized and transformative worldviews.

A Globalized View

The most well-established, mainstream ideology in the U.S. and many parts of the world (including China) is that of the globalized view. The universalization and homogenization of a commodified and commercialized globalized culture has expanded along with economic globalization since the 1980s. This globalized culture is increasingly being accepted and replicated among many in the Global Wave, with businesses encouraging consumerism as an embodiment of universal culture. For example, over 500,000 foreign students attend American universities. This education and socialization process enfolds foreign students into a globalized culture, which many enthusiastically embrace and take back with them to their country of origin. Millions of middle class Chinese and Indians enthusiastically purchase cars and other material goods that traditionally are associated with the West. Also, the ubiquitous satellite dishes perched on roofs around the world beam commercially laden television programs direct from Hollywood and Seoul, South Korea to the homes of billions around the world. Television programs implicitly extol the values of the globalized worldview in their programming selections and blatant commercialism.

A Transformative View

A challenge today and in the future is how to accommodate diverse opinions without losing social and national cohesiveness. There is a need to reduce the rigid dogma of fundamentalism without losing the sense of shared meaning and purpose that traditional religion offers. There is a need to embrace the technological wonders of the globalized worldview that connect people throughout the world, yet reject the rampant consumerism and social divide that economic globalization fosters. There is a need to counter the pessimism, obscurity, elitism, uninspiring and fragmenting effects of postmodern thought without losing the ability to probe below surface meanings. What worldview will emerge to replace the shattered worldviews that have failed to provide a framework that will enable us to address vast global problems?

A new perspective has been emerging in the Global Wave. Although still a minority view, what I have called the transformative worldview offers an alternative to the prevailing globalized, modern, and fundamentalist worldviews. After much research and reflection, I find this perspective offers the best hope for future well-being and planetary sustainability. The transformative worldview is a diverse, worldwide movement in which millions of people are reassessing the values of the other worldviews in order to find a more compassionate, community-focused value system. Although it is beyond the scope of this chapter to expand upon all the facets of the transformative worldview, I have organized 10 aspects that characterize the emerging transformative worldview in the U.S. and across the world.

The Transformative Worldview: 10 Characteristics

1. **Interdependent Ideals** rather than greed, aggression, independence, and segmentation. New ideals are emerging: interdependence, cooperation, community, connections, support, and altruism. Other descriptors include simultaneity, uncertainty, relationship, networks, webs, integration, and diversity.

2. **Community-Focused Social Values** come from contemporary culture, from ancient traditions, and from our own imaginations. We can learn to draw upon the wisdom of our elders and their experiential insights. Also, intense individualism is a learned, aggressive behavior, historically created and promoted by Western society, especially the U.S. A shift to a worldview emphasizing greater cooperative, supportive, and life-enhancing attributes is a viable alternative. Clark notes: "We urgently need to reinstate feelings of relatedness and community into our social vision."[107]

3. **Natural Capitalism** places priority on the

well-being and sustainability of the Earth. It includes socially responsible investing, social entrepreneurship, micro-credit banking, community development, local businesses, self-managed worker-run enterprises, cooperatives, non-profit organizations, and more. Since the 2008 financial crisis, there is a renewed call for governmental oversight of financial markets, a cap on excessive executive compensation, and break up of large corporate holdings.

4. **Ecological Awareness** has awakened our insight into the interdependence of everything in nature, where every event has an effect on everything else. Humans are part of the mystery of the Universe and not isolated, separate, superior entities. With this awareness comes the desire to repair environmental damage and halt its further destruction. For example, ecological tourism is an option for many travelers.

5. **Renewable Energy** in the form of wind and solar energy is important in countering the dire effects of climate change. The devastation caused by a fossil fuel-dependent lifestyle has galvanized world citizens to start shifting from oil and coal dependence. Many citizens are rethinking their car-dependent city configurations and urban sprawl to include more energy efficient modes of public transportation and urban revitalization. Also, the alienating nature of suburbs has sparked some people to consider more community-focused neighborhoods that reduce commuting time and conserve valuable suburban land for agriculture and biodiversity.

6. **Peace and Justice Movements** have experienced renewed vigor with world-wide communication that connect millions of people instantly. Among a few of the many causes and issues advocated by this diverse and widespread movement include democratic reforms, peace efforts, nuclear disarmament, population control, human rights, animal rights, LGBT rights, environmental issues, educational reforms, equality, indigenous people's rights, women's and children's issues, and others.

7. **Sustainable Agriculture** that also includes local and organic farming is an alternative to industrial agricultural that is no longer able to meet the world's food needs. Along with its enormous demands for irrigation water, its chemical inputs deplete the fertility of the soil and its fossil fuel dependency contributes to climate change. Organic farming has expanded significantly in the last several years and connects what one eats to how one lives. It also considers the person charged with spraying destructive chemicals on foods and the considerable harm done to his/her health.

Sustainable agriculture in Vincente Guerrero Mexico. Photo by Denise Ames

8. **Holistic Health** offers alternatives to Western medicine that is often dominated by a for-profit pharmaceutical industry. It encourages health and well-being and a way to cure diseases ranging from cancer to heart disease. Organizations such as the Slow Food Movement encourage us to enjoy moderate portions of healthy, nutritious organic foods that give us sustenance, instead of the mass-produced foods that contribute to our chronic health and obesity woes.

9. **Spirituality** has alternative practices that depart from traditional religious practices. Many traditional religions have adjusted their services to accommodate the desire expressed by many people for more connected and personal spiritual experiences rather than rote adherence to prescribed creeds and rituals. Many women have resurrected feminist spirituality that connects them with the sacred feminine and goddess that they

claim male-dominated universal religions have suppressed. The field of ecopsychology, connecting psychology and ecology, and integrates the human psyche with the Earth.

10. **Holistic Education**. Some people who promote a transformative worldview believe that education is the key to ushering in alternative changes. Holistic educational practices encourage multi-culturalism, open-mindedness and diversity, inquiry-based learning, activities to connect with our multiple intelligences, a global perspective, and a holistic world history!

Insights: Learning from the Past

Cultural Currents

The Global Wave poses a huge challenge for us. The challenges have been discussed in this chapter: environmental degradation, a huge socio-economic gap, unchecked individualism, a political system out of touch with reality, and a worldview unable to deal with future challenges. Our innate behaviors and historical experiences have not prepared us well for the urgency of the global issues that confront us; we do not have a firm track record that we can draw on. Our innate behaviors as a species have equipped us to deal with a threat such as a marauding lion or the needs of our immediate 25 member group, but now we must deal with the threat of planet-wide environmental devastation and the needs of our immediate 7+ billion member group!

We often turn to our political or religious leaders as potential saviors. However, they are also overwhelmed with the issues. Our political leaders in the U.S. are adept (somewhat) at dealing with isolated problems in a legally, deliberative, cumbersome way with built in mechanisms to stymie impulsive actions. But they have failed to provide a vision of where we need to head and what we need to do. With their enslavement to corporations for their campaign donations and their intransigent bi-partisanship, many politicians are unable to provide the leadership so desperately needed. Some of our religious leaders have also failed us, although many are working hard to bring about change. Many religious people have scoffed, for example, at the idea of climate change, although some evangelical leaders are now alarmed that we humans are contaminating God's creation and are calling for action. Other religious people continue to disbelieve the hard scientific findings.

Our faith in and reliance on technology can perhaps help us deal with some of the urgent issues. As we have found in world history, one thing that we humans are really good at is making things. Sometimes we don't think of the repercussions of our tool-making creations; the atomic and nuclear bombs come to mind as inventions that have few, if any, redeeming qualities. But many inventions have definitely been beneficial—the Internet has certainly benefited me. Many new innovations are underway to help "clean-up" the environment and bring more energy efficiency to our way of life today. Perhaps technology will provide the tools we need to save ourselves, but not without the vision to tell us how to use them.

The modern and globalized worldviews, the dominant views currently, are incapable of addressing the challenges we face. In fact, they exacerbate the problems! Paradoxically, the competitive individualistic behaviors that served us in the Modern Wave are the opposite behaviors we need to deal with problems such as environmental catastrophe. This problem requires collective action, long-term commitment, giving up our addiction to immediate gratification, and cooperation among diverse people. The reward, saving our planet for future generations, is well worth any sacrifices we may have to make. Unfortunately, that goal seems too remote and disconnected from the everyday lives of many people. For them, the transition to a new way of thinking and acting is difficult to make. But many others are inspired to make the world livable for our children and grandchildren. Although we eagerly install fluorescent light bulbs or turn off our computers at night, deep structural, systemic changes are difficult to accomplish on our own. Our whole worldview is embedded in the way society is structured; it is hard to make the leap to another worldview. Writers have written of a "tipping point," where things quickly make a dramatic shift to something different. The signals that we need to shift to a different worldview are becoming ever more readily apparent. The leap to a transformative worldview is ever more urgent.

Questions to Consider

1. What worldview do you most closely identify with? Why?

Insights: Learning from the Past

THE GLOBAL WAVE: CONCLUDING INSIGHTS

We must create a different worldview that can enable us to avert environmental collapse and deal with the myriad of issues facing us today and in the near future. That is why I have written this holistic world history from a transformative worldview perspective. I firmly believe that transformation is necessary to help us make the shift to a new way of thinking that will move us into a new and more productive, relationship with each other and our world.

One step in formulating and expanding a transformative worldview is one that you have just accomplished: to re-imagine our past and see it through a holistic lens. By imagining, writing, communicating, teaching, and thinking about the past as a holistic and interdependent system, we can put into action new ways of thinking to help shape a sustainable, life-enhancing future in which all people have a crucial stake. The ability to think critically, comparatively, globally and holistically helps us actively engage in the process of change. Identifying commonalities that link all humans together into an interdependent web affirms our shared humanity. Through the study of a holistic world history, alternative social myths emerge from which we can develop our visions of a shared future. Clark notes, "The study of history is to our civic self-image what theology is to religious faith—a means for redefining our worldview."[108] Embracing a comparative, holistic, interdependent historical imagination will help us to analyze our own culture by comparing and linking it to alternatives. It is my intent and hope that with this holistic world history, a step has been taken towards developing a new consciousness based on a holistic, transformative worldview. We can make that leap!

ENDNOTES

1. Lester Brown, *World on the Edge: How to Prevent Environmental and Economic Collapse* (New York: W.W. Norton & Company, 2011) 78.
2. "Why Population Matters," *World Overpopulation Awareness* (Sept.10, 2007). *www.overpopulation.org/* and Michele L. Swartz and Jessica Notini, "Desertification and Migration in Mexico and the U.S.," *US Commission on Migration* (2000) 7.
3. Donella and Dennis Meadows, Jorgen Randers, *Limits to Growth: the Thirty Year Update* (White Rive Junction, VT: Chelsea Green Publishing, 2004) 75.
4. Clive Ponting, *A Green History of the World* (New York: Penguin Books, 1991) 257-258 and "Deforestation," *Earth Observatory/NASA. www.earthobservatory.nasa.gov/Library/Deforestation/*
5. "Deforestation," *Earth Observatory/NASA.*
6. Mark A. Sircus, "Water: The World is Facing a Dire Shortage," *Natural News.com* (May 20, 2008). *http://www.naturalnews.com/023267.html*
7. David Simm, "World War Day 2015 Report," *IB Times* (March 2015), ret. 6/15/15. *http://www.ibtimes.co.uk*
8. Simm, "World War Day."
9. Tony Clarke and Maude Barlowe, "The Battle for Water," *Yes Magazine* (Winter, 2004) 1. *http://www.futurenet.org/article.asp?id=669*
10. Clarke and Barlowe, "Battle for Water," *Yes*, 1.
11. Katherine Boehner, "This Is How Much Water It Takes To Make Your Favorite Foods," *Huffington Post* (Oct. 10, 2013), ret. 6/15/15. *http://www.huffingtonpost.com/2014/10/13/food-water-footprint_n_5952862.html*
12. Lester Brown, "As Countries Over-Pump Aquifers, Falling Water Tables Mean Falling Harvests," *Business and Corporate Responsibility* (June 18, 2008), ret. 6/16/15. *http://www.treehugger.com/corporate-responsibility/as-countries-over-pump-aquifers-falling-water-tables-mean-falling-harvests.html*
13. Adam Nagourney, Jack Healy, and Nelson D. Schwartz, "California Drought Tests History of Endless Growth," *New York Times* (Apr. 4, 2015). *http://www.nytimes.com/2015/04/05/us/california-drought-tests-history-of-endless-growth.html?_r=0*
14. "Food and Agriculture Organization United Nations Report," *Age* (Mar. 22, 2007).
15. Lester Brown, "Water Deficits Growing in Many Countries," *Earth Policy Institute* (Aug. 6, 2002). *http://www.earth-policy.org/*
16. "Landmark Climate Report: Clock is Ticking," *The Associated Press* (Feb. 2, 2007). *http://www.msnbc.msn.com/id/16904988/*
17. Environmental Fact Sheet, *Environmental and Energy Study Institute* (2015), ret. 6/16/15. *www.eesi.org/publications.*
18. "Why Population Matters," *World Overpopulation Awareness* (Sept. 10, 2007). *www.overpopulation.org/* and Anders Levermann, et.al., "The Multimillennial Sea-Level Commitment of Global Warming," *PNAS* (June 13, 2013). *http://www.pnas.org/content/110/34/13745.abstract?sid=26fd1d37-7276-46e2-9192-0931e6ebf6ab*
19. Ian Sample, "Global food crisis looms as climate change and population growth strip fertile land," *The Guardian* (Aug. 31, 2007), ret. 7/23/08. *http://www.theguardian.com/environment/2007/aug/31/climatechange.food*
20. "Dirt Poor: Have Fruits and Vegetables Become Less Nutritious?" *Scientific American* (Apr. 27, 2011). *http://www.scientificamerican.com/article/soil-depletion-and-nutrition-loss/*
21. Meadows & Rander, *Limits to Growth*, 57 and 61. (1950 and 2000 world grain production more than tripled, from around 590 to more than 2000 million metric tons per year).
22. Julie Wilson, "Organic farming thrives in India as growers revert back to traditional methods," *Natural News* (June 7, 2015), ret. 6/19/15. *http://www.naturalnews.com/049993_organic_farming_India_traditional_agriculture.html#ixzz3d8lJrsyk*
23. Meadows & Rander, *Limits to Growth*, 1 and 3.

24. "Living Planet Report," *World Wildlife Foundation* (Oct. 24, 2006).
25. *The Columbus Dispatch*, Columbus, Ohio (Feb. 20, 2007).
26. Meadows & Rander, *Limits to Growth*, 174-176 and list of symptoms.
27. *Belfast Telegraph*, Belfast Ireland (June 27, 2007) and Meadows & Rander, *Limits to Growth*, 177.
28. *http://www.poodwaddle.com/worldclock.swf*, and other interesting facts.
29. United Nations figures from *Optimum Population Trust* (Mar. 13, 2007).
30. *United Nations News*, (Mar. 19, 2007), reported in *World Overpopulation Awareness. www.overpopulation.org/*
31. *Christian Science Monitor* (Oct. 10, 2006).
32. *Belfast Telegraph*.
33. Elizabeth Kolbert, *The Sixth Extinction: An Unnatural History* (New York: Picador, 2014).
34. "Species Extinction," *Rainforest Action Network* (2004). *http://www.rainforestweb.org/*
35. "Species Extinction," *Rainforest Action Network*.
36. "Genuine Progress Indicator," *Redefining Progress. http://www.rprogress.org/sustainability_indicators/genuine_progress_indicator.htm*
37. *World English Dictionary. http://dictionary.reference.com/browse/neoliberalism*
38. Richard Robbins, *Global Problems and the Culture of Capitalism* (Allyn and Bacon, 1999) 100.
39. "Privatization in Mexico: Telemex," *50 Years is Enough. http://www.50years.org/factsheets/telmex.html* and Matthew DiLallo, *Motley Fool* (June 20, 2015), ret, 6/23/15. *http://www.fool.com/investing/general/2015/06/20/who-is-the-richest-man-in-the-world.aspx*
40. Ian Bremmer, *The End of the Free Market: Who Wins the War Between States and Corporations?* (New York: Portfolio, 2010) 33 and 40.
41. Bremmer, *End of the Free Market*, cover jacket.
42. Bremmer, *Free Market*, 21 and 42.
43. Bremmer, *Free Market*, 20-21.
44. Andrew Soergel, "Asian Infrastructure Bank," *U.S. News* (June 20, 2015), ret. 6/23/15. *http://www.usnews.com/news/articles/2015/06/10/asian-infrastructure-investment-bank-chinas-answer-to-western-marginalization*
45. Index Mundi, ret. Feb. 2010. *http://indexmundi.com/iran/unemployment_rate.html*
46. Walden Bello, "The Global Financial System in Crisis," *Speech at People's Development Forum*, University of the Philippines (Mar. 25, 2008). *http://www.waldenbello.org/index2.php?option=com_content&task=view&id=86&pop=1&page*
47. Walden Bello, "A Primer on the Wall Street Meltdown," *Focus on the Global South* (2008). *http://www.waldenbello.org/index2.php?option=com_content&task=view&id=98&pop=1&page*
48. ranking information found at website: *http://www2.le.ac.uk/ebulletin/news/press-releases/2000-2009/2006/07/nparticle.2006-07-28.2448323827*
49. Samir Amin, *Capitalism in the Age of Globalization* (London: Zed Books Limited, 1997) 3-5. Amin listed 5 monopolies; I have expanded it to 6 and elaborated on them.
50. James Gustave Speth, *The Bridge at the Edge of the World: Capitalism, the Environment, and Crossing from Crisis to Sustainability* (New Haven: Yale University Press, 2008), 161 and "Consumerism," *Wikipedia. http://en.wikipedia.org/wiki/Consumerism*
51. Madeline Levine, "Challenging the Culture of Affluence," *Independent School* (2007) 28-36. *http://www.nais.org/publications/ismagazinearticle.cfm?ItemNumber=150274*
52. Barber, Benjamin R., *Consumed: How Markets Corrupt Children, Infantilize Adults, and Swallow Citizens Whole* (New York: Norton & Co., 2007).
53. Barber, *Consumed*, 167.
54. Robert Costanza, "Toward a new Sustainable Economy," *Real World Economics Review* (Mar. 26, 2009) 1, in *Common Dreams.org. www.commondreams.org/print/40015*

55. Speth, *The Bridge*, 121 and 59-60.
56. Paul Samuelson as cited in Robert M. Collins. *More: The Politics of Economic Growth in Postwar America* (Oxford: University Press, 2000) 229.
57. Speth, *Bridge*, 46-47.
58. Collins, *More*, 21.
59. Collins, *More*, 23.
60. Robbins, *Global Problems*, 1.
61. Meadows & Rander, *Limits to Growth*, 6.
62. Andrew Simms, Victoria Johnson, and Peter Chowla, "Growth Isn't Possible: Why Rich Countries Need a New Economic Direction," *New Economics Foundation* (2010). *http://www.neweconomics.org/sites/neweconomics.org/files/Growth_Isnt_Possible.pdf.*
63. Meadows & Rander, *Limits to Growth*, 27, 41, and 42.
64. Rajesh Makwana, "The Follies of Growth and Climate Denial," *Share the World's Resources* in *Common Dreams. www.commondreams.org/print/56760*
65. Martin Carnoy, Manuel Castells, Stephen S. Cohen, Fernando Henrique Carduso. *The New Global Economy in the Information Age: Reflections on our Changing World* (University Park, PA: The Pennsylvania State University Press, 1993). 1-3 and 5-6; and Michael Perelman, *Class Warfare in the Information Age* (New York: St. Martin's Press, 1998) 16.
66. "Uber May be Worth $50 billion. Really?" *CNN Money*, (July 8, 2015), ret. 7/8/15. *http://money.cnn.com/2015/05/11/investing/uber-50-billion-valuation/index.html*
67. Jeffry A. Frieden, *Global Capitalism: Its Fall and Rise in the Twentieth Century* (New York: W.W. Norton, 2006) 110.
68. Nayan Chanda, *Bound Together: How Traders, Preachers, Adventurers, and Warriors Shaped Globalization* (New Haven: Yale University Press, 2007) 290.
69. Alejandro Reuss, "Do Lower Tax Rates Really Increase Government Revenue?" *Dollars & Sense* (June 2011) 2. *http://www.dollarsandsense.org/ archives/2011/0611reuss.html*
70. Robert Reich, "How to End the Great Recession," *New York Times* (Sept. 2, 2010). *http://www.nytimes.com/2010/09/03/opinion/03reich.html?r=1&emc+eta1&pagewanted=print*
71. James M. Cypher, "Nearly $2 Trillion Purloined from U.S. Workers in 2009," *Dollars & Sense* (July/Aug. 2011). *http://www.dollarsandsense.org/archives/2011/0711cypher.html Cypher.*
72. Robert Kuttner, *The Squandering of America: How the Failure of Our Politics Undermines our Prosperity* (New York: Alfred A. Knopf, 2007) 21 and 76.
73. "Economics," *About.com. http://economics.about.com/od/economicsglossary/g/stolper.htm* and Thomas Palley, "Labor Threat," *Tom Paine* (Oct, 4, 2005) 1. *www.zmag.org/content/print_articles.cfm?itemID=8867§ion ID=1*
74. Palley, "Labor Threat," *Tom Paine*, 1.
75. Samuelson quoted in Palley, "Labor Threat," *Tom Paine*, 2.
76. Chanda, *Bound Together*, 294.
77. Wendell Berry, "Decolonizing Rural America," *Audubon* (Vol. 95, No. 2, March-April, 1993), 105.
78. Peter F. Drucker, *Post-Capitalist Societies*, (New York: Harper Collins Publishers, 1993) 153-155.
79. Meadows & Rander, *Limits to Growth*, 41-42.
80. Meadows & Rander, *Limits to Growth*, 44-45.
81. Don Peck, "Can the Middle Class be Saved," *The Atlantic* (Sept. 2011) 63. *http://www.theatlantic.com/magazine/print/2011/09/can-the-middle-class-be-saved/8600*
82. Joseph E. Stiglitz, *Freefall: America, Free Markets, and the Sinking of the World Economy* (New York: W.W. Norton & Co., 2010) 191.
83. Nouriel Roubini and Stephen Mihm, *Crisis Economics: A Crash Course in the Future of Finance* (New York: Penguin Press, 2010) 299.
84. Mai Ling, "Housing," *MSN Real Estate* (Oct. 14, 2010). *http://realestate.msn.com/blogs/listed-blogpost.aspx?post=1816304>1=35006*

85. "Globalization and Inequality," *Business Maps of India.*
86. Sam Pizzigati, "Mapping Global Wealth," report from Credit Suisse, *OtherWords* (Sept, 2011). *http://www.otherwords.org/articles/mapping_global_wealth*
87. Chrystia Freeland, The Rise of the New Global Elite," *Atlantic Magazine* (Jan./Feb., 2011). *http://www.theatlantic.com/magazine/print/2011/01/the-rise-of-the-new-global-elite/8343/*
88. Joseph E. Stiglitz, "Of the 1%, for the 1%, by the 1%," *Vanity Fair* (May 2011). *http://www.vanityfair.com/society/features/2011/05/top-one-percent-201105*
89. Jon Jeter, *Flat Broke in the Free Market* (New York: W.W. Norton & Co., 2009) xiii.
90. Pizzigati, "Mapping Global Wealth," *OtherWords.*
91. Pizzigati, "Mapping Global Wealth," *OtherWords.*
92. Jeter, *Flat Broke*, xiii.
93. Shachua Chen, et.al. "A Dollar a Day Revised" *World Bank* (Aug. 2008).
94. "Globalization and Inequality," *Business Maps of India.*
95. Pizzigati, "Mapping Global Wealth," *OtherWords.*
96. Jeter, *Flat Broke*, xii.
97. Jeter, *Flat Broke*, xii-xiii.
98. Jeter, *Flat Broke*, xii.
99. Rajesh Makwana, "The Follies of Growth and Climate Denial," *Share the World's Resources* (June 2, 2010). *http://www.stwr.org/climate-change-environment/the-follies-of-growth-and-climate-denial.html*
100. Simms, Johnson, and Chowla, "Growth Isn't Possible," *New Economic Foundation.*
101. Farouk Mawlawi, "New Conflicts, New Challenges: The Evolving Role for Non-Governmental Actors," *Journal of International Affairs* (Winter, 1993), 392.
102. Robert Jervis, "The Future of World Politics: Will it Resemble the Past?" *International Security* (Vol. 16, No. 3, Winter, 1991) 50.
103. Jeffrey Record, "Bounding the Global War on Terrorism," *U.S. Army War College* (Dec. 1, 2003).
104. Barber, *Consumed*, 102.
105. Clark, Mary E., *Ariadne's Thread: The Search for New Modes of Thinking* (New York: St. Martin's Press, 1989) 473.
106. Norman F. Kantor, *The American Century: Varieties of Culture in Modern Times* (New York: Harper Perennial, 1997) 510.
107. Clark, *Ariadne's Thread*, 490-492.
108. Clark, *Ariadne's Thread*, 497.

WORLD HISTORY GLOSSARY

The terms below are those highlighted in the book.
For an expanded glossary, which includes many other terms related to world history, go to www.global-awareness.org/worldhistory and look for the bibliography link.

absolute monarchy strong, authoritative monarchs who ruled with little oversight or limit imposed by other bodies of government. (7)

achieved status based on criterion such as wealth, hereditary, and special abilities, is primarily found in stratified societies. Rules of succession are attached to status and it is also a method for maintaining social order. (3)

abimsa Hindu belief and practice of non-violence toward all living things. (6)

ambush a long-used military tactic in which ambushers strike their enemies from concealed positions such as behind dense underbrush or hidden by hilltops. The purpose is to launch a surprise attack. (5)

American Revolution pitted the independent-minded American colony, what would become the United States, against her British colonial masters in 1776. Inspired by Enlightenment political ideas. Won a battlefield victory against the British in 1781. Passed the constitution with more centralized government in 1787, which is still in place today, provided for a separation of powers between three branches of government: judicial, legislative, and executive. In 1789 ten amendments, Bill of Rights, added to the Constitution. (7)

ancestral spirits or souls of ancestors are active spirits from the past that influence present life and remain interested and involved in affairs of their descendants. They provide a sense of continuity with the past, present, and future.(3)

animism the belief that everything in nature—humans, animals, plants, ornaments, weapons, rocks, rivers, woods, and mountains—contains personified, animated, conscious spirits or souls. (3, 4)

apartheid a legal and institutional segregation of blacks and whites in the Union of South Africa. This system lasted until the election of Nelson Mandela, an African president, in 1994. (7)

archaic Homo sapiens a term applied to hominids living between 400,000 years ago until the appearance of modern humans; these hominids were ancestors to both Homo sapiens sapiens and Neanderthals. (2)

archetypes are universal, collective, primordial images or concepts that, together with instincts, form the collective unconscious according to Carl Jung. Archetypes are not fully developed pictures in the mind, but can be compared to a photograph waiting to be developed by an individual's experiences. (3)

Aristotle (384-322 BCE), a leading Greek philosopher, a student of Plato, he was more interested in the meaning of life than politics and produced over 200 different written volumes. He was also a master of logic and argued, logically and rationally, for the concept of a single god. (6)

artisan a craft person. (5)

ascribed status social positions that one is assumed to occupy by virtue of the group into which one happens to be born – for instance, one's sex, age, kinship, or race. Ascribed status is found in both stratified societies and egalitarian societies. (3)

Asoka, King (r. 273-232 BCE), the most notable rulers of the Mauryan Empire in India and is considered to be one of India's greatest rulers. He conquered many territories but after one particular brutal battle he became a pacifist and turned his concerns to human suffering, a long-lasting tradition in Indian culture. (6)

asymmetric warfare between nations or groups that are uneven in their economic, political, and military power and development. (8)

attitude statements of preferences, likes, and dislikes; a subjective reaction to an experience expressed in positive or negative terms. (3)

Augustus Caesar (r. 27 BCE-14CE), first known as Octavian, first emperor of the Roman Empire, laid the social, economic, military, and political foundation for the empire. (6)

Australopithecus extinct hominid that walked erect and had humanlike teeth but apelike skull, jaw, and brain size. Evidence of species – *afarensis, africanus, robustus*, and *boisei* – has been found in Africa, when they lived from about 6 million to 1 million years ago. (2)

Avestas a compilation of texts based on teachings of a prophet named Zoroaster, an ancient Persia and founder of Zoroastrianism. (6)

Axial Age named by Karl Jaspers, a time period occupying most of the first millennium BCE, and especially during the centuries between 800--500 BCE, the emergence of universal religions or worldviews takes place during this age. (6)

Aztec nomadic people who invaded and conquered the short-lived Toltec civilization in central Mexico around 1300, and ruled for 200 years. Apparently part of a nomadic group, the *Mexica*. Founded their major city, Tenochtitlan, on the site of present-day Mexico City. (6)

band a small kinship group that usually numbers between 20 and 50 and rarely exceed 100 people, with no full-time government and economically based on a foraging, subsistence technology. (3, 4)

Bantu meaning people in many Bantu languages, is the label for over 400 ethnic groups stretching across sub-Saharan Africa. (6)

barter form of exchange of goods by trading that does not involve money, but some other token of value. (4)

Big Bang about 15 billion years ago an originating power, a singularity exploded into the Universe from a vacuum or void. Each and every thing in the Universe had its roots in this originating force. (2)

bipedalism upright walking on the two hind legs, as humans' habitual mode of locomotion. (2)

bilateral trade one-on-one, country-to-country agreements of trade. (8)

black holes thought to be a replication of the state of the Universe before the Big Bang. Believed to form when the core of a star cluster or the nucleus of a galaxy becomes unstable and collapses. They are the end states of very immense stars with masses equal to thousands, millions, or even billions of solar masses. (2)

Body of Civil Law compiled by Justinian, emperor of the Byzantine Empire, during his reign 527-565. This reinitiated the Roman legal tradition, which remained a legal standard in Europe well into the 19th century. (6)

Buddhism a universal religion, an offshoot of Hinduism, started with the birth of Siddhartha Gautama in northern India in 563-483 BCE. Buddha taught there were Four Noble Truths: first, all people suffer; second, people suffer because of their desires; third, they can end their suffering by eliminating desires; and fourth, to eliminate those desires, the Eightfold Path should be followed. (6)

Byzantine Empire (395-1453) refers to the eastern portion of the Roman Empire, which had been divided administratively in 395 from the western portion and continued until its collapse in 1453. The term is an invention by historians and was never used during at the time, but commonly used since the 19th century. Capital city was Constantinople. (6)

camping groups a primary kinship group consisted of closely related families, less permanent than nuclear families, they typically pastured all or part of the year together and lent support to each other. Range in number from ten to over 100 individuals. (6)

capitalism an economic system in which private parties make their goods and services available on a free market and seek to make a profit on their activities. Private parties, either individuals or companies, own the means of production --land, machinery, tools, equipment, buildings, workshops, and raw materials. Private parties decide what to produce. The center of the system is the free market in which business people compete, and the forces of supply and demand determine the prices received for goods and services. Businesses may realize profits from their endeavors, reinvest profits gained, or suffer losses. (7)

carrying capacity is the maximum number of individuals of a species that an area can support. Refers to the size of a population that can live indefinitely in an environment without doing that environment any harm. This applies to plants, animals and people. (3, 8)

cash crops such as coffee, tea, fruits, sugar, cotton, and others grown for the world market and price determined by supply and demand on the world commodity market. (7)

caste system found in India, are hierarchically organized, occupation-specific groups. The members of individual castes perform certain economic tasks and exchange their own production or services for those of other castes. They must also marry within their caste. (6)

centralized governments have strong, concentrated, formal authority that is located in a centralized center and wield considerable power, with a strong military and bureaucracy to back up that power. (6)

chief presiding political official of a chiefdom society or of a subdivision of a chiefdom society, who legal authority extends in at least some areas over members of families other than his or her own. (5)

chiefdom is a political unit of permanently allied tribes and villages under one recognized leader. (3, 5)

Christianity founded by Jesus of Nazareth. His disciples provided many details of his life and teachings in the four gospels that make up the New Testament of the Bible, the Christian's holy book. Jesus about the power of love and compassion, the greatest commandment was to love your neighbor as yourself. He proclaimed the poor as the salt of the earth. After Jesus' was crucified on the cross, Paul of Tarsus was instrumental in spreading Christianity's message to gentiles, or non-Jews, and helped make Christianity a universal religion. (6)

city-states consist of an independent city that has sovereignty over contiguous territory and serves as the center of the region's political, economic, and cultural life. (6)

civilization designates a loose configuration of peoples who share a common culture or political rule and usually form urban centers in which large populations live. It is characterized by a state government, large populations and economic specialists, social classes, draft labor and government-sponsored public works projects, markets and long distance trade, an increased emphasis on residence location over family ties in determining social roles and usually, urban centers, writing, and mathematics. (6)

Clean Election an alternative way to elect political candidates, who must collect a certain number of small qualifying contributions, some as little as five dollars, from registered voters. In return their campaigns are paid a flat sum by the government and the candidates agree not to raise money from private sources. Opponents not running as Clean Election candidates may outspend publicly financed candidates, who then may receive additional public matching funds. (8)

climate change takes place when the climate is altered during two different periods of time, with changes in average weather conditions as well as how much the weather varies around these averages. (8)

Cold War (1945-1989) between the Soviet Union and the United States was a story of confrontation between two contrasting ideologies that were both a product of the modern worldview. Unlike World War II, there was not direct conflict between the two super-powers and the Cold War did not escalate into an unlimited, total war; instead, conflict was conducted in proxy wars in many regions around the world including Korea, Guatemala, Vietnam, Afghanistan, Nicaragua, Cuba, Cambodia, and Chile. (7)

collective unconscious a concept developed by Carl Jung proposing that we inherit certain personality characteristics from our ancestors, including even our prehuman ancestry. The repository of these inherited psychic characteristics, which transcends cultures, individual differences, and is the cumulative experience we inherit from our ancestors. (3)

colonialism is the extension of a powerful country's control over a dependent, weaker country, territory, or people. Colonizers generally dominate the resources, labor, and markets of their colonial territory, and may also impose religious, socio-cultural, and linguistic structures on the native populations and intervene in their political affairs. (7)

Columbian Exchange the exchange of disease, plants, animals, and metals between the Western hemisphere and Europe after Columbus' initial contact with the Americas. (7)

commercial capitalism in the early modern era, production and trade in primary industries along with an increase in commercial agricultural productivity were the most dynamic sectors of the European economy creating wealth. (7)

commodification is the process of turning something with little or no economic value into a product or service that has a specific value or a higher monetary value. (8)

communism a system of social and political organization in which all economic and social activity is controlled by a totalitarian state dominated by a single and self-perpetuating political party. (7)

communist economy the state or government owns the means of production and "commands" or determines the supply, demand, and price of goods produced (contrast with capitalist economy). Emphasis on government planning and less response to supply and demand pressures. (7)

Confucius lived (551-470 BCE) established a social and moral philosophy for China that highlighted familial piety and correctness of social relationships. (6)

consciousness is a feature of the mind usually regarded to include traits such as subjectivity, self-awareness, sentience, the capacity to perceive the relationship connecting oneself and one's environment, and the ability to reflect upon these. (3, 4)

conservatives in the Modern Wave (1500s to 1900s) were monarchs, the landowning aristocracy, military elites, and church leaders who had a self-interest in continuing policies that supported tradition, stability, and obedience to political authority and organized religion. They were generally unfriendly toward revolution, liberal reform, individual rights, and representative government. In the 20th and 21st centuries conservatives tend to be the traditional religious people, businesspeople, and military. (7)

constitutional monarchy the monarchy is limited by the laws of a written constitution. (7)

continuity the persistence of cultural elements in a society. (1)

consumerism is a social and economic order that is based on the systematic creation and fostering of a desire to purchase goods or services in ever greater amounts. (8)

conventional thinking sometimes called traditional, linear or mechanistic thinking, seeing simple sequences of cause and effect that are limited in time and space, which assumes that cause and effect occur within a close time frame. (1)

core where early urban, modern, or global development takes place. An urban core is a city, or city-state at the center of a larger surrounding area called the periphery. A modern core is an industrialized center of wealth creation. A global core is where financial transactions and wealth creation is located. (6)

corporation a legalized form of economic organization. They extended their operations globally in order to gain cheap or hard-to-find raw materials and more markets. Commercial expansion required additional capital for investments in factories, ports, warehouses, and transportation networks. Considerable investment funds were raised for corporate formation through an expanding stock market, partnerships, financial institutions, speculation, and government programs. (7)

corvee labor extracted from peasants by rulers in the Urban Wave for the construction of monumental projects built by the state. (6)

cottage industries also called a "putting out" system. A merchant bought raw materials, most commonly wool and flax at the time, and "put them out" or sent them to rural workers, who spun the raw materials into yarn and then wove it into cloth on simple looms. The merchants collected the finished products from the textile workers, paid them according to a piecework wage, and then sold the cloth for a profit. Spinners and weavers worked in their own cottages where families—women, men, and children—all worked to supplement their family's agricultural income. The work was done in the rural countryside to bypass the regulations of the city's guilds. (7)

courage cultures physically strong males bound to each other through ties of kinship and personal loyalty. A premium was placed on personal honor, physical courage, and heroic deeds. (6)

creative destruction term coined by economist Joseph Schumpeter that applies to capitalism. Competition under capitalism brings technological and institutional creativity and increased productivity, creating a more comfortable standard of living for some. But technological innovations and economic expansion also demolish traditional institutions, and those who do not follow the capitalist precepts lose out. Capitalism destroys foraging and farming societies, their traditional cultures, stability in the periphery regions, and the ecosystem itself. (7)

culture system of learned behaviors, symbols, customs, beliefs, institutions, artifacts, and technology characteristic of a group, transmitted by its members to their offspring. The term culture often conveys an image of bounded entities that have distinct boundaries, for example one culture is considered distinct from another. But cultures are imagined constructs and do not have rigid boundaries. People living within these imagined boundaries do not have fixed identities; people change and identities reconfigure. Imagined cultural boundaries are porous, and ideas, goods, and other people easily flow in and out. The term culture is merely a tool for conveying a broad generalization, an idea, or abstraction. Using the term culture is analogous to using a map; the map is merely a tool and not the actual territory. (3)

Cyrus (r. 559-530 BCE), united various Persian tribes from central Asia and over the course of three decades established the Persian Empire as his armies conquered most of the Middle East by 525 BCE. (6)

customs informal norms that define desirable or acceptable behavior in a society or a subgroup within a society. (3)

Daoism (Taoism) the belief that people attain happiness and wisdom by seeking the dao, or mystical path, in all things. The yin and yang symbols represent the Daoist theory of harmony that can be found in following nature. Founded by Lao Tzu in China in 6th century BCE. (6)

Dao De Jing Lao Tzu's ideas were recorded by his followers. Believed that people attained happiness and wisdom by seeking the *dao*, or mystical path, in all things. (6)

Darwin, Charles applied Newton's mechanistic explanations to his theory of evolution, ranked as an important contributor to 19th century thought. Darwin's theory postulated material causation as the explanation for how life formed and evolved over time. Natural selection was the key. (7)

decentralized governments power is diffused and precarious, with a weak military and bureaucracy to back up that power. Often subordinate groups such as the nobility or warlords rival decentralized governments. (6)

deforestation is the conversion of forests to cropland and pasture for growing crops or raising livestock to meet the daily needs of burgeoning populations and selling for export. (8)

delay in feedback in systems thinking terms we are not yet in a situation where the stresses on the Earth have sent strong enough signals to force us to shrink our ecological footprint. Overshoot is possible because there are accumulated resource stocks that can be drawn down. (8)

Delhi Sultanate (1206-1526) refers to the many Muslim dynasties that ruled in India. (6)

democracy a type of political system in which sovereignty is vested in the people. Contrast with autocracy, oligarchy, and theocracy. It is often used to refer to a representative system in which the adult population is permitted at intervals to choose among a limited number of candidates for public office. (7)

desertification results from deforesting land and overstocking and overgrazing grasslands. (8)

development in holistic world history context means the common ways in which humans fashion their ways of living, interact with the environment, develop political, economic, and social systems, and create cultural and religious expressions. (1)

distribution the movement of resources or goods from where they are located or produced to where they are ultimately used. (3)

division of labor the rules, customs, or traditions that govern how the day-to-day work of life is divided among the holders of various statuses such as age and gender. (4)

domestic mode of production or domestic economy the reproductive, economic, and social behaviors that characterize life within the family or household. (5)

dowry money, goods, or estate that a wife brought to her husband in marriage. (6)

Eastern Orthodox Church official Christian church of the Byzantine Empire. A schism in Christianity in 1054 permanently divided it the from the Roman Catholic Church in the West. (6)

ecological footprint calculates the amount of land

required to supply needed resources (grain, food, water, wood, urban land, etc.) and the land required to absorb the resulting wastes (carbon dioxide, pollutants). (8)

economic globalization refers to the increasing expansion of the global economy around the world, integrating world economies into a world economic system. Even though countries may have different versions of capitalism, they still participate in the world economy. Trade, investment, business, capital, financial flows, production, management, markets, movement of labor (although somewhat restricted), information, competition, and technology are carried out across local and national boundaries on a world stage, subsuming many national and local economies into one integrated economic system. There is also a growing concentration of wealth and influence of multi-national corporations, sovereign wealth funds, and huge financial institutions. (1, 8)

economic growth is the process in which wealth increases over time as new value is added to goods and services in the economy. Growth is an essential component of the capitalist economic system, which must expand constantly to generate new wealth. (8)

economic system is a method by which people procure, distribute, and consume valued food, material goods, and services. An economic system includes subsistence methods that are related to the production of food and other needed goods, as well as the customs or rules that control what is done with these goods once they are produced and how they are utilized. (3)

ecosystem the interacting community of all the organisms in an area—including humans and the non-human world— and their physical environment. (3)

educational institutions formal organizations with the primary function of educating society's members into its specific worldview. For example, religious training is conducted for the purpose of inculcating the religious worldview. (3)

egalitarian is where everyone has equal access to food, to the technology needed to acquire resources, and to the paths leading to prestige. Societies in which there is little differentiation between groups, either by age, sex, or kinship. (3)

Eightfold Path teachings of the Buddha that include right view or knowing the truth, right intention or resisting evil, right speech or saying nothing to hurt others, right action or respecting life, right livelihood or working for the good of others, right effort or freeing the mind from evil, right mindfulness or controlling thoughts, and right concentration or practicing meditation. (6)

Einstein, Albert most influential scientist of the 20th century, developed theory of relativity. (7)

elite democracy in which elites manipulate the democratic process for their own self-interest and control. (8)

empires are states that expand beyond their city or provincial boundaries to encompass expansive territories and either politically, militarily, or economically control diverse people. Usually these territories are conquered by a centralized state military and annexed to the empire's center both politically and economically. (3, 6)

enclosure farms, as well as shared areas called "the commons," were converted to privately owned plots marked with clear boundaries and specific ownership. Efficiency and productivity became primary. (7)

Enlightenment a cultural movement that took place in 18th century Western Europe, particularly France, among educated elites who reasoned that scientific methods drawn from the natural sciences also applied to social and intellectual sciences. The key ingredients -- optimism and rationality -- distinguished Enlightenment thinking. (7)

ethnocentrism an example of an attitude in which an individual imagines his/her own particular culture is superior to others. (3)

evolutionary psychology a field of study that merges the disciplines of psychology and anthropology and helps explain individual and group commonalities. It is informed by our 2.5 million year history as hunters and gatherers. (3)

exchange refers to a common human pattern of giving and receiving valuable objects, commodities, and services. (3)

external areas that have not been incorporated into the core-and-periphery world system; they remain outside urban, modern, or global developments. (6)

externalizing costs when corporations transfer social, medical, and environmental costs to the general public instead of paying them from their profits. (8)

family is a basic and enduring form of human organization found in diverse domestic settings around the world. The particular family type is related to its social, historical, and environmental circumstances. Families provide such valuable functions as protecting a female during her long pregnancy and childcare years, and acculturating family members with the group's values, beliefs, and worldview. (3)

family, extended is a domestic group that includes various combinations of brothers, sisters, their spouses, nieces, nephews, aunts, uncles, grandparents, cousins, unmarried children, and others. (3)

family, nuclear generally includes a male/s, female/s, and dependent children, which, in turn, is part of a larger and more inclusive kinship group known as an extended family. (3)

farm wilds plants or animals in certain abundant regions were so dense that people were able to live in one place and intensely harvest the wild plants and animals as if they were domesticated. Their lifestyles were similar to farmers, and some have called them sedentary collectors. (4)

feedback process by which a change in one component in a system affects other components, which in turn bring about changes in the first component. (1)

feedback, balancing limits, restricts, and opposes change and keeps the system stable. Sometimes called negative feedback, it is neither good nor bad but merely means the system resists change. All systems have balancing feedback loops to stay stable so all systems have a goal, even if it is to remain as they are. (1)

feedback, reinforcing when changes in the whole system feeds back to amplify the original change. Change goes through the system producing more change in the same direction as the initial change. Reinforcing feedback drives a system in the way it is going. Reinforcing feedback is often referred to as positive feedback but this can be confusing since not all feedback is always positive or beneficial. (1)

feminist movement launched in mid 19th century US and Britain. Advocated for more rights for women, including right to vote, own property, and use birth control. Revived along with the civil rights movement in the 1960s and 1970s. (7)

feud hostility between kinship groups initiated by one group to avenge a wrong, usually the murder of one of its members by another group. Occur between kinship groups who live in the same or adjacent communities. (4, 5)

feudalism a system of obligations that bound lord and their subjects. In theory, the king owned all or most of the land and gave it to his leading nobles in return for their loyalty and military service. The nobles, in turn, held land that peasants, including serfs (unfree peasants), were allowed to farm in return for a portion of their produce and labor and protection from outside attacks. System in place in post-classical era in Europe and similar developments in Japan. (6)

financial sector encompasses a broad range of organizations that deal with the management of money: banks (commercial and investment), credit card companies, insurance companies, consumer finance companies, stock brokerages, investment funds, foreign exchange services, real estate, and some government sponsored enterprises. (8)

Five Pillars of Islam found in the Qur'an, represent the core of the practices that each member of the faith must follow: 1. faith, recited as "There is no God but Allah; Muhammad is His prophet." 2. pray five times daily facing Mecca; 3. almsgiving, or giving to the poor; 4. fasting during the holy month of Ramadan; 5. undertaking, if possible, a pilgrimage to Mecca, or *hajj*, once during one's lifetime. (6)

five relationships a Confucian, Chinese concept in which the individual subject was subordinate to the emperor, the family to its male head, the son to the father, the younger brother to the elder, and always, females to males. (6)

folk religions are religious customs, traditions, beliefs, superstitions, and rituals of a particular group, band, village, tribe, or ethnic group. The religion is transmitted from generation to generation in a specific culture. They are not organized or universal religions but particular to a group. (5)

foraging is where the primary subsistence method involves the direct procurement of edible plants and animals from the wild, without recourse to the domestication of either. Small mobile populations subsist on whatever resources are available within their territory. They adapt to conditions as they find them, using what is already there. Also known as hunting and gathering or food collecting. (4)

Four Noble Truths from the teachings of the Buddha: first, all people suffer; second, people suffer because of their desires; third, they can end their suffering by eliminating desires; and fourth, to eliminate those desires, the Eightfold Path should be followed. (6)

Fourteen Points post-World War I plan drawn up by the American President Woodrow Wilson for post-war order. One of the points was the right to self-determination by nations and another the formation of the League of Nations. (7)

free-market economy government laws and regulations that interfere with the natural laws of a self-governing economy—or, as Adam Smith called it, the "invisible hand of the marketplace"—should be repealed. Smith, disagreed with the mercantilists' regulations on trade and protective tariffs. Smith believed that tariffs should not protect home industries from competition from exporting countries but the home industries should be left to freely compete in the marketplace. (7)

freeloader a person that takes more from the group then contributes. (4)

French Revolution 1789, reached a conclusion in 1815. Inspired by the American Revolution, and influenced by Enlightenment ideals, the French Revolution arose amidst an outdated social structure, rising commercialization, destabilization resulting from population growth, an inefficient monarchy, and a large tax burden from a series of wars that fell disproportionately on the middle class and peasants. Ended with Napoleon Bonaparte rise and fall. (7)

fundamentalism a belief in a strict adherence to a set of basic principles (often religious in nature), sometimes as a reaction to perceived compromises with modern social, ideological and political life. (1)

gender a set of characteristics distinguishing between male and female. An important distinction is made between sex, which is biological, and gender, which is cultural. (3)

Ghana (750-1076) a kingdom that flourished in West Africa as a result of commerce and trade in gold, ivory, and salt that were transported by camel to the Middle East, north Africa, and Europe in exchange for manufactured goods. (6)

global warming change in the global average surface temperature. The world will not warm uniformly, even though the term implies that it will; some areas warm more than others, such as the North and South poles. Some areas will even become cooler. But the term is still in use, despite its flaws. (8)

globalization a complex, multi-dimensional phenomenon that interconnects worldwide economic, political, cultural, social, environmental, and technological forces that transcended former national boundaries. Greatly intensifying since 1980s, it reflects the many ways in which people are being drawn together not only by their own movements but also through the flow of goods, services, capital, labor, technology, ideas, and information. Globalization refers to the worldwide compression of space and time and reduction in importance of the state. In globalization the world becomes a single place that serves as frame of reference to everyone and it influences the way billions of people around the world conduct their everyday lives. (1)

globalized worldview holds to globalized attitudes, values, and principles. (1)

Glorious Revolution (1688-1689) in England, established principle that Parliament not the monarch, had supreme power. (7)

Greek philosophy/philosophers ancient Greeks created new ways of thinking based on humanism and rationalism, expounding upon the supremacy of logical thought while diminishing the importance of the traditional gods. The new discipline of philosophy developed by three notable Greek philosophers: Socrates (470-399 BCE), Plato (427-347 BCE) and Aristotle (384-322 BCE). All three had a profound influence on Western philosophy. (6)

greenhouse gases natural system that regulates the temperature on Earth, just as glass in a greenhouse keeps heat in. Sunlight passes through the atmosphere to warm our Earth, but the warmed Earth also emits heat energy back to the atmosphere, thus keeping the earth's energy budget in balance. (8)

Gross Domestic Product (GDP) economic measurement method that measure's national spending in the US without regard to economic, environmental, or social well-being of the good produced. (8)

Genuine Progress Indicator (GPI) created by the organization Redefining Progress in 1995, measures the general economic and social well-being of all citizens. (8)

guild a mutual aid association of merchants and artisans in the same trade that protected their members' interests by restricting competition, regulating apprenticeships, and establishing uniform prices and quality. Guilds prevented, with some success, the disruptive forces of a market economy by tightly and mutually regulating their economic system for the benefit of themselves and their customers. (6)

Hellenistic civilization a hybrid of elements composed of classical Greek and west Asian influences, was located on territory conquered by Alexander the Great of Macedonia around 330 BCE. Greek language, architecture, traditions, and ideals were disseminated from Greece and Egypt, to Asia up to the borders of India. (6)

Hinduism built upon the spiritual and contemplative compilations of the Vedic folk traditions of the earlier Aryan religion around 800 BCE. Collected new religious beliefs in writings called the Upanishads, ancient Sanskrit scriptures of India that transformed Hinduism into a universal religion. These writings advanced the idea that there is one eternal spirit called Brahma. (6)

holistic all the traits of a culture—economic, technological, social, political, cultural--reinforce each others. It also emphasizes the full range of relations among parts of a system and the ways the operation of those parts helps to perpetuate the whole system. (1)

holistic world history offers an alternative to the familiar chronological and linear approach to world history. A "big picture" vision of the past drawn from various disciplines—history, sociology, anthropology, political science, geography, economics, psychology, and the sciences. The model helps to connect seemingly disparate strands of the past and present into a holistic process that provides a workable, intelligible framework for understanding our shared history. (1)

home base where either hunting or scavenging and foraging activities were centered. From here rich cultural developments evolved. (2)

Homer, the author of the Greek classics the *Iliad* and *Odyssey*, lived in the 8th century BCE and extolled what are known as the Homeric principles —self-assertion, courage, craftiness, and joy in material gain. These values were passed on through oral tradition and became deeply embedded in Greek, Roman, and later Western thought. (6)

Homo A genus within the hominid family which includes modern human and extinct species of Homo such as Homo erectus. By 2.5 million years ago, utilized tools and left an enduring archaeological legacy. (2)

Homo erectus extinct human species that probably lived from about 1.9 million to 300,000 years ago. Had a medium brain size, stood fully erect, and was associated with fire and tool use. (2)

Homo habilis gracile, or delicate-boned toolmaker that probably lived from about 2.3 million to 1.5 million years ago and direct ancestor of modern humans. (2)

Homo sapiens sapiens modern humans; most recent subspecies of Homo sapiens, believed to have first appeared sometime around 100,000 years ago in South Africa. (2)

Holocaust Germany, led by Adolph Hitler, exterminated six million Jews during World War II. (7)

horticulture cultivation of crops using simple hand tools such as the hoe and digging stick and without fertilization of the soil, crop rotation, and often without irrigation. (5)

household consist of families or a group of people whose members may or may not be related and in which cooperation, such as economic production, consumption, child rearing, and shelter, are organized and carried out. Often share a common residence. (3)

human development means the common ways in which humans fashion their ways of living, interact with the environment, cultivate political, economic, and social systems, and create cultural and religious expressions. Thus, the development of people, rather than a strictly chronological periodization plan used in most history, is the master organizer of this world history narrative. (1)

humanism emphasizes the essential goodness of human beings and the optimistic belief in their potential for growth. It affirms the dignity and worth of all people. (6)

identity is used here to mean an umbrella term to describe an individual's understanding of him or herself as a distinct separate entity. An individual usually identifies with a particular ethnicity, nation, or gender. (3,8)

imperialism political and economic control by a greater power over a less powerful territory or country. Usually dates from 1873-1914 when the West embarked on a form of aggressive intervention in the non-Western world. It includes colonialism as well as indirect rule by outsiders over local people. (7)

Incas from the region of Cuzco in the Andes Mountains of present-day Peru, the Incas consolidated their powerbase around 1200. By 1442 they had defeated and conquered all of the surrounding neighbors to create a large and powerful state that extended from Columbia to the tip of South America with a population of 12 million. A civil war broke out between two brothers vying for the throne in 1527. Conquered by Pizarro in 1532. (6)

indigenous people a people whose occupation of an area precedes the state political system that now controls that area and who usually have little or no influence within that political system. (1)

individualism special emphasis placed on the worth and dignity of the individual. Individual stands apart and separate from the community or group. Emphasis on human potential, pursuit of happiness, and ownership of private property. (7)

Industrial Revolution revolution in technology that began in England in the middle to late 18th century, has since spread to most of the world, and is still continuing. (7)

industrialization the process of change from an economy based on home production of goods to one based on large-scale, mechanized factory production with a wage-based labor force. (7)

infanticide practice of killing newborn infants. (3)

information specific data or particular services applied to a product, service, or activity that adds value. Some examples include advertising, marketing, accounting, insurance, financial advisers, lawyers, efficiency experts, health care costs, etc. (8)

in-group group to which an individual belongs. (3)

institution system of social relationships and cultural elements that develops in a society in response to some set of basic and persistent needs. Institutions are formal organizations that carry out social functions in a procedural manner. Institutions are formed when societies become more complex, such as in the Urban, Modern, and Global Waves. (3)

intermediary third party, who act on their behalf and enforce the government's rule. here were two kinds of intermediaries: those who directly advised, controlled access to resources, and carried out the leader's orders; and those at a local level who transmitted and implemented decisions on the leader's behalf. (5)

Islam messenger Muhammad in the 6th century CE. Follows the Five Pillars of Islam found in the Qu'ran: 1) There is no God but Allah; Muhammad is His prophet. 2) prayer five times daily facing Mecca, 3) almsgiving, or simply giving to the poor, 4) fasting during the holy month of Ramadan, 5) a pilgrimage to Mecca, or *hajj*, once during one's lifetime. (6)

Jainism universal religion in India. Founded by Mahavira who died 477 BCE, taught that all life has a soul, so all life is sacred and should not be destroyed. To liberate oneself Mahavira taught the necessity of right faith, right knowledge, and right conduct. At the heart of right conduct for the Jains lie the five vows: non-violence, not to cause harm to any living being; truthfulness, to speak the harmless truth only; non-stealing, not to take anything not properly given; chastity, not to indulge in sensual pleasure; and non-attachment, complete detachment from people, places, and material things. (6)

Jesus (5 BCE-30CE) teachings are the basis of Christianity. Born in Nazareth in present day Israel, and was a carpenter by trade. His disciples provided many details of his life and teachings in the four gospels that make up the New Testament of the Bible, the Christians' holy book. (6)

joint stock companies European monarchies granted royal charters to joint-stock companies for trade with their colonies. Investors could pool their capital to lessen their possible losses from risky ventures. One individual was not required to raise all the capital for entrepreneurial activities. (7)

Judaism the covenant with Abraham, the Ten Commandments from Moses, and the Torah, Jewish holy writings, formed the foundation for this universal religion that reinforces the idea of social justice and individual worth and dignity. (6)

karma is the Hindu belief that actions performed in one stage of a person's life determine the next stage of one's existence. (6)

Keynes, John Maynard (1883-1946) argued that the government must accept more responsibility for regulating capitalist economies. He advocated regulation through a number of controls: running government surpluses or deficits when necessary; creating public works projects for the unemployed during economic downturns; adjusting the flow of money and credit; and raising or lowering interest rates. The purpose of these interventions was to make capitalism work better through government planning. (7)

Khmer Empire during the 9th century a kingdom called Angkor emerged to dominate the Khmer people in the area of present-day Cambodia. The kingdom was renamed the Khemer Empire in 802 and ruled until 1432. (6)

kingdom describes regions under a king's control. (6)

kinship a set of interpersonal relations which unite individuals on the basis of descent and marriage and which are maintained by a system of socially recognized obligations, rights, and customs. (3)

kinship group a basic human configuration, consist of people who are related to each other through descent or some bond that links them together such as marriage. (3)

labor denotes work or physical/mental exertion to complete a specific task. (3)

labor productivity is the amount a worker produces in a unit of time, usually per hour; whether wages rise with productivity depends on the bargaining power of workers and their employers. (8)

***laissez-faire* economics** advocated by the English economist Adam Smith, also known as free trade. Laws and regulations that interfere with the natural laws of a self-governing economy or as Smith referred to it as the "invisible hand of the marketplace" should be repealed. Smith, therefore, disagreed with the mercantilists' regulations on trade and protective tariffs. (7)

language a system of symbols. Currently about 5,000 languages in the world. Evolved primarily to foster social cohesion and not necessarily to communicate truth, beauty, or honesty. (3)

law cultural rules that regulate human behavior and maintain order. (3)

Law of Cultural Dominance coined by historian Dave Kaplan, tendency in which the cultural system that more effectively exploits a given territory will tend to spread into the territory at the expense of the less effective systems. (6)

LBGT movements have been achieving human rights for lesbian, bisexual, gay, transgender and transsexual people around the world. (8)

legends semi-historical narratives that account for heroic deeds, movements of people, and local customs mixed with the supernatural or extraordinary. Legends usually serve to entertain, instruct, inspire, and bolster pride in a family, tribe, or nation. (3)

leveling mechanisms societal obligations compelling members to distribute goods and services equally and preventing certain members from gaining too much recognition. (3, 4)

leverage intervention so that a small effort can get a huge result. To apply leverage first ask what stops the change, and then look at the connections that are holding in place the part you want to change. Cut or weaken these connections and the change may be easy. (1)

liberalism an alternative to absolutism, evolved during the 17th and 18th centuries in Britain and the Netherlands. The English political philosopher, John Locke (1632-1704), helped to formulate Enlightenment principles that maintained that all men possessed certain natural rights based on their innate ability to reason. The state acted as protector of the individual's basic rights of life, liberty, and property; at the same time, the monarchs' powers were to be controlled and limited by an independent Parliamentary branch. (7)

local capitalism reduces dependency on multinational corporations, while creating wealth-accumulating enterprises at the local level. Local economies can produce, market, and process many of their own products for local or regional consumption, reducing transportation and middleman costs. (8)

Mahavira founder of Jainism, lived 549 to 477 BCE, taught that all life has a soul, so all life is sacred and should not be destroyed. (6)

male dominance situation in which men have highly preferential access, although not always exclusive rights, to those activities to which the society accords the greatest value, and permits a measure of control over others. (4)

Mali (1235-1600) kingdom in West Africa. Its economic prosperity was garnered in part from heavy taxes imposed on the merchants who transported gold, salt, and slaves across the Sahara. The largest city of the kingdom, Timbuktu. (6)

managed or regulated capitalism generally the government closely regulated the financial sector to prevent wild financial speculation and insure transparency of the system. Tariffs protected manufacturing jobs in the home country; therefore, wages and prices were set according to supply and demand at the national level rather than global level. For the most part, education, health care, the military, and prisons were government run and paid for through taxes, and the state sometimes owned companies such as airlines and transportation networks. Private enterprise existed but was carefully regulated, with tax brackets for the wealthiest individuals hovering around 90 percent. Corporations also paid a larger share of their profits in taxes than today. (7, 8)

Manifest Destiny westward imperialist expansion by the United States in the 19th century. Settlers gobbled up land and destroyed native peoples who resisted their encroachment. (7)

manoralism self-sufficient, local, domestic economy that was part of feudalism in Europe during the Middle Ages or post-classical era. (6)

market economy an economy based on capitalist principles but is smaller in scale than a modern economy and mostly locally based. According to this world history the market economy is found in the Urban Wave and continues in the Modern and Global Waves but is largely subsumed by capitalism. (6)

marriage a cross-cultural response to the common human need to belong. It is a reproductive alliance that has a mutual obligation of parental investment in their children, is recognized by people in the larger community, and is backed by customs, rules, or laws. The marriage institution publicly recognizes sexual access by males to childbearing females. (3)

Marx, Karl proposed a communist alternative to capitalism in the short book, the *Communist Manifesto* in 1848. Emphasis on more government planning by state officials than in capitalist societies and less response to supply and demand pressures. (7)

materialism is an approach to life and social well-being that elevates the material conditions of life over the spiritual and social dimensions. (8)

matrilineal descent and inheritance traced through the female line. (4)

Maya (250 CE to 900 CE) replaced the collapsed Olmec civilization and occupied an extensive area of Central America. At its apex it was one of the most densely populated and culturally dynamic civilizations in the world. Accomplishments such as writing, mathematics, architecture and its long-lasting influence in the Western hemisphere. (6)

mercantilism based on the economic relationship between a European country, called the "mother country," with the colonies that it had established throughout the Western hemisphere and beyond. The colonial ruler strove to maintain a favorable balance of trade by importing cheap raw materials from its colonies and in turn exporting back to its colonies the more profitable manufactured goods that it produced. Similar system in operation in the Global Wave as China and other countries follow an "export driven" economy that restricts their imports and exports as much value added manufactured items as possible. (7)

merchant an intermediary in the exchange of goods and services and extracted a portion of the profits or surplus of an exchange as payment for their services. (6)

Mesopotamia often referred to as the "cradle of civilization," developed along the banks of the Tigris and Euphrates rivers in the Middle East and by 3000 BCE city states dotted the landscape. (6)

Ming dynasty (1368-1644) in China, strengthened the Great Wall to ensure the Mongols would not return to rule again. Created a highly efficient bureaucracy, using the civil service exam to fill bureaucratic positions. Even a national school system was devised to help recruit able students, completed the Grand Canal that provided shipment of agricultural products from north to south. Launch naval expeditions under command of voyager Zheng He. (7)

Mitochondrial Eve hypothesis that argues for a recent sub-Saharan African origin of modern humans, followed by movement into the rest of Eurasia and total replacement of existing archaic populations; based on genetic evidence. (2)

modern folk societies a social type of modern rural farmer who is associated with preindustrial civilization, but dominated by the city and its culture, although marginal to both. (5)

modern worldview traces its historical origins more than 500 years to the expansion of Western European power and its influence and/or ultimate dominance around the world. Especially powerful over the last two centuries, it has expanded to the farthest reaches of the world. It extols scientific reasoning, exalts individualism, treats nature as a commodity, promotes liberal political traditions, separates church and state, and places faith in technological solutions. (1)

money standard medium of value that is itself not usually consumed. In more complex societies money is a standard medium of value that is mutually agreed upon to be exchanged, but not consumed itself. (6)

Mongol Empire (1206-1405) nomadic tribes lived around Gobi Desert and steppes of central Asia united under Genghis Khan to form a formidable military might that terrorized opposition into submission. Created a capital city at Karakorum. Grandsons—Batu, Hulegu, and Kublai—continued the conquest and plunder in the 13th century. (6)

monoculture or monocrop growing just one crop to the exclusion of others for the world market, displaces subsistence agriculture during the Modern Wave. (7)

monogamy marriage in which an individual has a single spouse. (3)

Mughal Empire (1526-1739) imposed control in India. Mughal, the Persian word for Mongol, generally refers to the Central Asians who claimed descent from the Mongol warriors of Genghis Khan. The Mughals divided their territory into regional political units that succumbed to Muslim rule and later fell to British domination. (7)

Muhammad (570-632 CE) messenger of Islam, (which means, submission), taught that there is only one God, Allah. (6)

multiregional evolutionary model Homo erectus populations migrated out of Africa close to two million years ago and settled throughout Eurasia. Genetic continuity was maintained by gene flow between local populations so that an evolutionary trend towards modern humans occurred in concert wherever populations of Homo erectus existed. In this model modern races have deep genetic roots. (2)

multinational corporations (MNCs) have services in at least two countries, have maneuvered to gain access and authority, defining the rules of economic globalization by exerting powerful influence over international rule-making institutions like the World Bank, World Trade Organization (WTO) and International Monetary Fund (IMF). (8)

myth have an explanatory function that typically provides a rationale for religious beliefs and practices, depict an orderly Universe, describe appropriate behavior, express a group's worldview, show a group's place in nature, and reveal the limits and workings of the world. Diverse people express similar and recurring themes in myths. (3)

nation or **nation-state** a social, cultural, and political community with defined national boundaries and usually a shared common identity and origin, and a sense of history and ancestry that extends across past, present, and future generations. Those determined to legally reside in nations are called citizens. (3, 7)

nationalism is the political movement that holds that a nation has the right to form an independent political community based on a common destiny, identity, and shared history. (7)

natural selection is a self-selecting process by individual organisms, which select characteristics most advantageous for their survival. It steers the addition of design modifications over generations according to reproductive success. (2)

Nazi an ideology created by Adolph Hitler that borrowed from Mussolini in Italy, rejected and assaulted reason, democracy, individualism, and liberalism. Carried out in Germany in the 1930s and into World War II. (7)

Neanderthal subspecies of Homo sapiens inhabiting Europe, Asia, and Africa from 200,000 to 35,000 years ago and reached its classic form around 75,000 years ago. (2)

neoliberalism the revival of liberal laissez faire, free market theory and practice in the 1980s. Led by the University of Chicago, "Chicago School" of economics and Milton Friedman. Championed by President Ronald Reagan and Prime Minister Margaret Thatcher in the 1980s. It is the modern politico-economic theory favoring free trade, privatization, minimal government intervention in business, and reduced public expenditure on social services, etc. (7, 8)

Neolithic the New Stone Age; usually associated with the beginnings of agriculture 10,000 to 12,000 years ago. (5)

nirvana a state of freedom from the cycle of reincarnation in Hindu and Buddhist beliefs. (6)

no man's land a term for contested land that is not occupied or is under dispute between warring parties. The two parties do not occupy the land for fear that warfare will ensue. (5)

non-governmental organizations (NGOs) privately created organizations with an international scope, unaffiliated with a particular nation. (8)

nuclear family the form of family that consists only of married persons and their children. (7)

oligarchy rule of the few, it is composed of competitive subgroups all vying for power. Usually this internal strife is non-violent, but on occasion it can turn violent and civil war may result. (3)

Olmec (1200 – 400 BCE) developed in the lowlands along the coast of the Gulf of Mexico in present day Mexico. Developed somewhat later than the river valley civilizations of the Eastern hemisphere, the Olmec is considered an ancient civilization because it provided a foundation for other civilizations in the Western hemisphere. (6)

open field system a form of agricultural organization practiced for centuries in Europe, in which peasants farmed large tracks of land for elite landlords. Peasant farmers produced food for their own subsistence needs, and paid a required amount of the surplus as tribute to the landowner. In this system efficiency and productivity were largely secondary, with the tribute payment to the landowner and the subsistence needs of the peasants as primary. (7)

Opium Wars (1839-1942 and 1856-1860) between Britain and China. In the first half of the 19th century, the British were engaged in an unfavorable balance of triangular trade with China and India, in which the British shipped manufactured goods to India, Indian cotton to China, and Chinese tea, porcelain, silk, and other luxuries to Britain. The British corrected this imbalance of trade by selling opium to China. The Chinese forcibly resisted this intervention but were unable to turn back a technologically superior British military and finally succumbed to British encroachment. (7)

oracle bones etched with early forms of Chinese writing, were recovered at the Shang dynasty capital of An Yang in 1600 BCE. (6)

Osiris and Isis deities in ancient Egypt, symbols of resurrection and renewal that offered salvation for all and reflected a fundamental cosmic harmony. (6)

overshoot means to go too far, to go beyond limits accidentally or on purpose, without intention, and without consideration for the consequences. Usually refers to overshooting the carrying capacity of our Earth. (8)

Out of Africa evolutionary model Homo erectus, as well as subsequent species of Homo sapiens, dispersed out of Africa. Actually, three migrations occurred: first Homo erectus, second archaic Homo sapiens, and later modern Homo sapiens. Eventually the travelers from Africa replaced existing populations of Homo erectus and archaic Homo sapiens. Populations thus have shallow genetic roots and all derive from a single recently evolved population in Africa. (2)

out-group group to which an individual does not belong, sometimes referred to as "the other." (3)

outsourcing involves contracting out a business function to an external provider, usually to a low-wage country. (8)

Paleolithic commonly referred to as the Old Stone Age; starting with the first appearance of stone tools, 2.5 million years ago, and ending with the origins of agriculture, 10,000 years ago. (4)

participatory democracy attempts to check the abuses of elite democracy and corporate economic and political power regulatory legislation and chronicle corporate abuses through the media. (8)

pastoralism a food procurement strategy based on animal domestication, found in environments where agriculture is insufficient to support a sedentary population. (6)

patriarchy describes the dominance of males in a society where they occupy the positions of power and authority. Patriarchy is a historic, not a biological, creation. (6)

patrilineal descent and inheritance through the male line. (4)

Paul of Tarsus follower of Jesus and was instrumental in spreading Christianity's message to gentiles, or non-Jews, and helped make Christianity a universal religion. (6)

periphery surrounds core areas. Periphery regions serve the core by providing raw materials, agricultural produce, and forced labor from these areas to provide for the core's many needs ranging from necessities to luxuries. Peripheries exist in the Urban, Modern, and Global Waves. (6)

philosophes 18th century Enlightenment thinkers or philosophers mainly entered in France. They reasoned that scientific methods drawn from the natural sciences also applied to the social and intellectual sciences. (7)

Plato (427-347 BCE) Greek philosopher, student of Socrates, examined the politics of the Greek city-states, whose ideal ruler, he thought, should be a philosopher-king. He stressed the importance of ideals and ultimate truths. (6)

plow agriculture intensive form of agriculture, replaced horticulture as the dominant method of food production in areas surrounding urban centers. The plow was invented in Egypt and Mesopotamia around 3000 BCE. (6)

polyandry type of polygamy in which a wife is married to more than one husband. (3)

polygamy plural marriage, where a person permitted to have more than one spouse at the same time. (3)

polygyny a type of polygamy in which a husband is married to more than one wife at a time. (3)

prestige reputation, influence, or high standing arising from success, achievement, rank, or other favorable attributes. (3)

priest/priestess full-time religious practitioner believed to have supernatural powers bestowed on him/her by an organized religious group; performs rituals for the benefit of groups; one who mediates between deity or deities and humans. (3)

primary industries the sector of the economy that focuses on mining, agriculture, forestry, trapping animals, and fishing, changes natural resources into primary products. Also, the manufacturing industries that amass, pack, package, clean or process the raw materials close to the primary producers. (7)

protectorate a state or nation that is dominated or controlled by a much stronger state or nation. (7)

quern artisans invented these flat slabs of stone with indentations for grinding harvested grains into flour. (5)

Qur'an (also spelled Koran) holy book of Islam revealed to Muhammad. (6)

Qing dynasty (1644-1911) Manchu from Manchuria overthrew the Ming dynasty. Like the Yuan (Mongol) dynasty before them, the Manchu ruled as outsiders but did adopt many Chinese customs and culture. (7)

raid organized violence by one group against another to obtain an economic advantage. It is usually a repetitive and ongoing act motivated by economic gain. The goal is not to exterminate or even conquer the enemy permanently, but to accomplish the limited goal of seizing such goods as food, cattle, women, or other valuables. (5)

rank refers to differences in prestige but not to political power. Some societies give special privileges called rank to those who have more prestige. In ranked societies prestige is rarely translated into power or control over others, but it has responsibilities along with privileges. (3)

rationalism is the doctrine that knowledge comes from reason without the aid of the senses and that humans and the universe are understandable, predictable, and follow determined laws. (6)

reciprocity an economic system in which goods or services are exchanged passed from one individual or group to another as gifts without the need for payment. (4)

redistribution commodities are contributed by all members of a group to a common pool from which they will be distributed to where they will be used. (5, 6)

religion beliefs concerning supernatural powers and beings and rituals designed to influence those beings and powers; a system through which people interpret the nonhuman realm as if it were human and seek to influence it through symbolic communication. Often contains a moral code governing the conduct of human affairs. (3)

Renaissance meaning rebirth, extended roughly from the 14th to the 17th centuries in Europe. It began as a cultural movement among an educated elite class in the prosperous northern Italian city states of Florence, Genoa, and Milan. Involved both socio-economic changes and artistic and cultural innovations. Espoused the values of individualism, humanism, secularism and human progress, encouraged the revival of classical Greek and Roman traditions, and extolled the advancement of knowledge. (7)

republic not led by a hereditary monarch, instead the people or at least some of the people have some impact on the governmental policies. (6)

retribution the redressing of a wrong committed by an individual or group that does not have a centralized governmental authority for the enforcement of its rules. (4, 5)

Roman Catholic Church the Christian church that evolved in Europe, first centered in the city of Rome, then spread throughout western Europe. (6)

Roman Empire (31 BCE-476 CE) Rome first formed as republic then failed to govern the far-flung territorial conquests and gave way to an empire. Although Rome liberally borrowed Greek culture and ideas, its main contributions to Western society were in government, law, engineering, and imperialism. Roman law, political institutions, engineering skills, and the Latin language spread throughout the empire. (6)

Safavid dynasty (1501-1722) united Iran into a magnificent empire, the first since the Sassanian Empire that had ended in 651CE. The Safavids established the societal and territorial foundations for the modern state of Iran; Shi'a Islam became the official religion and it spread throughout the region. Isfahan was the capital city. (7)

samurai Japanese warriors hired by aristocrats to protect people and lands. They followed a code of conduct called the "way of the warrior," to guide their actions. (6)

sanctions externalized social controls that are formal and enforced by official political regulations called laws. (3)

scientific method theories regarding the nature of reality were evaluated by careful observation and systematic experimentation based on those observations. Interpretation of the experiments used mathematical measurements as the chief evaluating tool for arriving at new conclusions and knowledge. (7)

Scientific Revolution a major cultural development that took place in the 16th and 17th centuries (Modern Wave) in Europe. It advanced a proliferation of scientific ideas and challenged the authority of the Catholic Church. Noted scientists such as Copernicus, Galileo, Descartes, and Newton led the way. (7)

scramble for Africa took place between 1880 and 1914. European nations met at the Berlin conference in 1885 to carve out their territorial claims upon Africans. Colonial borders were haphazardly drawn with no attention to boundaries established by native customs, tribal affiliation, or economic relations; about 175 million Africans were subject to colonial control. (7)

secondary industries the sector of the capitalist economy that focuses on manufacturing and construction. The industry converts, with a great input of energy, raw materials into finished, usable products. (7)

serf a peasant farmer under feudalism in Europe who was bound to the land and subject to the owner of the land. (6)

service industry also called tertiary industry, is a form of wealth in a capitalist economy. A sector of industry that provides intangible goods or services to businesses and final consumers. The focus is on serving the customer rather than transforming physical goods. Examples of services may include retail, insurance, government, tourism, banking, education, public utilities, and social services. (7)

sexual revolution broke sexual barriers wide open in the U.S. and Western Europe. Later in the 20th century, female sexuality, homosexuality, and sexual activity outside marriage became more socially acceptable but were vigorously rejected by religious social conservatives. (7)

shaman part-time religious specialists who possess special spiritual gifts of healing or divination. (3, 4)

sharia body of Islamic religious law based on the Qur'an. (6)

sharing economy takes many forms, leveraging information technology to enable individuals, corporations, non-profits and government with information to efficiently distribute, share and reuse the excess capacity in goods and services. (8)

Shiites branch of Islam, known as the party of Ali, they believed that Ali was the rightful successor to Muhammad because he was a cousin and son-in-law. (6)

Shinto Japanese indigenous religion, means the "sacred way," started as the worship of spirits, living in trees, rivers, and mountains, and then later included ancestor worship. Eventually, became a state religion; the emperor was considered divine and the state sacred. (6)

shogun a Japanese commanding military authority who ruled by the sword. (6)

silent trade a trading method that minimized possible conflict between two groups. (4)

sixth extinction the alarming extinction of species today, follows upon the five previous known extinctions in the Ordovican, Devonian, Permian, Triassic and Cretaceious periods. (8)

slavery developed during the Urban Wave. With hierarchical social structures, warfare, property ownership, and the demand for more workers, slavery became an entrenched institution. Slaves were the lowest of all on the social status ladder. Those captured and not slaughtered by conquerors during warfare were forced into slavery; others were born into slavery. (6)

Slavic people settled in Russia, a branch that originally came from the steppes of Asia. Eastern Slavic people encountered different Viking groups out of Scandinavia from 800 to 1100, who soon came to dominate them. (6)

Smith, Adam an Englishman, he outlined a free trade economy in his seminal book the *Wealth of Nations* in 1776. He argued that the economy is governed by natural laws, especially the law of supply and demand. In classical economic theory, the relation between these two factors determines the price of a commodity. (7)

socialism an economic system that denotes the combination of some state owned enterprises and private capitalism. the government owns and operates large industries such as military, education, transportation, health care, utilities and others, while small businesses are privately owned and operated. (7)

socialization a continuing process whereby an individual acquires a personal identity and learns the norms, values, and social skills appropriate to his social position and that of his/her society. (3)

Socrates (470-399 BCE) leading Greek philosophers, studied human behavior, ethics, and the field of logic. He was famous for his ability to argue and challenge ideas through questioning that became known as the Socratic method. (6)

soil depletion occurs when the nutrients contributing to soil fertility are removed and not replaced. (8)

Songhay, the kingdom of West Africa bore the name of its leading ethnic group, rose to power after the decline of Mali. The capital city was located at Gao. (6)

sovereign wealth funds state-owned investment funds composed of financial assets such as stocks, bonds, property, precious metals or other financial instruments that invest globally using these pools of excess capital. (8)

Soviet Union or Union of Soviet Socialist Republics

(USSR) the world's first communist nation lurched into existence in 1917. (7)

spirituality humans generally believe in something beyond the visible and palpable that is expressed in the form of spirituality. The essence of spirituality is to evoke a mysterious feeling of communion with a sacred realm. (3)

stagflation high inflation coupled with stagnant economic growth. (8)

stars after swirling for several billion years, great clouds of hydrogen and helium collapsed into stars. In star formation, it is theorized, a cloud of cold gas condenses under its own weight. (2)

state a centralized political unit encompassing many communities and possessing coercive power. A state has legitimacy, assumes moral authority, claims its right to exist, commands sovereignty, and encompasses territory within defined boundaries. (3, 6, 7)

state capitalism a version of capitalism in which the state plays the role of leading economic actor and uses markets primarily for political gain. (8)

state religion reinforced the primacy of the state, king, elite, reigning priesthood, and class hierarchies through festival, commemorations, monumental buildings, and repetitive rituals. (6)

state terrorism terrorist acts are generally considered illegitimate because they are not sanctioned by governments. But some governments even sponsor terrorist acts. (8)

status a culturally defined relationship in which one individual may have greater stature in the group than another. (3)

stratified societies individuals with higher social status exercise real power over individuals of lower status. Low-status individuals have less access to the material fruits of society. Social stratification signifies institutionalized inequality. (3)

Structural Adjustment Policy (SAP) rules mandated by the International Monetary Fund (IMF) that indebted nations to the World Bank must open their markets to development, thus inviting foreign corporations to participate in their national economies, and they must sell their natural resources at world market prices. They are also expected to cut social programs—which usually means medical care and education. Money generated from these efforts is used for repaying the debt to the World Bank. (8)

subsistence economy self-sufficient, few specialized economic activities, and people consume what they produce. Each family basically produces enough for its own consumption and families turn out more or less the same number of goods. (4)

sultan a title given to a certain Muslim ruler in India. (6)

Sunni branch of Islam, descended from Abu Bakr who was regarded as the first caliph or successor to Muhammad. Muawiyah, unrelated to Muhammad, claimed that he was the next in line as the rightful caliph. A majority of Muslims accepted his rule, and became the Sunni (currently about 80% of all Muslims are Sunni). (6)

supply and demand in classical economic theory, the relation between these two factors determines the price of a commodity. This relationship is thought to be the driving force in a free market. As demand for an item increases, prices rise. When manufacturers respond to the price increase by producing a larger supply of that item, this increases competition and drives the price down. (7)

Swahili a Bantu term meaning "mixed" is the syncretism of languages and cultures of the horn of east Africa. (6)

system an entity that maintains its existence and functions as a whole through the interaction of its parts. (1)

systems thinking is where all the parts and the connections between the parts is studied in order to more fully understand all the parts and the whole system. It is the opposite of reductionist thinking, where the whole is seen as simply the sum of its divisible parts. Parts are seen as interconnected and functioning as a whole, if one piece of the whole is taken away the whole system changes. All parts are interconnected and work together with the behavior of each part depending on the total structure. (1)

Tang dynasty (618-907) in China, expanded westward and south, even incorporating Tibet into their dynastic realm. Restored the civil service examinations, broke up the powerful landed aristocracy and redistributed land to the peasant population. Overthrown in 907 by Turkish-speaking nomadic people from central Asia. (6)

tariff an import tax that protects the domestic industry from competition abroad. (7)

technology is defined as information for converting material resources of the environment in order to satisfy human needs. (3)

Ten Commandments in 1200 BCE Moses introduced a written moral code of conduct for the tribes of Israel. (6)

terrorism any act intended to cause death or serious bodily harm to civilians or non-combatants with the purpose of intimidating a population or compelling a government or an international organization to do or abstain from doing any act. (8)

Tokugawa Ieyasu premier political power in Japan in 1603 and took the title shogun. Successors continued in power until 1868, called the period of "Great Peace," the shogun's politically unified Japan and eliminated feudalism. Trade and industry flourished, the economy prospered, and culture thrived. In 1543 Portuguese traders landed in Japan. (7)

trade more complex than simple exchange, involves money, merchants, and rules governing the transactions. (3)

traditional family values in the US are promoted by those who define these values, among others, as against abortion and homosexuality, favor prayer in the schools, promote strict moral limits, and advocate abstinence before marriage. (8)

transformative worldview diverse and alternative paths for the future. Millions of people around the world are promoting alternative ideas and diverse options for a different worldview and voicing their convictions in a forceful, yet peaceful fashion. (1)

Treaty of Westphalia in 1648 that concluded the Thirty Years' War (1618-1648) in Europe and signaled the primacy of the sovereign state as the acknowledged form of European political organization. (7)

Triangle Trade in the 18th century developed between Africa, Europe, and the Americas. European ships carried guns, knives, metal ware, manufactured items, beads, colored cloth, and liquor to the West African coast to be exchanged for captured slaves who were shipped to the Americas in exchange for raw materials such as sugar, tobacco, furs, precious metals, and raw cotton that were in turn transported to Europe to be made into finished goods that either were shipped back to the colonies or to Africa to begin the trading network again. (7)

tribalism political philosophy found in the Global Wave based on tribes, which are ethnic groups that share a common ideology, history, language, traditions, and religion. Tribes may not accept the political philosophy of a multi-cultural, multi-ethnic nation; some strive to establish nations based on their own exclusive ethnicity. (8)

tribe is a unit of sociopolitical organization—families, several bands, clans, or lineage groups—who are united by ties of descent from a common ancestor, adherence to agreed upon customs and traditions, and loyalty to the same leader. A tribe has a similar language and lifestyle and occupies a distinct territory. (3, 5)

tribute taxation collected from the peasants that took the form of rents, interest on debts, compulsory labor service (corvee), tithes, fines, and obligatory gifts to the elite. Commodities contributed to a common pool, then distributed to certain members of the community. (6)

universal religions or worldviews with urbanization and the collection of diverse people into urban centers, spiritual needs were redirected from folk religions that had appealed to people of a particular band or tribe to universal religions that served the needs of a diverse urban population. A universal worldview appealed to different classes of individuals and reconfigured these diverse groups into a broader and more expansive collectivity. (6)

Upanishads ancient Sanskrit scriptures of India. These writings transformed Hinduism into a universal religion by advancing the idea that there is one eternal spirit called Brahma, yet many manifestations of the one spirit. (6)

Upper Paleolithic the cultural period beginning about 40,000 years ago and ending 10,000 years ago. (4)

Vietnam War after end of World War II, France

attempted to reestablish its former colonial rule in Vietnam, only to be defeated. The U.S. took over the French role and attempted to oust the communist government led by Ho Chi Minh in the north, only to meet defeat in 1975. (7)

war organized, armed conflict between political communities or combat between groups who represent separate territorial contingents or political affinities. (3)

waves a metaphor in this world history for five major human transformations in human development. Critical turning points or watersheds that signify deep structural change in our human historical process. (1)

well-field system peasants in China worked lands owned by their landlord but also cultivated their own small plots. (6)

wergild an example of a peace making strategy, a compensation practice that is a regular payment made to the victims or to the victim's family for a harm done. (3)

white man's burden many misguided, but well-meaning people firmly believed that Western culture, European people, and Christianity were superior to non-Western culture, people, and religion and thought it was their duty to "civilize the heathens." This philosophy was popularized by Rudyard Kipling's poem of the same name. (7)

worldview an overall perspective from which one sees and interprets the world; a set of simplifying suppositions about how the world works and what we see and don't see. It is an internal collection of assumptions, held by an individual or a group, that we believe are self-evident truths. These assumptions shape our beliefs, ideas, attitudes, and values, which, in turn, affect our behaviors and actions. A paradigm, a fundamental way of looking at reality. (1)

World War I or the Great War (1914-1918) pitted the main antagonists--Germany, Ottoman Empire, Austria-Hungary against Great Britain, France, Italy, Japan, and United States. (7)

World War II (1939-1945) pitted the main antagonists—Germany, Italy, Japan, against Great Britain, France, Soviet Union and the United States. (7)

writing started in the Urban Wave, enables language to be stored and transmitted through time and space. With writing, the length and complexity of communication expands, and wisdom is conveyed increasingly in written, rather than oral, form, available only to those who read. (6)

Yahweh the monotheistic god of Judaism (6)

Zoroastrianism from the teachings of a prophet named Zoroaster in ancient Persia and a compilation of texts based on his teachings called the *Avestas*. Only one god to be worshipped: Auhra Mazda. There is a cosmic struggle between gods of good and evil. (6)

Index

I

J

K

L

M

N

O

P

Q

R

Z